365 Days *of*
GARDEN COLOR

Keeping Your Garden In Bloom

By Philip Edinger, Susan Lang, Janet H. Sanchez, Vicki Webster, Hazel White,
and the Editors of Sunset Books

Menlo Park, California

Sunset Books

10 9 8 7 6 5 4 3 2 1
First printing January 2010
Copyright © 2010, Sunset
Publishing Corp., Menlo Park,
CA 94025. First edition. All rights
reserved, including the right of
reproduction in whole or in part
in any form.

Library of Congress Catalog Card
Number: 2008942793

ISBN-13: 978-0-376-03422-9
ISBN-10: 0-376-03422-X

Printed in the United States.

Front cover photograph by
Friedrich Strauss/Mise au Point

Page 1 photograph by Rob D.
Brodman

Page 2 photograph by Rob D.
Brodman

CONTENTS

ANNUALS AND PERENNIALS

BY PHILIP EDINGER, JANET H. SANCHEZ,
AND THE EDITORS OF SUNSET BOOKS

SUNSET BOOKS · MENLO PARK, CALIFORNIA

CONTENTS

Whether you stage your garden show in grand beds and borders or in a modest collection of containers on the patio, annuals and perennials can make each season's performance beautiful.

ANNUALS
AND PERENNIALS
ON STAGE

These plants offer a wealth of colorful choices—so many, in fact, that narrowing the field down to just those that are right for you can be quite a challenge. In the next chapter (pages 12–45), we offer advice on matching plants to your garden conditions—soil type, exposure, available water, and so on. Before you begin that process, though, you'll find it useful to know just what the words "annual" and "perennial" mean to botanists (and to gardeners). We'll start by defining those terms—and discussing the less familiar category of biennials, as well. We'll then focus on the many ways to present these plants, using the photos at left and on the next four pages to illustrate the possibilities. You'll see traditional beds of annuals and perennials, cottage gardens featuring a charming jumble of all sorts of plants, and plots of brilliant flowers just right for showy bouquets. There are graceful ornamental grasses, fast-growing annual vines ideal for decorating trellises, and even lush gardens grown entirely in containers.

Photographed in autumn, this garden features a striking mix of late-flowering annuals and perennials, including asters, sedums, and nicotiana. A variety of plants with handsome foliage make the scene even brighter.

WHAT ARE ANNUALS AND PERENNIALS?

"Annual," "perennial," and "biennial" all have fairly straightforward botanical definitions. In gardening usage, though, the category lines can become somewhat blurred. For example, some plants a botanist would categorize as perennials can be grown most successfully as annuals.

ANNUALS

Botanically, an annual is a plant that completes its life cycle in a year or less. In the course of a single growing season, the seed germinates and the plant grows, blooms, goes to seed, and dies. Because they must complete their life cycle in such a short time, annuals grow and bloom quickly in their rush to set seed, bringing their joyous color to the garden in only a few months from sowing. They are reliable bloomers: if spent blossoms are removed, most kinds flower for a long period, persisting in their quest to produce seed.

Depending on the varieties you choose, annuals can decorate your garden for much of the year. Cool-season types (calendula and viola, for example) prosper in cool soils and mild temperatures—from fall through spring in mild-winter climates, from early to late spring elsewhere. Following the cool-season show are warm-season annuals such as cosmos and zinnia, which are typically planted after the year's last frost and, in most climates, bloom generously throughout summer and fall.

PERENNIALS

In botanical terms, perennials are nonwoody plants that live for more than 2 years. Unlike annuals, they return to grace the landscape year after year, requiring no replanting—though many grow at a somewhat relaxed pace and may require a season or two to settle in and reach their full potential.

Among perennials, you'll find plants with various growth habits. Some, such as hosta and peony *(Paeonia),* die down to the ground at the end of each growing season, then reappear at the start of the next; these are often referred to as "herbaceous" plants. Others, including Shasta daisy *(Chrysanthemum maximum)* and coral bells *(Heuchera),* go through winter as low tufts of leaves, ready to grow when spring arrives. A third type of perennial is truly evergreen, with foliage that persists almost unchanged throughout the winter months. New Zealand flax *(Phormium),* some daylilies *(Hemerocallis),* and perennial pinks *(Dianthus)* are familiar examples.

A few plants, though technically perennials, may be grown as annuals. Examples include certain tender plants (those that cannot survive freezing temperatures) such as common geranium *(Pelargonium),* fibrous begonia, marguerite *(Chrysanthemum*

Paeonia
'Festiva Maxima'

TOP: This bright group of warm-season annuals includes gloriosa daisies *(Rudbeckia hirta),* marigolds *(Tagetes),* and zinnias.

MIDDLE: Pansies *(Viola × wittrockiana)* grow and bloom best in cool weather.

BOTTOM: Though they're perennial in mild climates, garden geraniums *(Pelargonium × hortorum)* are treated as annuals in colder regions.

Surrounded by smoothly mowed lawn, this perennial island bed can be viewed from all sides.

In this mixed border, low-growing moss pink *(Phlox subulata)* and white evergreen candytuft *(Iberis sempervirens)* enhance the springtime blossoms of a dogwood tree.

frutescens), and some kinds of salvia and verbena. These flower year after year in mild-winter climates, but where winters are cold they're typically treated like annuals and discarded at the end of the growing season. Others, such as snapdragon *(Antirrhinum)*, are hardy enough to live through frost—but because older plants don't perform as well as young ones, such hardier types too are usually grown as annuals.

BIENNIALS

By definition, these are plants that complete their life cycle in 2 years. During their first year, they grow from seed to form a foliage rosette, but they do not bloom. They live through the winter, experiencing the period of cold temperatures that many require to induce flowering; then, in the following spring or summer, they bloom, set seed, and die. Familiar biennials include foxglove *(Digitalis)*, Canterbury bells *(Campanula medium)*, hollyhock *(Alcea)*, and sweet William *(Dianthus barbatus)*. Note that for some biennials, breeders have developed strains that behave like annuals; that is, they bloom the first year from seed sown early in spring. Such plants are noted in the encyclopedia beginning on page 86.

Usually grown as biennials, tall hollyhocks *(Alcea)* are standouts in a sunny garden.

This cottage-style garden features an eclectic assortment of annuals, perennials, and ornamental grasses, as well as shrubs and small trees.

TOP: Salvia, spider flower *(Cleome)*, petunias, and impatiens mingle in this pink-and-blue design. White-flowered phlox adds a refreshing accent.

RIGHT: Annuals such as larkspur *(Consolida)* and cosmos are ideal for bouquets.

ABOVE: Glowing orange and gold marigolds *(Tagetes)* in bright blue pots line a path.

LEFT: Intense purple petunias, red verbena, and red garden geraniums *(Pelargonium × bortorum)* bring summertime interest to container-grown evergreens and ornamental grasses.

RIGHT: Built on a raised bed, a cedar trellis cloaked in vining sweet peas (Lathyrus) offers a beautiful way to divide a large garden into smaller spaces.

BELOW: Featuring colorful annuals such as sunflowers (Helianthus), salvia, and coleus, this cheerful cottage garden looks great all summer.

LEFT: Violas and butter lettuce are charming companions in borders or—as here—in a vegetable garden.

BELOW: A sunny border of petunias and salvia softens the edges of a walkway.

ABOVE: Impatiens is a popular choice for bringing bright color to areas in dappled sunlight or shade. Here, the vivid blooms are set off by a tidy edging of annual lobelia.

LEFT: Ornamental grasses, including blue oat grass (Helictotrichon), feather reed grass (Calamagrostis), and red Japanese blood grass (Imperata) bring this border alive with their texture, color, and movement.

Inch for inch, pound for pound, planting bed for planting bed—by any measure, annuals and perennials give you the greatest volume of beauty for your effort. For lavish production in a hurry, nothing compares with many annuals; and for year-after-year performance with minimal fussing,

Annuals and Perennials in the
GARDEN

nothing touches perennials. And in all climates, you can find annuals and perennials that will deliver the goods, annually.

In the following pages, you'll first learn how to choose the plants best suited to your particular garden. Next, we discuss how to combine them effectively, reviewing elements such as size, shape, texture, and color. Throughout, we provide lists of annuals and perennials with specific characteristics. You'll find plants that prefer shade, tolerate dry soil, and enjoy life in boggy spots; you'll learn which ones provide flower color in each season. Other lists group plants by growth habit and foliage type—you'll see which ones are tall or short or bulky, which ones have bold or lacy or brightly colored leaves. We've also noted some "special-purpose" plants: those with enticing fragrance, flowers ideal for cutting, and blossoms that are magnets for butterflies and birds.

As varied as a Dutch still life, this artful combination of annuals and perennials features a white Siberian iris attended by *Geranium* 'Johnson's Blue', gray-leafed lamb's ears *(Stachys byzantina)*, purple pansies *(Viola × wittrockiana)*; and pink snapdragon *(Antirrhinum)*. Design by Kristin Home.

CHOOSING FOR SUCCESS

Some gardeners don't spend much time selecting plants: they already know which ones they want to grow, and devote their efforts to choosing spots where those plants are likely to flourish. Just as often, however, a gardener—particularly one confronting bare patches of earth!—focuses on location first, then seeks out plants that might thrive there. Either way, success hinges on matching the plants to the site. As you build your garden, start by thinking about your climate; then consider exposure, soil type, and the amount of water available.

If you're utterly determined to grow plants not suited to the native conditions, you can go to great lengths to modify the environment. But for lovely results with the least amount of struggle, choose plants that are likely to prosper with what your garden naturally offers.

To create a luxuriant garden in a shady spot, choose shade lovers such as hosta and yellow-flowered lady's-mantle *(Alchemilla)*.

CLIMATE

Summer heat, winter cold, degree of humidity—these are just a few basic features of climate. Add to these the amount and timing of rainfall, length of growing season, presence or absence of wind—and you begin to see the countless combinations that result in vastly different gardening conditions as you move from one region to another. In the encyclopedia beginning on page 86, each annual and perennial is zoned according to *Sunset*'s climate zones, which cover Alaska, Hawaii, and the contiguous 48 states, including adjacent areas of Canada and Mexico. Mapped and described on pages 644–648, these zones are unique entities, each combining a wide variety of climatic factors that affect gardening. Find your zone, then choose plants suited to it.

EXPOSURE

Every plant has a preferred exposure. A plant that needs a full day of sun will languish or fail if planted in a shaded place; conversely, one needing shelter from direct sun will certainly disappoint if given a sunny spot. In some cases, exposure needs vary according to climate: certain plants thrive in full sun where summers are cool or overcast but must have partial shade in hot-summer regions. In the encyclopedia, we note the best exposure for each plant. Observe your garden carefully, noting its sun and shade patterns; then choose plants accordingly. Remember, too,

ABOVE: Containers give you control over soil and exposure. Featured here are white impatiens and pink-flowered annual phlox *(Phlox drummondii)*.

LEFT: Blazing with color, these summer-flowering perennials adapt well to the wind and cold of the eastern Rockies. Pink Mexican evening primrose *(Oenothera speciosa* 'Rosea') fronts carmine Jupiter's beard *(Centranthus)*, orange penstemon, and purple *Salvia* × *sylvestris* 'Blauhügel'.

that exposure can change with the seasons. A patch receiving afternoon shade in early spring may be considerably sunnier during the summer, while one getting plenty of sun in the warmer months may be too shaded early in the year for sun-loving spring annuals and perennials.

SOIL

Some soils retain water so well they're likely to be on the soggy side. Others drain relatively quickly, while still others are so porous they dry out in no time. Knowing just what type your garden holds is important when you're choosing plants, since some demand fast drainage and others prefer a really retentive soil. Another factor to consider is soil pH: if your soil is notably acid or alkaline, it's likely to be unsatisfactory for many plants.

Of course, soil can be modified to some degree to accommodate a broader range of plants—and if it's truly inhospitable, you can do an end-run around it by filling raised beds, planters, or containers with good, plant-friendly soil. For the simplest path to success, though, choose plants that appreciate your native soil, either "as is" or with only minor modifications. For more on soils and soil preparation, see pages 64–67.

WATER

All plants require water for survival—some more, some less. Whether you need to water frequently, occasionally, or never depends in part on soil type (moisture-retentive soils let you go longer between waterings than sandy ones do), in part on the usual rainfall pattern in your region and the needs of the plants in your garden. Where summer rainfall is the norm (and the rainfall is well timed), even plants requiring regular moisture may get through a growing season with little or no supplemental watering. However, many regions typically experience long dry periods during spring, summer, and early fall. In these areas, you have two choices. You can plant annuals and perennials that need regular water, then make sure you give them enough to grow well; or you can choose low-water-use plants and save yourself considerable trouble. Do be sure, though, that you don't locate plants with differing water requirements side by side; this makes it virtually impossible to give each one what it prefers.

COLD HARDINESS

In order to live up to their name, perennials must be able to survive the expected winter low temperatures in your area. The climate zones noted for each plant let you know the degree of cold tolerance you can expect. However, certain factors can moderate winter cold and lessen the chance of damage to plants, especially marginally hardy ones. A good snow cover provides an insulating blanket, keeping the ground—and thus plant roots—a bit warmer than the air above. And every garden has its warm spots, such as wind-sheltered locations and planting beds near surfaces that absorb and radiate heat (such as south-facing walls).

A lightly shaded spot with constantly moist to boggy soil brings out the best in perennial cardinal flower *(Lobelia cardinalis)*.

Plantings near a lake, river, or ocean must be able to endure the winds that sweep unimpeded across the water. This sturdy planting contains yellow cosmos and African marigolds *(Tagetes erecta)*, coral zinnias, red petunias, and rosy purple coneflower *(Echinacea)*.

Pale, delicate blossoms are suspended beneath the elegant leaves of Solomon's seal (*Polygonatum odoratum* 'Variegatum').

Helleborus orientalis

PLANTS FOR SHADE

ANNUALS

Ageratum houstonianum. Zones 1–45

Cerinthe major. Zones 1–24, 32, 34–45

Cleome hassleriana. Zones 1–45

Coleus × hybridus. All zones

Gomphrena. Zones 1–45; H1, H2

Impatiens. All zones

Lobelia erinus. All zones

Matthiola. Zones 1–45

Myosotis sylvatica. A1–A3; 1–24, 32–45

Nicotiana. All zones

Nigella damascena. All zones

Tropaeolum majus. All zones

Viola. Zones vary

* = grows as perennial in warmest zones (see encyclopedia)

PERENNIALS

Acanthus. Zones vary

Aconitum. Zones A1–A3; 1–9, 14–21, 34–45

Adenophora. Zones A2, A3; 1–10, 14–24, 30–43

Agapanthus. Zones vary

Agastache. Zones vary

Alchemilla mollis. Zones A2, A3; 1–9, 14–24, 31–43

Alstroemeria. Zones 5–9, 14–24, 26, 28, 31, 32 (warmer parts), 34; H1

Amsonia. Zones vary

Anemone. Zones vary

Aquilegia. Zones vary

Aruncus. Zones vary

Astilbe. Zones 1–7, 14–17, 32–43

Begonia, Semperflorens group. Zones 14–28; H1, H2

Bergenia. Zones vary

Brunnera macrophylla. Zones 1–24, 31–45

Calibrachoa. Zones 2–43

Campanula. Zones vary

Cimicifuga. Zones 1–7, 17, 32–45

Corydalis. Zones 2–9, 14–24, 32–35, 37, 39–43

Dicentra. Zones vary

Dictamnus albus. 1–9, 31–45

Digitalis. Zones vary

Erigeron. Zones vary

Eupatorium. Zones vary

Filipendula. Zones vary

Geranium (some). Zones vary

Helleborus. Zones vary

Heuchera, × *Heucherella.* Zones vary

Hosta. Zones vary

Ligularia. Zones vary

Lobelia (most). Zones vary

Myosotis scorpioides. Zones A1–A3; 1–24, 32–45

Nepeta. Zones 1–24, 30, 32–43

Oenothera (some). Zones vary

Ornamental grasses (some). See pages 128–131

Phlox (some). Zones vary

Phormium. Zones 5–9, 14–28; H1, H2

Physostegia virginiana. Zones A3; 1–9, 14–24, 26–45

Polygonatum. Zones A1–A3; 1–9, 14–17, 28–45

Primula. Zones vary

Pulmonaria. Zones 1–9, 14–17, 32–43

Rodgersia. Zones 2–9, 14–17, 32–41

Solidago. Zones 1–11, 14–23, 28–45

Stachys. Zones vary

Thalictrum. Zones vary

Viola odorata. Zones vary

Shady spots may be a bit dark—but that's no reason for shaded plantings to be dull or colorless. In the planting above, warm pink plumes of astilbe are complemented by the bold leaves of two hostas ('Janet Craig' and 'Ginko Craig') and the bright green, paddle-like foliage of *Bergenia cordifolia*.

Winsome violets *(Viola odorata)* carpet a shaded garden in early spring.

In another color-sparked shade garden, 'Rheinland' astilbe and fringed bleeding heart *(Dicentra eximia)* combine with contrasting leaves of *Hosta* 'Gold Standard' and *Hosta sieboldiana* 'Elegans'.

PLANTS THAT NEED LITTLE WATER

ANNUALS

Eschscholzia californica. Zones 1–45; H1

PERENNIALS

Achillea. Zones A1–A3; 1–24, 26, 28–45

Agapanthus. Zones vary

Artemisia. Zones vary

Baptisia. Zones 1–24, 28–45

Centranthus ruber. Zones 2–9, 12–24, 28–43; H1

Coreopsis (some). Zones vary

Erigeron karvinskianus. Zones 8, 9, 12–28; H1, H2

Euphorbia (many). Zones vary

Gaura lindheimeri. Zones 2b–35, 37, 38 (coastal), 39

Lobelia laxiflora. Zones 7–9, 12–24

Oenothera. Zones vary

Ornamental grasses (some). See pages 128–131

Penstemon (some). Zones vary

Perovskia. Zones 2–24, 28–43

Phlomis. Zones vary

Phormium. Zones 5–9, 14–28; H1, H2

Verbena (some). Zones vary

Zauschneria (most). Zones vary

Western native California fuchsia *(Zauschneria californica latifolia)* takes heat in stride and can survive on rainfall alone.

ABOVE: California poppy *(Eschscholzia),* the state's signature flower, offers silken beauty in orange as well as yellow, white, and assorted pastel colors.

RIGHT: Choose the right plants, and you'll get maximum color for just moderate amounts of water. Fluorescent purple *Verbena rigida* and red *Penstemon* × *gloxinioides* 'Firebird' steal this scene.

PLANTS FOR CONSTANTLY MOIST SOIL

ANNUALS

Myosotis sylvatica. Zones A1–A3; 1–24, 32–45

PERENNIALS

Aconitum. Zones A1–A3; 1–9, 14–21, 31–45

Aruncus. Zones vary

Chelone. Zones 1–9, 14–24, 28–43

Eupatorium. Zones vary

Filipendula (some). Zones vary

Hosta. Zones vary

Iris, Japanese. Zones 1–10, 14–24, 32–45

Ligularia. Zones vary

Lobelia (many). Zones vary

Monarda. Zones vary

Myosotis scorpioides. Zones A1–A3; 1–24, 32–45

Ornamental grasses (some). See pages 128–131

Primula (some). Zones vary

Rodgersia. Zones 2–9, 14–17, 32–41

For beautifying a damp swale, you can't go wrong with indestructible annual forget-me-nots *(Myosotis sylvatica).* These plants require little maintenance after the initial planting, and volunteer seedlings keep new plants coming along year after year.

Hosta sieboldiana

Japanese iris 'Caprician Butterfly' (above left) revels in pondside soil, even shallow water. Bee balm *(Monarda)* cultivars also perform best where the soil never dries out; shown above right is 'Cambridge Scarlet'.

DESIGNING WITH PLANTS

Whether you envision a garden that's all annuals, exclusively perennials, or a combination of both, a few basic principles of design will help you compose an attractive floral "painting." One simple statement sums it up: rather than focusing on color alone, consider the entire plant. Though color may be the most obvious component of a planting (see pages 30–33), other features work with it to create a pleasing, interesting, and memorable whole.

Complete with brick-wall backdrop, this classic English-style perennial border exemplifies artful plant combination, with flower colors, plant sizes and shapes, foliage textures, and bloom seasons all taken into consideration.

PLANT SIZE

Annuals and perennials vary enormously in size. In both categories, you'll find plants that grow just ankle high, giants that overtop all but the exceptional basketball player, and individuals at every possible height in between.

Size matters in several ways. The standard advice is to locate tall plants at the back of a bed, short ones in front. This rule is a foolproof one, but nonetheless, it can be broken to great effect. Placing a tall plant in the foreground can provide a telling accent, perking up the surrounding flatness—an especially effective tactic if the accent plant differs markedly in shape or texture from its companions.

In addition to considering sizes of plants relative to each other, think about plant size relative to planting-area size. In a relatively narrow bed (3 to 5 feet deep) or a small area, you won't want to use the very tallest, largest individuals—such as hollyhock *(Alcea)* and rose-mallow *(Hibiscus)*. Instead, scale down the heights and widths of the plants you use to keep them in proportion to the space. Reserve the true colossi for large planting areas, where they'll contribute to the design rather than overwhelming it.

Contemporary, pocket-size perennial border shows the classic attention to colors, shapes, and textures, forming a garden that presents an harmonious overall picture yet showcases each plant.

Lavish sweep of mixed perennials gains distinction from its striking complementary colors (yellow and violet), contrasting leaf and flower shapes, and use of vertical-growing plants as accents among spreading and billowy individuals.

Bear in mind that some perennials, in particular, grow dramatically higher at bloom time, sending up tall flowering stems from relatively low foliage masses. In these cases, height is a seasonal accent, not a permanent design element; if the plants are fairly wispy looking (as are *Verbena bonariensis* and *Anemone × hybrida*, for example), they can be used even in smaller beds, since their overall bulk is slight.

PLANT SHAPE

Spreading, rounded, vertical, fountainlike, vaselike—annuals and perennials come in as many shapes as they do sizes. And to spice up any planting, aim for variety in shape as well as size. Letting just one shape dominate will lead to monotony, whereas choosing contrasting ones automatically calls attention to the individuality of each plant or group of plants.

As noted under "Plant Size" (facing page), many plants become taller when in bloom. This increased height is accompanied by a change in form. In some cases, the entire foliage mass rises, making the plant taller and bulkier; in others, stems simply shoot up from leafy clumps that remain low. When you use these plants, think about how their changes will affect the garden's design over the course of the growing season.

PLANT DENSITY

Some plants look solid, opaque, and weighty; others are airier, with an openness to their structure that lets you see into or right through the foliage mass. A planting composed entirely of dense plants looks lumpy and impenetrable, while one using exclusively see-through plants seems insubstantial. It's a balance between the two types that makes for a dynamic composition. Some plants present a combination of density and openness, particularly those that send up flowering stems high above a thick foliage mass. Many ornamental grasses and clumping plants with narrow or swordlike leaves—New Zealand flax *(Phormium)*, for example—are solid looking near the base but much less so toward the leaf tips.

Ligularia stenocephala 'The Rocket'

FOLIAGE SIZE AND TEXTURE

Though all leaves serve the same function, they are far from uniform in appearance. Just compare *Hosta* 'Sum and Substance' with threadleaf coreopsis *(Coreopsis verticillata)*—the former has broad, plate-sized leaves, while the latter's fine, feathery foliage is reminiscent of green threads. Adding to the variety is the fact that leaf size and texture don't necessarily correspond to plant size and shape. There are big plants with small, fine leaves, small plants with big, coarse leaves, bulky plants with filmy foliage, and open-looking ones with large leaves.

In designing a planting area, make use of the vast array of leaf widths, lengths, shapes, and textures. Remember that large, bold leaves are attention-getters, regardless of plant size; use them carefully, as accents. Small- and filmy-leafed plants are more subtle and retiring, fine choices for buffering and highlighting bolder-leafed individuals.

FOLIAGE COLOR

Green is the color we automatically associate with leaves. But there are hundreds of different greens—some lighter, some darker, some blended with varying amounts of yellow, blue, or gray. And some plants depart quite markedly from the usual, offering leaves in "unconventional" colors: gray (sometimes so pale as to be near-white), blue, yellow, red, bronze, purple, and variegated combinations. Such colored-leaf plants (listed on pages 28–29) are first-rate accents, adding sparkle to the garden's greenness and working in concert with floral color.

FOLIAGE SURFACE QUALITY

Combining elements of both texture and color, the quality of a leaf's surface is a subtle design feature that can be used to great advantage, particularly in plantings that emphasize foliage rather than flowers. Some leaves look polished, shiny enough to reflect light; others have a matte finish, like slate, or have a whitish bloom like that on the skin of a plum. Still others are covered with silky hairs that give them a silvery sheen. And some leaves are thickly furred and totally nonreflective.

ABOVE: Brilliant 'Sunrise' coleus is highlighted by the slim foliage of ornamental grass and the spent flower heads of lily-of-the-Nile *(Agapanthus)*.

RIGHT: Vividly striped leaves of 'Pretoria' canna (right) have a bold shape that contrasts with adjacent perennials—but their colors harmonize with orange Mexican sunflower *(Tithonia)* and blue floss flower *(Ageratum)*.

LEFT: More than color catches the eye in this varied composition. The flowers differ markedly in shape, too, blooming in tall spires, loose clusters, tight bunches, and flat-topped heads.

TOP: Pleasant mixed planting of annuals and perennials is accented by a fountainlike clump of eulalia grass (*Miscanthus sinensis* 'Variegatus').

BOTTOM: Varied colors and shapes of leaves and blossoms provide nonstop interest. Design by Landcraft Environments.

FLOWER SIZE AND PRESENTATION

Though color plays an important role in defining floral impact, it's only one part of the picture. A flower's size and shape, the way it is carried on the plant—these too are features to consider.

Viewed individually, a large flower attracts more attention than a small one. But floral abundance can tip the scale the other way: a plant smothered in small blossoms can be showier than one with just a scattering of large blooms. Likewise, a smaller cluster of packed-together flowers may carry more visual weight than a larger but looser cluster.

Besides thinking about abundance and density, consider just how the blossoms are presented on the plant. Some, such as peony *(Paeonia)*, are borne singly, each at the tip of an individual stem. Others, like hollyhock *(Alcea)*, are carried in upright, many-flowered spikes, with the blooms set so close to the stem they look almost pasted on. Still others come in clusters that may be round, dome shaped, or flat topped. You'll find flowers in open sprays, blossoms arrayed like bursting fireworks, and some—like baby's breath *(Gypsophila)*—that are sprinkled over the plant like a shower of confetti. All these variations let you produce textural effects quite independent of color.

PLANT CHARACTER

A dynamic planting relies on variety in plant habit as much as it does on creative use of color. On these two pages, we list plants that depart from the typical rounded, well-foliaged shape—tall types good for accents, large, bulky sorts, and see-through kinds with an airy, open look.

VERTICAL PLANTS

Though their heights vary, the following plants all provide strongly vertical effects. In some cases, the entire plant is spire-like; in others, only the flowering stems are tall and slim.

For a stunning vertical accent in an easy-to-grow plant, nothing touches stately foxgloves. Shown here are blossom spires of *Digitalis purpurea*, Excelsior strain.

ANNUALS

Alcea rosea. Zones 1–45

Antirrhinum majus. Zones A3; 1–45

Celosia, plume kinds. Zones A3; 1–45; H1, H2

Consolida ajacis. Zones 1–45

Moluccella laevis. Zones 1–45; H1, H2

PERENNIALS

Acanthus. Zones vary

Aconitum. Zones A1–A3; 1–9, 14–21, 34–45

Adenophora. Zones A2, A3; 1–10, 14–24, 30–43

Astilbe (some). Zones 1–7, 14–17, 32–43

Baptisia. Zones 1–24, 28–45

Campanula (some). Zones vary

Delphinium. Zones vary

Digitalis. Zones vary

Aconitum napellus

Liatris. Zones A2, A3; 1–10, 14–24, 26, 28–45

Ligularia (some). Zones vary

Lobelia (some). Zones vary

Lupinus. Zones A1–A3; 1–7, 14–17, 34, 36–45

Ornamental grasses (some). See pages 128–131

Penstemon (many). Zones vary

Physostegia virginiana. Zones A3; 1–9, 14–24, 26–45

Salvia (some). Zones vary

Verbascum. Zones vary

Veronica (some). Zones vary

Given the conditions they need, hybrid lupines *(Lupinus)* bloom lavishly, bearing spikes of sweet pea–shaped blossoms in a wide range of colors.

Verbena bonariensis sends sprays of violet flowers skyward on a network of needle-thin branches.

Though they differ in form, eulalia grass (*Miscanthus sinensis* 'Variegatus') and purple-flowered spotted Joe Pye weed *(Eupatorium purpureum maculatum)* both contribute mass to this planting.

LARGE, BULKY PLANTS

Their shapes vary—some are upright growing, others broader and more rounded—but all these plants contribute solidity and mass to a planting. You can consider them the annual and perennial equivalents of shrubs.

ANNUALS

Cleome hassleriana. Zones 1–45
Helianthus annuus. All zones
Lavatera trimestris. All zones
Ricinus communis. Zones 1–45; H1, H2
Tithonia rotundifolia. All zones

PERENNIALS

Aruncus dioicus. Zones A2, A3; 1–9, 14–17, 31–43
Baptisia. Zones 1–24, 28–45
Canna. Zones 6–9, 12–31, warmer parts of 32; H1, H2
Eupatorium (most). Zones vary
Filipendula rubra. Zones A1–A3; 1–9, 14–17, 31–45
Hibiscus moscheutos. Zones 2–24, 26–41; H1
Ornamental grasses (many). See pages 128–131
Phormium. Zones 5–9, 14–28; H1, H2
Rodgersia (most). Zones 2–9, 14–17, 32–41

Big, bold, and beautiful—this hybrid New Zealand flax *(Phormium)* is a real traffic stopper.

FILMY, SEE-THROUGH PLANTS

In contrast to the bulky-looking plants listed at left, the following individuals have a see-through structure. In a few cases, the entire plant has an open look; in the rest, intricate or wispy flower stems rise above the main foliage mass, giving the impression of floral lace.

PERENNIALS

Anemone. Zones vary
Aster (some). Zones vary
Cimicifuga. Zones 1–7, 17, 32–45
Eryngium. Zones vary
Filipendula. Zones vary
Foeniculum vulgare 'Purpurascens'. Zones 2b–11, 14–24, 29–41; H1, H2
Gaura lindheimeri. Zones 2b–35, 37, 38 (coastal), 39
Gypsophila paniculata. Zones A2, A3; 1–10, 14–16, 18–21, 31–45; H1
Heuchera (many). Zones vary
Kniphofia. Zones 2–9, 14–24, 28–41
Limonium. Zones vary
Ornamental grasses (some). See pages 128–131
Perovskia. Zones 2–24, 28–43
Thalictrum. Zones vary
Verbena bonariensis. Zones 8–24, 26 (northern), 28
Verbena bonariensis. Zones 8–24, 28–31, warmer parts of 32

FOLIAGE CHARACTER

Flowers typically put on a show for just part of the growing season—but foliage enhances your garden from spring until frost, if not beyond. Use leaves of various shapes, sizes, and textures to add long-lasting appeal to your plantings.

FERNLIKE FOLIAGE

Like maidenhair fern, the plants listed below have leaves composed of numerous small leaflets that are more or less rounded or oval.

PERENNIALS

Aquilegia. Zones vary

Aruncus. Zones vary

Astilbe. Zones 1–7, 14–17, 32–43

Cimicifuga. Zones 1–7, 17, 32–45

Corydalis. Zones 2–9, 14–24, 32–35, 37, 39–43

Delphinium. Zones vary

Dicentra. Zones vary

Filipendula. Zones vary

Thalictrum. Zones vary

NARROW, GRASSLIKE, OR SWORDLIKE LEAVES

Varying from fountainlike to stiffly upright, these clumping perennials have leaves that contrast sharply in form with all other foliage shapes.

PERENNIALS

Agapanthus. Zones vary

Dianthus. Zones vary

Hemerocallis. Zones 1–45; H1, H2

Iris. Zones vary

Kniphofia. Zones 2–9, 14–24, 28–41

Liatris. Zones A2, A3; 1–10, 14–24, 26, 28–45

Ornamental grasses. See pages 128–131

Phormium. Zones 5–9, 14–28; H1, H2

Swordlike leaves of 'Yellow Wave' New Zealand flax *(Phormium)* rise above a riotous mix of coleus. Design by David Culp.

Demure pink flowers of fringed bleeding heart *(Dicentra eximia)* are beautifully set off by the finely divided, fernlike foliage.

Arching leaves of zebra grass (*Miscanthus sinensis* 'Zebrinus') almost seem to embrace the sweet William (*Dianthus barbatus*) and gloriosa daisies (*Rudbeckia hirta*) planted below.

Hostas are classic foliage plants, including a world of choices in an incredible array of leaf shapes, sizes, and colors.

LARGE LEAVES

The sheer size of their leaves gives these plants a real garden presence. The plants vary in overall size and shape, but any one of them makes a dramatic statement in the landscape.

ANNUALS

Ricinus communis. Zones 1–45; H1, H2

PERENNIALS

Acanthus. Zones vary
Bergenia. Zones vary
Canna. Zones 6–9, 12–31, warmer parts of 32; H1, H2
Helleborus. Zones vary
Hosta (some). Zones vary
Ligularia. Zones vary
Phlomis. Zones vary
Rodgersia. Zones 2–9, 14–17, 32–41
Salvia sclarea. Zones 2–24, 27–41
Verbascum (many). Zones vary

FILIGREE FOLIAGE

Threadlike leaves or leaf segments give these plants a soft, filmy look. In mixed plantings, they provide a nice contrast to large-leafed plants.

ANNUALS

Consolida ajacis. Zones 1–45
Cosmos. Zones A3; 1–45
Eschscholzia californica. Zones 1–45; H1
Nigella damascena. All zones
Tagetes. All zones

PERENNIALS

Achillea. Zones A1–A3; 1–24, 26, 28–45
Aconitum (some). Zones A1–A3; 1–9, 14–21, 34–45
Artemisia. Zones vary
Chrysanthemum (some). Zones vary
Coreopsis verticillata. Zones 1–24, 26, 28–45
Foeniculum vulgare 'Purpurascens'. Zones 2b–11, 14–24, 29–41; H1, H2
Perovskia. Zones 2–24, 28–43
Verbena (some). Zones vary

LEFT: Leaves of open, airy love-in-a-mist *(Nigella)* resemble delicate netting.
RIGHT: Threadleaf coreopsis *(Coreopsis verticillata)* is a more compact plant with threadlike foliage.

FOLIAGE COLOR

Flowers don't have a monopoly on color! As you design your garden beds, don't overlook the contributions that plants with colored foliage can make to any composition. Though leaves are typically green, there are plenty of plants with foliage in other colors: near-blue, yellow, red, pink, bronze, purple, gray, even white. In addition to these, you'll find variegated combinations that range from subtle to vividly showy. Colored-leaf plants are perfect accents for a green background, and gray-foliaged types also make lovely companions for bright or pastel flowers.

'Halcyon' hosta creates a startling patch of blue.

BLUE LEAVES

ANNUALS

Cerinthe major 'Pupurascens'.
Zones 1–24, 32, 34–45

PERENNIALS

Dicentra (several). Zones vary
Eryngium. Zones vary
Hosta (some). Zones vary
Ornamental grasses (some).
See pages 128–131

YELLOW LEAVES

ANNUALS

Coleus × *hybridus*. All zones

PERENNIALS

Chrysanthemum parthenium 'Aureum'.
Zones 2–24, 28–45
Helichrysum petiolare 'Limelight'.
Zones 16, 17, 22–24
Hosta (some). Zones vary
Phormium (some). Zones 5–9, 14–28;
H1, H2
Stachys byzantina 'Primrose Heron'.
Zones 1–24, 29–43

GRAY LEAVES

PERENNIALS

Achillea (some). Zones A1–A3; 1–24,
26, 28–45
Artemisia. Zones vary
Centaurea cineraria. Zones 8–30
Cerastium tomentosum. Zones A1,
A2; 1–24, 32–45
Dianthus (some). Zones vary
Nepeta. Zones 1–24, 30, 32–43
Ornamental grasses (some).
See pages 128–131
Perovskia. Zones 2–24, 28–43
Salvia argentea. Zones 1–24, 26,
28–45
Stachys byzantina. Zones 1–24,
29–43
Verbascum (some). Zones vary
Zauschneria (most). Zones vary

LEFT: Among colored-leaf plants, coleus offers some of the brightest choices. These varieties sport foliage in shades of yellow to chartreuse.

RIGHT: Gray-leafed plants such as this *Artemisia schmidtiana* 'Silver Mound' add a soft, cool touch to the garden.

Colored foliage can be subtle—but 'Tropicana' canna is downright gaudy, with leaves striped in purple, green, yellow, pink, and red.

VARIEGATED LEAVES

ANNUALS

Coleus × hybridus. All zones
Euphorbia marginata. Zones 1–45
Impatiens, New Guinea Hybrids (some). All zones
Tropaeolum majus (some). All zones

PERENNIALS

Agapanthus (some). Zones vary
Aquilegia (some). Zones vary
Aurinia saxatilis 'Dudley Nevill Variegated'. Zones 1–24, 32–43
Begonia, Semperflorens group (some). Zones 14–28; H1, H2
Brunnera macrophylla (several). Zones 1–24, 31–45
Canna (some). Zones 6–9, 12–31, warmer parts of 32; H1, H2
Filipendula ulmaria 'Variegata'. Zones 1–9, 14–17, 31–45
Gaura lindheimeri 'Corrie's Gold'. Zones 2b–35, 37, 38 (coastal), 39
Helichrysum petiolare 'Variegata'. Zones 16, 17, 22–24
Heuchera (several). Zones vary
Hosta (many). Zones vary
Pelargonium (some). Zones 8, 9, 12–24
Phormium (some). Zones 5–9, 14–28; H1, H2

Physostegia virginiana 'Variegata'. Zones A3; 1–9, 14–24, 26–45
Polygonatum odoratum 'Variegatum'. Zones A1–A3; 1–9, 14–17, 28–43
Pulmonaria. Zones 1–9, 14–17, 32–43
Sedum (several). Zones vary

BRONZE, RED, PURPLE, PINK LEAVES

ANNUALS

Celosia (some). Zones A3; 1–45; H1, H2
Coleus × hybridus. All zones
Eschscholzia californica, Thai Silk strain. Zones 1–45; H1
Impatiens, New Guinea Hybrids (some). All zones
Perilla frutescens purpurascens. All zones
Ricinus communis (some). Zones 1–45; H1, H2

PERENNIALS

Begonia, Semperflorens group (some). Zones 14–28; H1, H2
Bergenia (some). Zones vary
Canna (some). Zones 6–9, 12–31, warmer parts of 32; H1, H2
Cimicifuga simplex (several). Zones 1–7, 17, 32–45
Eupatorium rugosum 'Chocolate'. Zones 1–10, 14–17, 28–45

Euphorbia (some). Zones vary
Foeniculum vulgare 'Purpurascens'. Zones 2b–11, 14–24, 29–41; H1, H2
Gaura lindheimeri 'Siskiyou Pink'. Zones 2b–35, 37, 38 (coastal), 39
Heuchera (several). Zones vary
Ligularia dentata 'Dark Beauty'. Zones 1–9, 14–17, 32, 34, 36–43
Lobelia (some). Zones vary
Ornamental grasses (some). See pages 128–131
Penstemon digitalis 'Husker Red'. Zones 1–9, 14–24, 29–43
Phormium (some). Zones 5–9, 14–28; H1, H2
Sedum telephium (some). Zones 1–24, 29–43

TOP: Glowing burgundy leaves of 'Dark Star' coleus
BOTTOM: 'Yellow Wave' New Zealand flax *(Phormium)*

This assortment of warm colors features bicolored gloriosa daisies *(Rudbeckia hirta)* surrounded by petite orange zinnias and yellow celosia and calendulas.

DESIGNING WITH COLOR

Annuals and perennials are a reliable and tremendously varied source of garden color—probably the main reason for their immense popularity. To guarantee color groupings that are sure to please, take time to study the basics outlined here before you finalize your design. When you're ready to make your choices, take a look at the charts on pages 34–39, where every flowering annual and perennial described in the plant encyclopedia is listed according to the colors it offers and the time of year it blooms.

THE COLOR WHEEL

The color display shown at left arranges the spectrum in a wheel, making it easy to see the relationships between colors. Refer to it as you review the discussion below.

HUE. A pure hue is an undiluted color, with no addition of white, gray, or black. Three hues are *primary colors*: red, yellow, and blue. No mixture of colors can produce them. Three other hues, each resulting from mixing two primary colors, are *secondary colors*: violet (red plus blue), green (yellow plus blue), and orange (yellow plus red).

VALUE. As the color wheel shows, each pure hue can become lighter (as you go toward the wheel's center) or darker (as you approach the perimeter). These gradations are called *values*. Adding white to a hue produces the lighter values referred to as *tints*; the addition of black results in darker *shades*.

SATURATION. Hues can be bright or dull, a condition described as degree of *saturation* (also called *intensity*). Differences in saturation result from the amount of gray added to a hue: the more gray you add, the duller and less saturated the color. Gray values are called *tones*.

WARM VERSUS COOL COLORS. When you draw a line across the color wheel between green and yellow-green on one side, between red and red-violet on the other, you divide the colors into two groups: one *warm*, the other *cool*. The warm colors are yellow, orange, and red; the cool ones are violet, blue, and green.

COLOR COMBINATIONS

The color wheel lets you view all sorts of color combinations at a glance. Three possible schemes are described on the following two pages: monochromatic, harmonious, and contrasting. Also discussed are white and gray, two "colors" not

Shade
Hue
Tint
Tone

Their colors are harmonious—but the red-violet lobelia and warm red scarlet sage *(Salvia splendens)* shown here are so rich and intense they almost seem to contrast with each other.

A horticultural heat wave, this landscape sizzles with shimmering, summery shades of yellow, orange, and red from African marigolds *(Tagetes erecta),* zinnias, and bedding begonias.

TOP: Featuring lighter, softer values of the red-and-violet combination shown on the facing page, this planting of pink bee balm *(Monarda)* and blue-violet speedwell *(Veronica)* is purely harmonious.

BOTTOM: Leaves of 'Palace Purple' coral bells *(Heuchera)* and blue blossoms of catmint *(Nepeta × faassenii)* are another harmonious pairing.

represented on the wheel but widely found in flowers and foliage. Both can be used in virtually any color combination.

MONOCHROMATIC. The simplest color scheme is centered on a single hue—blue, for example—and includes flowers in all that hue's tints, shades, and various saturations. The result is almost automatically pleasant, though monochromatic schemes based on warm colors run the risk of being overassertive. To avoid monotony, select plants with different forms and a variety of foliage colors, textures, and shapes.

The all-white garden is another application of the monochromatic idea, though white, strictly speaking, is not a color (see page 33).

HARMONIOUS. On the color wheel, harmonious colors are those that lie between any two primary hues. Moving from yellow to red, for example, you'll find yellow-

ABOVE: Pairing primary colors with similar values creates an effective contrast—as here, where yellow coneflower (*Rudbeckia fulgida sullivantii* 'Goldsturm') combines with 'Blue Fortune' agastache.

RIGHT: Coleus foliage in red and near-yellow offers another example of contrasting primary colors. Orange-red impatiens makes the picture even brighter.

Full-strength yellow gloriosa daisies *(Rudbeckia hirta)* complement lavender-blue penstemon and purple coneflowers *(Echinacea)* in rosy violet.

orange, orange, and orange-red. A broadly harmonious composition includes the full range of colors between the two primaries as well as one of those two hues; the most limited harmonious scheme encompasses just two adjacent colors on the wheel (yellow and yellow-orange, for example). Thanks to the close relationship between the colors used, harmonious combinations are pleasing to the eye. And because two hues are involved rather than just one, they're a bit livelier than monochromatic schemes.

CONTRASTING. Color contrasts occur between two totally unrelated colors. The primary hues provide an obvious example of vivid contrasts. Another contrast is formed by *complementary* colors—those opposite each other on the color wheel, such as blue and orange or yellow and violet. In most cases, you'll be aiming for contrasting flower colors; but note that the complement to red is green. Vivid red scarlet sage *(Salvia splendens)* against a backdrop of green foliage creates as true a contrast as blue delphiniums behind orange daylilies *(Hemerocallis)*.

Contrasts involving fully saturated colors are most effective when used in moderation, as accents or foils for quieter, more harmonious schemes. Used in large quantity, these vivid contrasts both jar the eye and lose their impact. Also keep in mind that contrasting colors are typically more effective if used in unequal amounts: rather than composing a planting bed of half yellow iris and half violet ones, use one color sparingly, as an accent to greater amounts of the other.

Contrasting colors need not be bright. For a softer look, use tints: cream and lavender, for example, instead of yellow and violet. You can also mix values when you create contrast, combining a fully saturated color with a softer, paler one—intense blue with pale peach, for instance, or bright green foliage as a foil for soft pink flowers.

WHITE. Gardeners think of white as a color, but to color theorists, it's atonal—the complete lack of color. As white is added to a color, it produces lighter and lighter tints, until—at the center of the color wheel—only white remains. White, then, can assort with all colors, light or dark. Combined with lighter values, it is harmonious; its lack of color seems closely related to the paleness around it. Used with fully saturated colors or darker shades, it offers a sharp contrast. (Use it sparingly in this role—overuse of contrast will give the planting a discordant, uneasy feel.)

GRAY. Though you won't find truly gray flowers, there are plenty of gray-leafed plants. Usually thought of as a cool color, gray actually results from mixing any two complementary colors. This explains its unique ability to fit into virtually any scheme, warm or cool. Gray is the great moderator: its soft neutrality tones down brilliance, highlights every color, and imparts softness to the overall picture.

ABOVE, LEFT: Used in combination with fully saturated colors, white creates an effective contrast.

ABOVE: Paired with green foliage alone, white looks bright yet cool.

Yellow marigolds *(Tagetes)* and red verbena look cooler and less assertive when separated by a drift of gray dusty miller *(Centaurea cineraria)*.

FLOWER COLOR BY SEASON

Many annuals and some perennials have notably long flowering periods, but none blooms for the entire growing season. The charts on these six pages give bloom seasons and flower colors for all the annuals and perennials described in the encyclopedia beginning on page 86. Use them to find the plants that will give you flowers when you need them, in the colors you want.

The exact onset and end of flowering depends somewhat on climate. Cold-winter regions (other than parts of Alaska) have shorter bloom seasons; in hot-summer climates, flowering usually starts earlier in the season and comes to an end more quickly. In mild-winter and Southwest desert regions, some spring flowers reliably bloom in winter. Be sure to read the encyclopedia descriptions and heed the zone recommendations.

ANNUAL NAME	BLOOM SEASON				ZONES
	SP	SU	F	W	
Ageratum houstonianum ✿ ❀ ✿ ✿		■	■		1–45
Anchusa capensis ✿		■			All zones
Antirrhinum majus ✿ ❀ ✿ ✿ ✿ ✿	■				A3; 1–45
Asarina (see page 182) ✿ ❀ ✿		■			1–45
Calendula officinalis ❀ ✿ ✿		■			1–45; H1
Calibrachoa ✿ ✿ ✿ ❀ ✿ ✿ ✿			■		2–43
Callistephus chinensis ✿ ❀ ✿ ✿ ✿		■			1–45
Catharanthus roseus ✿ ❀ ✿ ✿ ✿		■	■		1–45; H1, H2
Celosia ✿ ❀ ✿ ✿ ✿ ✿		■			A3; 1–45; H1, H2
Centaurea (some) ✿ ✿ ❀ ✿ ✿ ✿	■				Zones vary
Cerinthe major ✿ ✿		■			1–24, 32, 34–45
Chrysanthemum (some) ✿ ❀ ✿ ✿ ✿ ✿		■			Zones vary
Clarkia ✿ ❀ ✿ ✿ ✿ ✿	■				1–45
Cleome hassleriana ✿ ❀ ✿ ✿		■			1–45
Cobaea scandens (see page 182) ✿ ❀		■			3–41
Consolida ajacis ✿ ✿ ❀ ✿	■				1–45
Convolvulus tricolor ✿ ✿ ✿ ❀ ✿ ✿		■			1–45
Coreopsis tinctoria ✿ ✿		■			1–45; H1, H2
Cosmos ✿ ❀ ✿ ✿ ✿ ✿			■		A3; 1–45
Dianthus (some) ✿ ❀ ✿ ✿	■				A2, A3; 1–24, 30–45
Dolichos lablab (see page 182) ✿		■			All zones
Eschscholzia californica ✿ ❀ ✿ ✿ ✿ ✿	■			■	1–45; H1
Euphorbia marginata ❀		■			1–45
Gaillardia pulchella ❀ ✿ ✿ ✿		■			1–45; H1, H2
Gomphrena ✿ ❀ ✿ ✿ ✿		■	■		1–45; H1, H2
Helianthus annuus ❀ ✿ ✿ ✿		■			All zones
Helichrysum bracteatum ✿ ❀ ✿ ✿ ✿ ✿		■	■		All zones
Iberis (some) ✿ ❀ ✿ ✿		■			1–45

Annual Name	Bloom Season				Zones
	SP	SU	F	W	
Impatiens ✿ ❀ ✿ ✿					All zones
Ipomoea (see page 182) ✿ ✿ ❀ ✿ ✿					All zones
Lathyrus odoratus ✿ ✿ ❀ ✿ ✿					All zones
Lavatera trimestris ❀					All zones
Limonium sinuatum ✿ ✿ ❀ ✿ ✿					All zones
Lobelia erinus ✿ ❀ ✿					All zones
Lobularia maritima ✿ ❀					All zones
Matthiola ✿ ❀ ✿ ✿					1–45
Moluccella laevis ✿					1–45; H1, H2
Myosotis sylvatica ✿ ❀					A1–A3; 1–24, 32–45
Nicotiana ✿ ❀ ✿ ✿					All zones
Nigella damascena ✿ ✿ ❀					All zones
Papaver ✿ ✿ ❀ ✿ ✿					Zones vary
Petunia × hybrida ✿ ✿ ❀ ✿ ✿					All zones
Phlox drummondii ✿ ✿ ❀ ✿ ✿					A2, A3; 1–45; H1
Portulaca ✿ ❀ ✿ ✿ ✿					All zones
Rudbeckia hirta ✿ ✿ ✿					1–24, 28–43
Salpiglossis sinuata ✿ ✿ ✿ ✿					1–45
Salvia (some) ✿ ✿ ❀ ✿ ✿					All zones
Sanvitalia procumbens ✿ ✿					1–45
Scabiosa atropurpurea ✿ ✿ ❀					1–45; H1, H2
Tagetes ❀ ✿ ✿ ✿					All zones
Thunbergia alata (see page 183) ❀ ✿ ✿					All zones
Tithonia rotundifolia ✿ ✿					All zones
Tropaeolum ❀ ✿ ✿ ✿					All zones
Verbena (some) ✿ ✿ ❀ ✿					All zones
Viola (some) ✿ ✿ ❀ ✿ ✿ ✿					Zones vary
Zinnia ✿ ❀ ✿ ✿ ✿ ✿					1–45; H1, H2

TOP: *Petunia × hybrida,* Primetime series
BOTTOM: *Antirrhinum majus*

Matthiola incana

TOP: *Tagetes patula*
BOTTOM: *Calendula officinalis*

Amsonia tabernaemontana

Perennial Name	Bloom Season				Zones
	SP	SU	F	W	
Acanthus ✿ ❀ ✾	●	●			Zones vary
Achillea ✿ ❀ ✾ ✿ ❀ ✾		●	●		A1–A3; 1–24, 26, 28–45
Aconitum ✿ ✾ ❀ ✾		●	●		A1–A3; 1–9, 14–21, 34–45
Adenophora ✿ ❀		●	●		A2, A3; 1–10, 14–24, 30–43
Agapanthus ✿ ❀		●			Zones vary
Agastache ✿ ✾ ✿ ❀ ✿ ✾		●	●		Zones vary
Alcea rosea ✿ ❀ ✾ ✿ ❀ ✾ ✾		●			1–45
Alchemilla mollis ✾	●	●			A2, A3; 1–9, 14–24, 31–43
Alstroemeria ✿ ❀ ✾ ✿ ❀ ✾	●	●			5–9, 14–24, 26, 28, 31, warmer parts of 32, 34; H1
Amsonia ✾	●				Zones vary
Anchusa ✾		●			Zones vary
Anemone ❀ ✾			●		Zones vary
Aquilegia ✿ ✾ ❀ ✿ ❀ ✾ ✾	●	●			Zones vary
Artemisia lactiflora ❀		●	●		1–9, 14–21, 29–41
Aruncus ❀		●			Zones vary
Asclepias tuberosa ✿ ✿ ❀ ✾		●			Zones 1–45
Aster ✿ ✾ ❀ ✿ ✾			●		Zones vary
Astilbe ✿ ❀ ✿ ✾		●			1–7, 14–17, 32–43
Aurinia saxatilis ✿ ✾	●				1–24, 32–43
Baptisia ✿ ✾ ❀	●	●			1–24, 28–45
Begonia, Semperflorens group ❀ ✿ ✾		●	●		14–28; H1, H2
Bergenia ✿ ✿ ❀ ✾	●			●	Zones vary
Brunnera macrophylla ✾	●				1–24, 31–45
Campanula ✿ ✾ ✿ ❀ ✾	●	●			Zones vary
Canna ❀ ✾ ✿ ❀ ✾		●	●		6–9, 12–31, warmer parts of 32; H1, H2
Centaurea ✿ ✾ ✾	●	●			Zones vary
Centranthus ruber ❀ ✿ ✾	●	●			2–9, 12–24, 28–43; H1

Perennial Name	Bloom Season				Zones
	SP	SU	F	W	
Cerastium tomentosum ✿		■			A1, A2; 1–24, 32–45
Chelone ✿ ✿ ✿ ✿		■	■		1–9, 14–24, 28–43
Chrysanthemum ✿ ✿ ✿ ✿ ✿ ✿	■				Zones vary
Cimicifuga ✿		■	■		1–7, 17, 32–45
Coreopsis ✿ ✿ ✿		■			Zones vary
Corydalis ✿ ✿ ✿	■	■			2–9, 14–24, 32–35, 37, 39–43
Delphinium ✿ ✿ ✿ ✿		■			Zones vary
Dianthus ✿ ✿ ✿ ✿		■			Zones vary
Dicentra ✿ ✿ ✿	■				Zones vary
Dictamnus albus ✿ ✿ ✿		■			1–9, 31–45
Digitalis ✿ ✿ ✿ ✿		■			Zones vary
Echinacea purpurea ✿ ✿ ✿ ✿		■			A2, A3; 1–24, 26–45
Echinops ✿			■		A2, A3; 1–24, 31–45
Erigeron ✿ ✿ ✿ ✿		■			Zones vary
Eryngium ✿ ✿ ✿ ✿		■			Zones vary
Eupatorium ✿ ✿ ✿ ✿			■		Zones vary
Euphorbia ✿ ✿ ✿ ✿	■		■		Zones vary
Filipendula ✿ ✿		■			Zones vary
Gaillardia × grandiflora ✿ ✿ ✿		■	■		1–45; H1, H2
Gaura lindheimeri ✿ ✿		■			2b–35, 37, 38 (coastal), 39
Geranium ✿ ✿ ✿ ✿		■			Zones vary
Gypsophila paniculata ✿ ✿		■			A2, A3; 1–10, 14–16, 18–21, 31–45; H1
Helenium ✿ ✿ ✿		■			1–45
Helianthus ✿		■			1–24, 28–43
Helleborus ✿ ✿ ✿ ✿ ✿ ✿	■			■	Zones vary
Hemerocallis ✿ ✿ ✿ ✿ ✿		■			1–45; H1, H2
Heuchera, × Heucherella ✿ ✿ ✿		■			Zones vary
Hibiscus moscheutos ✿ ✿ ✿		■			2–24, 26–41; H1

Bergenia cordifolia

Chrysanthemum
× morifolium

Heuchera sanguinea

Hemerocallis 'Oodnadatta'

Perennial Name	Bloom Season				Zones
	SP	SU	F	W	
Hosta ✿ ❀		■			Zones vary
Iberis sempervirens ❀	■				1–24, 31–45
Iris ✿ ✿ ❀ ✿ ✿ ✿	■				Zones vary
Kniphofia ❀ ✿ ✿ ✿ ✿ ✿		■			2–9, 14–24, 28–41
Liatris ✿ ❀ ✿		■			A2, A3; 1–10, 14–24, 26, 28–45
Ligularia ✿ ✿		■			Zones vary
Limonium ✿ ❀		■			Zones vary
Lobelia ✿ ✿ ❀ ✿ ✿ ✿		■			Zones vary
Lupinus ✿ ✿ ❀ ✿ ✿ ✿		■			A1–A3; 1–7, 14–17, 34, 36–45
Malva ✿ ✿ ❀		■	■		1–9, 14–24, 31–45
Monarda ✿ ❀ ✿ ✿		■			A1–A3; 1–11, 14–17, 30–43
Myosotis scorpioides ✿ ❀	■				A1–A3; 1–24, 32–45
Nepeta ✿ ✿ ❀ ✿		■			1–24, 30, 32–43
Oenothera ❀ ✿ ✿		■			Zones vary
Paeonia ❀ ✿ ✿ ✿	■				A1–A3; 1–11, 14–20, 30–45
Papaver ✿ ✿ ❀ ✿ ✿ ✿		■			Zones vary
Pelargonium ✿ ✿ ❀ ✿ ✿		■			8, 9, 12–24
Penstemon ✿ ✿ ❀ ✿ ✿ ✿ ✿		■			Zones vary
Perovskia ✿		■			2–24, 28–43

RIGHT: *Kniphofia* hybrid
FAR RIGHT: *Liatris spicata* 'Kobold'

Perennial Name	SP	SU	F	W	Zones
Phlomis	●	●			Zones vary
Phlox	●	●			Zones vary
Phormium	●				5–9, 14–28; H1, H2
Physostegia virginiana		●	●		A3; 1–9, 14–24, 26–45
Platycodon grandiflorus		●			1–10, 14–24, 26, 28–45
Polygonatum	●				A1–A3; 1–9, 14–17, 28–45
Primula	●			●	Zones vary
Pulmonaria	●				1–9, 14–17, 32–43
Rodgersia		●			2–9, 14–17, 32–41
Rudbeckia		●			Zones vary
Salvia	●	●			Zones vary
Scabiosa	●	●			Zones vary
Sedum		●	●		Zones vary
Solidago, × Solidaster		●	●		1–11, 14–23, 28–45
Stachys		●			Zones vary
Thalictrum		●			Zones vary
Verbascum	●	●			Zones vary
Verbena		●			Zones vary
Veronica		●			Zones vary
Viola odorata	●			●	Zones vary
Zauschneria		●	●		Zones vary

Papaver orientale

Scabiosa columbaria
'Pink Mist'

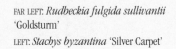

FAR LEFT: *Rudbeckia fulgida sullivantii* 'Goldsturm'
LEFT: *Stachys byzantina* 'Silver Carpet'

SPECIAL-PURPOSE PLANTS

Many annuals and perennials have appealing blooms—and quite a few have a little something extra. Some bear flowers ideal for displaying in bouquets; others are sweetly fragrant; still others are irresistible lures for birds and butterflies. And many bloom happily in containers as well as in the garden.

CUT-FLOWER PLANTS

ANNUALS

Ageratum houstonianum. Zones 1–45
Antirrhinum majus. Zones A3; 1–45
Calendula officinalis. Zones 1–45; H1
Callistephus chinensis. Zones 1–45
*Celosia. Zones A3; 1–45; H1, H2
Centaurea (some). Zones vary
Chrysanthemum (some). Zones vary
Clarkia. Zones 1–45
*Cleome hassleriana. Zones 1–45
Consolida ajacis. Zones 1–45

Coreopsis tinctoria. Zones 1–45; H1, H2
Cosmos. Zones A3; 1–45
Dianthus (some). Zones A2, A3; 1–24, 30–45
Gaillardia pulchella. Zones 1–45; H1, H2
*Gomphrena. Zones 1–45; H1, H2
Helianthus annuus. All zones
*Helichrysum bracteatum. All zones
Iberis (some). Zones 1–45
Lathyrus odoratus. All zones
*Limonium sinuatum. All zones
Matthiola. Zones 1–45
*Moluccella laevis. Zones 1–45; H1, H2
Nicotiana. All zones
*Nigella damascena. All zones
Papaver. Zones vary
Scabiosa atropurpurea. Zones 1–45; H1, H2
Tagetes. All zones
Tithonia rotundifolia. All zones
Tropaeolum majus. All zones
Viola (some). All zones
Zinnia. Zones 1–45; H1, H2

PERENNIALS

Achillea. Zones A1–A3; 1–24, 26, 28–45
Alcea rosea. Zones 1–45
Alstroemeria. Zones 5–9, 14–24, 26, 28, 31, warmer parts of 32, 34; H1
Anemone. Zones vary
Aquilegia. Zones vary
Asclepias tuberosa. Zones 1–45
Aster. Zones vary
Astilbe. Zones 1–7, 14–17, 32–43
*Baptisia. Zones 1–24, 28–45
Campanula (some). Zones vary

Cosmos bipinnatus

Centranthus ruber. Zones 2–9, 12–24, 28–43; H1
Chrysanthemum. Zones vary
*Cimicifuga. Zones 1–7, 17, 32–45
Coreopsis (some). Zones vary
Delphinium. Zones vary
Dianthus. Zones vary
Digitalis. Zones vary
Dictamnus albus. Zones 1–9, 31–45

Campanula medium

Helianthus annuus

Echinacea purpurea. Zones A2, A3;
   1–24, 26–45

Echinops. Zones A2, A3; 1–24, 31–45

Eryngium. Zones vary

Euphorbia (some). Zones vary

Gaillardia × grandiflora. Zones 1–45;
   H1, H2

Gypsophila paniculata. Zones A2, A3;
   1–10, 14–16, 18–21, 31–45; H1

Helenium. Zones 1–45

Helianthus. Zones 1–24, 28–43

Helleborus. Zones vary

Heuchera, × Heucherella. Zones vary

Iberis sempervirens. Zones 1–24,
   31–45

Iris. Zones vary

Liatris. Zones A2, A3; 1–10, 14–24, 26,
   28–45

Limonium. Zones vary

Lupinus. Zones A1–A3; 1–7, 14–17, 34,
   36–45

Monarda. Zones A1–A3; 1–11, 14–17,
   30–43

*Ornamental grasses (many).
   See pages 128–131

Paeonia. Zones A1–A3; 1–11, 14–20,
   30–45

Papaver. Zones vary

Penstemon. Zones vary

Phlomis. Zones vary

Phlox (some). Zones vary

Physostegia virginiana. Zones A3; 1–9,
   14–24, 26–45

Platycodon grandiflorus. Zones 1–10,
   14–24, 26, 28–45

Primula. Zones vary

Rudbeckia. Zones vary

Scabiosa. Zones vary

*Sedum (some). Zones vary

Solidago, × Solidaster. Zones 1–11,
   14–23, 28–45

Veronica (some). Zones vary

Viola odorata. Zones vary

* = flowers and/or seed heads can
   be dried

Single-flowered herbaceous peony *(Paeonia)* with petals surrounding a cluster of stamens.

FRAGRANT FLOWERS

ANNUALS

Dianthus (some). Zones A2, A3; 1–24,
   30–45

Iberis amara. Zones 1–45

Lathyrus odoratus. All zones

Lobularia maritima. All zones

Matthiola. Zones 1–45

Nicotiana. All zones

Phlox drummondii. Zones A2, A3;
   1–45; H1

Two old-fashioned cultivars of sweet pea *(Lathyrus):*
'Cupani' (left) and 'Painted Lady' (right).

PERENNIALS

Dianthus (some). Zones vary

Hemerocallis lilioasphodelus. Zones
   1–45; H1, H2

Hosta plantaginea. Zones 1–10, 14–21,
   28, 31–45

Iris, bearded. Zones 1–24, 30–45

Paeonia. Zones A1–A3; 1–11, 14–20,
   30–45

Phlox paniculata. Zones 1–14, 18–21,
   27–43

Viola odorata. Zones vary

Early-blooming lemon daylily, *Hemerocallis lilioasphodelus,* is one of the few daylilies renowned for its fragrance.

A female broad-tailed hummingbird arrives to enjoy blossoms of a violet delphinium.

TO ATTRACT BIRDS

ANNUALS

Calendula officinalis (seeds). Zones 1–45; H1

Centaurea cyanus (seeds). Zones 1–45; H1, H2

Clarkia (nectar). Zones 1–45

Cleome hassleriana (nectar). Zones 1–45

Coreopsis tinctoria (seeds). Zones 1–45; H1, H2

Cosmos (seeds). Zones A3; 1–45

Eschscholzia californica (seeds). Zones 1–45; H1

Gaillardia pulchella (seeds). Zones 1–45; H1, H2

Helianthus annuus (seeds). All zones

Impatiens (nectar). All zones

Lobularia maritima (seeds). All zones

Nicotiana (nectar). All zones

Nigella damascena (seeds). All zones

Petunia × *hybrida* (nectar). All zones

Phlox drummondii (nectar). Zones A2, A3; 1–45; H1

Salvia (nectar). Zones vary

Scabiosa atropurpurea (seeds). Zones 1–45; H1, H2

Tagetes (seeds). All zones

Tithonia rotundifolia (seeds). All zones

Tropaeolum majus (nectar). All zones

Zinnia (nectar, seeds). Zones 1–45; H1, H2

PERENNIALS

Agastache (nectar). Zones vary

Alcea rosea (nectar). Zones 1–45

Alstroemeria (nectar). Zones 5–9, 14–24, 26, 28, 31, warmer parts of 32, 34; H1

Aquilegia (nectar, seeds). Zones vary

Asclepias tuberosa (nectar). Zones 1–45

Coreopsis (seeds). Zones vary

Delphinium (nectar). Zones vary

Dicentra (nectar). Zones vary

Digitalis (nectar, seeds). Zones vary

Echinacea purpurea (seeds). Zones A2, A3; 1–24, 26–45

Eupatorium (seeds). Zones vary

Heuchera, × *Heucherella* (nectar). Zones vary

Kniphofia (nectar). Zones 2–9, 14–24, 28–41

Lobelia, red-flowered (nectar). Zones vary

Lupinus (nectar). Zones A1–A3; 1–7, 14–17, 34, 36–45

Monarda (nectar). Zones A1–A3; 1–11, 14–17, 30–43

Pelargonium (nectar). Zones 8, 9, 12–24

Penstemon (nectar). Zones vary

Phlox (nectar). Zones vary

Phormium (nectar). Zones 5–9, 14–28; H1, H2

Rudbeckia (seeds). Zones vary

Salvia (nectar). Zones vary

Solidago (seeds). Zones 1–11, 14–23, 28–45

Veronica (nectar). Zones vary

Zauschneria (nectar). Zones vary

Wide-open penstemon flowers offer an irresistible invitation to hummers.

Farewell-to-spring *(Clarkia amoena)* is a flashy nectar source for hummingbirds.

TO ATTRACT BUTTERFLIES

ANNUALS

Antirrhinum majus. Zones A3; 1–45

Consolida ajacis. Zones 1–45

Dianthus (some). Zones A2, A3; 1–24, 30–45

Gaillardia pulchella. Zones 1–45; H1, H2

Iberis (some). Zones 1–45

Lathyrus odoratus. All zones

Lobularia maritima. All zones

Phlox drummondii. Zones A2, A3; 1–45; H1

Salvia. Zones vary

Scabiosa atropurpurea. Zones 1–45; H1, H2

Tagetes. All zones

Tithonia rotundifolia. All zones

PERENNIALS

Achillea. Zones A1–A3; 1–24, 26, 28–45

Agapanthus. Zones vary

Aquilegia. Zones vary

Asclepias tuberosa. Zones 1–45

Aster. Zones vary

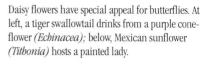

Daisy flowers have special appeal for butterflies. At left, a tiger swallowtail drinks from a purple coneflower *(Echinacea)*; below, Mexican sunflower *(Tithonia)* hosts a painted lady.

Astilbe. Zones 1–7, 14–17, 32–43

Centranthus ruber. Zones 2–9, 12–24, 28–43; H1

Chrysanthemum maximum. Zones A1–A3; 1–24, 26 (northern part), 28–43; H1

Coreopsis. Zones vary

Delphinium. Zones vary

Dianthus. Zones vary

Echinacea purpurea. A2, A3; 1–24, 26–45

Echinops. A2, A3; 1–24, 31–45

Erigeron. Zones vary

Eryngium. Zones vary

Eupatorium. Zones vary

Gaillardia × grandiflora. Zones 1–45; H1, H2

Iberis sempervirens. Zones 1–24, 31–45

Liatris. Zones A2, A3; 1–10, 14–24, 26, 28–45

Lobelia. Zones vary

Monarda. Zones A1–A3; 1–11, 14–17, 30–43

Penstemon. Zones vary

Phlox. Zones vary

Rudbeckia. Zones vary

Salvia. Zones vary

Scabiosa. Zones vary

Sedum. Zones vary

Solidago, × Solidaster. Zones 1–11, 14–23, 28–45

Verbena. Zones vary

Late-summer flower heads of *Sedum* 'Autumn Joy' are convenient landing strips for butterflies.

ANNUALS AND PERENNIALS
FOR CONTAINERS

A great many annuals and perennials are well suited to life in containers. Annuals are unsurpassed for container color in a hurry, while numerous perennials feature season-long attractive foliage in addition to lovely flowers. You can create stunning displays from annuals or perennials alone—and imaginative combinations of the two can be just as impressive.

Among containers, traditional terra-cotta is still a favorite; the standard design is available everywhere, and designer pots in European and Asian styles are becoming widely available. Other options include glazed ceramic, lightweight plastic (some of these mimic terra-cotta), and decay-resistant wood. For more on growing annuals and perennials in containers, see pages 70–71.

TOP: Ornamental grasses assort with blanket flowers *(Gaillardia × grandiflora),* purple coneflowers *(Echinacea),* and gloriosa daisies *(Rudbeckia hirta).*

BOTTOM: Silvery *Artemisia* 'Powis Castle' joins *Zinnia angustifolia* 'Crystal White'.

ANNUALS

Ageratum houstonianum. Zones 1–45

Anchusa capensis. All zones

Antirrhinum majus. Zones A3; 1–45

Calendula officinalis. Zones 1–45; H1

Calibrachoa. Zones 2–43

Catharanthus roseus. Zones 1–45; H1, H2

Celosia. Zones A3; 1–45; H1, H2

Cerinthe major. Zones 1–24, 32, 34–45

Cleome hassleriana. Zones 1–45

Coleus × hybridus. All zones

Convolvulus tricolor. Zones 1–45

Cosmos. Zones A3; 1–45

Dianthus. Zones vary

Gomphrena. Zones 1–45; H1, H2

Iberis. Zones 1–45

Impatiens. All zones

Lathyrus odoratus (bush kinds). All zones

Lobelia erinus. All zones

Lobularia maritima. All zones

Matthiola. Zones 1–45

Myosotis sylvatica. Zones A1–A3; 1–24, 31–45

Nicotiana alata (shorter kinds). All zones

Nigella damascena. All zones

Petunia × hybrida. All zones

Phlox drummondii. Zones A2, A3; 1–45; H1

Portulaca. All zones

Primula malacoides. Zones 1–9, 12–24, 31–41

Rudbeckia hirta. Zones 1–24, 28–43

Salpiglossis sinuata. Zones 1–45

Salvia splendens. All zones

Sanvitalia procumbens. Zones 1–45

Tagetes. All zones

Tropaeolum majus. All zones

Verbena (some). All zones

Viola (some). Zones vary

Zinnia. Zones 1–45, H1, H2

PERENNIALS

Acanthus. Zones vary

Agapanthus. Zones vary

Alchemilla mollis. Zones A2, A3; 1–9, 14–24, 31–43

Alstroemeria. Zones 5–9, 14–24, 26, 28, 31, warmer parts of 32, 34; H1

LEFT: Impatiens teams with sweet alyssum and licorice plant *(Helichrysum petiolare* 'Limelight').

BELOW: Versatile impatiens—the all-purpose container annual—dominates a window box; sweet alyssum *(Lobularia)* shows beneath. Design by Jonathan Plant.

Astilbe. Zones 1–7, 14–17, 32–43

Aurinia saxatilis. Zones 1–24, 32–43

Begonia, Semperflorens group. Zones 14–28; H1, H2

Brunnera macrophylla. Zones 1–24, 31–45

Campanula (some). Zones vary

Canna. Zones 6–9, 12–31, warmer parts of 32; H1, H2

Centaurea cineraria. Zones 8–30

Chrysanthemum (some). Zones vary

Coreopsis. Zones vary

Corydalis. Zones 2–9, 14–24, 32–35, 37, 39–43

Delphinium (shorter kinds). Zones vary

Erigeron. Zones vary

Gaillardia × *grandiflora.* Zones 1–45; H1, H2

Geranium. Zones vary.

Helichrysum petiolare. Zones 16, 17, 22–24

Hemerocallis (smaller kinds). Zones 1–45; H1, H2

Heuchera. Zones vary

Hosta. Zones vary

Iberis sempervirens. Zones 1–24, 31–45

Wire hanging basket is covered with pansies *(Viola* × *wittrockiana),* stock *(Matthiola),* and sweet alyssum *(Lobularia).* Design by Roger's Garden.

Limonium. Zones vary

Lupinus. Zones A1–A3; 1–7, 14–17, 34, 36–45

Nepeta. Zones 1–24, 30, 32–43

Ornamental grasses (smaller kinds). See pages 128–131

Papaver nudicaule. Zones A2, A3; 1–6, 10, 32–45

Pelargonium. Zones 8, 9, 12–24

Penstemon. Zones vary

Phormium. Zones 5–9, 14–28; H1, H2

Polygonatum. A1–A3; 1–9, 14–17, 28–45

Primula (many). Zones vary

Salvia (some). Zones vary

Scabiosa. Zones vary

Verbena. Zones vary

Lovely when viewed individually, annuals and perennials are perhaps even more beautiful in combination. A mixed planting delights the eye with its complements and contrasts in color and texture— and the best features of each plant are emphasized. A stately hollyhock looks still more imposing when fronted by a frothy mound of baby's breath or fernleaf yarrow; a blue aster is startlingly brilliant when set amid blossoms in gold and orange.

Garden DESIGNS

The preceding chapter covers factors to consider when you combine plants: their flower color, foliage character, and overall shape and size. In the following pages, you'll see those principles put into practice. The 12 garden designs presented here all use a wide variety of annuals and perennials, and their themes are just as varied. Some focus on particular colors or plants, others on seasonal beauty; still others are designed for "trouble spots" such as shady or dry areas. There's even a garden intended to draw butterflies and birds to your home—and one planted exclusively in containers. Use the plans as blueprints, or just let them inspire you to create similar designs perfectly suited to your own garden.

With not a square inch left unplanted, this summer garden offers a brilliant show that invites close appreciation from the garden path. Design by Kristin Home.

CREATING A
GARDEN PLAN

Some gardeners compose beautiful plantings without ever putting pencil to paper. They take small plants still in their containers, shuffle them around in the planting bed until the arrangement looks "right," and plant them then and there. More often than not, though, successful gardens—even the most casual-looking ones—begin on paper.

This sort of planning can begin during the drear winter months, effectively starting the gardening year a season early (if only in the mind!). Blocking out a design also lets you make unlimited changes before you actually dig the first hole, thus minimizing mistakes that might require hours of tedious transplanting later on.

Start by gathering a tape measure, graph paper (a ¼-inch grid is convenient), a ruler or T-square, and pencils (both ordinary lead and colored). Then measure the intended planting site, noting the location of shrubs and trees as well as any hardscape elements such as paths and fences. Transfer these measurements to your graph paper, letting one ¼-inch square equal 1 foot (if the garden is very large, you may want to double the scale). Keep this plot outline as your master sheet; make photocopies of it to use for your design ideas.

Once you have a scale drawing of the plot, you can start the creative work. With a plain lead pencil, sketch in the placements of the plants you want to include, using circles, ovals, or elongated drifts. As you plan, think about the plant combination tips in the preceding chapter and the ultimate size of each plant (see the encyclopedia beginning on page 86). To work out pleasing color schemes, use colored pencils to shade in the hues of flowers and leaves.

Young nursery-grown perennials, ready to be set out according to plan

R E A D I N G   T H E   P L A N S

For each of the following 12 planting designs, we provide a watercolor illustration showing the garden at its peak. Accompanying the illustration is a plot plan, with each plant shaded in the basic color of its flowers or foliage and labeled by a letter. These letters identify the plants for you: just find the corresponding letter in the plant list provided. For every plant in the list, we give botanical name and common name (if there is one); the number in parentheses indicates the total number of that plant used in the garden shown. For details on how to read these plans, review the example below (taken from page 54).

PLAN ILLUSTRATION AND DESCRIPTION

Botanical name

Common name

PLANT LIST

A. Artemisia lactiflora. White mugwort (1)

B. Echinacea purpurea 'White Swan'. Purple coneflower (7+)

C. Achillea millefolium, Summer Pastels strain. Common yarrow (3+)

D. Coreopsis verticillata 'Moonbeam'. Threadleaf coreopsis (1)

E. Verbena 'Homestead Purple' (4)

F. Dianthus × allwoodii 'Doris' (or other dark pink selection). Pink (3)

G. Liatris spicata 'Kobold'. Gayfeather (4)

H. Cerastium tomentosum. Snow-in-summer (7)

Cultivar name

I. Coreopsis auriculata 'Nana' (3)

J. Limonium platyphyllum. Statice (3)

K. Achillea 'Moonshine'. Yarrow (4)

Number of plants used in plan

Letter corresponds to plant location in plot plan

SUMMER OPULENCE

Spring may usher in the flowering year, but summer's show is no less dazzling—and many summer bloomers mount a longer-lasting display than the spring crowd. In keeping with the season's balmy temperatures, many of these blossoms come in distinctly warm colors. In this planting, sunny hues of yellow and rosy red are balanced by cooling blue, purple, and white. Give the garden a place in the sun (of course) and a climate with at least some winter chill.

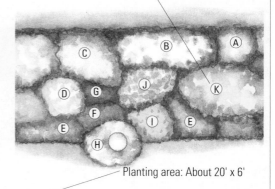

Planting area: About 20' x 6'

Dimensions of planting

PLANT LIST

A. **Hibiscus moscheutos 'Blue River'.**
   Rose-mallow (1)

B. **Centranthus ruber 'Albus'.**
   Jupiter's beard (3)

C. **Panicum virgatum 'Heavy Metal'.**
   Switch grass (1)

D. **Gaura lindheimeri** (1)

E. **Echinops 'Taplow Blue'. Globe thistle** (2)

F. **Chrysanthemum maximum 'Esther Read'.**
   Shasta daisy (4)

G. **Liatris spicata 'Silvertips'. Gayfeather** (1)

H. **Gypsophila paniculata 'Bristol Fairy'.**
   Baby's breath (1)

I. **Geranium phaeum. Mourning widow** (1)

J. **Aster × frikartii 'Mönch'** (3)

K. **Scabiosa caucasica.**
   Pincushion flower (6)

L. **Stachys byzantina 'Silver Carpet'.**
   Lamb's ears (5)

M. **Salvia × sylvestris 'Blauhügel'** (7)

N. **Dianthus deltoides 'Albus'.**
   Maiden pink (3)

O. **Iberis sempervirens 'Snowflake'.**
   Evergreen candytuft (4)

P. **Limonium platyphyllum. Statice** (2)

Q. **Veronica austriaca teucrium
   'Crater Lake Blue'. Speedwell** (1)

R. **Veronica spicata 'Icicle'. Speedwell** (2)

S. **Verbena 'Homestead Purple'** (1)

T. **Festuca amethystina.**
   Large blue fescue (4)

U. **Lobularia maritima. Sweet alyssum** (8)

COOL SUMMER ISLAND

In the heat of the summer, this oasis of cool, fresh color invites you to spend a bit of time on the chaise longue with an iced drink and a good book. The planting is anchored by a tall, white-blossomed rose-mallow (A) and an upright clump of switch grass (C). Weaving around and between these two foundations are blue and white flowers in variety, and leaves in gray, silver, and green. Flowering starts in spring with the evergreen candytuft (O), Jupiter's beard (B), and sweet alyssum (U), reaches a crescendo in midsummer—and continues into fall, weather permitting. You'll have the best success with this island in a full-sun location receiving regular water.

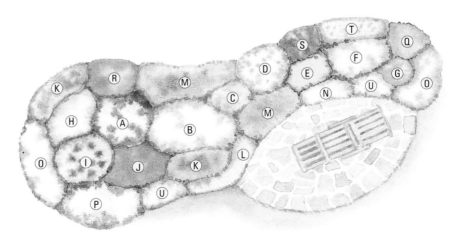

Planting area: About 20' × 8'

A WHITE GARDEN

White has an uplifting sparkle, a clean, pure look that's soothing to both eyes and spirit. What better place to relax, then, than a garden bearing only white flowers? Most of these plants are green foliaged, but the lamb's ears (S) has distinctive woolly white leaves that echo the planting's pristine blossoms. Floral offerings start in spring with the climbing rose (U), Siberian iris (K), peony (E), and dianthus (R); the remaining plants carry the show on into summer. This garden is best with at least some winter chill; the rose will need protection if winter temperatures drop below 10°F/−12°C.

PLANT LIST

A. Hibiscus moscheutos 'Blue River'.
Rose-mallow (1)

B. Digitalis purpurea 'Alba'. Foxglove (4)

C. Phlox maculata 'Miss Lingard'.
Thick-leaf phlox (5)

D. Delphinium elatum 'Galahad' (4)

E. Paeonia (herbaceous), white cultivar.
Peony (1)

F. Artemisia lactiflora. White mugwort (1)

G. Liatris spicata 'Floristan White'.
Gayfeather (2)

H. Baptisia alba. White false indigo (1)

I. Centranthus ruber 'Albus'.
Jupiter's beard (2)

J. Chrysanthemum maximum
'Esther Read'.
Shasta daisy (9)

K. Iris, Siberian, 'White Swirl' (4)

L. Filipendula vulgaris 'Flore Pleno'.
Dropwort (3)

M. Physostegia virginiana 'Summer Snow'.
False dragonhead (2)

N. Limonium platyphyllum, white form.
Statice (1)

O. Salvia × sylvestris 'Schneehügel' (5)

P. Geranium sanguineum 'Album'.
Bloody cranesbill (2)

Q. Iberis sempervirens 'Snowflake'.
Evergreen candytuft (2)

R. Dianthus × allwoodii 'Aqua'.
Pink (4)

S. Stachys byzantina 'Silver Carpet'.
Lamb's ears (6)

T. Cerastium tomentosum.
Snow-in-summer (3)

U. Rosa 'Climbing Iceberg'.
Climbing rose (1)

V. Buxus microphylla koreana.
Korean boxwood

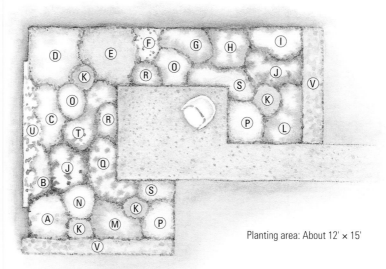

Planting area: About 12' × 15'

WARM-SEASON SIZZLER

The warmest time of year comes from late spring through summer—and this planting features a palette to suit the season, with flowers in yellow, orange, red, and mahogany. Foliage gets in on the act, too, in the reddish bronze leaves of shiso (R). Moderating the heat are a hollyhock (E), daylily (I), and sunflower (W) in pale yellow and cream, plus verbena (K) in cool, contrasting purple. A tranquil pool of water, inspired by Moorish gardens in Spain, is another soothing feature. Nearly two-thirds of the plants are perennials, giving the planting a permanent structure. The remaining annuals grow quickly and easily, amply repaying the effort required to plant them anew each year.

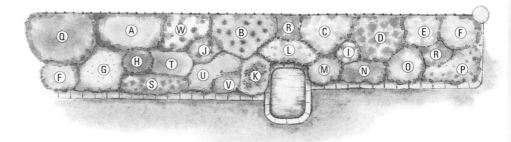

Planting area: About 24' × 5'

PLANT LIST

A. Achillea filipendulina 'Coronation Gold'. Fernleaf yarrow (3)

B. Gaillardia × grandiflora 'Mandarin'. Blanket flower (3)

C. Asclepias tuberosa. Butterfly weed (3)

D. Achillea millefolium 'Fireland' (or other red cultivar). Common yarrow (1)

E. Alcea rosea, light yellow selection. Hollyhock (3)

F. Chrysanthemum frutescens, yellow cultivar. Marguerite (2)

G. Coreopsis verticillata 'Moonbeam'. Threadleaf coreopsis (2)

H. Hemerocallis, red cultivar. Daylily (1)

I. Hemerocallis, cream cultivar. Daylily (1)

J. Canna 'Wyoming' (1)

K. Verbena, Tapien hybrid, purple selection (1)

L. Coreopsis grandiflora 'Sunray' (3)

M. Oenothera macrocarpa. Ozark sundrops (1)

N. Gaillardia × grandiflora 'Goblin'. Blanket flower (3)

O. Phlomis russeliana (1)

P. Gaillardia × grandiflora 'Baby Cole'. Blanket flower (3)

Q. Tithonia rotundifolia. Mexican sunflower (2)

R. Perilla frutescens purpurascens. Shiso (4)

S. Tagetes patula, Aurora strain. French marigold (5)

T. Celosia 'Apricot Brandy'. Plume cockscomb (5)

U. Tagetes erecta, Galore strain, yellow selection. African marigold (4)

V. Portulaca grandiflora, orange selection. Rose moss (2)

W. Helianthus annuus 'Moonshadow'. Annual sunflower (4)

BREATH OF SPRING

As the chill and gloom of winter slowly give way to brighter days, nothing is more heartening than flowers. At first, blossoms appear in scattered bursts; but as spring settles in for good, the garden is soon awash in waves of color. The cheery (and cheering) assortment of perennials shown here captures the spirit and bounty of spring in all its colors—compressed into one simple cottage-garden planting. This plan works best in a climate with some winter chill; site it in a sunny location.

All of these plants blossom in spring, and at least half of them are likely to continue to bloom into the summer months.

Kniphofia 'Shining Scepter'

PLANT LIST

A. Kniphofia, yellow cultivar. Red-hot poker (1)

B. Baptisia australis. Blue false indigo (1)

C. Paeonia (herbaceous), white cultivar. Peony (2)

D. Centranthus ruber 'Albus.' Jupiter's beard (4)

E. Penstemon barbatus 'Rose Elf' (3)

F. Aster × frikartii 'Mönch' (4)

G. Chrysanthemum coccineum. Painted daisy (3)

H. Iris, Siberian, 'Caesar's Brother' (1)

I. Hemerocallis, cream cultivar. Daylily (2)

J. Hemerocallis 'Stella de Oro'. Daylily (4)

K. Gaura lindheimeri 'Siskiyou Pink' (1)

L. Geranium 'Johnson's Blue' (4)

M. Papaver orientale, pink cultivar. Oriental poppy (1)

N. Coreopsis grandiflora 'Early Sunrise' (2)

O. Heuchera 'Palace Purple'. Coral bells (6)

P. Iberis sempervirens 'Snowflake'. Evergreen candytuft (2)

Q. Campanula portenschlagiana. Dalmatian bellflower (2)

R. Aurinia saxatilis. Basket-of-gold (3)

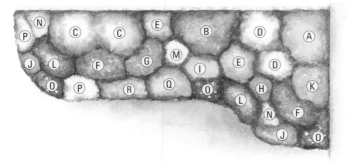

Planting area: About 20' × 8'

PLANT LIST

A. **Artemisia lactiflora.** White mugwort (1)

B. **Echinacea purpurea 'White Swan'.** Purple coneflower (7+)

C. **Achillea millefolium, Summer Pastels strain.** Common yarrow (3+)

D. **Coreopsis verticillata 'Moonbeam'.** Threadleaf coreopsis (1)

E. **Verbena 'Homestead Purple'** (4)

F. **Dianthus × allwoodii 'Doris' (or other dark pink selection).** Pink (3)

G. **Liatris spicata 'Kobold'.** Gayfeather (4)

H. **Cerastium tomentosum.** Snow-in-summer (7)

I. **Coreopsis auriculata 'Nana'** (3)

J. **Limonium platyphyllum.** Statice (3)

K. **Achillea 'Moonshine'.** Yarrow (4)

L. **Hemerocallis, cream cultivar.** Daylily (2)

M. **Dictamnus albus 'Albiflorus'.** Gas plant (2)

N. **Chrysanthemum maximum 'Aglaya'.** Shasta daisy (5+)

O. **Veronica 'Goodness Grows'.** Speedwell (4+)

SUMMER OPULENCE

Spring may usher in the flowering year, but summer's show is no less dazzling—and many summer bloomers mount a longer-lasting display than the spring crowd. In keeping with the season's balmy temperatures, many of these blossoms come in distinctly warm colors. In this planting, sunny hues of yellow and rosy red are balanced by cooling blue, purple, and white. Give the garden a place in the sun (of course) and a climate with at least some winter chill.

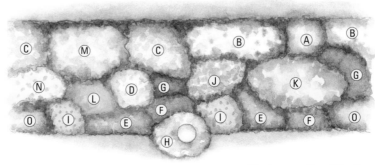

Planting area: About 20' × 6'

AUTUMN ASSEMBLY

Designed for fall—the last act of the gardening year, in many regions—this planting features the warm hues typical of the harvest season. Prominent is an assortment of daisy-flowered plants with wide-open, circular blossoms that offer a striking contrast in form to the fine foliage and filmy seed heads of the four featured ornamental grasses (A through D). Two of these daisies, both of them New York asters (F and L), bring lovely touches of autumn-sky blue to the composition.

There's no need to tidy up the planting before winter; let the daisies and grasses go to seed, providing tempting fare for birds.

Calamagrostis × acutiflora 'Karl Foerster'

PLANT LIST

A. Calamagrostis × acutiflora 'Karl Foerster'. Feather reed grass (1)

B. Miscanthus sinensis 'Malepartus'. Eulalia grass (1)

C. Muhlenbergia rigida. Purple muhly (2)

D. Festuca glauca 'Blausilber'. Common blue fescue (4)

E. Phormium tenax 'Bronze Baby'. New Zealand flax (1)

F. Aster novi-belgii 'Climax'. New York aster (4)

G. Solidago 'Goldenmosa'. Goldenrod (4)

H. Helenium 'Crimson Beauty'. Sneezeweed (2)

I. Achillea filipendulina 'Coronation Gold'. Fernleaf yarrow (3)

J. Gaillardia × grandiflora 'Burgundy'. Blanket flower (4)

K. Sedum 'Autumn Joy' (4)

L. Aster novi-belgii 'Professor Anton Kippenburg'. New York aster (4)

M. Hemerocallis 'Stella de Oro'. Daylily (1)

N. Chrysanthemum × morifolium, light yellow pompom type. Florists' chrysanthemum (3)

O. Tithonia rotundifolia. Mexican sunflower (3)

P. Helianthus annuus 'Italian White'. Annual sunflower (3)

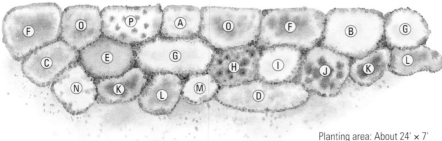

Planting area: About 24' × 7'

A COTTAGE-GARDEN BORDER

The original cottage garden was a riotous plot where "one of everything"—flowers, vegetables, even fruit trees—mingled in an apparently artless jumble. In Edwardian times, this humble garden was elevated to an actual landscape style, formalized in the English border. Variety is still paramount, and the look is still casual, but the sizes, colors, textures, and bloom periods of the plants are carefully calculated to keep things looking good from spring straight through fall. This candy cane–shaped border brings the spirit of cottage garden to a bed that will fit easily into most contemporary gardens.

PLANT LIST

A. Digitalis purpurea, Foxy strain. Foxglove (4)

B. Gypsophila paniculata 'Bristol Fairy'. Baby's breath (1)

C. Alcea rosea, Chater's Double strain. Hollyhock (6)

D. Foeniculum vulgare 'Purpurascens'. Bronze fennel (1)

E. Paeonia (herbaceous). Peony (1)

F. Aster × frikartii 'Mönch' (2)

G. Geranium endressii (1)

H. Iris, Siberian, white cultivar (1)

I. Physostegia virginiana 'Variegata'. False dragonhead (1)

J. Kniphofia 'Little Maid'. Red-hot poker (1)

K. Sedum 'Autumn Joy' (1)

L. Achillea 'Moonshine'. Yarrow (2)

M. Chrysanthemum maximum 'Alaska'. Shasta daisy (4)

N. Scabiosa caucasica. Pincushion flower (2)

O. Dianthus plumarius. Cottage pink (3)

P. Heuchera 'Palace Purple'. Coral bells (3)

Q. Phlox subulata, lavender cultivar. Moss pink (2)

R. Hemerocallis 'Stella de Oro'. Daylily (2)

S. Coreopsis rosea (2)

T. Iberis sempervirens. Evergreen candytuft (3)

U. Stachys byzantina 'Silver Carpet'. Lamb's ears (3)

V. Aquilegia, McKana Giants strain. Columbine (1)

W. Heuchera sanguinea. Coral bells (4)

X. Hemerocallis lilioasphodelus. Lemon daylily (1)

Y. Aurinia saxatilis. Basket-of-gold (3)

Z. Nepeta × faassenii. Catmint (2)

AA. Cosmos bipinnatus, Sonata series (6)

BB. Lobularia maritima. Sweet alyssum (6)

CC. Cleome hassleriana. Spider flower (1)

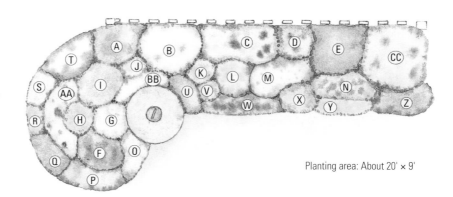

Planting area: About 20' × 9'

A SHADY GARDEN OF PERENNIALS

There's no shortage of choices for that tree-shaded patch of your domain. It's true that shade-loving plants aren't as numerous as those that like sun, but they still offer plenty of variety—both in foliage and in flower. In this planting, blossoms are spread out over a period that runs from late winter (in milder regions) clear into summer, and foliage is a constant source of beauty from spring through fall. Most of these plants can remain in place for many years, requiring only an annual late-winter cleanup. For best success, use this plan in regions with at least some winter chill.

Helleborus orientalis

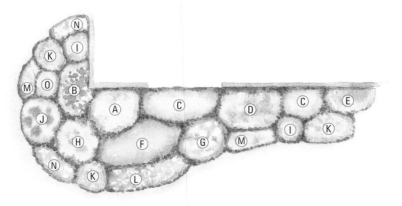

Planting area: About 24' × 12'

PLANT LIST

A. **Thalictrum rochebrunianum.** Meadow rue (1)

B. **Campanula persicifolia.** Peach-leafed bluebell (3)

C. **Alchemilla mollis.** Lady's-mantle (3)

D. **Digitalis × mertonensis.** Foxglove (6)

E. **Adenophora confusa.** Lady bells (3)

F. **Helleborus orientalis.** Lenten rose (4)

G. **Hosta 'Francee'** (1)

H. **Hosta 'Gold Standard'** (1)

I. **Hosta 'Blue Wedgwood'** (2)

J. **Brunnera macrophylla** (2)

K. **Bergenia 'Abendglut'** (4)

L. **Pulmonaria saccharata 'Janet Fisk'.** Lungwort (3)

M. **Heuchera americana 'Pewter Veil'.** Coral bells (5)

N. **Carex morrowii 'Variegata'.** Variegated Japanese sedge (5)

O. **Polygonatum odoratum 'Variegatum'.** Solomon's seal (1)

UNTHIRSTY ISLAND

Eschscholzia californica

As originally conceived, the "island bed" was a sizable group of plants rising from a sea of turf. In semiarid regions, seas of turf are a troublesome extravagance—but even there, the island concept still works. Just make it an oasis of flowers and foliage in an otherwise dry expanse (such as gravel or raked bare earth). With its colorful blossoms, foliage in gray and silver as well as green, and wide assortment of leaf sizes and shapes, this unthirsty island looks interesting throughout the growing season. The plants used here do best in the West and Southwest.

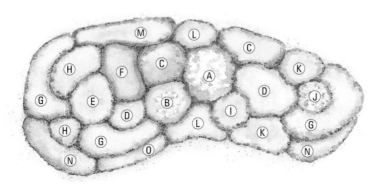

Planting area: About 20' × 9'

PLANT LIST

A. **Centranthus ruber 'Albus'.** Jupiter's beard (2)

B. **Gaura lindheimeri 'Whirling Butterflies'** (1)

C. **Phlomis russeliana** (4)

D. **Panicum virgatum 'Heavy Metal'.** Switch grass (3)

E. **Euphorbia characias wulfenii** (2)

F. **Artemisia absinthium.** Common wormwood (2)

G. **Artemisia 'Powis Castle'** (5)

H. **Muhlenbergia emersleyi.** Bull grass (3)

I. **Achillea filipendulina 'Coronation Gold'.** Fernleaf yarrow (2)

J. **Gaura lindheimeri 'Corrie's Gold'** (1)

K. **Oenothera macrocarpa.** Ozark sundrops (5)

L. **Verbena bipinnatifida** (5)

M. **Coreopsis grandiflora 'Sunray'** (5)

N. **Zauschneria californica 'Etteri'.** California fuchsia (5)

O. **Eschscholzia californica.** California poppy (from seed scattered over the area)

FOR BIRDS AND BUTTERFLIES

Plant it and they will come! Birds and butterflies are drawn to plants that supply them with food: nectar for butterflies and hummingbirds, seeds for seed-eating birds. This colorful group of late-spring and summer bloomers offers treats for all comers, with some plants providing both nectar and seeds. While the garden won't guarantee you a swallowtail or an oriole—that depends on where you live—you can still be assured of an array of winged visitors. This is a widely adapted planting, suitable for much of the country (steamy-summer Deep South excepted).

Achillea millefolium

PLANT LIST

A. Agastache rugosa. Korean hummingbird mint (1)

B. Alcea rosea. Hollyhock (6)

C. Centranthus ruber 'Albus'. Jupiter's beard (1)

D. Asclepias tuberosa. Butterfly weed (3)

E. Achillea filipendulina 'Coronation Gold'. Fernleaf yarrow (2)

F. Achillea millefolium, Summer Pastels strain. Common yarrow (4)

G. Echinacea purpurea 'Bravado'. Purple coneflower (3)

H. Chrysanthemum maximum 'Alaska'. Shasta daisy (7)

I. Coreopsis grandiflora 'Early Sunrise' or 'Sunburst' (12)

J. Liatris spicata. Gayfeather (1)

K. Sedum 'Autumn Joy' (3)

L. Salvia nemorosa 'Ostfriesland' (3)

M. Heuchera sanguinea. Coral bells (9)

N. Cleome hassleriana. Spider flower (1)

O. Dianthus gratianopolitanus. Cheddar pink (4)

P. Iberis sempervirens 'Purity' or 'Snowflake'. Evergreen candytuft (4)

Q. Antirrhinum majus, Rocket strain. Snapdragon (6)

R. Tagetes erecta, Sweet Cream strain. African marigold (4)

S. Tagetes patula, Aurora or Sophia strain. French marigold (6)

T. Nicotiana alata, Nicki strain. Flowering tobacco (10)

U. Salvia splendens. Scarlet sage (4)

V. Cosmos bipinnatus, Sonata series (4)

W. Petunia × hybrida (5)

X. Lobularia maritima. Sweet alyssum (8)

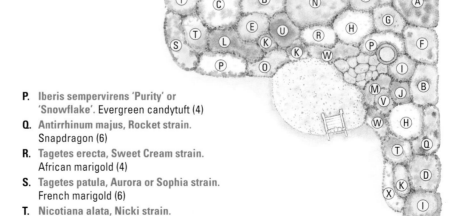

Planting area: About 15' × 18'

PLANT LIST

A. **Miscanthus sinensis 'Strictus'.**
Porcupine grass (2)

B. **Calamagrostis × acutiflora**
'Karl Foerster'. Feather reed grass (2)

C. **Panicum virgatum 'Haense Herms'.**
Switch grass (2)

D. **Pennisetum orientale.**
Oriental fountain grass (2)

E. **Miscanthus sinensis 'Yaku Jima'.**
Eulalia grass (1)

F. **Helictotrichon sempervirens.**
Blue oat grass (1)

G. **Pennisetum alopecuroides 'Hameln'.**
Fountain grass (1)

H. **Imperata cylindrica 'Red Baron'.**
Japanese blood grass (3)

I. **Deschampsia cespitosa.**
Tufted hair grass (2)

J. **Festuca glauca 'Elijah Blue'.**
Common blue fescue (5)

K. **Rhynchelytrum nerviglume**
'Pink Crystals'. Natal ruby grass (2)

L. **Rudbeckia fulgida.** Coneflower (3)

M. **Phlomis russeliana** (2)

N. **Hemereocallis 'Stella de Oro'.** Daylily (4)

O. **Tithonia rotundifolia.**
Mexican sunflower (1)

P. **Ricinus communis 'Dwarf Red Spire'.**
Castor bean (1)

Q. **Celosia, Castle series.**
Plume cockscomb (7)

FEATURING
ORNAMENTAL GRASSES

If you think of grass as nothing more than a flat green surface demanding hours of tedious watering and mowing, this planting will be a revelation. The decorative grasses used here come in all forms: foliage in fountains, shafts, and tussocks, blossoms and seed heads in spikes and plumes. And not all are green. You'll see steely blue-gray, near-red, and variegated leaves—and many change color in autumn, adding still more variety to the landscape. To highlight the grasses, the planting also includes a number of bright flowers and a shrubby annual with big, tropical-looking burgundy leaves.

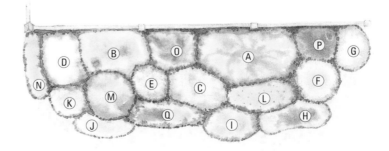

Planting area: About 25' × 8'

A GARDEN IN CONTAINERS

Deck the deck with lots of pots! You can achieve a bountiful display of annuals and perennials without a real plot of ground—great news for flower lovers limited to deck or patio gardening. And even if you do have a garden, you can create a colorful transition zone from house to yard with plants growing in pots carefully chosen to enhance the living bouquets they hold. Many of the plants shown here are described in the encyclopedia beginning on page 86; for still more good container choices, see pages 44–45. Try other annuals and perennials as well, such as the sweet-scented heliotrope and dainty twinspur shown in container G.

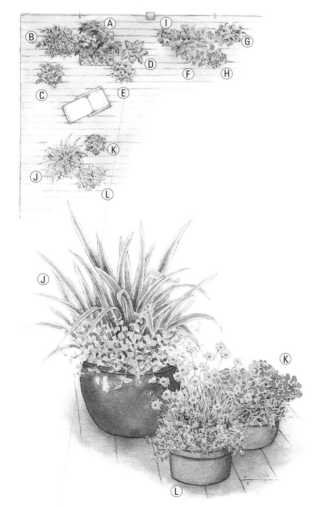

PLANT LIST

A. **Acer palmatum 'Bloodgood'.** Japanese maple (1)

AS UNDERPLANTING: **Viola odorata.** Sweet violet (4)

B. **Polygonatum odoratum 'Variegatum'.** Solomon's seal (1)

AS UNDERPLANTING: **Campanula poscharskyana.** Serbian bellflower (2)

C. **Coleus × hybridus** (mixed colors) (4)

D. **Hosta 'Gold Standard'** (1)

E. **Impatiens, New Guinea Hybrid 'Tango'** (1)

F. **Limonium perezii.** Statice (1)
Chrysanthemum paludosum (3)
Verbena, Tapien hybrid, purple selection (1)

G. **Heliotropium arborescens.** Common heliotrope (1)

AS UNDERPLANTING: **Diascia rigens.** Twinspur (3)

H. **Catharanthus roseus, Mediterranean series, apricot selection.** Madagascar periwinkle (2)

I. **Begonia, Semperflorens Group, Cocktail series** (3)

J. **Phormium 'Apricot Queen' or 'Duet'.** New Zealand flax (1)

AS UNDERPLANTING: **Helichrysum petiolare 'Limelight'.** Licorice plant (2)

K. **Tagetes patula, Aurora strain.** French marigold (5)

L. **Coreopsis grandiflora 'Early Sunrise'** (2)

AS UNDERPLANTING: **Lobelia erinus 'Crystal Palace'** (4)

PLANTING AND CARE

Flourishing garden beds, brimming with dazzling flowers and healthy foliage—that's what most gardeners envision when they plant annuals and perennials. In this chapter, you will discover how to make that picture a reality. As a first step, learn about your soil: its type, how to work it, and how to improve it with organic amendments. It's just as important to prepare the beds well and set out the plants properly.

Once your annuals and perennials are safely in the ground, they'll require attention to basic care such as watering, mulching, fertilizing, staking, and/or pruning. We also discuss common-sense pest and disease control (including photographs of a number of troublemakers) and offer suggestions for dealing with pesky weeds.

At the end of the chapter, we cover ways to start your own annuals and perennials (and biennials, too). These plants can all be grown from seed—sown directly in garden beds, in a wildflower meadow, or in containers (to transplant later to the garden). Perennials can also be propagated by division and by taking stem and root cuttings.

In spring, set out annuals around blooming tulips (or other springtime bulbs). As the tulips fade, the annuals will take over, carrying the flower show into summer.

Preparing the Soil

It's no secret that the healthiest and most attractive annuals and perennials grow in "good" soil. On these pages, we discuss the composition of garden soil, then move on to instructions for making compost to improve your soil; preparing planting beds; and using raised beds to deal with soil problems.

LEARNING ABOUT YOUR GARDEN'S SOIL

All soils are based on mineral particles formed by the natural breakdown of rock. They also contain varying amounts of organic matter, air, and water, as well as numerous living creatures—earthworms, nematodes, bacteria, fungi, and many others. The size and shape of a soil's mineral particles determine its basic characteristics.

Clay soils, also called heavy soils, are made up of very small particles that pack together tightly, producing a compact mass with microscopic pore spaces (the area between soil particles). Drainage is usually slow, since water and nutrients percolate slowly through the tiny pores. Clay soil is not easy for roots to penetrate, and during prolonged rainy spells (or if overwatered), it remains saturated, even to the point of causing root rot. Working clay soil is a miserable job: it's sticky when wet and rock-hard when dry. On the plus side, its slower drainage does allow you to water and fertilize less often.

While some annuals and perennials thrive in perpetually moist areas (see the list on page 19), most require well-drained soil. To check drainage, dig a 1½- to 2-foot-deep hole and fill it with water. After it drains, fill it again. If this second amount of water drains away in an hour or less, the drainage is good. If it remains for several hours or more, the soil drains poorly. To help improve drainage, you can add organic matter—but if drainage is extremely slow, you may need to plant in another (better-drained) part of the garden or in raised beds (see page 67).

At the other end of the spectrum are sandy (light) soils, with large, irregularly rounded particles and large pore spaces that allow water and nutrients to drain away freely. Plants growing in sand are unlikely to suffer root rot, but you will need to water them more often to keep their roots moist. You'll be fertilizing more often, too, to replace nutrients leached away by the necessary frequent watering.

Fortunately, most garden soils fall somewhere between the extremes of clay and sand. The best ones for plant growth, referred to as loam, have mineral particles in a mixture of sizes. They also contain a generous proportion of organic matter—and in fact, adding organic amendments (see "Making a Planting Bed," page 66) is one basic way to bring both clay and sand closer to loam in structure. These materials gradually loosen clay soils, improving drainage; in sandy soils, on the other hand, they enhance moisture retention by wedging into the large pore spaces between soil particles.

MAKING COMPOST

Composting is a natural process that converts raw organic materials into an invaluable soil amendment. You can make compost in several ways. The simplest method, called *slow* or *cold* composting, is to pile garden debris such as leaves, branches, and other trimmings in an out-of-the-way corner; eventually, the pile will decompose.

If you'd like to speed up the process, you can employ *hot* composting. This takes a bit more effort than cold composting: you provide optimum conditions for the organisms responsible for decay (by giving them the mixture of oxygen, water, and carbon- and nitrogen-rich nutrients they need), causing the pile to heat up quickly and decompose in a few months. Hot composting has the additional advantage of destroying many (though not all) weeds and disease pathogens.

You can make hot compost in a freestanding pile or use an enclosure, such as a wire cylinder or wooden bins. In both cases, the fundamentals of the process are the same.

GATHER MATERIALS. You will need more or less equal amounts by volume of brown matter and green matter. Brown matter is high in carbon and includes dry leaves, hay, and woody prunings. Green matter is high in nitrogen; it includes grass clippings, green leaves, fruit and vegetable trimmings, and manure. *Do not* compost bones, cat or dog waste, badly diseased plants or plant parts, or pernicious weeds such as bindweed and quackgrass.

CHOP MATERIALS. Shredding or chopping your raw materials into smaller pieces (ideally no more than an inch or two long) allows decay-producing organisms to reach more surfaces, speeding up the composting process. Use a lawn mower or shredder-chipper; or chop the materials with a machete on a large wooden block.

When you build a freestanding compost pile, make it at least 3 feet high and wide. This provides a mass of material great enough to generate the microbial activity needed for heating the pile thoroughly. When siting the pile, be sure to allow space alongside for turning.

BUILD THE PILE. Building the pile like a layer cake makes it easier to judge the ratio of brown to green materials. Start by spreading a 4- to 8-inch layer of brown matter over an area at least 3 feet square; then add 2 to 8 inches of green matter. Make layers of grass clippings only 2 inches deep; less-dense green materials can be layered more thickly. Add another layer of brown matter and sprinkle with water. Mix these first three layers with a spading fork. Continue adding layers (about two at a time), watering, and mixing until the pile is about 3 feet tall.

TURN THE PILE. In just a few days, the pile will heat up. In time, it will decompose on its own, but you can hurry things along considerably by turning the contents to add more oxygen—which is needed by the organisms responsible for decomposition. Using a spading fork or pitchfork, restack the pile, placing materials originally on the outside in its center; also add water to keep the pile moist. Continue turning the pile weekly, if possible, until most of the materials have turned into dark, crumbly compost, ready to add to planting beds or to spread as mulch.

THREE-BIN COMPOSTING SYSTEM

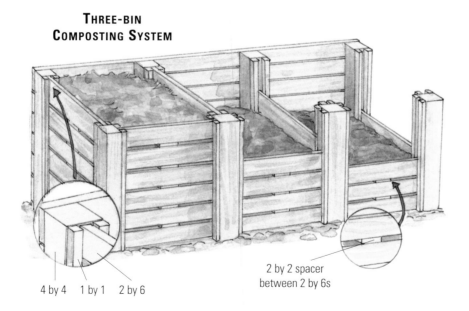

4 by 4   1 by 1   2 by 6

2 by 2 spacer between 2 by 6s

ACID OR ALKALINE SOIL: THE PH SCALE

Soil may be acid, neutral, or alkaline. A pH of 7 indicates a neutral soil; soils with a pH below 7 are acid, while those with a pH above 7 are alkaline. In general, alkaline soils are found in dry-summer regions with low rainfall, while acid types are associated with high rainfall and humid summers.

Most annuals and perennials grow well in soils ranging from moderately acid to somewhat alkaline; a few, as noted in the plant encyclopedia beginning on page 86, *require* somewhat acid or alkaline soils. Extreme acidity or alkalinity, however, causes problems, since it makes some nutrients chemically unavailable to plant roots. If poor plant growth makes you suspect that your soil is strongly acid or alkaline, have it tested. The kits sold in nurseries and garden centers will give you a ball-park reading. For more precise information, send a soil sample to a laboratory (look under "Laboratories—Analytical" in the Yellow Pages or check with your Cooperative Extension Office). Such tests can also uncover any nutrient deficiencies. The lab will tell you how and when to collect the sample and will give advice on correcting any problems the analysis reveals.

In a three-bin composting system, the left bin holds new green and brown material; the center bin contains partially decomposed material, while the right one holds finished or nearly finished compost. Turn the material in each bin weekly, moving decomposed material to the right. The right bin will be empty for a few weeks at the start.

MAKING A PLANTING BED

You may already have well-prepared garden beds and borders, ready to receive annual and perennial plants or seeds. However, if you're planting in a new area (such as a former lawn) or in a new garden, you'll need to put some time and effort into soil preparation to encourage your new plants to grow quickly and robustly. Begin by removing sod and controlling weeds; then loosen the soil and work in amendments.

1 Use a sharp spade to cut sod into sections, then push the spade under each section to sever the roots. Lift the sections away with your hands. (For more information on eliminating weeds and sod, see page 79.)

2 In small areas, you can use a spading fork to loosen the soil; for larger beds, you may wish to use a rotary tiller. The soil should be slightly damp when you work it; don't try to dig soil that's too wet or completely dry. Dig to a depth of 10 to 12 inches, breaking up clods of earth and removing stones as you go.

3 The next step is to amend the soil with organic matter, fertilizer, and any materials needed to correct pH. As mentioned on page 64, organic matter improves both clay and sand—and it helps plants grow even better in loam, too. Organic materials include compost (homemade or purchased), nitrogen-fortified wood by-products (such as ground bark and sawdust), aged manure, and peat moss; other choices may be available locally.

   Use generous quantities of organic matter, spreading at least a 3- to 4-inch-thick layer over the loosened soil. (Aged manure can be an exception; too much can burn roots and leach excess nutrients into the groundwater. To be on the safe side, spread it in a layer just 1 inch thick.) As a rule of thumb, a cubic yard of organic material should cover 100 square feet of planting bed to a depth of 3 inches.

   Phosphorus and potassium (two of the major plant nutrients) should be placed near plant roots to have the greatest benefit (see "Fertilizing," page 72), so it's best to work a fertilizer high in these nutrients, such as a 5-10-10 product, into the soil before planting. Spread the fertilizer over the soil, using the amount indicated on the label. Also add any amendments needed to alter soil pH at this time (see page 65).

4 With a spading fork or tiller, incorporate all the amendments evenly into the soil. Then level the bed with a rake and water well. If possible, let the soil settle for a few weeks before setting out plants or sowing seed. When you do plant, the soil will be easy to work, and planting will be a pleasure.

LEFT: Interlocking concrete blocks form the sides of this raised bed.

BELOW: A raised bed bursting with flowers is enclosed with boards held in place by sturdy posts.

BUILDING RAISED BEDS

Many gardeners choose to plant annuals and perennials in some sort of raised bed. This arrangement has a number of advantages. Such beds offer a good way to cope with problem soils. If the native soil is heavy clay, for example, the increased height will allow for better drainage. If your soil is too acidic or alkaline to grow favorite annuals or perennials, you can fill the bed with imported topsoil with a more neutral pH. In addition, raised beds made of decorative materials add interest to a garden's overall design. They bring plants closer to eye level, define boundaries, and, when filled with tall-growing plants, can help provide privacy by enclosing a deck, patio, or seating area.

The simplest raised beds are made by piling amended soil on the area you want to plant. For a slightly more formal look, though, you can enclose the bed with some sort of border; this helps contain the soil, as well. Good choices for borders include wooden boards (1½ to 2 inches thick), bricks, or stone. Whatever method you choose, loosen the existing soil first to ease penetration by roots and water. Then create the planting mound or fill the enclosure with good topsoil (either purchased or dug from pathways or other parts of your garden) amended with plenty of organic matter.

A low, brick-edged raised bed filled with perennials and other favorite plants adds color and structural variety to a courtyard garden.

SELECTING AND PLANTING

Choose your annual and perennial plants wisely, set them out carefully in well-prepared soil, and you'll soon have a flourishing garden. For information on starting plants from seed, see page 80.

CHOOSING PLANTS

Nurseries and garden centers sell annuals and perennials in various containers. Annuals are most often available in cell-packs or 4-inch pots, though you'll sometimes find them sold in gallon-size containers. Perennials are also sold in smaller containers as well as in gallon-size (or occasionally larger) pots.

Small plants are generally the best buy, and once in the ground, they usually become established more quickly and put out new growth sooner than larger ones. When you shop, look for compact plants with good foliage color and a root ball that holds together well but is not tangled or matted. Try to avoid plants in full bloom; they have already put so much energy into producing flowers that they will have little left to establish new roots in your garden. Once you bring the plants home from the nursery, put them in a shaded location and keep the soil moist until planting time.

WHEN TO PLANT

As noted at right, the ideal planting time depends upon the particular plant. Whatever the season, though, try to set out your plants during cool, cloudy, calm weather; they will get established more quickly if not subjected to stress from heat, bright sun, and wind. It's best to avoid planting in the heat of summer—but if you must do so, be sure to shade the new plants temporarily and pay special attention to watering once they are in the ground.

1-gallon pot

4-inch pot

Cell-pack with 1-inch cells

In addition to the containers shown above, you may find annuals and perennials sold in jumbo packs with six 2½-inch cells.

ANNUALS. These plants fall into two groups, cool-season and warm-season, differing in their bloom season and preferred planting time.

Cool-season annuals include calendula, pansy *(Viola)*, sweet pea *(Lathyrus)*, and many others (see the plant encyclopedia beginning on page 86). Also called hardy annuals, these plants perform best in the cool soil and mild temperatures of fall and early spring. They can withstand fairly heavy frosts; indeed, if they are to bloom vigorously, they must develop roots and foliage during cool weather. Gardeners in cold-winter areas should plant them in very early spring, as soon as the soil can be worked. Where winters are mild, they can be planted in fall for bloom in winter and early spring. To ensure winter flowers in these regions, timing is important: plant while the days are still warm enough to encourage growth but when day length is decreasing. If you plant too early in fall, the plants will rush into bloom before they become established; if planted too late, they may not flower until spring. Where winters are mild, cool-season annuals can also be planted in late winter or very early spring for spring blooms.

Warm-season annuals include cosmos, sunflower *(Helianthus)*, zinnia, and numerous other favorites. They grow and flower best in the warm months of late spring, summer, and early fall. They are tender to cold and may perish in a late frost if planted too early in spring. In cold-winter climates, set them out after all danger of frost is past; in mild-winter climates, plant in midspring. (In desert regions of the Southwest with very hot summers, however, certain warm-season annuals, such as petunias, are typically planted in early fall for bloom in later fall and winter.)

BIENNIALS. Most biennials are set out as small plants in fall to bloom the following spring or summer. However, larger plants may be available at nurseries in spring; set these out in the garden immediately for bloom within a few months.

PERENNIALS. If you're planting an entire new bed of perennials, do so in early spring or early autumn. If you are adding just a few new plants, try to set out summer- or autumn-flowering sorts in early spring, so that they will be well established by bloom time. For the same reason, plant spring bloomers in early fall.

SETTING OUT PLANTS FROM CONTAINERS

Before planting, prepare a bed as described on page 66—or, if you are setting out plants in an existing bed, work a shovelful of organic matter into the soil before planting each one. Then set out plants as illustrated below, spacing them far enough apart to prevent crowding. Once you've finished planting, spread a thin layer of mulch (see page 72) around the plants to keep the soil cool, conserve moisture, and discourage weeds. To lessen the possibility of rot, be sure to keep the mulch an inch or two away from each plant's crown.

1 Soak the plant, still in its pot, in a bucket of water for about 30 minutes or until the soil is completely dampened.

2 Dig a hole for each plant, making it the same depth as the container and an inch or two wider.

3 With your fingers, lightly separate matted roots. If there's a pad of coiled white roots at the pot bottom, cut or pull it off so the new roots will form and grow into the soil.

4 Place each plant in its hole so that the top of the root ball is even with the soil surface. Firm soil around the roots; then water each plant with a gentle flow that won't disturb soil or roots.

PLANTING BARE-ROOT PERENNIALS

Nurseries and mail-order companies sell some perennials as bare-root plants. These have most or all of the soil removed from around the roots, which are then surrounded with organic packing material and enclosed in plastic bags. If you'll be setting out such plants within a day or two after receipt or purchase, open the bags slightly, add a little water, and store in a cool place. If planting must be delayed by more than a few days, pot up the plants in small containers or heel them in—that is, plant them temporarily in a shallow trench in the garden.

Before planting bare-root perennials in their permanent position, prepare a planting bed as shown on page 66. If you are adding plants to an existing bed, work a shovelful of organic material into the soil for each perennial.

Remove the packing material and soak the roots in water for about 30 minutes. Dig a hole about twice as wide as the root system, as shown below. Then make a cone of soil in the center to support the roots. Set the plant on the cone of soil and spread the roots evenly. Fill the hole with soil so that the crown of the plant is level with or slightly above the soil, then water well. Finally, spread a thin layer of mulch around the plant.

INSTALLING A WINDOW BOX

Window boxes overflowing with annuals and perennials dress up your home, painting a colorful picture whether you're working outside or enjoying the view from indoors. And it's easy to change the plants with the seasons.

The boxes may be constructed of fiberglass, metal, or wood. If you opt for a wooden box, choose (or make) one of decay-resistant redwood or cedar. Be sure the box has drainage holes; one ½- to ¾-inch hole per foot of box length is ideal. Since water must drain away from house walls and foundations when the box is mounted, make certain that the holes are near the front of the box. To keep the soil from washing out, put a piece of plastic mesh or a layer of gravel in the box bottom.

Window boxes are heavy when planted, so it's essential to provide adequate support, such as sturdy brackets. If the box is to decorate a wooden wall, you'll need to take steps to discourage dry rot. Rather than attach the box directly to the wall, bolt one or two pressure-treated 2 by 2s or 2 by 4s to the wall, then fasten the back of the box to these horizontal runners.

PLANTING ANNUALS AND PERENNIALS IN CONTAINERS

Containers of all sorts—pots in varying sizes, window boxes, hanging baskets—offer a wonderful way to showcase annuals and perennials. The best choices for this sort of display are plants that bloom over a long period or have good-looking foliage throughout the growing season. On pages 44 and 45, you'll find lists of annuals and perennials well suited to container gardens.

In general, container-grown plants are more effective if spaced more closely than they would be in the ground. Place taller plants near the center; set lower-growing and cascading sorts around the edge. Be sure to think about how much sun or shade the plants need, then position the containers accordingly.

Note: Make sure that any container you use has at least one drainage hole.

SOIL MIXES. Plants in containers need fast-draining yet moisture-retentive soil, with a structure loose enough to allow roots to grow easily. Quick drainage means roots won't run the risk of suffocating in soggy soil; good moisture retention saves you from having to water constantly. Regular garden soil, even if it's good loam, is too dense for container use; it forms a solid mass that roots cannot penetrate easily, and it remains soggy for too long after watering. A better bet is one of the packaged potting mixes sold at nurseries or garden centers.

WATERING. Because they have only a limited amount of soil from which to draw moisture, container-grown plants require more frequent watering than those grown in the ground. During hot or windy spells, this can mean daily attention; in cool weather, it may be sufficient to water weekly or even less often. Check the soil in containers and water when the top inch or two is dry. When you do water, be sure to moisten the entire soil mass. A drip irrigation system can make watering container plants almost effortless; kits designed for this purpose are widely available.

Chosen for their attractive foliage, the plants in this container provide color and interest over a long season.

You can reduce watering frequency somewhat by adding soil polymers to your potting mix or by using a mix that already includes them. These tiny, gel-like granules absorb hundreds of times their weight in rain or irrigation water, holding it (and the dissolved nutrients it contains) for plants to use. Follow package instructions carefully for the amounts to add; if you use too much, some of the particles may ooze to the surface.

FERTILIZING. Because frequent watering leaches nutrients from the potting mix, container plants need regular feeding. Liquid fertilizers are easy to use; start right after planting and repeat at least every 2 weeks. You can also mix a controlled-release fertilizer into the potting mix before planting.

PLANTING A HANGING WIRE BASKET

Hanging baskets bring plants to eye level, decorating entryways, arbors, and patio overheads. Wire baskets are traditionally lined with loose sphagnum moss, but you can also purchase preformed liners made of sphagnum or coco fiber (a by-product of coconut farming).

Choose a wire basket at least 12 inches in diameter, since smaller baskets are more difficult to keep moist. Use a high-quality potting mix and add a controlled-release fertilizer and soil polymers (see facing page) to it. Small plants from cell-packs are easiest to insert in the basket.

1 Push soaking-wet sphagnum moss through the mesh from the inside to make an inch-thick lining that extends 1 inch above the basket rim.

2 Place enough potting mix in the basket to fill it by about one-third. Poke holes through the moss every

few inches all around the circumference of the pot, just above the potting mix. Gently push one plant, root ball first, through each hole, so that the roots sit atop the soil. Add more mix, covering the roots; gently tamp down.

3 Continue planting and adding potting mix in tiers. Finish by filling the basket almost to the top with mix; then plant the top surface. Water the basket well, then keep it moist but not soggy. In warm weather, you may need to water daily.

CASCADING PLANTS FOR HANGING BASKETS AND WINDOW BOXES

A few favorite trailing plants are listed here; check the encyclopedia beginning on page 86 for other choices.

Calibrachoa
Coleus
Convolvulus tricolor
Helichrysum petiolare
Impatiens walleriana
Ipomoea tricolor

Lobelia erinus
Lobularia maritima
Pelargonium peltatum
Petunia × *hybrida*
Tropaeolum majus
Verbena × *hybrida*

Ivy geranium *(Pelargonium peltatum)* cascades from a hanging planter.

CARING FOR ANNUALS AND PERENNIALS

Like other garden plants, annuals and perennials need basic care such as watering, mulching, fertilizing, pruning, and staking. Some perennials may need winter protection, as well; and most will need periodic dividing and rejuvenating (see page 83).

WATERING

All plants, even drought-tolerant sorts, must have water to grow and bloom. General moisture requirements for specific plants are noted in the encyclopedia beginning on page 86; in addition, you'll find a list of good choices for dry soil on page 18 and for perpetually moist conditions on page 19.

Also be sure to take climate, soil type, and the age of the plant into account when you're deciding how much and how often to water. If you garden where summers are long, hot, and dry, you will of course need to water more often than you would in a cool, moist climate. Likewise, if your soil is light and sandy, it will require more frequent irrigation than clay or highly organic soil. Young plants (including those that can withstand dry conditions when mature) need more frequent watering than do those with deeper and more extensive root systems.

APPLYING WATER. How you choose to water your plants depends on how often they need watering and how much water you have at your disposal. If watering is only necessary during the occasional dry spell, hand watering or a hose-end sprinkler will usually suffice. (However,

ABOVE: A minisprayer (also called a micro-sprayer) gently showers plants with water.

BELOW: A soaker hose lets water ooze slowly and steadily into the soil.

sprinklers that give off a strong spray may topple taller plants.) Where regular irrigation is needed all summer, use soaker hoses laid among the plants; or install a drip system outfitted with emitters (spaced to water each plant) or minisprayers. Drip irrigation is an especially good choice where water is scarce or expensive: it allows you to apply water only where it is needed, with no loss to runoff or wind.

If you're growing long, regular rows of plants, as in a cutting garden, you may opt to water in furrows. Dig a 6- to 8-inch-deep furrow along one or both sides of the row. Then let a hose run at one end of the furrow until the furrow is full.

Regardless of the watering system you choose, test the soil for moisture before you turn on the faucet by digging down a few inches with your fingers or a trowel. For small, newly transplanted annuals and perennials and those that require regular to ample moisture, water when the top inch or so of soil is dry. For established plants that require only moderate water, you can wait until the top 3 to 4 inches are dry.

Aim to soak the root zone when you water. Most annuals and perennials send their roots down to a foot or so, and large-growing sorts have even deeper roots. By watering the entire root zone rather than just the top few inches, you'll encourage the roots to grow deeply. Deeper roots have access to more moisture, letting the plants go longer between waterings; they are also less subject than shallow roots to the drying effects of heat and wind.

MULCHING

A layer of mulch around and between annuals and perennials serves several purposes. It helps conserve water, aids in suppressing weed growth, and, as it decomposes, improves the soil. Good mulches include compost (homemade or commercial), bark (ground, shredded, or chips), wood chips, pine needles, and various agricultural by-products such as ground corncobs and apple or grape pomace. Apply the mulch in a layer 1 to 2 inches thick, keeping it away from the plants' crowns (where the stems and roots join) to avoid the possibility of rot.

FERTILIZING

When plants are actively growing, they need a steady supply of nutrients. Most of the necessary nutrients are already present in soil, water, and air, but gardeners may sometimes need to supplement them—particularly the major nutrients nitrogen (N), phosphorus (P), and potassium (K). The label on a package of fertilizer notes the percentage (by weight) of each major nutrient the product contains, always presenting them in N-P-K order. For example, a 5-10-10 product contains 5 percent nitrogen, 10 percent phosphorus, and 10 percent potassium, while a 12-0-0 fertilizer contains 12 percent nitrogen but no phosphorus or potassium.

Products containing all three major nutrients are known as *complete* fertilizers. Those lacking in one or two of them are called *incomplete* and can be useful when a soil test indicates a deficiency in a certain nutrient. Of the three major nutrients, nitrogen is most likely to be in short supply: not only is it water-soluble and easily leached from soil by rainfall and watering, but it's also the nutrient used most extensively by plants. Phosphorus and potassium, in contrast, cannot move through the soil in solution and must be placed near the root zone to do the most good. The best way to get them there is to dig fertilizer thoroughly into the soil when you prepare it for planting. These two nutrients won't need to be supplemented as often as nitrogen.

For best results, plant annuals and perennials in a well-prepared bed enriched with organic matter and fertilizer.

NATURAL AND CHEMICAL FERTILIZERS. You can buy fertilizers in either natural (organic) or chemical (synthetic) form. *Natural* fertilizers are derived from the remains of living organisms and include blood meal, bone meal, cottonseed meal, and some animal manures, such as bat guano. Most contain lower levels of nutrients than chemical products. They release their nutrients more slowly, as well: rather than dissolving in water, they are broken down by microorganisms in the soil, providing nutrients as they decay. Most are sold and applied in dry form; you scatter the fertilizer over the soil, then dig or scratch it in. A few (fish emulsion, for example) are available as concentrated liquids to be diluted before application.

Many natural fertilizers are high in just one of the three major nutrients. For example, blood meal and cottonseed meal are good sources of nitrogen; bone meal is high in phosphorus, while greensand is a natural source of potassium. Some manufacturers combine a variety of organic products in one package to make a complete fertilizer.

Chemical fertilizers are manufactured from the chemical sources listed on the label. They may be sold as dry granules or as soluble crystals or concentrated liquids to be diluted in water before use. Because their nutrients are for the most part water soluble, they act faster than organic sorts (though only nitrogen moves through the soil to any extent); types used in liquid form provide nutrients especially quickly, making them a good choice for giving plants a quick boost. You apply the dry kinds as you would natural fertilizers, scratching or digging them into the soil. If you want gradual nutrient delivery rather than quick action, choose controlled-release sorts: they act over a relatively long period (3 to 9 months, depending on the brand) if the soil receives regular moisture.

A FERTILIZING SCHEDULE

As mentioned above, phosphorus and potassium are most effective when placed near plant roots. Thus, it's important to work a fertilizer containing these nutrients (as well as some nitrogen) into the soil before setting out annuals and perennials; a 5-10-10 product is a good choice. This job is easy to do when you're preparing a new planting bed (see page 66). If you're setting out just a few plants in an existing bed, sprinkle a little fertilizer into each planting hole and work it in well, taking care that it does not come in contact with plant roots. In either case, dig in organic matter along with the fertilizer.

For most perennials, this initial fertilizing will be adequate for the first year's growth. After that, you may need to replenish the soil's nutrients. Many gardeners find that a yearly application of compost, spread over the soil as an inch-thick mulch in spring or fall, takes care of all or most nutrient needs, though other gardeners add fertilizer anyway. If you decide to fertilize, do so in spring, as your perennials begin growing. Use a nitrogen-only (or predominantly nitrogen) product for this pick-me-up, since nitrogen is the nutrient most needed when growth begins and the only one that will leach into the root zone.

Annuals make more demands on soil nutrients than perennials do: they grow much faster, proceeding from seedling to flower in a matter of weeks. An application of fertilizer at planting time should carry the plants through the first half of the growing season. In cool-winter areas, give a second feeding after bloom begins, using a nitrogen fertilizer. Where winters are warmer and the growing season is longer, give supplemental feedings of nitrogen after flowering starts and again in late summer.

Take care not to overfertilize. Too much feeding can result in rank, lanky growth and sparse bloom. In addition, any excess fertilizer can simply wash away, often contaminating the groundwater.

PRUNING

Annuals and perennials aren't woody plants, but some still need pruning, in the form of pinching, deadheading, thinning, and/ or cutting back. Besides controlling growth, this sort of pruning often encourages more profuse bloom. To do most of these jobs, you can use small hand pruners (or even just your thumb and forefinger), but you may prefer hedge or grass shears for large-scale cutting back.

PINCHING. Nipping off growing tips increases branching from buds lower on the stem, making for a compact, bushy plant with more branches and therefore more flowers. Since pinching reduces a plant's height, it can make staking unnecessary in

PRUNING TECHNIQUES

Pinching growing tips makes plants more compact and bushy.

Deadhead spent flowers to encourage more bloom and prevent seeding.

Thinning helps control the size of plants and improves air circulation.

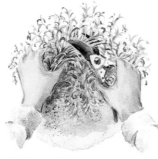

Cutting back improves appearance and may promote more bloom. Hold the stems together in a bunch and cut them all at once.

some cases. The branches of petunias and some geraniums *(Pelargonium)* should be pinched back by about one-third two or three times during the growing season to prevent legginess, give denser growth, and encourage repeat flowering. Florists' chrysanthemum *(Chrysanthemum × morifolium)*, too, should be pinched several times from spring until late summer to produce dense, leafy growth.

Perennials with a tendency toward ranginess benefit from a single pinching in late spring to early summer; these include the taller asters and artemisias, eupatorium, sneezeweed *(Helenium)*, phlox, and false dragonhead *(Physostegia)*. This type of pinching can also delay bloom; if you pinch back half a clump of asters in early summer, for instance, that section will come into blossom a bit later than the unpinched section, prolonging the flowering season by a few weeks.

DEADHEADING. This rather grim-sounding term simply refers to removing spent flowers. It's done partly for aesthetic reasons: the plant looks fresh and full of vigor without a drab load of dead flowers. Beyond this, however, deadheading prevents plants from setting seed. It thus keeps prolific self-sowers from swamping you with volunteer seedlings; and in many cases, it induces longer bloom, since a deadheaded plant often continues to produce flowers in an attempt to form seed and complete its life cycle. Of course, if you want to save seed for future planting, you'll avoid deadheading. In addition, some annuals and perennials and most ornamental grasses have attractive seedheads that many gardeners leave in place until winter or early spring, both to decorate the garden and to provide food for seed-eating birds.

THINNING. When you thin a plant, you cut out stems at or near the base. Thinning is sometimes done to reduce the size of a plant that is impinging on its neighbors. It's also a useful way to improve air circulation around and within a plant, thus discouraging powdery mildew in susceptible annuals and perennials such as bee balm *(Monarda)*, border phlox *(Phlox paniculata)*, and zinnia.

CUTTING BACK. This involves shearing or clipping off rangy growth and spent flowering stems, all at once. It improves the plant's appearance and often promotes new bushy growth and flowering stems. Cut back spreading, low-growing annuals such as lobelia and sweet alyssum *(Lobularia)* by about half when flowering diminishes; then water and apply fertilizer to stimulate another round of bloom.

Most perennials should be cut back at some point after flowering ends but before growth gets underway the following spring. This yearly removal of old growth makes the garden look neater, provides space for fresh new stems and leaves to grow, and deprives certain pests (especially snails and slugs) of potential hiding places.

PROVIDING WINTER PROTECTION FOR PERENNIALS

In colder climates, perennials sometimes need winter protection—not so much to shield them from cold (as is often thought) as to protect them from abrupt fluctuations in temperature. Assuming you have chosen plants hardy to the low temperatures typical for your region, winter damage generally occurs when the plants are subjected to alternate spells of freezing and thawing, a process that ruptures their cells, which then decay. Newly planted perennials without firmly established roots may be heaved from the ground by freeze-thaw cycles; the exposed roots are then likely to be killed by cold and desiccation.

Snow provides excellent protection for garden plants, but if you can't count on a good snow cover for most of the winter, it's best to lay down an insulating blanket of an organic material. Evergreen boughs, salt hay, marsh hay, and pine needles are all good choices; avoid materials such as leaves, which can pack down into an airtight mass. Wait until the soil freezes; then put the protection in place. Use two layers of evergreen boughs (setting the top layer at right angles to the bottom one) or about 6 inches of hay or pine needles. When spring arrives, remove the material gradually, taking it off before the plants put on much growth but not so soon that emerging leaves and shoots can be killed by a late freeze.

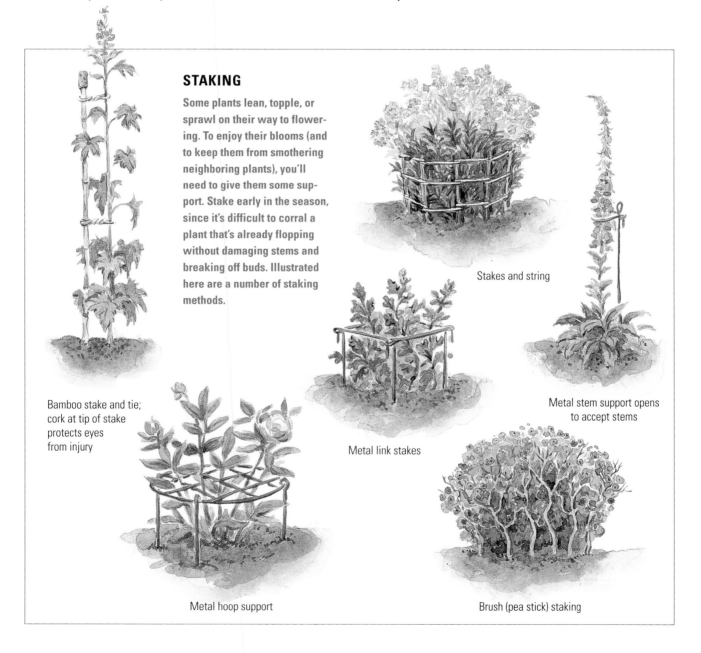

STAKING

Some plants lean, topple, or sprawl on their way to flowering. To enjoy their blooms (and to keep them from smothering neighboring plants), you'll need to give them some support. Stake early in the season, since it's difficult to corral a plant that's already flopping without damaging stems and breaking off buds. Illustrated here are a number of staking methods.

Stakes and string

Bamboo stake and tie; cork at tip of stake protects eyes from injury

Metal link stakes

Metal stem support opens to accept stems

Metal hoop support

Brush (pea stick) staking

Diseases, Pests, and Weeds

Most garden problems caused by diseases, pests, and weeds can be prevented through careful culture—and the problems that do occur can usually be managed without resort to chemicals, as noted on these pages.

DISEASES AND PESTS

Prevention is the most important step in managing diseases and pests: you won't have to solve problems that don't get a chance to crop up in the first place. Do your best to keep plants healthy and stress free. Set them out at the recommended planting time in well-prepared soil, and give them the care they need throughout the growing season. Be sure to choose plants adapted to your growing conditions; a plant that requires a cool, moist climate, for example, is quite likely to fall prey to diseases and pests if grown in a hot, dry region. Whenever possible, select varieties resistant to pests or diseases; some of these are described in the encyclopedia beginning on page 86. When you buy plants, look them over carefully to be sure you won't be importing problems to your garden. Finally, keep the garden free of debris that can harbor pests and disease-causing organisms. A thorough fall or winter cleanup is especially effective.

Check the plants growing in your garden frequently; regular tours give you a good opportunity to notice problems before they get out of hand. If you do spot trouble, take action only if the infestation is severe. A few aphids or chewed leaves are not cause for alarm, and problems often disappear quite quickly on

---

BENEFICIAL INSECTS

Hundreds of species of beneficial insects help gardeners keep pests at bay. The half-dozen we describe here are likely to be naturally present in your garden; some (as noted) can be purchased from nurseries or mail-order firms. To encourage beneficials, set out flowering plants that provide food for them. Good choices include yarrow *(Achillea)*, feverfew *(Chrysanthemum parthenium)*, coreopsis, cosmos, and sweet alyssum *(Lobularia)*, as well as herbs such as cilantro, dill, and fennel.

ASSASSIN BUGS. Slim, ½- to ¾-inch-long insects; may be red, black, brown, or gray. They feed on a wide variety of pests.

DAMSEL BUGS. Dull gray or brown, ½-inch-long, very slender insects with a long, narrow head. Nymphs resemble the adults but are smaller and have no wings. Both nymphs and adults feed on aphids, leafhoppers, and small worms.

GROUND BEETLES. Shiny black insects from ½ to 1 inch long. Smaller species eat other insects, caterpillars, cutworms, and grubs; some larger species eat slugs and snails and their eggs.

LACEWINGS. Adults are inch-long flying insects that feed only on nectar, pollen, and honeydew, but larvae devour aphids, leafhoppers, thrips, and many other insects, as well as mites. They resemble ½-inch-long alligators and are commercially available.

LADY BEETLES. Also known as ladybugs, these beetles and their larvae (which look like ¼-inch-long, six-legged alligators) feed on aphids, mealybugs, and the eggs of many insects. You can buy lady beetles, but they often fly away as soon as you release them. Freeing them at night or keeping them in cages for a few days after purchase may encourage them to remain in your garden.

SYRPHID FLIES. Adults, also known as flower or hover flies, look a bit like bees but have just one set of wings; they feed only on nectar. Larvae (tapered green or gray maggots with small fangs) consume dozens of aphids each day.

Assassin bug   Lacewing

Damsel bug   Lady beetle

Ground beetle   Syrphid fly

their own as pests die out naturally or move on. In many cases, natural predators will take care of infestations for you; some of the most important beneficial insects are shown on the facing page. Because damaging pests and beneficial or harmless creatures are often quite similar in appearance, it's crucial to identify the organisms you find accurately. For help with identification, check the photos and descriptions on these pages or consult your Cooperative Extension Office or a local nursery.

MANAGING DISEASES AND PESTS. You have a range of options for managing problems. Start with physical and/or biological solutions; turn to chemical controls only when all other methods fail.

Among the simplest of *physical* controls is handpicking: you just remove and destroy pests, infected leaves, or even whole plants, if necessary. Other physical approaches include strong water jets, which can knock pests from plants and often kill them, and various barriers and traps (see the descriptions of individual pests). *Biological* controls are effective in some cases, and they do not harm nontarget creatures. A familiar biological control is *Bacillus thuringiensis (Bt)*, a bacterium which, once ingested by susceptible pest larvae, causes them to stop feeding and eventually die.

As a last resort, turn to *chemical* controls, focusing on less toxic pesticides such as insecticidal soap, neem-based products, and products containing pyrethrins (the active ingredient is derived from a dried flower). Be aware that, despite their relatively low toxicity, these products will still kill beneficial and harmless insects. Use them only on plants that are being attacked and only when pests are present, and follow the label directions exactly. The management suggestions given below and on page 78 do not include recommendations for more toxic chemicals, since their registration and availability change frequently. If you feel you need stronger controls, consult your Cooperative Extension Office for advice.

DISEASES

DISEASE	DESCRIPTION	MANAGEMENT
Botrytis (gray mold)	Fungal disease. Soft, tan to brown spots or blotches appear on flowers and leaves; these later become covered with coarse gray mold.	Remove and discard dead or infected plant parts. Clean planting area thoroughly in autumn, disposing of all dead and fallen leaves and stems.
Powdery mildew	Fungal disease. Shows up as a powdery white to gray coating on leaves, stems, and flower buds. Heavy infestations debilitate and disfigure plants. Favored by moist air, poor air circulation, and shade—but needs dry leaves to become established.	Improve air circulation by thinning crowded plants. Spray with water to wash off fungus. Discard infected plant parts. Spray with copper soap fungicide, neem oil, or potassium bicarbonate.
Root rot	Fungal disease; sometimes called water mold. Active in warm, wet, or poorly drained soils. Young leaves turn yellow and wilt; plants may be stunted or may wilt and die, even in moist soil.	Keep soil moist, but do not overwater plants. Improve drainage or plant in raised beds. Remove and discard diseased plants.
Rust	A great many rust fungi exist, each specific to a certain plant. Yellow, orange, red, or brown pustules appear on leaf undersides; the powdery spores are spread by wind and water.	Plant resistant varieties. Improve air circulation. Remove infected leaves immediately; in winter, clean up all fallen leaves and debris. If watering from overhead, be sure plants will dry before dusk.

Botrytis

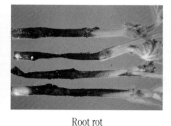

Powdery mildew

Root rot

Rust

PESTS

PEST	DESCRIPTION	MANAGEMENT
Aphids	Soft-bodied, rounded insects that range from pinhead to matchhead size. May be black, white, pink, or pale green. They cluster on new growth, sucking plant juices; heavy infestations distort growth. Some kinds transmit viral diseases.	Hose off with strong jets of water. Spray with insecticidal soap or a natural pesticide containing pyrethrins.
Cutworms	A variety of soil-dwelling caterpillars of various colors. They feed at night and on overcast days; during daylight hours, they hide underground, curled up in a C shape. Most cut the stems of young plants.	Protect young transplants from cutworms by encircling each with a can (with both ends removed) or a paper cup with the bottom cut out. Handpick at night.
Geranium budworms (tobacco budworms)	Striped caterpillars up to ¾ inch long; may be greenish, tan, or reddish. Besides geraniums, they attack petunias and other flowers, burrowing into buds and feeding from the inside. They also eat leaves and stems.	Remove dried-up buds and flowers that may harbor the pests. In fall, clear away dead annuals and infested parts of other plants to remove eggs. *Bt* kills budworms if applied before the caterpillars enter buds.
Japanese beetles	Half-inch-long beetles with a distinctive metallic green sheen; attack foliage of many plants. Major pests in the eastern U.S., they have been gradually moving westward.	Don't bring infested plants or soil (containing larvae) into unaffected areas. Handpick, use traps, or spray with a natural pesticide containing pyrethrins.
Leaf miners	A catchall term for certain moth, beetle, and fly larvae that tunnel within plant leaves, leaving a nearly transparent, twisting trail on the surface.	Pick off and destroy infected leaves. Neem extract may discourage adults from laying eggs on leaf surfaces, but once the insect is inside the leaf, sprays are not effective.
Mites	Tiny spider relatives found on leaf undersides (webbing is often present); leaf surface is pale and stippled. Foliage eventually dries out, turns brown. To spot them, hold a piece of white paper under affected foliage and tap plant. Disturbed mites drop onto the paper; they look like specks of pepper. Infestations increase rapidly in hot weather.	Hose off plants with strong jets of water. You can purchase predatory mites that feed on harmful mite species; lacewing larvae are also effective. Spray with insecticidal soap, sulfur, or neem oil.
Slugs and snails	Both are night-feeding mollusks; snails have shells, slugs do not. They feast on leaves, stems, and flowers, leaving tell-tale trails of silvery slime.	Handpick and destroy. Containers filled with beer and set at ground level attract the pests, which then fall in and drown. Use barriers: surround plants or beds with rings of diatomaceous earth, or enclose containers and raised beds with copper strips. Use bait containing nontoxic iron phosphate (Sluggo), which is not hazardous to other creatures.
Thrips	Near-microscopic pests that feed by rasping soft flower and leaf tissue. Leaf surfaces take on a shiny, silvery or tan cast.	Hose off plants with strong jets of water. Spray with insecticidal soap.
Whiteflies	Tiny white pests that fly up in a cloud when disturbed; they suck plant juices from leaf undersides. Damaged foliage is sometimes stippled with yellow and may eventually curl and turn brown.	Handpicking heavily infested leaves helps reduce populations. Yellow sticky traps (available commercially) can trap significant numbers. Hose off plants frequently with jets of water. Spray with insecticidal soap, neem extract.

Aphids

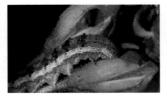

Geranium budworms

Leaf miners

Whiteflies

WEEDS

Weeds are plants growing where gardeners don't want them to grow. Besides being unsightly in the garden, they rob desirable plants of water, nutrients, and sunlight; some may also harbor diseases or harmful insects. Management does take effort, but working at it consistently for several years can significantly reduce the weed population in your garden.

MANAGING WEEDS. Winning the battle against weeds starts with prevention. Weed seeds often hitchhike into the garden in mulches, animal manure, or purchased topsoil, so ask about possible weed problems before you buy these products. After applying any of them, check frequently for new weeds and dispatch them immediately. Also check the soil of container-grown nursery plants and reject any with visible weeds.

Besides working to prevent weeds from showing up in the first place, you'll need to control those already present in your garden. For best success at this job, learn to distinguish between annual, biennial, and perennial weeds. *Annual* weeds—like annuals grown for ornament—grow shoots and leaves, come into flower, set seed, and die within a period of less than a year. Familiar examples include crabgrass, purslane, and spotted spurge. *Biennial* weeds, such as mullein, produce a cluster of leaves in their first year, then flower, set seed, and die the following year. *Perennial* weeds live for several years; they reproduce by setting seed and, in most cases, by producing spreading roots, bulbs, or tubers, making control more difficult. Common perennial weeds include bindweed, quackgrass, and dandelions.

You can control weeds by physical means or, if absolutely necessary, by chemical methods. Once you have destroyed them, take steps to prevent them from returning. Mulching bare soil around plants is an effective deterrent; see page 72 for more on organic mulches.

Landscape fabrics (above right) also help discourage weeds.

Physical controls, especially hand pulling and hoeing, are your first line of defense against annual and biennial weeds. Be sure to remove weeds before they set seed to prevent future generations. These methods will also help control perennial weeds, but you'll need to catch the plants while they're young. Once they have passed the seedling stage, it is usually necessary to dig out their roots—just pulling them up by hand (or cutting off the tops with a hoe) leaves behind root fragments, which will resprout. Even with assiduous digging, you'll probably have to repeat the process several times.

Spotted spurge

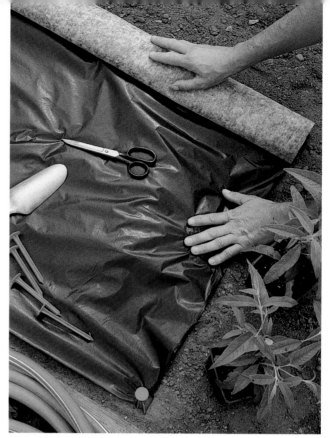

Landscape fabrics, unlike plastic, are porous, allowing air, water, and dissolved nutrients to reach the soil. Sold in nurseries and garden supply centers, these fabrics are best used to prevent weed growth around fairly permanent plantings of perennials; they aren't suited for beds of annuals where you change plants often. To install, unroll the fabric and use a knife or scissors to cut slits where you want to set out plants. After planting, cover the fabric with a 2-inch layer of mulch.

Smothering is another physical control. This technique effectively kills sod and weeds in areas earmarked for future planting. After mowing or cutting off the top growth, put down a layer of heavy cardboard, newspapers (make the layer at least three dozen sheets thick), or black plastic. Overlap these materials so weeds can't grow through the cracks. Anchor the covering with a layer of bark chips or other organic mulch. Leave the smothering materials in place for at least a full growing season; allow a year or more for tough perennial weeds.

Presprouting is a physical control useful for preparing planting beds for annuals or perennials in weedy areas. Dig out existing weeds and spread amendments over the soil. Till or dig the soil, water, and then wait a week or two for weed seeds to germinate. When they're only a few inches high, scrape them away. Then sow or transplant, disturbing the soil as little as possible to avoid bringing more weed seeds to the surface.

Chemical control of weeds with herbicides poses serious risks and, in most cases, should be used only when other methods have failed. Many herbicides can damage desirable plants if they drift through the air or run off in irrigation or rainwater. Some persist in the soil, hindering the growth of later plantings. If you do use herbicides, read the label carefully and follow directions exactly.

PROPAGATION

In gardening usage, "propagation" is a general term for the many ways of starting new plants. Annuals, biennials, and perennials can all be started from seed. For perennials, other options include division and taking root, stem, or basal cuttings; either of these methods will give you an increased supply of plants to expand your own beds and borders and to share with friends and neighbors. A greenhouse or cold frame (see page 84) is the ideal place to raise young plants resulting from division or cuttings—and to harden off those grown from seed.

SOWING SEEDS

Starting from seed is an economical way to get lots of plants. It also allows you to experiment with new and unusual varieties, since most seed catalogs and nursery seed racks offer more choices than you are likely to find among ready-to-plant young plants in pots and cell-packs. You can sow seeds directly outdoors—in a planting bed or cutting garden, for example—or in containers for later transplanting to the garden. Or, if you're planting wildflower seeds, you may want to create a natural meadow; this is a distinct garden style that involves a particular planting method (see page 82).

SOWING SEEDS IN THE GARDEN. Many fast-growing annuals and a few perennials can be sown right where they are to grow, either to cover an entire bed or to fill in empty patches among other plants. This is also a good way to grow a garden of flowers for cutting. Direct sowing saves the trouble of starting seeds indoors and transplanting the young plants. And some annuals grow better when sown directly in the garden, since they have delicate root systems or taproots that make successful transplanting difficult (though not impossible). Such plants include clarkia, California poppy *(Eschscholzia)*, sweet pea *(Lathyrus)*, love-in-a-mist *(Nigella)*, some poppies *(Papaver)*, and nasturtium *(Tropaeolum)*.

Plan to sow cool-season annuals and hardy perennials as soon as the soil can be worked in spring (some may also be sown in fall); wait until after the last frost to sow warm-season annuals and tender perennials. (For more on cool- and warm-season annuals, see page 68.)

Start by preparing a planting bed as described on page 66—even if you're planting only a small area. You can broadcast seeds, creating a natural-looking planting, or plant them in orderly rows. To broadcast, scatter seeds evenly over the prepared soil; then rake lightly, barely covering the seeds. To sow in rows, make furrows with a hoe or rake, following the seed packet instructions for depth and spacing. Sow seeds evenly, then cover them with soil to the recommended depth, patting them into the soil with your hands. Water the bed or rows of seeds with a fine spray, keeping the soil surface moist but not dripping wet. After the seedlings are up and growing, gradually cut back on watering, being sure to keep the root zone moist. When the seedlings have developed two sets of true leaves, thin them to the spacing recommended on the seed packet.

GROWING BIENNIALS

As noted on page 9, biennials typically complete their life cycle in 2 years. During their first year, they grow from seed into leafy but nonblooming plants. They live through the winter (experiencing the cold temperatures that most require if they are to bloom), then flower, set seed, and die in the following year.

To grow biennials, sow seeds in containers or directly in the garden at the time indicated on the seed packet—typically in mid- to late spring or in summer. Transplant seedlings started in containers into the garden in early fall, setting them in well-prepared soil; water as needed. In areas where the ground freezes, place a protective mulch of straw or chopped leaves around the plants, taking care not to smother the foliage rosettes. In spring, pull back the mulch and feed with a high-nitrogen fertilizer as soon as new growth begins.

The first-year foliage clump of biennial foxglove *(Digitalis purpurea)*.

In the second year, flowering spikes appear.

SOWING SEEDS IN CONTAINERS. Many annuals and perennials turn in the best performance when started in containers indoors, then transplanted outside later in the season. It's easier to provide young plants in containers with the warm temperatures and bright light they need for quick growth, and it's also easier to protect them from insects and birds. The information on the packet will help you decide when to plant. Timing does vary, but most annuals should be sown at some point from late winter to midspring—somewhere between 4 and 10 weeks before it's time to set them outdoors. Sow seeds of most perennials within this same winter-to-spring time period. Many kinds will be ready to transplant by early summer or fall (avoid planting in the heat of midsummer). Others, though, may not be mature enough until the following spring.

You can select from a variety of containers, including flats or trays (with or without dividers), small individual pots, and cell-packs. If you're reusing old containers, scrub them out and soak them for half an hour in a solution of 1 part household bleach to 9 parts hot water to destroy any disease organisms. Then proceed as directed below.

SEEDS TO SEEDLINGS

1 Fill each container to within ½ inch of the rim with damp seed-starting or potting mix, firming it gently. Scatter seeds thinly over the surface. Check the seed packet for recommended planting depth and cover with the proper amount of mix. (As a rule of thumb, cover seeds to a depth equal to twice their diameter.) Label each container with the plant's name and the date. Moisten lightly. Covering containers loosely with damp newspaper helps keep soil moist—but don't cover if the seed packet informs you that the seeds need light to germinate.

Place the containers in a warm spot. When the seeds sprout, uncover the containers, if necessary; then move them to a location where they'll be in bright light, such as a greenhouse or sunny window. (Or give them 12 to 14 hours of fluorescent light each day, setting the light 6 to 8 inches above the tops of plants.) Water with a fine mist when the soil surface feels dry.

2 When the seedlings develop their second set of true leaves, it's time to transplant them to larger containers, such as 3-inch plastic pots. Fill the new containers with moist potting mix. Remove the seedlings from their original pots by squeezing each pot's sides and turning it upside down, keeping one hand around the soil ball. Once the soil ball is out of the pot, carefully pull it apart with both hands and set it down on a flat surface.

3 To separate the seedlings, separate the fragile roots with a toothpick or skewer or tease them apart with your fingers.

4 Poke a hole in the new container's potting mix. Handle each seedling by the leaves to avoid damaging the tender stem; support the soil ball with your finger. Place each seedling in its new container and firm the mix around it. Water immediately, then set the pots in bright light (but keep them out of direct sunlight for a few days). Fertilize weekly with a fertilizer sold for starting seeds or with a liquid type diluted to half-strength.

About 10 days before the seedlings are ready to plant outdoors, harden them off so they can withstand bright outdoor sun and cooler temperatures. Stop fertilizing and set the seedlings outside for a few hours each day in a wind-sheltered spot in filtered light. Over the next week, gradually increase exposure until plants are in full sun all day. (Plants that prefer shade are an exception; they should not be exposed to day-long sun.) Alternatively, you can harden off seedlings by placing them in a cold frame (see page 84), opening its cover a bit more each day (as well as at night). Set out seedlings in the garden as shown on page 69.

PLANTING A WILDFLOWER MEADOW

For a carefree, natural look, gardeners turn to mixes of wildflowers and other easy-to-grow annuals and perennials. Though the word "meadow" conjures up the image of a sweeping, grassy expanse, a meadow-type garden can also be established in more confined spaces—in a small planting bed, around a mailbox, even in a container. Planted in a carefully prepared site, a wildflower meadow can give you months of pleasure, and provide food and nectar for butterflies and beneficial insects at the same time.

If you garden in a mild-winter climate, sow wildflowers in fall or early winter. In cold-winter areas, spring planting is more successful. Many sorts of wildflower mixes are available; most contain both native and non-native annuals and perennials, though you can find native-only mixtures. It's a good idea to choose a mix geared to your region—a so-called Midwestern wildflower mix, for example. Most wildflowers grow best in a sunny spot, but mixes for partially shaded sites are available. Local nurseries and mail-order firms sell wildflower seed mixes.

Follow these steps to sow and care for your meadow.

1. Cultivate the soil, removing all weeds. Most garden soils need no additional organic matter to support wildflowers successfully, but if your soil is very heavy clay or very sandy, spread on an inch or two of compost and work it in. Soak the soil thoroughly, then wait for weed seeds to germinate. When they do (allow about 3 weeks), hoe or pull them.

2. Rake the soil lightly to form shallow grooves. Broadcast the wildflower seeds over the soil according to package directions (you'll need about 1 ounce per 100 square feet). Rake lightly again to cover the seeds; water well. Continue watering just enough to keep the surface of the soil moist until seedlings appear.

3. Pull out any weeds as soon as they germinate. To help you tell the difference between weeds and wildflowers, sow some of the wildflower seeds in a nursery flat at planting time. When the seedlings in the flat come up, compare them with seedlings in the meadow planting; any seedlings that show up in the meadow but not in the flat are probably weeds.

4. Water and weed regularly during growing season. As the flowers fade, cut the plants back, shaking seeds from the faded blooms over the ground to provide a new flowering meadow next year.

Brilliant poppies *(Papaver)*, clarkias, and bachelor's buttons *(Centaurea cyanus)* glow in this wildflower meadow.

DIVIDING PERENNIALS

To divide a perennial, you dig it up, separate it into sections, and replant the pieces. Besides giving you new plants, division rejuvenates overgrown plants, improving bloom and overall appearance. Most perennials can be divided either in fall or in early spring. If you plan to divide in fall and you live in a cold-winter climate, do the job early enough in the season to let roots get established before freezing weather arrives (generally 6 to 8 weeks before the first hard frost).

Step-by-step instructions for dividing perennials are given below. A day or two before dividing, thoroughly moisten the soil around the clump. To make the plants easier to handle, many gardeners cut back the stems of larger perennials, leaving about 6 inches of foliage. If you'll be planting in a new bed, prepare the area (see page 66) in advance, so you can replant the divisions promptly. If you're replanting in the same location, place the divisions in a shady spot and cover them with damp newspapers while you replenish the soil.

To divide large, tough, or overgrown perennials such as these daylilies *(Hemerocallis)*, pry the roots apart with two spading forks inserted back to back in the center of the clump.

1 Loosen the soil in a circle around the clump, cutting 6 to 12 inches beyond the plant's perimeter with a shovel or spading fork. Then dig under the roots to free them from the soil. Lift the whole clump out of the ground; or, if it's too heavy to lift, cut it into sections. Set the clump (or pieces) in a convenient working spot, such as a path.

2 Gently tease some soil from the root ball so you can see what you are doing. For larger, fibrous-rooted perennials such as daylilies *(Hemerocallis)*, hose off as much of the soil as possible.

3 Now make the divisions. Look at the plant, noting natural dividing points between stems or sections. You can easily divide some perennials by pulling the clumps apart by hand. Those with mats of small, fibrous roots can be cut with a knife, small pruning saw, or trowel; types with thick, tough roots may require a sharp-bladed shovel or an ax. Try to divide the clumps into good-sized sections, which will grow and bloom more quickly than small divisions. Trim any damaged roots, stems, or leaves from the divisions.

4 Replant the divisions as soon as possible, then keep them well watered while they get established. You can also plant divisions in containers (a good idea if they're very small) to set out later or share with other gardeners.

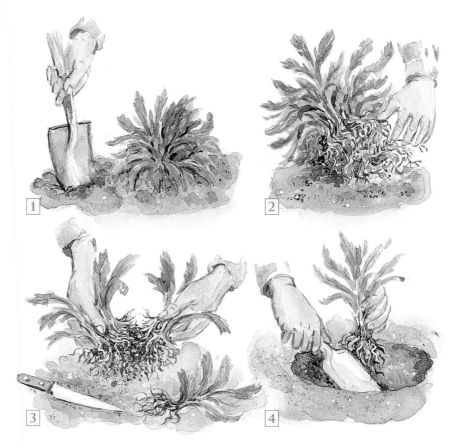

TAKING ROOT CUTTINGS

Some fleshy-rooted perennials—acanthus, sea holly *(Eryngium)*, and phlox, for example—can be increased from root cuttings. For most perennials, root cuttings are best made in late winter to early spring, when the plant is still dormant but close to beginning growth. (Exceptions are bleeding heart, *Dicentra*, and Oriental poppy, *Papaver orientale*; these are dormant in late summer or fall, and you should take root cuttings then.)

To obtain roots for cuttings, you can dig up an entire plant or just a section of its roots. Using a sharp knife, remove vigorous, healthy pieces of root. Those growing closest to the plant's crown will form new plants most quickly. Being sure to note which end was closest to the crown, cut the pieces into 2- to 4-inch-long sections. If you have only a few cuttings, you can insert them upright in a container filled with damp potting mix, with the top cut ends just at soil level. For larger numbers of cuttings (or for very thin pieces of root), fill a flat to within an inch of the top with potting mix. Lay the cuttings flat on top of the mix, then cover them with ½ inch more mix.

Water the planted containers well, then place them in a growing area such as a greenhouse or cold frame and provide protection from direct sun. Once stems and green leaves have formed, move the containers into full light and water them as needed. When the young shoots are several inches tall and new roots have formed (check by gently digging up a cutting), transplant them to individual pots and feed with liquid fertilizer.

COLD FRAMES

Used to protect tender plants or rooted cuttings during the colder months, as well as to harden off seedlings, a cold frame is simply a box with a transparent lid or cover. It acts as a passive solar energy collector and reservoir. During the day, the sun's rays heat the air and soil in the frame; at night, the heat absorbed by the soil radiates out, keeping the plants warm.

You can buy a ready-made cold frame or build your own, using rot-resistant lumber. For the cover, use a recycled window or staple polyethylene film to a wooden frame. Make the cold frame about 3 feet wide (so you can reach all the plants) and as long as you like; a longer frame will need several covers. The frame should slope from back to front to allow water to run off and to capture more heat. Place the frame in a site protected from harsh winds; if possible, orient it to face south. Sinking the frame 8 to 10 inches into the ground increases heat retention.

Ventilation is vital to prevent overheating. Open the cover when the temperature inside reaches 70 to 75°F/21 to 24°C; keep a minimum-maximum thermometer inside the frame to help keep track of temperature fluctuations. Close the cover in late afternoon to trap heat. On very cold nights, drape the frame with an old blanket to provide extra insulation.

TAKING STEM OR BASAL CUTTINGS

Most perennials, including tender ones often grown as annuals (such as begonia, coleus, and *Pelargonium*), can be propagated from stem or basal cuttings.

Stem cuttings, also called softwood cuttings, are taken from pieces of the stem or shoot. Basal cuttings, recommended for a few perennials, are quite similar; they consist of entire young shoots, cut from the parent plant so that each retains a piece of firm tissue at its base. They are rooted in the same way as stem cuttings, shown below. Take stem and basal cuttings during the active growing season from spring until late summer; the plant encyclopedia beginning on page 86 notes the best time to take them for each perennial.

1 Prepare containers first. Use clean pots or flats with drainage holes. Fill them with a half-and-half mixture of perlite and peat moss, or with perlite or peat moss alone. Dampen the mixture.

2 Gather material for cuttings early in the day, when plants are full of moisture. The parent plant should be healthy and growing vigorously. With a sharp knife or bypass pruners, snip 5- to 6-inch-long pieces from the plant, choosing vigorous young tip or side shoots.

    Remove and discard any flower buds, flowers, and small shoots growing laterally from the main stem. Then trim the stems into 3- to 4-inch lengths, each with at least two nodes (growing points). Make the lower cut just below a node, since new roots will form at this point. Remove leaves from the lower half of the cutting.

3 Dip the lower cut ends of the cuttings in liquid or powdered rooting hormone; shake off any excess. (Many gardeners omit this step and still get good results.)

    Using the end of a pencil, make 1- to 1½-inch-deep holes in the rooting medium, spacing them 1 to 2 inches apart; then insert the cuttings. Firm the medium around the cuttings and water with a fine spray. Label each container (or group of plants within a container) with the name of the plant and the date.

    Enclose each container in a plastic bag. Close the bag to maintain humidity, but open it for a few minutes every day to provide ventilation. Set the containers in a warm, shaded (but not dark) location.

4 The cuttings will usually take hold and begin growing roots in 1 to 5 weeks. To check, gently pull on a cutting; if you feel resistance, roots are forming. At this point, expose the cuttings to drier air by opening the bags; if the cuttings wilt, close the bags again for a few days (opening them briefly each day for ventilation).

    When the plants seem acclimated to open air, transplant each to its own 3- to 4-inch pot of lightweight potting mix. When they're well rooted and growing new leaves, they're ready to go into the ground.

ENCYCLOPEDIA OF ANNUALS AND PERENNIALS

The realm of annuals and perennials is a vast one, including enough plants to keep gardeners busy and happy for years—and each spring, nurseries introduce even more enticing choices. The following pages present a diverse selection that includes long-time favorites as well as promising newer varieties. You'll also find special features on ornamental grasses (pages 128–131), varieties of vegetables attractive enough to decorate beds and borders (page 153), and flowering annual vines (pages 182–183).

Each entry in this encyclopedia begins with the plant's botanical name; any alternate botanical names (former names that are still widely used or new ones that haven't yet taken hold) appear in parentheses. Entries that describe a number of species and hybrids are headed simply by the plant's genus—*Achillea*, for example. Other entries cover only a single species and are headed by both genus and species, as in the case of *Ageratum houstonianum*.

Next, we give the plant's common name or names (if there are any) and its botanical family. The plant is then identified as a perennial, biennial, or annual; annuals are further identified as cool-season or warm-season (see page 68). The following line notes the *Sunset* climate zones (see pages 644–648) in which the plant will succeed.

Recommended exposure is indicated next. *Full sun* means the plant grows best with day-long bright, unshaded sun. *Partial shade* and *light shade* refer to spots that are sunny in the morning but shaded in the afternoon, or to those that receive no direct sun but still get plenty of light. *Full shade* indicates that the plant prefers little or no direct sunlight.

Moisture needs are identified as well. *Moderate water* and *little water* apply to plants that need some moisture but prefer to have the soil go somewhat to quite dry between waterings. *Regular water* means the plant requires steady moisture, but the soil shouldn't remain saturated. A few plants need *ample water;* these grow happily in soggy soil.

Finally, we note the range of flower colors and the main bloom season for each plant.

ACANTHUS

ACANTHUS, BEAR'S BREECH
Acanthaceae
PERENNIALS
ZONES 4–24, 28–32, 34, 39, EXCEPT AS NOTED
FULL SUN OR PARTIAL SHADE
MODERATE TO REGULAR WATER
✿❀✿ FLOWERS IN LATE SPRING, SUMMER

A good choice for a garden accent, a thriving clump of acanthus has a bold, sculptural look—and when bloom time comes, it provides a strong vertical effect as well. Borne on arching stems, the dark green, 2-foot-long leaves are attractively lobed; in some species, the leaf margins are spiny. Rigid flower spikes rise to a height of 3 to 4 feet, set with tubular blossoms surrounded by spiny bracts (modified leaves). ***A. balcanicus (A. hungaricus)*** has deeply lobed leaves with wide gaps between the lobes; it blooms profusely in summer, bearing white or pale pink blossoms with purple bracts.

The most commonly grown species, ***A. mollis*** (Zones 5–24, 28–32), has shiny deep green leaves that are not as deeply lobed as those of the other two species described here. White flowers with purple-flushed bracts bloom from late spring to early summer. **'Latifolius'** has larger leaves than the species, flowers less freely, and reputedly tolerates more cold. ***A. spinosus,*** another species that blooms from late spring to early summer, has finely cut, spiny-margined leaves and white blossoms with purple bracts.

CULTURE. Where hardy, acanthus are almost too easy to grow. The roots spread rapidly underground, especially in loose, moist, well-enriched soil. To save yourself the task of constantly fighting the plants back, either allow them plenty of space or confine the roots with an 8-inch-deep barrier. Where summers are hot, locate acanthus in

Acanthus spinosus

partial shade; hot sun causes the leaves to wilt. In dry-summer regions, plants go dormant if not regularly watered.

Propagate acanthus by dividing the clumps. In mild-winter regions, do the job at some time from fall through late winter; in cold-winter regions, wait until spring. Note that any roots left in the soil will sprout, forming new clumps.

ACHILLEA
YARROW
Asteraceae (Compositae)
PERENNIALS
ZONES A1–A3; 1–24, 26, 28–45
FULL SUN
LITTLE TO MODERATE WATER
✿ ❀ ✿ ✿ ✿ FLOWERS IN SUMMER,
EARLY FALL

Ranging from foot-tall front-of-the-border plants in soft pastels to 5-footers with brillaint yellow flowers, yarrows are carefree, generously blooming perennials. Most species have aromatic gray or green leaves that are narrow, fernlike, and finely dissected. The flowers, appearing in summer and early fall, are tiny daisies packed tightly into flattened or somewhat rounded heads. They make good fresh cut flowers and also dry nicely for winter arrangements.

A. filipendulina 'Gold Plate' is one of the tallest yarrows, producing 6-inch-wide, deep yellow flower clusters on 5-foot stems that may require staking. A related hybrid, '**Coronation Gold**', tolerates a wide range of soils and climates; its shiny golden flower heads are 3 to 4 inches across, carried on strong, 2- to 3-foot stems.

Common yarrow, *A. millefolium,* forms a spreading mat of green to gray-green leaves. The species is a roadside weed with off-white flowers on 1- to 2-foot stems. Gardeners grow various selected forms and hybrids, including '**Cerise Queen**', a 1½-footer with magenta flowers; 2- to 3-foot-tall '**The Beacon**' ('**Fanal**'), with rich red blossoms centered in yellow; 3-foot-tall '**Fireland**', with flowers that open red, then fade to pink and gold; and 3- to 4-foot '**Credo**', bearing light yellow blooms that fade to creamy white. The **Summer Pastels** strain features 2-foot plants that flower the first year from seed in a range of colors, including white, purple, apricot, and yellow.

A. '**Moonshine**', a popular hybrid with gray-green, filigreelike foliage, has deep lemon yellow flowers on 1- to 2-foot stems. The related hybrid '**Anthea**' bears light yellow blooms on plants that tend to be more erect in habit.

A. ptarmica goes by the common name "sneezeweed" (note that it isn't the same plant as another sneezeweed, *Helenium*). The species can be quite invasive, but selected forms such as '**Angel's Breath**' and double-flowered '**The Pearl**' are less aggressive. They grow about 2 feet tall and produce white blossoms that are often used in bouquets as a substitute for baby's breath *(Gypsophila)*.

CULTURE. Yarrows grow best in reasonably good, well-drained soil. They are drought tolerant once established but look more attractive with moderate watering. Cut out the spent stems after flowering. Divide crowded clumps in spring.

Achillea 'Moonshine'

ACONITUM
MONKSHOOD, ACONITE
Ranunculaceae
PERENNIALS
ZONES A1–A3; 1–9, 14–21, 34–45
FULL SUN OR PARTIAL SHADE
REGULAR WATER
✿ ✿ ❀ ✿ FLOWERS IN SUMMER, FALL

Aconitum

The curious helmet- or hood-shaped flowers of monkshood are set closely along tall, leafy spikes that rise above attractive clumps of dark green, deeply lobed foliage. These plants can substitute for delphiniums in shady locations; they are effective in borders or near a bog garden. Keep in mind, however, that all parts of monkshood are poisonous, and be especially careful not to locate it where the tuberous roots could be mistaken for edible roots.

Summer-blooming *A.* × *cammarum* '**Bicolor**' grows to 4 feet and produces two-tone blossoms of white and violet blue. Flowering later (in late summer and early autumn) is *A. carmichaelii (A. fischeri),* bearing dense, branching clusters of deep purple-blue flowers on 2- to

Aconitum napellus

4-foot stems. An early-summer bloomer is **A. 'Ivorine',** a compact, 1½-foot-tall form topped with many clusters of creamy white flowers. Common monkshood, **A. napellus,** flowers in late summer; it grows 2 to 5 feet tall and is available in blue, violet, pink, and white forms.

CULTURE. Plant monkshood in moist, fertile soil enriched with compost. Plants grow best in cool-summer regions with some winter chill; they are difficult to establish in warm, dry climates. Clumps can remain undisturbed for years with no loss of vigor and bloom quality—and in fact, it's best not to disturb established plants. If you want to increase your plantings, however, you can carefully separate and replant the tuberous roots in very early spring. Mulch new plants and transplanted roots the first winter.

ADENOPHORA
LADY BELLS
Campanulaceae (Lobeliaceae)
PERENNIALS
ZONES A2, A3; 1–10, 14–24, 30–43
FULL SUN OR LIGHT SHADE
MODERATE TO REGULAR WATER
✿ ❀ FLOWERS IN SUMMER

These are slim, erect plants with narrow, leafy stems that bear rows of charming, fragrant, bell-like, typically blue flowers along their upper portions. They look much like campanulas (to which they are related) and may substitute for them in the hot, humid climates where campanulas often fail. Group several plants together for the showiest display.

Common lady bells, **A. confusa,** grows 2 to 3 feet tall and 2 feet wide. The nodding flowers are deep blue. Lilyleaf lady bells, **A. liliifolia,** is similar but smaller, just 1½ feet high and a foot wide; its blooms are pale lavender blue or, in some forms, white.

CULTURE. Plant lady bells in rich, well-drained soil. When buying container-grown plants, look for young ones, since older plants have deep, fleshy roots that do not transplant readily. For the same reason, it's best not to divide clumps— division harms the roots and is rarely successful. Instead, propagate lady bells by sowing the fine seeds outdoors in containers in fall (as soon as seed ripens) or indoors in late winter. Plants may self-seed abundantly; pull out seedlings you don't want.

Adenophora confusa

AGAPANTHUS
AGAPANTHUS, LILY-OF-THE-NILE
Amaryllidaceae
PERENNIALS
ZONES VARY
FULL SUN OR LIGHT SHADE
LITTLE TO REGULAR WATER
✿ ❀ FLOWERS IN SUMMER

These elegant, stately, summer-blooming plants feature fountainlike clumps of handsome, strap-shaped foliage that send up sturdy, 1- to 5-foot stems topped with rounded clusters containing dozens of tubular flowers. Colors include almost every shade of blue, from the palest tints to deep midnight, as well as sparkling white.

A number of species and hybrids are available. Two typically evergreen choices are **A. africanus (A. umbellatus)** and **A. praecox orientalis (A. orientalis);** both are successful in Zones 6–9, 12–24, 28–31, H1, H2. A. africanus has leaves that reach about a foot long and 1½- to 2-foot flower stalks carrying 6-inch-wide clusters of 20 to 50 blue flowers. **'Albus'** is a white-flowered cultivar that looks especially showy in the night garden.

A. praecox orientalis grows altogether larger than A. africanus, with 1- to 2-foot-long leaves and 4- to 5-foot stems carrying 8- to 12-inch-wide heads of up to 100 blue or white flowers. Hybrid selections include 3- to 4-foot-tall **'Midknight Blue',** with exceptionally deep blue flowers, and the outstanding dwarf **'Peter Pan',** with foliage clumps just 1 foot tall and profuse blue flowers atop 1- to 1½-foot-high stems.

Agapanthus 'Peter Pan'

The more cold-hardy **Headbourne Hybrids** and *A. inapertus* (both suitable for Zones 4–9, 12–21, 28–31, warmer parts of 32) are deciduous in winter. The Headbourne Hybrids have fairly narrow, upright leaves and 2- to 3-foot-tall stems bearing 6-inch-wide flower heads; colors include many shades of blue as well as white. *A. inapertus* is taller, reaching 4 to 5 feet in bloom, and features deep blue blossoms in drooping, 4- to 6-inch-wide clusters.

CULTURE. Tough and durable, agapanthus thrive in loamy soil with regular water, but they tolerate poor soils, and, once established, can get along with little or no irrigation. They flower most freely in sun but also grow and bloom fairly well in light shade. Clumps can remain in place for many years before they need dividing; when it's time to divide, do the job in early spring.

In zones too cold for in-ground planting, grow agapanthus in containers placed in the garden, around a pool, or on a deck or patio. When winter weather comes, move the containers to a frost-free place and allow the crowns to dry out; as spring approaches, move them into bright light and begin to water again.

Agapanthus praecox orientalis

These showy mint-family members have aromatic foliage, often delightfully reminiscent of licorice; in summer and fall, they send up blossom spikes set with whorls of small, tubular flowers. Though frequently planted in herb gardens, they are equally at home in borders and large containers.

A. barberi (Zones 2–24, 29–32, 34, 39), reaching 2 feet tall, has 6- to 12-inch spikes of reddish purple flowers. Its ovate green leaves are about 2 inches long. Anise hyssop, **A. foeniculum** (Zones A3; 1–24, 28–41), forms an erect, bushy plant to 5 feet tall, clothed in lance-shaped, gray-green, 2- to 3-inch leaves with downy undersides. Its dense clusters of lilac-blue flowers are borne in 4-inch spikes. It blooms the first year from seed and reseeds freely. Korean hummingbird mint, **A. rugosa** (Zones 4–24, 28–33), bearing purplish blue blossoms, grows about 5 feet tall. Its ovate, tooth-edged, 2½- to 3-inch-long leaves are glossy green with a purplish tinge.

Among hybrid agastaches are **'Blue Fortune'**, to 3 feet tall, with blue blossom spikes; and the shorter **'Firebird'**, which grows just 1½ to 2 feet tall and bears coppery orange-red blooms. Both grow in Zones 4–24, 28–33. **'Apricot Sunrise'** (Zones 2–24, 29–32, 34, 39) is a 2½-footer with pale orange flowers.

CULTURE. Plant agastaches in well-drained soil. They tolerate some drought but grow and bloom best with regular water. A full-sun location will yield the most prolific flower show, but you'll get a good performance in light shade as well. Propagate by seed sown indoors in late winter, division in spring, or stem cuttings.

AGASTACHE
AGASTACHE, HYSSOP
Lamiaceae (Labiatae)
PERENNIALS
ZONES VARY
FULL SUN OR PARTIAL SHADE
MODERATE TO REGULAR WATER
✿ ✿ ❀ ✿ ✿ ✿ FLOWERS IN SUMMER, FALL

Agastache 'Blue Fortune'

Floss flower is a reliable favorite for color from summer until frost, a good choice for edging borders and for use in beds and containers. In mild-winter areas, it can be grown as a fall- and winter-flowering annual. The plants have a mounded form, with soft, hairy green leaves that are usually heart shaped at the base. Individual flowers are tiny but are borne in dense clusters resembling powder puffs. Among the many blue-blossomed varieties are some of the truest blues available to gardeners. These include dwarf sorts (about 6 inches in height) such as **'Blue Danube' ('Blue Puffs')**, **'Dwarf Blue Bedder'**, and **'Royal Delft'**; 8- to 10-inch-high **'Blue Lagoon'**, with masses of navy blue flowers; and foot-tall **'Capri'** and **'Southern Cross'**, bearing blue blossoms with brightly contrasting white centers. **'Blue Horizon'**, to 2½ feet tall, is an excellent

AGERATUM
houstonianum
FLOSS FLOWER
Asteraceae (Compositae)
WARM-SEASON ANNUAL
ZONES 1–45
FULL SUN, EXCEPT AS NOTED
REGULAR WATER
✿ ❀ ✿ FLOWERS IN SUMMER AND FALL,
    EXCEPT AS NOTED

Ageratum houstonianum 'Blue Horizon'

choice for the middle of a border; it's also a popular cut flower. Floss flowers with blossoms in other colors include **'Pink Powder-puffs'** and white **'Summer Snow'**, both 9 inches high.

CULTURE. Plant floss flower in rich, moist soil. Choose a full-sun location except in hot-summer climates, where filtered shade is best.

Sow seeds indoors 8 to 10 weeks before warm weather is expected. (In mild-winter regions, you can sow or set out young plants in late summer or early fall.) The seeds need light to germinate, so barely press them into the potting mix. Be sure soil has warmed thoroughly in spring before setting out transplants. Pinch back after planting to promote bushiness. To help keep the plants looking neat and encourage continuous bloom, deadhead regularly.

ALCEA rosea
(Althaea rosea)
HOLLYHOCK
Malvaceae

PERENNIAL, BIENNIAL, OR WARM-SEASON
ANNUAL

ZONES 1–45

FULL SUN, EXCEPT AS NOTED

REGULAR WATER

✿❀✿✿✿❀ FLOWERS IN SUMMER

An old-fashioned favorite now enjoying a revival, hollyhock forms a clump of big, rough, more or less lobed leaves with a rounded heart shape. At bloom time, it sends up spikes of 3- to 6-inch-wide, funnel-shaped flowers that may be single, semidouble, or double. The blossom spikes of some older single-flowered varieties can reach 9 feet tall, but newer selections tend to be quite a bit shorter. A fine background plant, hollyhock is especially attractive planted against a fence or near a gate. It's generally grown as a biennial but often lives over for several years, making it a short-lived perennial. Some strains are grown as annuals; they bloom the first year from seed, provided seed is started indoors early in spring.

Chater's Double strain grows 6 to 8 feet tall and has ruffled double flowers in a wide range of colors. **'Nigra'**, a classic single-flowered type, bears deep chocolate maroon blossoms on 6- to 8-foot spikes; the 5-foot-tall **Country Romance** strain, also single flowered, offers a mix of colors. Mixed-color strains that bloom the first year from seed include double-flowered **Summer Carnival**, which grows 5 to 6 feet tall, and 2½-foot-tall **Majorette**, with semidouble flowers.

CULTURE. Hollyhock grows best in moderately rich, well-drained soil. Give it full sun except in the hottest climates, where partial shade is better. The tall flowering spikes may need staking in windy sites. Rust (see page 77) can damage leaves and shorten the life of the plants. Pick off infected leaves as soon as you notice them.

For blossoms in the current year, sow seed indoors in early spring; transplant seedlings into the garden as soon as warm weather arrives. To grow hollyhock as a biennial, sow seed in the garden (in the spot where plants are to grow) from spring into summer, up to 8 weeks before the first frost. Or sow in pots and transplant into the garden in late summer or in spring. Plants often self-sow, providing plenty of volunteers.

Alcea rosea

Alcea rosea

Alchemilla mollis

A soft-looking plant for the front of the border, lady's-mantle forms a mound of rounded, velvety gray-green, about 6-inch-wide leaves that glisten when beaded with droplets of dew or rain. In late spring or summer, frothy sprays of yellow-green blossoms offer a soothing contrast to brighter flowers. The plant reaches 1½ to 2 feet high and spreads 2 to 2½ feet across. **'Thriller'** is a floriferous selection with larger, pleated-looking leaves.

ALCHEMILLA mollis
LADY'S-MANTLE
Rosaceae
PERENNIAL
ZONES A2, A3; 1–9, 14–24, 31–43
FULL SUN OR LIGHT SHADE
REGULAR WATER
✿ FLOWERS IN LATE SPRING, SUMMER

CULTURE. Lady's-mantle requires good soil that is moist but well drained. In regions with mild summers, plant in sun or light shade. In warm-summer areas, a location in partial shade is important—but even if given a shady spot, plants tend to be short lived where summers are long, hot, and dry. Lady's-mantle doesn't require division to stay healthy, but you can divide in early spring (before flowering) to increase your supply of plants. Self-sown seedlings often appear.

Growing from tuberous roots, alstroemerias form spreading clumps of wiry, upright, 1- to 4-foot stems topped in late spring and summer by clusters of long-lasting, lilylike blossoms. Bright colors, bicolor combinations, and beautiful markings give the flowers an exotic appearance; they are excellent for cutting. Evergreen varieties bloom for a longer season if spent flower stems are removed. Gently pull the stems away from the root; this encourages new growth. (Don't simply cut them off at the base, since this slows new growth and bloom.)

Cordu and **Meyer** are hybrid strains that are evergreen where temperatures remain above freezing. They form compact, 1- to 3-foot-tall clumps and bloom over a long season, in colors including white, pink, red, lilac, and purple, usually bicolored and spotted. Another evergreen alstroemeria is 3- to 4-foot-high ***A. aurea (A. aurantiaca),*** bearing blossoms in yellow, orange, or orange red, liberally marked with dark stripes and flecks; **'Lutea'** is a named selection with yellow flowers marked in carmine. Both the species and 'Lutea' do best in mild-winter areas of the West Coast, and both tend to spread widely, sometimes becoming invasive.

Parrot lily, ***A. psittacina (A. pulchella),*** also evergreen, grows to 2½ feet tall and sports dark red flowers tipped with green and spotted with deep purple.

Deciduous alstroemerias are represented by the **Ligtu** hybrids, which produce leafy shoots 2 to 5 feet tall in late winter and into spring. As the leaves begin to brown, the flowering shoots appear, with blooms following in early to midsummer. Flowers come in colors including orange and orange shades (peach, salmon, shrimp) as well as red and near-white; all are flecked and striped with deeper colors. Plants go dormant after flowering.

ALSTROEMERIA
ALSTROEMERIA, PERUVIAN LILY
Liliaceae
PERENNIALS
ZONES 5–9, 14–24, 26, 28, 31, 32 (WARMER PARTS), 34; H1
LIGHT SHADE, EXCEPT AS NOTED
REGULAR WATER, EXCEPT AS NOTED
✿✸✿✿✿ FLOWERS IN LATE SPRING, SUMMER

CULTURE. Alstroemerias require well-drained soil enriched with organic matter. Plants do well everywhere in light shade (and must have afternoon shade where summers are hot); in cool-summer areas, they'll also take full sun. Handle the brittle roots carefully, setting them 6 to 8 inches deep and 1 foot apart. In warm regions, it's a good idea to mulch with ground bark, shredded leaves, or other organic material to help keep the soil cool. The plants tolerate some drought but grow best if given regular moisture (the Ligtu hybrids are exceptions: after they become dormant, they need no water unless winter rains fail). Mulch to protect the roots over winter.

Listing continues>

Alstroemeria aurea

Established clumps can be divided, but because plants reestablish slowly after transplanting, it's usually best to start new plants from seed. Sow in fall, winter, or earliest spring, either directly in the garden or in individual pots for later transplanting

Note that contact with alstroemeria foliage may cause an allergic skin reaction in some people.

AMSONIA

BLUE STAR FLOWER

Apocynaceae

PERENNIALS

ZONES VARY

FULL SUN OR LIGHT SHADE

MODERATE TO REGULAR WATER

✿ FLOWERS IN LATE SPRING, SUMMER

Amsonia ciliata

These elegant perennials form handsome, bushy clumps of 2- to 3-foot stems. The small (½- to ¾-inch), star-shaped blue blossoms are borne in clusters during late spring and summer. The foliage turns a lovely golden yellow in autumn; it hangs on until frost, then drops. *A. ciliata* (Zones 2–24, 28–41), with pale blue blooms, grows 2½ to 3 feet tall, its stems crowded with 2-inch leaves that look needlelike but are soft and silky to the touch. *A. tabernaemontana* (Zones 2–24, 28–45) reaches 2 to 2½ feet; it has shiny, willowlike leaves and bears nodding clusters of slate blue flowers.

Amsonia ciliata

CULTURE. Easy to grow and undemanding, these plants thrive in average, well-drained soil in full sun or light shade. In very shady sites, they may become leggy and require staking. They are tolerant of occasional lapses in watering. Clumps increase steadily in size but seldom require division to maintain top appearance; however, you can dig and divide in early spring to increase your plantings. You can also propagate blue star flowers by taking stem cuttings in summer.

ANCHUSA

Boraginaceae

PERENNIALS, BIENNIALS, AND

   WARM-SEASON ANNUALS

ZONES VARY

FULL SUN

MODERATE TO REGULAR WATER

✿ FLOWERS IN SUMMER

Anchusa capensis

Clusters of blue summer blossoms, larger and showier than those of the related forget-me-not (*Myosotis*), characterize these plants. Cape forget-me-not, *A. capensis*, is grown as an annual in all zones; in Zones 6–24, it can also be treated as a biennial (see "Culture," below). Rich blue blossoms with white centers are clustered on hairy, branching stems to 1½ feet tall; the narrow, 5-inch-long leaves are rough in texture. 'Blue Angel' is a free-flowering, compact selection (to 9 inches high).

Bearing bright blue flowers, Italian bugloss, *A. azurea* (*A. italica*; Zones 1–24, 29–45), is a short-lived perennial with flower stems that grow as tall as 4 feet in some selections; they rise from clumps of hairy, lance-shaped, 4- to 16-inch-long leaves. 'Dropmore' is a widely available cultivar with deep blue flowers; it grows 4 feet high. 'Loddon Royalist', to 3 feet tall, is a bushier, sturdier plant with lovely gentian blue blooms. Dark blue–flowered 'Little John' is a compact selection reaching just 1½ feet.

CULTURE. These plants need well-drained soil. Provide enough water to keep the roots moist but not saturated; they tend to rot in overly wet soil. Deadhead spent flowers to encourage a second bloom flush. Taller varieties may need staking. *A. azurea* declines after its second year; to rejuvenate the clump, divide and replant it. You can also propagate it by root cuttings taken in early spring.

To grow *A. capensis* as an annual, sow seed indoors 8 to 10 weeks before the last frost; keep temperatures at about 85°F/29°C during the day, 70°F/21°C at night. When the soil is warm, transplant seedlings into the garden. In warmer regions, where this plant can be grown as a biennial, sow seed in the garden in summer or early fall; keep soil moist until germination occurs. Plants will bloom the following summer.

Anemone tomentosa 'Robustissima'

Prized for late-season bloom, these graceful perennials are especially effective in front of a dark hedge or near the back of a border. They can be slow to establish, but once settled in, they spread widely. Japanese anemone, **A. × hybrida** (Zones 2b–24, 30–43), produces clumps of dark green, deeply veined, divided leaves at the ends of long leafstalks. The wiry, somewhat leafy flower stems typically reach 3 to 5 feet tall and bear loose sprays of cupped, gold-centered flowers resembling wild roses. Classic varieties include 3- to 4-foot **'Honorine Jobert'**, with single white flowers, and 3-foot **'Königin Charlotte'** (**'Reine Charlotte', 'Queen Charlotte'**), with semidouble pink blooms. **'Alice'** is a shorter selection (to about 2 feet tall) with semidouble light pink blossoms.

A. tomentosa 'Robustissima' (*A. vitifolia* 'Robustissima'; Zones 2b–9, 14–21, 30–43) forms a spreading clump of three-leafleted leaves. At bloom time, branching stems to about 3½ feet tall rise from the foliage clump, bearing single pale pink flowers.

CULTURE. Both *A. × hybrida* and *A. tomentosa* 'Robustissima' grow best in well-drained soil enriched with organic matter. Plant in light or partial shade or in filtered sun; where summers are cool, plants will also do well in full sun. Clumps don't need dividing for rejuvenation, but you can dig and transplant rooted shoots in spring to increase your supply of plants. Or propagate by root cuttings taken in late winter.

ANEMONE
Ranunculaceae
PERENNIALS
ZONES VARY
LIGHT SHADE, EXCEPT AS NOTED
REGULAR WATER
❀ ☆ FLOWERS IN LATE SUMMER, FALL

Delightful for sunny gardens and for cutting, snapdragons bloom abundantly, bearing solid-colored as well as bicolored blossoms that come in every shade but blue. In most climates, they are at their best in spring and early summer, but in mild-winter regions, they'll bloom in winter and early spring and may even live for several years. In addition to the familiar "snapping" snapdragon with upper and lower "jaws," you'll find types with double, bell-shaped, and azalea-shaped flowers. The flowers are borne in spikes above medium green, lance-shaped leaves. Dwarf forms are suitable for edging, small beds, and containers, while taller sorts provide vertical accents and are among the choicest annuals to include in perennial beds and borders. Snapdragons are most often sold in mixed colors (as both transplants and seeds), but some strains and varieties are also offered in separate colors.

Dwarf "snapping" snapdragons (6 to 12 inches tall) include **Floral Showers, Palette,** and rust-resistant **Royal Carpet** strains. Among intermediate types (1 to 2 feet tall) you will find strains such as **Rainbow, Sonnet, Ribbon,** and rust-resistant **Monarch;** others include **'Night and Day'**, with scarlet-and-white blooms, and heirloom **'Black Prince'**, with bronze foliage and deep crimson flowers. Tall-growing sorts (to 3 feet) include **Rocket** and double-flowered **Double Supreme** strains.

Bell-flowered snapdragons include **Bells Mixed** (8 to 12 inches tall), **La Bella** (to 1½ feet), and **Bright Butterflies** (2½ feet high). Among azalea-flowered types are

ANTIRRHINUM majus
SNAPDRAGON
Scrophulariaceae
PERENNIAL GROWN AS COOL-SEASON ANNUAL
ZONES A3; 1–45
FULL SUN
REGULAR WATER
✿ ❀ ✿ ✿ ✿ ☆ FLOWERS IN SPRING AND SUMMER, EXCEPT AS NOTED

Antirrhinum majus

Antirrhinum majus

foot-tall **Sweetheart** (which is resistant to rust) and 2½-foot **Madame Butterfly.** In a class of their own are the cascading snapdragons, grown for a trailing growth habit that makes them ideal for hanging baskets; these include **Cascadia** and **Lampion** strains.

CULTURE. Grow snapdragons in well-drained soil enriched with organic matter. Sow seed from late summer to early spring, about 10 weeks before you plan to set plants out in the garden. Press seeds into the surface of the potting mix rather than covering them. Keep pots or flats at fairly low temperatures—around 50°F/10°C at night, about 65°F/18°C during the day. Pinch young plants to encourage bushy growth and more flowers. In colder climates, set out plants in spring; in mild-winter regions, set out in early fall. If snapdragon seedlings are set out early enough in fall to reach bud stage before night temperatures drop below 50°F/10°C, they'll start blooming in winter and continue until weather gets hot. If set out later, they usually won't bloom until late winter or early spring.

Snapdragons are susceptible to rust, a disease which disfigures the leaves (see page 77). To help prevent this problem, plant rust-resistant varieties (note that these are resistant, not immune) and fertilize regularly. Also keep plants well watered—but avoid overhead watering (or water only in the morning or on sunny days, so foliage will dry before nightfall). If rust persists, change planting locations from one year to the next.

AQUILEGIA
COLUMBINE
Ranunculaceae
PERENNIALS
ZONES VARY
LIGHT SHADE, EXCEPT AS NOTED
REGULAR WATER
✿ ✿ ✿ ✿ ✿ ✿ FLOWERS IN SPRING,
  EARLY SUMMER

Graceful and full of charm, columbines have lacy foliage and intricate, delicate flowers. Heights vary from only a few inches to 4 feet; leaves are typically lobed and gray green, with a shape reminiscent of maidenhair fern foliage. The erect or nodding blossoms, carried on slender, branching stems, appear in spring and early summer. Many sorts have sepals and petals in contrasting colors, and most have backward-projecting spurs. There are also short-spurred sorts, spurless types, and kinds with double flowers.

Three North American species are especially noted for their stately form. Rocky Mountain columbine, *A. caerulea* (Zones A1–A3; 1–11, 14–24, 32–45), has classic long-spurred, blue-and-white flowers on 1½- to 3-foot stems; the blooms are held erect and reach about 2 inches wide. Canadian columbine, *A. canadensis* (Zones A1–A3; 1–10, 14–24, 30–45), is a 1- to 2-footer with nodding red-and-yellow flowers about 1½ inches wide. A selected form, *A. canadensis* 'Corbett', bears creamy yellow blooms. Golden columbine, *A. chrysantha* (Zones 1–11, 14–24, 31–45), forms a many-branched plant 3 to 4 feet high; its pure yellow flowers are 1½ to 3 inches across.

The Japanese native *A. flabellata* (Zones A2, A3; 1–9, 14–24, 31–45) forms a compact mound growing 8 inches to 1½ feet high; it is well suited to the front of the border. It bears nodding, 1½-inch-wide, lilac-blue or creamy white flowers and has thicker, darker leaves than other columbines. European columbine, *A. vulgaris* (Zones A2, A3; 1–10, 14–24, 32–45), grows 1 to 2½ feet tall and has nodding, 2-inch blossoms in blue, violet, or white; the species has blooms with very short spurs, but some selected forms are spurless.

Aquilegia,
McKana Giants strain

Many hybrid columbine strains are available. Among these are double-blossomed **Spring Song,** with flowers in a range of colors, and the graceful, long-spurred **McKana Giants,** in bicolors and solid colors that include white, blue, purple, pink, peach, red, and yellow. Both Spring Song and the McKana Giants reach 3 feet tall and grow in Zones A2, A3, 1–10, 14–24, 32–45.

Aquilegia chrysantha

CULTURE. Columbines are not fussy about soil type, but they must have good drainage. Plant them in light shade or filtered sun; where summers are cool, plants also grow well in sun. Cut back old stems for a second crop of flowers. Most columbines are not long lived; plan on replacing them every 3 to 4 years. If you let the spent flowers form seed capsules, you'll get a crop of volunteer seedlings—but if you're growing hybrids, the seedlings may differ from the parents. Seedlings from species (if grown isolated from other columbines) should closely resemble the parents, however.

Leaf miners (see page 78) are a potential pest, especially on hybrids. Cut off affected foliage; new leaves will soon appear.

ARTEMISIA
ARTEMISIA, WORMWOOD
Asteraceae (Compositae)
PERENNIALS
ZONES VARY
FULL SUN
LITTLE TO MODERATE WATER,
  EXCEPT AS NOTED
❀ FLOWERS IN LATE SUMMER; MOST
  ARE GROWN PRIMARILY FOR GRAY
  OR WHITE FOLIAGE

Artemisias are valued for their interesting leaf texture and for the aromatic, silvery gray or white foliage that always enhances its surroundings—providing an admirable foil for vivid flower colors and blending subtly with soft blues, lavenders, and pinks. In height, the plants vary from about 1 foot to over 4 feet tall; some are shrubby (woody based), while others die back in winter.

Among the taller shrubby species is southernwood, *A. abrotanum* (Zones 2b–24, 27–41), with finely cut gray-green foliage on a spreading, bushy plant 3 to 5 feet high. Common wormwood, *A. absinthium* (Zones 2–24, 29–41), grows 2 to 4 feet tall and has silvery gray, finely divided leaves. **'Lambrook Silver'** is a 2-foot form with especially finely cut foliage. A related hybrid is *A. **'Powis Castle'*** (Zones 2–24, 29–34), with soft, silvery gray-green foliage that forms a splendid lacy mound to 3 feet tall and 6 feet wide.

Two other shrubby species are shorter, useful when you want a foreground accent in soft, shimmering silvery gray. *A. stellerana* **'Silver Brocade'** (Zones A1–A3; 1–10, 14–24, 29–45), with beautiful felted, lobed leaves, is one of several plants called dusty miller. It forms a dense, low-growing mound to 1 foot tall and 2 feet wide. *A. schmidtiana* **'Silver Mound'** (Zones A1–A3; 1–10, 14–24, 29–41), is another dense, low grower, reaching just 1 foot high and wide. In hot, humid climates, its foliage tends to rot in summer.

Unlike the plants described above, *A. ludoviciana* **'Silver King'** (Zones 1–24, 29–41) is deciduous, with stems that die down at the onset of frost. During the growing season, it reaches 2 to 3½ feet, with many slender, spreading branches covered in silvery white, 2-inch leaves. **'Silver Queen'** is a shorter selection with slightly larger leaves. Both spread widely and can be seriously invasive in a small garden. Plant them where they can colonize freely; or confine them with an 8-inch-deep barrier around the roots.

White mugwort, *A. lactiflora* (Zones 1–9, 14–21, 29–41), also dies down in winter. This is the only artemisia grown primarily not for foliage, but for its attractive flowers: elegantly plumed spikes of small, creamy white blossoms that appear in late summer atop upright, 4- to 6-foot stems clad in dark green, lobed leaves. Plants in the **Guizhou Group** (often sold as *A. lactiflora* **'Guizho'**) feature handsome purple-red stems.

CULTURE. All artemisias require well-drained soil, and all tolerate drought except for *A. lactiflora,* which needs regular moisture during the growing season. Cut back stems of shrubby kinds fairly heavily in late winter or early spring to keep growth compact. For the two deciduous species, cut spent stems down to the basal rosette of leaves in autumn or early spring.

Propagate clump-forming artemisias by division in early spring. The tall, shrubby kinds may propagate themselves by layering (that is, stems that come in contact with the soil may form rooted sections); these layers can then be separated from the parent plant in spring. All artemisias can be propagated by stem cuttings in spring or summer.

TOP: *Artemisia schmidtiana* 'Silver Mound'
BOTTOM: *Artemisia* 'Powis Castle'

ARUNCUS
GOATSBEARD
Rosaceae
PERENNIALS
ZONES VARY
SUN OR SHADE, EXCEPT AS NOTED
REGULAR TO AMPLE WATER
❀ FLOWERS IN SUMMER

Well suited to woodland gardens, the goatsbeards resemble airy astilbes, with elegant, feathery plumes of tiny white summer flowers rising above slowly spreading clumps of finely divided leaves.

At just 1 foot tall and wide, *A. aethusifolius* (Zones 1–9, 14–17, 31–43) is an excellent choice for the front of the border. The deep green, finely divided foliage gives the plant a delicate look; the flower plumes add a graceful note at bloom time.

A much larger species is *A. dioicus* (Zones A2, A3; 1–9, 14–17, 31–43). It forms a 4-foot-tall, shrublike mound of broad, fernlike leaves topped with a foam of blossoms in many-branched clusters to 20 inches long. **'Kneiffii'** is only half as tall as the species, with leaves finely divided into threadlike segments. **'Child of Two Worlds' ('Zweiweltenkind')** reaches about 5 feet tall; its branched flower clusters droop gracefully.

Aruncus dioicus

CULTURE. Plant goatsbeards in moist soil. You can grow them in sun or shade except in hot-summer regions, where they require shade throughout the day. They do not thrive where summers are both hot and dry.

A. dioicus has large, deep roots that make the plant difficult to move or divide once established. The smaller *A. aethusifolius* is easier to divide (do the job in spring). Both species can be propagated by seed sown indoors in late winter.

ASCLEPIAS tuberosa
BUTTERFLY WEED
Asclepiadaceae
PERENNIALS
ZONES 1–45
FULL SUN
LITTLE TO MODERATE WATER
✿ ✿ ✿ ✿ FLOWERS IN SUMMER

Asclepias tuberosa, Gay Butterflies strain

The common name may label it a weed—but gardeners (and butterflies too!) count this rugged, easy-to-grow plant a desirable one. Each spring, the dormant root sends up many stems clothed in lance-shaped leaves to 4 inches long. Stems reach 2 to 3 feet tall by bloom time in summer, when many small, starlike flowers are carried in broad, flattened clusters at the stem tips. Vivid orange is the usual color, but other bright hues also occur naturally. The aptly named **Gay Butterflies** strain is a mix containing red, orange, pink, yellow, and bicolored flowers; **'Hello Yellow'** bears vibrant yellow blossoms.

In some regions, butterfly weed is a favorite food of monarch butterfly caterpillars, which can quickly eat plants almost to the ground. In these parts of the country, some gardeners like to set out other perennials nearby, providing a temporary screen for the demolished butterfly weed (the plants grow back rapidly).

CULTURE. Plant butterfly weed where you want it to grow permanently; the plants establish slowly but are long lived. Plant in well-drained soil, since too much moisture around the roots, especially in winter, can lead to rot. Butterfly weed is drought tolerant but performs best with moderate watering. Because the stems emerge later in spring than those of many other plants, mark the location of your plantings (or leave the old stems in place as markers).

The easiest way to increase a planting is to raise new plants from seed sown indoors in late winter, but you can also take root cuttings or divide clumps in spring. When dividing, dig deeply, removing as much of the root system as possible.

Typically blooming in late summer and autumn, asters bear cheerful daisy flowers (usually just ½ to 1 inch wide) in a wide variety of colors, on plants that range from low front-of-the-border mounds to imposing 6-footers. White wood aster, *A. divaricatus* (Zones 1–10, 14–24, 31–43), is a spreading plant up to 2 feet high with dark stems and a generous show of flowers in pure white aging to pink. Unlike most asters, it grows well in shade. Heath aster, *A. ericoides* (Zones 1–10, 14–24, 31–43), reaches 3 feet high; it has narrow leaves and a strong horizontal branching pattern. It's a profuse bloomer with blossoms in white, pink, or blue. Often sold as a form of *A. ericoides* is *A. pringlei* 'Monte Cassino', successful in Zones 1–24, 31–43. An especially good cut flower, it produces tall stems—up to 5 feet—set with short branches bearing clouds of starry white blossoms.

The hybrid *A. × frikartii* (Zones 2b–24, 31–43) has produced excellent selections with exceptionally long flowering seasons. 'Mönch' and 'Wonder of Staffa' are bushy plants in the 3-foot range; both bear clear lavender-blue, 2- to 3-inch-wide blossoms from early summer to fall in most areas, almost all year in mild-winter areas (with regular deadheading). These plants may be short lived.

Smooth aster, *A. laevis* (Zones 1–10, 14–24, 31–45), grows 3½ feet tall and has blue or purple blossoms. The selection 'Bluebird' bears charming clusters of violet-blue flowers on arching stems. Cultivars of calico aster, *A. lateriflorus* (Zones 1–10, 14–21, 31–45), are attractive and easy to grow. 'Horizontalis' is a bushy, mounding 2½-footer with spreading branches bearing white flowers with reddish centers; in fall, the tiny dark green leaves take on a reddish tint that echoes the bloom colors. 'Prince' has even darker foliage and bears flowers centered in deeper red.

An old-fashioned classic fall bloomer is New England aster, *A. novae-angliae* (Zones 1–24, 31–43). It rises to 6 feet or more in its basic form, bearing great, airy sprays of violet-blue flowers; the stems are clothed in grayish green, hairy leaves. Several pink and nearly red selections are available, including 3- to 4-foot-tall, bright rose 'Andenken an Alma Pötschke' ('Alma Pötschke') and 3-foot 'Honeysong Pink'. 'Purple Dome' is a compact selection that forms a 1½- to 2-foot mound covered in violet-blue flowers.

Another old favorite is New York aster, also known as Michaelmas daisy (*A. novi-belgii*; Zones 1–24, 31–42). Like *A. novae-angliae*, it blooms primarily in violet blue, but it grows only 3 to 4 feet high and has smooth foliage. Its hundreds of cultivars range in height from about 1 foot to well over 5 feet. A few choice selections are foot-tall 'Professor Anton Kippenburg', with semidouble lavender-blue blossoms; 2- to 3-foot 'Winston Churchill', sporting handsome red flowers; and 'Climax', a 5- to 6-foot giant bearing outstanding medium blue blooms that measure 2 to 3 inches across.

CULTURE. Asters are undemanding plants, needing only a sunny location (except for *A. divaricatus*, which prefers shade), and reasonably good, well-drained soil. *A. novi-belgii* is particularly susceptible to powdery mildew; keeping it well watered helps minimize this problem. Most of the taller asters flop over by flowering time. To deal with this problem, either stake them early in the season or cut back the stems by about one-third in early summer (early to mid-June) to make them more compact (plants cut back this way may bloom a bit later than unpruned plants). While most asters don't need winter protection, the cultivars of *A. × frikartii* may benefit from a blanket of evergreen boughs in the colder zones.

Especially vigorous asters, notably *A. novae-angliae* and *A. novi-belgii*, spread rapidly and can become invasive. Dig and divide the roots at least every other year in spring, replanting only the strong divisions from the clump's perimeter. Other kinds of asters need dividing only when vigor diminishes and the center of the clump becomes bare and woody. Asters can also be propagated by stem cuttings taken in summer.

ASTER

Asteraceae (Compositae)
PERENNIALS
ZONES VARY
FULL SUN, EXCEPT AS NOTED
REGULAR WATER
✿ ✿ ✵ ✿ ✿ FLOWERS IN LATE SUMMER
    AND FALL, EXCEPT AS NOTED

TOP: *Aster × frikartii* 'Wonder of Staffa'
BOTTOM: *Aster novae-angliae* 'Purple Dome'

ASTILBE
ASTILBE, FALSE SPIRAEA,
MEADOWSWEET
Saxifragaceae
PERENNIALS
ZONES 1–7, 14–17, 32–43
  (BUT SEE "CULTURE," BELOW)
PARTIAL SHADE, EXCEPT AS NOTED
REGULAR WATER
✿✸✿✿ FLOWERS IN LATE SPRING,
  SUMMER

Airy and plumelike, astilbe's flower clusters are an invaluable addition to summer borders and woodland gardens—and they're good for cutting, as well. Either upright or gracefully arching, the floral plumes rise above clumps of handsome, fernlike leaves; they are held on wiry stems that range from 6 inches to 5 feet high. By selecting varieties carefully, making sure that bloom times overlap, you can enjoy flowers from late spring or early summer right through to summer's end.

Most astilbes sold in nurseries are listed as **A. × arendsii,** though some have been reclassified into other species. **'Deutschland'** flowers in late spring—early in the season for an astilbe—bearing dense plumes of white flowers on 1½-foot stems. **'Fanal'** also blooms quite early, carrying its blood red flowers on 1½- to 2½-foot stems. Blooming in mid- to late summer, **'Ostrich Plume'** (**'Straussenfeder'**, often listed as a hybrid of **A. thunbergii**) features drooping pink clusters on 3- to 3½-foot stems. Among A. × arendsii selections, those with deeper flower colors tend to have bronzy new leaves.

Astilbe × arendsii 'Fanal'

A. chinensis is a late-summer bloomer that tolerates somewhat drier soils than other astilbes. One of its well-known cultivars is **'Pumila',** with rosy lilac flower spikes on foot-tall stems held stiffly upright over spreading mats of foliage. Pink-flowered **'Finale',** to 20 inches tall, is one of the latest to bloom. Another late-blooming selection is **A. c. taquetii 'Superba'** (**A. taquetii 'Superba'**), which grows 4 to 5 feet tall and has bright pinkish purple flowers.

Summer-blooming **A. simplicifolia 'Sprite',** an excellent front-of-the-border plant, has bronze-tinted foliage and abundant shell pink, drooping spires on 1-foot stems. The blossoms are followed by attractive, long-lasting rust-colored seed heads.

CULTURE. Grow astilbes in moist but not saturated soil enriched with plenty of organic matter. They thrive in light shade, though they can take full sun in cool-summer climates if given plenty of moisture. Tall kinds are self-supporting and require no staking. When bloom production declines noticeably (after 3 to 5 years), divide the clumps in early spring. Survival in the coldest zones (1, 2a, 43) depends on good snow cover.

Astilbe × arendsii 'Ostrich Plume'

AURINIA saxatilis
(Alyssum saxatile)
BASKET-OF-GOLD
Brassicaceae (Cruciferae)
PERENNIAL
ZONES 1–24, 32–43
FULL SUN
MODERATE WATER
✿✿ FLOWERS IN SPRING

Providing a welcome splash of bright color in spring, basket-of-gold forms a spreading mound (9 to 12 inches high and 1½ feet wide) of narrow, gray-green, lance-shaped leaves 2 to 5 inches long. Individual flowers are small, but they come in many rounded, 1-inch clusters that virtually cover the plant. Basket-of-gold is a traditional component of large-scale rock gardens, and it also looks good at the front of a sunny border or spilling over a wall.

In addition to the basic bright yellow form, you can choose **'Citrina',** with pale yellow blossoms; **'Compacta',** which forms a smaller, tighter-growing clump; **'Silver Queen',** a compact grower with pale yellow blooms; and **'Dudley Nevill Variegated'** (**'Dudley Neville Variegated'**), an apricot-flowered form with leaves handsomely edged in creamy white.

Aurinia saxatilis 'Dudley Nevill Variegated'

CULTURE. Plant basket-of-gold in a sunny location in average, well-drained soil (if soil is too rich, the plant tends to become sprawling and untidy). After the flowers finish, shear the plant back by about a third to keep it compact and to divert energy from seed production (thus preventing excess volunteer seedlings). Basket-of-gold is short lived in hot, humid areas; gardeners in such regions often treat it as a biennial, setting out new plants in fall for spring bloom, then removing them once the show is over. Propagate basket-of-gold by division in fall or by stem cuttings taken in spring or summer.

Baptisia australis

Reliable, long-lived, large-scale perennials native to the eastern and midwestern U.S., the false indigos bloom in late spring and early summer, carrying spires of sweet pea–shaped flowers above clumps of bluish green, cloverlike foliage. Dark brown to black, inflated-looking seedpods add interest later in summer and on into fall. Plants emerge early in spring and grow quickly to their full size.

White false indigo, *B. alba*, grows 2 to 3 feet tall and spreads to about 3 feet wide. Foot-long spikes of white blossoms (sometimes blotched with purple) contrast well with the charcoal gray stems. The more widely grown blue false indigo, *B. australis*, is a larger plant, reaching 3 to 6 feet tall and 4 feet wide. Its flowers are deep indigo blue. **'Purple Smoke'**, a hybrid between *B. alba* and *B. australis*, grows 4½ feet tall and has violet blooms with dark purple centers.

CULTURE. False indigos are easy to grow, needing only moderately fertile, nonalkaline soil. Their deep taproots make them drought tolerant once established. Clumps gradually increase in size but do not require division—and in fact, established plants resent transplanting. To start more plants, sow seed in early spring, after danger of frost is past; or transplant volunteer seedlings.

BAPTISIA
FALSE INDIGO
Fabaceae (Leguminosae)
PERENNIALS
ZONES 1–24, 28–45
FULL SUN
MODERATE WATER
✿ ✿ ❀ FLOWERS IN LATE SPRING, EARLY SUMMER

Bearing abundant clusters of single or double blossoms, fibrous begonias form mounding, 8- to 12-inch tall plants with succulent stems and glossy green or bronze leaves. In most regions, they bloom from spring straight through until frost; in the hottest climates, though, gardeners grow them as winter-blooming annuals. Use them in beds and borders, as an edging, or as superb container plants; they can also be grown as houseplants. Many varieties are offered. The foot-tall **Cocktail** series has rounded dark bronze leaves and single flowers in scarlet, rose, pink, white, and bicolors; the **Lotto** series features extra-large (2-inch-wide) flowers in red or pink on compact, 8-inch-high plants with green leaves. Plants in the early-blooming **Super Olympia** series also grow 8 inches high and have green foliage; they bear flowers in pink, red, white, coral, and bicolors.

Begonia, Semperflorens group

Listing continues>

BEGONIA,
Semperflorens group
FIBROUS, BEDDING, OR WAX BEGONIAS
Begoniaceae
PERENNIALS OFTEN GROWN AS WARM-SEASON ANNUALS
ZONES 14–28, H1, H2 AS PERENNIALS; ANNUALS ANYWHERE
PARTIAL SHADE, EXCEPT AS NOTED
REGULAR WATER
❀ ✿ ✿ FLOWERS IN SPRING, SUMMER, AND FALL, EXCEPT AS NOTED

Begonia, Semperflorens group

CULTURE. Grow fibrous begonias in rich, moisture-retentive soil. Give them partial shade except in cool-summer areas, where they'll thrive in full sun (dark-foliaged kinds, however, will take full sun even in warm climates if well watered).

Fibrous begonias take 3 to 4 months to grow from seed to transplanting size. Sow the dustlike seeds thinly on the potting mix; do not cover them with mix. Lay plastic wrap loosely over the container so the mix stays moist, then keep at 70°F/21°C. After the seedlings sprout (in 2 to 3 weeks), make sure night temperatures don't drop below 60°F/18°C. You can also propagate these plants from stem cuttings. Take them in late summer and grow over winter indoors; or take in spring from indoor plants.

BERGENIA
Saxifragaceae
PERENNIALS
ZONES A1–A3, 1–9, 12–24, 30–45,
EXCEPT AS NOTED
LIGHT TO FULL SHADE, EXCEPT AS NOTED
MODERATE TO REGULAR WATER
✿ ❀ ✿ ✿ FLOWERS IN WINTER,
EARLY SPRING

Even if bergenias never flowered, they'd be worth planting for their handsome foliage alone. Growing in informal rosettes 1 to 1½ feet high, the substantial, oval to nearly round leaves are leathery and deeply veined; they grow up to a foot long and are borne on equally long leafstalks. They often take on purple tints in cold weather. Graceful clusters of small flowers appear on thick, leafless, 1- to 1½-foot stalks.

B. ciliata is the most elegant-looking species, though it's less hardy than the rest (Zones 5–9, 14–24, 29–34, 39). Its lustrous light green leaves are covered with short, silky hairs; they are damaged by frosts and die down completely in the colder zones of the range. The early-spring flowers are light pink or white, often darkening with age.

Also blooming in early spring is heartleaf bergenia, *B. cordifolia,* with glossy, wavy-edged leaves that partially conceal the rose or lilac flowers. Winter-blooming bergenia, *B. crassifolia,* bears its dense clusters of rose, lilac, or purple flowers any time from midwinter to early spring, depending on climate. The blossoms are held above clumps of glossy, rubbery leaves.

Named hybrid bergenias are increasingly available from specialty nurseries. Choices include **'Abendglut' ('Evening Glow')**, a slightly shorter selection with dark red blooms and leaves that turn dark red in cold weather; **'Baby Doll'**, which grows about 1 foot tall and has soft pink flowers; **'Bressingham White'**; **'Bressingham Ruby'**; and **'Bressingham Salmon'**.

Bergenia 'Bressingham Salmon'

CULTURE. Though bergenias tolerate dry shade and poor soil, their foliage and flowers are much more attractive when the plants are given good soil and regular watering. In mild- and warm-summer areas, they prefer filtered sun to full shade; where summers are cool, they can also take full sun. Divide crowded clumps and replant vigorous divisions in late winter or early spring.

BRUNNERA macrophylla
BRUNNERA, SIBERIAN BUGLOSS,
PERENNIAL FORGET-ME-NOT
Boraginaceae
PERENNIAL
ZONES 1–24, 31–45
LIGHT SHADE, EXCEPT AS NOTED
REGULAR WATER
✿ FLOWERS IN EARLY SPRING

In early spring, airy sprays of little (¼-inch) azure blue flowers resembling forget-me-nots *(Myosotis)* rise above lush clumps of heart-shaped dark green leaves to 4 inches wide and 6 inches long. As the season progresses, the leaves become larger and the stems grow taller, reaching 1½ to 2 feet by the time flowering is over. The foliage stays attractive for the rest of the growing season, making brunnera a good choice for a small-scale ground cover under high-branching shrubs or near a shady pool or stream. Several selections offer variegated foliage; among these is **'Dawson's White' ('Variegata')**, with elegant creamy white bands along the leaf margins.

Brunnera macrophylla
'Dawson's White'

CULTURE. Brunnera looks best when grown in well-drained, moisture-retentive soil. It's at home anywhere in light shade; where summers are cool, you can also plant it in sun. Keep in mind, however, that variegated forms always require shade to keep their leaves from scorching. Brunnera self-sows freely once established; it can also be propagated by dividing clumps in fall or taking root cuttings in late winter.

Easy to grow and long blooming, calendula brings glowing color to the garden from spring to midsummer (from fall through spring, where winters are mild). The plant grows 1 to 2½ feet tall, with aromatic, slightly sticky green leaves and single or double, daisylike flowers 2½ to 4 inches across.

Besides making excellent cut flowers, the blossoms have edible petals that add a tangy flavor to salads, egg dishes, and fish. When cooked with rice, they give the grain a saffron color. In times past, both leaves and petals went into vegetable stews—hence the common name "pot marigold."

Dwarf strains (12 to 16 inches high) include early-blooming **Bon Bon,** with 2½-inch-wide flowers in a mix of bright and soft yellows, oranges, and apricots; and **Calypso,** which has larger (3- to 4-inch) blossoms in orange or yellow with black centers. **Touch of Red** grows 16 to 18 inches tall and features 2½-inch-wide flowers in cream, yellow, and orange; the petal tips and backs are mahogany red. The **Kablouna** series (20 inches tall), bearing 3-inch-wide flowers with a crested, pompomlike center, comes in all the calendula colors. The **Prince** series grows 2 to 2½ feet high and bears long-stemmed, 3-inch-wide blooms in golden yellow and orange.

CULTURE. Calendula thrives in full sun and rich soil; it also does well in average soil as long as drainage is good. Deadheading helps prolong bloom. The plants will self-sow, though seedlings' flowers may differ from those of the parents.

Sow seeds in place in the garden as soon as soil can be worked in spring. Or start seeds indoors in late winter, then set out seedlings in early spring. In mild-winter areas, you can sow seed or set out transplants in late summer or early fall.

CALENDULA officinalis
CALENDULA, POT MARIGOLD
Asteraceae (Compositae)
COOL-SEASON ANNUAL
ZONES 1–45; H1
FULL SUN
MODERATE WATER
❀ ✿ ✿ FLOWERS IN SPRING AND SUMMER, EXCEPT AS NOTED

Calendula officinalis, Touch of Red strain

Introduced to gardeners in the 1990s, these petunia relatives are long blooming and easy to grow. They're smaller overall than petunias, with finer foliage, wiry, slender stems, and trumpet-shaped blooms about an inch across. The plants are "self-cleaning"—the spent flowers drop off cleanly, eliminating the need for deadheading. Two basic forms are available: low-growing trailers and more mounding types that reach 10 inches tall. Plant calibrachoas in containers and hanging baskets; or use them as bedding plants. In most regions, gardeners grow them as annuals that bloom from early summer to autumn, but in mild-winter climates they are truly perennial.

The low-growing **Liricashower** series offers blooms in pink-blushed white, blue, pink, and rose, while the mounding **Colorburst** series has flowers in violet, rose, and red. Plants sold under the common name "million bells" include trailing types in white, blue, and pink, as well as mounding ones in pink, terra-cotta, and yellow.

CULTURE. Plant calibrachoas in moist, well-drained soil. To keep them blooming over a long season, fertilize container-grown plants every 2 weeks and those in the ground once a month. Growers propagate the plants through tissue culture; seed is not available.

CALIBRACHOA
CALIBRACHOA, MILLION BELLS
Solanaceae
PERENNIALS USUALLY GROWN AS WARM-SEASON ANNUALS
ZONES 2–43
FULL SUN OR PARTIAL SHADE
REGULAR WATER
✿ ✿ ❀ ✿ ✿ ✿ FLOWERS IN SUMMER, FALL

Calibrachoa

CALLISTEPHUS chinensis

CHINA ASTER

Asteraceae (Compositae)

WARM-SEASON ANNUAL

ZONES 1–45

FULL SUN

REGULAR WATER

✿ ❀ ✿ ✿ ✿ FLOWERS IN SUMMER

Callistephus chinensis

Treasured by gardeners for its brilliant colors and usefulness as a cut flower, summer-blooming China aster is a fast-growing, bushy annual related to perennial asters. The 1½- to 4-inch flowers come in white, yellow, and shades of pink, purple, and red, and are available in a variety of forms. You'll find blossoms resembling chrysanthemums or daisies (both single and double) and those that look like peonies or pin-studded pincushions; and the flowers may have quilled, spidery, incurved, or ribbonlike petals or crested centers. Plant height varies from 8 inches to about 2½ feet; the medium green leaves are coarsely toothed and reach 3 inches long.

Low-growing varieties include the 8-inch-tall, double-flowered **Pinocchio** series, bearing dense, rounded, 1½-inch-wide flowers with incurved petals; it comes in a wide range of colors. Another low-growing double form is the 10-inch **Asteroid** series, with larger (4-inch) blossoms in mixed as well as many individual colors. Taller sorts especially well suited for cutting include the 20-inch **Massagno** series, bearing 3½-inch double flowers with thin, spidery petals, and **Single California Giant,** which features 3-inch single blooms on 2½-foot plants. Both are sold in mixed colors.

CULTURE. Plant China aster in rich, loamy or sandy soil with a neutral to slightly alkaline pH. Taller varieties may need staking, which should be done while plants are young.

After the danger of frost is past, sow seed in place in the garden. For earlier blooms, you can start seed indoors 6 to 8 weeks before the last-frost date. Transplant seedlings carefully, since they are very sensitive to root disturbance.

China aster (along with many other kinds of plants) is subject to aster yellows, a viral disease transmitted by leafhoppers. Symptoms include yellowed foliage and pale leaf veins; flowers may be small, deformed, or nonexistent. To control the disease, spray to keep the leafhopper population in bounds; also discard infected plants (to prevent further spread) and destroy nearby weeds, which may harbor the disease. China aster is also susceptible to aster wilt or stem rot, caused by a parasitic soil-dwelling fungus that enters plants through their roots; many varieties are at least somewhat resistant to this disease. Overwatering (especially in heavy or poorly drained soil) produces ideal conditions for both aster yellows and aster wilt. To prevent a buildup of disease organisms, don't plant China aster in the same location in successive years.

CAMPANULA

CAMPANULA, BELLFLOWER

Campanulaceae (Lobeliaceae)

PERENNIALS, BIENNIALS, AND BIENNIALS
  GROWN AS ANNUALS

ZONES 1–9, 14–24, 31–45, EXCEPT
  AS NOTED

FULL SUN, EXCEPT AS NOTED

MODERATE TO REGULAR WATER

✿ ✿ ❀ ✿ ✿ FLOWERS IN SPRING, SUMMER

A vast and varied group, campanulas range in form from stately back-of-border plants to low, spreading or compact mounds suitable for use at the front of the border, in rock gardens, and as small-scale ground covers. The five-petaled flowers are typically bell-shaped, but some kinds have upward-facing, cup-shaped blossoms, while others are star-shaped.

Canterbury bells, *C. medium,* is the popular campanula of cottage gardens. Though it is usually grown as a biennial (it flowers the second year from seed, then dies), some varieties can be grown as annuals. The narrow, lance-shaped, 6- to 10-inch-long leaves form a clump that sends up erect, leafy, 2- to 3-foot flowering stems in spring and summer. Borne in loose spikes, the

Campanula medium 'Calycanthema'

upward-facing bells reach 2 inches across; colors include blue shades, purple, pink, and white. The popular cup-and-saucer version, 2½-foot-tall **'Calycanthema'**, has an unusual flower form: each cuplike flower is seated on a flattened corolla that forms the "saucer." Forms of *C. medium* grown as annuals tend to be shorter in stature and include the 14-inch-tall **Dwarf Bells** strain, which has flowers in mauve, lilac, pink, and white, and **'Russian Pink'**, to 15 inches high.

The perennial campanulas discussed here are divided into two groups—those with upright flowering stems and those that form spreading mounds. In the descriptions that follow, the second category is represented only by Dalmatian and Serbian bell-flowers, *C. portenschlagiana* and *C. poscharskyana*.

Tussock bellflower, **C. carpatica,** is the shortest of the upright campanulas, topping out at about 1 foot. Wiry, branching stems rise from low clumps of narrow, 1½-inch-long leaves in late spring, bearing cup-shaped, 1- to 2-inch-wide flowers in white and various blue shades; bloom continues into summer if the spent flowers are removed. **'White Clips'** and **'Blue Clips'** are reliable selections. Somewhat taller (1 to 2 feet or more) is summer-blooming clustered bellflower, **C. glomerata** (Zones A1, A2; 1–10, 14–24, 31–45). Its dense clusters of flaring, typically blue-violet, inch-wide bells are carried on erect stems above clumps of broadly lance-shaped, 2- to 4-inch-long leaves. Named selections vary in flower color and plant height. **'Crown of Snow'** is a 1½- to 2-foot plant with white flowers; **'Superba'**, to 2½ feet, bears blossoms in an intense, glowing violet; purple **'Joan Elliott'** grows to 1½ feet.

Tallest of the widely grown campanulas is **C. lactiflora** (Zones 1–9, 14–24, 31–34, 39). Its upright stems, clothed with 3-inch, pointed leaves, top out in the 3- to 5-foot range. Large, conical clusters of open, starry-looking, 1-inch-wide bells bloom in summer. Named selections include pale pink, 3- to 4-foot-high **'Loddon Anna'**; 3-foot-tall, blue-violet **'Prichard's Variety'**; and dwarf **'Pouffe'**, which forms a mound of pale blue flowers just over 1 foot tall.

Campanula persicifolia

Graceful peach-leafed bluebell, **C. persici-folia,** has leafy, 2- to 3-foot stems above low clumps of narrow, 4- to 8-inch-long leaves. In summer, each stem bears loose spires of cupped, outward-facing, inch-wide bells in blue, pink, or white. Named selections include **'Chettle Charm'**, with white flowers edged in pale violet blue, and **'Telham Beauty'**, with larger (3-inch) blue blossoms. Spotted bellflower, **C. punctata,** forms a rosette of heart-shaped, 3- to 5-inch basal leaves. In summer, arching stems to 2 feet high bear nodding, elongated, 2-inch bells in white, lilac, or pink, typically marked with spots on the inside. **'Cherry Bells'** has reddish flowers edged in white.

Campanula punctata

Forming a low (6-inch-high) mound of roundish, ¾- to 1½-inch-wide leaves, easy-to-grow Dalmatian bellflower, **C. portenschlagiana** (Zones 2–9, 14–24, 31–41), produces purplish blue, bell- to cup-shaped, inch-wide flowers from late spring through summer. The more aggressive Serbian bellflower, **C. poscharskyana,** has clumps of heart-shaped, about 1-inch-long leaves and spreads by rooting runners to form a solid foliage carpet. Starlike, ½- to 1-inch-wide blooms in soft blue or white appear along semi-upright, foot-tall stems in spring to early summer.

Listing continues>

Campanula portenschlagiana

CULTURE. Plant campanulas in well-drained soil that has been enriched with organic matter. Most need regular watering for good performance, though *C. portenschlagiana* and *C. poscharskyana* are somewhat drought tolerant. Campanulas grow well in full sun except in warm-summer areas, where they need partial shade. Tall kinds require staking. To encourage repeat bloom, remove spent flowers. Slugs and snails can be serious pests; for controls, see page 78.

To grow *C. medium* (Canterbury bells) as a biennial, sow seeds outdoors in late spring or early summer, either in place or in a nursery bed for later transplanting; transplant, if necessary, in fall or early spring. In colder regions, protect plants over winter with a mulch of evergreen boughs or salt hay. Start seed of annual varieties indoors in early spring; most kinds require 16 to 20 weeks to reach blooming size. Barely press seeds into the soil surface—they need light to germinate.

To propagate perennial campanulas, dig and divide crowded clumps in early spring. Plants can also be propagated by stem cuttings or, for the species and some named varieties, by seed sown indoors in late winter.

CANNA

CANNA LILY, INDIAN SHOT

Cannaceae

PERENNIALS

ZONES 6–9, 12–31, WARMER PARTS OF 32;
H1, H2; OR DIG AND STORE

FULL SUN

AMPLE WATER

❀ ✿ ✿ ✿ ✿ FLOWERS IN SUMMER, FALL

Bringing a bold, tropical accent to borders and container gardens from summer into autumn, cannas flaunt spikes of big, showy, irregularly shaped flowers and large leaves that may be rich green, bronzy red, or variegated. In size, the plants range from dwarfs only a few feet high to giants that reach 6 feet or taller. Numerous varieties (most are hybrids between several species) are available. Just a few of the many choices are **'Pretoria' ('Bengal Tiger')**, a 6-footer with dramatic green-and-yellow striped leaves and bright orange flowers; 4-foot **'Wyoming'**, with bronzy purple foliage and orange blooms; and the lower-growing **'Pfitzer Chinese Coral'** and **'Pfitzer Crimson Beauty'**, both just 2½ to 3 feet tall.

Canna 'Pretoria'

CULTURE. Cannas require moist soil enriched with organic matter. They thrive in hot, bright locations. Cut stems to the ground as they finish flowering; new stems will continue to appear throughout summer and early fall. Every 3 or 4 years, divide crowded clumps in early spring. Dig the rhizomes and cut them apart; let the cuts heal (this takes about 24 hours), then replant, covering with 2 to 4 inches of soil.

In the colder parts of their range, protect cannas with a 6-inch layer of mulch over winter. Beyond their hardiness limit, cut off the stalks and dig the rhizomes after the first frosts have killed the leaves. Let rhizomes dry in a warm place for a few days; then place in a box, cover with dry peat moss, and store in a frost-free location over winter. In spring, plant the rhizomes indoors in pots about 4 weeks before the usual last-frost date. Transplant to the garden after weather has warmed.

Creating a colorful show throughout the heat of summer and on into late autumn, Madagascar periwinkle flourishes in dry as well as humid conditions. The bushy plant typically reaches 1 to 2 feet high and wide. Single, phloxlike, 1- to 2-inch-wide flowers, often featuring a contrasting eye, are set off perfectly by glossy green, 1- to 3-inch-long leaves. Depending on the variety you choose, you can plant Madagascar periwinkle to edge a border, as a small-scale ground cover, or to trail over the sides of a pot or window box.

The **Pacifica** and **Cooler** series form compact, 15-inch plants with 2-inch-wide flowers; both are available in mixed colors and in a wide range of individual colors. Plants in the trailing **Mediterranean** series spread to 2½ feet wide but grow only 5 to 6 inches high. Colors include white, deep rose, lilac, and apricot (some apricot varieties have a large deep rose eye).

Catharanthus roseus

CULTURE. Madagascar periwinkle thrives in well-drained, average to rich soil. Sow seed indoors 12 weeks before the usual last-frost date. To avoid disease, take care not to overwater seedlings. Transplant to the garden after the weather has warmed in spring. To increase your supply of a favorite color (of either seed-raised or nursery plants), take cuttings in spring or early summer.

CATHARANTHUS roseus (Vinca rosea)
MADAGASCAR PERIWINKLE
Apocynaceae
PERENNIAL USUALLY GROWN AS
WARM-SEASON ANNUAL
ZONES 1–45; H1, H2
FULL SUN OR PARTIAL SHADE
MODERATE WATER
✿ ❀ ✿ ✿ ✩ FLOWERS IN SUMMER, FALL

Brilliant and long lasting, celosias are stunning in the summer garden and equally striking for indoor arrangements—both as fresh cut flowers and dried for winter bouquets. In the garden, they're effective massed as well as in combination with other annuals in vivid colors; they also make good container subjects.

Three popular kinds of celosias are derived from **C. argentea,** a white-flowered tropical species with narrow leaves to 2 inches or more long. Plume cockscombs (often sold as **C. 'Plumosa'**) range in height from 10 inches to 3 feet; as the name indicates, they have feathery flower plumes. Low-growing varieties include the **Kimono** series, only 10 inches tall, and the 14-inch-high **Castle** series; both are available in a wide variety of individual colors and as mixtures. Among the taller sorts, 20-inch-tall **'Apricot Brandy'** has deep orange plumes; the 3-foot-tall **Sparkler Mix** is a popular choice for cut flowers.

Crested cockscombs (often sold as **C. 'Cristata'**) grow from 6 inches to over 3 feet high and feature velvety, fan-shaped flower clusters that are often strangely contorted or fluted, resembling enormous rooster combs. The **Amigo** series features 6-inch-wide flower heads in magenta, red, rose, scarlet, and yellow on plants only 6 inches high; most have green leaves. **'Amigo Mahogany Red',** however, boasts dark purple foliage topped by dark maroon flower heads. **'Prestige Scarlet'** is a dense, branching plant 15 to 20 inches tall and wide.

CELOSIA
CELOSIA, COCKSCOMB
Amaranthaceae
WARM-SEASON ANNUALS
ZONES A3; 1–45; H1, H2
FULL SUN
MODERATE WATER
✿ ❀ ✿ ✿ ✩ FLOWERS IN SUMMER

Celosia 'Apricot Brandy'

Listing continues>

Celosia 'Flamingo Feather'

Wheat celosias (often sold as **C. 'Spicata'**) include upright, branching plants to 2½ feet tall with slim, cylindrical flower spikes. Varieties include **'Flamingo Feather'**, with blossoms in soft pink and white, and **'Purple Flamingo'**. All may reseed.

CULTURE. Plant celosias in moist but well-drained soil that has been enriched with organic matter. They thrive in hot, humid weather but not in chilly conditions—so don't sow or transplant too early. Tall varieties may need staking. To dry the flowers, cut them just as they open fully and hang them upside down in a warm, dry, airy place.

Sow seed indoors 6 to 8 weeks before the last expected frost. To avoid shocking the seedlings, use lukewarm water when watering; once the plants are up, keep them out of cold drafts. Set out transplants when they are still fairly young (or purchase small plants); older plants do not transplant as successfully and generally produce fewer flowers.

CENTAUREA
Asteraceae (Compositae)
PERENNIALS AND COOL-SEASON ANNUALS
ZONES VARY
FULL SUN
MODERATE WATER
✿ ✿ ❀ ✿ ✿ ☆ FLOWERS IN SPRING AND
    SUMMER, EXCEPT AS NOTED

Among these easy-to-grow plants for the border or wild garden, the best known is the annual bachelor's button or cornflower (**C. cyanus;** Zones 1–45, H1, H2). In most areas, it blooms in spring and early summer, but in desert areas it is planted for flowers in winter and early spring. The plant grows 1 to 1½ feet high, with gray-green, narrow, 2- to 3-inch-long leaves and 1½-inch, thistlelike flowers in white, blue, purple, pink, rose, or wine red (blue varieties are traditional favorites for boutonnières). **'Jubilee Gem'** is a bushy, compact 1-footer with deep blue flowers; the 16-inch **Polka Dot** strain features all the bachelor's button colors.

C. cineraria, one of a number of plants called dusty miller, is grown for its clumps of lobed, velvety white leaves. Perennial only in Zones 8–30, it is popular as an annual in regions beyond its hardiness range. Though its foliage is the main attraction, it also bears yellow blooms in summer.

Showy-flowered perennial centaureas include two species hardy in Zones 1–9, 14–24, 29–43. Summer-blooming Persian cornflower, **C. dealbata** (usually offered in the cultivar **'Steenbergii'**), forms spreading clumps of lobed, 8- to 12-inch-long leaves that are soft green on the upper surfaces, gray green beneath. It bears thistle-like purple flowers with white centers on slender, 2-foot stems. **C. hypoleuca 'John Coutts'** (sometimes listed as a variety of *C. dealbata*) is more compact, with deep rose pink blooms from late spring to mid-

Centaurea hypoleuca 'John Coutts'

summer. It has the same foliage color as *C. dealbata,* but the lobed, wavy-edged leaves are smaller (6 to 8 inches long) and lance shaped.

CULTURE. Plants grow vigorously in moderately fertile, well-drained soil. For best performance, add lime to acid soils. Taller varieties usually require staking.

While perennial species (including *C. cineraria*) are most easily grown from purchased plants, annual *C. cyanus* is easy to start from seed sown in place in spring, at about the time of the last expected frost. Or sow indoors 6 to 8 weeks before the last frost. (In desert regions, sow seed in fall for flowers in winter and spring.) When you plant, be sure to cover seed with ⅛ to ¼ inch of soil; darkness helps germination. Transplant seedlings grown in pots carefully, since too much root disturbance stunts the plants.

With the exception of *C. cineraria,* clumps of perennial species spread easily and may need to be divided every 3 to 4 years to renew growth and keep plantings in bounds.

Centaurea cyanus

Trouble-free Jupiter's beard has naturalized in the far western U.S. and in parts of England and continental Europe. Its upright stems, clothed in bluish green, 4-inch leaves, form bushy clumps to about 3 feet high; in spring and summer, tiny carmine red to rosy pink flowers appear in elongated, fluffy clusters at stem ends. **'Albus'** has pure white flowers.

CULTURE. Though Jupiter's beard will grow in poor, dry soils, it looks best if given reasonably good, well-drained soil and moderate watering. Cut off spent flower stems to shape plants, encourage repeat bloom, and prevent excessive self-seeding. The plant will bloom the first year from seed, with the seedlings usually producing flowers in reddish hues as well as white. To propagate a selected color, take basal cuttings during spring and summer; or divide plants in spring.

Centranthus ruber 'Albus'

CENTRANTHUS ruber
JUPITER'S BEARD, RED VALERIAN
Valerianaceae
PERENNIAL
ZONES 2–9, 12–24, 28–43; H1
FULL SUN OR LIGHT SHADE
LITTLE TO MODERATE WATER
❀✿☆ FLOWERS IN SPRING, SUMMER

Forming a silvery gray, 6- to 8-inch-high mat of stems clothed in narrow, ¾-inch leaves, snow-in-summer is covered in small, snowy white flowers in early summer—hence the common name. It makes an excellent edging and is especially effective setting off a border of brightly colored flowers. Or use it between stepping-stones or as a ground cover.

CULTURE. As long as drainage is good, snow-in-summer will grow in any soil. Where summers are hot, it looks best with some afternoon shade. Shear off faded flowers after bloom ends. Start with nursery plants; or sow seed outdoors in early spring after danger of frost is past, either in place or in containers for later transplanting. When a planting begins to show bare patches, divide and replant in fall or early spring.

Cerastium tomentosum

CERASTIUM tomentosum
SNOW-IN-SUMMER
Caryophyllaceae
PERENNIAL
ZONES A1, A2; 1–24, 32–45
FULL SUN, EXCEPT AS NOTED
MODERATE TO REGULAR WATER
❀ FLOWERS IN EARLY SUMMER

Honeywort grows 1 to 2 feet tall, with gray-green, 2½-inch leaves that seem to clasp its sturdy stems. Small, nodding clusters of unusual tubular flowers surrounded by showy bracts (modified leaves) appear at the stem tips from spring until early summer in most climates—but in mild-winter areas, bloom often begins in late winter and continues until hot weather arrives. The species has bicolored flowers in yellow and maroon. More widely grown, however, is **'Purpurascens'**; its flowers, bracts, and upper leaves are purplish blue, making the top of each stem look as though it's been dipped in purple dye.

CULTURE. Give honeywort full sun and well-drained, average soil. In mild-winter climates, sow seed outdoors in autumn, in the spot where the plants are to grow. In colder regions, sow seed outdoors in spring, just after the last-frost date; or sow indoors 8 weeks before the last-frost date. The plant may self-sow but does not do so profusely enough to become a pest.

Cerinthe major 'Purpurascens'

CERINTHE major
HONEYWORT
Boraginaceae
COOL-SEASON ANNUAL
ZONES 1–24, 32, 34–45
FULL SUN OR LIGHT SHADE
REGULAR WATER
✿☆ FLOWERS IN SPRING AND SUMMER,
   EXCEPT AS NOTED

CHELONE

TURTLEHEAD

Scrophulariaceae

PERENNIALS

ZONES 1–9, 14–24, 28–43

FULL SUN OR LIGHT SHADE

AMPLE WATER

✿ ❀ ✿ FLOWERS IN LATE SUMMER, FALL

These natives of the southeastern U. S. bear inch-long, puffy, two-lipped flowers of a vaguely reptilian appearance—hence the common name "turtlehead." From spring into summer, the plants are clumps of good-looking, glossy foliage; then, as bloom time approaches, leafy, branching stems rise 2 to 3½ feet, bearing blossoms in branching spikes. *C. glabra* has white flowers tinged with rose. *C. lyonii*, the most widely available species, produces rose pink flowers. *C. obliqua* has rosy purple blossoms; its cultivars include deep rose **'Bethelli'**, more floriferous than the species, and white **'Alba'**.

Chelone obliqua

CULTURE. Grow turtleheads in naturally damp places, such as in bog gardens or along stream banks. They also succeed in borders if grown in soil enriched with organic matter and given plenty of water. In general, turtleheads do well in full sun or light shade, though *C. lyonii* needs partial shade in hot-summer regions. *C. obliqua* is more tolerant of heat and sun.

When clumps become crowded, divide them in spring; or increase your supply of plants by stem cuttings taken in spring or summer.

CHRYSANTHEMUM

Asteraceae (Compositae)

PERENNIALS AND COOL-SEASON ANNUALS

ZONES VARY

FULL SUN, EXCEPT AS NOTED

REGULAR WATER, EXCEPT AS NOTED

✿ ❀ ✿ ✿ ✿ FLOWERS IN SPRING,
SUMMER, AND FALL, EXCEPT AS NOTED

While the name "chrysanthemum" is often associated with fall-blooming mums, the genus also includes other favorite spring- and summer-flowering daisies, among them annuals such as tricolor chrysanthemum and crown daisy. Perennial sorts include brightly colored painted daisy, feverfew, and the popular Shasta daisy. Taxonomists have split *Chrysanthemum* into a number of new genera—and in certain cases, changed their minds and returned some species to the original genus. In the following descriptions, the former, often more familiar names are given first, followed by the new names in parentheses.

ANNUAL CHRYSANTHEMUMS

Tricolor chrysanthemum, *C. carinatum* (*Glebionis carinatum*; Zones 1–45, H1, H2), is an erect, 1- to 3-foot-tall plant with deeply cut bright green foliage. Appearing in early summer in most climates (winter and spring in mild-winter regions), the 3- to 4-inch-wide flowers feature a dark center ringed with contrasting zones of white, purple, red, orange, or yellow. Crown daisy, *C. coronarium* (*Glebionis coronarium*; Zones 1–45, H1, H2), to 2½ feet tall, has coarsely cut light green leaves and 2-inch-wide yellow daisies in spring and summer. **'Primrose Gem'** is lower growing (1 to 1½ feet tall), with golden-eyed semidouble flowers in a softer yellow. *C. paludosum* (*Leucanthemum paludosum, Melampodium paludosum*; Zones A1–A3, 1–24), forms a 2- to 6-inch-tall clump of dark green, toothed leaves. In summer, the foliage mound sends up 8- to 10-inch stems topped by yellow-centered, inch-wide, white or yellow blossoms.

Chrysanthemum coronarium

CULTURE. Grow these annuals in full sun, in average to rich, well-drained soil. All can be sown in place in early spring, as soon as the soil can be worked. Or start seed indoors about 8 weeks before the usual last-frost date. (In mild-winter regions, sow *C. carinatum* in fall for winter and spring flowers.) Pinch young plants to encourage bushiness; deadhead to prolong bloom.

PERENNIAL CHRYSANTHEMUMS

The first species described below, *C. frutescens,* is grown as an annual in many parts of the country. The remaining species are raised as perennials everywhere.

Marguerite, *C. frutescens (Argyranthemum frutescens),* is a short-lived shrubby perennial in Zones 14–24, 26, 28, H1, H2; elsewhere, it is grown as an annual. It is an excellent container plant in any region. It grows fast—a young plant can expand to a dense, 4- by 4-foot mound of coarsely cut green leaves in just a few months. Summer brings a generous show of 2½-inch flowers. The typical form has single white blossoms with yellow centers, but named selections offer variations; among these are double-flowered **'Snow White'**, pale yellow **'Jamaica Primrose'**, and **'Vancouver'**, with anemone-centered, semidouble pink blooms.

CULTURE. Plant marguerites in a sunny spot, in loose-textured, well-drained soil. Cut plants back lightly and frequently to maintain bushiness, encourage rebloom, and limit size. Even in climates where marguerites are perennial, individual plants last just a few years; start replacements from cuttings taken in spring or summer. In cold climates, you can take cutings in late summer and overwinter them indoors in a bright, cool spot.

Chrysanthemum frutescens 'Vancouver'

Painted daisy, *C. coccineum (Tanacetum coccineum, Pyrethrum roseum)* grows in Zones A1, 1–24, 32–41. It forms a bushy, 2- to 3-foot plant with bright green, very finely divided leaves. The long-stemmed, 3-inch-wide blooms are single or double and come in pink shades, red, and white. Flowering starts in midspring where winters are mild, in late spring in colder regions. If you cut the stems to the ground after flowering, plants will sometimes rebloom in late summer. Cultivars include dark red **'James Kelway'** and the double-flowered **Robinson's Hybrids,** available in white, pink, and red.

CULTURE. Painted daisy grows best where summers are warm to hot, but it does not tolerate high humidity. Divide clumps or sow seeds in spring (seedlings flower in their second year).

Shasta daisy, *C. maximum (C. × superbum, Leucanthemum maximum, L. × superbum),* succeeds in Zones A1–A3, 1–24, 26 (northern part), 28–43, H1. A charming and versatile summer-flowering perennial for the border, it forms robust clumps of toothed, linear dark green leaves from which rise leafy flower stalks, each topped with one to several showy white daisies. The original forms featured 2- to 4-foot stems bearing 3- to 4-inch single flowers with big yellow centers; **'Alaska'** and **'Polaris'** are good examples, as is the more recently introduced **'Becky'**, which grows exceptionally well in hot, humid regions. **'Esther Read'** is a widely grown, long-blooming cultivar with double white blossoms on 2-foot stems. **'Aglaya'**, another 2-footer, has fringed double flowers. A popular dwarf is 15- to 18-inch **'Snowcap'**.

CULTURE. Shasta daisies thrive in fairly rich, moist soil. They prefer sun but do well in partial shade in hot-summer climates; the double-flowered kinds hold up better in very light shade in all regions. Deadhead to keep the flowers coming. In the coldest zones, mulch around the plants for winter, taking care not to smother the foliage. Clumps increase quickly and usually need division every other year or so. Divide in early spring (in fall in mild-winter areas). Shasta daisies are easy to grow from seed. Catalogs offer many strains, including some that bloom the first year.

TOP: *Chrysanthemum coccineum*
BOTTOM: *Chrysanthemum maximum*

Florists' chrysanthemum, *C. × morifolium (Dendranthema × grandiflorum),* is the mainstay of the autumn perennial flower show—both in the garden and in containers. It succeeds in Zones 2–24, 26 (northern part), 28–41, H1. Also known simply as garden mum, it's available in an incredible array of flower forms, flower colors, and growth habits. Popular among gardeners are types with single, semidouble, and double

Chrysanthemum × *morifolium* 'Debonair'

flowers, in a basic daisy shape or with a pompom, shaggy, or quilled form in colors including white and many shades of yellow, orange, bronze, red, purple, and pink. For general garden display, opt for the lower-growing kinds (usually under 1½ feet) with smaller flowers and a bushy, compact habit; large-flowered exhibition types are often rangy and require staking, even if you pinch them often to control growth. It's also important to consider your climate when choosing mums. The shorter the growing season, the more important it is to select early-flowering types, since fall frosts will destroy late bloomers before the flowers have a chance to open.

CULTURE. Plant florists' chrysanthemum in good, well-drained soil improved with organic matter; also dig in a complete fertilizer before planting. In hot climates, provide shade from afternoon sun. Set out young plants in early spring. Water deeply as needed to keep the soil moist but not saturated: too little water leads to woody stems and loss of lower leaves, while overwatering causes leaves to yellow, then blacken and drop. Several times during the growing season, pinch back all but the lowest-growing mums (the "cushion" type): as soon as a stem reaches 5 inches long, nip out the tip to force branching and create a dense, leafy plant. In cold-winter regions, stop pinching in early summer; in less severe climates (where lows seldom dip below 0°F/−18°C), continue pinching into August. After flowering has finished, cut stems down to about 8 inches; in cold regions, use the cut stems as a mulch over the plants. When growth begins the next year, cut the remaining portion of the stems to the ground. Clumps will need dividing about every other year. Do the job in early spring, replanting small, single-stem divisions from the outside of the clump and discarding the woody center.

Feverfew, ***C. parthenium*** (***Tanacetum parthenium*;** Zones 2−24, 28−45) is an old-fashioned favorite that makes a useful filler in the perennial border and provides excellent cut flowers. Clumps of bright green, somewhat feathery leaves with a pungent, peppery scent send up 2- to 3-foot stems in summer; these produce clusters of white daisies less than an inch across. **'Aureum'** grows 8 to 12 inches tall and has chartreuse foliage; **'Snowball'** reaches 1 to 2 feet and bears double flowers.

CULTURE. Plant this adaptable perennial in full sun in well-drained, average soil. It isn't long lived, but an ample supply of volunteer seedlings usually allows you to maintain your planting. You can also propagate feverfew by dividing the clumps in spring or by sowing seeds in spring for bloom by midsummer.

Chrysanthemum parthenium 'Snowball'

Listed in catalogs as cultivars of ***C.* × *rubellum*** or ***Dendranthema zawadskii*** are two other pretty chrysanthemums; both grow about 2 feet tall, have finely cut leaves, and succeed in Zones 1−24, 28−43. They bear 2- to 3-inch-wide daisies over a long season, beginning earlier than garden mums and continuing into fall. **'Clara Curtis'** has bright pink flowers; blossoms of **'Mary Stoker'** are an unusual soft yellow with apricot touches.

CULTURE. Give plants full sun and moderate water. When clumps become crowded (usually every other year), divide them in spring.

Tall, slender plants with an airy, delicate texture, the bugbanes are at home in woodland gardens or in borders. Clumps of coarse, fernlike dark green leaves may reach 2½ feet; from these rise slim, branching stems that terminate in spikes of small, bristly white flowers. One of the tallest species is black snakeroot, *C. racemosa*, a North American native which easily reaches 6 feet when in bloom—in midsummer in southern regions, in late summer or early fall further north. It has erect flower spikes. The floral plumes of Kamchatka bugbane, *C. simplex*, in contrast, are arching; they appear in autumn on 4-foot stems. Among this species' selections are '**White Pearl**', with especially large, dense flower spikes; '**Atropurpurea**', with 4- to 6-foot blossom stalks and dark reddish purple foliage; and '**Brunette**' (3 to 4 feet tall) and '**Hillside Black Beauty**' (5 to 6 feet tall), with even more richly colored foliage. (The last three selections are sometimes listed as selections of *C. racemosa.*)

Cimicifuga simplex

CULTURE. Plant bugbanes in soil enriched with organic matter. Where summers are cool or mild, they can be planted in full sun or partial shade; in hot areas, they require some shade (as at the edge of a woodland, for example). Plants seldom need division, but if you want to divide to increase your planting, do so in early spring.

CIMICIFUGA
(Actaea)
BUGBANE, SNAKEROOT
Ranunculaceae
PERENNIALS
ZONES 1–7, 17, 32–45
FULL SUN OR PARTIAL SHADE,
  EXCEPT AS NOTED
REGULAR WATER
❀ FLOWERS IN SUMMER, FALL

Named for Captain William Clark of the Lewis and Clark expedition, these slender-stemmed annual wildflowers are grown for their clusters of satiny blossoms. They make good cut flowers; cut the stems when the top bud opens (others open successively). Plants range in height from well under a foot to as tall as 4 feet; they grow and bloom best in cool climates and do not tolerate heat and humidity.

Farewell-to-spring, *C. amoena (Godetia amoena)* has two forms in the wild. One is coarse stemmed and sprawling, only 4 to 5 inches high; the other is a slender-stemmed, 1½- to 2½-foot plant. The tapered leaves are ½ to 2 inches long. On both forms, the buds grow upright along the stems, opening into 2-inch-wide, cup-shaped pink or lavender flowers, often with central blotches of contrasting colors. The **Grace** series has lavender, pink, red, or salmon blossoms on 20-inch plants.

C. pulchella is a slim, upright, 1- to 1½-foot plant with reddish stems and narrow, 1- to 2-inch-long leaves. The bright pink to lavender flowers are single or semidouble; each petal has a distinctive three-lobed tip. '**Snowflake**' is a pure white form that grows 12 to 15 inches high.

Mountain garland, *C. unguiculata (C. elegans)*, grows from 1 to 4 feet high and has lance-shaped, 1- to 2-inch-long leaves; the inch-wide flowers have petals that are narrow at the base, rounded or lobed at the tip. Wild forms bloom in rose, purple, and white. Varieties include '**Apple Blossom**', with fully double flowers in soft apricot pink, and the **Royal Bouquet** strain, also with double flowers, in colors including white, purple, pink, rose, salmon, orange, and creamy yellow.

CULTURE. Clarkias grow best in sandy soil without added fertilizer. Sow seed in place in the garden—in fall in mild-winter regions, in early spring in colder areas. Plants often self-sow, producing volunteers for next year's garden.

CLARKIA
Onagraceae
COOL-SEASON ANNUALS
ZONES 1–45
FULL SUN
MODERATE WATER
✿❀✿✿✿ FLOWERS IN SPRING,
  EARLY SUMMER

Clarkia amoena

CLEOME hassleriana
(C. spinosa)
SPIDER FLOWER

Capparidaceae

WARM-SEASON ANNUAL

ZONES 1–45

FULL SUN

MODERATE TO REGULAR WATER

✿ ❀ ✿ ✿ FLOWERS IN SUMMER, FALL

Growing as tall as 5 feet, this substantial annual produces leafy spikes topped in summer and fall by open clusters of blossoms with extremely long, protruding stamens—a feature that gives the flowers a distinctly spidery look. Long, narrow, pointed seedpods follow the blossoms, adding to the plant's unusual appearance. The lower leaves are divided, with leaflets radiating out from the center like fingers of a hand; the upper ones are undivided. Both leaves and stems have a pungent odor and feel somewhat clammy to the touch. The stems are usually set with short spines, so be careful when cutting the flowers for indoor display.

Cleome hassleriana

Spider flower provides a colorful, unusual background for a large border; it is also attractive grown as an annual hedge or in a large container. Seeds are sold in mixed or individual colors; the latter group includes **'Helen Campbell'**, with pure white blooms, and **'Purple Queen'**, **'Pink Queen'**, **'Cherry Queen'**, and **'Rose Queen'**.

CULTURE. Spider plant grows well in warm weather, in light, well-drained soil. It self-sows, sometimes to the point of becoming invasive. For flowers earlier in the season, sow seeds indoors 6 to 8 weeks before the last-frost date. Or sow outdoors after the last frost. In either case, mix the seeds with moist potting mix in a plastic bag and chill in the refrigerator for 5 days before planting.

COLEUS × hybridus
(Solenostemon
scutellarioides)
Lamiaceae (Labiatae)

PERENNIAL USUALLY GROWN AS
  WARM-SEASON ANNUAL

ALL ZONES

LIGHT SHADE, EXCEPT AS NOTED

REGULAR WATER

FLOWERS ARE INSIGNIFICANT; GROWN
  FOR FOLIAGE IN PURPLE, RED, BUFF,
  BROWN, SALMON, ORANGE, YELLOW,
  CHARTREUSE, BICOLORS

Valued for its brilliant foliage, coleus forms a bushy plant 1 to 3 feet high. Leaves vary from 1 to 7 inches long and may be toothed or ruffled; in most selections, each leaf displays two or more colors, with contrasting edges, splotches, or veins. The blue flower spikes are attractive, but they're usually pinched out in bud to make the plant more rounded and compact.

Coleus are classic plants for shaded borders and containers, but varieties more tolerant of sun are becoming available. In general, the more red or purple pigment the foliage has, the greater the sun tolerance; examples include **'Cranberry Sun'**, with reddish purple foliage, and **'Plum Parfait'**, featuring ruffled plum-colored leaves edged in pink. Both of these grow 2 to 3 feet high and have 1½- to 3-inch-long leaves. They are sold as cutting-grown plants—as are **'Black Magic'**, a 1½- to 2-footer with 1½- to 2-inch, dark velvety purple leaves bordered in green, and 2-foot **'Saturn'**, bearing pur-

Coleus × hybridus 'Plum Parfait'

ple, 2½- to 3-inch-long leaves sporting a vivid lime center. Many other cutting-grown coleus are offered; all tend to be more uniform in habit than seed-grown sorts.

Among seed-grown coleus, **The Wizard** is a well-known self-branching dwarf strain. It reaches 10 to 12 inches tall and has heart-shaped, 2- to 2½-inch leaves in a wide range of color combinations. Another seed-grown strain is **Giant Exhibition**, featuring 12- to 15-inch plants with huge (6- to 7-inch-long) leaves in a great variety of colors.

CULTURE. Grow coleus in rich, loose, evenly moist, well-drained soil. As noted above, most (though not all) varieties require some shade. Fertilize regularly.

Sow seeds indoors 10 weeks before the last frost. Barely press seeds into the potting mix; they need light to sprout. Pinch seedlings as well as older plants frequently to encourage bushy growth. Set out plants in the garden after all danger of frost is past. You can easily propagate coleus from cuttings—and this method provides a simple way to overwinter favorite varieties. Take cuttings in late summer and keep the resulting plants indoors through winter; then, in early spring, take more cuttings to produce plants for outdoor use.

Consolida ajacis

Prized for its resemblance to the stately perennial delphinium and for its ease of culture, larkspur is an erect, 1- to 4-foot-tall plant with deeply cut, almost fernlike leaves and showy blossom spikes set thickly with single or double, 1- to 1½-inch-wide blossoms. It blooms best in the cool weather of spring and early summer, dying out when hot temperatures arrive. Tall varieties make excellent back-of-border plants and provide charming cut flowers; shorter ones are a good source of color at the front of beds and borders. Note that all parts of this plant are poisonous (especially the seeds).

The **Dwarf Hyacinth Flowering** series offers neat, foot-tall plants with double flowers in white, blue, lilac, violet, and pink. Growing 20 inches tall, the **Earlibird** series is available in white, blue, lilac, or rose. Taller larkspurs include **'Blue Cloud'**, to 3½ feet tall, and 4-foot **'Earl Grey'**, with double flowers in an unusual shade of silvery mauve. The double-blossomed **Giant Imperial** series produces 4-foot plants in colors including white, blue, lilac, pink, salmon, and rose.

CULTURE. Larkspur grows best if sown in place directly in the garden, in a well-prepared planting bed enriched with organic matter. Sow in autumn except in heavy, slow-draining soils; in these soils, plant in spring, about 2 weeks before the last frost. Thin seedlings to avoid crowding; tall varieties may need staking. Larkspurs often self-sow.

CONSOLIDA ajacis (Consolida ambigua, Delphinium ambiguum)
LARKSPUR, ANNUAL DELPHINIUM
Ranunculaceae
COOL-SEASON ANNUAL
ZONES 1–45
FULL SUN
REGULAR WATER
✿ ✿ ❀ ✿ FLOWERS IN SPRING, EARLY SUMMER

Intensely colored, trumpet-shaped blossoms, their throats highlighted by jagged bands of white and yellow, make dwarf morning glory a striking choice for the summer garden. It's a mounding, somewhat trailing plant to 1 foot or a little taller, 2 feet wide. Its flowers, like those of the related annual morning glory vine (*Ipomoea tricolor*, page 182), last only a day and do not open in cloudy weather. Dwarf morning glory is a reliable summer bloomer; in mild-winter climates, it can also be planted in fall for spring flowers. It's effective in a large rock garden, as an edging, draped over the top of a wall, or in hanging baskets.

The **Ensign** series, growing 12 to 14 inches tall, is available in mixed or individual colors. **'Royal Ensign'** has blooms of the classic deep royal blue; **'Red Ensign'** and **'Rose Ensign'** are also offered. **Choice Mixed,** to 16 inches, blooms in white and shades of pink and blue.

Listing continues>

CONVOLVULUS tricolor
DWARF MORNING GLORY
Convolvulaceae
WARM-SEASON ANNUAL
ZONES 1–45
FULL SUN
MODERATE WATER
✿ ✿ ❀ ✿ FLOWERS IN SUMMER, EXCEPT AS NOTED

CULTURE. Grow dwarf morning glory in a sunny area, in average to moderately rich soil. The seed coat (outer covering) is very hard, preventing the seed from absorbing moisture; nicking each seed with a sharp knife or soaking seeds overnight in warm water before planting will improve germination. Sow seeds in place in the garden after the last-frost date (in mild-winter areas, sow in fall).

Convolvulus tricolor 'Royal Ensign'

COREOPSIS

COREOPSIS, TICKSEED

Asteraceae (Compositae)

PERENNIALS AND WARM-SEASON ANNUALS

ZONES VARY BY SPECIES

FULL SUN

LITTLE TO MODERATE WATER, EXCEPT
   AS NOTED

✿ ✿ ✿ FLOWERS IN SPRING, SUMMER, FALL

Coreopsis tinctoria

Brightening the garden with sunny daisies over a long season, species and varieties of coreopsis range from a few inches to several feet in height. One annual species, summer-blooming *C. tinctoria* (Zones 1–45; H1, H2), is widely grown. Known as annual coreopsis and native to much of North America, it's a slender, upright, 1½- to 3-foot-tall plant with wiry stems and lacy-looking leaves to 4 inches long. The species bears the solid yellow blooms common to most other coreopsis, but its cultivars offer variations with maroon centers and petals strikingly striped or marked in dark red, maroon, or purplish-brown. The flowers are 1 to 2 inches wide.

The following perennial choices are native to the southern and eastern U. S. At only 6 inches tall, *C. auriculata* 'Nana' (Zones 1–24, 26–45) is the shortest of the group, useful as an edging at the front of a border. It blooms from spring to early fall, sending up stems bearing vivid orange-yellow, 1- to 2½-inch blossoms above a mat of 2- to 5-inch-long leaves. *C. grandiflora* (Zones 2–24, 26, 28–43; H1, H2), with narrow, 2- to 4-inch-long leaves, includes several excellent selections that bloom from late spring through summer. 'Early Sunrise' is a 1½- to 2-footer with semidouble bright yellow, 2-inch-wide flowers; 'Sunray' is similar but has double blooms in a deeper yellow. *C. lanceolata* (Zones 1–24, 26, 28–45; H1, H2) grows 1 to 2 feet high; it has narrow basal leaves to about 6 inches long. Bright yellow, 1½- to 2-inch-wide blossoms bloom in late spring and summer; they are excellent for cutting.

C. rosea (Zones 2b–24, 31–41), reaching 1½ to 2 feet tall, is a fine-textured plant with linear bright green leaves to about 2 inches long. Yellow-centered pink blossoms appear from summer to fall.

As the common name indicates, threadleaf coreopsis, *C. verticillata* (Zones 1–24, 26, 28–45), has finely divided, very narrow leaves. Ranging from 1 to 2½ feet tall, the bushy, mounding plant bears bright yellow, 2-inch daisies over a long summer-to-autumn season. 'Moonbeam' features blossoms of a soft pale yellow on a 1½- to 2-foot plant; foot-tall 'Zagreb' has golden yellow flowers.

CULTURE. Coreopsis are trouble-free plants, thriving even in relatively poor soil (as long as it is well drained). Once established, they grow well with relatively little water—with the exception of *C. rosea*, which prefers moist soil. Remove spent blossoms to prolong flowering. Most of the perennials spread rapidly and may need frequent division (as often as every 2 to 3 years) to stay in bounds. Both annual and perennial coreopsis can be propagated from seed. Sow seed of annual coreopsis, *C. tinctoria*, in place in the garden after the last frost. Start seed of perennial sorts indoors in late winter.

Coreopsis lanceolata

These shade-loving perennials carry their charming little spurred flowers above handsome clumps of dainty, divided, fernlike leaves much like those of bleeding heart (*Dicentra*, to which they are closely related) or maidenhair fern (to which they are not).

C. cheilanthifolia, growing 8 to 10 inches high, has green foliage and clusters of deep yellow, ½-inch-long flowers in spring. *C. flexuosa* (sometimes called blue corydalis), an introduction from western China, forms a 9- to 12-inch mound of blue-green foliage. Narrow, erect clusters of beautiful sky blue, long-spurred, 1-inch flowers bloom in early spring, often continuing into summer. The plant may go dormant in summer, especially in hot climates, but it will reappear the following spring. Selected forms include '**Blue Panda**', with brilliant gentian blue flowers, and '**Père David**', with lavender to light blue blooms.

A many-stemmed plant with masses of gray-green foliage, *C. lutea* reaches 15 inches tall and bears golden yellow, ¾-inch-long, short-spurred flowers throughout the summer. It often self-sows, popping up in shady places throughout the garden.

CULTURE. Give corydalis rich soil that is moist but well drained. Plants grow well and look good in shady areas among rocks, in open woodland, or near a pool or stream. Divide clumps or sow seed in spring or fall (seed germinates best if freshly collected).

CORYDALIS

Fumariaceae
PERENNIALS
ZONES 2–9, 14–24, 32–35, 37, 39–43
PARTIAL SHADE
REGULAR WATER
✿ ✿ ✿ FLOWERS IN SPRING, SUMMER

Corydalis lutea

Long-time cottage-garden favorites, cosmos are airy, graceful plants with daisylike, satiny-petalled blossoms. The plants range from 1½ to 4 feet high (or even taller) and have bright green, finely divided leaves. Cosmos are useful for mass color in beds and borders, as background plants, and mixed with other annuals in big containers; they're also first-rate cut flowers (gather them as soon as the blossoms open and immediately place them in cool water).

C. bipinnatus produces 3- to 4-inch-wide flowers in white and shades of lavender, purple, pink, rose, and red; all have tufted yellow centers. The species has single flowers with flat petals, but there are also double-flowered sorts and kinds with quilled petals. The dwarf **Sonata** series produces bushy plants just 2 feet tall; it's available in mixed colors and in single shades including pure white, pink, pink-blushed white, and carmine. The **Seashells** strain has rolled or quilled petals, giving the flowers greater depth and substance; plants grow 3 to 4 feet tall and are usually offered in mixed colors that range from white through pink to red. Also reaching 3 to 4 feet, **Psyche** offers frilly semidouble flowers in pink as well as soft or deep rose. Bred for cut flowers, the **Versailles** strain features 3½-foot-tall, vigorous, strong-stemmed plants with blossoms in a variety of colors.

Yellow cosmos, *C. sulphureus*, produces 2- to 3-inch-wide blossoms in bold shades of yellow, golden orange, and scarlet orange. The dwarf **Ladybird** series packs a lot of color into plants only 12 to 14 inches tall; its semidouble flowers come in vivid shades of scarlet, orange, and yellow. '**Lemon Twist**' offers softer yellow blossoms on plants growing about 2½ feet high; the 3-foot-tall **Polidor** mix flaunts flowers in glowing red, orange, and yellow.

CULTURE. Grow cosmos in well-drained, average soil; if planted in rich soil, they produce foliage at the expense of flowers. Stake taller varieties to keep them upright. Removing spent flowers will encourage more blossoms.

Sow seed in place after danger of frost is past; or, for earlier blossoms, sow indoors 6 weeks before the usual last-frost date. Seed germinates quickly—in only 5 to 10 days. Cosmos often self-sow.

COSMOS

Asteraceae (Compositae)
WARM-SEASON ANNUALS
ZONES A3; 1–45
FULL SUN
MODERATE WATER
✿ ✿ ✿ ✿ ✿ FLOWERS IN SUMMER, FALL

Cosmos bipinnatus

DELPHINIUM

Ranunculaceae

PERENNIALS

ZONES VARY

FULL SUN, EXCEPT AS NOTED

REGULAR WATER

✿ ✿ ❀ ✿ FLOWERS IN SUMMER

Delphinium elatum,
Magic Fountains strain

Stately and aristocratic, delphiniums epitomize both the classic English border and the cottage garden. Though these old-fashioned favorites are most often associated with blue flowers, they're available in a range of colors, including white, pink, lilac, and purple. Some of the hybrids have bi- or even tricolored blooms, with the center petals (the "bee") offering a white, black, or gold contrast to the outer petals. Ranging in height from 15-inch dwarfs to 8-foot giants, the plants bear their rounded blossoms on spikes; the lobed or fanlike leaves are variously cut and divided. All delphiniums require considerable effort from the gardener if they are to grow to perfection.

D. × belladonna (Zones 1–9, 14–24, 32, 34, 36–43) is a hybrid group of plants that reach 3 to 4 feet when in bloom. Unlike the well-known *D. elatum* hybrids (see below), which have a central flower stem followed later in the season by smaller branches, these delphiniums produce many flower stems at the same time; they also have airier, more loosely arranged flower clusters than *D. elatum* hybrids and are somewhat longer lived. Selections include light blue **'Belladonna'**, dark blue **'Volkerfrieden' ('People of Peace')**, white **'Casa Blanca'**, and deep turquoise **'Cliveden Beauty'**.

D. elatum is a Siberian native reaching 3 to 6 feet tall; it has small purple flowers and is among the parents of the familiar tall modern delphiniums—complex *D. elatum* hybrids that grow in Zones A1–A3, 1–10, 14–24, 32, 34, 36–41. **Pacific strain** delphiniums (also known as **Pacific Hybrids, Pacific Giants,** and **Pacific Coast Hybrids**) reach 5 to 8 feet under optimal conditions. They're available as seed-raised mixed-color plants and in named series that produce specific colors, including light blue **'Summer Skies'**, medium blue **'Blue Bird'**, dark violet **'Black Knight'**, white **'Galahad'**, and **'Percival'**, which has white flowers with a black center. Many other named varieties in purple, lavender, and pink are sold. Shorter choices include the 2- to 2½-foot-tall **Blue Fountains, Blue Springs,** and **Magic Fountains** strains. Even shorter is the 15- to 20-inch **Stand Up** strain.

CULTURE. Delphiniums grow best in the classic English climate—that is, in regions with cool to warm (not hot), humid summers. They are much less successful where summers are hot, dry, or both. In marginal locations, shelter plants by placing them in dappled sunlight, and take care to provide sufficient moisture. These plants require soil that is cool, moist yet well drained, and slightly acid to slightly alkaline. Add lime to strongly acid soils. Dig plenty of organic matter and a complete fertilizer into the soil a few weeks before planting time. To prevent rot, take care not to cover the crown of the plant. Taller varieties require staking. Slugs and snails can ruin young plants; see page 78 for controls.

During the bloom season, cut off spent blossom spikes just below the lowest flower, leaving part of the stalk and its foliage. Then, when new basal shoots reach about 6 inches tall, cut the old spikes to the ground and apply a complete fertilizer around the plant. The new stems should flower in late summer or early autumn.

Even with the best care, hybrid delphiniums tend to be short lived. You can take basal cuttings in spring or divide clumps and set out individual plants in well-prepared soil—but most gardeners find it easier to start fresh with young seedlings or cutting-grown plants from a nursery. You can also treat delphiniums as annuals by planting them in autumn (in mild-winter regions) or early spring (in all regions) to flower in summer. This is the best tactic in areas that have hot summers and/or mild winters.

Delphinium elatum, Pacific strain,
'Summer Skies'

For centuries, gardeners have enjoyed the many sorts of dianthus for their cheerful flowers and, in most species, delightful clove fragrance. Borne singly or in clusters, the circular, ½- to 1-inch-wide flowers may be single, semidouble, or double; they are often fringed at the edges and may have eyes and petal margins in contrasting colors. All are delightful in low borders, in rock gardens, and as edgings. Annual and biennial sorts are also good choices for containers.

The China pink, **D. chinensis,** may live for more than a year as a biennial or short-lived perennial in warm-winter climates, but it's generally grown as an annual everywhere. Ranging from 6 inches to 2½ feet tall, the dome-shaped plants have stems that branch near the top. The basal leaves are medium green, up to 3 inches long (they often wither before flowering time); the narrow stem leaves are 1 to 3 inches long. Fringed-looking flowers in white and shades of pink and red are produced in loose clusters in late spring or early summer; unlike most other dianthus, they have little or no scent. The **Ideal** series produces foot-tall plants that flower better than most others in summer heat; the blossoms often feature a charming contrasting eye. **Telstar** is a bushy, 6- to 8-inch-tall strain; its blossoms, often with intricately marked eyes, may have smooth-edged or fringed petals.

Sweet William, **D. barbatus,** is generally grown as a vigorous biennial—but some newer fast-maturing varieties are treated as annuals, blooming the first year from seed. These cottage-garden classics reach 20 inches tall and have light to dark green, 1½- to 3-inch-long leaves. In late spring and early summer, dense clusters of small, fragrant flowers bloom in white, pink, rose, red, and bicolors. '**Harlequin**', to 1½ feet tall, produces large flower heads that contain blossoms in a mix of colors, ranging from white to deep pink. The **Rondo** series (6 inches tall) and **New Era Mixed** (1½ feet tall) are two sweet Williams that have been bred to bloom the first year if sown in early spring. Both have flowers in white and shades of pink and red, quite often with contrasting central rings or outer edges.

The Allwood pinks, **D. × allwoodii,** are perennial hybrids developed early in the 20th century; they vary somewhat, but most have gray-green foliage and two blossoms per stem. Among the many varieties are '**Aqua**', with double blooms in pure white, and '**Doris**', with salmon pink flowers accented by a deep pink eye; both grow 10 to 12 inches high. '**Horatio**', to just 6 inches tall, has double pink flowers with a dark eye.

Maiden pink, **D. deltoides,** also a perennial, grows well in light shade. The green-foliaged plants spread to form broad, loose mats about 6 inches high, making a good small-scale ground cover. Branched stems bear flowers at their tips in summer. The species has purple to rose-colored flowers. Available varieties include pure white '**Albus**'; deep red '**Vampire**'; and '**Zing Rose**', bearing rosy red blossoms with a darker ring around the eye.

Perennial Cheddar pink, **D. gratianopolitanus (D. caesius),** forms a ground-hugging mat of blue-green leaves; pink flowers appear in summer on 6- to 10-inch stems. Selected forms vary in size and flower color. '**Bath's Pink**' sends up 12- to 15-inch stems bearing fringed soft pink blossoms; smaller-growing cultivars include 6-inch-tall, red-and-white '**Spotty**' and 4-inch '**Tiny Rubies**', with small double blooms in ruby red. The species as well as its varieties grow well in hot, humid areas.

Perennial cottage or grass pink, **D. plumarius** (Zones A1; 1–24, 30–45), forms a loose mat of gray-green foliage. It blooms in early summer, carrying its blossoms on stems 10 to 18 inches tall. Some of the oldest dianthus are classified here, including the legendary 17th-century '**Dad's Favorite**', with ruby-edged double white flowers centered in maroon, and '**Musgrave's Pink**', a classic at least two centuries old that bears intensely fragrant single white flowers with a green eye.

Listing continues>

DIANTHUS
Caryophyllaceae
PERENNIALS, BIENNIALS OFTEN GROWN
    AS COOL-SEASON ANNUALS
ZONES A2, A3, 1–24, 30–45,
    EXCEPT AS NOTED
FULL SUN, EXCEPT AS NOTED
MODERATE TO REGULAR WATER
✿ ❀ ✿ ✾ FLOWERS IN SPRING, SUMMER

Dianthus chinensis 'Telstar Scarlet'

Dianthus chinensis 'Telstar Picotee'

Dianthus × allwoodii 'Horatio'

CULTURE. All kinds of dianthus thrive in fast-draining soil. *D. barbatus* and *D. plumarius* need fairly rich soil; the others described here require a light, even gritty, soil. All prefer neutral to slightly alkaline soil; add lime to acidic soils. In hot-summer regions, place plants where they will receive a little afternoon shade. To encourage more flowers throughout summer, remove faded blossoms, breaking or cutting the stems at the nodes where new growth is starting. In colder regions (where winter lows dip to −10°F/−23°C), protect perennial varieties with a loose cover of evergreen boughs.

Most dianthus are easy to grow from seed, and many self-sow. Sow seed of perennials in containers in a cold frame in spring or fall. You can sow seed of annual dianthus (*D. chinensis,* annual forms of *D. barbatus*) outdoors a few weeks before the last frost; or, for earlier flowering, sow indoors 8 weeks before the last frost. To grow *D. barbatus* as a biennial, sow seed in late spring or early summer in a nursery bed; in fall, transplant the young plants to the desired garden location for bloom the following year.

After several years, most perennial dianthus begin to decline. Replace them with plants grown from seed or cuttings. Take stem cuttings in spring from new growth that has not flowered; the cuttings should be about six nodes in length. Stems that spread along the ground may take root where nodes touch the soil; cut these rooted plants from the parent and transplant them.

DICENTRA
BLEEDING HEART
Fumariaceae
PERENNIALS
ZONES 1–9, 14–24, 31–45, EXCEPT
    AS NOTED
LIGHT SHADE, EXCEPT AS NOTED
REGULAR WATER
❀ ✿ ✿ FLOWERS IN SPRING, SUMMER

Dicentra spectabilis

Delicate wands of heart-shaped flowers and finely dissected, almost feathery foliage make bleeding heart a favorite. Eastern and western North America are home to two similar low-growing species. The eastern species is fringed bleeding heart, ***D. eximia;*** it forms a tidy, non-spreading, 1- to 1½-foot clump of blue-gray foliage. The bare stems rise just above the leaves, carrying dangling deep pink flowers from mid-spring into summer. **'Alba'** is a white-flowered selection. Foot-tall Western bleeding heart,

Dicentra spectabilis 'Alba'

D. formosa, has blue-green foliage; in spring, pale to deep rose flowers are clustered on slim stems that rise 6 to 8 inches above the leaves. Under favorable conditions, this species spreads widely, but it is not invasive. **'Zestful'** is a long-blooming variety with deep rose flowers. ***D. f. oregana*** is shorter than the species and bears cream blossoms tipped in pink.

Nurseries offer a number of superior 12- to 15-inch selections of uncertain ancestry; they may be hybrids of the above two species or selected forms of one of them. **'Bacchanal'**, bearing deep red blooms, is nearly everblooming during the growing season, as is pink-flowered **'Bountiful'**. The hardy selection **'Luxuriant'** (Zones A1–A3; 1–9, 14–24; 31–45) can endure drier soil and stronger light than most; its deep pink flowers appear in spring and early summer.

Common bleeding heart, ***D. spectabilis*** (Zones A1–A3; 1–9, 14–24, 31–45), native to Japan, is the showiest and largest leafed of the bleeding hearts. Clothed in soft green foliage, the plants grow 2 to 3 feet high; in late spring, branched stems carry nearly horizontal sprays of pendulous, heart-shaped rose pink flowers with protruding white inner petals. **'Alba'** is pure white. Plants begin to die down after flowering and are generally dormant by midsummer, though they tend to last longer in cool-summer climates if given adequate moisture. To fill the gap they leave, plant summer-maturing perennials (such as hostas or ferns) or annuals such as impatiens nearby.

CULTURE. Plant bleeding hearts in light, well-drained soil enriched with organic matter. The roots should be kept cool and moist, but not soggy. Most of these plants prefer filtered sunlight to partial shade, but in cool regions, *D. spectabilis* and the hybrid 'Luxuriant' will tolerate full sun. All but *D. spectabilis* may need dividing after several years. Do this in earliest spring, before growth is really underway. (*D. spectabilis* has brittle roots and is best left undisturbed, though you can divide it during dormancy to increase your plantings.) All can be propagated by root cuttings taken in summer or fall.

Dictamnus albus

Sturdy and long lived, this handsome perennial forms bushy, 2½- to 4-foot-tall clumps of glossy, citrus-scented foliage on sturdy stems; the leaves are composed of 3-inch-long, pointed leaflets. At bloom time in late spring and summer, loose spires of narrow-petaled blossoms with prominent, greenish stamens appear at the stem tips; they are reminiscent of wild azaleas. Pink is the basic color, but nurseries also offer lilac '**Purpureus**' and white '**Albiflorus**'. The seedpods that follow are also attractive. In warm, humid weather, volatile oils from the immature seed capsules may briefly ignite if you hold a lighted match immediately beneath a flower cluster—hence the common names "gas plant" and "burning bush." (This "ignition test" does not harm the plant.)

Gas plant contains phototoxins, chemical substances that make the skin of susceptible people hypersensitive to sunlight following direct exposure to plant parts.

CULTURE. Give gas plant well-drained, moderately fertile soil. It grows best in regions with cool nights. Plants may take 2 to 3 years to settle in and start blooming well, but they can remain in place indefinitely (and should, in fact, be left in one place; they reestablish slowly if divided). Start new plants from seed or from root cuttings taken in late winter.

DICTAMNUS albus
GAS PLANT, BURNING BUSH,
FRAXINELLA
Rutaceae
PERENNIAL
ZONES 1–9, 31–45
FULL SUN OR LIGHT SHADE
MODERATE TO REGULAR WATER
✿ ❀ ✿ FLOWERS IN LATE SPRING, SUMMER

These old-fashioned favorites feature tubular flowers shaped like the fingertips of a glove, carried in erect spikes that rise above a rosette of lance-shaped leaves. The classic garden sort, **D. purpurea** (Zones A2, A3; 1–24, 31–41), is a biennial: it develops a clump of large, furry light green leaves during its first year, sends up stately, 4- to 6-foot spires of pendulous blossoms in spring and early summer of the second year, and then usually dies. The 2- to 3-inch-long flowers come in creamy yellow, white, rose purple, or pink, all spotted with purple inside. Garden strains include 5-foot-tall **Excelsior,** with outward-facing flowers in creamy yellow, white, purple, and pink; 3½-foot , apricot pink '**Sutton's Apricot**'; and '**Alba**', a pure white form lacking the typical interior spots. As is the case with many other biennials, breeders have developed a fast-growing strain that can be grown as an annual: 3-foot-tall **Foxy,** which flowers in just 5 months from seed and offers a range of colors.

DIGITALIS
FOXGLOVE
Scrophulariaceae
PERENNIALS AND BIENNIALS
ZONES VARY
LIGHT SHADE, EXCEPT AS NOTED
REGULAR WATER, EXCEPT AS NOTED
✿ ❀ ✿ ✿ FLOWERS IN LATE SPRING,
SUMMER

Digitalis purpurea, Foxy strain

Listing continues>

Digitalis grandiflora

Other species are perennial (though sometimes short lived); they produce the typical clumps of bold leaves but feature somewhat shorter flower spikes. Yellow foxglove, ***D. grandiflora (D. ambigua),*** succeeds in Zones 1–10, 14–24, 31–43. It grows 2 to 3 feet tall and has 2-inch-long pale yellow flowers lightly spotted brown on the inside. Its cultivar '**Carillon**' grows only 12 to 15 inches high. Grecian foxglove, ***D. lanata*** (Zones 2b–10, 14–24, 31–41), has dark green leaves and narrow, 3-foot-tall spikes of 1¼-inch, cream-colored flowers with purplish veining and a small near-white lip. ***D. × mertonensis*** (Zones 1–10, 14–24, 31–41) bears 2- to 3-foot spikes of 2½-inch flowers in a deep pink shade often described as strawberry. Though it is a hybrid, it comes true from seed.

Narrow-leaf foxglove, ***D. obscura*** (Zones 2–10, 14–24, 31–41), grows 1½ feet high; it has lance-shaped leaves and unusual brown-and-yellow flowers just ¾ to 1¼ inches long. ***D. thapsi*** (Zones 2–10, 14–24, 31–41) reaches only a foot high and features drooping, inch-long pink flowers over furry foliage.

Note that all parts of all foxglove species are poisonous if ingested.

CULTURE. Most foxgloves are at their best in filtered sun to light or partial shade; where summers are cool, however, you can plant them in sun. Most kinds also need good soil enriched with organic matter and do best with regular watering. *D. obscura* and *D. thapsi,* however, are exceptions: they prefer full sun to light shade, well-drained soil that is not too rich, and occasional deep watering.

For all species, remove spent flower spikes to encourage repeat bloom in late summer or autumn. If you want seeds to start new plants, leave a few spikes.

Sow seed of biennial foxgloves in late spring or summer—in place in the garden, in an outdoor nursery bed, or in containers. Transplant seedlings from beds or containers to their final location in early fall or in spring. To grow foxgloves as annuals, start seed indoors in midwinter. Set out plants of perennial foxgloves (and biennials bought from a nursery) in early spring. You can divide clumps of perennial kinds in spring.

ECHINACEA purpurea
PURPLE CONEFLOWER
Asteraceae (Compositae)
PERENNIAL
ZONES A2, A3; 1–24, 26-45
FULL SUN, EXCEPT AS NOTED
MODERATE WATER
✿ ❀ ✿ ✿ FLOWERS IN SUMMER

Purple coneflower bears showy, 4-inch-wide daisies with dark, beehivelike centers and rosy purple petals that are typically slightly drooping. Bristly, oblong, 3- to 4-inch-long leaves form dense clumps; from these, sparsely leafed flowering stems rise 2 to 4 feet and bear flowers over a long summer season. '**Bright Star**' is a free-flowering, 2½-foot-tall cultivar with rose-colored blossoms; '**Crimson Star**' reaches 2 feet high, as does '**Bravado**', bearing the typical rosy purple blooms. '**Magnus**', to 3 feet tall, has rose pink flowers with petals that do not droop, but are held horizontally. '**White Swan**' and '**White Lustre**' feature white blooms with an orange-yellow cone.

Echinacea purpurea

CULTURE. Purple coneflower is a trouble-free plant that needs only a sunny spot in average, well-drained soil. In hot-summer regions, it also does well in light shade. It is drought tolerant but performs better with moderate watering. Deadheading encourages repeat flowering and keeps plants looking neat, but many gardeners leave some of the seedheads for birds to enjoy. The clumps spread slowly and may become crowded after 4 years or so. The fleshy rootstocks can be difficult to separate; divide them carefully, making sure that each division has a shoot and roots. You can also increase your supply of plants by taking root cuttings in fall, sowing seed, or transplanting self-sown seedlings (note that these may not bloom true to the parent plants).

Though related to common thistles, these plants have none of their roadside relatives' weediness. Reaching up to 1 foot long, the prickly, deeply cut leaves are usually green on the upper surface, gray and woolly beneath. Upright, well-foliaged stems rise to about 4 feet by bloom time, bearing distinctive spherical flower heads that look like golf ball–size pincushions stuck full of tubular, metallic blue pins.

You'll find globe thistles sold under various species names—*E. exaltatus, E. humilis, E. ritro, E. sphaerocephalus*—but by any name, plants are likely to fit the description above, particularly if you buy **'Taplow Blue'** (which may be sold as a selection of any of those species). **'Veitch's Blue'** offers darker blue flowers on stems just 2½ to 3 feet tall. Globe thistles bloom from summer to late fall and are excellent in everlasting arrangements; cut the stems just before flowers open, then hang them upside down to dry.

CULTURE. Given a warm, sunny site, globe thistles thrive with moderate water in well-drained soil of just average fertility. (With rich soil and regular moisture, they can grow too lushly, producing taller stems that require support.) Clumps can flourish undisturbed for years, but to increase your plantings, you can dig and separate them in spring or take root cuttings in early spring.

Echinops

ECHINOPS
GLOBE THISTLE
Asteraceae (Compositae)
PERENNIALS
ZONES A2, A3; 1–24, 31–45
FULL SUN
MODERATE WATER
✿ FLOWERS IN SUMMER, FALL

At first glance, you could mistake these leafy, fine-textured, mounding or spreading plants for perennial asters—but the fleabanes have threadlike petals rather than the flattened ones of asters. Mexican or Santa Barbara daisy, *E. karvinskianus* (Zones 8, 9, 12–28; H1, H2), is a semitrailing, wiry-stemmed plant that can reach 1½ feet high and spread to 3 feet wide, rooting as it spreads. Its pink-tinted white flowers are small (no more than ½ inch wide) but profuse, thickly dappling the foliage over a long, midspring-into-summer period—or virtually all year, in frost-free climates. Tough and adaptable, it grows with little to regular water and self-sows readily. For larger, pale lavender flowers on a more compact plant, look for **'Moerheimii'**.

The other popular fleabanes are selections and hybrids of *E. speciosus* (Zones 1–9, 14–24, 31–43). All are bushy growers to about 2 feet high and wide, with clusters of 1½- to 2-inch, single to double blossoms in summer. Violet-blue **'Darkest of All'** has double flowers; **'Azure Fairy'** (**'Azurfee'**) is slightly taller (to 2½ feet), with semidouble lavender-blue blooms. **'Förster's Liebling'** (**'Förster's Darling'**), only 1½ feet tall, has semidouble carmine pink blossoms; fully double **'Quakeress'** is light mauve pink; **'White Quakeress'** is a double-flowered choice with off-white flowers.

CULTURE. All fleabanes grow best in well-drained, fairly light soil (*E. karvinskianus* will even grow in crevices in rock walls). *E. karvinskianus* thrives with any amount of moisture, from little to regular; *E. speciosus* prefers moderate watering. Where summers are cool to moderately warm, all thrive in full sun; in hotter-summer regions, *E. speciosus* and its selections prefer some light shade (and even then will have a shorter bloom season than in cooler climates). All types benefit from cutting back. With the *E. speciosus* group, cut plants back halfway after the first flush of bloom to encourage a repeat performance; for *E. karvinskianus*, cut back plants hard (nearly to the ground) at the start of the growing season. Divide crowded clumps in spring.

ERIGERON
FLEABANE
Asteraceae (Compositae)
PERENNIALS
ZONES VARY
FULL SUN, EXCEPT AS NOTED
WATER NEEDS VARY
✿ ✿ ✿ ✿ FLOWERS IN SPRING AND SUMMER, EXCEPT AS NOTED

Erigeron karvinskianus

ERYNGIUM

SEA HOLLY

Apiaceae (Umbelliferae)

PERENNIALS AND BIENNIALS

ZONES 2–24, 29–43, EXCEPT AS NOTED

FULL SUN

MODERATE WATER, EXCEPT AS NOTED

✿ ✿ ✾ ✿ FLOWERS IN SUMMER

Eryngium alpinum

I n contrast to the many soft and billowy perennials, sea hollies offer a stiff, sculptural look that borders on the artificial. In summer, a branched flowering stem rises from a rosette of 3- to 6-inch-long leaves; each branch bears at its tip a cone-shaped flower head sitting on a spiny starburst of bracts (modified leaves). Bracts are narrow and jagged in some species, broad and deeply cut in others. The usual flower and bract colors are silvery gray, steel blue, sea green—a palette that adds to the "fake flower" air!

Biennial Miss Willmott's ghost, *E. giganteum,* is a green-leafed plant to 4 feet or taller. Pale green to blue flower heads are surrounded by silvery white bracts; the whole inflorescence reaches about 4 inches across. The plant forms a foliage rosette in its first year from seed; the next year, it sends up flowering stems, blooms, and dies—but not before scattering seeds for a new generation of plants. By sowing seeds in two successive years, you can have flowering plants each year.

The remaining sea hollies discussed here are perennials. Despite its prickly appearance, *E. alpinum* is soft to the touch. Clumps of spiny-edged leaves give rise to 2½-foot, blue-tinted stems bearing 1½-inch-tall, silvery violet flower heads surrounded by intricately cut violet-blue bracts. Handsome *E. amethystinum* (Zones 1–24, 26, 28–45), another 2½-footer, has medium green leaves, silvery blue stems, and violet, 1-inch-tall flower heads encircled by a spiny ruff of silvery blue bracts.

Surrounded by spiky blue-green bracts, the light blue flower heads of many-branched, 3-foot-tall *E. planum* are only ¾ inch tall, but their profusion makes up for their small size. Foliage is deep green. Cultivars differ in flower color and/or plant height. Choices include 3- to 4-foot 'Silverstone', with creamy white flower heads; dark blue, 2-foot 'Flüela'; and 1½-foot 'Blue Diamond', also with deep blue blooms.

Hybrid *E.* × *zabelii* resembles its *E. alpinum* parent but has rounded flower heads and more deeply lobed leaves; 'Jewel' is a selection in dark steel blue.

CULTURE. Because sea hollies have long taproots, they are best planted in deep, fairly light soils; a sandy or gravelly soil that is not too fertile suits them well. All do well with moderate watering except *E. giganteum,* which prefers regular moisture. Clumps prefer to be left undisturbed, though you can take root cuttings in late winter to get new plants of perennial species (or grow them from seed). Plant seeds of biennial *E. giganteum* in fall or early spring, in the location where you want the plants to grow.

ESCHSCHOLZIA californica

CALIFORNIA POPPY

Papaveraceae

PERENNIAL OFTEN GROWN AS
    COOL-SEASON ANNUAL

ZONES 1–45; H1

FULL SUN

LITTLE TO REGULAR WATER

✿ ✾ ✿ ✿ ✿ FLOWERS IN LATE WINTER
    AND SPRING, EXCEPT AS NOTED

I n its native western states, California poppy blooms from late winter through spring, adorning grassy hillsides and fields with patches of blazing orange and yellow. Each plant forms a foot-high clump (branching from the base) of green to silvery bluish green leaves that are divided into fine, nearly threadlike segments. Tapered buds open to four-petaled, satiny, 2-inch flowers on stems to 2 feet high. The typical colors are orange and orange-centered yellow, but cream to white variants also appear in the wild. Seed strains include a much wider range of colors; some also offer semidouble and double blossoms. Among widely available strains offering the full range of colors are **Sunset;** semidouble **Mission Bells;** semidouble **Ballerina,** with fluted petals; and **Thai Silk,** with semidouble, fluted-looking blooms and bronze-tinted foliage.

Named selections feature specific colors. Semidouble 'Apricot Flambeau' has fluted pale yellow petals tipped in coral orange; 'Carmine King' bears creamy white blooms heavily brushed with deep rosy red. 'Dalli' has orange-red flowers (some with yellow centers); 'Inferno' is solid scarlet orange. Other choices include 'Cherry Ripe', 'Milky White', and 'Purple Cup'. 'Golden Tears' has trailing, 2-foot stems.

CULTURE. In nature, this plant's seed capsules scatter copious amounts of seed with the onset of summer heat, after which the taprooted plant becomes semidormant. With the arrival of fall and winter rains, the seeds germinate and the parent plant resumes growth to flower the next year. In the garden, however, California poppy is usually treated as an annual, enjoyed for its flashy blooms in spring (in summer, in cold-winter regions), then discarded after it sets seed. Except in cool-summer climates, second-year plants rarely perform as well as new seedlings.

California poppy grows best in average, well-drained soil loose enough to let its taproot penetrate easily. It tolerates drought but performs best with moderate to regular water during growth and bloom. Sow seed in fall where winters are mild, in early spring in regions where temperatures dip to 0°F/−18°C or lower. If you remove spent flowers, the bloom period will last longer, but you'll want to let some flowers set seed to provide new plants for the next year. In mild-winter regions, let plants self-sow; in colder areas, collect seeds and sow them the following year.

Eschscholzia californica

Their bulk, density, and large leaves give these perennials a shrublike appearance that doesn't quite match their summer-to-fall blossoms: the flowers are tiny, carried in large, loose clusters that suggest puffs of smoke. Stems are strong and erect, bearing whorls of lance-shaped leaves.

Known as hardy ageratum, ***E. coelestinum*** (***Conoclinium coelestinum***; Zones 1–9, 14–17, 25–43) bears broad clusters of fluffy blue blossoms resembling those of floss flower *(Ageratum)*. The many-branched plant reaches 3 feet high; dark green, 4-inch leaves are carried in opposite pairs. Smaller cultivars include pure blue, 2-foot-tall **'Cori'**, blooming later than the species; white **'Album'**, also 2 feet high; and blue **'Wayside Variety'**, reaching a compact 15 inches.

Joe Pye weed, ***E. purpureum*** (Zones 1–9, 14–17, 28–45), is a giant that can reach 9 feet high. Its hollow, upright stems are clothed in dark green, foot-long leaves and topped with domes of pale purple blossoms. Spotted Joe Pye weed, ***E. p. maculatum***, is similar but shorter (6 to 7 feet high), with smaller leaves and purple-mottled stems. **'Atropurpureum'** has purple stems and leaf veins; **'Gateway'** (sometimes listed as a form of *E. fistulosum*) bears dusky rose flowers atop stems only 4 to 5 feet tall.

White snakeroot, ***E. rugosum*** (Zones 1–10, 14–17, 28–45), reaches 3 to 5 feet and bears fluffy white flower clusters; both the stems and the 5-inch leaves are heavily marked in brownish red. **'Chocolate'** has bronze to dark maroon leaves and stems.

CULTURE. Native to moist meadows, these plants are at their luxuriant best in good soil with plenty of water. *E. coelestinum* spreads to form broad clumps; dig and divide every 3 to 4 years in early spring. The remaining species can remain undisturbed for many years. For all species, it's wise to remove spent flower heads to prevent self-sowing.

EUPATORIUM
Asteraceae (Compositae)
PERENNIALS
ZONES VARY
FULL SUN OR LIGHT SHADE
REGULAR TO AMPLE WATER
✿ ✿ ❀ ✿ FLOWERS IN SUMMER, FALL

Eupatorium purpureum maculatum 'Gateway'

This amazingly varied group of plants includes lush, tropical-looking individuals (like the familiar holiday poinsettia) as well as desert natives that resemble cacti. What unites them is their floral structure: all have petal-like bracts (modified leaves), often quite colorful and showy, surrounding insignificant true flowers. Another common feature is a milky sap which can irritate the eyes and skin.

Annual snow-on-the-mountain, ***E. marginata*** (Zones 1–45), a slender plant to about 2 feet high, is an old-fashioned favorite for the summer garden. Along the upper parts of the stems, the oval light green leaves are margined and striped white—and may sometimes be solid white. Even the bract clusters are white and green. **'Summer Icicle'** is shorter, just 1½ feet high. Plant close together for good mass effect (stems become bare at the base, so use shorter annuals in the foreground). Listing continues>

EUPHORBIA
SPURGE
Euphorbiaceae
PERENNIALS AND WARM-SEASON ANNUALS
ZONES VARY
FULL SUN, EXCEPT AS NOTED
MODERATE WATER
❀ ✿ ✿ ✿ FLOWERS IN WINTER, SPRING, SUMMER

Euphorbia marginata

Euphorbia × martinii

The following five evergreen species and hybrids (and their subspecies and cultivars) all have unbranched stems, domelike clusters of typically chartreuse to lime green bracts in late winter and early spring, and narrowly elliptical leaves that are usually bluish green. In 3-foot-tall *E. amygdaloides* (Zones 2b–24, 31–41), leaves have red undersides and stems are red tinged; the red shades intensify in winter. (For leaves and stems in solid reddish bronze, look for the cultivar 'Purpurea'.) Showy *E. characias* (Zones 4–24, 31, warmer parts of 32) forms an upright, shrubby clump to 4 feet high and has dark-centered bract clusters; more commonly grown is *E. c. wulfenii (E. veneta),* with broader clusters of bracts that lack a dark center. *E. c.* 'Portuguese Velvet' has shorter leaves on a shorter plant (2 to 3 feet high) and features coppery gold bracts. *E. × martinii* (Zones 3–24, 31, 32), to 2½ feet tall, has bronze-tinted leaves and brown-centered bract clusters.

Trailing stems of *E. myrsinites* (Zones 2–24, 31–41) look something like bottlebrushes: they're thickly clothed in leaves and turn up just at the tips to bear flattish bract clusters. The plant grows about 6 inches tall and spreads to a foot wide. *E. rigida* (*E. biglandulosa;* Zones 4–24, 31) is another species with "bottlebrush" branches: its gray-green leaves sit directly on the stems and spiral around them. The stems sprawl outward, then turn upright to produce a clump 3 to 5 feet across but just 2 feet high.

Unlike the preceding spurges, the following three have branching stems. All are deciduous. *E. dulcis* 'Chameleon' (Zones 2b–24, 31–34), a mounding plant just 1 to 2 feet high and wide, has leaves that emerge purple in spring and mature to bronzed green by summer; in fall, all parts of the plant turn a rich purple. Purple-tinged, greenish yellow bract clusters appear at stem ends in summer. Another summer bloomer is *E. griffithii* (Zones 2–10, 14–24, 28–41), which forms clumps that expand by creeping rhizomes; its stems grow upright to 3 feet. The species has lance-shaped medium green leaves with pink midribs and bears open, branching clusters of orange-red bracts. 'Fireglow' has brick red bracts; 'Dixter' offers orange bracts and red-flushed foliage. A fine choice for borders is cushion spurge, *E. polychroma* (*E. epithymoides;* Zones A2, A3, 1–24, 26, 28–45). Dense, rounded foliage clumps to 1½ feet high and wide are covered from late spring into summer with flattened clusters of greenish yellow bracts. The dark green leaves turn red in autumn.

CULTURE. Sun, well-drained average soil, and moderate watering satisfy the spurges. *E. amygdaloides* and *E. griffithii* also take light shade; *E. polychroma* needs some shade in the hottest regions. When perennials' bract clusters turn brown, cut out the entire stem (by then, new stems will have grown from the base). Only *E. griffithii* needs periodic dividing or curbing; all the others form discrete clumps. Many self-sow.

Sow seed of annual *E. marginata* after the danger of frost has passed, in the spot where plants are to grow.

FILIPENDULA
MEADOWSWEET
Rosaceae
PERENNIALS
ZONES VARY
LIGHT SHADE, EXCEPT AS NOTED
REGULAR TO AMPLE WATER,
 EXCEPT AS NOTED
❀ ✿ FLOWERS IN SUMMER

Their dense plumes of tiny summer flowers floating above handsome clumps of large, jagged-lobed leaves, the meadowsweets look like pumped-up versions of their astilbe relatives. Their size puts them at the back of the border; their love of moisture recommends them for planting beside pools and streams.

Siberian meadowsweet, *F. palmata* (Zones A2, A3; 1–9, 14–17, 31–45), features pale pink blossoms on 3- to 4-foot stems that rise above coarse, palmately lobed leaves. Its selection 'Nana' is much smaller, reaching just 8 to 10 inches. Japanese meadowsweet, *F. purpurea* (Zones 3b–9, 14–17, 31–34, 39), forms broad clumps of maplelike leaves that send up reddish, 4-foot stems topped with dark pink blossom plumes. 'Elegans' has white blossoms accented by red stamens.

North American native queen of the prairie, **_F. rubra_** (Zones A1–A3; 1–9, 14–17, 31–45), is the most imposing species: it reaches 6 to 8 feet if given ample moisture. Leaves are deeply lobed, with jagged edges. The species has bright pink flowers; **'Venusta'** bears darker, purplish pink blossoms on a smaller plant (4 to 6 feet). **'Alba'**, also growing 4 to 6 feet high, has white blooms.

Queen of the meadow, **_F. ulmaria_** (Zones 1–9, 14–17, 31–45), is a European native that resembles _F. rubra_ but grows a little shorter (to 6 feet tall) and has creamy white blossoms. A bit showier is its 3-foot-tall, double-flowered selection **'Flore Pleno'**. **'Variegata'** has leaves margined in light yellow. **'Aurea'** has solid bright yellow foliage; its flowers are insignificant.

Standing apart from the other species in appearance and cultural needs is dropwort, **_F. vulgaris_** (_F. hexapetala_; Zones A1–A3, 1–9, 14–17, 31–45). Leaves are fine textured, almost fernlike, in low, spreading mounds. Slender stems rise 2 to 3 feet high, bearing branched sprays of white blossoms. **'Flore Pleno'** has double flowers resembling small roses.

CULTURE. With the exception of _F. vulgaris,_ the meadowsweets need good, organically enriched soil and a steady water supply; they prefer partial or light shade in most regions, though they can take full sun in northern latitudes and cool-summer areas. Plant _F. vulgaris_ in full sun except in the warmest regions (where it needs light shade). It tolerates dry soils but looks better with moderate watering.

You can propagate all meadowsweets by dividing the clumps in early spring.

Filipendula ulmaria 'Flore Pleno'

These showy, easy-to-grow daisies feature warm, bright colors and a tough constitution. Native to the central and western U. S., they're unfazed by heat, wind, and capricious watering.

Annual **_G. pulchella_** blooms in summer, producing 2-inch-wide blossoms on long, whiplike stems that rise as high as 2 feet above a clump of narrow, deeply cut, downy gray-green leaves. Flower colors range from cream and yellow through orange and red, and there are bicolor combinations as well. Blossoms are typically single to semidouble, but double-flowered types are available, including **'Red Plume'** and **'Yellow Plume'** (both just 12 to 14 inches high).

Perennial **_G. × grandiflora_** blooms from early summer until frost, flaunting single or semidouble, 3- to 4-inch flowers on slender stems above clumps of gray-green, dandelionlike foliage. Flowers may be solid colored or bicolored; they typically have a dark center surrounded by red, maroon, or bronze petals tipped in yellow. Named selections vary in flower color and plant height. Among types reaching 2 to 3 feet in bloom are **'Dazzler'**, with yellow petals tipped in crimson; **'Torchlight'**, bearing yellow blossoms bordered with red; pure orange **'Tokajer'**; **'Mandarin'**, with orange petals and a maroon center; wine red **'Burgundy'**; and solid yellow **'Yellow Queen'**. For front-of-the-border plants, look for foot-tall **'Goblin'**, with yellow-bordered red petals, and its all-yellow counterpart **'Goblin Yellow'**. Shortest of all (to about 8 inches) is red-and-yellow **'Baby Cole'**.

CULTURE. Blanket flowers need well-drained, preferably sandy to loam soil; in heavier, claylike soils, perennial kinds may rot over winter. To start either annuals or perennials from seed, sow indoors 4 to 6 weeks before the usual last-frost date. You also can sow seeds directly in the garden as soon as soil is workable in spring. Nursery plants of _G. × grandiflora_ can be set out in early spring; when established clumps become crowded or show bare centers, divide in early spring. Or start new plants from stem cuttings taken in spring and early summer.

GAILLARDIA
BLANKET FLOWER
Asteraceae (Compositae)
PERENNIALS AND WARM-SEASON ANNUALS
ZONES 1–45; H1, H2
FULL SUN
MODERATE WATER
❀ ✿ ✿ ✿ FLOWERS IN SUMMER, FALL

Gaillardia × *grandiflora* 'Goblin'

GAURA lindheimeri

Onagraceae
PERENNIAL
ZONES 2B–35, 37, 38 (COASTAL), 39
FULL SUN
MODERATE WATER
❀ ✿ FLOWERS IN SPRING,
   SUMMER, FALL

Gaura lindheimeri
'Siskiyou Pink'

Gaura doesn't put on a traffic-stopping display—but its grace, prolific spring-to-fall bloom, and toughness make it deserving of a spot in the garden. Numerous slender stems clothed in narrow, 3-inch leaves rise from a carrotlike taproot, forming a shrubby, vase-shaped plant 2 to 4 feet high and 3 feet across. In late spring, flower spikes rise above the foliage, bearing pink buds that open to starry white, 1-inch blossoms. Spikes open just a few flowers at a time, so established plants will give you the best show. Among selected forms, 3-foot-high **'Whirling Butterflies'** offers spikes of slightly larger, showier blossoms; **'Siskiyou Pink'** features maroon-mottled leaves and pink blooms that open from maroon buds; and 2½-foot **'Corrie's Gold'** has leaves conspicuously edged in gold.

CULTURE. Hailing from the dry Southwest, gaura handles adversity well. Give it deep, well-drained, preferably sandy to loam soil. (Where summers are hot, humid, and rainy, good drainage is essential.) This plant self-sows, sometimes to the point of being a nuisance; to curb this tendency, cut out spent flower stems. Gaura can remain in place indefinitely, and the deep taproot makes division difficult in any case. For additional plants, count on volunteer seedlings; or, to propagate named selections, take stem cuttings in summer.

GERANIUM

GERANIUM, CRANESBILL
Geraniaceae
PERENNIALS
ZONES VARY
FULL SUN OR LIGHT SHADE, EXCEPT
   AS NOTED
REGULAR WATER
✿ ✿ ❀ ✿ FLOWERS IN SPRING,
   SUMMER, FALL

Geranium × *cantabrigiense*
'Biokovo'

Not to be confused with *Pelargonium* (the well-known common and Martha Washington "geraniums"), these hardy true geraniums encompass an assortment of modestly pretty to frankly showy plants that remain attractive from spring through fall. In size and habit, they vary from ground-hugging spreaders to bushy 4-footers, but all have similar features: lobed, maplelike to finely cut leaves carried on long stalks; five-petaled flowers, circular in outline; and beaklike fruits that account for the common name "cranesbill." Flower colors range from subtle to vibrant; leaves of some species turn a striking orange to red in autumn. Specialty nurseries offer a great many species and named hybrids; those described below are among the most widely sold.

Among the lowest-growing geraniums is *G.* × *cantabrigiense* (Zones 1–24, 31–43), best known through two selections with ¾- to 1-inch-wide flowers: pink-tinged white **'Biokovo'** and bright bluish pink **'Cambridge'**. Both bloom from late spring to early summer. The dark green plants reach just 6 inches high but eventually spread widely, making a good small-scale ground cover. Another low, wide spreader is *G. cinereum* (Zones 1–24, 31–43), forming a dense, 8- to 12-inch-high mat of gray-green, deeply cut leaves. Appearing in early to midsummer, the pale pink, dark-veined flowers reach 1½ inches across; **'Ballerina'** has a longer season, bearing dark-centered lilac blossoms throughout summer and on into fall. *G. macrorrhizum* (Zones 1–24, 30–43) grows 8 to 10 inches high and spreads into sizable patches; lobed, pale green, 3- to 4-inch leaves offer good color in fall. Inch-wide white, pink, or magenta flowers bloom from spring through early summer. Selections include pink-flushed white **'Album'**, vibrant deep magenta **'Bevan's Variety'**, and soft lilac-pink **'Ingwersen's Variety'**.

The following three geraniums are all about 1 foot high. The hybrid *G.* **'Ann Folkard'** (Zones 2b–9, 14–24, 31–41) is a billowing, spreading plant to 5 feet across. Showy, 1½-inch magenta-purple flowers with black veins and centers bloom from spring into fall, set off nicely by the chartreuse to light green leaves. *G. himalayense* (*G. grandiflorum;* Zones 1–24, 31–43) is a spreading plant with deeply lobed medium green leaves that turn rich red in fall. It blooms from late spring into summer. The species has red-veined blue blossoms to about 2 inches in diameter; **'Plenum'**

('**Birch Double**') has lavender-blue double flowers. Hybrid **G. × _riversleaianum_** (Zones 2b–9, 14–24, 31–41) makes a broadly spreading, silvery green carpet dotted with ¾-inch flowers from late spring into fall. Two popular selections are soft pink **'Mavis Simpson'** and magenta **'Russell Prichard'**.

The remaining geraniums described here range from about 1½ feet high to as tall as 4 feet. **G. _clarkei_** 'Kashmir White' (Zones 2b–9, 14–24, 31–41) is a 2-footer with medium green, long-stalked leaves to 6 inches wide; it spreads widely by rhizomes. Pink-veined white, 1½-inch-wide flowers bloom from late spring into summer. **G. _endressii_** (Zones 1–9, 14–24, 31–43) is best known through its selection **'Wargrave Pink'**—a dense, bushy, 1½-foot-tall, mounding plant with soft light green leaves and vivid warm pink, 1½-inch flowers. It blooms from late spring into fall where summers are cool, from spring into early summer in hot-summer areas. The **G. _himalayense_** hybrid **G. 'Johnson's Blue'** (Zones 2–9, 14–24, 30–41) produces intense violet-blue, 2-inch flowers from spring to fall on a mounding, 1½-foot plant with deeply cut medium green leaves that, like those of the parent, turn vibrant red in autumn. Vigorous **G. × _oxonianum_** (Zones 2–9, 14–24, 30–41) is a _G. endressii_ hybrid; best known is its selection **'Claridge Druce'**, a 2- to 3-foot plant with deeply cut gray-green leaves and cool lilac-pink, 1½-inch flowers in spring and early summer.

Geranium 'Johnson's Blue'

Mourning widow, **G. _phaeum_** (Zones 2b–9, 14–24, 32–41), is a bushy 2-footer bearing clusters of dark maroon or purple, ¾- to 1-inch blossoms from spring to fall; **'Samobor'** features white-centered maroon flowers and leaves with brown markings. **G. 'Philippe Vapelle'** (Zones 3–9, 14–24, 31–39), a rounded plant growing 1 to 1½ feet high, has gray-green foliage and blue-purple, 1¾-inch flowers from spring to midsummer. Meadow cranesbill, **G. _pratense_** (Zones 2–7, 14–24, 32–41), forms a bushy dark green clump to 2 feet high and 3 feet across. Blue, inch-wide flowers with red veins bloom in spring and early summer; fine selections are white **'Galactic'** and light blue **'Mrs. Kendall Clark'**. Reaching 4 feet high and wide, **G. _psilostemon_** (**G. _armeneum;_** Zones 2b–9, 14–24, 30–41) could fill in for a small shrub! The deep green leaves sometimes reach 8 inches across and turn flaming red in fall. Black-centered magenta, 1- to 1½-inch blossoms appear in early summer.

Geranium sanguineum striatum

Adaptable and easy-to-grow bloody cranesbill, **G. _sanguineum_** (Zones A2, A3; 1–9, 14–24, 30–45), reaches 2½ feet high and can spread to 3 feet or more; the deeply lobed dark green leaves turn bright red in fall. Blossoms about 1½ inches wide appear from spring into summer. Good selections include white **'Album'**, dark-veined pink **'John Elsley'**, red-purple **'Max Frei'**, and dark purple **'New Hampshire'**. A much lower version is **G. s. _striatum_ (G. s. _lancastriense)_;** it forms a spreading, 8-inch-high carpet decorated with salmon pink flowers.

Geranium psilostemon

CULTURE. These geraniums grow best where summers are cool to just mildly warm; in these climates, they'll thrive in full sun or light shade. For success in hotter-summer regions, be sure plants get filtered sunlight or light shade. They prefer moist, well drained, average to good soil. Set out plants in early to midspring—even late winter in mild-winter areas. Most can remain in place for many years before they become over-crowded and start to decline. When this occurs, dig, divide, and replant in early spring. If you want to increase an established planting, dig and transplant rooted portions from the edge of the clump.

ANNUAL AND PERENNIAL ORNAMENTAL GRASSES

Texture, color, height, graceful motion—when you plant ornamental grasses, you add all of these features to your garden. These plants highlight and enliven groups of more traditional annuals and perennials. And because their size range is so great (they vary from low tufts to giants reaching 8 feet or more), you'll find choices to use as edgings, combine with medium-size plants in a border, or plant as accents or focal points. Most are excellent for containers and cutting, as well. Many have variegated or colored foliage in addition to interesting flower heads; foliage and flowering stems often persist into autumn and winter, adding interest to the garden at a typically stark time of year.

Annual species complete their life cycle in a single year and require little maintenance. Perennial species need a bit more attention. Tidy up clumps in early spring before new growth begins, cutting back dead foliage; this is also the best time to divide crowded clumps and to set out new plants.

Note that a few annual and perennial ornamental grasses can be invasive, both in the garden and in nearby wild lands. Before trying a species new to you, ask suppliers whether it could cause problems in this regard.

ANNUAL GRASSES

Delicate, graceful rattlesnake or quaking grass, ***Briza maxima*** (Zones 1–45), grows 1 to 2 feet tall and has ¼-inch-wide leaves to 6 inches long. It blooms in summer, bearing clusters of nodding, heart-shaped green spikelets that somewhat resemble rattlesnake rattles; they dangle from threadlike stems and quake in the lightest breeze. As the spikelets mature, they develop a purplish tinge, then eventually turn straw colored. Rattlesnake grass is valued for dried arrangements; cut the stems when green and hang them to dry, or cut them after they have dried on the plant.

Sow seed in place in the garden in spring, after the last-frost date. Choose a sunny spot with average, well-drained soil. Thin seedlings to stand a foot apart.

Two species of Natal ruby grass, ***Rhynchelytrum (Melinis)***, are usually grown as annuals. They succeed in all zones and may become perennials in mild-winter climates. Both form

1- by 1-foot clumps of narrow blue-green leaves that are erect, then arching. At bloom time, the clumps send up 2-foot spikes of flowers that open deep pink to purplish red, then gradually fade to light pinkish tan. A selection of ***R. nerviglume*** is sold as **'Pink Crystals'**; it blooms in late summer. ***R. repens*** is similar; it flowers in summer or early autumn (and may continue throughout winter in mild climates).

Sow seed indoors 6 to 8 weeks before the last frost. Set out seedlings in a full-sun location; soil type is not important, but drainage must be good. In the warm-winter climates where this grass is a perennial, plants are sometimes available in nurseries. Once these have put on some size, they can be divided in early spring to increase your plantings.

An annual grasslike plant popular in Victorian times is striped maize, ***Zea mays japonica*** (all zones). **'Variegata'**, with green leaves boldly striped in white, grows about 3 feet tall. **'Harlequin'**, to 4 feet high, has even showier foliage—it's striped in green, red (or pink), and cream. Both varieties

Briza maxima

Rhynchelytrum nerviglume
'Pink Crystals'

Zea mays japonica

are striking at the back of a border or massed as a focal point in a large bed of annuals.

Sow seed outdoors after the danger of frost has passed. Or sow indoors 6 weeks before the last-frost date, using individual peat pots to avoid root disturbance. Give plants full sun and well-drained soil enriched with organic matter. The plants may produce ears of corn; these are not edible, but they can be dried and used as decorations.

PERENNIAL GRASSES

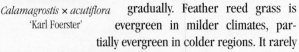

Feather reed grass, **Calamagrostis × acutiflora,** succeeds in Zones 2b–24, 29–41. The well-known selection **'Karl Foerster'** (**'Stricta'**) has a strong vertical form, with narrow, reedlike, 1½- to 4-foot stems rising over lustrous deep green foliage. Flowering stems appear in early summer, growing to 6 feet high; they bear feathery purplish plumes that age to buff and remain attractive for much of the winter. **'Overdam'** is similar but has variegated foliage: each leaf has a central creamy white stripe. Clumps are compact and expand gradually. Feather reed grass is evergreen in milder climates, partially evergreen in colder regions. It rarely produces volunteer seedlings.

Calamagrostis × acutiflora
'Karl Foerster'

Choose a location in sun or partial shade. Performance is best with good soil and regular watering, but the plants will also grow in soil that is heavy, damp, and poorly drained.

Though members of the genus **Carex** are sedges rather than true grasses, their long, narrow leaves give them a grasslike appearance. Some species have striped or unusually colored foliage. Of the plants described here, all but *C. elata* 'Aurea' are evergreen. Leather leaf sedge, **C. buchananii** (Zones 2b–9, 14–24, 28–41), forms an upright, 2- to 3-foot clump of arching leaves that are slightly curled at the tips; foliage is a striking reddish bronze, offering a fine-textured color contrast to other plants. It needs moderate water. Bowles' golden sedge, **C. elata 'Aurea'** (**'Bowles Golden'**; Zones 2–9, 14–24, 28–43), is just 2 feet tall, with an upright yet fountainlike habit. Its narrow leaves are brilliant yellow from spring well into summer, then turn green

for the remainder of the season. Give it ample moisture. Variegated Japanese sedge, **C. morrowii 'Variegata'** (Zones 3–9, 14–24, 28–32, warmer parts of 33), forms a 1-foot mound of drooping, green-and-white striped leaves. It does best with regular water.

Carex morrowii 'Variegata'

Where summers are cool, grow these plants in full sun; in warmer areas, give them partial shade.

Tufted hair grass, **Deschampsia cespitosa** (Zones 2–24, 28–41), forms a 1- to 2-foot clump of narrow dark green leaves; it's evergreen in mild regions but goes dormant in colder climates. Delicate, arching, 3-foot stems bearing clouds of airy, green to greenish gold flower heads appear in early summer; the flowers persist into winter, turning straw colored as weather cools. Tufted hair grass prefers partial shade but will tolerate full sun where summers are cool. Provide regular moisture for the best performance.

The fescues form tight, tufted, evergreen clumps of narrow foliage. Nomenclature is confusing; you many find the following plants sold under different botanical names. Large blue fescue, **Festuca amethystina** (Zones 2–10, 14–24, 29–45), forms a clump of foot-tall, threadlike bluish green foliage; drooping flowering stems reach 2 feet high. The selection **'Superba'** has attractive amethyst pink flowers. Common blue fescue, **F. glauca** (**F. cinerea, F. ovina glauca;** Zones 1–24, 29–45), is available in a number of similar selections with foliage in various shades of blue; they grow from 8 to 12 inches tall, with the flowering stems reaching slightly higher.

Fescues tolerate partial shade in all regions and require it where summers are hot. Plant them in average, well-drained soil and provide moderate water.

TOP: *Deschampsia cespitosa*
BOTTOM: *Festuca glauca*

Japanese forest grass, **_Hakonechloa macra_** (Zones 2b–9, 14–24, 31–41), somewhat resembles a tiny bamboo. The widely grown variety '**Aureola**' has graceful, slender, lax or arching green leaves striped with gold; they reach about 1½ feet long. Foliage of '**All Gold**' is solid yellow. These grasses spread slowly by underground runners; they are dormant in winter. Plant in partial shade, in well-drained soil enriched with organic matter. Water regularly.

Hakonechloa macra 'Aureola'

Blue oat grass, **_Helictotrichon sempervirens_** (Zones 1–24, 30–41), forms a 2- to 3-foot, evergreen fountain of narrow foliage in a bright blue gray. Small, straw-colored flower plumes appear in late spring, held a foot or two above the leaves on slim stems. This grass is clump forming and does not spread. Provide a full-sun location and well-drained, average to good soil; give

Helictotrichon sempervirens

moderate water. Poor drainage during the winter months can cause root rot.

Japanese blood grass, **_Imperata cylindrica_** '**Red Baron**' ('**Rubra**'), Zones 2b–24, 26, 28, 31–34, 39, is one of the most colorful ornamental grasses. Clumps of upright leaves grow 1 to 2 feet high; the top half of each leaf blade is red. The color is most intense in full sun and is especially striking if plants are located where sunlight can shine through the blades. Japanese blood grass

Imperata cylindrica 'Red Baron'

spreads slowly by underground runners. It is dormant in winter. Provide average to good soil; give moderate to regular water.

Eulalia grass, **_Miscanthus sinensis_**, grows in Zones 2–24, 29–41. The species and its many named selections all form tall, robust yet graceful clumps with stately flowering stems that rise well above the foliage in late summer or fall. Leaves and stems turn golden tan in winter, providing interest until you cut them down at cleanup time in early spring. One of the most compact selections is '**Yaku Jima**', a 2- to 3-footer with narrow green leaves and tan flower heads. '**Malepartus**', to 3 feet, has rose pink flower plumes borne on 6- to 7-foot stems; they appear earlier in the season than those of most selections. '**Strictus**', also known as porcupine grass, grows upright to 6 feet; it has coppery plumes and green leaves horizontally striped in white. '**Cabaret**' grows 6 to 7 feet tall and bears pink blossoms and broad green leaves with a creamy central stripe.

Miscanthus sinensis 'Cabaret'

Whether planted in sun or light shade, eulalia grasses make dense clumps. Given moderate to regular water, they'll grow in any well-drained soil. The tallest varieties may need staking if grown in rich soil. In warm, moist regions with long growing seasons, varieties selected for early bloom may self-sow aggressively.

Purple moor grass, **_Molinia caerulea_** (Zones 1–9, 14–17, 32–41), forms a neat, dense, 1- to 2-foot-high clump. Narrow, spike-like clusters of yellowish to purplish flowers bloom in summer, rising 1 to 2 feet or more above the green foliage; the flowering stems are quite numerous, but they have a narrow structure that gives the clump an unusual see-through quality. The blossom clusters turn tan in fall and last until

Molinia caerulea arundinacea 'Skyracer'

late in the season, when both they and the leaves break off and blow away. A favorite selection of the subspecies *M. c. arundinacea* is 'Skyracer', with foliage clumps to 3 feet high and upright flowering stems reaching 7 to 8 feet.

Native to wet moorlands, these grasses prefer regular water and neutral to acid soil enriched with organic matter. Plant in full sun or light shade. They are long lived but slow growing, taking a few years to reach their full potential.

Native to the southern U. S. and Mexico, grasses in the genus *Muhlenbergia* are drought tolerant and sun loving. Most are large and showy, standing out in the garden whether used as specimens or planted in groups. They are evergreen in mild winters, though they turn tan or brown with hard freezes. Bull grass, *M. emersleyi* (Zones 2–24, 30, 33, 35), forms a 1½-foot-tall, 3-foot-wide mound of glossy green leaves; in summer and fall, spikes of purplish or reddish flowers rise 2 to 3 feet above the foliage. Purple muhly, *M. rigida* (Zones 6–24, 30, 33), forms a clump 2 feet high and wide; its 3-foot spikes of brownish to deep purple flowers appear in late summer and fall. Plant these grasses in well-drained, average soil. They will survive in dry conditions but look better and grow larger if given supplemental water.

Switch grass, *Panicum virgatum* (Zones 1–11, 14–23, 28–43), native to the tall grass prairie of the Midwest, forms an upright clump of narrow leaves. In summer, the foliage clump is topped by slender flower clusters opening into loose, airy clouds of pinkish blossoms that age to

Muhlenbergia emersleyi

Panicum virgatum

Pennisetum orientale   *Stipa gigantea*

white and finally to brown. Clumps reach 4 to 7 feet when in bloom. Foliage turns yellow in fall, gradually fading to beige. Both foliage and flowers persist all winter. The 4-foot-tall selection 'Hänse Herms' is grown for its red fall foliage; 'Heavy Metal', with metallic blue foliage, forms a stiffly upright clump to 5 feet high. Switch grasses are easy to grow, tolerating wet or dry soil and flourishing in both full sun and partial shade.

The fountain grasses, belonging to the genus *Pennisetum,* form graceful clumps of gently arching leaves; slender stems carrying furry, foxtail-like flower plumes rise above the foliage in summer. Hardiest is 4-foot-tall *P. alopecuroides* (Zones 2b–24, 31–35, 37, 39), with bright green leaves and pinkish plumes. Its leaves turn yellow in fall, brown in winter. The selection 'Hameln' is more compact (to just 1 to 1½ feet); its white plumes are carried on stems to 3 feet tall. 'Moudry' bears dramatic black plumes that rise to about 3 feet, held above a 2-foot clump of glossy foliage. *P. alopecuroides* and its varieties may self-sow to some extent, but they are usually not weedy—with the exception of 'Moudry', which self-seeds heavily and can be weedy.

Oriental fountain grass, *P. orientale* (Zones 3–10, 14–24, 31–35, 37, 39), forms a dense, rounded, 1½-foot clump of narrow gray-green leaves that turn straw colored in fall. The fuzzy pink flowers arch a foot or more above the foliage.

Plant fountain grasses in sun or light shade, in average soil; provide regular water.

Giant feather grass, *Stipa gigantea* (Zones 4–9, 14–24, 29–34, 39), forms 2- to 3-foot-tall clumps of narrow, arching leaves. During the summer bloom season, it lives up to its name, producing stems up to 6 feet high that carry large, open, airy sheaves of yellowish flowers that shimmer in the breeze. This stately grass is evergreen in mild climates. Give it full sun and good soil. Water regularly when young; established plants will take some drought.

GOMPHRENA
GLOBE AMARANTH
Amaranthaceae
WARM-SEASON ANNUALS AND PERENNIALS
GROWN AS ANNUALS
ZONES 1–45; H1, H2
FULL SUN OR PARTIAL SHADE
MODERATE WATER
✿✿✿✿✿ FLOWERS IN
SUMMER, FALL

Gomphrena globosa
'Lavender Lady'

Reveling in the heat of summer and early fall, globe amaranths make a bright splash—both in garden beds and in containers. They're also good cut flowers for fresh as well as dried arrangements. The more common species is *G. globosa,* an upright 2-footer with narrowly oval, 2- to 4-inch leaves and ½-inch flower heads that look like clover. Colors include purple, red, pink, lavender, and white. You can buy seeds of specific colors as well as named selections such as **'Lavender Lady'** and red **'Strawberry Fields'.** Dwarf selections, growing just 8 to 10 inches high, include purple **'Buddy'**, white **'Cissy'**, and rosy purple **'Gnome'**.

Technically a perennial but generally grown as an annual, *G. haageana* produces orange-and-yellow flowers resembling inchwide pinecones; selections with flowers in red and apricot are sometimes available. Like *G. globosa*, this species is an upright, 2-foot-tall plant.

CULTURE. Globe amaranths prefer well-drained, sandy to loam soil. Sow seeds in place after all danger of frost is past. For an earlier start, sow indoors 4 to 6 weeks before the last-frost date.

GYPSOPHILA paniculata
BABY'S BREATH
Caryophyllaceae
PERENNIAL
ZONES A2, A3; 1–10, 14–16, 18–21,
31–45; H1
FULL SUN
MODERATE WATER
✿✿ FLOWERS IN SUMMER

Gypsophila paniculata 'Bristol Fairy'

Bearing a summertime froth of small flowers that almost appear to float in midair, baby's breath is a much-branched, rounded plant reminiscent of a tumbleweed, its stems set rather sparsely with narrow leaves. In the garden, it's used as an airy filler—the role it also plays in bouquets. The basic species grows about 3 feet high and wide, with white, ⅛-inch single flowers. More popular are a number of showier cultivars. **'Bristol Fairy'**, reaching 3 to 4 feet, is the classic double-flowered white baby's breath, bearing flowers about ¼ inch wide. **'Perfecta'**, the florists' favorite, is about the same size but features ½-inch double blossoms. **'Compacta Plena'** is a double-flowered white form just 1½ feet tall. Other short cultivars, all with double pink flowers, include **'Pink Fairy'** (1½ to 2 feet high and wide), **'Pink Star'** (to 1½ feet), and **'Viette's Dwarf'** (12 to 15 inches). **Double Snowflake** and **Early Snowball** are seed strains that produce 3-foot plants with double white flowers.

CULTURE. This taprooted plant needs deep, well-drained, nonacid soil; if soil is acid, add lime to neutralize it (the name *Gypsophila* can be roughly translated as "lime loving"). If you want the plant to remain spherical, provide some sort of support (see page 75) to counteract the flattening effects of overhead watering, rain, and wind. Once planted, baby's breath is a permanent plant that never needs dividing or replanting.

Note: In coastal parts of the Great Lakes region, baby's breath has naturalized and become invasive, crowding out native vegetation. If you live in this area, check with your Cooperative Extension Office or a local nursery before you plant.

HELENIUM
SNEEZEWEED
Asteraceae (Compositae)
PERENNIAL
ZONES 1–45
FULL SUN
REGULAR WATER
✿✿✿ FLOWERS IN SUMMER, FALL

Bright daisies in autumnal colors light up the garden from midsummer well into fall—a time when many other flowers are on the wane. Each 1- to 2-inch blossom has a nearly spherical yellow or brown center that sits on a "wheel" of notched petals. Most widely available are hybrids (often sold—incorrectly—as selections of *H. autumnale*). These are available in specific colors and in sizes ranging from 2 to nearly 5 feet; all are upright, branching plants with narrow, linear leaves. At the short end of the height scale is **'Crimson Beauty'**, with bronzy red flowers on a 2- to 3-foot plant. Reaching 3 feet or a bit taller are **'Butterpat'**, with solid yellow blooms; dark-centered mahogany **'Moerheim Beauty'**; and brown-centered yellow **'Wyndley'**. Taller

Helenium 'Moerheim Beauty'

cultivars (4 to 5 feet high) are **'Baudirektor Linne'** (brownish red with brown center), **'Riverton Beauty'** (tawny gold with brown center), and **'Waldtraut'** (coppery brown with dark center).

CULTURE. Sneezeweeds turn in their best performance in hot-summer climates, with average soil and regular watering. They bloom more profusely if you're stingy with fertilizer. Taller kinds may need staking. Clumps become crowded fairly quickly; dig and divide every 2 or 3 years in early spring.

HELIANTHUS
SUNFLOWER
Asteraceae (Compositae)
PERENNIALS AND WARM-SEASON ANNUALS
ZONES VARY
FULL SUN
REGULAR WATER
❀ ✿ ✿ ✿ FLOWERS IN SUMMER, FALL

The annual sunflower is recognized all around the world: a big, dark disk surrounded by a single row of yellow petals. Native to central North America, it is grown worldwide for its edible seeds and the oil they produce. Both the familiar annual species and the perennial types have the same general appearance: brash blossoms on coarse, upright plants with oval, sandpapery leaves. All bloom in summer and autumn.

The classic yellow annual sunflower, **H. annuus** (all zones), includes the familiar yellow-flowered plants of towering size—traditional seed-producing sunflowers such as **'Kong'**, **'Mammoth Russian'**, and **'Russian Giant'**, all reaching at least 10 feet high and bearing foot-wide (or larger!) blossoms with short petals and broad disks. (**'Sunspot'** is a much shorter version, with 10-inch flowers on a plant just 2 to 2½ feet tall.)

Plant breeders have also produced an assortment of smaller cultivars in a wider color range, intended more for simple garden ornament and cut flowers than for seed crops. Among these, most of the following bear 4- to 8-inch-wide flowers. Pollenless kinds (generally classed as **H. × hybridus**) are better for cutting, since they won't shed pollen on furniture. The **Large Flowered Mix** features yellow, red, and bronze flowers on 6- to 10-foot plants. Among named cultivars are 4- to 7-foot **'Bright Bandolier'** (yellow-and-mahogany bicolor), 5- to 7-foot **'Cinnamon Sun'** (rosy bronze), and 6- to 8-foot **'Velvet Queen'** (bicolor combination of brown and wine red). Deep garnet **'Prado Red'** reaches only 4 feet; light yellow **'Valentine'** grows no more than 5 feet tall.

In the pollen-bearing category of *H. annuus*, **Parasol Mix** gives yellow, orange, red, and bicolored blossoms on 4- to 5-foot plants; **'Soraya'**, to 6 feet, has dark-centered orange blooms. For pale colors, try 5-foot **'Italian White'** (cream to nearly white), 4-foot **'Moonshadow'** (pale yellow to cream), and 4- to 6-foot **'Lemon Eclair'** (light yellow). **'Indian Blanket'** grows 4 to 5 feet tall and bears blossoms with yellow-tipped red petals. **'Pacino'**, reaching only 2½ feet high, bears 8-inch-wide yellow flowers with yellow centers. **'Teddy Bear'** is smaller still, with fully double, bright yellow, 6-inch-wide flowers on 1½-foot plants.

Perennial sunflowers may have single, semidouble, or double blossoms, but the color is always yellow. Best known is **H. × multiflorus** (Zones 1–24, 28–43), a hybrid group of narrow, bushy plants to about 5 feet high. **'Loddon Gold'** (**'Flore Pleno'**) has fully double, 4-inch blossoms. Lemon yellow **'Capenoch Star'** has 4-inch-wide single blooms—but its disk flowers are rolled into tubes, giving the blossom's center a pincushionlike look. (Nurseries sometimes offer the above as selections of *H. decapetalus*.) Another noteworthy perennial is 8-foot-tall willowleaf sunflower, **H. salicifolius** (**H. orgyalis**; Zones 1–24, 28–43), with narrow, 8-inch, gracefully drooping leaves and dark-centered, 2-inch flowers in branched clusters.

CULTURE. All sunflowers perform best with good soil and regular watering. Plant the large seeds of annual sunflower directly in the garden after all danger of frost is past. Thin plants to 1½ feet apart; stake the tallest, seed-producing kinds as flower heads form. Set out young perennial plants in early spring. They increase fairly rapidly; you'll need to dig and divide clumps every 3 to 4 years in early spring.

TOP: *Helianthus* 'Velvet Queen'
BOTTOM: *Helianthus* × *multiflorus* 'Capenoch Star'

Helichrysum bracteatum

HELICHRYSUM
Asteraceae (Compositae)
WARM-SEASON ANNUALS AND PERENNIALS
    USUALLY TREATED AS ANNUALS
ZONES VARY
FULL SUN
MODERATE WATER
✿❀✿✿✿ FLOWERS IN SUMMER, FALL

The two helichrysums discussed here are strikingly different plants—one is a staple for dried flower arrangements, the other an invaluable filler for container plantings.

Annual strawflower, **H. bracteatum** (all zones), is probably the most popular flower for use in everlasting arrangements. What appear to be petals are actually papery bracts (modified leaves) surrounding a central disk of true flowers; the flower head resembles a prickly, pompomlike double daisy with flat to incurved petals. The plant grows upright to 3 feet tall and 1 foot wide, with medium green, straplike leaves to 5 inches long. About 2½-inch-wide flowers in a range of bright colors bloom from summer until frost. Though fine in fresh bouquets, they're much more widely used in their dried form—in which they can remain "fresh" for well over a year. Various named strains are available, featuring mixed pastels, mixed bright colors, and individual colors. Dwarf types, such as **Bright Bikini** and **Dwarf Spangle**, reach just 1 foot high.

Licorice plant, **H. petioliare,** can be perennial in Zones 16, 17, 22–24, but it grows so rapidly it is usually treated as an annual in all zones. Lax stems bear rounded, inch-long grayish green leaves with a woolly white coating; tiny flowers are inconspicuous. Where the growing season is long, the plant can reach 1½ to 3 feet high and spread to 4 feet. It's most often used in combination with other plants; you'll see it spilling from mixed container plantings or meandering through the foreground of a border. Several cultivars vary in foliage color, though all retain the woolly white coating. '**Limelight**' has light chartreuse leaves; '**Licorice Splash**' is variegated in yellow and green; '**Variegatum**' has green-and-white variegation.

Helichrysum petiolare 'Limelight'

CULTURE. Both species need well-drained, light to medium soil and moderate watering. Set out plants of *H. petiolare* after danger of frost is past. Where plants will be killed by frosts, take stem cuttings in late summer; then overwinter the started plants indoors for planting out the next year. To grow *H. bracteatum* in mild-winter regions, sow seeds outdoors at any time after the danger of frost is past. In colder regions, sow outdoors after weather has warmed; or sow indoors 6 to 8 weeks before the last-frost date, preferably at a temperature of 65 to 70°F/18 to 21°C. Indoors or out, simply press seeds onto the soil surface, but do not cover them; they need light for germination. Tall kinds may need staking to remain upright.

HELLEBORUS
HELLEBORE
Ranunculaceae
PERENNIALS
ZONES VARY
PARTIAL TO FULL SHADE, EXCEPT AS NOTED
REGULAR WATER, EXCEPT AS NOTED
✿❀✿✿✿ FLOWERS IN WINTER,
    EARLY SPRING

Elegant plants with an air of understated sophistication, the hellebores flower in winter and early spring—a time when not much else is in bloom, and their beauty is especially appreciated. All bear blossoms consisting of five petal-like sepals surrounding a large cluster of stamens; they look a bit like single roses, a fact reflected in the common names of several species. Each long-stalked leaf is composed of large, leathery leaflets grouped together like fingers on an outstretched hand.

Two growth habits are possible. Most hellebores form tight clumps with leafstalks seeming to rise directly from the ground; separate (typically leafless) flower stems arise from the same growing points. These are the *acaulescent* types. A few species and hybrids—the *caulescent* types—form clumps of stems set with leaves all along their length; the stems produce dome-shaped flower clusters at their tips, then die back as new stems rise from the ground.

The caulescent group includes the largest species: Corsican hellebore, **H. argutifolius** (**H. corsicus;** Zones 3b–9, 14–24, 31, 32), an almost shrublike plant with numerous stems rising to as high as 3 feet. Each pale blue-green leaf has three leaflets with sharply toothed edges. In milder zones, the light chartreuse, 2-inch flowers may appear in late fall or winter; in colder areas, bloom comes in early spring. Unlike the other hellebores, this one will take some sun; it is also fairly drought-tolerant once established. Bear's-foot hellebore, **H. foetidus** (Zones 2b–9, 14–24, 30–34, 39), bears the most graceful foliage of the group, with each leafstalk carrying 7 to 11 narrow, blackish green leaflets. In late winter and early spring, clusters of inch-wide, purple-marked green flowers appear atop leafy, 1½-foot stems. In the **Wester Flisk** strain, all plant parts are strikingly infused with red. **H. × sternii** (Zones 4–9, 14–24, 31, 32) is a hybrid group derived from *H. argutifolius* and another, similar species. Plants have bluish green leaves netted with white or cream; pink-tinted greenish flowers to 2 inches wide come in winter to early spring, carried on stems to about 2 feet tall.

Among the acaulescent types, Christmas rose, **H. niger** (Zones 1–7, 14–17, 32–45), is the first to bloom. Depending on the severity of the winter, flowers can appear from early winter to early spring. Each leafless, 1½-foot stem usually holds one upward-facing flower to 2 inches across; the blossoms open white, then age to purplish pink. Dark green, lusterless leaves have seven to nine leaflets. Blooms of **'Potter's Wheel'** have a conspicuous green center; **'White Magic'** has white flowers that blush pink with age. **Sunrise** (with pink-infused flowers) and **Sunset** (near-red) are two seed strains available as both seeds and plants.

Lenten rose, **H. orientalis** (Zones 2b–10, 14–24, 31–41), is an easy-to-grow plant that resembles *H. niger* but blooms a bit later, from the end of winter into spring. Each 1- to 1½-foot stem bears a few modified leaves and branched clusters of nodding, 2- to 3-inch, downward-facing flowers. Colors range from greenish or buff-tinted white through pinkish tones to maroon and liver purple; blossoms frequently show dark spots in the center or a freckling of spots overall. Leaves have 5 to 11 broad, glossy leaflets. Many plants sold as *H. orientalis* actually are hybrids—derived in large part from *H. orientalis* but also involving other, similar species. In plant, flower, and zone adaptation, these hybrids are similar to *H. orientalis,* but they have a wider range of blossom colors and patterns, including near-yellow, blackish red, mauve gray, and various color combinations with contrasting dotting.

CULTURE. Though established plants of *H. argutifolius* and *H. foetidus* withstand some drought and prosper with just moderate water, all hellebores appreciate good, organically enriched soil and regular watering. Choose a planting spot in filtered sun to partial or full shade (*H. argutifolius* will also take full sun). Clumps can remain in place indefinitely with no need for division. You can, however, divide clumps in early spring—but divisions reestablish slowly, and some of them may not survive. An easier way to increase a planting is to transplant volunteer seedlings. Keep in mind that seedlings' flowers may differ somewhat from those of the parent plants.

Helleborus argutifolius

Helleborus foetidus

I n the hands of dedicated amateur and professional breeders, the old yellow or orange daylily has been transformed: today's hybrids offer a dazzling color array (including patterns of two or more colors), increased petal width and thickness, and, in some cases, blossoms that remain open well into the evening or even overnight. In size, plants range from foot-high miniatures to giants that can hit 6 feet when in bloom. But all produce linear, arching leaves in flat sprays that account for another of this plant's common names—"corn lily."

Daylilies may be deciduous, semievergreen, or evergreen. Deciduous types die back completely in winter and are the hardiest, withstanding −35°F/−37°C with little

HEMEROCALLIS
DAYLILY
Liliaceae
PERENNIALS
ZONES 1–45; H1, H2
FULL SUN, EXCEPT AS NOTED
REGULAR WATER
✿❀✿✿✿ FLOWERS IN SPRING, SUMMER, FALL

TOP: *Hemerocallis* 'Oodnadatta'
BOTTOM: *Hemerocallis* 'Black-eyed Stella'

or no snow protection; in mild-winter regions, however, they may not get enough chill for top performance. Evergreen kinds grow well in both mild and cold regions but need a protective winter mulch where temperatures normally dip below $-20°F/-29°C$. Semievergreen types are intermediate between the other two in hardiness; some perform better than others where winters are mild.

The majority of daylily hybrids reach 2½ to 4 feet high in bloom. Carried on stems that branch near the top, the blossoms are lily or chalice shaped, in widths ranging from 3 to 8 inches (1½ to 3 inches in smaller and miniature types). A typical flower has six overlapping, petal-like segments, but there are also double kinds (with an indeterminate number of segments) and spider types with long, narrow segments that are frequently twisted. Though each flower lasts just one day, stems produce many buds that open sequentially over a long period. Flowering typically runs from midspring into early summer—but cultivars bloom at the beginning, middle, or end of this period, so if you choose carefully, you can enjoy an extended display. Scattered bloom may also come in summer, and some cultivars reliably rebloom in fall. A few types flower throughout the growing season, notably the 2-foot-tall **'Stella de Oro'** and **'Happy Returns'** (both yellow), **'Black-eyed Stella'** (yellow with red eye), and **'Pardon Me'** (red).

A few daylilies are fragrant. The old favorite **'Hyperion'**, a 4-footer with yellow blooms, is notably sweet scented, as is *H. lilioasphodelus (H. flavus)*, the lemon daylily, with 3-foot stems and pure yellow blossoms.

CULTURE. Few perennials are as easy to grow as daylilies, but extra attention reaps rewards. Plant in well-drained, organically amended, average to good soil. Full sun is best, but partial shade is a good idea where summers are hot and dry. Set out bare-root plants in fall or early spring, or plant from containers at any time during the growing season. Water regularly throughout the growing season. Divide clumps when they become crowded—usually every 3 to 6 years, though reblooming types should be divided every 2 or 3 years. In hot-summer regions, do the job in fall or early spring; in areas with cool summers or a short growing season, divide in summer.

HEUCHERA
(and × HEUCHERELLA)
CORAL BELLS, ALUM ROOT
Saxifragaceae
PERENNIALS
ZONES VARY
FULL SUN, EXCEPT AS NOTED
MODERATE TO REGULAR WATER
❀✿☆ FLOWERS IN SPRING, SUMMER, FALL

Heuchera sanguinea

Coral bells are old-fashioned favorites, long prized for their good-looking foliage and graceful spikes of showy flowers. And in recent years, hybrids and selections of species with quite understated blossoms have become popular for their strikingly attractive leaves. Whether grown for flowers, foliage, or both, all kinds have nearly round to heart-shaped leaves on long leafstalks and form low, mounded clumps that gradually spread as the woody rootstocks branch and elongate. Leaves are typically hairy and may have scalloped margins and decorative dark or silvery mottling. Wiry, branching stems rise above the leaves, bearing open clusters of small, bell-shaped blossoms.

Of the showy-flowered kinds, the hybrid *H. × brizoides* (Zones 1–10, 14–24, 31–45) has spawned a number of named cultivars. The rounded leaves are shallowly lobed, with scalloped edges; flowers in white, pink shades, and red come in spring or summer on 1- to 2½-foot-tall stems. Representative are **'Firefly' ('Leuchtkäfer')**, with fragrant scarlet flowers; rosy pink **'Freedom'**; white **'June Bride'**; and **'Snowstorm'**, with reddish pink flowers and white-variegated leaves. The seed-grown **Bressingham Hybrids** offer the full color range of white through pink to red; some have been named, including **'Bressingham White'**.

H. sanguinea (Zones A1–A3; 1–11, 14–24, 31–45) is a favorite from times past. Round, scallop-edged green leaves are 1 to 2 inches across; nodding bells in bright red to coral pink bloom from spring into summer, carried on stems that reach 1 to 2 feet high. Selections are available with blooms in white, pure pink, and red shades. Two red-flowered varieties are **'Cherry Splash'**, with foliage variegated in white and gold, and **'Frosty'**, with silver leaf variegation.

Good choices for gardeners in the western U.S. are hybrids of *H. sanguinea* with Western native species. The following three succeed in Zones 14–24. All bloom from spring through summer and into fall and are somewhat drought tolerant. **'Santa Ana Cardinal'** has light green, 3- to 4-inch leaves that make a sizable foliage mound; massive clusters of bright rosy red flowers come on 2- to 3-foot stems. **'Genevieve'** has pink-centered white bells and gray-mottled, 2- to 3-inch leaves, while **'Wendy'** has peachy pink blossoms and lightly mottled light green leaves 3 to 4 inches wide.

H. sanguinea hybrids belonging to the spring-blooming **Canyon Series** grow in Zones 2–11, 14–24. Medium green, 1½-inch leaves form matlike mounds to 6 inches high and 2 feet across. Red **'Canyon Belle'**, rosy **'Canyon Delight'**, and **'Canyon Pink'** have 20-inch stems; smaller overall, with 1-foot stems, are **'Canyon Chimes'**, **'Canyon Duet'**, and **'Canyon Melody'**, all with pink-and-white blossoms.

Two species account for the growing number of coral bells with showy foliage. *H. americana* (Zones 1–9, 14–24, 32–43), a mounding plant to 2 feet high, has green leaves to 4 inches across with attractive silver-and-white veining and mottling. Tiny greenish white flowers appear in early summer on thread-thin stems to 3 feet tall. Many of this species' cultivars feature purple leaves variously flushed and veined in silver; these include **'Chocolate Veil'**, **'Persian Carpet'**, **'Pewter Veil'**, **'Plum Pudding'**, and **'Ruby Veil'**. **'Ring of Fire'** has maroon-veined silver leaves that turn red at the edges in cold weather. **'Chocolate Ruffles'** (chocolate above, wine red beneath) and **'Velvet Night'** (bluish purple) are dramatic solid-colored choices.

H. micrantha (Zones 1–10, 14–24, 31–43) is best known in its form (or hybrid) **'Palace Purple'**, with maplelike, brownish to purplish, 3-inch leaves that color best in sun. This is now a seed strain, so color saturation will vary. In late spring and early summer, tiny greenish white flowers come on red-tinged 2-foot stems.

The plants known as × *Heucherella* (Zones 1–10, 14–24, 31–45) are a group of hybrids between *Heuchera* × *brizoides* and related *Tiarella* species. All form mounded, foot-wide clumps of heart-shaped to maplelike, hairy leaves that send up wiry spikes of tiny, starlike pink flowers. Widely available × *H. alba* **'Bridget Bloom'**, to 16 inches high, flowers from spring to midsummer. **'Pink Frost'**, to 2 feet, blooms from spring to fall.

CULTURE. Give *Heuchera* and × *Heucherella* well-drained soil enriched with organic matter. Plants prefer full sun except where summers are hot and dry; in those areas, they need light or partial shade, especially in the afternoon. Moderate to regular watering is suitable for *Heuchera*; × *Heucherella* does best with regular moisture. Clumps become crowded after 3 or 4 years, with the foliage clustered at the ends of short, thick, woody stalks. Divide crowded clumps in early spring (in fall, where winters are mild), replanting divisions so crowns are even with the soil surface.

Heuchera × brizoides

× *Heucherella alba* 'Bridget Bloom'

Flamboyant rose-mallow brings a touch of the tropics to temperate gardens. Blossoms reminiscent of giant morning glories (up to a foot wide) decorate upright, shrubby plants that can reach as tall as 8 feet in the basic species. The oval leaves, dark green above and nearly white beneath, are correspondingly large—to 10 inches long and 4 inches wide. Bloom begins in early summer and continues until frost, after which stems die to the ground.

Named cultivars come in specific colors. The following choices are all about 4 feet tall. Sporting 10-inch flowers are pure white **'Blue River'**, **'George Riegel'** (ruffled

HIBISCUS moscheutos
ROSE-MALLOW
Malvaceae
PERENNIAL
ZONES 2–24, 26–41; H1
FULL SUN, EXCEPT AS NOTED
REGULAR WATER
❀ ✿ ☆ FLOWERS IN SUMMER, FALL

Hibiscus moscheutos

pink with red center), and dark red **'Lord Baltimore'**. **'Turn of the Century'** boasts 5- to 10-inch pink-and-white flowers with red centers; **'Lady Baltimore'** and **'The Clown'** have 8-inch-wide pink blossoms centered in red.

Seed strains offer shorter plants with 8- to 12-inch-wide flowers in white, pink, and red, often with red centers. **Southern Belle** grows 4 feet high; **Disco Belle, Frisbee,** and **Rio Carnival** reach only 2½ feet. You can sometimes find specific color selections of these; Disco Belle, for example, is available in white and pink.

CULTURE. Rich soil and plenty of water help these plants achieve full magnificence. Liberally amend the soil with organic matter before planting; mulch to conserve moisture. Avoid planting in windswept locations where leaves and flowers will burn. Where summers are hot and dry, give plants a bit of afternoon shade to prevent wilting. Fertilize plants every 6 to 8 weeks during the growing season. Clumps gradually increase in size but do not need division for good performance. You can start new plants from stem cuttings taken in summer. To raise from seed, sow indoors 6 to 8 weeks before the last-frost date; plants may flower the first year from seed.

HOSTA
HOSTA, PLANTAIN LILY
Liliaceae
PERENNIALS
ZONES 1–10, 14–21, 28, 31–45,
    EXCEPT AS NOTED
PARTIAL TO FULL SHADE, EXCEPT AS NOTED
REGULAR WATER
✿❀ FLOWERS IN LATE SPRING, SUMMER;
    MOST ARE GROWN PRIMARILY FOR
    FOLIAGE IN BLUE, GREEN, YELLOW, AND
    VARIEGATED COMBINATIONS

Though hostas bear spikes of modest trumpet-shaped flowers in spring and summer, the blossoms pale in significance when weighed against the season-long show of exceptionally handsome foliage. Named cultivars and species offer a bewildering assortment of colors, markings, and shapes. Leaves may be lance shaped, heart shaped, oval, or nearly round, with smooth or gracefully undulating margins; the surface may be smooth, quilted looking, or puckered, either glossy or dusted with a grayish bloom like that on the skin of a plum. Colors range from light to dark green to chartreuse, near-yellow, and virtually blue; you will also find color combinations, including variegations with white, cream, or yellow.

The leaves are carried on long stalks that rise from the ground, radiating from a central point; plants increase to form tight clumps. In some hostas, the clump has an elegant vase shape, but most make mounds of leaves that overlap like shingles. In size, plants range from demure 4- to 6-inch specimens to showpiece types that can reach 3 to 4 feet high with equal or greater spread. Flowers come in white or purple shades; they rise well above the foliage in some kinds but barely show in others. Some are pleasantly fragrant.

Hosta specialists offer a dazzling array of cultivars, and even well-stocked nurseries may carry quite a range of sizes and colors. Even so, there are a number of tried-and-true, widely available plants that are good, inexpensive choices for the neophyte. One word of caution: the names of many hosta species have been changed over the years, with the result that the same plant may go by one name in older references, by another in more recent ones.

Hosta species. The following six species are long-time garden favorites; they and their selected forms offer a sampler of these plants' variability.

Plants sold as ***H. fortunei*** (Zones A1–A3; 1–10, 14–21, 28, 31–45) may actually be hybrids involving *H. sieboldiana* (see facing page). Many named selections are sold, in colors ranging from gray green to yellow green to variegated combinations. Leaves are typically broadly heart shaped, up to a foot long; they form clumps to 2 feet high and somewhat wider. Lilac flowers bloom on stems to 3 feet tall. **'Albomarginata'** has dark green leaves with a creamy white margin; *H. f. hyacinthina* features slightly puckered gray-green leaves thinly edged in white.

As the name indicates, ***H. lancifolia*** has narrow leaves—dark green, about 6 inches long, tapering to long leafstalks. The entire clump mounds to about 1 foot.

Hosta fortunei

Outward-facing lavender flowers come on 2-foot stalks. Fragrant plantain lily, ***H. plan-taginea,*** offers scented, 4-inch white flowers on short spikes rising just above a 2-foot-high foliage mound. Leaves are typically quilted-looking, bright apple green ovals to 10 inches long.

H. sieboldiana (H. glauca) is a big plant with puckered, broadly heart-shaped blue-green leaves that can reach 15 inches long; an established clump may reach 2½ feet high, 4 feet or more wide. The small flowers are palest lavender, barely showing above the leaves. **'Elegans'** has foliage covered with a gray-blue bloom; its sport **'Frances Williams'** adds a broad chartreuse edge to the leaves, while another sport, **'Great Expectations'**, features a creamy flame pattern in the center of each leaf.

Hosta sieboldiana 'Frances Williams'

The appropriately named ***H. undulata*** has narrow, oval, 8-inch leaves with undulating margins; it forms lively-looking clumps about 1½ feet high. The species has green leaves with a white central stripe; ***H. u. albo-marginata*** has green leaves with a white margin, while ***H. u. erromena*** features solid green foliage. Blue plantain lily, ***H. ventricosa,*** forms a mound to 2 feet tall of deep green, 8-inch-long, deeply veined leaves with a broad heart shape. Showy blue-violet blossoms are carried on 3-foot stems above the foliage. **'Aureomarginata'** has leaves margined in creamy white.

Hosta hybrids. The majority of available named hostas fall into this group. Among proven performers, **'Blue Angel'** makes an impressive clump to 4 feet high and 5 feet wide; the broadly heart-shaped, steel blue leaves have a veined, corrugated surface. White flowers come on 4- to 5-foot stems. **'Francee'**, forming a clump to 1½ feet high, has rich green, broadly oval leaves with a crisp white margin; light lavender blossoms appear above the foliage. In its sport **'Patriot'**, the white leaf margins are much wider. **'Ginko Craig'** forms a 7- to 12-inch mound of narrow dark green leaves edged in white; lavender flowers are held above the foliage. **'Halcyon'** has foliage in a fetching silvery blue, the heart-shaped and deeply veined leaves making an arching clump to about 15 inches high. Bluish lilac blossoms are carried several inches above the foliage.

'Honeybells' has deeply veined, wavy-edged, oval bright green leaves in a clump to 2½ feet high; pale lilac blooms come on 3-foot stems. **'Krossa Regal'** is an elegant vase-shaped plant to about 2½ feet high, with lance-shaped, powdery blue gray leaves on long stalks; spikes of lavender flowers can rise to 5 feet. **'Sum and Substance'** forms a massive mound—to 3 feet high and 5 feet across—of chartreuse, very broadly heart-shaped leaves to 20 inches long. Lavender blossoms appear just above the foliage.

Hosta sieboldiana 'Elegans'

CULTURE. All hostas grow most luxuriantly in good, organically enriched soil, with regular moisture and periodic feeding during the growing season. They are, however, tough and durable enough to take leaner diets and occasional lapses in watering, though growth in such conditions will of course be less impressive. They perform best in regions with frosty or freezing winters followed by humid summers.

In general, hostas prefer a spot in partial or even full shade, though they'll also take sun where summers are cool and humid. Plants with a considerable amount of white or yellow in their leaves tend to be the most sun sensitive. The more sun a hosta receives, the more compact it will be and the more flowers it will produce; grown in shade, the same plant is likely to be taller and broader.

Watch for snails and slugs, which zero in on hosta leaves, especially emerging new growth. Cultivars with a waxy "bloom" on the leaves are more resistant to slug and snail damage. Foliage of all hostas collapses and withers after frosts.

Hostas are permanent perennials, remaining vigorous without periodic division—and in fact, they gain in beauty as they put on size. To increase your supply of a favorite plant, carefully remove rooted pieces from the clump's perimeter; or cut a wedge-shaped piece from the clump and transplant it (the resulting gap will fill in quickly).

Hosta 'Ginko Craig'

IBERIS
CANDYTUFT

Brassicaceae (Cruciferae)

PERENNIALS AND COOL-SEASON ANNUALS

ZONES VARY

FULL SUN, EXCEPT AS NOTED

REGULAR WATER

✿ ❀ ✿ ✿ FLOWERS IN SPRING, SUMMER, FALL

TOP: *Iberis umbellata,* Dwarf Fairy strain
BOTTOM: *Iberis sempervirens*

B oth annual and perennial candytufts are dense, low-growing plants that bear small flowers massed together in tight clusters. Profuse bloom and overall charm make them delightful front-of-the-border plants; many are good cut flowers as well.

Two annual species grow in Zones 1–45. Both flower in spring and summer, performing best with moderate daytime temperatures and cool nights. Hyacinth-flowered candytuft, *I. amara,* is accurately described by its common name: the fragrant white flowers are borne in a tight, domed cluster that eventually elongates into a hyacinthlike spike. The plant grows upright to 15 inches high but just 6 inches wide; leaves are narrow and slightly fuzzy. Globe candytuft, *I. umbellata,* is a bushy plant to 15 inches tall and about 9 inches wide. Blossoms are borne in clusters shaped like flattened cones; colors include white, pink shades, rosy red, purple, and lavender. Low-growing strains **Dwarf Fairy** and **Magic Carpet** offer the full color range on 6-inch plants; **Flash** is a few inches taller.

Perennial evergreen candytuft, *I. sempervirens* (Zones 1–24, 31–45), smothers itself in 2-inch clusters of sparkling white flowers from early to late spring. Even when not in bloom, the plants are attractive, their narrow, glossy dark green leaves forming dense mounds to 1 foot high, up to 2 feet wide. Named cultivars are lower and more compact. **'Little Gem'** grows just 4 to 6 inches high; **'Alexander's White'** (with very narrow leaves) and **'Kingwood Compact'** top out at 6 inches. **'Purity'** ranges from 4 to 12 inches high and spreads widely. **'Snowflake'** offers larger-than-normal flowers and broader leaves on a plant 4 to 12 inches high and up to 3 feet wide; it blooms sporadically throughout the year where summers and winters are mild. **'Autumnale'** and **'Autumn Snow'** reliably rebloom in fall.

CULTURE. Both annual and perennial candytufts need well-drained soil. Plant them in full sun except in hot-summer regions; in those areas, they'll benefit from a little afternoon shade. In all regions, you can plant *I. sempervirens* in spring; where winters are fairly mild, plants set out in fall will get established over winter and come into bloom earlier the following spring. After the main flowering burst, cut or shear back plants to encourage compactness. You can start new plants from stem cuttings taken in summer.

Sow seeds of annual *I. amara* and *I. umbellata* in place in the garden—in early spring in cold-winter climates, in late fall where winters are mild. Or sow indoors 6 to 8 weeks before the last-frost date.

IMPATIENS

Balsaminaceae

PERENNIALS USUALLY GROWN AS WARM-SEASON ANNUALS

ALL ZONES

EXPOSURE NEEDS VARY

REGULAR WATER

✿ ❀ ✿ ✿ ✿ FLOWERS IN SPRING, SUMMER

A vailable in a range of brilliant and soft colors lacking only true blue and yellow, impatiens have become *the* premier summer bedding plants for lightly or partially shaded gardens. In frost-free areas, they'll live from one year to the next, self-sowing to ensure a permanent presence in the garden. In all other areas, plants die with a touch of frost. Even where they can live over, though, they are typically grown as annuals. Two kinds are sold almost everywhere: *I. walleriana* (sometimes called busy Lizzie) and the New Guinea Hybrids. Both are bushy, fleshy-leafed, succulent-stemmed plants that branch from the base. The flat, roughly circular flowers have petals that are not quite uniform in size; a slender spur projects from the blossom's back. Ripe seed capsules burst open at the slightest touch, scattering seeds in all directions.

I. walleriana includes plants in a range of sizes, from 6- to 12-inch dwarfs to 2-foot-tall strains. It has 1- to 2-inch flowers and semiglossy dark green, spade-shaped, 1- to 3-inch-long leaves set on light green stems. Plant breeders have developed many strains that offer particular flower characteristics or plant habits. Unless otherwise indicated, the following strains come in mixed colors and, usually, in individual colors as well (**Accent Coral**, for example).

Among the smallest strains are **Firefly,** with ½-inch flowers, and **Neon,** both on 6- to 8-inch plants. **Super Elfin** grows 8 to 10 inches high and offers blended colors— pink with a wash of red, for instance—in addition to mixed and single hues. Ten-inch-high choices include **Accent; Accent Star,** bearing blossoms with a white central blaze; and **Tempo,** especially good in hanging containers (flowers of **Tempo Butterfly** have a butterfly-shaped central marking in a contrasting color). Strains with plants in the 10- to 16-inch range are **Bruno** and **Pride,** with large (2½-inch) flowers; **Mosaic,** featuring rose and lilac tones irregularly splashed white; **Stardust,** in which flowers have a central white star; and **Swirl,** in pastel colors with darker picotee margins.

Double-flowered impatiens, with blossoms resembling small roses, include **Confection, Fiesta,** and **Tioga,** all growing 10 to 12 inches high. '**Victorian Rose**' is the same size; it bears frilled, rose pink semidouble flowers.

New Guinea Hybrids are as valued for foliage as they are for flowers. They grow larger than *I. walleriana*—usually 1 to 2 feet tall and wide—and bear dark green, lance-shaped leaves to as much as 8 inches long. Some have foliage with striking cream or red variegation, and a few have bronze leaves. Plants don't produce the mass of flowers that the *I. walleriana* types do, but the 2½-inch blossoms are showy nonetheless, in colors including pure lavender, purple, pink, salmon, orange, red, and white. A number of strains are sold, some available as seeds, some only as cutting-grown plants. '**Tango**', with glowing orange flowers and bronzy green leaves on a 2-foot plant, is sold as seeds; other seed strains are **Java,** with bronze foliage, and **Spectra (Firelake),** with cream- or white-variegated leaves. **Paradise** and **Pure Beauty** are sold as cutting-grown plants, as is **Celebration,** with 3-inch flowers.

CULTURE. All impatiens appreciate plenty of water, especially during hot weather. These are premier container plants, needing a highly organic potting mix that is moisture retentive but fast draining. Plants also can be grown in lightly shaded borders, given soil liberally amended with organic matter. Though *I. walleriana* will take morning sun in cool- and mild-summer regions, it's usually grown in light shade. New Guinea Hybrids are a bit more sun tolerant. Nursery plants of both kinds are readily available, but you can also grow them from seed sown indoors 4 to 6 weeks before the last-frost date. For best germination, keep the planted containers in a warm spot (70 to 75°F/21 to 24°C).

Impatiens walleriana

Impatiens, New Guinea Hybrid

The mainstays of the spring flower border, irises bear showy flowers that rise above fans of swordlike leaves. An iris blossom is composed of three true petals *(standards)* and three petal-like sepals *(falls);* standards may be upright, arching, or flaring to horizontal, while falls range from flaring to drooping. Popular garden irises are separated into two broad categories. *Bearded* irises have a caterpillarlike ridge of hairs on each fall; *beardless* irises lack this feature.

BEARDED IRISES

The various bearded irises (Zones 1–24, 30–45) are more widely grown than beardless types. Available in a dazzling array of colors, patterns, and color combinations, these hybrids typically bloom in spring, though the growing category of rebloomers (often called remontants) flowers a second time in summer, fall, or winter. Bearded irises are classified according to stem height—as tall, median, or miniature dwarf. Most familiar are the *tall bearded* kinds; these flower in midspring, bearing large blossoms on branching stems ranging from 28 inches to 4 feet tall. The flowers, many with elaborately ruffled or fringed petals, bloom in all colors but true red and green (and breeders are coming close to these).

Listing continues>

IRIS

Iridaceae
PERENNIALS
ZONES VARY
FULL SUN, EXCEPT
  AS NOTED
REGULAR WATER, EXCEPT
  AS NOTED
✿ ✿ ❁ ✿ ✿ ✿ ✿ FLOWERS
  IN SPRING, EXCEPT
  AS NOTED

Tall bearded iris 'Orange Harvest'

Median irises comprise four classes that cover the height range from 8 to 28 inches. *Border bearded* and *miniature tall bearded* irises flower at the same time as the tall beardeds, on stems from 15 to 28 inches tall; *standard dwarf bearded* irises are early-spring bloomers with 8- to 15-inch stems. *Intermediate bearded* irises bloom midway between the standard dwarf beardeds and tall beardeds; they have 15- to 28-inch stems.

Miniature dwarf bearded irises are at the low end of the size range: they are 2- to 8-inch-high plants that flower at the first breath of spring.

Given the huge number of named cultivars, choices can be bewildering. A great way to get an idea of what's available is to visit a commercial iris garden during the bloom season; lacking that opportunity, you can turn to mail-order catalogs, some of which have plenty of color photographs.

CULTURE. Bearded irises need good drainage, since the rhizomes may rot if kept too wet. They'll grow in a range of soils—sandy to claylike, somewhat acid to somewhat alkaline—but if you plant in clay, make planting ridges (or plant in raised beds) to assure good drainage. Amend any soil with organic matter before planting. In cool- and mild-summer climates, choose a full-sun location; in the hottest-summer regions, a bit of afternoon shade is beneficial (though too much shade reduces the amount of bloom). Plant in July or August in cold-winter areas, in September or October where summers are hot. Where both winters and summers are mild, plant at any time from July to October.

Set rhizomes with their tops barely beneath the soil surface. New growth proceeds from the leafy end of the rhizome, so place the foliage fan in the direction you want growth to proceed initially. Bearded irises grow best if watered regularly from the time growth begins until about 6 weeks after the blooms fade; during summer, they need less moisture, though the smaller types (with smaller, shallower root systems) need a little more attention than larger growers do. After 3 to 4 years, clumps become crowded and bloom decreases in quantity and quality. When this occurs, dig and divide at the best planting time for your climate.

BEARDLESS IRISES

Of the many classes among the beardless category, Japanese and Siberian irises are the most widely grown. Both types have long, narrow, almost grasslike leaves and slender rhizomes with fibrous roots (rather than the fleshy roots of bearded types). In other respects, they differ considerably from one another.

Japanese irises (Zones 1–10, 14–24, 32–45) are derived solely from *I. ensata* (formerly *I. kaempferi*). Slender stems up to 4 feet high rise above clumps of graceful foliage, bearing sumptuous, single to double, relatively flat flowers 4 to 12 inches across. Colors include purple, violet, pink, rose, red, and white, often with contrasting veins or edges. Japanese irises bloom later than most tall beardeds, typically in late spring or early summer.

CULTURE. Set out plants in fall or spring, being careful not to let roots dry out (soak newly received mail-order plants overnight in water). Plants need organically amended, acid to neutral soil. Plant them in a sunny spot where summers are cool, in dappled sun or light afternoon shade where summers are hot. They revel in plenty of moisture, so give them a well-watered garden bed—or grow them at pond margins or in containers sunk halfway to their rims in water during the growing season. Divide crowded clumps in late summer or early fall; replant immediately so roots remain moist.

Siberian irises (Zones 1–10, 14–23, 32–45) are, for the most part, named hybrids derived from *I. sanguinea* and *I. sibirica*. In midspring, slender stems 2 to 4 feet tall (depending on the cultivar) rise above clumps of grasslike foliage, each bearing two to

Japanese iris 'Caprician Butterfly'

five blossoms with upright to splayed standards and flaring to drooping falls. Colors include white, light yellow, and various shades of blue, lavender, purple, wine red, and pink. Foliage turns an attractive tawny gold in autumn.

CULTURE. Plant in full sun or partial shade, in neutral to acid soil well amended with organic matter. In cold-winter regions, plant in early spring or late summer; in milder regions, plant in fall. Be sure to keep roots moist (see facing page, under Japanese iris culture). Water liberally from the time spring growth begins until several weeks after bloom ends; regular water will suffice for the rest of the growing season. Clumps may remain in place for many years but will eventually become hollow in the center; when this happens, dig and divide at the best planting time for your climate.

Siberian iris

Thick, fountainlike clumps of coarse, narrow leaves give these plants a decidedly grassy appearance. At flowering time, though, they're far more flamboyant than even the most ornamental of grasses: spearlike stems rise above the foliage, each bearing a thick, bottlebrush-style "torch" of drooping tubular flowers.

Old-fashioned favorite **K. uvaria** forms a hefty clump that sends up flower spikes to 6 feet tall; blossoms at the bottom of each cluster are yellow, those closer to the top orange red. Bloom comes at some point during spring.

Modern selections and hybrids—with *K. uvaria* and other species in their ancestry—offer an expanded color palette and a greater range of plant sizes; they generally bloom in late spring or summer. At the short end of the scale are 2-foot **'Little Maid'**, with creamy white flowers above notably thin leaves; 2- to 2½-foot **'Vanilla'**, with yellow buds opening to cream blossoms; and 2½-foot **Flamenco**, a seed-grown strain that offers the full range of colors. In the 3-foot range are **'Bee's Sunset'** (yellow flowers opening from near-orange buds), **'Gold Mine'** (amber yellow), and **'Primrose Beauty'** (light yellow). At 4 to 5 feet are **'Border Ballet'** (coral pink and cream), **'Peaches and Cream'** (peach pink and cream), and **'Percy's Pride'** (color varies from greenish yellow to cream). **'Malibu Yellow'** is about the size of *K. uvaria* and produces bright yellow flowers from green buds.

CULTURE. Give red-hot pokers good, organically enriched, fast-draining soil. Water regularly in spring and summer; cut back later in the year. Be particularly careful not to overwater in winter, since plants cannot tolerate saturated soil then. Choose a spot in full sun except in hot-summer regions, where plants need afternoon shade. Where winter temperatures drop to 0°F/−18°C or lower, tie the leaves together over the clump to protect the growing points from freezes; in warmer regions, you can cut old foliage to the ground in fall. Clumps can remain in place indefinitely; to increase your planting, just dig and relocate young plants from the clump's edge.

Sweet peas have been cherished for hundreds of years for their memorable fragrance and clean, fresh colors. In most climates, they flower from spring into summer, but in mild-winter regions they can be planted in late summer for bloom in winter and early spring.

Traditional vining sweet peas are described on page 183; here, we focus on the more recently introduced nonvining, bushy strains that can be used in borders and containers. All have the familiar banner-and-keel flower shape. The taller types may need some support to remain upright; brush staking, shown on page 75, is a simple solution.

Listing continues>

KNIPHOFIA
RED-HOT POKER
Liliaceae
PERENNIALS
ZONES 2–9, 14–24, 28–41
FULL SUN, EXCEPT AS NOTED
REGULAR WATER, EXCEPT AS NOTED
❀ ✿ ✿ ✿ ✿ ✿ FLOWERS IN SPRING, SUMMER

Kniphofia uvaria

LATHYRUS odoratus
SWEET PEA
Fabaceae (Leguminosae)
COOL-SEASON ANNUAL
ALL ZONES
FULL SUN
REGULAR WATER
✿ ✿ ❀ ✿ ✿ FLOWERS IN LATE WINTER, SPRING, EARLY SUMMER

Lathyrus odoratus, Knee-Hi strain

At 2 to 3 feet, **Jet Set** is potentially the tallest bush sweet pea. **Knee-Hi** reaches about 2½ feet in the open garden, though plants against a wall or fence will grow taller. Topping out at about 2 feet are **Explorer** and **Supersnoop. Snoopea** grows 12 to 15 inches high; **Bijou** reaches about 1 foot. Still shorter is the little **Little Sweethearts** strain, with rounded, bushy, mounding plants to 8 inches high and wide. Plants of the **Cupid** strain grow a mere 4 to 6 inches high and spread to about a foot; they're excellent for window boxes and hanging containers.

CULTURE. Sweet peas revel in the best "vegetable garden" treatment, flourishing with good soil and regular moisture. Dig soil thoroughly and deeply before planting, incorporating plenty of organic matter. If soil is on the heavy side, mound it a bit to ensure that water will drain away from the plants' bases.

Like their vining kin, bush sweet peas are cool-season performers, ending their run with the onset of hot weather. For this reason, your climate determines the time of year you should plant. Where winters are mild and summers are warm to hot, plant seeds at some point from late summer through early January; you'll get flowers as early as late winter and on into spring, depending on when you planted. Where winters are cool and summers warm to hot, plant seed as early as possible in spring for flowers in later spring and into summer. In cold-winter areas with cool or short summers, also plant as soon as soil is workable in spring.

To hasten germination, soak seeds in lukewarm water overnight before planting.

LAVATERA trimestris
ANNUAL MALLOW
Malvaceae
WARM-SEASON ANNUAL
ALL ZONES
FULL SUN
REGULAR WATER
❀ ✿ FLOWERS IN
    SUMMER, FALL

Reaching 2 to 6 feet tall, these shrubby plants bear satiny, 2- to 4-inch-wide flowers that resemble smaller versions of tropical hibiscus. Quick to grow from seed, they will flower from midsummer until frost if you remove spent blossoms faithfully. Named selections and strains are the most widely sold annual mallows. Few of these reach the upper end of the height range; the tallest, at 3 to 4 feet, is deep rose **'Loveliness'.** Compact kinds (to about 2 feet) include white **'Mont Blanc',** rose pink **'Mont Rose',** soft pink **'Pink Beauty',** bright pink **'Silver Cup',** and **'Ruby Regis',** in cerise pink with darker veins.

Lavatera trimestris
'Mont Blanc'

CULTURE. Give plants average soil; overly rich soil promotes foliage at the expense of flowers. Sow seeds in place, a little before the last-frost date (or in early spring, in mild-winter climates). In cold-winter areas, you also can sow indoors 6 to 8 weeks before the last-frost date.

LIATRIS
GAYFEATHER
Asteraceae (Compositae)
PERENNIALS
ZONES A2, A3; 1–10, 14–24, 26, 28–45
FULL SUN
MODERATE TO REGULAR WATER
❀ ❀ ✿ FLOWERS IN SUMMER

For relatives of chrysanthemum and perennial aster, the gayfeathers look amazingly un-daisylike. Rising in summer from tufts of grassy foliage, leafy stems bear spikes of small, tightly clustered blossoms with prominent stamens. An unusual feature is that the blossoms open from the top of the spike downward—rather than from the bottom up, as flowers in spikes usually do.

Two species produce stems up to 5 feet high. *L. ligulistylis* has dark red buds opening to reddish purple flowers. Kansas gayfeather, *L. pycnostachya,* has purplish pink blossoms; its variety **'Alba'** is pure white. The most widely sold species, light purple *L. spicata,* reaches about 4 feet high. Attractive variants are **'Floristan White'** and **'Floristan Violet',** both 3 feet tall; 2- to 2½-foot **'Kobold',** with bright rose pink blossoms; and 3-foot **'Silvertips',** bearing silvery lilac blooms with white tips.

Liatris pycnostachya

CULTURE. The gayfeathers need moderately fertile soil and good drainage; their thick, almost tuberous roots are especially prone to rot if soil is soggy during the winter dormant period. Plants are moderately drought-tolerant but perform best with regular watering during the growing period. After a number of years, when performance declines, divide crowded clumps in early spring.

Given their preferred conditions of rich soil, ample water, and moist air, ligularias will reward you with bold clumps of handsome foliage, topped in summer by spikes or clusters of bright, daisylike flowers. Leaves are usually heart-shaped to nearly circular and a foot or more across, with margins that may be strongly toothed, wavy, or deeply dissected.

Dramatic foliage is the main selling point of **L. dentata** (Zones 1–9, 14–17, 32, 34, 36–43): its leathery, tooth-edged, rounded medium green leaves can reach 16 inches across. The foliage forms a clump to 2 feet high; at bloom time, 3- to 5-foot stems rise above the leaves, bearing orange, 4-inch flowers in branched clusters. **'Dark Beauty'** has leaves in a particularly dark purple; **'Desdemona'** and **'Othello'** have green leaves with purple stalks, veins, and undersides.

Elegant blossom spires adorn clumps of **L. stenocephala** (Zones A2, A3; 1–9, 14–17, 32, 34, 36–45), usually represented in catalogs by its selection (or hybrid) **'The Rocket'**. Heart-shaped, deeply toothed green leaves to 1 foot wide send up 5-foot-tall purple stems carrying yellow, 1½-inch daisies in foxtail-like spikes.

CULTURE. Ligularias grow best in good, organically enriched soil with plenty of moisture and some shade. They're ideal for shady pondside plantings. They don't take kindly to heat or dry air, and even with humidity and ample water, leaves may wilt somewhat during the warmest part of the day. Slugs and snails can ravage the foliage. Clumps can remain in place for many years, though you can divide for increase in early spring.

Tough and trouble free, the various species of statice give you garden color that can be cut and dried for everlasting bouquets. Though the plants do vary, all have similar blossoms: each consists of an outer, petal-like, papery envelope that surrounds the very tiny true flowers. The two parts often differ in color. Though individually small, the blossoms are carried in showy clusters or impressive, airy sprays.

Annual **L. sinuatum** (all zones) is a summer bloomer 1½ to 2 feet high, up to 1 foot wide. The basal leaves are deeply lobed, while the many-branched flower stems have distinctive leaflike "wings." Tight, flat-topped blossom clusters come in white and shades of blue, purple, yellow, orange, and pink; seeds are sold in both mixed and individual colors. **Pastel Shades** is a mixed-color strain; **Pacific, Soirée Improved,** and **Turbo** are all sold in mixed and single colors. **Forever Gold** has bright yellow flowers; **Sunset** offers blossoms in orange, yellow, apricot, peach, and rose.

Perennial species are taprooted plants that produce clumps of leathery leaves and multibranched blossom stalks bearing clouds of flowers. Summer-flowering **L. gmelinii** (Zones 1–10, 14–24, 32–43) forms clumps of oblong, 5-inch leaves and somewhat flattened sprays of tiny white-and-lavender flowers that float above the foliage like a haze of lavender baby's breath *(Gypsophila)*. On established plants, the flower "cloud"

LIGULARIA
Asteraceae (Compositae)
PERENNIALS
ZONES VARY
PARTIAL TO FULL SHADE
REGULAR TO AMPLE WATER
✿ ✿ FLOWERS IN SUMMER

Ligularia stenocephala 'The Rocket'

LIMONIUM
STATICE, SEA LAVENDER
Plumbaginaceae
PERENNIALS AND WARM-SEASON ANNUALS
ZONES VARY
FULL SUN
LITTLE TO MODERATE WATER
✿ ✿ ✿ ✿ ✿ ✿ FLOWERS IN SPRING, SUMMER

Limonium sinuatum

may reach 2 feet across. ***L. platyphyllum*** (***L. latifolium;*** Zones 1–10, 14–24, 26, 28, 31–43, H1) is essentially a larger version, with leaves to 10 inches long and a blossom cloud to 2 feet high and 3 feet across.

Blooming in spring and summer, ***L. perezii*** (Zones 13, 15–17, 20–27) grows quickly enough to be used as an annual in zones too cold for its year-round survival. Clumps of broad, wavy-edged leaves to 1 foot long are topped by dense clusters of purple-and-white flowers on wiry stems to 3 feet tall.

CULTURE. The perennial forms of statice need only average, well-drained soil. They withstand drought but bloom profusely with moderate water. Clumps may remain in place indefinitely; to increase a planting, take root cuttings in late winter or divide clumps in early spring. All can also be raised from seed sown indoors 6 to 8 weeks before the last-frost date.

Like its perennial kin, annual *L. sinuatum* performs well in average, well-drained soil, but it doesn't take drought and needs consistent moderate watering. Sow seeds outdoors after all danger of frost is past; or sow indoors 6 to 8 weeks before the last-frost date.

LOBELIA
Campanulaceae (Lobeliaceae)
PERENNIALS AND WARM-SEASON ANNUALS
ZONES VARY
PARTIAL SHADE, EXCEPT AS NOTED
WATER NEEDS VARY
✿ ✿ ❀ ✿ ✿ FLOWERS IN SUMMER,
EXCEPT AS NOTED

Lobelia cardinalis

The lobelias are a varied group: there are perennials for perpetually damp soil and one that will colonize dry ground, plus an annual beloved for its abundant bloom. All bear tubular blossoms that flare into five unequal lobes—but beyond that, they can differ quite markedly.

Flowering during the hot times of year, annual ***L. erinus*** (all zones) is an invaluable source of cool blue color. The 3- to 6-inch-high plant consists of many slender, branching stems clothed in small green to bronze leaves; its dense foliage as well as its generous bloom make it a topnotch choice for borders and containers. Each ½-inch flower has the standard five unequal lobes and a dot of white or yellow in the throat; blue shades, white, and lilac pink are the basic colors. In mild-winter regions, the plant blooms from spring until frost; performance is best where summer nights are cool. In mild-winter desert zones, grow it for bloom in winter or early spring. Two old seed-grown cultivars still are popular. '**Cambridge Blue**' has lettuce green leaves and soft blue blossoms; '**Crystal Palace**' offers vivid deep blue blooms and bronzy green foliage. '**Rosamund**' provides a change of pace, bearing flowers in cherry red. The **Riviera** series features low, compact, mounded plants with flowers in various blue shades, white, and pink. Plants in the **Cascade** series are trailing, making them especially good for hanging baskets and window boxes; you'll find mixed as well as individual colors, including light and dark blue, white, pink, and purplish red.

The following moisture-loving perennial lobelias all form clumps of lance-shaped leaves that give rise in summer to flowering stems 2 to 5 feet high. Best known is cardinal flower, ***L. cardinalis*** (Zones 1–7, 14–17, upper half of 26, 28–45), with foliage rosettes sending up leafy, 3- to 4-foot stems bearing spikes of vivid red, 1½-inch blossoms. White and pink forms are sometimes available. ***L. siphilitica*** (Zones 1–9, 14–17, 31–45) resembles *L. cardinalis* but has flower stems just 2 to 3 feet high and bears rich blue to blue-violet blossoms. ***L. × gerardii*** (Zones 2–9, 14–17, 31–43), a hybrid between *L. cardinalis* and *L. siphilitica,* is available in several named cultivars. Red-flowered '**Ruby Queen**' reaches about 3 feet high; 4-foot '**Vedrariensis**' carries royal purple flowers above clumps of copper-infused leaves.

Breeding between various moisture-loving perennial species (including those discussed above) has produced a number of excellent plants in a range of colors. These may be offered as cultivars of ***L. × speciosa,*** though more often you'll find them simply listed by cultivar name. All flourish with ample water and succeed in Zones 2–9,

14–17, 31–43. Spectacular **'Bees Flame'** features beet red foliage and bright scarlet blooms on spikes to 5 feet. The **Compliment** series, available from seed, produces 2½-foot-tall plants with blooms in red, pink, or purple. Unusual **'Cotton Candy'**, also about 2½ feet tall, has white flowers tinged with pink. **'Dark Crusader'**, to 3 feet high, has deep magenta blossoms and dark purple leaves; another 3-footer, **'Tania'**, produces magenta purple blossoms and silvery green foliage. **'Sparkle DeVine'** carries its blue-flushed fuchsia blooms on stems to 4 feet high.

Unlike the preceding plants, Southwestern native ***L. laxiflora*** (Zones 7–9, 12–24) is notable for its drought tolerance. Upright stems reach 2 feet high, set somewhat sparsely with dark green, very narrow leaves and topped by loose clusters of tubular orange-red flowers over a long summer season.

CULTURE. Annual *L. erinus* is rather slow growing after germination, taking about 2 months to reach planting-out size; for this reason, most gardeners prefer to buy nursery-grown young plants. To raise from seed, sow indoors 8 to 10 weeks before the last-frost date. Simply press seeds into the potting mix, being careful not to cover them; they need light to germinate. Give regular water; provide partial shade except in cool-summer areas, where the plant does well in a sunny spot.

Perennial lobelias (*L. laxiflora* excepted) need ample water, good soil liberally enriched with organic matter, and a location in partial shade (in all but cool-summer regions, where they'll take full sun). Left unattended, clumps will dwindle and disappear; divide them every couple of years to keep the plants vigorous. You also can take stem cuttings just after flowering or layer stems to start new plants. If soil is constantly damp, volunteer seedlings may appear. Where winter temperatures dip to −10°F/−23°C or lower, protect plants with a layer of mulch; remove it as weather warms in spring.

L. laxiflora takes full sun and thrives with little water; it is unparticular about soil quality, growing well even in poor soil. Clumps spread by underground stems and can become invasive, especially in good soil with moderate to regular water.

Lobelia siphilitica

Sweet alyssum blooms throughout the growing season, bearing its tiny, honey-scented flowers in dense, dome-shaped clusters that literally cover the plant. Leaves are very narrow, at most a little over 1 inch long; the plant is bushy and spreading, reaching 1 foot high and wide. Sweet alyssum is excellent as an edging or small-scale ground cover, for planting between paving stones, and as a filler in containers. The basic flower color is white, but you can find named selections in lilac pink (**'Pink Heather'** and **'Rosie O'Day'**) and violet (**'Oriental Night'** and **'Violet Queen'**); these are compact plants that reach no higher than 6 inches. **'Pastel Carpet'** features a mixture of white, pink, lavender, violet, and cream flowers on spreading plants about 4 inches high. Low, compact white selections include **'Carpet of Snow'**, **'Little Gem'**, and **'Tiny Tim'**. At the other end of the size scale is foot-high **'Tetra Snowdrift'**, featuring larger flowers on long stems.

CULTURE. Nothing is easier to grow than sweet alyssum. The simplest method is to sow seeds where you want plants to grow, then thin seedlings to about 8 inches apart. Sow seeds in fall (even winter, in mild-winter regions), pressing them onto the soil without covering them; they need light to germinate. You also can sow in spring, a few weeks before the last-frost date (while soil is still cool). After the first flush of bloom, shear plants back about halfway to promote compactness and another round of flowers.

Sweet alyssum self-sows freely. Where colored- and white-flowered types grow together, the first volunteer seedlings will be in white and in paler shades of the parents' colors; in years to come, white flowers will prevail. Even volunteers from all-colored plantings usually lack the color depth of the parent plants.

LOBULARIA maritima
SWEET ALYSSUM
Brassicaceae (Cruciferae)
WARM-SEASON ANNUAL
ALL ZONES
FULL SUN
REGULAR WATER
✿ ❀ ✿ FLOWERS IN SPRING, SUMMER, FALL

Lobularia maritima

LUPINUS

LUPINE

Fabaceae (Leguminosae)

PERENNIALS

ZONES A1–A3; 1–7, 14–17, 34, 36–45

FULL SUN, EXCEPT AS NOTED

REGULAR WATER

✿ ✿ ❀ ✿ ✿ ✿ ✿ FLOWERS IN SPRING, SUMMER

Lupinus, Russell Hybrids

Magnificent perennial lupines, their stately spires packed with colorful blossoms, evoke images of romantic cottage-garden plantings and Victorian perennial borders. Nonetheless, they derive from a number of species native to the western U.S.—though the original hybrids were developed in England during the early 20th century. These plants—the **Russell Hybrids**—set the standard for beauty and appearance. Some of them still are sold, but other, more recent hybrids have captured the Russell look in vigorous, more widely adapted plants that lack the Russell susceptibility to powdery mildew.

A typical lupine forms a bushy clump of attractive leaves that resemble, in both shape and size, a hand with fingers spread. At bloom time in spring and summer, vertical flower spikes rise to 4 to 5 feet, with sweet pea–shaped blossoms encircling each spike's upper portion. You'll find individual solid colors as well as lovely bicolor combinations; plants usually are sold as mixed colors, though some specialty nurseries offer named cultivars in specific colors. The **New Generation Hybrids** give you the Russell style and color range on sturdier, mildew-resistant, 4-foot-tall plants that need no staking. **Gallery, Little Lulu, Popsicle,** and **Minarette** are mixed-color strains that produce Russell-type flowers on plants to about 20 inches high.

CULTURE. Lupines grow best in regions with fairly cool summers, where they flourish in sunny locations. Where summers are warm and dry, they can be grown with some success if planted in light shade and kept moist. In regions with hot, humid summers, they are likely to fail even with shade and regular water. Set out plants in spring, in well-drained, neutral to acid soil enriched with organic matter. Clumps are not long lived, but you can revitalize them by division in early spring or start new plants from stem cuttings taken in spring. Or start from seed sown indoors 6 to 8 weeks before the last-frost date or outdoors 2 to 3 weeks before that time. To hasten germination, soak seeds overnight in lukewarm water before planting.

MALVA

MALLOW

Malvaceae

PERENNIALS

ZONES 1–9, 14–24, 31–45

FULL SUN, EXCEPT AS NOTED

REGULAR WATER

✿ ✿ ❀ ✿ FLOWERS IN SUMMER, FALL

Malva moschata 'Alba'

Several long-blooming, easy-to-grow mallows are popular in gardens. All offer deep green, rounded, lobed or cleft leaves and hollyhock-like, typically 2-inch-wide blossoms from summer into fall. *M. sylvestris,* an erect, bushy plant reaching 2 to 4 feet tall, is a short-lived perennial more often grown as a biennial. Often flowering until stopped by autumn frost, it bears rosy purple flowers with darker stripes on the petals. **'Zebrina'** has pale lavender blossoms with pronounced deep purple veins. Two 1½- to 2-foot-tall choices with 1¼-inch flowers are **'Primley Blue'**, with soft blue, dark-veined flowers on a somewhat spreading plant, and **'Marina'**, bearing dark-veined violet blooms on a less spreading plant.

Two other species are truly perennial. Neither is quite as large or tall as hollyhock *(Alcea),* but the plants are bushier and bloom more profusely. Hollyhock mallow, *M. alcea,* is usually represented by its cultivar **'Fastigiata'**: an upright, narrow, many-branched plant 3 to 4 feet high, with deeply lobed leaves and dark pink blossoms. Musk mallow, *M. moschata,* is a broader plant—to around 3 feet high and 2 feet wide—with rose pink flowers and leaves cut into threadlike segments. **'Alba'** has blossoms in sparkling white.

CULTURE. The mallows don't demand good soil, but they do need good drainage. Give them full sun except in the hottest regions, where light shade is appreciated. Even the truly perennial sorts are fairly short lived, but volunteer seedlings usually provide replacement plants. All species are easy to grow from seed sown outdoors where plants are to grow, several weeks before the usual last-frost date. You can also start new plants from stem cuttings taken in summer.

A fragrance both sweet and spicy has endeared stock to generations of gardeners. With hints of clove and cinnamon, the perfume alone makes the plants worth growing—but fortunately, the flowers are as lovely as the scent. In the mildest climates, plants bloom from late winter into spring; in cooler ones, you can plant for flowers in summer.

The more widely grown species is *M. incana,* typically a bushy plant with narrow gray-green leaves. Carried in upright spikes at stem ends, the inch-wide, single or double flowers come in cream, white, and shades of pink, red, and purple. Many strains are available, ranging in size from under a foot to 3 feet tall. At the high end of the range, the **Giant Imperial** strain grows to 2½ feet; unbranched **Column** and **Double Giant Flowering** strains can reach 3 feet high. **Ten Weeks** (to 1½ feet) and the shorter **Dwarf Ten Weeks** (to 1 foot) flower in 10 weeks from seed; **Trysomic Seven Weeks** (to 15 inches) beats them into bloom by 3 weeks. Lower-growing strains abound, among them **Vintage** (to 15 inches high), **Brilliant Double Purpose** (1 foot), **Cinderella** (10 inches), and **Midget** (10 inches). Strains may be available as both mixed and single colors.

Foot-tall evening scented stock, *M. longipetala bicornis,* with lance-shaped green leaves and spikes of small lilac-purple flowers, is considerably less showy than *M. incana.* But its wonderful fragrance (most pronounced during the evening) is even more potent.

CULTURE. For success with stock, provide moderately rich, preferably neutral to slightly alkaline soil. Plants prefer cool weather and do not perform well where summers are hot or nights are warm. These preferences influence planting times. In regions where days are mild and nights are cool in summer, you can grow stock for summer flowers; sow seeds indoors 6 to 8 weeks before the last-frost date, or sow outdoors just after the last frost. Where spring is mild but summer is hot, grow stock for spring flowers, starting seeds indoors in winter for planting out in very early spring. In mild-winter areas, you can sow seeds in early fall for flowers in late winter and spring.

When sowing seeds, just press them onto the soil surface; they need light in order to germinate.

MATTHIOLA
STOCK
Brassicaceae (Cruciferae)
COOL-SEASON ANNUALS
ZONES 1–45
FULL SUN OR LIGHT SHADE
REGULAR WATER
✿ ❀ ✿ ✿ FLOWERS IN LATE WINTER, SPRING, SUMMER

Matthiola incana

G reen leaves are commonplace, but green flowers are a rarity—one reason bells-of-Ireland has been a favorite with generations of flower arrangers. What look like petals are in fact prominent, white-veined apple green calyxes; these form a cup-shaped "flower" that surrounds the true flowers, which are tiny, white, and fragrant. Blossoms appear in whorls of six, stacked in tiers along the upper one-third of 2- to 3-foot stems. Leaves are rounded and coarsely toothed; by the time plants come into bloom, the lowest leaves will have started to shrivel. You can use bells-of-Ireland in fresh arrangements or dry the stems for use in everlasting bouquets.

CULTURE. Bells-of-Ireland prefers a well-drained soil but doesn't need a particularly fertile one. The best way to grow this plant is to sow seeds in place in the garden, then thin seedlings to about a foot apart. The seeds need chilling to germinate well. Where winters are moderately cold (to about −10°F/−23°C), sow seeds outdoors several weeks before the normal last-frost date; in mild-winter regions, sow in late fall. You can also start seeds indoors (the preferred method where winter lows dip below −10°F/−23°C), but it's best to chill them for about 2 weeks in the refrigerator before planting. Then sow seeds in containers about 10 weeks before the last-frost date. Indoors or out, seeds may take up to 4 weeks to germinate.

Moluccella laevis

MOLUCCELLA laevis
BELLS-OF-IRELAND
Lamiaceae (Labiatae)
WARM-SEASON ANNUAL
ZONES 1–45; H1, H2
FULL SUN
REGULAR WATER
✿ FLOWERS IN SUMMER

MONARDA

BEE BALM, WILD BERGAMOT

Lamiaceae (Labiatae)

PERENNIALS

ZONES A1–A3; 1–11, 14–17, 30–43

FULL SUN, EXCEPT AS NOTED

REGULAR WATER

✿ ❀ ✿ ✿ FLOWERS IN SUMMER

Monarda didyma

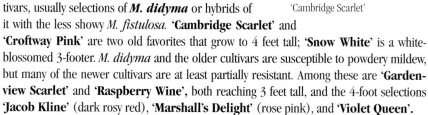

Monarda didyma
'Cambridge Scarlet'

Crush or rub the foliage, and you'll instantly recognize bee balm's kinship with mint. Spreading clumps of aromatic, lance-shaped, 6-inch-long leaves send up numerous leafy, branching stems crowned with one or two dense, shaggy-looking whorls of tubular, two-lipped flowers that are magnets for hummingbirds. Catalogs carry numerous named cultivars, usually selections of **M. didyma** or hybrids of it with the less showy *M. fistulosa.* **'Cambridge Scarlet'** and **'Croftway Pink'** are two old favorites that grow to 4 feet tall; **'Snow White'** is a white-blossomed 3-footer. *M. didyma* and the older cultivars are susceptible to powdery mildew, but many of the newer cultivars are at least partially resistant. Among these are **'Gardenview Scarlet'** and **'Raspberry Wine'**, both reaching 3 feet tall, and the 4-foot selections **'Jacob Kline'** (dark rosy red), **'Marshall's Delight'** (rose pink), and **'Violet Queen'**.

CULTURE. With good, organically enriched soil and regular watering, bee balm grows vigorously. Give full sun except in hotter regions, where partial shade is better. Overly dry soil and poor air circulation increase susceptibility to mildew, so be attentive to watering and make sure air circulation is good. Clumps spread rapidly and may even be invasive; divide them every 2 to 3 years in spring.

MYOSOTIS

FORGET-ME-NOT

Boraginaceae

PERENNIALS AND COOL-SEASON ANNUALS

ZONES A1–A3; 1–24, 32–45

PARTIAL SHADE

REGULAR TO AMPLE WATER

✿ ❀ ✿ FLOWERS IN LATE WINTER, SPRING

Myosotis sylvatica

In appearance, there's little difference between annual and perennial forget-me-nots. Both have bright green, lance-shaped leaves to about 4 inches long—hairy in annual *M. sylvatica,* glossy in perennial *M. scorpioides.* And both bear elongated, curving clusters of ¼- to ⅓-inch-wide, sparkling sky blue flowers. At bloom time, the blossoms form a cerulean cloud in lightly shaded and woodland plantings. *M. sylvatica* in particular is a favorite choice for underplanting spring-blooming bulbs such as daffodils and tulips.

Annual **M. sylvatica** reaches up to 1 foot high and spreads as wide as 2 feet. Its yellow-eyed blossoms appear in winter or early spring, depending on the severity of the winter, and continue to bloom as long as weather remains cool to mild. Variations include **'Rosylva'**, with pure pink flowers on a more compact plant; **'Blue Ball'**, with 6-inch, almost spherical plants well suited to containers; and the **Victoria** series, featuring blue, pink, and white blossoms.

Perennial **M. scorpioides** generally remains under a foot high but reaches 2 feet or more across, spreading by creeping roots. The blue springtime flowers typically have a yellow eye, though white- and pink-eyed forms exist. Named cultivars in white and various blue shades have been cataloged, but except for the long-blooming **'Mermaid'** (**'Semperflorens'**), they are not in general circulation.

CULTURE. As long as you can give them organically enriched soil and regular to ample water, forget-me-nots offer no cultural challenges. They'll even thrive in the always-moist soil beside a pond or stream. Both annual and perennial species look and perform best in cool weather and where summers are not excessively hot.

To increase plantings of *M. scorpioides,* divide clumps in early spring. Grow *M. sylvatica* from seed; it self-sows prolifically, so one planting can be a lifetime investment! Where winter lows hit 0°F/−18°C or below, sow outdoors several weeks before the last-frost date; or sow indoors 8 to 10 weeks before the last-frost date. In milder areas, sow seeds in fall for spring bloom (plants may overwinter to bloom a second year).

Planted at the edge of a path or border, the catmints provide a refreshing haze of cool color over a long period, beginning in midspring. Loose spikes of small (¼- to ½-inch), clustered blossoms cover billowy plants that usually are broader than tall; oval, slightly rough-textured, typically grayish leaves grow ¾ to 1½ inches long. Many of the catmints are as attractive to felines as catnip *(N. cataria)*; susceptible cats will roll frenziedly on the plants and nibble the foliage. Young plants usually need protection until they're large and tough enough to withstand such ardent attentions.

Most widely available is ***N. × faassenii*** (sometimes sold as ***N. mussinii***). It forms a silvery gray-green mound about 2 feet wide and reaches 1 to 2 feet high in flower. The basic form bears loose spikes of soft lavender-blue blossoms; named selections include **'Porcelain'**, a 1½-foot plant with soft blue blossoms and blue-gray leaves, and white-flowered **'Snowflake'**. **'Dropmore'**, a 2-foot plant with longer spikes of rich blue flowers, may be sold as a *N. × faassenii* selection but is probably a hybrid. **'Six Hills Giant'**, to 2 to 3 feet high and 3 feet wide, is another probable *N. × faassenii* hybrid and looks like a larger version of it.

Husky ***N. grandiflora*** is an open, upright plant 2½ to 3 feet high and about 1½ feet wide; it has violet-blue flowers. Its cultivar **'Brandean'** bears lavender-blue blossoms emerging from purple calyxes; **'Dawn to Dusk'** has lilac-pink blossoms and purple calyxes. In both, the calyxes persist after flowers have finished.

Siberian catmint, ***N. sibirica,*** is another upright plant of about the same size as *N. grandiflora,* but its rich violet-blue blossoms are larger (to 1½ inches) and bloom later, appearing in summer. **'Souvenir d'André Chaudron' ('Blue Beauty')** appears to be a *N. sibirica* hybrid and has the same plant size and flower color, but it blooms over a longer period.

CULTURE. All catmints are easy to grow, needing only well-drained soil and a warm, sunny location (or a lightly shaded spot, where summers are hot). To keep plants more compact and encourage repeat bloom later in summer, shear off spent flowering stems. To propagate, divide clumps in early spring or take stem cuttings in spring or summer. You also may find new plants from stems that self-layer where they touch the soil; dig and transplant these as desired.

Nepeta × faassenii

NEPETA
CATMINT
Lamiaceae (Labiatae)
PERENNIALS
ZONES 1–24, 30, 32–43
FULL SUN, EXCEPT AS NOTED
MODERATE WATER
✿ ✿ ❀ ✿ FLOWERS IN SPRING, SUMMER

Nepeta × faassenii

These tender tropical natives have been cherished by generations of gardeners for their easy-to-grow nature and colorful, often sweet-scented spring and summer blossoms. Though technically tender perennnials, they are grown as annuals everywhere—even in the frost-free regions where they can live from year to year. Plants are upright and narrow, with large, soft, oval leaves; both stems and leaves are slightly sticky to the touch. The flowers are narrow tubes that flare out into a star-shaped blossom about 2 inches across; many are notably fragrant, and all attract hummingbirds.

The most widely available plants are derived from ***N. alata (N. affinis),*** sometimes known as flowering tobacco. The species reaches 2 to 4 feet or more tall, producing white blossoms that open as evening approaches, releasing a powerful perfume. Its hybrids, often cataloged as ***N. × sanderae,*** encompass a range of heights and colors. For guaranteed fragrance, choose white-blossomed **'Grandiflora'**, a night bloomer to 3 feet tall. For color variations (typically with reduced fragrance), you can choose from

NICOTIANA
Nyctaginaceae
PERENNIALS GROWN AS WARM-SEASON
   ANNUALS
ALL ZONES
FULL SUN, EXCEPT AS NOTED
REGULAR WATER
✿ ❀ ✿ ✿ ✿ FLOWERS IN SPRING, SUMMER

Nicotiana alata, Nicki strain

a number of day-blooming strains. Short plants (8 to 14 inches), good for containers and front-of-border plantings, include the mixed-color strains **Breakthrough, Domino, Havana,** and **Merlin.** The mixed-color **Nicki** strain grows to about 1½ feet; reaching the same height is red **'Crimson King'.** The **Daylight Sensation** strain produces flowers in white, lavender, purple, and pink on stems to 3 feet high. Taller still—to 3½ feet—is the **Heavenscent** series; this one offers strongly perfumed blossoms in white, pink, red, and purple.

Two 5-foot species make dramatic accents. *N. langsdorffii* is a branching, upright plant decorated with pendent clusters of bell-shaped flowers in bright green. Night-blooming *N. sylvestris* bears intensely fragrant, tubular white flowers in tiered clusters toward the tops of the plant.

CULTURE. Give nicotianas good, organically enriched, well-drained soil. They thrive in full sun except in hot-summer climates, where they appreciate dappled sun or light shade in the afternoon. Sow seeds indoors 6 to 8 weeks before the last-frost date. Where summers are fairly long, you can also sow seeds directly in the garden just after the last-frost date. In either case, merely press seeds into the soil without covering them; they need light to germinate. Deadhead spent blooms to prolong flowering.

NIGELLA damascena
LOVE-IN-A-MIST
Ranunculaceae
COOL-SEASON ANNUAL
ALL ZONES
FULL SUN OR PARTIAL SHADE
REGULAR WATER
✿ ✿ ❀ ✿ FLOWERS IN SPRING

Nigella damascena

An individual blossom of love-in-a-mist resembles the familiar bachelor's button *(Centaurea cyanus),* but it's framed in a ruff—a "mist"—of threadlike leaf segments. The same filigree foliage clothes the upright, 1½- to 2-foot-tall plant, giving it an airy, see-through appearance. The spring flowers are followed by conspicuous horned, papery-textured seed capsules that are decorative in the garden as well as in dried arrangements. Flowers come in blue, white, violet, and pink. The popular **Persian Jewels** strain features double blossoms in the complete range of colors. The **Miss Jekyll Hybrids** are a fine group with semidouble blossoms in bright blue, white, and pink. **'Mulberry Rose'** bears double blooms in rosy pink; **'Oxford Blue'** is taller than most (to 2½ feet), with double dark blue flowers and seedpods distinctly darker than those of the species.

CULTURE. Love-in-a-mist grows beautifully in average, well-drained soil. It is taprooted and does not transplant well, so it's best to sow seed directly where plants are to grow. Where winters are freezing to frosty, sow seeds outdoors 2 to 3 weeks before the last-frost date. In mild-winter regions, sow in fall for bloom in earliest spring—and if summers are also mild, you can sow every 4 weeks for continuous bloom until the plants are vanquished by heat. Love-in-a-mist self-sows readily, ensuring a good supply of replacement plants (if you're willing to take them wherever they happen to pop up).

OENOTHERA
EVENING PRIMROSE, SUNDROPS
Onagraceae
PERENNIALS
ZONES VARY
FULL SUN, EXCEPT AS NOTED
LITTLE TO MODERATE WATER
❀ ✿ ✿ FLOWERS IN SPRING, SUMMER

These adaptable, carefree plants provide a spring-and-summer bounty of silky, four-petaled flowers with a broad, flattened bowl shape. Some species bloom during the daylight hours, but others open in late afternoon and close the following morning.

Sundrops, *O. fruticosa,* grows in Zones 1–21, 30–45. A shrubby plant to 2 feet high and wide, it has shiny green leaves, reddish brown stems and buds, and clusters of 1- to 2-inch, bright yellow flowers that open during the day. Its form *O. f. glauca (O. tetragona)* bears light yellow blossoms on red stems. Cultivars of the basic species include **'Fireworks' ('Fyrverkeri'),** with red buds and purple-tinted foliage; **'Highlight' ('Hoheslicht'),** bearing slightly larger flowers; and **'Solstice' ('Sonnen-wende'),** with leaves that turn red in summer, then darken to wine purple in fall.

TOP: *Oenothera fruticosa*

BOTTOM: *Oenothera speciosa*

Ozark sundrops, ***O. macrocarpa (O. missouriensis),*** is suited to Zones 1–24, 30, 33–37, 39–45. It forms a spreading plant to 2 feet across, the stem ends arching upward to about 6 inches; bright yellow, 3- to 5-inch blossoms open in the afternoon, set off against the backdrop of soft, velvety gray-green leaves. Conspicuous winged seedpods follow the flowers.

Mexican evening primrose, ***O. speciosa,*** grows in Zones 2b–24, 29, 30, 33, 35, H1, H2. Rose pink, 2-inch-wide flowers with white centers darken with age; despite the plant's common name, they open in the daytime. Slender stems clothed in dark green foliage reach 10 to 15 inches tall on plants that can spread aggressively, colonizing large patches of ground. Selected cultivars include pure white **'Alba';** light pink **'Rosea'** (often incorrectly sold as ***O. berlandieri*** or ***O. speciosa childsii***); shorter (and less aggressive) pink **'Siskiyou';** and **'Woodside White',** with green-centered white flowers that are pink tinged when they unfurl.

CULTURE. These plants tolerate drought and poor soil, but do best with average, well-drained soil and moderate water. They prefer full sun, though *O. speciosa* also performs well in light shade. To rejuvenate crowded plantings or obtain new plants, divide clumps in early spring; you also can take stem cuttings at this time.

ORNAMENTAL VEGETABLES

A number of edible plants can bring beauty to beds and borders. Unless otherwise noted, grow these plants in well-amended soil, in a full-sun location; water regularly.

Several kinds of amaranth (warm-season annual; Zones 1–45, H1, H2) have bright-colored foliage or flowers. Young, tender leaves can be cooked or added to salads. Showy, 4-foot-tall selections of ***Amaranthus tricolor*** include **'Aurora',** with dark green lower leaves and warm yellow upper ones, and **'Molten Fire',** with deep brownish red foliage. Sow seed in place in early summer; soil temperature must be above 70°F/21°C for germination. Or start seed indoors in spring.

Decorative cultivars of Swiss chard (***Beta vulgaris;*** cool-season annual, all zones) include **'Rhubarb',** with dark green leaves and crimson stalks and leaf veins, and **'Bright Lights',** featuring leaves ranging from green to burgundy and leafstalks in white or various shades of yellow, orange, pink, red, purple, or green. Plants grow 1 to 2 feet high. Sow seed in place in the garden from early to midspring.

'Rhubarb' Swiss chard

Flowering cabbage and flowering kale (**Brassica;** cool-season annuals, all zones) are grown for their highly ornamental, 10- to 14-inch-tall leaf rosettes in deep, rich colors. Flowering kale forms a looser head and has more heavily fringed leaves than flowering cabbage. In most varieties, outer leaves are deep blue green, while inner ones may be cream, pink, rose, or purple. Leaves are edible raw or cooked. Plant in very early spring; or plant in late summer for fall color. In mild-winter regions, plants are attractive throughout winter.

Bronze fennel, ***Foeniculum vulgare*** **'Purpurascens',** is perennial in Zones 2b–11, 14–24, 29–41, H1, H2, but it is often grown everywhere as a biennial or annual. It features soft, ferny-looking, bronzy purple leaves on a 5- to 6-foot plant. Sow seed in its garden location in spring; give little to moderate water. This plant self-sows freely and can be invasive in mild-winter climates.

Shiso or beefsteak plant (***Perilla frutescens purpurascens;*** warm season annual, all zones) has large, slightly fuzzy, deep red-purple leaves resembling those of coleus. The plant grows fast to 2 to 3 feet. Shiso leaves make an unusual vegetable or flavoring (they taste something like mint, something like cinnamon). Grow in full sun to part shade, in moist soil. Sow indoors 10 weeks before the last frost; or sow outdoors after the last frost. Removing the spikes of white flowers (which are not showy) helps control excessive self-sowing.

PAEONIA
PEONY

Paeoniaceae

PERENNIALS

ZONES A1–A3; 1–11, 14–20, 30–45

FULL SUN, EXCEPT AS NOTED

REGULAR WATER

❀ ✿ ✿ ✿ FLOWERS IN LATE SPRING

Paeonia 'Festiva Maxima'

Herbaceous peonies are old-fashioned favorites, cherished for their spectacular late-spring blossoms—and for foliage that is almost as beautiful as the flowers. Each year, new shoots rise from the ground in early spring and develop into rounded, shrubby clumps of large, handsome leaves divided into numerous segments. At bloom time, round buds at the stem ends open into fragrant, satiny blossoms that range in diameter from 4 to 10 inches.

Such lovely and impressive flowers have naturally attracted the attention of breeders, and specialty catalogs now list multitudes of named hybrids in colors ranging from deep red through coral and all shades of pink to cream, white, and (more recently) yellow. These cultivars are classified by flower form and bloom time. Among forms, *double* peonies have countless petals, for a full, fluffy look. *Semidouble* types have a single row of petals and a center filled with stamens and smaller petals; *single* peonies also have just one row of petals, but they're centered with stamens only. *Japanese* (sometimes called bomb) peonies have a single row of petals and a large central mass of narrow, petal-like segments called staminodes. Bloom time is designated as early, midseason, or late; by choosing plants in each of these groups, you can enjoy flowers over a period of 4 to 6 weeks.

Because most peonies need definite winter chill to succeed, gardeners in the warmest of the zones listed above should look for varieties recommended for warmer-winter climates. In those areas, single or Japanese flower forms are generally more likely to turn in a good performance.

CULTURE. Planted the right way, in the right site, peonies can remain undisturbed indefinitely—good reason to pay careful attention to preparation. Choose a sunny but wind-sheltered spot; strong winds can break the blossom-heavy stems. (Where spring can be hot and dry, however, select only early-blooming kinds and plant in a location receiving light afternoon shade.) Be sure soil is well drained, and dig it deeply several days to several weeks before planting, adding plenty of organic matter. If soil is highly acid, incorporate lime when you prepare it.

Peony roots (technically rhizomes with tuberous roots) are usually planted in early fall, though in parts of the West they are also available for planting in early spring. Planting depth is critical, and it depends on your climate. In warm-winter regions, position the "eyes"—the growth buds at the top of the root—no deeper than 1 inch below the soil surface; this exposes the plant to as much winter cold as your climate offers. But where winter lows regularly reach 10°F/−12°C or lower, plant so that growth buds are 1½ to 2 inches beneath the soil. Be aware that, in any climate, planting too deeply reduces or eliminates flowering.

Peonies may not bloom the first spring after planting, but they'll start to hit their stride the following year. During periods of cool, humid weather, be on the alert for the fungal disease botrytis; symptoms include fuzzy, brown to gray spots on foliage and stems and buds that blacken and fail to open. To help prevent the problem, remove and discard dead or infected plant parts; clean up the planting area thoroughly in fall, disposing of all spent peony leaves and stems. As new growth emerges in spring, spray with a copper fungicide.

Though peonies can remain in the same place virtually forever, you can divide established clumps in early fall. Dig each clump carefully and hose off the roots; then divide it into rooted sections, making sure each has at least three growth buds. Replant divisions promptly.

TOP: *Paeonia* 'Chief Justice'

BOTTOM: *Paeonia* 'Largo'

Poppies are guaranteed attention getters, whether you choose the opulent Oriental type or the more modest Flanders Field poppies. The blossoms may be single or double, in bright or soft colors—but the petals are always silky and semitranslucent, with a pleated or crumpled texture. Single flowers are bowl shaped, often centered with a contrasting color; double blooms look like pompoms. The flowers are followed by decorative, nearly spherical (but flat-topped) seed capsules.

ANNUAL POPPIES

Flanders Field or Shirley poppy, *P. rhoeas* (Zones A1–A3; 1–24, 26, 28–45), blooms in spring and summer. In its wild form, this is the single bright red poppy of European fields. Modern versions, though, include a vast array of colors and combinations: white, soft blue, lilac, pink, salmon, red, orange, and bicolors. The single to double, 2- to 3-inch blossoms are carried on needle-thin, hairy, 2- to 3-foot-tall stems; leaves are pale green and deeply cut. The **Mother of Pearl** strain features mostly single flowers in muted, almost pearly-looking pastels and other colors; **Angels' Choir** offers a good array of colors and patterns in double flowers. **American Legion** and **Flanders Field** both bear brilliant scarlet blossoms with black centers.

Annual breadbox or opium poppy, *P. somniferum,* is a late-spring bloomer that succeeds in all zones. In its basic form, it's a striking plant with broad, jagged-edged gray-green leaves that clothe stems to 4 feet tall; the single, 4- to 5-inch blossoms are soft lilac pink. Thanks to selective breeding, however, colors now include not only pink shades but also white, red, plum, and blackish purple; flowers may be single, semi-double, or double. Spectacular double-flowered strains include **Frosted Salmon,** blackish maroon **Black Peony,** bright red **Oase,** and **White Cloud.** The large seed capsules of this poppy are the source of culinary poppy seed.

CULTURE. Sow seeds of annual poppies in well-drained, average to good soil. In areas where winter lows regularly drop below 10°F/−12°C, sow outdoors up to 4 weeks before the last-frost date. In warmer areas, sow in fall. The tiny seeds are difficult to distribute evenly; for best results, mix them with an equal amount of fine sand, then broadcast the mixture over the planting area. Barely cover the seeds with soil. In cool-summer climates, you can make successive sowings 6 weeks apart to get bloom over a long period. Remove spent flowers to prevent seed set; this will both prolong bloom and reduce the number of volunteer seedlings.

PERENNIAL POPPIES

Iceland poppy, *P. nudicaule,* grows as a summer-flowering perennial in Zones A2, A3, 1–6, 10, 32–45. But in mild-winter Zones 7–9, 12–24, 26 (upper half), 28, 31, it is grown as an annual for bloom in late winter and early spring. Clumps of blue-green, coarsely hairy, divided leaves send up thin stems bearing chalicelike blossoms 3 to 4 inches across. Colors include white, bright red, orange, and yellow, as well as softer shades of salmon, pink, and cream. Foot-tall **Champagne Bubbles** is a classic strain in pastel colors; **Partyfun** is the same size but includes many bright colors. **Wonderland** offers orange and pastel colors; its 10-inch stems are sturdier than most and resist wind. **Oregon Rainbows,** best adapted to the cool Pacific Northwest, features a full range of pastel colors on stems to 20 inches tall.

CULTURE. Plant Iceland poppies in well-drained, average soil. Where winter temperatures regularly drop below 10°F/−12°C, sow seeds outdoors for summer bloom as soon as soil can be worked; in milder regions, sow in fall for bloom in late winter or spring. If you're starting with young nursery-grown plants, set them out in fall in both cold- and mild-winter regions; they'll flower in summer or winter/spring, depending on climate.

Listing continues>

POPPY

Papaveraceae

PERENNIALS AND WARM-SEASON ANNUALS

ZONES VARY

FULL SUN, EXCEPT AS NOTED

MODERATE TO REGULAR WATER

✿ ✿ ❀ ✿ ✿ ✿ FLOWERS IN SPRING AND SUMMER, EXCEPT AS NOTED

Papaver rhoeas

Papaver orientale

Perennial Oriental poppy, **P. orientale,** is among the most spectacular of late-spring bloomers for Zones A1–A3, 1–11, 14–21, 30–45. Sumptuous, bowl-shaped blossoms to 8 inches wide (or wider) are carried on long, leafy stems that rise from clumps of finely divided, hairy green leaves. Foliage mounds grow about 2 feet high; stems can reach up to 4 feet, though height varies with the cultivar. The silken petals are tissue thin, with a crepe-paper texture; in many cultivars, they are black at the base, giving the flower a black center. The original Oriental poppies were neon orange or red, but the hundreds of cultivars sold today also offer blossoms in pastel shades, in white with colored edges, and with light rather than dark centers. The **Superpoppy** hybrids, with blossoms in red, pink, orange, and white, were developed to perform well in the mild-winter, hot-summer regions of the West Coast.

CULTURE. Oriental poppies perform best in zones with distinctly chilly winters. They need good drainage and will really flourish if you dig soil deeply and incorporate organic matter before planting. Choose a spot in full sun except in hot-summer areas, where light afternoon shade is better. Plant dormant roots in fall—3 inches deep in regions where soil freezes in winter, 1 inch deep in milder areas.

P. orientale and its various hybrids and strains all grow in spring, die down to the ground soon after flowering, send up new leaves in fall, and persist as small foliage tufts over winter. During growth and bloom, provide regular water; after bloom, moisture needs decrease (plants are fairly drought tolerant at that point). You can leave clumps in place for many years. If you need to divide for increase or to reduce crowding, do so in late summer. You also can take root cuttings in late summer; in fact, any cut roots left in the soil after digging may sprout.

PELARGONIUM

GERANIUM

Geraniaceae

PERENNIALS OFTEN GROWN AS
WARM-SEASON ANNUALS

ZONES 8, 9, 12–24 AS PERENNIALS;
ELSEWHERE AS ANNUALS

FULL SUN, EXCEPT AS NOTED

MODERATE TO REGULAR WATER

✿❀✿✿✿ FLOWERS IN SPRING, SUMMER

Pelargonium × domesticum

Bright and bountiful geraniums are mainstays of the summer garden, all-time favorites for pots and window boxes. Shrubby plants of various sizes, they are perennial in virtually frost-free, dry-summer climates—but they grow so fast and bloom so generously that they function as annuals in colder regions. Most have thick, almost succulent stems; long leafstalks carry rounded to heart-shaped leaves with edges that may be wavy, scalloped, toothed, or fluted. Five-petaled, somewhat to quite asymmetrical flowers are borne in large, rounded clusters.

Note: Though known by the common name "geranium," these plants should not be confused with the true or hardy geraniums described on page 126.

P. × domesticum goes by several names: Lady Washington pelargonium, Martha Washington geranium, regal geranium. Large, semiwoody plants 3 to 4 feet high and wide bear clusters of azalealike, 2- to 3-inch blossoms in white, lavender, pink shades, red, orange, or purple, usually with bright or velvety "thumbprints" in a darker color. Stiff dark green leaves are 2 to 4 inch inches across, with crinkled, sharp-toothed margins. Specialty growers offer many named cultivars.

Common or garden geranium, **P. × hortorum,** is the most widely grown of the tender geraniums, with the greatest available number of cultivars and strains. In frost-less regions, plants grown in the ground may reach 3 to 4 feet high and wide, but compared to *P. × domesticum* they're soft—both in appearance and to the touch—rather than stiff. Leaves have scalloped margins and a covering of soft hairs; in shape, they range from nearly circular to somewhat maplelike. Many show a noticeable ring of darker color inward from the edge; this is most pronounced in the group known as zonal geraniums. Flowers are single or double and about 1 inch across, packed into dense clusters 4 to 6 inches in diameter; the color range includes white, violet, pink, red, orange, and coral.

Specialty growers carry a great many named cultivars. A few of the named zonal types are also available in the general nursery trade. Examples include **'Mrs. Pollock'**, with clusters of bright red-orange blossoms and green, cream-margined leaves with a maroon red zone; and **'Golden Ears'** (perhaps identical to **'Vancouver Centennial'**), bearing coral pink blossoms and deeply cut (nearly star-shaped) leaves in bronzy red with a chartreuse border. But much of the mass-market production for seasonal planting features multicolored seed-grown strains developed for compact growth and freedom of bloom. Prominent among these are **Elite** (fast-blooming, compact, 10-inch plants), **Maverick** (15-inch plants with zonal leaves, large blossom clusters), **Multibloom** (early-blooming, 10-inch plants), **Orbit** (14-inch plants with heavily zoned leaves, broad flower clusters), **Sensation** (shade-tolerant plants about 1 foot high), and **Stardust** (8- to 12-inch plants bearing deeply lobed leaves and star-shaped flowers with pointed petals).

Ivy geranium, **P. peltatum,** produces trailing, branching stems that are perfect for draping from window boxes and hanging baskets; in frost-free regions, it is an excellent ground cover. Glossy, five-lobed, ivylike leaves reach 3 inches across and are thick textured and succulent. Single or double flowers resemble those of *P. × hortorum* and come in white, pink shades, red, magenta, lavender, and various striped combinations. Many named cultivars exist, though in nurseries plants are often sold simply by color. White-flowered **'L'Elegante'** is notable for its white-margined leaves. **Summer Showers** is a seed strain offering flowers in white, pink, red, maroon, and lavender.

CULTURE. All types grow best in well-drained soil. Set out plants as early as possible in spring but after all danger of frost is past. Choose a full-sun location except in hot-summer regions, where plants appreciate light shade in the afternoon. These geraniums perform best where summers are cool to mild and fairly dry; they dislike heat combined with humidity. If plants look like they're getting gangly, pinch stem tips periodically during the growing season to promote branching. Deadhead spent flower clusters both for neatness and to prevent seed set. Geranium budworm can ruin the flowers by eating buds before they open; see page 78 for controls.

New geraniums are easily started from stem cuttings taken in summer. To raise plants from seed, sow seeds indoors 14 to 16 weeks before the last-frost date. The plants will be killed by hard frosts, but you can overwinter potted specimens indoors or in a frost-free, well-lighted shelter.

Pelargonium × hortorum

Pelargonium × hortorum 'Golden Ears'

The penstemons are noted for showy blossom spikes that appear over a long spring-and-summer bloom season—a show made even more exciting by the hummingbirds the flowers attract. The plants typically form clumps of upright stems bearing narrow, pointed leaves and spires of tubular to bell-shaped, five-lipped blooms. Most species come from arid or semiarid parts of the Midwest and West and are poorly adapted to humid climates and well-watered gardens. The species and hybrids described below, however, succeed in a wider range of climates and garden conditions.

Despite its Rocky Mountain origins, **P. barbatus** (Zones 1–20, 31–43) has a high tolerance for humid summers, but it does need some winter chill. The plant is a bit open, to 3 feet high and half as wide, with bright green, 2- to 6-inch-long leaves and narrow pink to red bells to 1½ inches long. **'Elfin Pink'** has pure bright pink flowers on a 2-foot plant; dark pink **'Rose Elf'** grows to 2½ feet. Two-foot-high **'Schooley's Yellow'** offers an unusual color for a penstemon: soft lemon yellow. The seed-grown **Rondo** series has flowers in red, pink, lilac, and purple on plants to 16 inches high.

P. digitalis, native to the central and eastern U.S., is the best bet for humid-summer regions; it's adapted to Zones 1–9, 14–24, 29–43. Growing 3 to 5 feet tall, the

PENSTEMON
PENSTEMON. BEARD TONGUE
Scrophulariaceae
PERENNIALS SOMETIMES GROWN AS
   WARM-SEASON ANNUALS
ZONES VARY
FULL SUN, EXCEPT AS NOTED
WATER NEEDS VARY
✿ ✿ ❀ ✿ ✿ ✿ FLOWERS IN SPRING,
   SUMMER

Penstemon digitalis

plant has stems outfitted in leaves to 7 inches long and topped by clusters of white or pale pink, 1-inch bells. Its 2½- to 3-foot cultivar **'Husker Red'** has pinkish white blooms and rich maroon red foliage.

The showiest of these adaptable penstemons belong to the hybrid group designated *P. × gloxinioides*. Perennial in Zones 6–9, 12–24, these plants can be grown as annuals in other zones. They're compact, bushy growers 2 to 4 feet high, bearing 2-inch bells in almost all colors but orange and yellow; in many, the blossoms have white interiors. Among the many named selections are lavender **'Alice Hindley'**; deep purple **'Blackbird'** and **'Midnight'**; rosy pink **'Evelyn'**; dark scarlet **'Firebird'**; wine red **'Garnet'**; and pink-tinged **'Holly's White'**. **'Hopleys Variegated'** presents white-throated lilac-blue blossoms on plants with cream-margined leaves. The seed-grown **Kissed** series has flowers in various colors, all with white throats.

Penstemon × gloxinioides 'Firebird'

CULTURE. These penstemons grow easily in average soil as long as drainage is good; they won't tolerate saturated soil, especially in winter. *P. digitalis* takes regular watering. *P. barbatus* and *P. × gloxinioides* prefer moderate watering, though the latter will accept regular moisture if drainage is excellent. Where summers are hot, choose a site receiving a bit of shade during the heat of the day. After the first flush of flowers, cut plants back to encourage a second round of bloom.

Performance declines after 3 to 4 years. At that point, you can start replacement plants from stem cuttings taken in summer or by layering stems; some stems may even self-layer, providing replacement plants immediately.

PEROVSKIA
RUSSIAN SAGE
Lamiaceae (Labiatae)
PERENNIAL
ZONES 2–24, 28–43
FULL SUN
LITTLE TO MODERATE WATER
❀ FLOWERS IN SUMMER

Perovskia

In the shimmering heat of midsummer, Russian sage's cool blue haze of bloom is especially welcome. Many gray-white stems clothed in gray-green foliage form a shrubby, upright clump 3 to 4 feet high and wide. Along the lower parts of the stems, leaves are 2 to 3 inches long and deeply cut; higher up, they become smaller and are toothed rather than cut. Each stem terminates in a long, branching spray of small, tubular lavender-blue blossoms that seem to float over the foliage.

Though Russian sage is usually sold as *P. atriplicifolia*, the plants in general circulation are thought to be hybrids between that species and *P. abrotanoides*. Widely grown **'Blue Spire'** (sometimes sold as *P. atriplicifolia* **'Superba'** or *P.* **'Longin'**) has deep violet-blue blossoms on distinctly upright, 2-foot stems. Lighter blue choices include **'Blue Mist'**, which comes into flower earlier than other cultivars, and **'Blue Haze'**. **'Filigran'** is denser and more compact than the others, with light blue flowers held above silvery, filigreelike foliage. Lavender-blue **'Little Spire'** is a relatively dwarf cultivar reaching only about 2 feet high.

CULTURE. Russian sage will grow in almost any soil—poor to rich—as long as drainage is good. To keep the plants as bushy as possible, cut them nearly to the ground in early spring, leaving just one or two pairs of growth buds on each vigorous stem. Especially in lighter soils, established plants often will spread by underground stems to form colonies. Plants can remain in place indefinitely, but if you want to increase a planting, you can dig and transplant rooted stems from the clump's perimeter. Or take stem cuttings in summer.

In any contest for favorite annual, petunias would be top contenders. They're easy to grow, even in poor, sandy soil, and can produce color virtually nonstop from shortly after planting until stopped by frost. In the mildest areas, they'll live through the winter and grow as perennials, though their second-year performance seldom equals the first-year show. Flowers are pleasantly fragrant, single or double, ranging in size from under 1 inch to 6 inches across. Single flowers are shaped like trumpets; double types are so full and fluffy they look like carnations. You'll find a broad range of colors, and possible patterns vary widely, too. Blossoms may be solid colored, edged in white, marked with contrasting veins, or centered in a contrasting dark or light color; star-patterned bicolors sport a dark center and dark stripes radiating out onto each lobe of the flower.

Most petunias sold today fall into the four categories described below. Some are designated F_1—short for first-generation hybrids. These plants are more vigorous and more uniform in character than F_2 plants.

Hybrid Grandiflora. As the name suggests, these have the largest flowers among petunias. Plants reach 15 to 27 inches high and can spread to 3 feet. The majority have single flowers to 4½ inches across, with ruffled or fringed edges; colors include pink shades, red, blue, white, yellow, and striped combinations. **Double Hybrid Grandifloras,** with heavily ruffled flowers, come in all of those colors but yellow. Many strains are available. Among these, **Fluffy Ruffles** produces ultra-large flowers—up to 6 inches across. **Magic** and **Supermagic** are compact plants with 4- to 5-inch blooms in just white, pink, red, and blue. **Dream** and **Storm** hold up better in rainy weather than most Hybrid Grandifloras; **Aladdin** reaches blooming size from seed more quickly than most. **Hulahoop** and **Frost** have colored flowers with white picotee edges; the **Daddy** series features flowers with a network of darker veins on the petals. **'Prism Sunshine'** is a soft but bright yellow. **Cascade, Countdown,** and **Supercascade** have trailing stems.

Hybrid Multiflora (Floribunda). Plants of these strains resemble Hybrid Grandifloras, but they bloom much more profusely and tend to be denser and more compact. Blossoms are smaller (about 2 inches wide), single or double, with smooth petal edges. **Celebrity** and **Primetime** are two strains that offer a wide array of color choices, including yellow; plants of **Merlin** are profusely branched.

Hybrid Milliflora. Dwarf plants grow just 6 to 8 inches high and wide, forming neat mounds that stay compact without pinching or cutting back. Flowers are 1 to 1½ inches across. The **Fantasy** series offers flowers in white, blue, pink, and red.

Trailing petunias. Plants are low and wide spreading, suitable for containers as well as small-scale ground cover. The seed-grown, heavy-blooming **Wave** series bears flowers in pink shades and purple; plants reach just 6 inches high but can spread to 5 feet across. Cutting-grown types are available only as started plants. Among these, **Cascadias** have 1½-inch flowers in an extensive color range; **Surfinias** are similar but come only in white, pink, and bluish purple shades. **Petitunias** have the smallest flowers (just ¾ inch across); **Supertunias** have the largest, at 2½ inches wide.

CULTURE. Plant petunias in average to good, well-drained soil. To raise plants from seed, sow indoors 8 to 10 weeks before the last-frost date; simply press seeds into soil, since they need light in order to germinate. Plant outdoors after all danger of frost is past. After plants are established, pinch them back about halfway to promote compact growth. Fertilize monthly; deadhead to prevent seed set and promote continued flowering. As plants become leggy or straggly, cut them back to restore compactness; new growth will quickly fill in. The fungal disease botrytis can damage flowers and foliage in humid weather; geranium budworm can ruin the flowers. See pages 77 and 78 for controls. Smog can cause spots on leaves of young plants, especially those with white flowers.

PETUNIA × hybrida
Solanaceae
PERENNIAL GROWN AS
    WARM-SEASON ANNUAL
ALL ZONES
FULL SUN
REGULAR WATER
✿ ✿ ❀ ✿ ✿ FLOWERS IN SPRING,
    SUMMER, FALL

Petunia × hybrida, Daddy series

Petunia × hybrida 'Purple Wave'

PHLOMIS

Lamiaceae (Labiatae)
PERENNIALS
ZONES 2–24, 31–41, EXCEPT AS NOTED
FULL SUN, EXCEPT AS NOTED
LITTLE TO MODERATE WATER
✿❀✿✿✿ FLOWERS IN SPRING, SUMMER

Phlomis russeliana

These Mediterranean natives never fail to perform, even when given just a meager diet. All have the same basic appearance: upright stems are clothed with opposite pairs of hairy to furry, roughly arrow-shaped leaves and carry nearly ball-shaped whorls of tubular, two-lipped blossoms in their upper reaches.

P. russeliana, with furry olive green leaves to 8 inches long, spreads to form a low, ground-covering patch. Flower stems rise 2 to 3 feet tall in early summer, offering tiered whorls of soft yellow blossoms that age to cream. After the flowers fade, the dried stalks remain attractive until or even throughout winter. **P. samia** also forms a low-growing foliage mat; its scallop-edged, 4- to 8-inch-long leaves are medium green on top, white and woolly beneath. Flowers come all through summer on 2- to 3-foot stems; the standard colors are purple and dark lilac, but forms exist with white and nearly green blossoms.

Tuberous-rooted **P. tuberosa** (Zones A1–A3; 1–24, 31–45) forms a rosette of deep green, finely hairy leaves to 10 inches long; clumps remain discrete and do not spread widely. In late spring and early summer, flower stems rise 3 to 6 feet high, bearing tiered whorls of purple or lilac-pink flowers.

CULTURE. These plants are not particular about soil quality, but they must have good drainage. Give them full sun; *P. russeliana* will also succeed in light shade. All tolerate drought but look and perform better with moderate watering, especially where summers are hot and dry. To increase plantings, divide clumps in early spring; or remove and replant rooted pieces from a clump's perimeter.

PHLOX

Polemoniaceae
PERENNIALS AND COOL-SEASON ANNUALS
ZONES VARY
EXPOSURE NEEDS VARY
REGULAR WATER
✿✿❀✿✿✿ FLOWERS IN SPRING,
  SUMMER

Phlox drummondii, Phlox of Sheep strain

Ranging from low, spreading annual and perennial plants to taller, upright classics for the perennial border, the many phloxes are reliable sources of bright, pure color. All have blossoms that are quite similar in shape: a slender tube flares out to a flat, five-segmented flower that's circular in outline. In some of the low-growing sorts, the segments may be separate, giving the blossom the look of a star or pinwheel; in the tall kinds, the segments are usually overlapping, so that each blossom resembles an unbroken circle.

Annual phlox, **P. drummondii** (Zones A2, A3; 1–45; H1), blooms in spring and summer, bearing dense clusters of sweet-scented, ½- to 1-inch-wide flowers. It spreads to about a foot and grows from 6 to 18 inches high, depending on the strain; stems are somewhat sticky, clothed in nearly oval leaves 1 to 3 inches long. Flowers come in blue, purple, white, yellow, orange, red, and pink; some have a central eye, either in white or a darker shade of the blossom color. Annual phlox is excellent for borders, in containers, even as a small-scale ground cover. Many mixed-color strains are sold, including **Dolly, Beauty,** and **Globe** (all 6 inches); **Cecily** and **Fantasy** (8 inches); and 15-inch **Grandiflora. Phlox of Sheep** (1 foot) and **Unique** (10 inches) offer a mix of soft pastels; **Twinkle** (6 inches) has star-shaped flowers.

Perennial phloxes fall into two fairly distinct groups. One contains several low-growing, mostly spring-flowering species; these are spreading plants, good for foreground plantings or ground cover. The second group contains the summer-blooming sorts, typified by border phlox *(P. paniculata);* they grow 2 to 4 feet tall and bear showy flowers in dense terminal clusters.

Belonging to the first group, sweet William phlox, **P. divaricata** (Zones 1–17, 28–43), reaches about 1 foot high and spreads by creeping rhizomes. Its leafy stems are clothed in oval, 1- to 2-inch-long leaves; fragrant lavender-blue blossoms appear in open clusters at stem ends. Selections include icy blue '**Clouds of Perfume**' and '**Dirigo Ice**'; '**Eco Texas Purple**', with maroon-centered blue flowers; and white '**Fuller's White**' and '**White Perfume**'. The variant form **P. d. laphamii** reaches

1½ feet and offers bright blue blossoms (purple in the selection '**Louisiana Purple**'); its hybrid '**Chattahoochee**' has maroon-eyed lavender flowers on a 10-inch-high plant.

Another low grower is creeping phlox, *P. stolonifera* (Zones A2, A3; 1–17, 28–45). It mounds 6 to 8 inches high and spreads by stolons; stems are clothed in narrow leaves to 1½ inches long. Bloom time brings a lavish show of lavender, inch-wide flowers in small clusters. Named selections include '**Bruce's White**'; lavender-blue '**Blue Ridge**'; deep lavender '**Sherwood Purple**'; and '**Melrose**', '**Pink Ridge**', and '**Spring Delight**', all with pink flowers.

Moss pink, *P. subulata* (Zones 1–17, 28–45), is a favorite for growing on banks and in rock gardens. Creeping stems clothed in needlelike, ½-inch leaves form a 6-inch-high mat that is transformed into a sheet of brilliant color in late spring or early summer. The ¾-inch flowers range from white through lavender blue, violet, and magenta to some fairly neon shades of pink. Many named selections are available; the unusual '**Candy Stripe**' has deep pink blossoms margined in white.

The second perennial group—the tall, summer-blooming phloxes—is dominated by two species that produce large flower clusters atop lofty stems. Thick-leaf phlox, *P. maculata* (Zones 1–14, 18–23, 31–45), blooms in early summer, bearing ¾-inch flowers in elongated to nearly cylindrical clusters to 15 inches long. Colors include white and all shades of pink (from pale pink to magenta), often with a contrasting central eye. The plant reaches 3 to 4 feet high and has shiny green, lance-shaped, 2- to 4-inch leaves that resist powdery mildew. Nurseries offer named selections, including rose pink '**Alpha**', pink-and-white '**Natascha**', lavender-eyed white '**Omega**', and deep lilac-pink '**Rosalinde**'. Classic pure white '**Miss Lingard**' may be a selection or a hybrid with a similar species, *P. carolina*.

Blooming in midsummer, border or summer phlox, *P. paniculata* (Zones 1–14, 18–21, 27–43), boasts fragrant flowers in dome-shaped to pyramidal clusters up to 8 inches across. Colors include white, lavender, and soft pink as well as intense shades of salmon orange, magenta, red, maroon, and purple; many feature a contrasting eye. Plants reach 2 to 4 feet in bloom, depending on the cultivar. Leaves are a bit larger and duller than those of *P. carolina* and *P. maculata* and are notoriously susceptible to powdery mildew in late summer. Of the numerous available cultivars, some are resistant (but not immune) to mildew. These include '**Bright Eyes**', with crimson-eyed pale pink flowers; white '**David**' and '**Fujiyama**' ('**Mount Fujiyama**'); red-eyed pink '**Eva Cullum**'; and lilac-pink '**Franz Schubert**'.

CULTURE. *P. drummondii* prefers a sunny spot and fairly light, well-drained soil, thoroughly amended with organic matter. Sow seeds so that plants will flower during cool to mild weather, since heat—especially in combination with humidity—puts an end to performance. In mild-winter areas, you can sow seeds as early as fall for bloom in early spring; plants will continue flowering into summer if temperatures remain mild. Where winters are definitely cold and summers are hot, you can sow seeds outdoors 2 to 3 weeks before the last-frost date or indoors 6 to 8 weeks before that date. In cool-summer areas, sow indoors or outdoors, at the times just stated; plants should bloom throughout summer.

Among perennial phloxes, low-growing *P. divaricata* and *P. stolonifera* prefer light shade in most climates, but in cool-summer regions, they'll also prosper in full sun. *P. subulata* prefers full sun in all but the hottest climates. Plant all three of these species in well-drained, organically enriched soil. To increase your plantings, you can divide plants in early spring.

The tall phloxes need regular attention to remain healthy and attractive. They're at their best where summers are cool to mild and will take full sun there; in hot-summer regions, they fare better with more shade and a mulch to help retain moisture around

Phlox subulata

Phlox maculata 'Alpha'

Phlox paniculata 'Franz Schubert'

Phlox paniculata

the roots. Plant in well-prepared soil enriched with plenty of organic matter; water regularly throughout the growing season. To lessen problems with powdery mildew on *P. paniculata*, look for resistant cultivars and locate them where air circulation is good (away from walls and hedges), being sure not to crowd plants. Each clump will send up numerous stems; for the best display, cut out all but the strongest four to six of these. During bloom time, deadhead regularly. Besides encouraging a second flowering from side shoots, this will prevent seed set and a resultant crop of volunteer seedlings—which tend to produce purplish pink flowers, regardless of the parent's color. To maintain vigor, divide clumps every 2 to 4 years in early spring.

PHORMIUM

NEW ZEALAND FLAX

Agavaceae

PERENNIALS

ZONES 7–9, 14–28, H1, H2; PLANTS
   REGROW AFTER FREEZES IN ZONES 5, 6

FULL SUN OR PARTIAL SHADE

LITTLE TO MODERATE WATER,
   EXCEPT AS NOTED

✿ ✿ FLOWERS IN LATE SPRING, EARLY
   SUMMER; MOST ARE GROWN PRIMARILY
   FOR FOLIAGE IN SHADES OF GREEN,
   CREAM, BRONZE, RED, AND PURPLE,
   OFTEN IN MULTICOLORED COMBINATIONS

Phormium tenax 'Jack Spratt'

Dramatic accents for garden beds and containers alike, these striking evergreen perennials form irislike fans of sword-shaped leaves; established clumps are foliage fountains that look like grasses with very broad leaves. Multibranched spikes of tubular flowers come in late spring to early summer. Two species and a group of hybrids between the two offer a considerable choice of plant sizes and foliage colors.

P. cookianum (P. colensoi), forming clumps up to 5 feet high and 10 feet across, has gracefully arching, medium green, droopy-tipped leaves up to 3 inches wide and 5 feet long. Yellow flowers come on stems barely taller than the foliage. 'Dwarf', as the name implies, is a smaller-growing selection—just 3 feet high and 5 to 6 feet across. Leaves of **P. c. hookeri** 'Tricolor' are green with cream stripes and a thin red edge; in its sport 'Cream Delight', leaves feature a creamy yellow central stripe and a narrow green margin edged in dark red. Both cultivars will reach about 3 feet high and twice as wide.

P. tenax is a larger, bolder plant with bronzy green, stiffly upright leaves that can reach 5 inches wide and 9 feet long; mature clumps have a spread equal to or slightly greater than their height. Erect reddish brown stalks to 10 feet high develop a "hat rack" of branches holding many dull red to reddish orange blossoms. 'Variegatum', reaching 8 feet high and wide, has narrower leaves than the species, in grayish green with a cream margin. Two smaller versions of the same thing are 1-foot 'Tiny Tiger' ('Aurea Nana') and 2-foot 'Toney Tiger'. Other variegated cultivars include 6-foot 'Veitchianum' ('Radiance', 'Williamsii Variegatum'), with green leaves sporting a yellow central stripe, and 5-foot 'Pink Stripe' ('Pink Edge'), with purple-tinted gray-green leaves narrowly edged in bright pink.

Bronze- to purple-leafed selections to 8 feet high and wide are variously labeled 'Atropurpureum', 'Bronze', 'Purpureum', and 'Rubrum'; these are usually raised from seed, so there's some variation in leaf color regardless of the particular name. Smaller reddish- to bronze-leafed cultivars include 5-foot 'Atropurpureum Compactum' ('Monrovia Red'); 3-foot-tall 'Bronze Baby'; and brown, 5-foot 'Chocolate'. Two 1½-footers with red-brown foliage are 'Jack Spratt' (with twisting leaves) and 'Thumbelina' (with upright leaves). For other colors, try 6-foot 'Dusky Chief', with wine red leaves edged in coral, and purple-black 'Morticia', to 4 feet.

Many other cultivars noted for brightly colored foliage have been developed from *P. cookianum* and *P. tenax*. They're smaller than *P. tenax* and tend to be less tolerant of cold and heat than either parent; damage is likely at temperatures below 20°F/−7°C. This sampling is representative of the sizes and colors available. Three 3-foot-tall choices are 'Apricot Queen', forming a dense clump of yellowish green, apricot-blushed leaves with a green edge and hairline-thin red margin; 'Dazzler', with narrow, arching, twisting leaves in maroon striped with bright red; and 'Gold Sword', an upright grower with bright yellow leaves edged in green. 'Dark Delight' forms a 4-foot-tall clump of arching, bronzed red-purple leaves with an orange midrib. 'Yellow

Wave', reaching 4 to 5 feet high, has broad chartreuse leaves with a lime green margin. **'Maori Chief'** and **'Sundowner'** are both upright 6-footers with leaves in green shades, striped or margined in pink. Four-foot **'Maori Maiden'** reverses the color scheme: it has salmon pink leaves (fading to cream) with a narrow olive green margin. **'Rainbow Warrior'** is similar but darker; its leaves turn nearly blood red in winter.

CULTURE. Plant in well-drained, average soil. New Zealand flaxes do best where summers are cool to mild; in these climates, they'll grow in full sun to light shade and prosper with little to moderate water. In hot-summer areas, they need light shade during the hottest hours of the day (this is particularly true of hybrid cultivars) and moderate watering—even regular watering if soil is light. Where winters are too cold for these plants to survive in the ground, grow them in containers and move to a cool greenhouse over winter. Clumps can remain in place indefinitely with no need for division. However, to increase a particular plant, you can divide it in spring (or dig and transplant rooted pieces from the clump's perimeter).

Phormium 'Yellow Wave'

Physostegia virginiana 'Variegata'

Blossoms that resemble those of snapdragon *(Antirrhinum)* explain one of this plant's common names. The second name, "obedient plant," refers to a curious trait: the flowers will remain in place if twisted or pushed out of position. The plant forms a spreading clump, sending up 3- to 4-foot stems clothed in toothed, lance-shaped leaves to 5 inches long. In summer or early fall, each stem is topped by a tapering spike of inch-long flowers. The typical blossom color is bright bluish pink, but named cultivars offer other choices. **'Bouquet Rose'** has rose pink blossoms, while **'Red Beauty'** offers deeper rose blooms; both grow about 3 feet tall. Three 2-foot cultivars are **'Summer Snow'**, with pure white flowers; rose pink **'Vivid'**; and **'Variegata'**, bearing pink blossoms set off by foliage strikingly variegated in creamy white.

CULTURE. False dragonhead grows best with good soil and plenty of moisture. Under these conditions, it spreads rapidly and will require dividing and replanting every 2 to 3 years in spring.

PHYSOSTEGIA virginiana
FALSE DRAGONHEAD,
OBEDIENT PLANT
Lamiaceae (Labiatae)
PERENNIAL
ZONES A3; 1–9, 14–24, 26–45
FULL SUN TO PARTIAL SHADE
REGULAR WATER
❀ ✿ FLOWERS IN SUMMER, EARLY FALL

Physostegia virginiana

Balloonlike, nearly spherical buds open to star-shaped, 2-inch summer flowers like wide-open campanulas. Typically blue violet with purple veining, the blossoms are carried on slender stalks at the ends of upright, 3-foot stems clothed in broadly oval, 3-inch leaves. Named cultivars offer variations in plant size and flower color. White-blossomed **'Fuji White'** grows to 2 feet tall; **'Hakone Blue'**, with double bright blue flowers, and **'Shell Pink'** both reach 1½ to 2 feet high. Still shorter are two cultivars bearing blooms in the basic blue violet: **'Mariesii'** (1 to 1½ feet tall) and **'Sentimental Blue'** (just 10 inches high).

CULTURE. Balloon flower grows best in well-prepared, well-drained, fairly light soil. Give it full sun except in hot-summer regions, where light shade or filtered sunlight is

PLATYCODON grandiflorus
BALLOON FLOWER
Campanulaceae (Lobeliaceae)
PERENNIAL
ZONES 1–10, 14–24, 26, 28–45
FULL SUN, EXCEPT AS NOTED
REGULAR WATER
✿ ✿ ❀ ✿ FLOWERS IN SUMMER

preferable. If gophers are a problem in your garden, protect the plants' roots from them. Flowering will continue for 2 months or more if you regularly remove the spent blossoms (do so carefully, to keep from damaging new buds growing nearby along the stem). Plants die back completely in fall and new growth appears quite late the following spring, so mark locations carefully to avoid digging up roots by accident. Plants are a bit slow to establish and don't need division to maintain vigor—but if you want more plants, divide in spring, taking plenty of soil along with the deep roots.

Platycodon grandiflorus

POLYGONATUM
SOLOMON'S SEAL

Liliaceae

PERENNIALS

ZONES A1–A3; 1–9, 14–17, 28–45

PARTIAL TO FULL SHADE

REGULAR WATER

❀ FLOWERS IN SPRING

Polygonatum biflorum

Studies in elegance, these plants form gradually spreading clumps, sending up stems that grow upright for a distance and then arch outward. Broadly oval leaves are set on both sides of the stems, arranged in nearly horizontal planes. Where leaves join the stems, small, bell-shaped white blossoms are suspended on threadlike stalks; small blue-black berries may follow the flowers. In fall, leaves and stems turn bright yellow, then die back.

Sometimes called small Solomon's seal, ***P. biflorum*** has 4-inch leaves on stems to 3 feet tall; flowers come in twos or threes. The plant known as great Solomon's seal was once designated ***P. commutatum*** or ***P. canaliculatum,*** but it is now regarded simply as a large form of *P. biflorum*. Its stems can reach 5 feet tall, its leaves 7 inches long; flowers appear in groups of two to ten.

P. odoratum 'Variegatum' bears 4-inch leaves neatly margined in creamy white on 2- to 3-foot stems that are dark red until fully grown. Blossoms appear individually or in pairs.

CULTURE. These plants grow best in the moist, organically rich soil typical of woodlands, but they perform reasonably well in drier soils—even in competition with tree roots. Clumps can remain in place indefinitely, with no need for division. If you want to increase a planting, however, do so in early spring: remove rhizomes (each with at least one growth bud) from the clump's edge and replant immediately.

PORTULACA
Portulacaceae

WARM-SEASON ANNUALS

ALL ZONES

FULL SUN

MODERATE WATER

❀❀❀❀❀ FLOWERS IN SPRING, SUMMER, FALL

Flaunting silky-sheened blossoms in neon-bright colors, these plants add a definite sparkle to foreground plantings and containers. They have succulent leaves and stems and are at their best in warm weather, unfazed even by summer heat that stops many other plants in their tracks.

Old-fashioned favorite ***P. grandiflora,*** rose moss, is a spreading, trailing plant with reddish stems and narrow, virtually cylindrical, inch-long leaves. It blooms from spring into autumn, bearing single to double flowers that resemble inch-wide roses; they typically open in the morning and close by midafternoon. The mixed-color **Margarita** strain offers larger blossoms (to 1½ inches); deep pink '**Margarita Rosita**' is sold separately. Also available in a wide palette of both single and mixed colors (including some bicolors) is the **Sundial** strain, with still larger (2-inch) blooms that remain open later into the afternoon. The **Passion Fruit** strain contains flowers in cream and in fuchsia shades, irregularly marked and splashed with contrasting color.

Another portulaca resembles edible purslane *(P. oleracea)* and is widely known by the same common name, though in fact it's a different plant. Thick stems hug the ground and spread to 2 feet, bearing fleshy, oval leaves about 1 inch long; single, 1-inch-wide flowers last just a day but are produced over a long period in late spring and summer. Belonging to these "purslanes" are the **Wildfire** hybrids, which come in the full range of portulaca colors. Also included here is the **Duet** strain, offering several selections with yellow, pink, or white flowers with petal margins irregularly marked in another color.

CULTURE. These plants revel in hot weather and plenty of sunshine. Though they'll take more luxurious conditions, they perform brilliantly with just average soil (of any type) and moderate water. They're good choices for exposed, hard-to-water locations such as parking strips and hillsides. Both *P. grandiflora* and the purslanes are fine choices for containers and hanging baskets.

Sow seeds outdoors after the danger of frost is past; or sow indoors 6 to 8 weeks before the last-frost date. Just press seeds into soil, but do not cover them; they need light in order to germinate. All will self-sow readily, though seedlings tend not to show as wide a color range as the parents.

Portulaca grandiflora 'Sundial Peppermint'

W hether planted along a shaded path, in a border, or near a pond or stream, primroses provide an air of woodland or country-garden charm. Foliage rosettes send up stems bearing circular, five-petaled flowers, each petal notched or indented at its apex; blossoms may be borne individually, in clusters at the stem tips, or in tiered clusters along the stem. Primroses often are considered a symbol of spring, and most are in fact spring blooming—but some start flowering in mid- to late winter in mild climates, and a few bloom in early summer. The genus is a complex one, comprising hundreds of species and hybrids. The primroses described here are relatively common and relatively easy to grow, as long as they receive the conditions they need.

Fairy primrose, *P. malacoides*, will grow as a perennial in Zones 8, 9, 12–24, but even in those zones it is usually treated as an annual—as it must be in Zones 1–7, 31–41. Long-stalked, soft-textured leaves are pale green ovals to 3 inches long, with blunt-toothed margins. Stems reach 10 to 18 inches high, bearing tiered, loosely packed whorls of ½-inch flowers in white, lavender, pink, or rosy red. Depending on the mildness of winter, bloom can come at any time from midwinter to late spring. Fairy primrose is usually seen as a container plant, though in mild-winter areas it can be massed for an ephemeral flowering ground cover, looking especially fetching beneath early-flowering deciduous trees and with early-blooming daffodils.

Sometimes called drumstick primrose, perennial *P. denticulata* (Zones A2, A3; 1–6, 34–43) carries its dense, ball-shaped clusters of ½-inch flowers atop stout, foot-high stems. Colors run from blue to lavender to violet; there are white and lilac-pink forms as well. At bloom time in early spring, the medium green, spatula-shaped leaves are about 6 inches long; they later lengthen to about 1 foot. Polyanthus primrose, *P.* × *polyantha* (Zones 1–24, 32–41), is generally regarded as the most adaptable primrose. This hybrid group forms clumps of fresh green, tongue-shaped leaves to about 8 inches long; yellow-centered, 1- to 2-inch-wide flowers appear from winter to early or midspring, in an array of colors including everything but true green and black. The showy blossoms are carried in terminal clusters on stocky, 8- to 12-inch stems. Many strains are available, usually in mixed colors, though the **Gold Laced** strain has mahogany blossoms with yellow centers and edges.

P. sieboldii (Zones A2, A3; 2–7, 14–17, 34, 36–40) has downy, wrinkled, arrow-shaped light green leaves with scalloped margins. Each leaf is 2 to 4 inches long, carried on a slender leafstalk. In late spring, slender 4- to 8-inch stems bear clusters of

PRIMULA

PRIMROSE
Primulaceae
PERENNIALS, SOME GROWN AS
    COOL-SEASON ANNUALS
ZONES VARY
PARTIAL TO FULL SHADE, EXCEPT AS NOTED
REGULAR WATER, EXCEPT AS NOTED
✿ ✿ ✿ ✿ ✿ ✿ ✿ FLOWERS IN WINTER,
    SPRING, SUMMER

Primula denticulata

Primula × polyantha

Primula vulgaris

1- to 1½-inch-wide lavender flowers with a white eye. Named selections come in pure white as well as in purple shades ranging from lavender to wine violet. Leaves die back after flowering, helping this primrose endure hotter, drier summers more successfully than other species.

English primrose, *P. vulgaris* (*P. acaulis;* Zones A3, 2–6, 14–17, 21–24, 32–41), resembles *P. × polyantha* in general appearance, though it's a bit smaller. Bright green, wrinkled, 10-inch-long leaves shaped like canoe paddles form clumps to 8 inches high; in early spring, light yellow, fragrant, 1¼-inch flowers appear on individual stems just barely taller than the foliage. Garden strains may have two or three flowers per stem, in colors including white, yellow, red, blue, bronze, and wine red. The **Sweetheart** series has double flowers.

Though all primroses like regular watering, some are real moisture lovers, suited to boggy soil and even shallow water. These include the so-called Candelabra types, with tiered flower clusters on stems taller than those of other primroses. The most widely available of these is *P. japonica,* successful in Zones A3, 2–6, 15–17, 32 (cooler parts), 34, 36–40. During its bloom period in late spring to early summer, blossom stalks rise to as high as 2½ feet above clumps of tongue-shaped light green leaves to 9 inches long. The 1½-inch flowers typically come in purple, red, pink, and white; **'Miller's Crimson'** is a standard dark red cultivar, while **'Potsford White'** is a superior white selection with larger-than-usual blossoms. The skyscraper of these moisture lovers is *P. florindae* (Zones A2, A3; 3–6, 15–17). Stems to 3 feet tall carry nodding terminal clusters of up to 60 bell-shaped, ¾-inch, fragrant yellow flowers. Glossy, broadly oval medium green leaves are about 9 inches long, carried on long leafstalks.

CULTURE. Primrose species are native to woodlands and moist meadows, in cool, humid climates. They like the same conditions in gardens: organically enriched soil and a cool, moist atmosphere. In cool-summer areas, especially where foggy, overcast conditions are common, you can plant primroses in nearly full-sun locations. Elsewhere, plant them in full or part shade (be sure they receive protection from afternoon sun). Most of the primroses profiled above do best with regular watering, but the last two described—*P. japonica* and *P. florindae*—prefer even more moisture, thriving in squashy, marshy soil as well as in very shallow (even moving) water.

Primrose plants form tight clumps; when performance eventually declines, divide the clumps right after flowering finishes.

PULMONARIA
LUNGWORT
Boraginaceae
PERENNIALS
ZONES 1–9, 14–17, 32–43
PARTIAL TO FULL SHADE
REGULAR WATER
✿ ✿ ❀ ✿ ✿ FLOWERS IN SPRING

These charming woodland plants are decorative in both leaf and blossom, and their low stature and dense growth make them ideal for pathway edgings or even small-scale ground covers. Hairy, broadly oval to lance-shaped leaves form rosettes or clumps; in many kinds, the foliage is attractively dappled with gray or silver. Smaller leaves appear on the flowering stems, just beneath the clusters of nodding funnel- or trumpet-shaped flowers. The blossoms open just before or just as new growth emerges in spring. After bloom ends, the plants produce more foliage; with regular watering, they'll stay attractive throughout summer.

Blue lungwort, *P. angustifolia,* has bright blue flowers opening from pink buds; plants reach 8 to 12 inches high and have dark green, unspotted leaves to a foot long. Selected forms include **'Blaues Meer'**, with larger, brighter blue flowers than the species, and sky blue *P. a. azurea.* Silver-spotted dark green, slightly floppy leaves to 20 inches long distinguish *P. longifolia.* Its purplish blue flowers, borne on 8- to 12-inch stalks, bloom later in spring than those of other species. Its selection **'Bertram Anderson'** has vivid deep blue blossoms and fairly upright-growing foliage.

P. rubra, one of the earliest-blooming lungworts, has coral red flowers on 16-inch stems and pale green, unspotted, 6-inch leaves. **'Bowles' Red'** is an especially fine selection; **'Barfield Pink'** has brick red blossoms edged and veined in white. **'David Ward'** features coral-colored flowers and olive green foliage margined in cream.

Blue-flowered Bethlehem sage, ***P. saccharata,*** presents foot-long, beautifully spotted leaves on plants growing 1 to 1½ feet high. More widely available than the species are various choice selections, among them **'Margery Fish'** and **'Mrs. Moon'**, with pink buds opening to blue flowers; **'Janet Fisk'**, with similar flowers carried above heavily marbled leaves; **'Pierre's Pure Pink'**, salmon pink in both bud and open blossom; and **'Reginald Kaye'**, with rose pink buds that unfurl to violet blooms.

Many hybrid lungworts are also sold, most featuring especially beautiful foliage. **'Excalibur'** has violet-blue flowers and striking silvery white leaves margined in dark green. The sky blue blossoms of **'Roy Davidson'** are set off against long, narrow deep green leaves evenly marked with silver. **'Spilled Milk'** features foliage of an almost solid silver white, margined and sparsely flecked in dark green; blue flowers open from pink buds. Blue-flowered **'Golden Haze'** is named for its foliage: each leaf is irregularly edged in gold, and a golden overlay covers the entire leaf.

CULTURE. Lungworts need soil that's well drained but always moist. Incorporate plenty of organic matter before planting. Choose a spot in partial to full shade; even with moist soil, leaves tend to wilt in full sun. After a number of years, clumps will become crowded and require division. Do the job in early fall; be sure to keep the newly planted divisions well watered.

TOP: *Pulmonaria longifolia*
BOTTOM: *Pulmonaria* 'Excalibur'

Fast-growing castor bean is a dramatic accent for the summer garden—not for its flowers, which are inconsequential, but for the large leaves that lend a tropical air to any planting. Carried on long stalks, the leaves have 5 to 11 pointed lobes and can reach 1½ feet across (or even more) on young plants; foliage size decreases as the plant gets older and larger. Clusters of tiny white flowers come on foot-high stalks in summer, followed by conspicuous prickly reddish husks that contain attractively marked (and poisonous) seeds about the size of lima beans. In frost-free regions, castor bean lives from year to year, becoming treelike and woody. In colder areas, its annual bulk and height depend on the length of the growing season; expect it to grow anywhere from 6 to 15 feet tall and about half as wide.

A number of named cultivars exist, among them **'Carmencita'**, with reddish bronze foliage; **'Carmencita Pink'**, with pink seeds husks instead of the usual red ones; and **'Zanzibarensis'**, with green leaves that can reach 3 feet across. **'Dwarf Red Spire'** has bronzy red leaves on plants just to 6 feet high.

Note that the seeds ("beans") of castor bean are toxic if ingested.

CULTURE. Castor bean grows best in a sunny location with average to good soil and moderate to regular water. In all but frostless regions, you'll need to push it along quickly, with attentive watering and feeding, to get the maximum impact within a single growing season. To keep leaves from becoming tattered, choose a windless location; stake plants if they start to lean. In regions with a fairly long growing season, sow seeds outdoors after the last-frost date (to hasten germination, soak them in lukewarm water overnight before planting). Where the growing season is shorter, plant seeds indoors (in individual pots) 6 to 8 weeks before the last-frost date; plant seedlings outdoors when all danger of frost is past.

RICINUS communis
CASTOR BEAN
Euphorbiaceae
WARM-SEASON ANNUAL
ZONES 1–45; H1, H2
FULL SUN
MODERATE TO REGULAR WATER
❀ FLOWERS IN SUMMER; GROWN PRIMARILY FOR FOLIAGE

Ricinus communis 'Carmencita'

RODGERSIA

Saxifragaceae
PERENNIALS
ZONES 2–9, 14–17, 32–41
PARTIAL SHADE, EXCEPT AS NOTED
AMPLE WATER
❀✿✾ FLOWERS IN SUMMER

Rodgersia pinnata 'Superba'

Reminiscent of oversize astilbes, rodgersias form large mounds of handsome foliage that are decorative throughout the growing season; the airy summertime flower plumes are a bonus. Leafstalks rise directly from clumps of intertwined rhizomes, bearing leaves composed of jagged-edged leaflets. The flower stalks rise above the foliage, carrying tiny blossoms in many-branched spikes. Leaves usually take on bronze tones by fall, then disappear entirely over the winter.

The largest species is ***R. aesculifolia,*** bearing five- to seven-leafleted leaves to 2 feet across that resemble those of horsechestnut *(Aesculus).* It can reach as high as 6 feet in bloom, when pyramidal spikes of white flowers appear. ***R. pinnata*** is a bit smaller overall, with leaves to 16 inches across and reddish, 3- to 4-foot flower stems. Red is the usual flower color, but there are variations, including white '**Alba**'; creamy pink '**Elegans**'; and dark pink '**Superba**', which grows somewhat taller than the species and has bronzy foliage.

Each leaf of ***R. podophylla*** consists of five 10-inch leaflets that radiate from a central point; the foliage is bronze when new, maturing to green by summer. Flower stems can reach 5 feet, bearing nodding clusters of creamy white blossoms. ***R. sambucifolia*** differs from the others in foliage: its leaves have narrow leaflets arranged opposite one another in feather fashion (as many as five pairs of leaflets, plus a single terminal leaflet). Flat-topped plumes of creamy white flowers come on 3-foot stalks.

CULTURE. Rich soil and constant moisture are the secrets to success with rodgersias. They won't grow in standing water, but they're right at home in the marshy soil alongside a stream or pond. In the garden, provide the best and most retentive soil possible; liberally amend it with organic matter. Except in cool- and very mild-summer areas, where they'll take full sun, give these plants afternoon shade—or even light shade all day. The thick rhizomes form slowly spreading clumps that can remain in place indefinitely. If you want to increase your plantings, remove rhizomes from a clump's edge in late winter or early spring and replant immediately.

RUDBECKIA

CONEFLOWER
Asteraceae (Compositae)
PERENNIALS AND BIENNIALS
ZONES 1–24, 28–43, EXCEPT AS NOTED
FULL SUN
MODERATE TO REGULAR WATER
✿✿✿ FLOWERS IN SUMMER, FALL

Rudbeckia hirta
'Marmalade'

Showy, carefree plants for the summer and fall garden, these yellow daisies are descendants of North American species. They are more compact and longer blooming than their ancestors, but they retain the original flower form: the common name "coneflower" refers to the raised, typically dark cone in the center of each blossom.

Gloriosa daisy or black-eyed Susan, ***R. hirta,*** is by nature a biennial or even a short-lived perennial—but because it flowers the first summer from seed sown in early spring, it is often treated as an annual. Branching, 4-foot-tall plants are narrowly upright, with sandpapery stems and lance-shaped, 4-inch leaves. In the most basic form, flowers are 2 to 4 inches wide, with a row of orange-yellow petals surrounding a black-purple cone; seed strains offer variations in plant size and flower form and color, including double blossoms and bicolor patterns. '**Indian Summer**', to 3½ feet tall, bears golden yellow, single to semidouble blossoms 6 to 9 inches across. Three-foot '**Kelvedon Star**' has single yellow flowers with striking dark petal bases. '**Irish Eyes**' ('**Green Eyes**'), reaching 2½ feet, has the usual yellow petals, but they surround a light green cone that turns brown with age. Two-foot '**Marmalade**' has orange-yellow petals and a dark brown cone. For a mixture of colors—yellow, orange, bronze, and bicolors—try the **Gloriosa Daisy** strain, with single flowers to 6 inches across on 2½- to 3-foot stems. The **Gloriosa Double Daisy** strain produces double, 4½-inch blossoms in a more limited color range (just yellow and orange). At the short end of the scale are 20-inch '**Goldilocks**', with double, 4-inch yellow blossoms; 16-inch '**Sonora**', bearing 5- to 6-inch yellow-and-mahogany blooms; 10-inch '**Toto**', with semidouble, 4-inch yellow flowers; and the **Becky** strain, also 10 inches tall, bearing 4- to 6-inch-wide blossoms in yellow shades and bicolors.

Most widely grown of the perennial coneflowers is *R. fulgida sullivantii* **'Goldsturm'**. From midsummer through fall, clumps of lance-shaped, 4-inch leaves send up branching, 2- to 2½-foot stems bearing 3-inch, single yellow flowers with a black center. The **Goldsturm** seed strain has similar flowers, but plants may be taller.

R. laciniata is a bulky, 10-foot plant with deeply lobed, 4-inch leaves. Better suited to gardens, though, is its smaller selection **'Hortensia' ('Golden Glow')**, with double, 2- to 3½-inch blossoms on a 6- to 7-foot plant that can spread widely and quite aggressively. The hybrid **'Goldquelle'** has similar flowers, but it grows just 3 feet high and forms clumps that remain more compact. *R. nitida* (Zones 2–9, 14–24, 28–35, 37–41) looks like a shorter (6-foot) version of *R. laciniata*. More widely grown than the species is its selection (or possibly hybrid) **'Herbstsonne' ('Autumn Sun')**, a slender, 6-foot plant bearing 4- to 5-inch, single yellow flowers with a bright green central cone that ages to yellow.

CULTURE. All these plants are easy to grow, needing only average to good soil and moderate to regular watering. To raise *R. hirta* from seed, sow outdoors 2 weeks before the last frost; where the growing season is short, sow indoors 6 to 8 weeks before the last-frost date. Simply press seeds into the soil without covering them; they need light to germinate. To keep perennial types looking good, divide clumps in spring every 2 to 4 years. Curb the spread of *R. laciniata* 'Hortensia' as needed, either by division or by cutting away the edges of the clump.

Rudbeckia fulgida sullivantii 'Goldsturm'

P ainted tongue looks like a high-class, really dolled-up petunia, offering trumpet-shaped, 2- to 2½-inch flowers that feature an unusual combination of velvety texture, rich yet muted color, and delicate veining. The plant grows upright, carrying its exotic blossoms in clusters atop 2- to 3-foot stems. Both the stems and the narrow, oblong, 4-inch leaves are sticky. In most areas, bloom comes in late spring and early summer, but where summers are cool, the show will continue until frost if you remove spent blossoms regularly.

Several mixed-color strains are shorter than the species. Reaching 1½ to 2 feet are **Bolero**, bearing gold-veined flowers, and **Casino**, with low-branching plants that are bushier than most. **Royale**, just 15 to 20 inches high, is the best bet for growing in containers.

Salpiglossis sinuata,
Casino series

SALPIGLOSSIS sinuata
PAINTED TONGUE
Solanaceae
COOL-SEASON ANNUAL
ZONES 1–45
FULL SUN, EXCEPT AS NOTED
REGULAR WATER
✿ ✿ ✿ ✿ ✿ FLOWERS IN SPRING AND
   EARLY SUMMER, EXCEPT AS NOTED

CULTURE. Germination can be spotty, so in-ground sowing inevitably results in a planting with gaps. To avoid this problem, start seeds indoors in containers; sow 8 to 10 weeks before the last-frost date and keep pots at 70 to 75°F/21 to 24°C. Simply press the seeds into the potting mix without covering them, since they need light to sprout. Plant out seedlings a week or so before the last-frost date, being sure to harden them off first (see page 81). Give plants good, organically enriched soil. A sunny spot is best except in hot-summer regions, where light afternoon shade is preferable (and will prolong the bloom period).

SALVIA

SAGE, SALVIA

Lamiaceae (Labiatae)

PERENNIALS, BIENNIALS, AND
   WARM-SEASON ANNUALS

ZONES VARY

FULL SUN, EXCEPT AS NOTED

REGULAR WATER

✿ ✿ ✿ ✿ ✿ FLOWERS IN SPRING,
   SUMMER, FALL

Salvia coccinea 'Lady in Red'

Salvia coccinea 'Coral Nymph'

Sages are a large and useful group of garden plants—and gardeners' choices are expanding each year, as new species and hybrids are offered for planting in the milder West and Southwest. The plants presented here are the more widely adapted sorts, tried and true annual and perennial performers in both cold- and warm-winter regions. All have the characteristic two-lipped flowers of the mint family; some have colorful calyxes that add to the display. A number of sages are appreciated for aromatic foliage, and many offer that rarest of flower colors: true blue.

Annual clary, **S. viridis** (**S. horminum**; all zones), grows quickly to 1½ to 2 feet high and has 2-inch-long, oval medium green leaves. Bloom is in early summer, but the actual flowers are insignificant; the decorative elements are the 1½-inch, dark-veined bracts beneath each blossom, which are showy both fresh and dried. The **Claryssa** strain includes plants with bracts in white, blue, and pink; these colors also are available separately.

Several other sages are commonly grown as annuals everywhere, though most can be perennial in certain mild zones. Tropical sage, **S. coccinea**, is one of these—a short-lived perennial in Zones 12–24, 26–30, H1, H2. The bushy, upright plant grows to 3 feet tall and nearly as wide, clothed in hairy, oval dark green leaves to 2½ inches long. Spikes of 1-inch summer flowers come in white, pink shades, orange to red, and bicolors. Named seed-grown selections include **'Lady in Red'**; salmon **'Brenthurst'** (**'Lady in Pink'**); white **'Lactea'** (**'Lady in White'**) and **'White Nymph'**; and white-and-coral **'Coral Nymph'** (**'Cherry Blossom'**). Mealycup sage or Texas violet, **S. farinacea** (perennial in Zones 7–10, 12–24, 26–29; H1, H2), is a rounded, shrubby plant that grows quickly to 3 feet high. The narrow, pointed, 3-inch-long leaves are smooth gray green above, woolly and white beneath. From late spring to frost, ¾- to 1-inch blossoms appear on stems to about a foot long; colors run from deep violet blue through lighter blue shades to white. A number of shorter, more compact strains have been developed for bedding and container use. These include foot-tall **'Strata'**, bearing blue flowers with woolly, silver-white calyxes; 14-inch-high **'Cirrus'** (white) and **'Rhea'** (deep blue); and 20-inch-tall **'Victoria'**, with violet-blue blooms, and its white counterpart **'Victoria White'**.

Scarlet sage, **S. splendens** (perennial in Zones 21–25, 27; H2), has long been a mainstay of summer annual plantings. It's a bushy, 3- to 4-foot tall plant with bright green, 2- to 4-inch, heart-shaped leaves and spikes of fire engine red, 1½-inch flowers. Selections offer shorter plants (8 inches to 2 feet high) in a wider color range that includes some less assertive hues. You'll find flowers in orange, pink shades, purple, lavender, white, and bicolors that combine white with another color.

Two attractive sages grow as biennials or short-lived perennials. While most sages are planted for their colorful flowers, silver sage, **S. argentea** (Zones 1–24, 26, 28–45), is a striking foliage plant as well. It spends its first year developing into a 2-foot-wide clump of triangular, gray-green, 8-inch leaves covered with silvery hairs. In the summer of its second year, it produces multibranched, 3-foot stems carrying 1½-inch white flowers with silvery calyxes. If you let the plant set seed, it will usually die but leave you with volunteer seedlings; if you cut out the flowering stems after blooms fade, the clump may live for another year.

Clary sage, **S. sclarea** (Zones 2–24, 27–41), forms a handsome foliage clump 2 to 3 feet across, composed of wrinkled, oval to lance-shaped gray-green leaves to 1½ feet long. Multibranched, 3- to 4-foot flower spikes come in late spring to early summer of the second year; each 6- to 12-inch branch bears whorls of 1¼-inch lavender-blue blossoms with a white lower lip, and conspicuous purplish pink bracts continue the color show after the flowers fade. **'Alba'** has white flowers and bracts.

'Turkestanica' *(S. s. sclarea, S. s. turkestanica)* is a particularly vigorous form to 5 feet tall, with pink flowers and lilac bracts. Plants usually die after bloom, but volunteer seedlings provide replacement plants.

Reliably perennial sages are among the best sources of blue and purple for the summer and fall garden. Prairie or pitcher sage, **S. azurea grandiflora (S. pitcheri),** grows in Zones 1–24, 26 (northern part), 27–43. Each clump sends up multiple stems that need support to remain upright. Stems are set with narrow, 4-inch leaves and grow to 5 feet high, displaying foot-long spikes of sky blue flowers from summer until frost.

Three other species are similar enough to have created some name confusion in the nursery trade over the years; in fact, several of the named cultivars have been listed under more than one of these species. All three grow in Zones 2–10, 14–24, 30–41. **S. nemorosa** spreads by rhizomes, forming a 2- to 3-foot-wide clump of lance-shaped dull green leaves to 4 inches long. Upright, branched stems rise 1½ to 3 feet in summer and fall, bearing tiered, 3- to 6-inch clusters of ½-inch flowers. Nurseries offer named selections, including **'Lubecca'**, with gray-green leaves and violet flowers, and **'Ostfriesland'** (**'East Friesland'**), with blue-violet flowers and pinkish purple bracts. Both reach about 1½ feet high. **S. × superba** is found in nurseries as the cultivar **'Superba'**, but be aware that some plants sold by that name are not the genuine article (though they do resemble it). The plant is much like *S. nemorosa,* but it has green leaves with scalloped edges. From midspring until autumn, many-branched, 3-foot stems bear closely clustered, 6- to 8-inch tiers of violet-blue, ½-inch blossoms with red-purple bracts (the identifying feature) that persist long after flowers drop. **S. × sylvestris (S. deserta)** also resembles *S. nemorosa* but has wrinkled, medium green, slightly shorter leaves with scalloped edges. Flower stems have few or no branches and can reach 1 to 2½ feet, depending on cultivar; from spring through fall, ½-inch blossoms appear along the top 6 to 8 inches of the stem. Two taller cultivars are **'Blauhügel'** (**'Blue Hill'**), with medium blue flowers on 2-foot stems, and **'Mainacht'** (**'May Night'**), which starts flowering in midspring and has indigo, ¾-inch flowers on 2- to 2½-foot stems. In the 1- to 1½-foot range are **'Rosakönigin'** (**'Rose Queen'**), bearing purplish pink flowers with red bracts, and **'Schneehügel'** (**'Snow Hill'**), with green-bracted white blossoms.

Whorled clary, **S. verticillata,** is suited to Zones 2–10, 14–24, 30–41. The plant is a fine leafy presence in the garden, forming a clump to 2½ feet wide. The medium green, wavy-margined, softly hairy leaves are more or less oval, to 6 inches long. Leafy flower stems rise to 3 feet, carrying ½-inch blossoms in dense, widely spaced whorls. The flowers are typically violet to lavender, with conspicuous violet calyxes; with regular deadheading, they'll bloom from early summer through fall. **'Alba'** has white flowers and calyxes; 2-foot **'Purple Rain'** is particularly showy, with blossoms and calyxes in rich purple.

CULTURE. The sages need good drainage and moderately fertile soil; those described here require regular water (though *S. argentea* is particularly sensitive to overly moist soil in winter). In hot-summer areas, plants appreciate some shade in the afternoon. All perennial types (including those grown as annuals) can be propagated from stem cuttings taken in spring or summer. Those that form clumps can be divided in spring— and should be when performance starts to decline from overcrowding. For annual *S. viridis,* the perennials grown as annuals, and the biennial species *S. sclarea* and *S. argentea,* you can set out transplants in spring (after frost danger is past) or start from seed. Where winters are frost free or just slightly frosty, sow outdoors after the last-frost date; in colder regions, sow indoors 6 to 8 weeks before the last-frost date. Just press seeds into the soil, since they need light to germinate.

Salvia farinacea

TOP: *Salvia nemorosa* 'Ostfriesland'
BOTTOM: *Salvia verticillata* 'Purple Rain'

SANVITALIA procumbens
CREEPING ZINNIA

Asteraceae (Compositae)

WARM-SEASON ANNUAL

ZONES 1–45

FULL SUN

MODERATE TO REGULAR WATER

✿ ✿ FLOWERS IN SUMMER, FALL

Sanvitalia procumbens

As the common name indicates, this colorful annual could easily pass for a zinnia in flower and foliage. Leaves are sandpapery, to 2 inches long; the summer-into-fall blossoms are inch-wide yellow daisies with dark centers. The plant reaches just 4 to 6 inches high but spreads to 1½ feet or wider. For variations on the species, try **'Mandarin Orange'**, with orange flowers; **'Yellow Carpet'**, bearing blooms of a softer lemon yellow; or fully double **'Gold Braid'**, with blossoms showing no dark center. Creeping zinnia makes a showy small-scale ground cover and will spill attractively from pots, hanging baskets, and window boxes.

CULTURE. Sow seeds in light-textured, well-drained soil; just press them in, since light aids germination. Where frost is light or absent, you can sow seeds outdoors in fall; where winters are chilly but the growing season is fairly long, sow outdoors around the last-frost date. In colder areas, sow indoors 6 to 8 weeks before the last-frost date.

SCABIOSA
PINCUSHION FLOWER

Dipsacaceae

PERENNIALS AND WARM-SEASON ANNUALS

ZONES VARY

FULL SUN, EXCEPT AS NOTED

MODERATE TO REGULAR WATER

✿ ✿ ✿ ✿ ✿ FLOWERS IN SPRING AND
      SUMMER, EXCEPT AS NOTED

The blossoms' protruding stamens look something like pins bristling from a pincushion—hence these plants' common name. Each flower head is composed of countless tiny, closely packed tubular blooms. In the annual species, all of them are about the same size; in perennial types, the outer flowers are larger, giving the effect of a ring of petals around a central "cushion." Stems are smooth and knitting-needle thin.

Annual ***S. atropurpurea*** (Zones 1–45; H1, H2) may persist as a short-lived perennial where winters are mild. Clumps of oblong, coarsely toothed leaves send up numerous stems to 3 feet high, each bearing a 2- to 3-inch, sweetly fragrant flower; colors run from nearly black through dark red to pink shades, violet, lavender, and white. Mixed-color strains offering the full range of blossom colors include **Double Mixed** (to 3 feet), **Dwarf Double Mixed** (to 1½ feet), and **Sweet Scabious** (to 2½ feet). **'QIS Scarlet'**, **'Salmon Queen'**, and deep maroon **'Ace of Spades'** are 3-foot-tall, single-color seed strains.

Among perennial species, ***S. caucasica*** (Zones 1–10, 14–24, 32–43) forms clumps of long, narrow leaves that vary from smooth edged to finely cut. Flexible, 2-foot stems bear 3-inch flowers in blue or white; selected cultivars include lavender-blue **'Blue Perfection'**, darker blue **'Moerheim Blue'**, white **'Perfecta Alba'** (with 15-inch stems), and **'Bressingham White'**. Among seed strains, **'Fama'** produces lavender-blue flowers on 20-inch stems; **House's Mix (House's Novelty Mix)** grows to 2½ feet, with flowers in white and shades of blue and lavender.

Finely cut gray-green leaves distinguish ***S. columbaria*** (Zones 2–11, 14–24, 32–35). In spring and summer—or almost year-round in the mildest regions—2-foot stems bear 2-inch flowers in blue shades, white, and pink. Named cultivars include deep lavender-blue **'Butterfly Blue'** and soft pink **'Pink Mist'**.

CULTURE. All pincushion flowers do best in sandy to loam soil enriched with organic matter (and amended with lime, if the soil is acid). Good drainage is essential; perennial species are particularly sensitive to wet soil in winter. To start annual *S. atropurpurea*, sow seeds indoors about 5 weeks before the last-frost date, or sow outdoors just after that date. Among perennials, *S. caucasica* is best suited to regions with cool to mild summers, where it can grow in full sun; in warmer regions, it performs better with light shade during the afternoon. For hot-summer regions, *S. columbaria* is the better choice. To get additional plants, divide clumps or take basal cuttings in spring. With both annual and perennial types, regularly remove spent flowers to prolong bloom.

Scabiosa columbaria 'Pink Mist'

These undemanding perennials are succulents that bear large clusters of many tiny, star-shaped flowers. You'll find a multitude of ground-hugging sorts for rock gardens and for use as ground cover—but the plants profiled here are larger sorts, better suited to beds and borders. All form dense clumps that start the year as growth buds at ground level, develop into mounds of fleshy, rubbery foliage, and then send up leafy stems that terminate in nearly flat-topped flower clusters. After bloom ends, the stems die but dry out and remain standing until beaten down by rain or snow (or picked for dried arrangements). Botanists have reclassified all the following plants into the genus *Hylotelephium*, but catalogers and nurseries are still likely to list them under *Sedum*.

Sedum spectabile 'Brilliant'

S. spectabile (Hylotelephium spectabile) is suited to Zones 1–24, 28–43. Reaching about 1½ feet high, the erect to slightly spreading stems are set with oval, 3-inch blue-green leaves. Dense, 6-inch clusters of pink flowers open in late summer and gradually age to brownish maroon. Cultivars with different blossom colors include deep rose-red '**Brilliant**', soft rose '**Carmen**', pure white '**Iceberg**' (with lime-green leaves), coppery red '**Indian Chief**', and carmine red '**Meteor**'.

S. telephium (Hylotelephium telephium; Zones 1–24, 29–43) resembles *S. spectabile* in general appearance but has narrower, oblong gray-green leaves and taller stems (to 2 feet); its blossoms open purplish pink in late summer, then turn maroon brown with age. Most cultivars differ from the species in foliage color. '**Arthur Branch**' has purplish bronze leaves, wine red stems, and deep pink blooms; pink-flowered '**Matrona**' has red stems and red-blushed, pink-margined foliage; '**Munstead Red**' carries its deep rose flowers over purplish green leaves. Cultivars of **S. telephium maximum** include '**Atropurpureum**' (dusty pink flowers, burgundy leaves) and '**Gooseberry Fool**' (creamy green flowers, purple stems, purple-flushed foliage).

Ever-popular **S. 'Autumn Joy'** (Zones 1–10, 14–24, 29–43), reaching 1½ to 2 feet, is probably a hybrid between *S. spectabile* and *S. telephium*. It has blue-green, 2- to 3-inch leaves and bears broad, rounded clusters of pink flowers that age to coppery pink, then to rusty bronze. Another presumed hybrid, 1½- to 2-foot '**Frosty Morn**', has white-margined grayish green leaves and pale pink blossoms.

CULTURE. Stonecrops need well-drained soil but are not fussy about fertility. The *S. spectabile* cultivars will take moderate to regular watering, but all the others do better with a regular supply. When floppy stems and decreased bloom indicate overcrowding, divide clumps in early spring. To increase a favorite kind, dig out a rooted chunk from a clump's edge in early spring; or take stem cuttings in late spring and early summer.

SEDUM
STONECROP
Crassulaceae
PERENNIALS
ZONES VARY
FULL SUN
REGULAR WATER, EXCEPT AS NOTED
❀ ✿ ✿ ✿ FLOWERS IN SUMMER, FALL

Sedum 'Autumn Joy'

From mid- or late summer into fall, goldenrods *(Solidago)* brighten the garden with large, branching clusters of small yellow flowers carried on leafy stems that rise from tough, woody, spreading rootstocks. For all their flamboyant color and ease of care, they are not as widely planted as they deserve, largely because their pollen is incorrectly thought to cause hay fever. (The actual culprit is usually ragweed, which blooms at the same time.) Gardeners in the Midwest and East may also dismiss these plants as mere rangy roadside weeds—but a number of named cultivars are shorter and more compact than some of the wild forms, entirely suitable for cultivated gardens.

Listing continues>

SOLIDAGO (and × SOLIDASTER)
Asteraceae (Compositae)
PERENNIALS
ZONES 1–11, 14–23, 28–45
FULL SUN TO LIGHT SHADE
MODERATE WATER
✿ FLOWERS IN SUMMER, FALL

Solidago sphacelata 'Golden Fleece'

Solidago rugosa can reach 5 feet tall, bearing glowing gold fall flowers on arching, widely branching stems. Its cultivar **'Fireworks'** is a better garden bet: it grows to 3 feet tall and wide, with fluffy golden flower sprays on near-horizontal branches. For a foreground position, try 1½- to 2-foot **S. sphacelata** 'Golden Fleece', an arching, mounding clump that comes alive in late summer with sprays of golden yellow blossoms. You can use it as an individual accent or mass it for a fast-growing ground cover.

For a striking departure from other goldenrods, look for 2- to 3½-foot **S. flexicaulis** 'Variegata', with leaves brightly splashed in yellow. Narrow spikes of yellow flowers bloom in late summer.

A number of hybrid goldenrods are available in the short to medium height range. **'Cloth of Gold'**, just 1½ feet high, has a long bloom season that begins as early as midsummer. **'Crown of Rays'** ('Strahlenkrone') is a 2-footer with wide, flat, branched flower clusters. **'Goldenmosa'** bears mimosalike blossom clusters on stems to about 2½ feet tall. **'Goldkind'** ('Golden Baby') is another 2-foot plant; its flowers come in plumelike clusters.

× **Solidaster luteus** is a hybrid between *Solidago* and a hardy aster. It resembles goldenrod in habit, but the late-summer flowers are larger, reminiscent of small, primrose yellow asters. Plants grow to 2 feet high; unlike the generally self-supporting goldenrods, they require staking.

CULTURE. These undemanding plants grow as well in semiwild gardens as they do in highly cultivated ones. All they need is average soil and moderate watering. To rejuvenate clumps and control spreading, divide every 3 to 4 years in early spring.

STACHYS
Lamiaceae (Labiatae)
PERENNIALS
ZONES VARY
FULL SUN TO LIGHT SHADE
MODERATE WATER
✿ ❀ ✿ ✿ FLOWERS IN LATE SPRING, SUMMER, FALL

Stachys byzantina 'Silver Carpet'

Certain common features link these plants—square stems and aromatic foliage, for example—but beyond that they differ considerably.

Mexican native **S. albotomentosa** grows in Zones 7–10, 12–24, 29, 30. Its selected form **'Hidalgo'** has white, woolly stems and heavily veined, somewhat heart-shaped green leaves with white undersides; it reaches 2½ feet high and sprawls to as much as 5 to 6 feet across. Spikes of small summer flowers open salmon pink and age to brick red.

Old favorite lamb's ears, **S. byzantina** (**S. lanata**, **S. olympica**; Zones 1–24, 29–43), is a classic foreground plant and small-scale ground cover. The thick, soft, 4- to 6-inch-long, elliptical leaves do indeed resemble gray-white, furry lamb's or rabbit's ears. The plant increases rapidly, a single foliage rosette spreading into a clump as the stems root where they touch soil. In the basic species, upright, 1- to 1½-foot flower stems rise above the foliage in late spring or early summer, bearing small leaves and whorls of small purple blossoms. Massed plantings may become patchy after bloom. Cultivars vary significantly from the species. **'Big Ears'** ('Countess Helene von Stein') boasts leaves about twice as large as those of *S. byzantina;* it flowers only sparsely. **'Cotton Boll'** has the standard foliage, but in place of flowers, it produces wads of white, cottonlike fluff spaced along the stems. Sparse-flowering **'Primrose Heron'** has foliage covered in the usual white wool, but its leaves are yellow in spring, turning to chartreuse and then to gray green by summer. **'Silver Carpet'** blooms only rarely and forms a foliage cover that retains a solid, gap-free appearance for considerably longer than plantings of the flowering forms.

Scarlet hedge nettle, **S. coccinea** (Zones 7–10, 12–24, 29, 30), is a Southwestern native that forms a semishrubby clump to 1½ feet high and wide. The oval, 3-inch green leaves are heavily veined and wrinkled; spikes of small, brilliant red flowers appear in midsummer and continue into fall.

S. macrantha (*S. grandiflora;* Zones 1–24, 29–45) makes a dense, foot-high clump of long-stalked, heart-shaped dark green leaves with scalloped edges; wrinkled and roughly hairy, they reach 3 inches long. Slender stems rise above the foliage to 1½ to 2 feet, bearing smaller leaves and tiered whorls of showy purplish pink blossoms in late spring and summer. Available cultivars include white-flowered '**Alba**'; '**Hummelo**', with semiglossy leaves and rosy lavender flowers on 1½-foot stems; '**Robusta**', earlier to bloom and a bit larger in all parts; and '**Superba**', with violet flowers. A similar species, *S. officinalis,* also grows in Zones 1–24, 29–45; it differs primarily in having elongated rather than heart-shaped leaves and small lilac-pink flowers in more closely spaced whorls. It too has a white-blossomed cultivar '**Alba**'.

CULTURE. These are easy-to-grow plants, content with average, well-drained soil and moderate watering. *S. albotomentosa* and *S. coccinea* need full sun. The others will grow in full sun to partial shade—and may need some afternoon shade in hot-summer regions. When vigor declines or plantings show bare spots, divide and replant in spring. *S. byzantina* will need division more frequently than the others.

Stachys macrantha

Tagetes erecta,
Jubilee strain

Ｗith their warm, bright colors, marigolds just seem to say "summer." They light up the garden, growing quickly and easily and producing masses of bloom over several months; and their wide height range assures you of finding a marigold for any sunny garden (or container) location. Today's gardeners can also choose from an array of colors and flower types. In addition to the traditional yellow and orange, you'll find blooms in cream, near-white, bronzy red, maroon, and bicolors; forms vary from basic single daisies to double, drumstick-like pompoms. All types make long-lasting cut flowers. The finely cut, dark green foliage is typically strongly aromatic—some people like the fragrance, others emphatically do not.

Despite the nativities suggested by their common names, all marigolds are descended from New World species. So-called African marigold, *T. erecta,* was originally a 3- to 4-foot plant used strictly for middle and background planting—but breeders have developed a number of lovely strains in more useful heights that run from around 1 to 2½ feet. All have double flowers 3 to 5 inches across. Examples of taller mixed-color strains include **Climax** (2½ to 3 feet high) and **Odorless** (to 2½ feet, with scentless foliage and flowers). In the 16- to 20-inch range are mixed-color **Galore, Inca, Lady,** and **Perfection,** plus cream **Sweet Cream.** Mixed-color **Jubilee** is a bit taller at 1½ to 2 feet. Shortest of all are 16-inch **Antigua** and foot-tall **Discovery** and **Guys and Dolls.**

French marigold, *T. patula,* is the traditional small-flowered, front-of-the-border marigold, with single to double flowers in yellow, orange, copper, mahogany, and bicolors on plants that range from 6 to 18 inches high. Mixed-color, double-blossomed strains include 8-inch **Janie** (1¾-inch flowers), **Bonanza** (2-inch flowers), and the following foot-tall choices, all with 2- to 2½-inch blooms: **Aurora, Hero,** and **Sophia.** Two single-flowered strains are **Disco** (to about 1 foot) and 1- to 1½-foot **Mr. Majestic,** with blooms featuring a striking gold-and-mahogany pinwheel pattern.

TAGETES

MARIGOLD
Asteraceae (Compositae)
WARM-SEASON ANNUALS
ALL ZONES
FULL SUN
REGULAR WATER
❀ ✿ ✿ ✿ FLOWERS IN LATE SPRING,
SUMMER, FALL

Tagetes patula, Hero strain

Listing continues>

Tagetes tenuifolia 'Lemon Gem'

Triploid hybrids are an especially vigorous group derived from crosses between *T. erecta* and *T. patula*. In plant and blossom, they resemble *T. patula*, with 2½- to 3-inch flowers on foot-tall plants; because they are sterile, you don't need to remove spent blossoms to prevent seed set. Mixed-color strains are **Nugget, Trinity,** and **Zenith.**

Signet marigold, *T. tenuifolia (T. signata)*, produces 1-inch single flowers in amazing profusion on bushy plants to about 1 foot high. **Gem** and **Starfire** are mixed-color strains.

CULTURE. Given a sunny spot and average garden soil, marigolds are virtually foolproof (rich soil or overfertilization will encourage plants to produce leaves at the expense of flowers). In areas with a long growing season, sow seeds outdoors after the last-frost date. Where the growing season is shorter and winters are colder, start seeds indoors 6 to 8 weeks before the last-frost date. The tallest *T. erecta* types are likely to need staking. To make them sturdier—possibly strong enough to stand on their own—set them deep. Strip off any leaves from the lower 1 to 3 inches of stem, then plant so the stripped portion is below the soil line. Pinch taller types to promote bushy growth. During the bloom season, regularly deadhead all but the triploid hybrids to prevent seed set and prolong flowering.

THALICTRUM

MEADOW RUE

Ranunculaceae

PERENNIALS

ZONES 2–10, 14–17, 32–41,

    EXCEPT AS NOTED

LIGHT SHADE, EXCEPT AS NOTED

REGULAR WATER

✿ ❀ ✿ FLOWERS IN LATE SPRING, SUMMER

Thalictrum aquilegifolium

With their graceful, fernlike leaves and branching, open blossom clusters, airy-looking meadow rues are choice perennials for a shaded border or the edge of a wooded spot. Their foliage is similar to that of columbine *(Aquilegia)*, to which they are related, but they're generally much larger plants with leafy flower stems rising 2 to 6 feet high. Flower shape is different, too: the profuse small, petal-less blossoms have four sepals and a prominent cluster of stamens. Bloom comes in late spring and summer.

Thalictrum aquilegifolium

Earliest to bloom each year is *T. aquilegifolium*, a 2- to 3-foot-high clump with blue-tinted foliage. Flowers consist of clouds of rosy lilac, fluffy stamens carried just above the leaves; later, attractive seed heads develop. Forms featuring other colors include '**Thundercloud**', with particularly large purple flower heads, and *T. a. album*, with white blooms. Chinese meadow rue, *T. delavayi (T. dipterocarpum;* Zones 2–10, 14–17, 31–41) forms large clumps of especially delicate green leaves. From these rise dark purple, 3- to 6-foot stems bearing flowers that consist of lavender to violet sepals and yellow stamens. Blossoms of '**Hewitt's Double**' look double due to extra sepals and petal-like stamens; individual flowers are long-lasting, and the total display can go on for 2 months.

Light yellow flowers set *T. flavum glaucum (T. speciosissimum)* apart from the other meadow rues. Upright plants reach 5 feet when in flower, their fluffy pale yellow flower heads combining beautifully with the fernlike blue-green foliage. *T. rochebrunianum* has intricately branched flower stems that can grow to about 6 feet, bearing blossoms composed of lilac sepals and yellow stamens. Leaves are green.

CULTURE. Meadow rues thrive in good, well-drained, organically enriched soil. They do well anywhere in dappled sunlight or light shade; in cool-summer regions, they'll also grow in full sun. Flower stems may require staking to remain upright, especially in the case of *T. delavayi* and *T. flavum glaucum*. You'll need to divide clumps every 4 to 5 years in early spring.

Tithonia rotundifolia 'Fiesta del Sol'

Big and brassy, Mexican sunflower is impossible to overlook. The upright, bushy plant quickly grows to 6 feet high, blazing in summer and fall with 3- to 4-inch single, yellow-centered red-orange daisies. The largest leaves can reach 1 foot long; they are more or less oval, sometimes with several lobes. Thanks to its size and density, this plant makes a good annual hedge or background screen when set out in groups. **'Torch'** is an especially fine form. **'Goldfinger'** is a shorter plant, just 2½ to 3½ feet tall; compact **'Fiesta del Sol'** is shorter still (to about 2 feet) and comes into bloom earlier. Four-foot **'Aztec Sun'** has golden blossoms tinged with apricot; the **Arcadian Blend** strain, also to 4 feet, produces flowers in yellow, gold, and orange.

CULTURE. Well-drained, average soil suits Mexican sunflower. Where winters are fairly mild and the growing season is long, sow seeds outdoors after the last frost. Where the growing season is shorter, sow seeds indoors 6 to 8 weeks before the last-frost date. This plant is at its best in hot-summer regions. Stems are hollow, prone to bend or break in windy areas and when weighed down by overhead watering or rainfall; staking is a good idea, especially for the taller kinds. Remove spent flowers regularly to prevent seed set and keep bloom going.

TITHONIA rotundifolia
MEXICAN SUNFLOWER
Asteraceae (Compositae)
WARM-SEASON ANNUAL
ALL ZONES
FULL SUN
REGULAR WATER
✿ ✿ FLOWERS IN SUMMER, FALL

Fans of crayon-bright nasturtiums can choose between the familiar vining type (page 183) and the bushy, dwarf plants described here, good for foreground plantings and containers. The light green leaves are nearly circular, from 2 to 7 inches across, set off-center at the ends of long leafstalks; both leaves and immature seeds are edible and add a watercress-like tang to salads. The blossoms are nearly symmetrical five-lobed trumpets to 2½ inches across, with a spur projecting from the back. Nasturtiums' usual flowering season is spring, but in desert areas gardeners plant them for winter bloom.

Tropaeolum majus

A number of seed strains are available, in mixed as well as separate colors. Two strains to 1 foot high and wide are **Jewel,** offering the full range of colors as well as some bicolors, and **Whirlybird,** in separate and mixed colors. The mixed-color **Tom Thumb** strain is shorter—just 6 to 9 inches. The **Alaska** strain, with mixed colors on plants to 15 inches, is notable for its foliage: leaves are smaller than the usual and strikingly marbled in creamy white. **'Empress of India'** is a rather lax plant to 2 feet high and wide, with dark orange-scarlet flowers and dark green, purple-tinted foliage.

CULTURE. Well-drained soil is a must—preferably sandy soil of limited fertility (too-rich soil produces foliage at the expense of flowers). This plant does best in cool weather, dislikes warm, humid conditions, and literally burns out in summer heat.

Where summers are hot, sow seeds as early as possible for bloom in the cooler springtime; in the low desert and in virtually frost-free areas, sow in fall for bloom beginning in winter. It's best to sow outdoors, but where the growing season is fairly short, you can sow indoors 4 to 5 weeks before the last frost. Plant just one or two seeds in each small pot; plants resent disturbance, so this makes transplanting simpler. In mild-winter regions, plants may live over into a second year, and you are likely to get volunteer seedlings.

TROPAEOLUM majus
NASTURTIUM
Tropaeolaceae
COOL-SEASON ANNUAL
ALL ZONES
FULL SUN OR LIGHT SHADE
REGULAR WATER
✿ ✿ ✿ ✿ FLOWERS IN SPRING,
EXCEPT AS NOTED

Tropaeolum majus, Alaska strain

VERBASCUM

MULLEIN

Scrophulariaceae

PERENNIALS

ZONES VARY

FULL SUN

MODERATE WATER

✿❀✿✿✿ FLOWERS IN LATE SPRING,
SUMMER

Verbascum chaixii

Like delphinium and foxglove *(Digitalis)*, the mulleins are valuable for vertical accents in the landscape. Plants form rosettes of large, broad leaves (woolly in some species), above which rise 1- to 6-foot-tall spikes closely set with five-petaled, circular, nearly flat flowers about an inch across. Many mulleins—including the striking roadside weed *V. thapsus*—are biennial, but those presented here are reliably perennial.

Sometimes called nettle-leaved mullein, *V. chaixii* (Zones 2–11, 14–24, 31–41) forms a 2-foot-wide rosette of hairy green or slightly gray foliage. In late spring, flower spikes (branched, in older plants) rise to 3 feet, bearing red-centered yellow blossoms. '**Album**' bears white flowers with purple centers. Imposing *V. olympicum* (Zones 3–10, 14–24, 32–34, 39) produces a 3-foot-wide rosette of white leaves covered in soft, downy hairs. Branching stems appear in summer, growing as tall as 5 feet and carrying bright yellow flowers. Purple mullein, *V. phoeniceum* (Zones 1–10, 14–24, 32–43), forms a 1½-foot-wide rosette of dark green leaves that are smooth on top, hairy beneath. Slender, 2- to 4-foot spikes appear in spring; the usual flower color is purple, though rose, white, and yellow are also possible.

A number of hybrid mulleins (Zones 3–10, 14–24, 32–34, 39) offer 1- to 1½-inch flowers in the standard colors as well as appealing melon tints. The **Benary Hybrids** and **Cotswold Hybrids** are derived from *V. phoeniceum* and resemble it in general aspect. Coppery pink '**Cotswold Queen**' and rose pink '**Pink Domino**' reach 3 to 3½ feet tall; peach pink '**Helen Johnson**' grows about 2 feet high. '**Jackie**' has cantaloupe orange blossoms on 1½-foot stems.

CULTURE. Tough and undemanding, the mulleins do well with well-drained, average to fairly poor soil and just moderate watering. Regularly cut off spent flower spikes—both to induce a second round of bloom from new stems and to prevent seed setting, which can result in numerous volunteer seedlings (difficult to remove because of their taproots). To increase a planting, it's simplest to let just a few plants produce seeds; keep in mind, though, that seedlings of hybrid selections won't replicate the parent plant. To propagate hybrids (or any other mullein, for that matter), take root cuttings in early spring or separate and transplant rooted young rosettes from the clump.

Verbascum
'Helen Johnson'

VERBENA

Verbenaceae

PERENNIALS, SOME GROWN AS
WARM-SEASON ANNUALS

ZONES VARY

FULL SUN

MODERATE WATER, EXCEPT AS NOTED

✿❀✿✿ FLOWERS IN SPRING,
SUMMER, FALL

Easy to grow, reveling in sunshine and warmth, and bearing colorful flowers throughout much of the growing period, verbenas are understandably one of the mainstays of the warm-season garden. And offering a multitude of choices in blues, purples, and white, they provide a refreshing counterpoint to the yellows and oranges of many other warm-weather favorites. Strictly speaking, all are perennials—but many of the more tender types grow and bloom so quickly that they are almost always grown as annuals, even where they can survive the winter.

Garden verbena, *V. × hybrida (V. hortensis)*, is usually treated as an annual but can be a short-lived perennial in Zones 8–29, H1, H2. Plants in this hybrid group are freely branching and rather bushy, varying from 6 to 12 inches high and 1 to 3 feet across. Bright green, oblong leaves to 4 inches long form a dense backdrop for flat,

3-inch clusters of flowers that may be white, blue, purple, pink, or red; the colored forms often have a white eye. Mixed-color seed strains include 6-inch **Romance**, 9-inch **Sandy**, 10-inch **Quartz**, and 1-foot **Showtime**. As the name implies, pastel '**Peaches and Cream**' has blossoms in a blend of soft peach and cream on a plant to 9 inches high and about a foot wide. '**Blue Lagoon**', an upright grower to about 10 inches high and wide, bears flowers in pure bright blue.

V. peruviana (V. chamaedrifolia) is also typically grown as an annual, though it can be perennial in Zones 8–24, 29, 30. The species is a ground-hugging mat of spreading stems set with small dark green leaves and clusters of white-centered scarlet flowers. Nurseries usually offer named cultivars (usually hybrids of the species) that make a higher cover, up to about 6 inches. Widely grown '**Starfire**' has red blossoms; pink choices include '**Appleblossom**', '**Cherry Pink**', '**Little Pinkie**', '**Princess Gloria**', '**Raspberry Rose**', and '**St. Paul**'. Moss verbena, *V. pulchella gracilior (V. tenuisecta)*, is still another species that can be grown as an annual, though it is perennial in Zones 7–9, 14–24, 28–31. Finely divided dark green leaves cover a plant that may reach 6 inches high and spread as ground cover to as much as 5 feet. Clusters of blue, violet, or purple flowers appear from spring through fall in the mildest regions. '**Alba**' is a white-blossomed selection.

Hardy perennial verbenas include drought-tolerant *V. bipinnatifida* (Zones 1–24, northern part of 26, 27–43). It's a spreading plant to 16 inches high, 1½ to 2 feet wide, bearing clusters of blue blossoms over finely divided, lightly hairy green leaves. Among perennial hybrids is well-known *V.* '**Homestead Purple**' (Zones 2–24, 28–41), a dense, bushy grower 1 to 2 feet high and up to 3 feet wide, with dark green, deeply scallop-edged, 2-inch-long leaves and a lavish show of clustered bright purple blossoms from summer into fall. Other popular hybrids are the **Tapien** and **Temari** hybrids (Zones 4–9, 12–24, 28–31; H1, H2), both with dark green leaves. The former, growing 4 inches high and up to 1½ feet wide, has finely cut foliage and flowers in blue, purple, lavender, pink, and red. The latter has broadly oval leaves on plants to 3 inches high and 2½ feet wide; blossom colors are purple, wine red, and pink.

Two other perennial verbenas are quite different in appearance from the preceding. South American native *V. bonariensis* (Zones 8–24, 28–31, warmer parts of 32) is a large, dramatic-looking plant that sends up slender, branching, lightly leafy, 3- to 6-foot stems at bloom time; these rise above coarse, 2- to 4-inch leaves growing in a low clump. Each stem tip bears a cluster of small purple flowers that almost seem to float in the air; a clump of stems forms a see-through "fishnet." This species grows from a stout rootstock and increases by prolific seeding. It has naturalized in warmer regions of the U.S.—as has another South American native, *V. rigida* (*V. venosa*; Zones 3–24, 28–33). Stems reach 10 to 20 inches high, the clumps spreading into patches or colonies by means of underground shoots. Sandpapery, strongly toothed gray-green leaves to 4 inches long ascend stems that end in clusters of small purple flowers. Pale lilac '**Lilacina**', lavender-blue '**Polaris**', and scarlet '**Flame**' are selected forms.

CULTURE. All verbenas need average soil, good drainage (especially important in winter), and a location with good air circulation (to discourage powdery mildew). Moderate watering suits most; 'Homestead Purple' and the Tapien and Temari hybrids, however, are best with regular watering. To start any verbena from seed, sow indoors 8 to 10 weeks before the last-frost date; in warm-winter regions, you can also sow outdoors as soon as frost danger is past. You can start new plants of the low-growing and spreading types from stem cuttings in spring and summer (and from sections of stem that have rooted where they touch the soil). *V. bonariensis* readily self-sows, giving you a constant supply of new plants. To increase *V. rigida*, you can remove rooted shoots from the outside of a clump.

TOP: *Verbena × hybrida* 'Quartz Burgundy'
BOTTOM: *Verbena bonariensis*

VERONICA

SPEEDWELL

Scrophulariaceae

PERENNIALS

ZONES 1–9, 14–21, 32–43,
EXCEPT AS NOTED

FULL SUN, EXCEPT AS NOTED

REGULAR WATER

✿ ✿ ❀ FLOWERS IN SUMMER,
EXCEPT AS NOTED

Veronica austriaca teucrium 'Crater Lake Blue'

The speedwells are an invaluable summertime source of cool, soothing blue shades and white. A number of species are small-scale ground covers. The plants discussed below, however, are more upright, their tiny, starlike flowers held aloft in tapering spikes that rise like candles above shrubby clumps of narrow, pointed leaves. Shopping for these plants can be confusing. A few species may be listed under two (or more) names, and named cultivars are not always assigned to the same species. If the catalog descriptions—or the actual plants!—you see don't agree with the descriptions given here, don't worry. From the gardener's standpoint, it's easiest to make choices based simply on a plant's stated height and the color of its flowers and foliage.

V. austriaca teucrium '**Crater Lake Blue**', to 12 to 15 inches high and wide, bears dark green, 1½-inch leaves and short spikes of vivid medium blue flowers. Appropriately named *V. longifolia* has 3-inch leaves on a plant to around 2½ feet high. The basic blossom color is deep blue; selections include white-flowered '**Alba**' and bushy '**Blauriesin**' ('**Blue Giantess**'), with bright blue blooms. Old favorite *V. spicata* (Zones A2, A3; 1–9, 14–21, 28, 31–43) blooms over a long summer period, producing spikes of blue flowers that rise to 2 feet above rounded clumps of glossy green, 1- to 2-inch leaves. Two widely sold cultivars (both a bit shorter than 2 feet) are white '**Icicle**' and deep rose '**Rotfuchs**' ('**Red Fox**').

Several hybrid speedwells appear to be derived from *V. spicata* and resemble it in general habit. One popular choice is '**Sunny Border Blue**', to 2 feet high; it has crinkled dark green leaves and bears deep blue-violet blossoms in late spring to early summer, depending on climate. Three other hybrids, all successful in Zones 1–7, 14–17, 32–43, are 2-foot '**Blue Charm**', with lavender-blue flowers; foot-tall '**Goodness Grows**', a long-blooming plant (late spring to fall) with intense violet-blue blooms; and 1½-foot '**Noah Williams**', which resembles *V. spicata* 'Icicle' but has white-edged leaves.

CULTURE. Speedwells appreciate average soil with good drainage. In most climates, they prefer a full-sun location, but where summers are hot they do better with a little afternoon shade. Remove spent blossom spikes to encourage new flowering growth. When clumps decline in vigor, dig and divide them in early spring. You also can increase plants from stem cuttings taken in spring and summer.

VIOLA

Violaceae

PERENNIALS, SOME GROWN AS
COOL-SEASON ANNUALS

ZONES VARY

EXPOSURE NEEDS VARY

REGULAR WATER

✿ ✿ ❀ ✿ ✿ FLOWERS IN WINTER,
SPRING, SUMMER

Pansies, violets, and violas have been cherished by generations of gardeners for their jewel-like colors and, in the case of violets, for their sweet, distinctive perfume as well. Though all are perennials, pansies and most violas are grown as cool-season annuals. All have five-petaled flowers borne singly at the tips of slender stems. In pansies and many violas, the petals are nearly equal in size and shape, forming a flat blossom with a circular outline. In violets, however, petals differ in both shape and size, and the blossoms have an asymmetrical look.

Viola cornuta, Sorbet series

Viola or tufted pansy, *V. cornuta,* grows in Zones A2, A3, 1–24, 29–45 as an annual; perennial cultivars grow in Zones 1–10, 14–24, 29–43. Numerous seed-raised strains are available, featuring 1- to 2-inch flowers and broadly oval to elliptical, wavy-edged leaves on bushy plants to about 8 inches high and wide. Many solid colors are available—white, blue, purple, pink, red, orange, yellow; you'll also find numerous bicolor combinations, some of them with contrasting "whisker" patterns. The **Sorbet** series is particularly cold resistant, making it a good bet in zones where violas can be grown for winter color; plants also last longer into hot weather than most.

Specialty nurseries carry reliably perennial cultivars and hybrids of *V. cornuta* that form larger mounds than the species, growing about 2 feet wide. Among plants listed as hybrid violas are khaki-colored **'Irish Molly'** and virtually black **'Molly Sanderson'**. Another group of hybrids, the violettas, includes **'Raven'** (deep purple with orange eye), **'Rebecca'** (cream with violet-flecked margins), and creamy yellow, purple-whiskered **'Whiskers'**.

Pansy, **V. × *wittrockiana*,** grows in all zones. Plants look like slightly larger violas, reaching 10 to 12 inches high and wide, with broadly oval to heart-shaped leaves. Flowers, though, are notably larger—2 to 4 inches across—and come in an even more dazzling array of colors and patterns. The basic colors include white, blue, purple, lavender, pink, red, mahogany, brown, orange, apricot, yellow, and pink; you can find essentially solid-colored individuals, but far more widely grown are bi- and multicolored sorts. In many, the lower three petals are marked with dark, velvety blotches: the familiar pansy "face." Strains are too numerous to mention in detail, and new ones enter the market constantly. A few offer unmistakable, even startling flowers. **'Jolly Joker'** has a Halloween color scheme: bright orange lower petals, black-purple upper ones. The **Joker** series offers bicolored blooms in a variety of sharply contrasting colors. **'Padparadja'** is a solid tangerine scarlet; **'Springtime Black'** is a lustrous, velvety black. **'Brunig'** and **'Rippling Waters'** have dark flowers with striking petal edges: mahogany blooms with a yellow edge in the former, purplish black flowers edged with white in the latter.

Viola × wittrockiana 'Joker Poker Face'

Sweet violet, **V. *odorata*** (Zones 1–24, 29–43), grows just 4 to 8 inches high. An individual plant consists of a clump of long-stalked, nearly circular leaves—but one plant will spread in strawberry fashion, sending out long runners that root to produce new plants. Sweet-scented, ¾- to 1-inch flowers come in late winter to early spring, carried on stems just long enough to rise to the top of the foliage or barely above it; when bloom is at its peak, a violet patch is a sheet of color. Purple (or violet) is the color associated with these flowers, and **'Royal Robe'** is a widely sold example. But you'll also find violets in white, pink, lilac, and light to dark blue, and a few cultivars have double flowers. A small group of hybrids, the **Parma Violets** (Zones 4–9, 14–24, 29–31), features smaller, very double, highly fragrant flowers on plants that resemble a typical *V. odorata* but are less vigorous and spread more slowly. Named representatives include deep violet **'Marie Louise'** and lavender **'Duchesse de Parme'**.

CULTURE. Pansies and violas need good, organically enriched, well-drained soil and a location in sun or partial shade. In mild-winter regions, set out nursery plants in fall for winter-to-spring bloom; in cold-winter regions, set out plants as early as possible in spring for summer bloom. If you are starting from seed, timing depends on amount of winter cold. In mild-winter regions, sow seeds in late summer for planting out in fall; you'll get flowers in winter and spring. In colder areas, sow seeds indoors 10 to 12 weeks before the last-frost date for flowers by early summer. During the bloom period, remove spent flowers on pansies and violas to prevent seed set and prolong bloom. As weather warms, and particularly as night temperatures rise, performance declines; plants become ragged, unsightly, and start to fail at some point in summer in all but the coolest regions. In these cool-summer areas, you can cut back plants lightly in summer to control legginess; this can result in a passable display into fall.

Viola odorata 'White Czar'

Violets, too, appreciate good, organically enriched, well-drained soil, but they'll also thrive in fairly average soil with casual care. Give them partial to full shade, though in cool-summer regions they'll also grow in full sun. Set out plants in winter (in mild-winter regions) to spring (in colder areas). You can dig and divide for increase in early spring; or just dig rooted portions from a clump's perimeter.

ANNUAL VINES

A number of all-time favorite vines are annuals—and no wonder. Starting from seeds planted early in the year, these plants grow quickly to flowering size, giving you both color and bountiful foliage over a long season. Grow them on trellises, posts, walls, or fences; the largest ones can even cover an arbor. A few are also useful as fast-growing temporary ground covers. Unless otherwise noted, all do best in a sunny location. With a few exceptions (noted below), you should start seeds of these vines indoors in early spring; transplant seedlings to the garden after the weather has warmed. If you plan to train the vines on a temporary trellis or fence, be sure to set it up before setting out plants in the garden (or sowing seed in place); that way, you'll avoid damaging tender young growth.

Asarina scandens

Known as climbing snapdragon or chickabiddy, members of the genus ***Asarina*** (a tender perennial grown as an annual in Zones 1–45) have tubular flowers that resemble bell-shaped ("snapless") snapdragon *(Antirrhinum)* blooms. The twining stems, clothed in triangular to oval green leaves, will climb string, wire, or sticks, clamber over the ground, or spill over a retaining wall or the edges of a hanging basket. Largest is ***A. barclaiana,*** growing to 12 feet and bearing 2- to 3-inch flowers in white, pink, or purple. The same colors are available in the somewhat smaller-flowered ***A. scandens,*** which reaches just 4 to 8 feet. These plants require well-drained soil and prefer a location where their roots will be in shade, their tops in sun. They may live over winter and become perennials in Zones 17–27.

Cup-and-saucer vine, ***Cobaea scandens*** (a tender perennial grown as an annual in Zones 3–41), is extremely vigorous, reaching as much as 25 feet in a single season. The "cup and saucer" of the common name refer to the look of the flowers: the petals form a broad-based, 2-inch-long "cup," which rests on a circular, saucer-like, green calyx (the "saucer"). The cup is green at first, turning violet or rosy purple as it ages; **'Alba'** has white cups. Leaves are divided into two or three pairs of oval, 4-inch leaflets. At the end of each leaflet are curling tendrils that enable the vine to cling to string,

Ipomoea nil,
Early Call strain

wire, or rough surfaces. In cool-summer regions, flowering begins in late summer. In mild-winter areas (Zones 24–27; H1, H2), vines are perennial; they bloom in midsummer the first year from seed, from spring into fall in subsequent years.

Hyacinth bean (***Dolichos lablab,*** sometimes sold as ***Lablab purpurescens;*** all zones) grows quickly to 10 feet. It has purple stems and leaves composed of three broadly oval, 3- to 6-inch-long leaflets with purple veins. In late summer and early autumn, sweet pea–shaped purple flowers stand out from the vine on long stems; these are followed by edible, velvety magenta purple beans to 2½ inches long. Grow these plants

Dolichos lablab

as you would string beans, planting seeds in place in the garden after the last frost, in soil enriched with organic matter.

The genus ***Ipomoea*** includes several popular summer-blooming annual vines successful in all zones. They are related to dwarf morning glory *(Convolvulus tricolor,* described on page 113). The old-fashioned favorite vining morning glory, ***I. tricolor,*** twines vigorously to 10 to 15 feet, bearing heart-shaped leaves and the familiar funnel-shaped flowers 3 to 4 inches across. The traditional variety with sky-blue flowers is **'Heavenly Blue'; 'Pearly Gates'** has white flowers, while **'Crimson Rambler'** features blossoms in an intense magenta. There are also mixed-color strains including pink, purple, and lavender blooms. On sunny days, flowers open in the morning and close by afternoon; when weather is overcast, they'll remain open all day.

I. nil, also called morning glory, looks much like *I. tricolor* in plant and blossom. Selections include rosy red **'Scarlett O'Hara'** and pale red-brown **'Chocolate'**. The **Early Call** strain, featuring mixed colors of pink, magenta, blue, white, and lavender, blooms earlier than other members of the *I. nil* group, making it a good choice for short-summer regions.

The seed coat (outer covering) of morning glories is very hard, preventing the seed from absorbing moisture. Nicking each seed with a sharp knife or soaking seeds overnight in warm water before planting will improve germination. Where the growing season is long, seeds can be sown outdoors where the plants are to grow, 2 weeks after the last frost date.

Sweet pea, **Lathyrus odoratus** (all zones), is one of the best-known garden flowers, offering a delightful combination of beauty, color, and fragrance. Climbing to 5 feet or taller, it bears upright, long-stemmed clusters of flowers in cream, white, blue, purple, violet, red, and pink; there are also bicolor combinations featuring one of the usual colors plus white or cream. Seed companies offer a number of strains and varieties. For best success, plant seeds directly in the garden, in the spot where the vines are to grow.

Unlike many other annual vines, sweet peas are at their best in cool to mild weather; hot temperatures end their productivity. The planting time and variety best for you depend on your climate. In mild-winter, hot-summer areas, early-flowering strains will bloom in winter from seed sown in late summer; spring-flowering strains planted from October to early January will bloom from spring until hot weather arrives. In regions with cool winters and warm to hot summers, plant seeds of spring-flowering strains as soon as soil is workable in early spring. Summer-flowering strains are best for

Lathyrus odoratus

regions with cold winters and warm (but not hot) and/or short summers.

Like morning glories, sweet peas have a very hard seed coat (outer covering). To improve germination, pretreat the seeds as directed at left for morning glories. Plant in good, well-amended soil; keep soil moist but not saturated. To prolong bloom, remove all spent flower clusters.

Black-eyed Susan vine, **Thunbergia alata** (a tender perennial grown as an annual in all zones), reaches 10 feet tall, climbing by twining stems. The bright green, triangular leaves are about 3 inches long. Slender, 1-inch, tubular orange flowers with black throats bloom all summer; yellow- and white-flowered varieties are also available. In Zones 23–27 and H2, vines may live from year to year as perennials.

Thunbergia alata

Garden favorites everywhere, nasturtiums, **Tropaeolum majus** (all zones), are fast growing and easy to raise from seed. Vining types climb to about 6 feet, gripping their supports with coiling leafstalks; without support, they can serve as colorful ground covers. (See page 177 for information on dwarf, nonclimbing varieties.) The round bright green leaves grow on long stalks; the long-spurred flowers, blooming from summer into fall, reach 2½ inches across and have a refreshing fragrance. Orange is the traditional color, but choices also include creamy white, yellow, red brown, and maroon. Young leaves, flowers, and unripe seedpods have a peppery tang and are used in salads. In early spring, sow seed in place in the garden, in well-drained, average soil. The plants grow quickly and often reseed.

Canary bird flower, **T. peregrinum** (tender perennial grown as an annual in all zones), reaches 10 to 15 feet. Each leaf is deeply divided into five lobes. The inch-wide, canary yellow flowers have fringed petals and curved green spurs; they appear throughout summer until frost. Plant in light shade, in well-drained soil. Plants may become perennial in Zones 24–27, H1, H2.

Tropaeolum peregrinum

ZAUSCHNERIA
(Epilobium)
CALIFORNIA FUCHSIA
Onagraceae
PERENNIALS
ZONES 2–11, 14–24, EXCEPT AS NOTED
FULL SUN, EXCEPT AS NOTED
LITTLE TO MODERATE WATER,
   EXCEPT AS NOTED
✹ ✿ ✿ ✿ FLOWERS IN SUMMER, FALL

These plants are distantly related to true fuchsia and have somewhat similar blooms—hence the common name. However, the 1- to 2-inch, typically red or orange blossoms aren't pendent, but are instead carried in an almost horizontal position. Blossoms consist of a tube that flares out into an unequally lobed trumpet; leaves are narrow, ½ to 1½ inches long, and often gray or silvery in color. Growth varies from upright and almost shrublike to low and spreading. Thriving in hot, sunny locations, these natives of western North America typically grow best in areas of low humidity and sparse summer rainfall. They spread by underground stems and can be considered mildly invasive in manicured gardens; they excel in naturalistic plantings, on banks, and at the fringes of cultivated areas.

Botanists have recently reclassified these plants from *Zauschneria* to *Epilobium;* in nurseries and catalogs, you may find them listed under either name.

Z. californica (Epilobium canum canum) is the tallest species, with upright or arching growth to 2 feet. The leaves usually are grayish, the blossoms orange to scarlet. Selected forms include upright **'Bowman'**, semitrailing **'Calistoga'**, mounding **'Cloverdale'**, and compact **'Dublin'**; a white-flowered form is also occasionally sold. Leaves of **'Catalina'** are silvery white; **'Solidarity Pink'** has light pink blossoms. **'Etteri'**, forming a low mat of silvery foliage, is probably a hybrid with *Z. septentrionalis.*

The geographic variant ***Z. c. garrettii (Epilobium canum garrettii)*** is represented in nurseries by its selection **'Orange Carpet'**. A significant departure from the species, this is a low, compact plant to about 4 inches high and 16 inches wide. Another geographic variant, ***Z. c. latifolia (Epilobium canum latifolium)***, grows 1 to 1½ feet tall, its stems clothed in broadly elliptic green leaves. Its selection **'Arizonica'** ***(Z. arizonica)*** presents its bright orange flowers on stems to 3 feet high.

Humboldt County fuchsia, ***Z. septentrionalis (Epilobium septentrionale;*** Zones 5–7, 14–17, 19–24), is a mat-forming spreader to 8 inches high, with screaming scarlet flowers that stand in striking contrast to the gray-green to silvery leaves. **'Wayne's Silver'** has especially silvery leaves on a particularly dense plant.

CULTURE. California fuchsias usually flourish in poor, even rocky soil, though most also do well in more standard garden soil if drainage is good. Most prefer full sun and get along with little water. Exceptions are *Z. californica* 'Etteri', which requires moderate watering; *Z. californica garrettii* 'Orange Carpet', which does best with light afternoon shade and regular water; and *Z. septentrionalis*, which needs light afternoon shade and moderate water in hot-summer areas.

To curb a clump's spread, simply remove sections from the perimeter—and to increase a planting, transplant those sections to another location.

Zauschneria californica latifolia

ZINNIA
Asteraceae (Compositae)
WARM-SEASON ANNUALS
ZONES 1–45; H1, H2
FULL SUN
REGULAR WATER
✿ ✹ ✿ ✿ ✿ FLOWERS IN SUMMER

Hot stuff! With their showy blossoms in bright, pure, unshaded colors, zinnias are the perfect embodiment of their Latin American origins, enlivening the garden with bold brushstrokes straight from a Diego Rivera mural. True to their roots, they languish in cool, damp conditions but come alive in hot weather. Single-flowered individuals sport the basic daisy: a circular center surrounded by ray petals. Standard garden zinnias, however, are primarily semidouble- to double-flowered numbers resembling slightly shaggy pompoms.

Zinnia angustifolia 'Star White'

Looking like a domesticated wildflower, **Z. angustifolia** produces inch-wide single flowers; each bright orange petal is marked with a pale longitudinal stripe. Linear leaves to 2½ inches long cover a mounding, branching plant to 16 inches high and wide. **'Classic'** has 1½-inch blossoms on a plant to 1 foot high and 2 feet wide. White selections include **'Star White'** and **'Tropical Snow'** (both with 2-inch flowers) and **'Crystal White'** (with 1½-inch blooms). The **Star** series bears 2-inch flowers in orange, yellow, and white.

Zinnia elegans 'Whirligig'

The most familiar zinnia, **Z. elegans,** includes plants from under a foot high to 4 feet tall, with flowers from less than an inch to as much as 5 inches across. This group offers a zinnia for every conceivable sunny garden spot, containers included. Plants are upright but branching, bearing oval to lance-shaped leaves with a rough surface; leaf size is proportional to plant height and can reach 5 inches long in the tallest kinds. Flower forms include full double, cactus flowered (double with quilled petals), and crested (blossoms have a cushionlike center surrounded by rows of broad petals). Colors include white, lavender, purple, pink, red, orange, yellow, cream, and lime green (in the cultivar **'Envy'**), as well as bicolors and striped combinations.

Zinnia elegans, Candy Cane Mix

The tallest strains, all double flowered, are 4-foot **Benary's Giants** (also sold as **Blue Point** and **Park's Picks**), with 4- to 5-inch flowers; **Oklahoma,** with 1½-inch flowers on plants to 3½ feet tall; 3-foot **Dahlia-flowered Mix,** with 4- to 5-inch flowers; and 3-foot **'Big Red Hybrid',** with 5- to 6-inch blossoms. Strains of intermediate size (double flowered, unless otherwise noted) include 1½-foot **Candy Cane Mix,** with 4-inch white flowers striped in pink, rose, or red; the similar **Candy Stripe,** to 2 feet tall; 2- to 3-foot **Giant Cactus-flowered Mix** (semidouble, 4- to 5-inch flowers); 2½-foot **Ruffles Hybrids** (3½-inch flowers with ruffled petals); 2½-foot **Sun Hybrids** (flowers to 5 inches across); and **'Whirligig',** with 3- to 4½-inch bicolored blooms on 20-inch plants. Strains with plants to 1 foot tall and double flowers to 3 inches wide are **Dasher Hybrid Mixed, Parasol Mixed, Peter Pan Hybrid Improved,** and mildew-resistant **Small World.** The **Lilliput** and **Pompon** series reach 1½ feet tall and bear 1½-inch double blossoms.

Hybrids between *Z. elegans* and *Z. angustifolia* look like a slightly larger version of the *Z. angustifolia* parent, growing about 1½ feet high and wide and bearing narrow leaves and 2-inch flowers. The **Profusion** series comes in orange and cherry red, the flowers containing a second row of petals.

Upright-growing **Z. haageana** reaches 2 feet tall and has narrow, 3-inch leaves. Available strains bear double, 2-inch-wide flowers in yellow, orange, and mahogany red; all three colors are sometimes present in a single blossom. Foot-tall **Persian Carpet** and 16-inch **Old Mexico** are two popular choices.

CULTURE. Give zinnias a full-sun location with average to good, well-drained soil. These are hot-weather plants, and there's no point setting them out in cool weather: they won't start growing until temperatures are warm. In mild-winter regions, you can sow outdoors after the danger of frost is past and soil has warmed; in colder areas, sow indoors 6 to 8 weeks before the last-frost date. Powdery mildew is a potential problem in foggy regions, where plants are given overhead watering, and where nights are cool; it can also crop up in all areas as nights turn longer and cooler heading into fall.

Zinnia, Profusion series

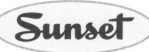

BULBS

BY PHILIP EDINGER, SUSAN LANG, AND THE EDITORS OF SUNSET BOOKS

SUNSET BOOKS · MENLO PARK, CALIFORNIA

CONTENTS

The beauty of bulbs touches us in varied ways. The experience may be grand and overpowering — the breathtaking sight of a sweep of tulips in a public planting, for example — or as simple and intimate as encountering a single blooming snowdrop or crocus where only unbroken snow had been the day before. Sometimes, we expect to find bulbs' bounty: what is a summer wedding without arrangements of gladiolus, or a springtime brunch without pots of daffodils?

HERE COME THE
BULBS

Visualize several popular bulbs — iris, hyacinth, tulip, daffodil, and lily — and you'll realize how greatly the plants we call "bulbs" can differ in appearance. They are so varied, in fact, that they raise an obvious question: what is the common thread drawing these seemingly unrelated plants together? The answer lies beneath the soil. All so-called bulbs grow from structures that serve as storage organs, depots where the plants accumulate nutrients to supply energy for growth and bloom in the year to come. Botanists draw firm distinctions between true bulbs and other structures with a similar function, but generations of gardeners have used "bulb" as a generic term both for true bulbs and for the plants that grow from bulblike organs: corms, tubers, rhizomes, and tuberous roots.

A sea of flowering bulbs proclaims that spring has come. Yellow narcissus
and peach pink hyacinths *(Hyacinthus)* provide a splashy foreground for an imposing
clump of orange-red crown imperial *(Fritillaria imperialis)*.

189

Where in the World...?

The bulbs in our gardens come from almost everywhere but Antarctica; their native lands represent virtually the complete range of habitable climates and encompass every combination of wet and dry, cold and hot. A look at these diverse climates explains the presence of bulbs in each: equipped with storage organs, the plants are well able to survive periods of less than hospitable weather. Knowing something of a particular bulb's native environment also makes it easier to understand that plant's needs in your garden.

DRY SUMMER, WET WINTER. The cradle of the world's bulb population is a broad latitudinal strip that extends from Spain and North Africa through the Mediterranean region, eastward through the Near East, Turkey, and Iran, and on into western China. Nearly all parts of this vast expanse experience winter precipitation (rain or snow) and hot, dry summers. In some areas (particularly the lands from central Asia into western China), winters are fairly cold, but much of this bulb-rich territory has the classic mild-winter Mediterranean climate. The same sort of climate reigns in California, parts of Chile, and South Africa's Cape Province; not surprisingly, these areas too are home to large bulb populations. Glory-of-the-snow (*Chionodoxa*), crocus, freesia, ixia, and harlequin flower (*Sparaxis*) are just a few of the many bulbs native to dry-summer, wet-winter regions.

In such climates, bulbous plants grow during the cooler, moister period of autumn through early spring. As spring days grow longer and warmer, they begin to flower, sometimes seeming to rush into bloom while conditions are still favorable for setting seed. Then, as flowers fade and seeds mature, the bulbs accumulate nutrient supplies that will sustain them, in a dormant state, after summer heat and dryness have withered foliage and put an end to the annual growing period.

WET SUMMER, DRY MILD WINTER. A smaller group of bulbs, most notably the summer-flowering African natives such as glory lily (*Gloriosa rothschildiana*) and common calla (*Zantedeschia aethiopica*), hail from regions where rainy weather comes during the hot summer months, while winters are cooler and drier. Growth occurs during the warm-season rainy period; plants go dormant or grow more slowly when rain ceases and weather cools.

Zantedeschia aethiopica

WET SUMMER, COLD WINTER. The wet-summer, cold-winter climate is a wide-spread one, found in northern and central Europe, in parts of China and the Himalayan foothills, and in much of the United States, Canada, Japan, and Russia. Technically, precipitation comes in varying amounts throughout the year—but in winter, that precipitation is likely to be snow, and even if snow is absent, winter temperatures are too low to encourage growth. Bulbs are dormant through the cold season, then reawaken when soil starts to warm; many flower in late spring or summer, retaining foliage until shorter

TOP: *Crocus* and *Chionodoxa*
BOTTOM: *Sparaxis tricolor*

Fritillaria meleagris

days and cooler temperatures trigger dieback in late summer to midautumn. Numerous lily species, the better-known species of *Erythronium,* and some fritillaries (such as *Fritillaria meleagris*) are native to this sort of climate.

Zephyranthes atamasco

INTERMITTENT RAIN. A few bulbs, such as habranthus and fairy lily *(Zephyranthes),* come from regions where moist and dry periods alternate irregularly. In this climate, the advantages of a bulb are obvious: the plant always has stored energy to carry it through unpredictable dry episodes. Bulbs native to these climates may flower more than once a year, whenever they receive enough rainfall (or watering) to stimulate another growth cycle.

Eucomis comosa

YEAR-ROUND RAINFALL. In an area where rain falls all year, why would a plant need any kind of bulb? Even in these benign, typically subtropical to tropical climates, there's often a distinct difference between moister times of year and drier periods—and bulbous plants can get by on less water during the drier season, which is nevertheless still warm enough to keep leaves green. Some true bulbs from these regions—such as crinum and pineapple flower *(Eucomis)*—belong to plant families rich in bulbous plants. Such individuals may represent not so much the development of a bulb in response to climate as the adaptation of a bulbous plant to a tropical environment.

Crinum × powellii

Leucojum

AMARYLLIDACEAE

Agapanthus	Leucojum
Amaryllis	Lycoris
Clivia	Narcissus
Crinum	Nerine
Cyrtanthus	Pancratium
Eucharis	Scadoxus
Galanthus	Sprekelia
Habranthus	Sternbergia
Hippeastrum	Tulbaghia
Hymenocallis	Zephyranthes
Ixiolirion	

Gladiolus

IRIDACEAE

Babiana	Iris
Belamcanda	Ixia
Crocosmia	Schizostylis
Crocus	Sparaxis
Dietes	Tigridia
Freesia	Tritonia
Gladiolus	Watsonia
Homeria	

Allium

LILIACEAE

Allium	Fritillaria
Alstroemeria	Galtonia
Brodiaea	Gloriosa
(and	Hemerocallis
Dichelostemma,	Hyacinthoides
Triteleia)	Hyacinthus
Calochortus	Ipheion
Camassia	Lachenalia
Cardiocrinum	Lilium
Chionodoxa	Muscari
Colchicum	Ornithogalum
Convallaria	Puschkinia
Eremurus	Scilla
Erythronium	Tulipa
Eucomis	Veltheimia

BULB TYPES

To a botanist, the word "bulb" refers only to true bulbs. Horticulturists and the general public, however, use the word as a generic term for plants that grow from five distinct types of underground structures: true bulbs, corms, tubers, rhizomes, and tuberous roots. Despite the technical differences, all serve the same function — they are storage organs, holding reserves of food that can keep the plant alive (often in a dormant or semi-dormant state) from one growing season to the next, through drought, heat, cold, or other climatic vagaries.

The characteristics of each bulb type are summarized here. The bulbs described in the encyclopedia (pages 215–291) are grouped by type on the facing page.

TRUE BULB

A true bulb is an underground stem base containing an embryonic plant complete with leaves, stems, and flower buds, ready to grow when conditions are right. Surrounding this embryonic plant are *scales* — modified leaves that overlap each other in a scalelike manner, giving the bulb as a whole a swollen, often pear-shaped contour. The *basal plate*, at the base of the bulb, holds the scales together and produces roots.

Many bulbs—narcissus and tulip *(Tulipa)* are familiar examples—are sheathed in a papery skin called a *tunic*, which protects against both injury and dehydration. Some bulbs, such as lily *(Lilium)*, lack a tunic; they need extra care in handling, and they cannot remain exposed to the air for long before they begin to dry and shrivel.

An individual bulb may persist for many years, periodically producing new, smaller bulbs *(increases)* from its basal plate.

CORM

Like a true bulb, a corm contains a stem base, but in this case the tissue is solid—purely a swollen underground stem base—rather than a series of overlapping modified leaves. Roots grow from a basal plate at the corm's bottom; the principal growth point "sits" at the top of the corm. Gladiolus and crocus are two favorite plants that grow from corms.

Some corms are covered in a tunic. Though superficially similar to the tunic covering a bulb, a corm's tunic is formed from the dried bases of the previous season's leaves rather than from a specialized layer of modified leaves.

THE FIVE BASIC BULB TYPES

Muscari   Iris (bulbous)   Leucojum   Narcissus

TRUE BULB

Watsonia   Freesia   Crocus

CORM

Begonia   Cyclamen

TUBER

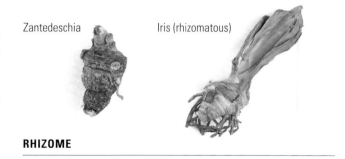

Zantedeschia   Iris (rhizomatous)

RHIZOME

Dahlia

TUBEROUS ROOT

Each corm lasts just one year, depleting its stored energies in the growth and bloom process. As it shrinks away, however, a new corm forms on top of it; numerous increases *(cormels)* may also be produced around the new corm's basal plate.

TUBER

Like corms, tubers are swollen stem bases. But whereas a corm has a fairly clearly organized structure, a tuber does not. There is no tunic of any kind, nor is there a basal plate; roots grow from the tuber's base and sides, and sometimes from the top as well. And instead of just one (or a few) growing points, a tuber has multiple growth points scattered over its upper surface; each one is really a scalelike leaf with a growth bud in its axil.

An individual tuber can last for many years. Those of some plants (cyclamen, for example) continually enlarge but never produce offsets. Other tuberous plants, such as caladium, form protuberances that can be removed and planted separately to become independent tubers.

RHIZOME

The best-known rhizomatous plant is doubtless the tall bearded iris; other familiar ones are calla lily *(Zantedeschia)* and canna. A rhizome is really a thickened stem that grows horizontally (in most cases), either partially or entirely underground. There is no basal plate; roots grow from the rhizome's underside. The primary growing point is at one end of the rhizome, encased (when dormant) in scalelike embryonic leaves. Additional growing points form along the rhizome's sides or on the upper surface.

Because growth proceeds in a straight line (usually horizontally) and because the increases give rise to full-fledged new plants, a planting that starts with a single rhizome can become more numerous and occupy more space as the years pass and the increases move into the soil around the point of the original planting.

TUBEROUS ROOT

Of the five bulb types, only the tuberous root is a true root, thickened to store nutrients, rather than a specialized stem. In a full-grown dahlia or daylily *(Hemerocallis)*, to cite the best-known examples, roots grow in a cluster, with the swollen tuberous portion radiating out from a central point. The growth buds lie on the roots' *necks* (at the top), on bases of old stems, or in a *crown* (the point where all the roots come together). Normal fibrous roots, for uptake of water and nutrients, grow from the sides and tip of each tuberous root structure.

An individual tuberous root can give rise to a separate plant as long as it is severed from the cluster of tuberous roots with a growth bud attached to its neck (as in daylilies) or to the base of an old stem just above it (as in dahlias).

WHICH BULB IS WHICH?

Here are all the entries in "An Encyclopedia of Favorite Bulbs," grouped according to type.

TRUE BULB
Allium
Amaryllis
Calochortus
Camassia
Cardiocrinum
Chionodoxa
Crinum
Cyrtanthus
Eucharis
Eucomis
Fritillaria
Galanthus
Galtonia
Habranthus
Hippeastrum
Hyacinthoides
Hyacinthus
Hymenocallis
Ipheion
Iris (some)
Ixiolirion
Lachenalia
Leucojum
Lilium
Lycoris
Muscari
Narcissus
Nerine
Ornithogalum
Oxalis (some)
Pancratium
Puschkinia

Scadoxus
Scilla
Sprekelia
Sternbergia
Tigridia
Tulipa
Veltheimia
Zephyranthes

CORM

Babiana
Brodiaea (and Dichelostemma, Triteleia)
Colchicum
Crocosmia
Crocus
Erythronium
Freesia
Gladiolus
Homeria
Ixia
Sparaxis
Tritonia
Watsonia

TUBER

Anemone (most)
Arisaema
Arum
Begonia
Caladium
Colocasia
Corydalis

Muscari

Cyclmen
Eranthis
Gloriosa
Oxalis (some)
Sinningia

RHIZOME

Achimenes
Agapanthus
Anemone (some)
Belamcanda
Bletilla
Canna
Convallaria
Dietes
Iris (many)
Oxalis (some)
Polianthes
Rhodohypoxis (but see encyclopedia, page 278)
Schizostylis
Tulbaghia
Zantedeschia

TUBEROUS ROOT

Alstroemeria
Clivia
Dahlia
Eremurus
Hemerocallis
Liatris
Ranunculus

Tulipa (left) and *Hyacinthus* (right)

Bulbs are easy to grow. That's a truth thousands of gardeners learn each year, as they admire the enchanting crocuses, tulips, irises, and lilies that looked like nothing more than lifeless lumps and bumps when they were planted months before. Pay conscientious attention to their few simple needs, and the bulbs in your garden will reward you with beauty for a long time to come.

GROWING BULBS

OUTDOORS

One cardinal rule to keep in mind is this: next year's performance is determined by this year's care. Bulbs purchased from nurseries or catalogs have been grown under optimum conditions to ensure a good initial display in your garden — though you will need to give them the overall climate, watering regime, and exposure they prefer (see "An Encyclopedia of Favorite Bulbs," pages 215–291). If they're to stage an equally dazzling show the following year, however, you must also satisfy their requirements after the blooming season ends. The following 12 pages outline the basics of bulb culture.

With the flowering of naturalized winter aconite *(Eranthis hyemalis)* and snowdrops *(Galanthus),* a lightly wooded hillside turns to a tapestry in yellow and white.

195

Buying Bulbs

A bulb is a ready-made floral factory, complete with embryonic leaf and flower buds and a supply of nutrients (stored during the previous year's growing season) to fuel its next growth cycle. For beautiful results the first year, buy top-quality bulbs — those that have been grown, shipped, and stored under the best possible conditions.

HOW TO CHOOSE, WHEN TO PLANT

As you select your bulbs and decide when and where to plant them, keep three guidelines in mind: appearance, size, and timing.

APPEARANCE. The look and heft of a bulb are clues to its general health. In most cases, look for plump, firm bulbs that feel heavy for their size. A soft, squashy feel usually indicates some sort of rot; lightweight and/or visibly shriveled bulbs may have lost too much moisture to recover well. (Two conspicuous exceptions are anemone and ranunculus; these usually look unpromisingly wizened.)

Ready-to-plant bulbs beckon from nursery bins.

SIZE. Big bulbs are likely to give the most impressive performance. The largest tulip *(Tulipa)* and hyacinth *(Hyacinthus)* bulbs, for example, produce larger flowers on taller, thicker stems; in the case of ranunculus, the largest roots will give you *more* flowers than will the smaller sizes. (If you're willing to give bulbs a year or two to build themselves up in your garden, though, you'll get fine results with smaller sizes — and their reduced cost makes them a good buy.)

TIMING. Finally, it's usually best to plant bulbs when they are dormant and fresh (they should not be dehydrated). The only exceptions to this rule are evergreen types such as clivia, which can be set out from containers at any time. In most cases, totally dormant bulbs are devoid of leaves and roots; in a few instances — iris and daylily *(Hemerocallis)*, for example — the bulb will have leaves and roots but will be sold at the least active period in its growth cycle. Responsible growers dig their stock at the optimum times, and retail outlets offer the bulbs as soon as they are received. Early shopping secures the freshest bulbs for planting.

SOURCES FOR BULBS

Nurseries and mail-order catalogs offer a tantalizing array of bulbs. Neither source is categorically better than the other, but each has its pros and cons.

RETAIL NURSERIES. In early autumn, retail nurseries and garden centers abound with bins and boxes of spring-blooming bulbs; the scene is repeated in early spring, when summer-flowering kinds become available. At these "hands-on" sources, you can easily check out the quality of the stock (while being seduced by the alluring color photos that accompany the display), and you can take your purchases home immediately. The only drawback to retail purchase is the limited selection: retailers tend to stock only tried-and-true best-sellers.

MAIL-ORDER SUPPLIERS. Colorful catalogs can be just as enticing as retail nurseries, but when you buy by mail, there's always a wait between order and receipt. Mail-order suppliers fall into three categories: the ultra-specialist, offering just one or a few kinds of bulbs; the general specialist, offering a broad range of different bulbs; and the general nursery catalog, which includes some bulbs among its varied offerings.

Ultra-specialists may carry a great assortment of varieties within their specialty, with prices ranging from modest to stratospheric. These catalogs appeal to specialists in the particular plants, who are willing to pay high prices for scarce novelties. The general gardener will enjoy browsing through the lower-cost offerings, which typically present more choices than retail nurseries do, at comparable prices. Many ultra-specialists grow their own stock, assuring shipment of fresh bulbs at the proper planting time.

General specialists carry more bulb types than you're likely to find at retail nurseries, though the selection within each type is more limited than that offered by an ultra-specialist. These suppliers usually do not grow the stock they sell; they buy it from specialty growers and bulb brokers. The quality of stock depends on the firm's integrity. The best ones offer top-quality bulbs shipped at the proper planting times — subject, of course, to receipt of stock from their suppliers. Freshness is comparable to that of bulbs in good retail nurseries.

General nursery catalogs, which sell bulbs in addition to a variety of other plants, are something of a calculated risk. Check shipping times to be sure they correspond with the best planting times for the bulbs offered; always look for guarantees and conditions under which you can receive a refund if quality or performance is unsatisfactory.

One final note: in any catalog, beware the words "tremendous bargain sale — end-of-season special!!" Reputable suppliers may offer genuinely good deals, but unscrupulous ones may simply be trying to unload poor-quality stock.

Match each bulb to its preferred growing conditions. Here, moisture-loving yellow flag *(Iris pseudacorus)* luxuriates in boggy pondside soil.

PLANTING

Buying top-quality bulbs assures you of the best potential first-year performance, but three other factors also influence the outcome: location, soil, and proper planting. By addressing these points at the start, you'll enjoy good performance not only in the first year, but also in the seasons to come.

LOCATION

Each entry in the encyclopedia (pages 215–291) notes a preferred exposure and year-round watering regime. Choose planting locations where the conditions match up to these needs.

SOIL

Assess the quality and condition of the soil where you want the bulbs to go. Because so many bulbs need good drainage, this is the quality to determine first (see "Soil types," above right). Many garden soils will pass muster for the majority of bulbs; any soil that grows good annuals or vegetables should be satisfactory, with no more preparation than digging and, perhaps, fertilizing (see page 201). But if you have sticky clay soil and want to grow more than common calla *(Zantedeschia aethiopica)* and yel-

low flag *(Iris pseudacorus)*, or if you have sievelike sand which would limit you to sea daffodil *(Pancratium maritimum)* or Oncocyclus irises, you'll need to make amends.

SOIL TYPES. Any soil is a dynamic combination of mineral particles, organic matter, air, and water. As water penetrates soil, it percolates through the pore spaces between particles; the air in these spaces is at first displaced, then restored as the water moves farther down or disappears through root uptake and evaporation. Poor drainage—too much water occupying the pores for too long—can drown roots and rot bulbs.

With their tiny, tightly packed particles, *clay soils* have greatly reduced pore space and, hence, poor drainage: the water-air exchange is slow, and these soils tend to remain too damp during and after rainfall or watering. *Sandy soils,* on the contrary, have good drainage in the extreme; their relatively large, loosely packed particles let water move through swiftly. Rot is seldom a problem; instead, roots can suffer from lack of moisture and nutrients unless watered and fertilized assiduously.

AMENDING THE SOIL. Both clay and sandy soils can be markedly improved with the addition of organic matter (compost, for example). In clay soils, organic materials literally force the soil structure apart; the tiny particles become grouped into larger aggregates, and water penetrates more easily. In sandy soils, organic materials become lodged in the relatively large pore spaces and function as sponges, slowing the passage of water and dissolved nutrients.

Remember that soil amendment isn't a one-time-only affair, since organic matter is always in the process of decomposition. In nature, this occurs fairly slowly: leaves and grasses, animal droppings and remains settle on the soil surface, then gradually rot away. In the artificial environment of gardens, though, we accelerate the process by intensive cultivation that involves watering and fertilizing. Thus, soil of any kind needs a periodic thorough amending, preferably done shortly before planting.

Well-composted organic matter is the champion soil amendment. Choices range from homemade compost to packaged products.

To speed up planting, use a bulb planter (TOP) or excavate the entire planting area to the correct depth (BOTTOM).

When soil is moist enough to be easily worked, dig it to a depth of 8 to 12 inches; then break up any large lumps and rake the surface smooth. Scatter fertilizer (see page 201) over the surface, then spread on a layer of organic matter. Be generous: use roughly 25 percent by volume of organic matter to soil, even more in problem soils. If you dig to a depth of 12 inches, for example, use a 3-inch-deep layer of organic material. Finally, dig or rotary-till the amendments into the soil and rake it smooth again. Ideally, let this prepared soil settle for a week before planting.

PLANTING TECHNIQUES

For each entry in the encyclopedia (pages 215–291), proper planting depth and spacing are specified under "Garden culture." With this information in your head and bulbs in hand, you're ready to plant.

For planting a small number of bulbs, nothing beats the familiar trowel. Simply dig the hole and set in the bulb so that it makes complete contact with soil at the bottom; then fill in, firming the soil around the bulb.

If you have quite a few bulbs to set out, though, planting by trowel requires too much time and effort: here, you're wiser to choose other devices and techniques. A bulb planter lets you remove plugs of soil easily: just insert, twist, and lift (and then drop in the bulb). When all bulbs are in place, rake the removed soil back into the holes. If you have a large area to plant, you may find it simpler to shovel out the soil to the proper planting depth, set out the bulbs in the arrangement you want, then cover them with the excavated soil. Follow the same plan to set out rows of bulbs: dig a trench to the correct depth, space the bulbs in it, and cover with soil.

After planting, water thoroughly to establish good contact between bulbs and soil and to provide enough moisture to initiate root growth. Subsequent watering depends on the particular bulb's needs; consult the encyclopedia.

FOILING THE SPOILERS

Underground animals can disturb bulb plantings—or even wipe them out altogether if the bulbs are especially tasty. Moles are notorious for pushing bulbs around; gophers and voles consider certain bulbs gourmet treats. In thwarting these pests, traps and poison baits have limited success. The most effective control is simply to keep the pests from reaching the bulbs—and the best way to do this is to plant your bulbs in wire baskets. A fairly small mesh (with ½-inch openings) will frustrate pillaging predators, yet easily allow bulb roots to penetrate the surrounding soil.

To make your baskets, you can use galvanized chicken wire or hardware cloth. Wire is easy to work with; hardware cloth is more difficult to cut and bend, but longer lasting. Cut a 12- by 36-inch strip of chicken wire or hardware cloth, form it into a cylinder (which will be about 12 inches in diameter), and twist or wire the ends together. To

make the bottom of the basket, cut a 12-inch square of wire or hardware cloth; attach it by folding the corners up over the sides of the cylinder and hooking them into the mesh.

Once the baskets are completed, dig holes in prepared soil and sink in the baskets. To discourage determined predators from gaining ground-level access, you can set baskets with their rims extending about 4 inches above the final soil level. Fill baskets with soil to the proper planting depth, firming the soil to prevent settling; then set in bulbs and fill in with soil the rest of the way.

You can use the same idea to construct predator-proof raised beds. After you've built the bed, tack ½-inch hardware cloth onto the bottom, then set the bed in the soil; or position the bed first, then line the bottom with hardware cloth, folding the edges to extend about 3 inches up the bed's sides. Fill the bed with soil, water well—and you're ready to plant.

Western pocket gopher

NATURALS FOR NATURALIZING

Allium (some)	*Homeria*
Anemone	*Hyacinthoides*
Brodiaea	*Hyacinthus* (some)
Calochortus	*Ipheion*
Camassia	*Ixia*
Chionodoxa	*Ixiolirion*
Colchicum	*Leucojum*
Convallaria	*Lilium* (some)
Crocosmia	*Muscari*
Crocus	*Narcissus*
Cyclamen	*Ornithogalum* (some)
Eranthis	*Puschkinia*
Erythronium	*Scilla*
Freesia	*Sparaxis*
Fritillaria	*Sternbergia*
Galanthus	*Tulipa* (some)
Habranthus	

Naturalizing Bulbs

Beds and rows of blooming bulbs are beautiful, but no less lovely are more casual plantings: a golden drift of daffodils across a grassy meadow, clumps of nodding bluebells in a woodsy clearing. If this sort of natural look is just what you want, follow the guidelines below.

CHOOSING WISELY

Not all bulbs are good naturalizers; the proven performers are listed on this page. To find out which ones will succeed for you, consult the encyclopedia (pages 215–291) for the climate each prefers. Then make sure you have an appropriate planting area—usually a sunny slope or meadow or a lightly shaded woodland, depending on the bulb. Finally, make sure the bulb's moisture needs are in sync with your region's natural rainfall (or with your ability to provide water when needed).

ACHIEVING THE EFFECT

The traditional naturalizing method is to broadcast a handful of bulbs over the desired planting area, then plant them where they fall. To achieve the most realistic effect, you may need to adjust the scatter pattern slightly: the drift should be denser at one end or toward the center, as if the bulbs began to grow in one spot, then gradually increased to colonize outlying territory. Wherever necessary, adjust spacing so bulbs will be able to grow and increase without immediate crowding.

Be sure to plant bulbs at their preferred depths, at the proper time of year. Thereafter, let nature take over. You can enhance performance, though, if you give plantings an annual application of fertilizer (see page 202).

After a number of years, you may notice a decrease in flower quantity and size. At this point, the planting is becoming overcrowded, and it's time to dig, divide, and replant. For more information on dividing, see pages 204–205.

Time-tested favorites for naturalizing include daffodil (*Narcissus;* TOP LEFT), crocus (TOP RIGHT), and hardy cyclamen (BOTTOM).

GENERAL CARE

Once your bulbs have been properly planted, they'll put down roots in preparation for their next round of growth and bloom. At this time, a little extra attention will bring rewards in the current season and build the bulbs up for a satisfying performance the year after that.

WATERING

From the moment it begins growing until some point after flowering has ceased, a bulb needs ample water. Its annual mission is to grow, flower, set seed (this step we gardeners thwart), and store nutrients for the next year. Depending on type, bulbs vary in the time over which they need water each year. Those native to areas with long, hot, dry summers typically need no water at all by summer, but many summer-flowering bulbs (native to summer-rainfall regions) need moisture until the plants shut down in autumn. Know the needs of the bulbs you grow, then tailor your supplemental watering schedule accordingly.

To do the greatest good, water must penetrate deeply. Think of a bulb—a daffodil *(Narcissus),* say—planted 6 inches deep. You can assume its roots extend at least 6 inches below that; therefore, each watering should moisten the soil to a depth of at least 1 foot. A casual sprinkling, whether provided by you or by rainfall, will not suffice.

In milder-winter regions, adequate deep watering may be furnished by rainfall in autumn, winter, and spring; in colder areas, snow melt followed by spring rains do the job. But whenever the natural supply is inadequate, be prepared to supplement it. As a general rule, *never let the root zone dry out during the growing and flowering period.*

For each bulb described on pages 215–291, you'll find information on water needs and timing. In general, *deciduous bulbs* start to enter dormancy a month or so after flowering; yellowing of foliage is a clue. At this point, you can usually reduce or withhold water (depending on the particular bulb's preference) until new root growth begins. For many spring-blooming bulbs, root growth resumes in autumn; for summer-flowering types, the next need for regular moisture usually comes the following spring.

Petite *Tulipa batalinii* 'Yellow Jewel' makes its appearance through a mulch of bark chips.

Evergreen bulbs have no true dormant period, so they can rarely go completely dry. No overall rule about water needs applies to all evergreen types, however, so be sure to consult individual encyclopedia descriptions for water requirements of the bulbs you grow.

One caution: when bulbs are in bloom, overhead watering can weigh down or topple stems of taller kinds. In rainy regions, it's wise to stake tall flowering stems; where rainfall is scant, you may want to devise an irrigation plan for use during the blooming season.

MULCHING

Mulches are nothing more than a layer of organic matter spread over the soil surface, but they bring numerous benefits. A mulch makes a planting look neat. It keeps the soil that lies beneath it cool; it conserves moisture by slowing evaporation. It helps suppress weeds by blocking the light their seeds need to germinate—and if any do sprout, they're easily pulled from the loose mulch. Finally, mulches decompose and, in the process, improve the condition of the soil.

Like many other plants, bulbs usually respond to mulching with improved performance. (Bearded irises are a notable exception; they will rot if mulched.)

The best mulches are loose or coarse enough for water to penetrate them easily, yet not so lightweight that wind can blow them away. Compost is a favorite choice; bark chips and wood chips are widely used. Pine needles are popular wherever they're available, and even thick-textured leaves (those from evergreen oaks, for example) can be satisfactory. In some areas, byproducts from regional agriculture are available as mulches: rice hulls, grape pomace (skins and crushed seeds), cotton burr compost.

FERTILIZING

Though bulbs will grow and bloom in most soils without the help of fertilizer, fertilized bulbs perform better: the plants are healthier and huskier.

FERTILIZER CHOICES. Two general forms of fertilizers are available: *dry (granular)* and *liquid*.

To apply *dry fertilizers*, you typically scatter them over the soil, then scratch them in (or dig them in, if you're preparing or reworking a planting area). If the fertilizer is the standard type, moisture quickly dissolves its granules, releasing the nutrients they contain. If the fertilizer is a timed-release sort, however, its soluble nutrients are contained in permeable synthetic pellets; a small amount of fertilizer dissolves with each watering, delivering the nutrient supply over a longer period of time. Such fertilizers are particularly convenient for container culture, since the necessary frequent waterings quickly leach nutrients from the soil.

Liquid fertilizers include both liquid and water-soluble dry concentrates. In either case, you dilute the concentrate in water, then apply the solution to the soil. Liquid fertilizers are most frequently used on container-grown bulbs, though they also give an instant boost to plants grown in the ground.

Whether dry or liquid, all fertilizers are either *complete* or *incomplete*. Complete fertilizers contain all three of the major nutrients essential for plant growth: nitrogen, phosphorus, and potassium. Incomplete types are lacking in one or two of these. For more information on the major nutrients, see "A Fertilizer Primer" (at right).

Fertilizers containing phosphorus and potassium have the greatest effect when dug into the soil before planting.

A FERTILIZER PRIMER

Most commercial fertilizers are *complete*, meaning that they contain the three major plant nutrients: nitrogen (N), phosphorus (P), and potassium (K). *Incomplete* fertilizers contain just one or two of these three; some of the so-called bulb foods, which contain only phosphorus and potassium, fall into this category, as do nitrogen-only fertilizers. The percentage of each element is stated as a number on the fertilizer label. The numbers 8-10-5, for example, identify a fertilizer that contains by volume 8 percent nitrogen, 10 percent phosphorus, and 5 percent potassium. A 10-0-0 formula contains by volume 10 percent nitrogen, but no phosphorus or potassium at all.

NITROGEN is the nutrient needed in greatest quantity for growth. It is also the element most likely to be deficient in garden soil, since it's water soluble and easily leached from soil by rain and watering. Nitrogen may be present in fertilizer in several forms, but it's usable by roots only in its nitrate form—so if you want quick results, buy a fertilizer containing nitrate nitrogen. Fertilizers containing nitrogen in organic or ammonium form (including nitrogen derived from urea or IBDU) provide a slower and more sustained release, since their nitrogen must be converted to the nitrate form in the soil before it can be assimilated.

PHOSPHORUS, the second of the three major nutrients, is expressed on fertilizer labels as phosphate (P_2O_5) and described there as "available phosphoric acid." Often billed as a bulb-builder, it is indeed important to the development of roots, bulbs, and seeds. Unlike nitrogen, it is not water soluble. Instead, the phosphoric acid binds chemically to soil particles in its immediate vicinity; from there, it is slowly released into the microscopic films of water surrounding those particles. Nearby roots can then absorb it. Thus, if phosphorus is applied to the soil surface, only roots in the top inch or two of soil will benefit.

POTASSIUM, the third major nutrient, is expressed on package labels as potash (K_2O) and described as "available" or "water-soluble" potash. In the soil, this water-soluble potash is quickly converted to insoluble *exchangeable potassium*, which roots can absorb by contact. Like phosphorus, therefore, potassium is least effective when applied to the soil surface. For greatest benefit, it must be applied near the root zone.

WHEN AND HOW TO FERTILIZE. There are three important times to fertilize bulbs: when you prepare a new planting or thoroughly rework an old one; when bulbs begin to grow each year; and after the year's bloom season has ended.

When you're preparing soil, simply scatter on dry fertilizer in the amount the package specifies, then dig or till it in. Use a high-phosphorus complete or incomplete fertilizer; so-called bulb foods are high-phosphorus types. Incorporating phosphorus and potassium into the soil gets these elements into the bulbs' root zone, where they can be assimilated. If you are planting bulbs individually, you can dig a bit of fertilizer into the bottom of each hole, then cover with 1 to 2 inches of soil before planting the bulb.

As bulbs begin to grow, they benefit from a feeding to enhance the quality of the current season's flowers. At this time, nitrogen is the needed element. Applied as a bulb is readying itself for bloom, it can increase the height of stems and the size of leaves and flowers. After flowering ends, make a second application: this will promote active root growth and improve assimilation of the other two major elements as bulbs stock up for the next year's growth.

For these second two applications—as growth begins and after bloom ends—use a dry nitrogen-only fertilizer with a modest amount of nitrogen, say 10-0-0. You also can use a complete fertilizer such as 10-10-5, but keep in mind that the phosphorus and potassium won't have much of an effect unless you can dig the fertilizer in (see below). Begin by watering the area so that soil and roots are moist; then scatter on fertilizer and water again to dissolve it. If you can lightly scratch or dig the fertilizer in, any phosphorus and potassium it contains will be more effective than they would be if applied only to the soil surface. If bulbs are planted in rows, it's easier to get these two largely immobile nutrients into the root zone: dig narrow, about 8-inch-deep trenches close to the plants (taking care not to damage roots); then scatter fertilizer in the trenches, cover it with soil, and water thoroughly.

For plantings of spring-blooming bulbs, you will apply fertilizer in early spring, then again in late spring or early summer; for summer-blooming types, the applications come in spring and again in late summer or early autumn. For autumn-flowering bulbs that grow during autumn, winter, and spring, fertilize once in autumn as foliage starts to grow, then perhaps again with a lighter application in early spring before leaves start to yellow.

Some evergreen bulbs may need fertilizing more than twice during the growing season, and perhaps at other times of year as well. For all bulbs (deciduous or evergreen) whose requirements differ from the general schedule above, specific instructions are noted in the encyclopedia (pages 215–291).

PESTS AND DISEASES

The truly trouble-free plant does not exist, but the presence of a predator doesn't always mean serious trouble. Some pests and diseases, however, can bother bulbs enough to warrant control; these are described on the facing page. Suggested controls for each pest are listed in order of increasing toxicity.

Be aware that new controls continue to be developed, while existing ones may be withdrawn from sale if research reveals that their use carries possible health or environmental hazards. For current recommendations, consult your Cooperative Extension agent or experienced nursery personnel.

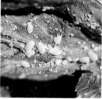

Iris borer   Mealybugs   Mites

Narcissus bulb fly   Powdery mildew   Squirrel

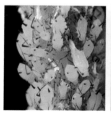

Aphids   Botrytis   Bulb rot

Snail   Thrips   Virus

PROBLEM	DESCRIPTION	CONTROLS
Aphids	Soft-bodied, rounded insects, ranging from pinhead to matchhead size; green, gray, pink, reddish brown, or black. Clustered on new growth, they suck plant juices; heavy infestations distort growth (and aid the spread of viruses).	Hose off with water; spray with insecticidal soap, pyrethrum, diazinon, malathion.
Botrytis	This fungal disease attacks leaves and flowers, weakens plants. Look for gray or brown spots, fuzzy mold spreading over decaying tissue. Damp early-spring weather favors growth; wind and rain spread spores.	Destroy infected leaves and flowers; spray with chlorothalonil.
Bulb rots	Basal rot, soft rot, and crown rot are fungal diseases that cause bulb decay; they are particularly serious in damp soil.	Plant in well-drained soils; water judiciously. Discard infected bulbs. For crown rot (white webbing with seedlike dormant spores), soak bulbs and soil with PCNB.
Iris borer	Burrowing grub attacks iris rhizomes; found from Iowa to Atlantic, Canada to Tennessee. Drab moths lay eggs in early autumn. Larvae hatch in May and June; they eat leaf edges, enter rhizomes and hollow them out.	Clean up garden in autumn; hand-pick borers; spray weekly with dimethoate from early spring through June.
Mealybugs	White, ⅛-inch insects, round to oval, fuzzy looking; cluster at bases of leaves and stems to suck plant juices. Found where air circulation is poor, particularly on house plants and container plants.	Spray with insecticidal soap, horticultural oil, diazinon, malathion, acephate; use spreader-sticker.
Mites	Tiny, spiderlike insects found on leaf undersides (often with webbing); leaf surface is pale and stippled. You'll need a magnifying glass to see them. Infestations increase rapidly in hot weather. Mites can destroy bulbs in storage.	Spray with insecticidal soap, horticultural oil, dicofol; dust stored bulbs with diazinon.
Narcissus bulb fly	Burrowing grub attacks *Narcissus*, also *Galanthus, Hymenocallis, Leucojum*. Beelike flies lay eggs in spring at leaf bases; grubs infest bulbs and hollow them out. Infested bulbs are soft, squashy.	Check bulbs before planting and destroy any grubs; dust leaves and soil with diazinon as leaves emerge.
Powdery mildew	Fungal disease leaves a powdery, white to gray covering on leaves, stems, and flower buds. Heavy infestation debilitates plant. Favored by poor air circulation, shade, weather with warm, dry days and cool, moist nights.	Avoid planting in mildew-prone locations; spray infected plants with triforine.
Rodents	Gophers and voles eat bulbs growing in the ground; mice chiefly dine on stored bulbs; chipmunks and ground squirrels dig up planted bulbs.	For gophers and voles, see "Foiling the Spoilers" (page 198); for mice, securely cover or enclose boxes of stored bulbs with screening or wire mesh; for chipmunks and ground squirrels, cover planted beds with screening or wire mesh.
Slugs and snails	Night-feeding mollusks (snails have shells, slugs do not) feast on leaves, stems, and flowers, leaving telltale trails of silvery slime. They live in cool, damp, shady places and in garden litter.	Hand-pick and squash; deter with copper strips; bait with metaldehyde, methiocarb (keep away from pets).
Thrips	Microscopic tan, brown, or black insects feed on petals, causing brown discoloration; heavy infestations distort blooms. To check, tap a flower over piece of white paper and look for moving specks.	Spray with diazinon, malathion, acephate, dimethoate.
Viruses	Microscopic organisms live in plant tissue, usually causing reduced vigor, flower distortion, streaks on flowers or leaves. Sucking insects (aphids, mealybugs) can spread viruses.	Discard all plants showing virus infection; control sucking insects.

OFF-SEASON CARE

Bulbs require the most attention from the moment they begin growth until the last flowers fade — but you'll also need to provide some care beyond the bloom season. During this post-flowering phase, your tasks will involve three main areas: dividing, storage, and (in cold-winter regions) winter protection of certain in-ground bulbs.

DIVIDING: MANY FROM ONE

With the exception of most tubers, bulbs produce increases which can be detached to establish new plantings. In fact, you will need to dig and divide periodically to keep plantings from becoming too crowded for good growth and bloom. Bulbs differ in their rate of increase: some can remain in place for years before crowding takes a toll, while others proliferate so rapidly that only frequent division will maintain quality. In general, the best time to dig and divide bulbs is at the proper planting time for your region.

STORAGE

Not all bulbs require annual digging and storage, and some need to be stored in some climates but not in others (check the encyclopedia, pages 215–291, for details on specific bulbs). Usually, though, storage is indicated when a bulb left in the ground cannot survive one of two conditions: winter cold or summer water.

In the first case, some bulbs can be grown in regions beyond their hardiness range if you dig them, then store them over winter under cool but not freezing conditions (35° to 55°F/2° to 13°C). Container-grown bulbs can remain in their pots in a dark, dry place.

In the second case, spring-flowering bulbs that demand dry summer conditions may succeed in rainy-summer areas if they are dug when leaves die back, stored dry over summer, and replanted in autumn. If you grow these bulbs in containers, you can simply withhold all moisture during the dormant phase.

The two storage methods presented below cover the needs of all popular bulbs. One cautionary note applies to both: if mice seeking shelter find your bulb storeroom, they'll have a banquet. If you suspect that mice may be a problem, securely cover or enclose the stored bulbs with screening or wire mesh.

VENTILATED STORAGE. Bulbs that have a protective tunic — such as narcissus and gladiolus — can be stored in mesh bags or piled loosely in boxes or baskets. Exposure to air keeps them dry and discourages rot, while the protective skin helps prevent dehydration.

To prepare bulbs for ventilated storage, follow this sequence (any exceptions are noted in the encyclopedia entries for individual bulbs). When foliage has yellowed, dig bulbs from the ground or knock them from their containers. Remove leaves and soil; then spread the bulbs on newspapers in a shaded location and let them dry for several days. It's best not to separate bulbs before storage, since broken surfaces offer easy entry for disease organisms and increase the chance of dehydration. Store the dried bulbs in a cool, dry, dark place (35° to 55°F/2° to 13°C) until the proper planting time for your area.

DIVIDING BULBS

When a bulb planting has become crowded, or when you want to make additional plantings of a favorite bulb, it's time to dig and divide. Because each of the five bulb types—true bulb, corm, tuber, rhizome, tuberous root—produces its increases in a diferent fashion, the division technique you use will depend on the bulb you're working with. The illustrations at right give instructions for dividing each of the five types.

True bulbs form increases that remain attached to a common basal plate. To divide, carefully break apart connected bulbs at base. For lilies, remove outer scales from basal plate, dip base ends in rooting hormone, and plant.

Corms renew themselves each growing season: a new corm and small increases (cormels) form on top of the old corm, which becomes flattened, shriveled, and worn out. To divide, separate healthy new corms and any cormels from the old corms.

COVERED STORAGE. A number of bulbs (caladium and begonia, for example) lack a protective covering; if exposed to the air for long after digging, they'll begin to shrivel. If dehydration continues during storage, the bulb may die or become severely debilitated before replanting time.

Dig and dry these bulbs as directed for "Ventilated storage" (facing page). Then place them in a single layer in a box or clay pot, making sure they don't touch one another (should any bulb rot during storage, the separation lessens the chance of decay spreading from one bulb to another). Cover with dry sand, vermiculite, sawdust, perlite, or peat moss, using enough to cover bulbs by about ½ inch. Replant bulbs at the proper time for your area, dividing them at that time if needed. If any appear dry or shriveled, plump them up in moist sand before replanting.

WINTER PROTECTION FOR IN-GROUND BULBS

Some bulbs may successfully remain in the ground in regions a bit colder than their preferred zones if you give them above-ground winter protection. A layer of insulating material spread over the soil surface has two benefits. First, it keeps the soil temperature from dipping as low as that of unprotected earth. Second, it *moderates* temperature—a critical point in snowless winters or in any region where weather is likely to alternate between warm and bitter cold. During bursts of springlike temperatures, protected ground remains colder than unprotected ground, and the bulbs under cover remain inactive; they aren't tricked into producing growth which would then be killed by a return to subfreezing weather.

It's important to apply winter protection at the right time. After the first hard frost in autumn, spread a 4- to 6-inch layer of protective material over the soil. A variety of materials can be used. Regional favorites include conifer boughs; marsh, prairie, and salt hay; and ground corn cobs. Whatever you use, make sure that winter snows and rains won't pack it into an airtight mass.

Leave the protection in place until just before the start of the normal spring growing period; then rake it aside.

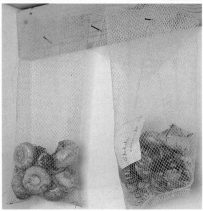

The kind of winter storage you provide for dormant bulbs depends on the particular bulb. Some need covered storage (TOP); others prefer ventilated storage (BOTTOM).

Tubers increase in size and number of growing points as they age, but most don't form discrete increases. To divide, cut a large tuber into two or more sections, making sure each section has one or more growing points.

Rhizomes produce new plants from growth points that form along their sides. To divide, break apart sections at the natural "waists" between them, making sure each division has at least one growing point.

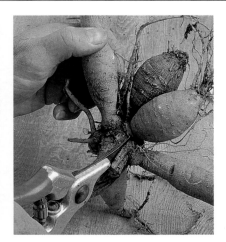

Tuberous roots form multiple growing points. Some, like daylily *(Hemerocallis),* form separate plants that can be pulled apart; others, like dahlia (above), do not. To divide the latter, cut apart so that each root has a growth bud.

BULBS IN CONTAINERS

Growing bulbs in containers entails no more effort than growing them in the ground. The few extra steps involved are balanced by reduced labor for soil preparation and planting. And since so many bulbs take well to container culture, you have a wide range of choices — though you may have some difficulty narrowing the field.

Planting bulbs with successive flowering times will let you enjoy months of uninterrupted bloom: as one colorful potful of flowers fades, bring on another that's just coming into blossom. This sort of portability also makes it easy to rearrange your garden — just move the pots to new locations.

CHOOSING CONTAINERS

Suitable containers for bulbs are so numerous that you should have no trouble finding the look you want. Six basic sorts are described at right.

Positioned atop a garden pedestal, delicate *Zephyranthes candida* stands out amid the surrounding foliage.

Potted springtime extravaganza features tulips *(Tulipa)* in red shades, daffodils *(Narcissus)* in both yellow and white with orange cups, and orange-red crown imperial *(Fritillaria imperialis)*.

Unglazed clay (terra-cotta) pots are the old stand-bys, available in a great assortment of sizes and shapes; some even have surface decoration. Because moisture evaporates through the pot as well as from the soil surface, plants in these pots need the closest attention to watering.

Glazed clay containers retain moisture much better than their unglazed counterparts. Choose color and decoration carefully — you don't want the pot to compete or clash with the flowers it displays.

Wooden containers offer a neutral, earthy-looking foil for plants of any sort. They retain moisture as well as glazed clay, and their thicker sides provide better insulation from extremes of temperature. Decay-resistant woods like cedar, cypress, and redwood make the longest-lasting containers.

Concrete and aggregate containers are heavier and costlier than other types, but their moisture retention is excellent and they provide the best insulation of any kind of container.

Plastic containers, ranging from purely utilitarian black or green nursery "cans" to red-brown imitations of unglazed clay pots, are as moisture retentive as glazed clay pots and usually less expensive than unglazed clay ones.

Paper pulp pots are lightweight and inexpensive; they come in earthy tones of tan to dark brown. They retain moisture better than unglazed clay, but not as well as other types. They last for about 3 years at best.

PLANTING

Some bulbs are nearly always grown in containers—achimenes and gloxinia *(Sinningia speciosa)*, for example. In these cases, you'll find detailed instructions for container culture in "An Encyclopedia of Favorite Bulbs" (pages 215–291). The majority of bulbs that may be grown in containers, however, fall into the three basic groups described below.

GROUP A. These are largely tropical and subtropical plants; many of them grow from tubers. All need a moisture-retentive but fast-draining soil mix. The following formula works well:

> *1 part peat moss*
> *1 part compost or leaf mold*
> *1 part perlite*

Mix a complete fertilizer (approximately 5-10-5 formulation) into the potting mix, using the quantity the label specifies. Plant bulbs at the depth and spacing recommended in their encyclopedia entries.

GROUP B. Bulbs in this group fall into two subgroups, based on the duration of their container lifetime.

Subgroup 1. These bulbs perform well in a container for one season, but should be set out in the garden at their next proper planting time. Narcissus, tulip *(Tulipa),* and crocus are three familiar examples. Because these bulbs will be in a container for just one flowering season, you can space them closely and plant them with their tips just beneath the soil surface.

Subgroup 2. The many bulbs in this subgroup can succeed in containers for more than one year, provided they receive the dormant conditions they need. Alstroemeria, lily-of-the-valley *(Convallaria majalis),* and freesia are a few of these. Plant them a few inches apart, at the depth recommended in their encyclopedia descriptions. Divide and repot when flower quality and quantity decline.

For either subgroup of group B, you can choose from two potting mixes.

For a mix that drains rapidly, use:

> *1 part peat moss*
> *1 part other organic material (compost, leaf mold,*
> *   ground bark)*
> *1 part builder's sand*

For a more moisture-retentive mix, use:

> *1 part soil (loam to sandy loam — not clay)*
> *1 part peat moss*
> *1 part builder's sand*

Mix a complete fertilizer (approximately 5-10-5 formulation) into either mix, using the quantity the label specifies.

GROUP C. These bulbs can remain in one container for several to many years. Agapanthus, clivia, amaryllis *(Hippeastrum),* and common calla *(Zantedeschia aethiopica)* are among the better-known individuals.

Because these plants will be contained for several years, be sure you choose fairly sizable containers—at least 8 inches across and 12 inches deep—to accommodate good root growth. Use either of the soil mixes suggested under group B; plant bulbs a few inches apart, at the depth recommended in their encyclopedia entries. Some of the bulbs in this group actually perform better when roots are crowded; they need repotting (and perhaps dividing) only when the containers are crowded almost to the bursting point.

WATERING

The water needs noted in the encyclopedia entry for each bulb apply to container-grown as well as in-ground bulbs. Remember, though, that container plants can dry out quickly, due to the limited amount of soil and the container's exposure. Be sure to keep soil moist during the growth and flowering period.

FERTILIZING

Bulbs in containers for just one flowering season (group B, subgroup 1) need no fertilizer beyond that which you add to the potting mix. Bulbs that will stay in containers for 2 years or more will appreciate further attention.

Liquid fertilizers and timed-release dry types (see page 201) are the fertilizers of choice. Liquids give plants an instant boost but have little staying power, since nutrients are quickly leached from the container with each watering. In general, apply them monthly during the growing season, diluted according to package directions; or apply every 2 weeks, diluted to half-strength. Always water the soil thoroughly before applying the fertilizer solution.

Parrot tulips spring from an equally flamboyant glazed clay container (TOP); strawberry pot houses a collection of crocus (BOTTOM).

Timed-release fertilizers can be applied less often than liquids, since they release nutrients gradually over time (the period of effectiveness depends on the particular formulation). One application at the start of the growing season may be sufficient; for evergreen bulbs in group C, a second application about 4 months later is often beneficial.

GROWING BULBS

INDOORS

If you enjoy bringing pots of blooming bulbs indoors to brighten and decorate your living space, why not grow bulbous plants specifically for interior use? It's easy — and what's more, it's fun to watch from close quarters as those bare, drab seemingly lifeless chunks of stem or root are transformed into full-fledged plants with dazzling flowers or foliage.

For seasonal color indoors, you can "force" many bulbs: by manipulating temperature and light, you can fool them into growing and flowering earlier than they would in nature. This technique lets you enjoy blooms in winter rather than waiting for spring — a welcome prospect anywhere, but especially in regions where winters are cold. In those frosty climates, forced bulbs provide a living source of color while the outdoor garden rests. The following pages offer simple directions for forcing popular bulbs as well as other smaller, less well-known bulbs. You'll also learn how to grow some types, such as hyacinth, directly in water.

You may find seasonal color from bulbs so pleasing that you decide to grow these plants indoors year-round. This is easily done in a greenhouse, but fortunately, quite a few bulbs thrive as house plants too. Some retain their foliage all year; others die down for a re-energizing respite, then grow back to delight you all over again.

Colorful flowering bulbs bring cheer on dreary winter days.

GIVE COLD TREATMENT

The following need cold treatment for forced early bloom.

Allium (small types no taller than 1 foot are best)

Anemone blanda

Camassia

Chionodoxa

Convallaria majalis

Crocus (nearly all spring-blooming types can be forced, but Dutch hybrids are best)

Eranthis hyemalis

Fritillaria meleagris

Galanthus

Hyacinthus orientalis

Ipheion uniflorum

Iris (Reticulata types)

Leucojum (Israeli-grown bulbs do especially well)

Muscari

Narcissus (trumpet, large-cupped, and small-cupped daffodils; Cyclamineus hybrids)

Scilla (except *S. peruviana)*

Tulipa (Single Early, Double Early, Double Late, Triumph, and species tulips)

KEEP OUT OF THE COLD

The following bulbs do not need cold treatment, since they are native to mild-winter areas.

Anemone coronaria

Colchicum

Crocus (fall-blooming types)

Freesia

Iris (Dutch hybrids)

Ixia

Narcissus (Tazettas identified as "Paper Whites" or "indoor narcissus")

Ranunculus asiaticus

Scilla peruviana

FORCING BULBS

Because newly purchased bulbs already contain the embryonic bloom for the following season, you can — with a bit of extra effort — manipulate conditions to induce flowering before the normal outdoor bloom season. This process, popularly known as "forcing," takes advantage of the fact that bulbs have certain minimum requirements for each stage prior to bloom. Because outdoor climate slows development, bulbs in the ground usually spend more than the minimally necessary time in these prebloom stages. Under a forcing regime, however, you can control conditions so each stage is completed as quickly as possible.

Not all bulbs respond well to forcing, though many of the most popular spring bloomers do (see list at left). When perusing catalogs, look for species and varieties described as "good for forcing." For the most satisfying results, buy the largest top-quality bulbs you can find: they have the most stored energy and thus are most likely to succeed in a process that draws heavily on their food reserves.

To make sure the bulbs bloom when you want them to do so, you'll need to calculate planting time carefully. Natives of mild-winter areas bloom the soonest after planting, since they don't need a prolonged period of cold. The more tender Tazetta narcissus varieties (often sold as "Paper Whites," though 'Paper White' is more properly the name of one variety) will bloom 5 to 7 weeks after planting. Hardy bulbs (those native to cold-winter regions) typically bloom after 13 to 15 weeks of cold treatment for root and early shoot development, followed by 3 to 4 weeks of warmth and light to induce flowering. Some of the hardy types that bloom earliest in nature—glory-of-the-snow *(Chionodoxa)*, winter aconite *(Eranthis hyemalis)*, and snowdrop *(Galanthus)*—may get by with only 12 weeks of cold before being brought into the light. Hardy bulbs are usually planted in October or November for bloom in January through April.

Some bulbs needing cold treatment, such as hyacinth *(Hyacinthus)* and lily-of-the-valley *(Convallaria majalis)*, can be purchased pre-chilled; you may see the terms "precooled" or

Various plants can fill a single pot.

Smaller-growing kinds of narcissus are excellent container subjects.

"pretreated." In fact, the bulbs are only partially chilled, saving you 3 or 4 weeks of cold treatment. The supplier should indicate how much longer the bulbs must be chilled after you receive them.

POTTING THE BULBS

Any kind of pot with drainage holes will do for forcing, though wider-than-tall bulb pots and bulb pans are ideal. Do make sure, though, that the pot is at least twice as tall as the bulb to allow adequate space for roots. Fill the pot loosely with either of the soil mixes described for group B on page 207; if you intend to transplant the bulb into the garden after bloom, add 1 tablespoon of 5-10-5 fertilizer per 6-inch pot.

Space the bulbs close together—for example, about 15 crocuses, 6 narcissus or tulips *(Tulipa)*, or 3 hyacinths *(Hyacinthus)* per 6-inch pot—and barely cover them with mix. Plant tulips with the flat side facing the outside of the pot, so that the first and largest leaf will also face that way and cover the rim of the pot. Water to settle the soil, but don't compact it. Label the pot with the bulb name and planting date.

Bulbs that do not need cold treatment can now be placed in a cool, well-lit spot (55° to 60°F/13° to 16°C), then moved to warmer conditions (65° to 75°F/18° to 24°C) when the buds begin to show color. For bulbs requiring cold treatment, follow the directions below.

PROVIDING COLD TREATMENT

The hardy bulbs need a prolonged period in dark, moist, chilly conditions (35° to 50°F/2° to 10°C) to get off to a good start; without this treatment, they tend to produce foliage and no flowers. Possible cooling sites include an old refrigerator, unheated basement or garage, service porch, cold frame, or trench dug in the ground and lined with wire mesh to keep mice away. Pots kept outdoors should be mulched with leaves, sawdust, straw, or other material to protect against freezing and to exclude light. If indoor pots will be exposed to light, put them in closed cupboards or cover them (by inverting baskets over them, for example). Make sure the bulbs don't dry out.

Start checking for top growth after 12 or 13 weeks. The bulbs are ready for forcing when shoots are about 1 inch high or a little taller. The emerging leaves will be white, since they formed in the dark, but they'll color up when exposed to light. Roots growing through the drainage holes are another sign that bulbs are ready for forcing, even if top growth isn't evident. Move the containers to a cool, well-lit spot (55° to 60°F/13° to 16°C); if you want to stagger bloom, bring them out a few at a time, every 2 weeks. When buds begin to show color, shift to a warmer, sunny location (65° to 75°F/18° to 24°C). Once flowers open, though, cooler conditions will lengthen their life. Keep plants well watered.

With the exception of amaryllis *(Hippeastrum;* see "Forcing Amaryllis," page 212), forced bulbs cannot be forced for a second

Dutch hybrid crocus poke through openings in a ceramic pot.

season. After bloom is over, you can set them out in the garden; in a year or two, they may build themselves up enough to flower at the normal time. Forced tulips, however, rarely bloom again.

WATER CULTURE

Some bulbs can be grown with their roots in water. Dutch hybrid hyacinth *(Hyacinthus)* and narcissus are the most familiar examples, though other choices are possible as well. Because bulbs cultivated in this manner expend all their energy, they should be discarded after bloom.

HYACINTH GLASS

The bulb most often grown this way is the hyacinth; in fact, it has lent its name to the special glass forcing vessel, which resembles an hourglass or egg cup. The bulb rests in the smaller upper section, while the roots grow in the larger, water-filled lower part. Other bulbs suited to this type of culture are Dutch hybrid crocus, dwarf early-flowering tulips *(Tulipa)*, snowdrop *(Galanthus)*, grape hyacinth *(Muscari)*, squill *(Scilla)*, and meadow saffron *(Colchicum)*. More petite containers are sold for smaller bulbs, which would fall through the opening of a traditional hyacinth glass.

Hyacinth in glass

To "plant" the glass, fill it with water to within ⅛ inch of the bulb base, then add a small piece of activated charcoal to discourage the growth of algae. Place the planted glass in a dark, cool place (around 55°F/13°C) until roots are well developed and top growth has begun; add more water as necessary during this time to keep the level just beneath the bulb's base. If the water looks murky, hold the bulb in place as you change the water; don't take the bulb out, since you won't be able to get the roots back into the glass without damaging them. When growth is underway, transfer the glass to a fairly cool spot (65° to 68°F/18° to 20°C) with plenty of light.

PEBBLES AND WATER

This method is most often used to force the fall- and winter-blooming Tazetta narcissus varieties ('Paper White' and similar types) that don't need a prolonged cool, dark period for root growth before they send up leaves. The interval between starting and blooming is 5 to 7 weeks. If you make your first planting in October and plant at 2-week intervals until December, you can have flowering narcissus indoors over a 2-month period. Hardy narcissus varieties and Dutch hybrid hyacinths are sometimes grown this way too.

Fill a shallow pan with pebbles, stone chips, or coarse sand. Crowd in the bulbs, anchoring them by heaping pebbles all around them, leaving only the top ½ inch or so of each bulb exposed. Then add water until the level reaches just below the base of the bulbs. As for bulbs in a hyacinth glass, start plants in a cool, dark spot, then move to a warmer, sunny spot when growth is underway. Add more water as needed.

Narcissus varieties are ideal candidates for growing in pebbles and water.

FORCING AMARYLLIS

With a minimum of effort, you can bring amaryllis (Hippeastrum) into bloom for the winter holidays. Nurseries and mail-order firms offer bulbs already planted in special plastic containers; if you buy one of these, all you have to do is water and wait. Or buy bulbs and pot them up yourself.

Nurseries usually offer one or more types of amaryllis bulbs: African, Dutch, Giant Dutch, or Royal Dutch Hybrids. For winter holiday bloom, choose those labeled African. These are grown to blooming size in South Africa, then stored and shipped under controlled conditions. When removed from cold storage, the bulbs sprout quickly and flower in 4 to 6 weeks. For sure bloom at Christmas, plant bulbs around November 15. Most Dutch varieties are dug and shipped from Holland in September; they will bloom 7 to 8 weeks after planting.

For each bulb, choose a container that allows 2 inches between all sides of the bulb and the container edges. Fill containers with one of the soil mixes recommended for group B (page 207); plant so that the neck and top half of the bulb protrude above the soil surface.

Water thoroughly after planting, then give just enough water to keep soil barely moist until active growth begins. Keep containers in a bright, warm room (70° to 75°F/21° to 24°C during the day, 60° to 65°F/16° to 18°C at night); turn them frequently so the flower stems will grow upright rather than leaning toward the light. As each bloom fades, cut it off to prevent seed formation. After all flowers have withered, cut off the entire stem at its base.

Leaves appear either during or after bloom. For good performance the following year, it's important to keep the plant growing vigorously; water regularly and give bimonthly applications of liquid fertilizer diluted to half strength. If you allow the leaves to wither naturally in fall, the plant will bloom at its normal time the following spring. If you'd like to schedule another holiday bloom, however, proceed as follows. Stop fertilizing 5 to 6 months after flowering ends; then taper off watering over the next 3 to 4 weeks. When foliage yellows, cut it off; then store the dry potted bulbs in a cool closet, basement, or garage where temperatures will remain above freezing (ideally around 40° to 50°F/4° to 10°C). About 4 to 8 weeks before bloom is desired, move the pots back into a bright, warm room and resume watering to start the next cycle of growth and flowering.

GROWING BULBS INDOORS YEAR-ROUND

A number of bulbs thrive indoors much or all of the year. In some cases, the climate dictates this treatment: the bulbs you want to grow may not succeed year-round in the garden. Other times, you may simply want to grow bulbs indoors for decorative purposes. Whatever your reasons, you'll enjoy having your favorites close up, where their flowers and foliage can be easily appreciated.

Cyrtanthus elatus 'Snow White'

BULBS AS HOUSE PLANTS

The bulbous plants most commonly grown indoors are the spring bloomers, such as hyacinth *(Hyacinthus)*, tulip *(Tulipa)*, and narcissus. Although they're breathtaking in bloom, their tenure as house plants is fleeting—especially if they must be hidden away for months of cold treatment before the floral display. After the flowers fade, most types must be planted in the garden or simply thrown away.

For bulbs with more staying power as house plants, look to those from mild-winter areas (many successful choices are native to South Africa). Such bulbs adapt better to indoor conditions than do those from colder regions. This group includes some evergreen kinds that look attractive all year; examples are clivia, Scarborough lily *(Cyrtanthus elatus)*, *Tulbaghia,* and some species of agapanthus. Others die down and should be stashed away for their dormant period; you can store the pot dry in a cool, dark place, then bring it out again after new growth appears.

Check the growing conditions specified for the various bulbs in the encyclopedia (pages 215–291). Plant at the appropriate time, in the soil mix recommended under "Container culture." Like most other house plants, bulbs grown indoors appreciate regular light feedings. Most need bright indirect sunlight during active growth and bloom; a location in a south-facing window is ideal, especially during the winter months, when light is often at a premium. If your house is very dry, raise the moisture level with a humidifier or place the potted plants atop pebbles in trays partially filled with water.

BULBS IN THE GREENHOUSE

You can grow just about any bulb in a greenhouse, though you probably won't want to do so for types that succeed perfectly well year-round in your garden. The value of a greenhouse is in providing growing conditions that your garden doesn't. In cold-winter areas, a greenhouse will protect tender bulbs from freezing; in moist-summer regions, it will keep rain away from bulbs that rot if they get too much moisture; in arid climates, it will elevate the humidity around tropical plants.

If you live in a mild-winter area and your goal is simply to keep rain at bay or provide humidity in summer, an unheated greenhouse may be sufficient. In all other regions, some heat is necessary for year-round use. A fairly cool greenhouse is useful for growing bulbs that experience cool, moist weather in winter and early spring, such as baboon flower *(Babiana)*, cape cowslip *(Lachenalia)*, and harlequin flower *(Sparaxis tricolor)*. Kept warmer, the greenhouse is an ideal place to grow tender bulbs such as achimenes, caladium, and gloxinia *(Sinningia speciosa)*.

HOUSE PLANT CANDIDATES

Agapanthus (some)
Begonia × **tuberhybrida**
Caladium bicolor
Clivia
Crinum
Cyclamen persicum
Cyrtanthus elatus
Eucharis × **grandiflora**
Eucomis
Gloriosa rothschildiana
Hippeastrum
Hymenocallis narcissiflora
Lachenalia
Ornithogalum thyrsoides
Oxalis
Scadoxus multiflorus katharinae
Sinningia speciosa
Sparaxis tricolor
Sprekelia formosissima
Tulbaghia
Veltheimia bracteata
Zantedeschia aethiopica
Zephyranthes grandiflora

Cyclamen persicum

Zantedeschia aethiopica

AN ENCYCLOPEDIA OF

FAVORITE BULBS

From Achimenes *to* Zephyranthes, *a dazzling world of bulbs awaits your discovery in the following 76 pages. Some of the plants presented here are favorites dear to generations of gardeners; others are well-known regional choices or less-familiar bulbs deserving of wider recognition. The descriptions in this chapter will help you decide how well each bulb suits your climate and garden conditions. Every entry begins with a list of at-a-glance information — a quick reference to the bulb's plant family, type, height, sun and water needs, and preferred climate. For a line-by-line explanation, see "Reading the entries" (page 216).*

Within each entry, you'll find comments on the plant's native territory and its typical appearance, followed by descriptions of the species and varieties you may encounter at nurseries or in catalogs. Next come ideas for using the plant in your garden. "Garden culture" discusses planting techniques and care for bulbs grown in the ground, while "Container culture" covers the same subjects for those in pots. Some entries lack a discussion of container care; for these bulbs, open-ground planting is the only successful treatment. A very few bulbs (Sinningia, *for example) are grown exclusively in containers. For these, no garden culture is given.*

Spring-blooming bulbs in full splendor include various tulips, dainty anemones, and a blue wash of grape hyacinths *(Muscari);* lofty red and yellow crown imperial *(Fritillaria imperialis)* presides over the scene.

THE YEAR IN FLOWERS

Throughout the year, bulbs of one sort or another are in bloom. The greatest number put on a show in spring and summer, but the other seasons are by no means bulb-free. Use these lists to guide your choices for seasonal color impact.

SPRING

Allium
Alstroemeria
Anemone
Arum
Babiana
Bletilla striata
Brodiaea
Calochortus
Camassia
Chionodoxa
Clivia miniata
Colchicum luteum
Convallaria majalis
Corydalis solida
Crinum
Crocus
Cyclamen
Dietes
Eranthis hyemalis
Eremurus
Erythronium
Freesia
Fritillaria
Galanthus
Gladiolus
Hemerocallis
Hippeastrum
Homeria collina

Hyacinthoides
Hyacinthus
Ipheion uniflorum
Iris
Ixia
Ixiolirion tataricum
Lachenalia
Leucojum
Lilium
Muscari
Narcissus
Ornithogalum
Oxalis
Puschkinia scilloides
Ranunculus asiaticus
Rhodohypoxis baueri
Scadoxus multiflorus
 katharinae
Scilla
Sparaxis tricolor
Tritonia
Tulbaghia
Tulipa
Veltheimia bracteata
Watsonia
Zantedeschia
Zephyranthes

SUMMER

Achimenes
Agapanthus
Allium
Alstroemeria
Amaryllis belladonna
Arisaema
Begonia
Belamcanda chinensis
Brodiaea
Caladium bicolor
Calochortus
Canna
Cardiocrinum giganteum
Colchicum
Crinum
Crocosmia
Cyclamen
Cyrtanthus elatus
Dahlia
Dietes
Eucomis
Galtonia candicans
Gladiolus
Gloriosa rothschildiana
Habranthus
Hemerocallis
Homeria collina
Hymenocallis

Iris
Liatris
Lilium
Lycoris
Oxalis
Pancratium maritimum
Polianthes tuberosa
Rhodohypoxis baueri
Scadoxus multiflorus
 katharinae
Sinningia speciosa
Sprekelia formosissima
Tigridia pavonia
Tulbaghia
Watsonia
Zantedeschia
Zephyranthes

AUTUMN

Begonia
Canna
Colchicum
Crocus
Cyclamen
Cyrtanthus elatus
Dahlia
Dietes
Gladiolus
Hemerocallis

Iris
Leucojum
Lycoris
Nerine
Oxalis
Polianthes tuberosa
Schizostylis coccinea
Sternbergia lutea
Tulbaghia
Zephyranthes

WINTER

Chionodoxa
Clivia miniata
Crocus
Cyclamen
Dietes
Eranthis hyemalis
Eucharis ×
 grandiflora
Galanthus
Iris
Lachenalia
Leucojum
Narcissus
Oxalis
Scilla
Tulbaghia
Veltheimia bracteata

READING THE ENTRIES

Each entry begins with the bulb's botanical name, followed by its common name (if one exists) and the name of its plant family. The next line identifies the bulb type: true bulb, corm, tuber, rhizome, or tuberous root. The following line, introduced by the symbol ▲, gives the plant's height range, covering all species and varieties mentioned in the entry.

Exposure needs are stated next. ☼ means bright, unshaded sun; ● means no direct sun at all. ◑ indicates light shade, part shade, or filtered sun. A location in *light shade* receives no direct sun but plenty of light; such a spot is brighter than one in full shade. A location in *part shade* is sunny during the cooler morning hours, shaded in the afternoon. A spot in *filtered sun* receives shade with shafts of light (as under a shade canopy or lath, for example).

Summer moisture needs are highlighted on the next line. ● means the bulb must have summer water to survive, while ○ means it must have dry conditions. ◑ means the bulb can take summer moisture or leave it.

✎ identifies the climate zones (see pages 644–648) where the bulb is known to succeed outside in the ground year-round. A number of bulbs, however, can be grown outdoors beyond the listed zones for the better part of the year if given special treatment, as noted under "Garden culture" and "Container culture" in individual entries.

If the plant or any of its parts is known to be poisonous, this is noted in the last line, next to the symbol ◊. Plants not so marked may have poisonous parts, but their toxicity is not well known.

Derived from species native to Central America and the Caribbean, these plants put on a lavish floral display throughout summer and early fall, often blooming so profusely that the slender stems and hairy, pointed oval leaves are almost obscured from view. Each flower is a five-lobed, flat-faced trumpet, 1 to 3 inches across; colors include purple, orchid, lavender, blue, white, pink, red, and orange. Nurseries offer plants in single as well as mixed colors; specialty growers sometimes carry named varieties and occasionally the species *A. longiflora*.

USES. This plant looks its best when displayed in containers—individual pots, planters, or hanging baskets.

CONTAINER CULTURE. Plant the small, irregularly shaped rhizomes in late winter or early spring, maintaining a minimum temperature of 60°F/16°C to encourage sprouting. Plant about 1 inch deep in a mixture of half moist peat moss, half sand; when plants are about 3 inches tall, transplant them to containers filled with a potting mix of equal parts peat moss, leaf mold, and perlite. Or plant rhizomes directly in their intended containers (using the potting mix just described), setting them ½ to 1 inch deep and about 2 inches apart (plant 6 to 12 in a 6-inch pot).

During the growing season, pinch back new growth if you want plump, bushy plants; leave growth unchecked for hanging basket specimens.

Water growing plants regularly. Once a month, apply a liquid fertilizer diluted to half strength. When day length shortens, flowering will lessen, then cease. As blooming ends, gradually cut back on water and let plants die down. Store dormant rhizomes over winter in a dry, cool location (but no cooler than 40°F/4°C). Leave rhizomes in their containers, or unpot them and store in dry perlite or vermiculite. Rhizomes stored in their containers should be unpotted and replanted in fresh potting mix at the proper planting time the following year.

ACHIMENES

Gesneriaceae

RHIZOME

- ▲ 1 TO 2 FEET (SOME TRAILING)
- ☽ LIGHT SHADE
- ◗ NEEDS SUMMER MOISTURE
- ✎ SOMETIMES GROWN IN BEDS IN ZONES 25, 26

Achimenes 'Minette'

Thanks to their fountainlike clumps of strap-shaped leaves, both evergreen and deciduous agapanthus are attractive foliage plants when not in flower. During bloom time, their cool blue or white blossoms provide a refreshing contrast to yellow and orange in the summer garden. Height of flowering stems ranges from 1 to 5 feet depending on the species or variety, but all plants are built along the same lines: thick stems, each topped by a rounded cluster of tubular to bell-shaped blooms, rise from the leaf clumps.

All agapanthus are native to South Africa's Cape Province. The two most commonly sold species, both evergreen, are *A. orientalis* and *A. africanus*. Both these species are also offered under the name *A. umbellatus*—and to confuse matters further, *A. orientalis*, now properly called *A. praecox orientalis*, is often sold as *A. africanus*. If you're intent on purchasing a particular species, buy blooming plants and check the appearance of the flower clusters carefully (see descriptions below).

A. orientalis is the tallest species, with the broadest leaves and the most flowers (up to 100) per cluster. Some nurseries sell named selections in white and various shades of light to fairly dark blue; 'Flore Pleno' has double blue blossoms. More often, you'll find plants labeled only as "white" or "blue." If you want a particular blue shade, choose plants while they're in bloom.

Narrower leaves, shorter stems (to about 1½ feet), and fewer flowers (up to 30) per cluster characterize *A. africanus*. Its blooms are deep blue.

The Headbourne Hybrids are a group of named varieties that include light through dark blue shades as well as white. Most are deciduous, with flowering stems rising to about 2 feet high. Some nurseries sell selections labeled simply by color.

Listing continues >

AGAPANTHUS

AGAPANTHUS, LILY-OF-THE-NILE

Amaryllidaceae

RHIZOME WITH FLESHY ROOTS

- ▲ 1 TO 5 FEET
- ☀ ☽ FULL SUN; PART OR LIGHT SHADE WHERE SUMMERS ARE HOT
- ◗ PREFERS SUMMER MOISTURE
- ✎ ZONES 3–9, 12–21, 28–31, WARMER PARTS OF 32 FOR DECIDUOUS KINDS; 7–9, 12–31 FOR EVERGREEN KINDS

Agapanthus 'Peter Pan'

Agapanthus orientalis

The deciduous species *A. inapertus* is as tall and nearly as many-flowered as *A. orientalis,* but its tubular deep blue blossoms are pendent.

For foreground plantings—even small-scale ground covers—choose from among a number of low varieties. Evergreen 'Peter Pan' has blue flowers carried on 1- to 1½-foot stems emerging from foliage clumps no more than a foot high. 'Tinkerbell' looks much the same, but its leaves are margined in creamy white. 'Peter Pan Albus' is white flowered and a bit larger overall than the preceding varieties; it's similar to or the same as 'Rancho White' (also sold as 'Dwarf White' and 'Rancho'). Deciduous 'Queen Anne' has blue flowers carried on 2-foot stems over foliage clumps to 15 inches high.

USES. Use the larger types as accent clumps or in mass or border plantings. Smaller kinds are fine for foreground or pathway plantings.

GARDEN CULTURE. Where summers are cool or mild, choose a planting area in full sun; in hot regions, plants need light shade all day (or at least some shade during the heat of the afternoon). Plants tolerate heavy soils and will put up with infrequent watering once established, but they perform best with good, well-drained soil and regular moisture during active growth and bloom. Protect from slugs and snails.

Agapanthus is sold only in containers. Set out plants in spring or summer, setting them about 1½ feet apart and at the same depth they were growing in their pots. Divide infrequently, only when clumps show a decline in vigor and flower quality—perhaps every 6 years. Early spring is the best time to divide all types, though evergreen types can also be divided in autumn.

CONTAINER CULTURE. All types are superb container plants, and as such are easily grown in areas beyond their hardiness range if given winter protection. All perform best when crowding the container to capacity. Follow directions "C" on page 207. Where winters are too cold for outdoor survival (evergreen types survive to about 20°F/−7°C, deciduous kinds to about 10°F/−12°C), move containers to a sheltered location where plants will receive some light and temperatures will remain above freezing. Water plants just often enough to keep leaves from wilting. Return containers outdoors in spring when danger of frost is past.

ALLIUM
ORNAMENTAL ALLIUM,
FLOWERING ONION
Liliaceae
TRUE BULB

- ▲ 6 INCHES TO OVER 5 FEET
- ☼ FULL SUN
- ◗ ○ WITHHOLD WATER AFTER BLOOM
- ✄ ZONES VARY BY SPECIES (SEE "GARDEN CULTURE")

Most people are acquainted with certain alliums without even realizing it: onions, garlic, shallots, chives, and leeks all belong to this genus. Native mainly to the Northern Hemisphere, the numerous species bear rounded, compact or loose clusters of small flowers—in blue, lavender, violet, red, pink, yellow, or white—at the tops of leafless stems in spring or summer. The tallest types reach 5 feet or more, while the shortest top out at under 1 foot; between these extremes are many of intermediate stature. Here, grouped according to height, are the most readily available species. Specialty bulb growers offer even more kinds.

Summer-blooming giant allium, *A. giganteum,* is the skyscraper of the group. Its softball-size clusters of lavender blossoms are borne on 5- to 6-foot stalks; leaves are a modest 1½ feet long. Nearly as tall are *A. macleanii (A. elatum)* and *A. rosenbachianum;* both are violet-flowered species that bloom in late spring. For green-tinted white flowers, look for *A. rosenbachianum* 'Album'. The hybrid 'Globemaster' produces long-lasting violet blossoms in spherical heads to 10 inches across. Spring-flowering *A. aflatunense* also resembles *A. giganteum,* but its stems are shorter (to 3 to 5 feet) and its heads of lilac blossoms are smaller.

Among the alliums of middling size are three strikingly colored species, all blooming in summer. *A. atropurpureum* and *A. sphaerocephalum* (the latter commonly called "drumsticks") both grow 2 to 2½ feet tall and bear 2-inch flower clusters; the former produces blossoms of dark purple to nearly black, while the latter has very tight clusters of red-purple blossoms. *A. carinatum pulchellum (A. pulchellum)* also has red-purple flowers, but its stems reach only 2 feet at the tallest.

The under-2-foot-tall category offers the greatest variety of floral colors and forms. Summer-blooming *A. narcissiflorum* bears bell-shaped, bright rose to wine red flowers in loose clusters atop foot-tall stems. *A. christophii* (star of Persia), blooming in late spring, has potentially the largest flower clusters of all alliums—from 6 inches to as much as 1 foot across. Individual blossoms are star shaped; color varies from lilac to amethyst purple. Stems are 1 to 1½ feet tall; the 1½-foot-long leaves have silvery white undersides.

Five other worthwhile small species also flower in late spring. The shortest of these is *A. oreophilum (A. ostrowskianum)*; its stems are just 8 to 12 inches tall, topped with 2-inch, rose-colored flower clusters. Its carmine red variety 'Zwanenburg' is only about 6 inches tall. *A. caeruleum*, blue allium, has cornflower blue blossoms in 2-inch rounded clusters on 1- to 1½-foot stems; rose pink *A. roseum* bears its 4-inch flower clusters on 12- to 14-inch stems. Two other species are yellow flowered. Golden garlic, *A. moly*, features loose, 2- to 3-inch clusters of bright yellow blossoms atop 9- to 18-inch stems; its gray-green leaves are nearly as long as the stems. Clusters of pendent straw yellow flowers on 12- to 15-inch stems characterize *A. flavum*.

Midspring flowers are provided by *A. karataviense*, the Turkestan allium. Its 5-inch clusters of pinkish beige to reddish lilac blossoms are carried on 8- to 12-inch stems. Each plant usually produces two purple-tinted leaves, each up to 4 inches wide and nearly prostrate.

Another midspring bloomer is pure white *A. neapolitanum*, with loose, 3-inch flower clusters; its stems are about 1 foot tall, rising above 1-inch-wide leaves. 'Grandiflorum' has larger individual flowers and begins blooming a bit earlier than the species.

Allium giganteum

Allium karataviense

'Cowanii' (often sold as *A.* 'Cowanii') is a superior form, with earlier flowers on longer stems.

USES. The tall and middle-size species provide attractive accents in mixed groupings of annuals and perennials. Shorter species are useful in foreground drifts or clumps and as pathway edgings. *A. caeruleum, A. flavum, A. moly,* and *A. neapolitanum* are the best choices for naturalizing.

GARDEN CULTURE. Grow *A. caeruleum* in Zones 1–24, 28–45; *A. flavum, A. karataviense, A. moly, A. oreophilum, A. sphaerocephalum* in Zones 1–24, 28–43; *A. aflatunense, A. christophii, A.* 'Globemaster', *A. rosenbachianum* in Zones 1–24, 29–43; *A. carinatum pulchellum, A. giganteum, A. macleanii, A. narcissiflorum* in Zones 3–24, 29–41; *A. atropurpureum, A. neapolitanum* in Zones 4–24, 28–34, 39; *A. roseum* in Zones 4–24, 28–32.

All types prefer well-drained soil (preferably on the sandy side), enriched before planting with organic matter. In fall or spring, plant bulbs as deep as their height or width, whichever is greater. Space smaller species 4 to 6 inches apart, larger ones 8 to 12 inches apart. Water regularly during growth and bloom, but when foliage begins to yellow after flowering, water less often or even let soil go dry. Leave plantings undisturbed until vigor and flower quality decline due to overcrowding. At that time, dig clumps after foliage has died down, divide bulbs, and replant in late summer or early autumn. If replanting in the same plot, dig plenty of organic matter into the soil.

Listing continues >

Allium moly

CONTAINER CULTURE. All alliums are suitable container subjects. By growing the plants in pots, you can easily let them dry off after flowering is finished. Container culture also lets you grow species in zones outside their stated hardiness range. The smaller types are good for display on patio or terrace. Pots of larger, taller kinds can be sunk into flower borders, where they can remain until bloom is completed. Follow directions "C" on page 207.

ALSTROEMERIA

ALSTROEMERIA, PERUVIAN LILY
Liliaceae
TUBEROUS ROOT

▲ 1 TO 4 FEET

☀ ◑ FULL SUN; FILTERED SUN OR PART SHADE WHERE SUMMERS ARE HOT

◉ NEEDS SUMMER WATER (EXCEPT AS NOTED)

✇ ZONES 5–9, 14–24, 26, 28, 31; WARMER PARTS OF 32, 34

Alstroemeria

This South American native's airy sprays of azalealike flowers enliven the garden as spring slips into summer. Viewed individually, young plants look rather wispy, so it's best to set them out in groups. As clumps become established, the leafy upright stems multiply, giving the planting a bulkier look.

Most alstroemerias sold in nurseries are hybrid strains with flowers in red, orange, yellow, cream, white, pink, or lavender, often speckled or blotched with a darker color. The older Ligtu and Chilean hybrids (both deciduous groups) are being supplanted by newer, shorter, stockier strains with longer bloom periods; these newer kinds, too, die to the ground after flowering. The Cordu and Meyer hybrids are evergreen; they keep blooming over an especially long season if the spent flowering stems are pulled (grasp each stem and gently twist while pulling upward). The deciduous Constitution Series, bred in Connecticut, makes it possible to grow alstroemerias in colder regions: if mulched heavily in winter, the plants succeed along the Atlantic seaboard.

Some nurseries offer species and named selections. Peruvian lily, *A. aurea (A. aurantiaca),* reaches 3 to 4 feet tall, bearing its flowers in loose sprays; varieties include 'Lutea' (yellow), 'Orange King' (yellow-orange petals with brown spots), and 'Splendens' (red). The Brazilian species *A. psittacina* is more or less evergreen, with exotic dark red blossoms marked in green and purple on 1- to 1½-foot stems; it can be invasive. For western dry-summer gardens that receive little or no supplementary water, *A. aurea* and the Ligtu Hybrids are the best choices.

USES. Alstroemeria is showy for weeks in late spring and summer. All kinds, especially the deciduous sorts, are best used in mixed plantings.

GARDEN CULTURE. Plants appreciate well-drained soil enriched with organic matter before planting. The ideal location is a spot where roots are in cool, moist soil during the growing season, while flowering stems receive full sun (in cool to moderate climates) or filtered sunlight or part shade (where summers are hot). To keep soil cool and moist, mulch the planting area or overplant it with nonaggressive ground cover annuals or perennials such as verbena or sweet alyssum.

Choose a site where plants can remain undisturbed for years. Plantings spread over time but usually don't need dividing, and plants reestablish slowly after replanting.

Tuberous roots may be sold bare root from late fall through winter; they're brittle, so handle with extreme care. Space them about a foot apart, setting the growth node about 4 inches beneath the soil surface. Carefully spread out roots as you plant; in time, they will grow to a considerable depth.

During the growing season, some nurseries also sell young plants in 1- or 2-gallon containers, ready for planting.

Water alstroemeria regularly during active growth and bloom, keeping water off flower heads to prevent stems from toppling. As flowers fade and plants enter their dormant period, water less often.

CONTAINER CULTURE. Follow directions "B" (subgroup 2) on page 207, using large, deep wooden boxes or tubs.

Native to the Cape Province of South Africa, this sturdy plant has strap-shaped dark green leaves that form good-looking, fountainlike clumps about 1 foot high and 2 feet wide. Foliage dies down and disappears in late spring or early summer; wine red, 2- to 3-foot flower stalks rise from bare earth about 6 weeks later. Each stalk bears a cluster of 4 to 12 trumpet-shaped, highly fragrant blossoms. Medium rose pink is the most common color, but paler and deeper variations exist; there is also a white-flowered form, 'Hathor'. (For the bulb with the common name "amaryllis," see *Hippeastrum*, page 252).

USES. Because of its tall, bare flower stems, belladonna lily is best planted among lower-growing perennials that will mask its leaflessness.

GARDEN CULTURE. Belladonna lily isn't particular about soil type, but it does require fairly good drainage. Plant bulbs in late summer, immediately after the blooming season ends; set them about 1 foot apart. Where winter temperatures remain above 15°F/−9°C, keep tops of bulb necks at or slightly above the soil line. In colder areas, set tops of bulb necks slightly below ground level and choose a planting location in a southern exposure, even against a south-facing wall. Established plants are quite tolerant of drought, though performance is better if they receive regular moisture until leaves start to die down.

Divide and replant infrequently. Crowded conditions don't hamper bloom, and reset plants may take a year or two to reestablish before they flower.

The words "bright" and "cheerful" are often applied to anemones. And for good reason: their clear, vivid colors—purple, blue, red, pink, and white—seem to capture the essence of springtime. The numerous species are native to many temperate climates of the world. The most widely available types can be separated into two groups, based on size, hardiness, and uses.

Daisylike flowers, stems no taller than 8 inches, and clumps of fernlike or parsley-like foliage characterize rhizomatous *A. apennina* and tuberous *A. blanda*. These are cold-tolerant plants, requiring distinct winter chill for good performance. The bloom period begins in early spring, with *A. blanda* starting several weeks before *A. apennina*. Blossoms of *A. apennina* are usually sky blue, though you may find white and violet variants (some of them with double flowers). Flowers of *A. blanda* also are typically blue, but numerous color variants exist, including 'Pink Star', 'Red Star', and purplish red 'Radar'.

The second group of anemones includes the taller, more frequently planted tuberous types with poppylike and double flowers. The poppy-flowered anemone, *A. coronaria*, has finely divided foliage and leafy stems to 1½ feet tall. Each stem bears a single 1½- to 2½-inch-wide blossom in red, pink, white, or blue, usually with blue stamens. The DeCaen strain of *A. coronaria* is single flowered; the St. Brigid strain has semidouble and double flowers. Specialty growers may offer single-color strains such as Blue Poppy and The Bride.

A. fulgens, the scarlet windflower, grows to 1 foot tall; it bears black-centered, brilliant red blossoms to 2½ inches across. The St. Bavo strain includes blooms in pink, rusty coral, and terra cotta as well as red.

USES. The smaller anemones, *A. apennina* and *A. blanda*, work well as underplanting for tulips, as ground cover drifts beneath deciduous shrubs and trees, and naturalized in short grass. The taller *A. coronaria* and *A. fulgens* make colorful mass plantings and

AMARYLLIS belladonna
BELLADONNA LILY, NAKED LADY
Amaryllidaceae
TRUE BULB

- ▲ 2 TO 3 FEET
- ☼ FULL SUN
- ◑ ACCEPTS SUMMER MOISTURE BUT DOESN'T NEED ANY
- ✿ ZONES 4–24, 28, 29
- ☦ BULBS ARE POISONOUS IF INGESTED

Amaryllis belladonna

ANEMONE
ANEMONE, WINDFLOWER
Ranunculaceae
TUBER; RHIZOME

- ▲ 2 TO 18 INCHES
- ☼ ◑ FULL SUN, PART SHADE, OR LIGHT SHADE
- ◑ ◌ SMALLER TYPES ACCEPT SUMMER MOISTURE
- ✿ ZONES VARY BY SPECIES (SEE "GARDEN CULTURE")

Anemone coronaria

Anemone blanda

accent clumps in borders of spring flowers. These two species and *A. blanda* are good container plants.

GARDEN CULTURE. Grow *A. blanda* in Zones 2–9, 14–23, 30–41; *A. apennina* in Zones 3–9, 14–24, 30–34, 39; *A. coronaria* in Zones 4–24, 30–34; *A. fulgens* in Zones 4–9, 14–24, 32–34.

All anemones need well-drained soil liberally amended with organic matter. Plant tubers or rhizomes top side up, 1 to 2 inches deep and 4 inches apart. To identify the top side (which can be difficult, given the irregular shapes of tubers and rhizomes), look for the depressed scar left by the base of last year's stem; the scarred side is the top.

Plant *A. apennina* and *A. blanda* in fall; where winter temperatures drop below −10°F/−23°C, apply winter protection (see page 205) annually after the first hard frost. Plant *A. coronaria* and *A. fulgens* in fall where they are hardy in the ground; in colder regions, plant in early spring.

Water plants regularly during active growth and bloom. *A. apennina* and *A. blanda* will take summer water, though they can do without it. They can be left undisturbed for many years to form large colonies; dig and divide only when vigor and bloom quality decline. For *A. coronaria* and *A. fulgens*, withhold moisture when foliage yellows; in dry-summer regions where they are hardy in the ground, you can leave them in place from year to year. But where there is summer watering or rainfall (and, for *A. fulgens*, in areas where winter lows dip below 0°F/−18°C), dig tubers when foliage yellows; then dry and store them as for tuberous begonia (page 244).

CONTAINER CULTURE. For *A. coronaria, A. blanda,* and *A. fulgens,* follow directions "B" (subgroup 1) on page 207.

ARISAEMA

Araceae
TUBER

- ▲ 1½ TO 4 FEET
- ☼● PART OR FULL SHADE
- ◖ NEEDS SUMMER MOISTURE
- ✂ ZONES VARY BY SPECIES (SEE "GARDEN CULTURE")

Arisaema triphyllum

These plants are related to the familiar calla *(Zantedeschia)* and have flowers that are much the same in form: a spikelike spadix sheathed by a petal-like bract called a spathe. But their green, purple, and mottled coloration gives these summer blossoms a curious, almost sinister beauty. As the flowers fade, the spathe withers and the spadix forms orange to red seeds, giving it the look of a small ear of red corn. Plants die to the ground in fall; new shoots emerge in the latter half of spring.

A. triphyllum, known as Jack-in-the-pulpit or Indian turnip, is a denizen of eastern North American woodlands. Each plant bears two 2-foot leafstalks that terminate in three 6-inch leaflets. The cobralike 6-inch spathe is green or purple with white stripes.

Three equally bizarre species hail from eastern Asia. The shortest of these, with two leafstalks to 20 inches tall, is the Japanese *A. sikokianum,* which features a white spadix enveloped by a 6-inch spathe that is purple outside, green inside. The showy cobra lily, *A. speciosum,* produces a single purple-mottled leafstalk to 1½ feet high, above which rises a 2- to 3-foot stem topped by an 8-inch spathe in purple with white stripes; this encloses a white spadix terminating in a thin 2-foot appendage. *A. tortuosum* is the tallest (to 3 to 4 feet) and leafiest species; it bears up to three leaves, each with as many as 15 narrow leaflets. The 6-inch, green or purple spathe curves strongly over the spadix, which bends to emerge from the spathe and rise above it.

USES. Because all species are conversation pieces, place them where their strange charm will be readily apparent. Use them in woodland plantings, but near pathways and with lower-growing plants that won't compete for attention.

GARDEN CULTURE. Grow *A. triphyllum* in Zones 1–6, 26, 28, 31–43; *A. sikokianum* in Zones 3–6, 31–41; *A. tortuosum* in Zones 4–6, 14–17, 31, 32; and *A. speciosum* in Zones 4–6, 14–17, 31.

In nature, these forest plants get a constant renewal of organic matter from fallen leaves and plant remains that decay each year. All prefer acid soil. In the garden, be sure to dig in plenty of organic matter at planting time in fall (set tubers 1 foot apart, about 2 inches deep); keep soil well mulched thereafter. Keep soil moist throughout the growing season, until plants begin to yellow and die down.

CONTAINER CULTURE. These plants make striking (if eerie) potted subjects for the shaded patio or terrace. Follow directions "C" on page 207.

L ike their relatives *Arisaema* and calla *(Zantedeschia)*, these plants have the signature flower structure of a cylindrical, vertical spadix loosely enclosed by a petal-like bract called a spathe. But the flowers of the arums are merely unusual or interesting—not unsettling like those of *Arisaema* or elegant like those of calla. Attractively veined leaves are one appealing feature; the bright fruits that follow the flowers are another.

Leaves of Italian arum, *A. italicum,* sprout from summer-dormant tubers in fall or early winter; when mature, the leaves reach about 1 foot long (on a leafstalk of about equal length), with a broad arrow shape and attractive pale veins. Short-stemmed, white to greenish white flowers appear in spring. At first, the 1-foot spathe remains erect—like a pale scoop—but later it folds over and conceals the short spadix. After bloom, the leaves die back to the ground, leaving just the flower stems, which hold tight, elongated clusters of bright red fruits. Plants offered as the selection 'Pictum' have foliage conspicuously veined in white.

Arum italicum

The fetchingly named black calla, *A. palaestinum,* doesn't disappoint: its 8-inch spathe is green on the outside, but it opens outward and curls back at the tip to reveal a purple interior and a black spadix. Veiny, arrow-shaped leaves reach about 8 inches long, carried on 1-foot leafstalks. Foliage starts growth from dormant tubers in winter; flowers come in spring and early summer. Leaves die to the ground after bloom.

Another species, *A. pictum,* is sometimes also called black calla, but its 8-inch spathe is violet with a white base and encloses a dark purple spadix. Flowers appear in fall—sometimes with the emerging new leaves, sometimes before them. The narrowly arrow-shaped leaves, light green with fine white veins, grow to 10 inches long and are borne on 10-inch leafstalks. Foliage dies to the ground with the onset of hot weather in late spring or early summer.

USES. All three species can be interesting components of a mixed border in shade; Italian arum can be used as a small-scale ground cover or "patch planting" if you don't mind its disappearance in summer.

GARDEN CULTURE. *A. italicum* is adapted to Zones 3–24, 28–34, 39; *A. pictum* to Zones 7–9, 14–24, 28–31; *A. palaestinum* to Zones 14–24. Plant in reasonably good soil amended with organic matter. Set out tubers in late summer or early fall toward the end of their dormant period, planting them 8 to 12 inches apart and about 2 inches deep. Plants can remain undisturbed for years; in favorable situations, Italian arum will spread or naturalize by volunteer seedlings.

CONTAINER CULTURE. Both of the black callas *(A. palaestinum* and *A. pictum)* are easy container subjects. In zones colder than their stated hardiness, container culture is the only way to enjoy their odd beauty. Follow directions "C" on page 207.

ARUM
Araceae
TUBER

- ▲ 1 TO 2 FEET
- ◑ ● PARTIAL OR FULL SHADE
- ◐ ACCEPTS SUMMER MOISTURE BUT DOESN'T NEED ANY
- ✎ ZONES VARY BY SPECIES (SEE "GARDEN CULTURE")

Arum italicum 'Pictum'

BABIANA

BABOON FLOWER

Iridaceae

CORM

- ▲ 6 TO 12 INCHES
- ☼ ◑ FULL SUN OR PART SHADE
- ◐ ACCEPTS SUMMER MOISTURE BUT DOESN'T NEED ANY
- ✺ ZONES 4–24, 29–31, WARMER PARTS OF 32

Babiana stricta

These natives of sub-Saharan Africa catch the eye with flowers in near-fluorescent shades of blue, lavender, purple, and red; there are also forms with white and blue-and-white blossoms. In mid- to late spring, each flowering stem produces six or more blooms, each up to 2 inches across and shaped like a shallow cup with six equal segments. The hairy, sword-shaped leaves have lengthwise ribbing and are borne in fans, like those of gladiolus. Baboons are said to enjoy eating the corms, hence the plant's common name.

Widely available *B. stricta* and its variously colored named selections bear their arresting blossoms on foot-tall stems. The ruby-throated royal blue blossoms of *B. rubrocyanea* appear on stems just half that height.

USES. Plant baboon flower to be viewed at close range—in rock gardens, along pathways, in foreground drifts.

GARDEN CULTURE. Plant in well-drained soil, in a location that receives sun for at least half the day. For a massed effect, set corms 4 inches deep and 4 to 6 inches apart. In Zones 8–24, 29, plant corms in autumn. In colder zones, plant in early spring, waiting until temperatures will remain above 20°F/−7°C.

Water plants regularly throughout growth and bloom, then taper off as leaves yellow after the bloom period ends. Trim foliage off after it dies back. Where corms can overwinter in the ground, leave them in place for several years—they'll increase and bloom more profusely with each passing year. In colder climates, dig and store corms as for gladiolus (see page 248).

CONTAINER CULTURE. Plant corms in a deep pot, setting them about 1 inch deep and 1 inch apart. Follow directions "B" (subgroup 2) on page 207.

BEGONIA

Begoniaceae

TUBER

- ▲ 1 TO 3 FEET
- ◑ FILTERED SUN OR LIGHT SHADE
- ● NEEDS SUMMER MOISTURE
- ✺ ZONES VARY BY SPECIES (SEE "GARDEN CULTURE")

Begonia grandis

The two familiar begonias that grow from tubers could hardly be more different. One is a flamboyant showstopper with masses of large blossoms in a great variety of colors and combinations; the other makes a case for subtle beauty, offering profuse small flowers in just two colors.

Hardy begonia, *B. grandis (B. evansiana, B. grandis evansiana),* an Asian species, reaches 2 to 3 feet tall, its upright, branching red stems bearing wing-shaped, coppery green leaves backed in red. Pink or white flowers, each slightly more than an inch across, bloom in drooping clusters during summer and early fall. Stems die to the ground with the onset of chilly weather; tubers resume growth the next spring after the danger of frost is past. After bloom—but before stems die down—small bulbils are produced where the leaves join the stems. You can detach these, store them over winter as for the tubers, and plant in spring for growth and bloom the same year.

For general magnificence and great range of hues (pink, red, orange, yellow, cream, white, and multicolors), tuberous begonias—sometimes sold as *B. × tuberhybrida*—are second to no other summer-flowering bulb. And for number of blossoms to size of plant, they clearly lead the pack. Starting with the original South American species, hybridizers have refined colors and patterns. Flower form has been tailored, too: a number of modern varieties have blossoms resembling those of other plants, such as rose, camellia, and carnation.

Well-grown plants of tuberous begonia may reach 1 to 1½ feet tall and produce saucer-size flowers. The irregularly shaped, pointed leaves grow to about 8 inches long. A special group of hybrids, sometimes sold as *B. × t.* 'Pendula', has drooping stems and downward-facing flowers. These are plants for hanging baskets and are best displayed at eye level, where their blossoms can be appreciated.

USES. Both types of begonias are useful as accents or in mixed plantings in the shady summer garden. For color impact, try mass plantings or groupings of tuberous begonias alone.

GARDEN CULTURE. *B. grandis* is hardy in Zones 3–33 (in colder zones, it can be grown in containers or dug and stored as for tuberous begonia). Tuberous begonias (those sometimes sold as *B. × tuberhybrida*) flourish when given an ideal combination of moist air and "tepid" temperatures: neither too hot nor too cool. They grow best in Zones 4–6, 15–17, 21–24, 38, 39, and 43, areas where bloom-time night temperatures remain above 60°F/16°C—along the Pacific and North Atlantic coasts, in the Great Lakes coastal areas, and in parts of northern Minnesota and Michigan. Heat plus high humidity, typical of summers in the Southeast and along the Gulf Coast, create the most trying conditions. At the end of the bloom season, when stems yellow and die, dig and store the tubers over winter as described below.

Although most gardeners grow both these begonias in containers (see below), the plants can also go directly in the ground for seasonal display. Amend the existing soil with the potting mix described below, using 1 part soil to 2 parts potting mix. With both begonias, sprout tubers in pots or flats as described below, then set them into the ground when plants have a few leaves. The leaves on sprouted tuberous begonias all point in one direction; when flowers come, they too will face that way. As you set these plants into the ground, position them so you'll see the fronts of the flowers.

For tuberous begonias planted in the ground (or hardy begonias to be stored over winter), follow the same regime of withholding water and fertilizer and of digging and storing as for container-grown plants.

CONTAINER CULTURE. Plant tubers of *B. grandis* about ¼ inch deep, 3 to 4 inches apart, directly into pots of potting mix (see directions "A" on page 207). Set the pots in light shade or dappled sun and keep soil moist but not saturated while tubers root and sprout. Apply a liquid fertilizer every 3 to 4 weeks during the growing season—through mid-August in colder zones, into mid- or late September where the season is longer. When growth and flowering cease, treat plants as outlined below for tuberous begonias.

Tuberous begonia plants can be set outdoors whenever night temperatures are sure to remain above 50°F/10°C. Start them 6 to 8 weeks in advance of the time you can put them outside, setting the tubers directly into pots of potting mix (see directions "A" on page 207); be sure the containers are large enough to leave 2 inches between all sides of the tubers and the container edges. Set tubers indented side up, covering them with no more than ¼ inch of mix. If you're planting a number of tubers, it's easiest to start them in a flat or shallow box, spacing them about 4 inches apart. Place pots or flats in a well-lit spot (but not in direct sun) where temperatures will remain above 65°F/18°C; keep soil moist but not saturated during the rooting period.

When the tubers have produced two leaves, you can move them outside if temperatures are warm enough; this is also the stage when plants sprouted in flats can be potted up.

Tuberous begonias need protection from wind but require freely circulating air: still, moist air will lead to mildewed foliage. Plenty of light (but no direct sun) is another requirement. Choose a spot in filtered sun or light shade—under high-branching trees, on the east or north side of a house, wall, or fence, or under light-modifying overhead structures of lath, shade cloth, or fiberglass.

As plants grow, keep soil moist but not soggy. Too much water will cause tubers to rot; too little will check growth. In dry climates, you'll also need to raise humidity around plants—set up a permanent mist or fog system, or use such attachments on your hose. Except for misting, however, keep water off leaves and flowers: the weight of the water droplets can topple blooming plants or break their stems.

Tuberous begonia hybrids

Listing continues >

Tuberous begonia hybrid

Begin applications of liquid fertilizer a week or two after young plants have reached the two-leaf stage. Gardeners who are going for the largest possible blossoms use a half-strength solution every other week, but you can easily grow fine plants with monthly regular-strength applications.

In late summer to midautumn, flower production will slow and then cease. When you notice this slowdown, stop fertilizing and cut back on water, keeping soil just moist enough to prevent foliage from wilting (you want tubers to store as much food as possible before they enter dormancy). When leaves begin to turn yellow, withhold water. If frosts are likely to occur before plants die down completely, move containers into a well-lit, frost-free location.

When leaves fall off and stems separate easily from tubers, the tubers are ready for storage. Place containers in a cool, dark spot where temperatures will remain above freezing (preferably in the range of 40° to 50°F/4° to 10°C). You can also store tubers out of their containers. Knock them from their pots, remove stems and all soil, and let them dry for several days in a shaded, dry location. Then give covered storage (see page 205) over winter.

BELAMCANDA chinensis, PARDANCANDA × norrisii
BLACKBERRY LILY, CANDY LILY
Iridaceae
RHIZOME

- ▲ 2 TO 3 FEET
- ☼ ◑ FULL SUN OR LIGHT SHADE
- ◓ NEEDS SOME SUMMER MOISTURE
- ✀ ZONES 1–24, 26, 28–43

Belamcanda chinensis

Native to China and Japan, blackberry lily (*Belamcanda chinensis*) produces iris-like foliage clumps which give rise to branched flowering stems 2 to 3 feet high. These bear swarms of 2- to 3-inch, red-spotted orange flowers, each with six petals arranged in pinwheel fashion. Though each bloom lasts just one day, each slender stem produces numerous flowers over several weeks in summer. When the seed capsules mature in fall, they split open to reveal clusters of shining black seeds resembling blackberries.

Plants cataloged as candy lily (designated as *Pardancanda × norrisii*) are hybrids between *Belamcanda chinensis* and its near relative *Pardanthopsis dichotoma*, a native of northern Asia. Candy lily resembles blackberry lily in plant habit and size, but its flowers come in blue, purple, pink, and yellow as well as orange.

USES. Blackberry lily and candy lily are good accent plants. Their vertical foliage clumps and masses of airy blossoms mix well with a variety of annuals and perennials.

GARDEN CULTURE. Plant rhizomes in well-drained soil in fall (early spring where winter temperatures fall below 10°F/–12°C); space them 1 foot apart, with their tops just beneath the soil surface. Fall planting is best in Zones 4–24, 26, 28, 29; plant in spring in Zones 1–3, 30–43. Water plants regularly during growth and bloom; after flowering, they'll get by with less frequent watering.

Established clumps give the best display, so divide and reset infrequently.

BLETILLA striata
CHINESE GROUND ORCHID
Orchidaceae
RHIZOME

- ▲ 1½ TO 2 FEET
- ◑ FILTERED SUN OR PART SHADE
- ◓ NEEDS SUMMER MOISTURE
- ✀ ZONES 4–9, 12–24, 26, 28–31, WARMER PARTS OF 32

This easy-to-grow plant from East Asia is unmistakably an orchid—its 2-inch flowers look much like the cattleya orchids of corsage fame. Lavender is the typical color, but a white-flowered variety ('Alba') is sometimes available. *B. s. albostriata* bears light pink flowers above leaves striped in green and white.

Plants break dormancy in early spring, sending up three to six lance-shaped, plaited-looking light green leaves. Bare flower stems to about 2 feet tall follow in late spring; each produces three to seven blossoms, spaced apart from each other toward the stem end.

USES. Plant in clumps, patches, or drifts. The delicate blooms look especially attractive in combination with rhododendrons or azaleas.

GARDEN CULTURE. Plant rhizomes at any time during the dormant period from late fall to early spring, setting them 1 inch deep and 1 foot apart in good, well-drained soil enriched with organic matter. When leaves emerge, put out bait for slugs and snails. Water regularly during growth and bloom, then taper off when leaves begin to yellow in fall. After foliage has died back completely, rhizomes become dormant and don't need much water.

Large, crowded clumps give the best display of blooms, but you may dig and divide as needed during dormancy.

CONTAINER CULTURE. A thriving clump of Chinese ground orchid makes a striking container plant, attractive during bloom and afterwards—until the leaves die back. Follow directions "C" on page 207.

Bletilla striata

I n recent years, botanists have transferred a number of species from *Brodiaea* to *Dichelostemma* and *Triteleia*. But because many nurseries still offer all these plants as *Brodiaea*—and many gardeners still refer to them as such—all are treated together here. The correct botanical name is given first; the old name appears in parentheses. For the plant once called *Brodiaea uniflora* (spring star flower), see *Ipheion uniflorum* on page 256.

The brodiaeas (and former brodiaeas) are native to the western United States, where they experience a hot, dry, and usually long summer dormant period. In the wild, these are field and meadow plants, often waving their heads of blue, purple, white, or yellow flowers above or among the dry grasses of fields and hillsides. Each plant produces a few grasslike leaves and a single slender stem topped by a loose cluster of bell-shaped or funnel-shaped blossoms in spring or summer.

Harvest brodiaea, *B. elegans,* bears 1-inch-wide dark blue blossoms on 10- to 20-inch stems in late spring and early summer; *B. coronaria* is very similar, but a bit smaller and shorter.

Dichelostemma capitatum (Brodiaea capitata) blooms in early to midspring, producing tight clusters of deep blue to violet flowers on 2-foot stems.

Two formerly separate *Brodiaea* species, *B. hyacinthina* and *B. lactea,* have been merged as one species with a totally new name: *Triteleia hyacinthina.* Flowering stems to 2½ feet tall arise in early to midsummer, bearing bell-shaped white flowers in open clusters. Golden brodiaea, *T. ixioides* (formerly *B. ixioides*), flaunts inch-long yellow blossoms on foot-tall stems in late spring. Ithuriel's spear, *T. laxa* (formerly *B. laxa*) flowers in mid- to late spring, its 2½-foot stems carrying profuse clusters of bluish purple flowers nearly 2 inches long. 'Queen Fabiola' is usually sold as a selected, superior form of *T. laxa.*

USES. The various brodiaeas are good choices for naturalizing at garden fringes and at the edges of uncultivated property. They can also be used to lend a wildflower-type accent to groupings of other drought-tolerant plants.

GARDEN CULTURE. Grow *B. elegans* and *T. hyacinthina* in Zones 1–9, 14–24, 29–43; *D. capitatum* in Zones 1–3, 5–12, 14–24; *T. laxa* and 'Queen Fabiola' in Zones 3–9, 14–24, 29, 30, 33; *B. coronaria* in Zones 4–9, 14–24, 29, 30; *T. ixioides* in Zones 5–9, 14–24. Under "native" conditions—hot, absolutely dry summer weather—these bulbs will accept heavy soils as well as light and well-drained ones. But if summer moisture is inevitable, good drainage is a necessity—and even then there's no guarantee of success. If you live in a moist-summer region and want to try growing

BRODIAEA, DICHELOSTEMMA, TRITELEIA
Liliaceae
CORM

▲ 10 TO 30 INCHES
☼ FULL SUN
◊ WITHHOLD SUMMER MOISTURE
✄ ZONES VARY BY SPECIES (SEE "GARDEN CULTURE")

Brodiaea 'Queen Fabiola'

any of these species in the garden, *T. hyacinthina* is probably your best bet. Container culture (see below) is another option.

Plant corms in fall, 2 to 3 inches deep and 2 to 4 inches apart. All species need regular moisture during their winter and spring growing period. Digging and dividing are necessary only infrequently, when clumps show a decline in vigor and bloom quality.

CONTAINER CULTURE. The various species aren't difficult to grow in containers, though they look rather wispy. Follow directions "B" (subgroup 2) on page 207.

CALADIUM bicolor
FANCY-LEAFED CALADIUM
Araceae
TUBER

▲ 2 TO 3 FEET

☼ FILTERED SUN OR LIGHT SHADE, EXCEPT AS NOTED

● NEEDS SUMMER MOISTURE

✂ ZONES 25–27

Caladium bicolor

No one would look twice at a caladium flower, which resembles a small calla *(Zantedeschia)*. What these tropical South American plants provide is crowd-stopping summer foliage in combinations of red, pink, white, green, silver, and bronze. Each tuber gives rise to numerous slim leafstalks, each of which supports a thin-textured leaf shaped like an elongated heart, up to 1 foot wide and 1½ feet long when well grown. Patterns are almost too varied to describe; veining, dotting, splashing, washing, and edging are some of the ways in which one color is contrasted against another.

Though all types need bright light, most do not tolerate direct sun. Varieties that do take sun include 'Fire Chief', 'Red Flash', 'Rose Bud', and 'White Queen'.

USES. Potted caladiums often decorate terraces and patios; they're greenhouse favorites, too. To simulate garden planting, you can sink the potted plants into the ground.

GARDEN CULTURE. Caladiums need a growing season of at least 4 months, with temperatures above 70°F/21°C during the day and ideally no lower than 60°F/16°C at night. As garden plants, they perform best in Florida and some areas of the Gulf Coast, where they can get rich soil, high humidity, heat, and plenty of water. Plant in early spring, in filtered sun or light shade (sun-tolerant types can take at least a half day of sun). Replace the top 6 inches of garden soil with the potting mix recommended for "A" on page 207. Set out plants (from the nursery or from tubers you started as for tuberous begonia, page 224) 8 to 12 inches apart, keeping tops of tubers even with the soil surface.

Keep soil moist but not soggy, and water more generously as more leaves develop. If humidity is low, mist foliage daily with a fine spray of water. For best performance, apply a liquid fertilizer diluted to half strength every other week. Put out bait for slugs and snails. Remove any blossoms, since these will divert energy from leaf production. When leaves begin to die down in late summer or early fall, cut back on watering. Tubers can stay in the ground where hardy; elsewhere, dig and store as for tuberous begonia (page 224).

CONTAINER CULTURE. Start tubers indoors a month before outside temperatures normally reach the levels noted under "Garden culture" (above), using soil mix described under "A" on page 207 and following directions for tuberous begonia (page 224).

CALOCHORTUS
Liliaceae
TRUE BULB

▲ 4 INCHES TO 3 FEET

☼ ☽ FULL SUN OR LIGHT SHADE

○ WITHHOLD SUMMER MOISTURE

✂ ZONES VARY BY SPECIES (SEE "GARDEN CULTURE")

Among bulbous plants, these rank near the top for delicacy and floral beauty in spring or early summer. However, the various species are also among the more challenging for the garden, since they demand the long, warm, dry summers of their native habitats in western North America.

Sparse, grasslike foliage is common to all members of the genus, but flower forms can be divided into three distinct groups. Globe tulips or fairy lanterns have nodding flowers, the petals turning inward to form a globe. Star tulips have upward-facing, cup-shaped flowers, with petal tips often rolled outward; those with long straight hairs on the inner flower parts are called "cat's ears" or "pussy ears." Mariposa lilies are generally the tallest types, with striking cup- or bowl-shaped flowers.

Bulb specialists may offer various species, representing some or all of the three basic flower types. Among the globe tulips are *C. albus* (white), *C. amabilis* (yellow), and *C. amoenus* (rosy purple). Star tulips and cat's ears include *C. nudus* (white or lavender), *C. tolmiei* (white or cream, tinged with purple), and *C. uniflorus* (lilac). Most variable of the mariposa lilies is *C. venustus;* its blossoms may be white, pink, light to dark red, purple, or yellow, usually centered with contrasting markings that sometimes extend onto the petals. Other mariposa lilies are *C. clavatus* and *C. luteus* (yellow), *C. splendens* (lilac with purple), *C. nuttallii* (white with purple), and *C. vestae* (white, lilac, or pink, with a contrasting color in the flower center).

USES. Where conditions favor success in the ground, all species can be conversation-piece ornaments in rock gardens or naturalized on sunny, grassy hillsides. As container plants, they are striking in bloom, but the foliage is rather wispy.

GARDEN CULTURE. Grow *C. nuttallii* in Zones 1–3; *C. splendens* and *C. venustus* in Zones 1–3, 7, 9, 14–24; *C. nudus* in Zones 1–3, 7–9, 14; *C. tolmiei* in Zones 1, 4–6, 7, 15–17; *C. amabilis* and *C. uniflorus* in Zones 4–7, 9, 14–24; *C. amoenus* and *C. vestae* in Zones 7, 9, 14–21; *C. albus, C. clavatus,* and *C. luteus* in Zones 7, 9, 14–24.

Plant bulbs in fall, setting them 3 to 4 inches deep and about 6 inches apart. The keys to success are well-drained soil and no water at all from the time leaves start to yellow after bloom until midautumn (when rainfall begins in native habitats). Under ideal conditions, plantings can remain undisturbed for years.

In areas with summer rainfall, try digging bulbs as soon as leaves turn yellow, then holding them in dry sand until fall. Some gardeners have successfully used this method year after year. An alternative is container culture; be sure to keep the soil mix completely dry during the long summer dormant period.

CONTAINER CULTURE. Follow directions "B" (subgroup 2) on page 207.

TOP: *Calochortus albus*
BOTTOM: *Calochortus luteus*

Camassia leichtlinii

You don't grow this western North American native for flamboyant, show-stopping floral displays. Instead, it offers the charm of a meadow wildflower—which is just what it is. Rosettes of grasslike to strap-shaped leaves send up slender spikes of loosely spaced, starlike blossoms in spring; after flowering, foliage dies down completely for the summer dormant period.

Bulb specialists offer several species and varieties. *C. cusickii* bears blue flowers on stems to 3 feet tall. *C. leichtlinii,* the tallest camass, reaches a height of 4 feet; its blossoms are creamy white. *C. l. suksdorfii* is blue flowered; *C. l.* 'Alba' is nearer to white than the species, while 'Plena' has double greenish white blossoms. For deep blue blooms on 1- to 2-foot stems, choose *C. quamash* or its varieties 'Orion' and 'San Juan Form'.

USES. Though camass is at home in meadowlike situations, the tall flower spikes also look attractive in mixed plantings of spring flowers. Since plants die down after bloom, set camass where the foliage of other plants will hide its yellowing leaves (and fill in the bare spots left after leaves are entirely gone).

GARDEN CULTURE. Camass never requires digging and dividing, so plant bulbs where they can remain undisturbed. In fall, set the large bulbs about 6 inches apart and 3 to 4 inches deep in good, moisture-retentive soil. Plants like ample water during growth and bloom, but can get by with less during the summer dormant period.

CAMASSIA
CAMASS
Liliaceae
TRUE BULB

▲ 1 TO 4 FEET
☼ ◑ FULL SUN OR LIGHT SHADE
◗ NEEDS SOME SUMMER MOISTURE
✄ ZONES 1–9, 14–17, 31, 32, 34, 39

CANNA

Cannaceae

RHIZOME

- ▲ 1½ TO 6 FEET
- ☼ FULL SUN
- ◗ NEEDS SUMMER MOISTURE
- ✂ ZONES 6–9, 12–31, WARMER PARTS OF 32

Canna

For showiness and productivity, you can't go wrong with cannas. Choose from several heights and a wide range of flower colors, including red, orange, yellow, pink, cream, white, and bicolors. Rhizomes produce clumps of upright stems sheathed in broad, lance-shaped, decidedly tropical-looking leaves that may be green, bronze, or variegated. In summer and fall, each stem bears a spike of large, bright flowers resembling irregularly shaped gladiolus.

Virtually all cannas in the nursery trade are hybrids of mixed ancestry, originating from species found in the American tropics and subtropics. The old-fashioned garden favorites reach 4 to 6 feet, but lower-growing, more compact strains are also available. The Grand Opera strain grows a bit over 2 feet tall, while the Pfitzer Dwarf strain reaches 2½ to 3 feet. Shortest of all is the 1½-foot Seven Dwarfs strain.

USES. Cannas are particularly dramatic as color accents, but their bright blossoms and bold leaves also add a striking tropical touch to the garden. They make stunning container plants.

GARDEN CULTURE. Cannas thrive in good, moist soil and a hot, bright location. Choose a sunny area where plants can receive regular moisture during growth and bloom; incorporate a generous amount of organic matter into the soil before setting out rhizomes.

Where rhizomes are hardy in the ground (they survive to about 0°F/−18°C), plant after the normal last-frost date in spring, spacing rhizomes 1½ to 2 feet apart and covering them with 2 to 4 inches of soil. In colder regions, start rhizomes indoors 4 to 6 weeks before the usual last-frost date, so that plants will bloom sooner after being planted outdoors.

As each stem finishes flowering, cut it to the ground; new stems will continue to grow throughout summer and early fall.

Where the climate is mild enough for cannas to remain in the ground from year to year, cut back faded flower stalks in fall after new flowering stems cease to appear. Clumps usually become overcrowded every 3 or 4 years; when this happens, dig in early spring and cut the rhizomes apart. Let the cuts dry and heal over (this takes about 24 hours), then replant in newly enriched soil.

In regions where winter temperatures fall below 0°F/−18°C, dig cannas after the first hard frost kills foliage. Cut off stems; knock soil from rhizomes and let them dry for several days in a dry, shaded spot. Give covered storage (see page 205) over winter.

CONTAINER CULTURE. Displayed in large pots or wooden planters, the shorter kinds of cannas are effective summer patio and terrace decorations. Follow directions "C" on page 207.

CARDIOCRINUM giganteum

Liliaceae

TRUE BULB

- ▲ 6 TO 12 FEET
- ☼ FILTERED SUN OR LIGHT SHADE
- ◗ NEEDS SUMMER MOISTURE
- ✂ ZONES 4–6, 14–17, 32

If ever a plant needed a common name, this Himalayan aristocrat is the one. It looks like a towering lily; and indeed, only small botanical niceties keep it from being classed as a lily species. One distinct difference is the foliage: the glossy dark green leaves are 1½ feet long, broadly oval to heart shaped, with a texture like that of spinach.

Every summer, the foliage rosette gives rise to a leafy, vertical stem. The stem is flowerless for several years, dying back to the ground each fall. In 3 or 4 years, however, a massive flowering stalk rises to bear its majestic beauty high overhead: a tier of up to twenty 6- to 8-inch, fragrant white trumpets with red markings in their throats, reminiscent of alien Easter lilies. The flowers set seed, after which the entire plant dies—but not before producing numerous small offset bulbs that will grow to flowering size within several years.

USES. This plant is the nonpareil of exclamation points in a woodland garden. Plant it among other shade-loving plants where you want a compelling late-summer floral display. It's best to set out bulbs of different sizes; this gives you a better chance of having one or more flowering stems each year while the immature plants build up strength for bloom in the future.

GARDEN CULTURE. Choose a location in light shade or dappled sun, with fertile, organically enriched soil that can be kept moist throughout the growing season. Set out bulbs in fall (in milder-winter regions) or early spring, spacing them about 2 feet apart and placing the tops just beneath the soil surface. Bulbs break dormancy early in spring; if late frosts are likely, mulch the planting location and protect emerging plants with cut conifer branches.

A plant that has flowered usually produces quite a few offset bulbs. If these are left in place, they will be too crowded to turn in a top-notch performance when they mature; for better results, dig, separate, and replant these offspring after the flowering stem dies, giving each enough space to grow to considerable size. You can also obtain new plants by sowing the seeds produced after flowering, but seedlings may take up to 7 years to reach blooming size.

Cardiocrinum giganteum

Chionodoxa sardensis

In their native lands of Crete, Cyprus, and Turkey, these charming little plants begin flowering as the snow melts at winter's end. Each bulb produces a stem to 6 inches tall, with blossoms spaced along its upper part: six-pointed blue, white, or pink stars about an inch across. The straight, narrow leaves are slightly shorter than the stem.

C. luciliae is the most frequently grown species. Each stem carries about 10 bright blue blossoms with white centers. Varieties include 'Alba', pure white and a bit larger flowered; 'Gigantea', with larger leaves and larger blossoms of violet blue; and pink-flowered 'Pink Giant' and 'Rosea'. *C. sardensis* produces blooms of deep gentian blue, each centered with a tiny white eye.

USES. Naturalized under deciduous shrubs, glory-of-the-snow will in time create a carpet of flowers. It's also good in rock gardens and pathway border plantings.

GARDEN CULTURE. Where summers are cool or mild, grow plants in full sun. In hot-summer climates, however, be sure the growing area is in filtered sun or light shade after the bloom period ends.

In fall, plant bulbs 2 to 3 inches deep and about 3 inches apart, in well-drained soil enriched with organic matter. Plants need regular moisture during growth and bloom, less when foliage begins to die back. If bulbs are planted where soil is shaded and relatively cool during summer, they can get by with little or no water during their summer dormancy. Where summers are hot and dry, make sure that any bulbs in full-sun locations receive moderate watering during summer.

Bulbs increase rapidly and may be dug and separated for increase in early fall, whenever plantings have declined in vigor and bloom quality. Plantings often also increase from self-sown seedlings.

CHIONODOXA
GLORY-OF-THE-SNOW
Liliaceae
TRUE BULB

▲ 6 INCHES

☼ ◑ FULL SUN; FILTERED SUN OR LIGHT SHADE AFTER BLOOM WHERE SUMMERS ARE HOT

◐ MAY NEED SOME SUMMER MOISTURE (SEE "GARDEN CULTURE")

✎ ZONES 1–7, 14–20, 31–43

Chionodoxa luciliae 'Pink Giant'

CLIVIA miniata

CLIVIA, KAFFIR LILY

Amaryllidaceae

TUBEROUS ROOT

- ▲ 2 FEET
- ◑ ● FILTERED SUN, PART SHADE, OR FULL SHADE
- ● NEEDS SUMMER MOISTURE
- ✂ ZONES 12–17, 19–27

Clivia miniata, Solomone Hybrid

This evergreen South African native is striking in both foliage and flowers. Broad, strap-shaped, lustrous dark green leaves grow to about 1½ feet long, arching outward to form a fountainlike clump. In winter and spring, the clump sends up thick stems to 2 feet tall, each crowned by a cluster of funnel-shaped, 2-inch blossoms, typically in vivid orange with a yellow center. Decorative red berries ripen after the flowers fade.

With a bit of nursery or catalog searching, you can find variations on the basic theme. 'Flame' has blooms of a particularly deep orange red; French and Belgian hybrids have notably wide leaves and thick flower stalks carrying blossoms ranging from yellow to orange red. The Solomone Hybrids offer yellow flowers in pale to deep shades.

USES. Clivia makes a good year-round accent plant for patio or shady garden—in a single clump or a mass planting, in containers or in the ground.

GARDEN CULTURE. Where winters are frost free (or nearly so), plant at any time of year, in filtered sunlight to shade. Dig a liberal amount of organic matter into the soil before planting. Set plants 1½ to 2 feet apart, at the depth they were growing in their pots (they are sold only in containers). Provide regular moisture from winter through summer; taper off when growth slows in autumn, but never let leaves wilt.

Plants will not need dividing for many years. When clumps do become overcrowded, dig and reset in spring, after flowering has ended.

CONTAINER CULTURE. Follow directions "C" on page 207. Apply liquid fertilizer monthly during spring and summer to enhance the next season's flowering.

Where winter temperatures drop below about 25°F/−4°C, container-grown plants can overwinter indoors in a brightly lit, cool room (night temperatures from 50° to 55°F/10° to 13°C). Clivia can also be treated as a house plant.

Clivia blooms best when rootbound, so repot (in spring) only when plants look as if they're about to burst out of the container.

COLCHICUM

MEADOW SAFFRON

Liliaceae

CORM

- ▲ 6 TO 8 INCHES
- ◌ FULL SUN
- ● NEEDS SOME SUMMER MOISTURE
- ✂ ZONES 1–9, 14–24, 29, 30, 33–43
- ◈ ALL PARTS ARE POISONOUS IF INGESTED

Colchicum 'Waterlily'

Meadow saffron's delicate flowers rise from bare earth in late summer to early autumn, holding the stage without accompaniment of foliage. The blooms are chalice shaped or starlike, in lavender, violet, pink, white, or yellow; each has six pointed petals atop a slim tube that acts as a stem. After the flowers wither, the plants essentially vanish until spring, when floppy, straplike leaves up to 1 foot long emerge; these aren't especially decorative, but last for just a few months and die back well before the blooming season. (An oddity among the meadow saffrons is yellow-flowered *C. luteum,* which blooms in spring.)

Many species of meadow saffron are native from the Mediterranean region to central Asia and India. Bulb specialists may offer several kinds, but most nurseries stock only *C. autumnale* (often referred to as "autumn crocus") and several named hybrids. Blossoms of *C. autumnale* are about 2 inches wide and typically pinkish lavender in color, though a white form exists (as do double-flowered kinds in both lavender and white). Available hybrids include 'Autumn Queen' (mottled purple on a paler background), 'The Giant' (lilac with a white center), 'Violet Queen' (rich purple with a white center), and 'Waterlily' (double violet).

USES. Meadow saffron looks best when naturalized along paths or walkways. Locate where flowers won't be obscured by taller plants, but where floppy leaves won't be too obtrusive.

GARDEN CULTURE. Plants aren't fussy about soil type, but they do need good drainage. Plant corms in summer, 6 to 8 inches apart and 3 inches deep. Provide some moisture all year: water regularly in spring while plants are in leaf, then more sparingly during the brief midsummer dormant period—but not so sparsely that soil dries out completely. Resume regular watering when flowers appear. Plantings may become overcrowded every 3 or 4 years. Dig and divide in midsummer as necessary.

CONTAINER CULTURE. These accommodating plants will flower even without benefit of a container: dormant corms placed on a sunny (but not hot) windowsill will bloom at the usual time. For standard container culture, see directions "B" (subgroup 2) on page 207.

T he common name "elephant's ear" provides a good description of this tropical plant's enormous (to 2½ by 3 feet), heart-shaped green leaves. Leathery to almost rubbery in texture, they are carried aloft at the ends of succulent stalks from spring through fall; an established clump of multiple tubers produces a display that can only be called junglelike. Inconspicuous flowers resembling greenish callas *(Zantedeschia)* appear only in the most temperate climates.

USES. Elephant's ear is a peerless choice for creating tropical effects in light shade. In native Hawaiian and other Polynesian cultures, the tubers are an important dietary source of carbohydrates.

GARDEN CULTURE. In mild-summer regions, plants can take full sun—but everywhere else, choose a location in filtered sun or light shade. Rich soil and plenty of moisture produce the most impressive leaves, but good drainage isn't a requirement; plants will grow in soggy soil, even in standing water.

Where winters are frost free, plant tubers in late winter or very early spring; elsewhere, wait until after the last-frost date. Enrich soil with organic matter before planting; then set out tubers 1 to 1½ feet apart and about 2 inches deep. Water frequently throughout the growing season; for the most impressive leaves, apply fertilizer periodically. When clumps become overcrowded, dig and divide in early spring.

In regions where soil freezes, plants cannot survive the winter outdoors. After foliage is killed by frost, dig and store tubers as for tuberous begonia (page 224).

CONTAINER CULTURE. In a suitably large container, elephant's ear is a spectacular summertime ornament for patio or terrace. Start tubers indoors 4 to 6 weeks before the expected last-frost date. Follow directions "C" on page 207. Fertilize bimonthly with a high-nitrogen liquid fertilizer such as fish emulsion. In zones too cold for year-round outdoor culture, you can move container-grown plants to a protected spot for the winter, then return them outside in spring after all danger of frost is past.

COLOCASIA esculenta
ELEPHANT'S EAR, TARO
Araceae
TUBER

- ▲ 6 FEET
- ☼ ◑ FULL SUN; FILTERED SUN OR LIGHT SHADE WHERE SUMMERS ARE HOT
- ◑ NEEDS SUMMER MOISTURE
- ⁍ ZONES 12, 16–28

Colocasia esculenta

CONVALLARIA majalis
LILY-OF-THE-VALLEY
Liliaceae
RHIZOME

- ▲ 6 TO 10 INCHES
- ◑ FILTERED SUN OR LIGHT SHADE
- ◑ NEEDS SUMMER MOISTURE
- ⁍ ZONES 1–7, 14–20, 31–45; BEST WITH SUBFREEZING WINTER TEMPERATURES
- ◊ ALL PARTS ARE POISONOUS IF INGESTED

L ily-of-the-valley is a favorite in regions providing enough winter chill for plants to prosper. Highly fragrant, delicate spring flowers account for part of this European native's popularity; good-looking foliage throughout the growing season is another asset.

Each rhizome (called a "pip") produces one slim flowering stem and two or three broad, lance-shaped leaves to 9 inches long. Along the length of the stem, 12 to 20 small, waxy white bells hang from threadlike stalks. Specialty bulb growers offer variations on the basic theme: sorts with double white blooms or light pink flowers, even a form with cream-striped foliage.

Convallaria majalis

Listing continues >

Convallaria majalis 'Aureo-variegata'

USES. Lily-of-the-valley makes a long-lived ground cover beneath deciduous shrubs and among other plants that need the same conditions.

GARDEN CULTURE. Choose a lightly shaded garden location (or one receiving only filtered sunlight) with good soil. Dig a generous quantity of organic matter into the soil before planting in fall; set out pips in clumps or drifts, 1 to 2 inches deep and 4 to 6 inches apart. Plants need regular moisture throughout the year, even during dormancy. Every year before new growth emerges, topdress the planting with compost, leaf mold, peat moss, or ground bark.

Divide plantings infrequently, only when performance starts to decline. Dig and separate rhizomes when leaves yellow in autumn.

CONTAINER CULTURE. Follow directions "B" (subgroup 2) on page 207. Potted lily-of-the-valley makes a charming patio decoration; it can even be kept indoors, as long as it is given bright indirect light (not direct sun) and fairly cool temperatures. Prechilled pips are available for forcing; see pages 210–211.

CORYDALIS solida
Fumariaceae
TUBER

- ▲ 6 TO 10 INCHES
- ☼ FILTERED SUN OR LIGHT SHADE
- ◗ NEEDS SUMMER MOISTURE
- ✂ ZONES 3–9, 14–24, 32–35, 37, 39–43

Corydalis solida 'George P. Baker'

This northern European native gives you all the beauty of a low-growing fern, with the bonus of charming blossoms. Spreading plants bear dissected foliage with rounded lobes, above which rise upright flowering stems to 10 inches tall in spring. The flowers—tubular with a curved spur, a bit less than an inch long—are borne in loose spikes of up to 20. Blossoms are typically light purplish red, but there are varieties in other colors, among them 'Blue Dream' and coral red 'George P. Baker'.

USES. Low growth and a spreading habit suit this plant to the foreground of woodland and shade garden plantings. It's effective spreading among rocks, draping over low walls, even growing from crevices in unmortared stone walls.

GARDEN CULTURE. Give corydalis good, well-drained, organically enriched soil and filtered sun or light shade. Plant tubers in fall, settting them 2 to 3 inches deep and 4 to 5 inches apart; keep soil moist, but not saturated, throughout the growing season. When clumps become crowded or whenever you want to increase your planting, dig tubers after foliage has died back in autumn; then separate and replant them right away.

CONTAINER CULTURE. Follow directions "C" on page 207. For the best display, reverse the container dimensions recommended: grow in a pot at least 1 foot wide and about 8 inches deep.

CRINUM, × AMARCRINUM
memoriacorsii
Amaryllidaceae
TRUE BULB

- ▲ 2 TO 4 FEET
- ☼ ◗ FULL SUN; PART SHADE WHERE SUMMERS ARE HOT
- ◗ NEEDS SUMMER MOISTURE
- ✂ ZONES 8, 9, 12–31; WARMER PARTS OF 32 AND 33
- ☣ ALL PARTS ARE POISONOUS IF INGESTED

Lush foliage and lilylike flowers of impressive size put crinums high on the list of garden attention-getters. Each bulb tapers to an elongated stemlike neck, from which radiate long, broad, strap-shaped leaves. At some point from late spring through summer—the exact time depends on the species or hybrid—thick stems to 4 feet tall rise from the foliage, each bearing a cluster of long-stalked flowers. The blossoms resemble those of belladonna lily *(Amaryllis belladonna)*, but they're twice as big and open out a bit wider. Most are highly fragrant; colors include white and many shades of pink, from light to dark.

Crinums are native to many warm and tropical parts of the world. Specialty bulb growers, especially those in the South and Southeast, may offer a number of species and hybrids, but only a few are widely available. *C. moorei*, found along streamsides in South Africa, is one of the better-known species; it has wavy-edged bright green leaves and pinkish red blossoms to 4 inches or more across. You may also be able to find forms with white or soft pink flowers. *C. bulbispermum,* also from moist areas of South Africa, has the same general appearance as *C. moorei,* but it is somewhat smaller in all parts and has narrower leaves. The typical flower color is white flushed with red on the outside, but pure white and pink forms also exist.

Among hybrids, the best known is *C. × powellii,* a cross between *C. bulbispermum* and *C. moorei.* It resembles *C. moorei,* but its flowers are deep rose pink, carried on shorter (2-foot-tall) stems. Its variety 'Album' is pure white. Another *C. moorei* hybrid is *C. × herbertii,* bearing flowers that are typically white with a rosy red stripe down the center of each flower segment—a coloration that explains the common name "milk and wine lily." Among hybrids of more complex ancestry, three widely available choices are rose to wine red 'Ellen Bosanquet', rose pink 'J. C. Harvey', and lavender pink 'Peachblow'.

Another hybrid occasionally offered by bulb specialists is the autumn-blooming × *Amarcrinum memoriacorsii* (sometimes sold as *Crinodonna corsii*), a cross between *Amaryllis belladonna* and *C. moorei.* It resembles *Crinum* in growth habit and foliage, but its flowers look more like those of belladonna lily, having a narrower funnel shape than the blooms of most crinums.

USES. These plants make attractive semipermanent accents among shrubs, perennials, and annuals.

GARDEN CULTURE. The bulbs may be planted in any season, but early spring and autumn are the preferred times of year. Where summers are mild, choose a full-sun location; in hot-summer climates, find a spot that receives midday or afternoon shade or a location in filtered sun. Soil need not be especially well drained, but it should be liberally amended with organic matter prior to planting. Set bulbs 2 to 4 feet apart, with tops of bulb necks even with the soil surface. Plants are somewhat drought tolerant, but for best performance, provide regular to copious moisture.

Divide crinums infrequently: the larger the clump becomes, the more impressive its display of foliage and flowers. Protect foliage from slugs and snails.

CONTAINER CULTURE. Follow directions "C" on page 207. Where winter temperatures fall below 20°F/−7°C, overwinter plants indoors in a bright, cool room (night temperatures from 50° to 55°F/10° to 13°C).

Crinum × powellii 'Album'

These South African natives clearly show their relationship to gladiolus, freesia, ixia, and harlequin flower *(Sparaxis tricolor).* The foliage clumps resemble those of gladiolus, with sword-shaped leaves growing in upright fans. In *C. × crocosmiiflora* (formerly *Tritonia × crocosmiiflora*), leaves may reach a height of 3 feet; the upright, branching stems grow in zigzag fashion to 3 to 4 feet. In summer, each branch bears flat sprays of vivid orange-scarlet blossoms similar in form to those of ixia.

Leaves of *C. masoniorum* are shorter (to 2½ feet) and broader than those of *C. × crocosmiiflora;* the 2½- to 3-foot flower stems bend at nearly a right angle, much like those of some freesias. The horizontal part of each stem carries a double row of ½-inch orange to scarlet blossoms.

Hybrid montbretias offer interesting variations. Three 2-foot-tall choices are 'Citronella', with yellow flowers; 'Emily MacKenzie', bearing red-throated deep orange blossoms; and 'Solfatare', with soft saffron yellow flowers above bronze foliage. 'Lucifer' is a robust 4-foot selection with bright red blooms.

Listing continues >

CROCOSMIA

MONTBRETIA

Iridaceae

CORM

- ▲ 2 TO 4 FEET
- ☼ ◑ FULL SUN; PART SHADE WHERE SUMMERS ARE HOT
- ● NEEDS SUMMER MOISTURE
- ✿ ZONES 5–24, 28–39; HYBRIDS ALSO GROW IN ZONES 4, 26

Crocosmia 'Lucifer'

CROCUS
Iridaceae
CORM

▲ 3 TO 6 INCHES

☼ ☽ FULL SUN; FILTERED SUN OR LIGHT SHADE AFTER BLOOM WHERE SUMMERS ARE HOT

◐ ACCEPTS SUMMER MOISTURE BUT DOESN'T NEED ANY

✎ ZONES 1–24, 30–45; BEST WITH SUBFREEZING WINTER TEMPERATURES

USES. Plants look attractive naturalized on sloping ground or set out to provide drifts of color among other plants. Single clumps also provide effective accents in mixed plantings.

GARDEN CULTURE. In cool- and mild-summer regions, grow in full sun; where summers are hot, give some afternoon shade. In spring, set out clumps of corms in well-drained soil enriched with organic matter, planting them about 2 inches deep and 3 inches apart. Once clumps are established, they'll perform with only casual watering—but for best results, water regularly throughout growth and bloom.

Where winter temperatures remain above 10°F/−12°C, corms are hardy in the ground; where lows range from 10° to −5°F/−12° to −21°C, protect plantings with a mulch of straw or cut conifer boughs. In colder regions, dig corms in early autumn after foliage yellows and store as for tuberous begonia (page 224).

Plantings increase in beauty as clumps grow thicker and larger; *C.* × *crocosmiiflora* can even become invasive. Divide and replant only when vigor and flower quality begin to deteriorate.

If you live in the right climate (one with some subfreezing winter temperatures), you can enjoy blooming crocuses for 7 months out of the year. Autumn-flowering species may come into bloom as early as late August; winter-blooming types continue the show where the climate allows. And as their season draws to a close, the species and hybrids that flower in late winter and early spring take the stage.

Most crocuses are native to the Mediterranean region. All have rather grasslike leaves, often with a silvery midrib. In the autumn-flowering group, flowers appear before foliage; the rest develop leaves before or during flowering. The flower tube flares at the top into a six-segmented, typically chalice-shaped blossom. The flowers appear to be stemless, since the short true stems are hidden underground.

Retail nurseries typically stock various named Dutch hybrids derived from *C. vernus*. These are the most vigorous kinds, bearing flowers in white, cream, and shades of purple, lavender, and yellow—often streaked or penciled with a contrasting color. They bloom in February where winters are mild, in April in the coldest regions.

The various crocus species and their hybrids generally are available from mail-order specialty bulb growers. These kinds usually have smaller blossoms than the familiar Dutch hybrids, but they often produce more flowers from each corm. Here are some of the more widely available species, beginning with the spring-blooming group.

C. ancyrensis. Orange-yellow blossoms; extremely early blooming.

C. angustifolius (formerly *C. susianus*). Called cloth-of-gold crocus for its brilliant orange-gold, starlike flowers; each segment has a dark brown stripe down the center.

C. biflorus. White or pale lilac flowers with purple striping on the exterior of the petals. Crossed with *C. chrysanthus* (below), it produced the hybrids 'Advance' (yellow petals with violet backs) and 'Blue Bird' (white petals with violet backs rimmed in white).

C. chrysanthus. The typical flower is sweet scented, with orange-yellow petals and black-tipped anthers. A number of named selections and hybrids are available, including 'Blue Pearl', palest blue; 'Cream Beauty', pale yellow; 'E. A. Bowles', bronzed yellow with a dark throat; 'Gipsy Girl', yellow with maroon-striped petal backs; 'Ladykiller', cold white with petal exteriors stained and marked in violet; and 'Snow Bunting', yellow-throated white with purple-feathered petal backs.

C. imperati. Saucer-shaped blossoms in bright lilac, with buff petal backs veined in violet.

C. korolkowii. Bright yellow blossoms (sometimes tinged buff or green) open out to a nearly flat star shape.

C. sieberi. Delicate lavender blue flowers with golden throats.

C. tomasinianus. Among the easiest to grow, with slender buds and star-shaped flowers in silvery lavender blue. Petal tips may be marked with a dark blotch. Named selections in solid violet or purple are available. Extremely prolific when well established, covering the ground with bloom.

Autumn-flowering species include:

C. goulimyi. Globe- to chalice-shaped blossoms are lilac to violet shading to a white throat. A native of southern Greece, this grows best where summers are hot and dry.

C. kotschyanus (formerly *C. zonatus*). Its blossoms usually are pale lavender with darker veins running the length of the petals; the flower center is either yellow or white.

C. speciosus. The showiest and largest of the autumn bloomers, this has blue-violet blossoms with brilliant orange stigmas; the petals may be as long as 3 inches. Named selections are available in pale blue, dark blue, lavender, and white.

Crocus tomasinianus

USES. For patches and drifts of color at ground level, crocuses are unsurpassed. Just a few corms can create small, jewel-like spots of color in rock gardens, between paving stones, in rock walls, and in gravel pathways. In addition, you can plant corms of Dutch *C. vernus* hybrids, *C. chrysanthus, C. speciosus,* and *C. tomasinianus* beneath deciduous trees and shrubs, or naturalize them in grassy areas that can remain unmowed until crocus foliage ripens.

GARDEN CULTURE. Crocuses are not particular about soil type, but they do require good drainage. All need sun when in bloom. In hot-summer climates, they will need a bit of light shade or filtered sun in summer; in cooler regions, summer sun is best in order to ripen the corms.

Plant corms as soon as they are available in autumn, setting them 2 to 3 inches deep and 3 to 4 inches apart. Provide regular moisture during growth and bloom; taper off when foliage begins to yellow. Crocuses prefer a dry dormant period, but they'll accept watering during that time if soil is well drained. The corms increase rapidly and will be ready for dividing after 3 to 4 years.

CONTAINER CULTURE. Follow directions "B" (subgroup 1) on page 207. You also can force crocuses for earlier bloom, following the methods outlined on pages 210–211.

TOP: *Crocus chrysanthus* 'Cream Beauty'
BOTTOM: *Crocus* 'Advance'

CYCLAMEN
Primulaceae
TUBER

- ▲ 3 TO 12 INCHES
- ☼ LIGHT SHADE OR FILTERED SUN
- ◉ NEEDS SUMMER MOISTURE
- ✄ ZONES VARY BY SPECIES
  (SEE "GARDEN CULTURE")

The large-flowered florists' cyclamen *(C. persicum)* is familiar to gardeners and nongardeners alike as a container-grown gift plant, often sold during the winter holiday season. Less well known, but much more successfully adapted to outdoor culture in many regions, are the various smaller species, most of them native to Europe, the Mediterranean region, and Asia.

All cyclamens have purple, lavender, pink, red, or white flowers resembling those of the perennial shooting star *(Dodecatheon):* elongated, somewhat twisted petals flare back sharply from a central ring that is often darker than the petals (or in a contrasting hue). Leaves are heart shaped to rounded, each carried at the end of a long, fleshy stalk. In many species, the foliage is marbled or patterned in silvery white or light green, and beautiful in its own right. Most cyclamens go through a leafless or near-leafless dormant period at some time during summer.

Listing continues >

TOP: *Cyclamen hederifolium*
BOTTOM: *Cyclamen coum*

C. persicum, the florists' cyclamen, is the largest (to 1 foot tall) and showiest of the group, available in the greatest color range: lavender, purple, red shades, pink shades, and white. Bloom begins in late autumn and continues until early spring. Leaves may be solid green or patterned in light green or silver. Dwarf or miniature strains, including Dwarf Fragrance and Mirabelle, are one-half to three-fourths the size of the standard plant. Careful gardeners can get these to bloom in 7 to 8 months from seed.

Though *C. persicum* can endure a bit of frost (to about 25°F/–4°C), it's usually grown as a container plant, spending its winter bloom period indoors in a bright, cool room.

The hardier species of cyclamen, smaller than *C. persicum,* will survive to about 0°F/–18°C. Two easy-to-grow types, both flowering on 4- to 6-inch stems, are widely available. *C. hederifolium (C. neapolitanum)* blooms in late summer or early autumn, its rose pink or white flowers appearing before the leaves. The ivylike foliage—light green marbled with silver and white—is especially handsome. *C. coum* and its numerous subspecies begin flowering with the new year and continue to bloom until earliest spring. A typical plant has solid green leaves and rosy crimson flowers, but pink- and white-blossomed forms and subspecies are also sold, some with silver-patterned foliage.

With a little nursery searching, you may also be able to find several other hardy cyclamens. Spring-blooming *C. repandum* has narrow-petaled crimson flowers on 6-inch stems; its ivylike, tooth-edged leaves are marbled with silver. The same description nearly covers midsummer-blooming *C. purpurascens (C. europaeum),* but its blossoms are fragrant and its red-backed leaves are nearly evergreen. *C. cilicium* blooms from early autumn into midwinter; its pale pink flowers (or white blooms, in the case of 'Album') are carried on 3- to 6-inch stems. Leaves are marked with silver and appear very early in the blooming season.

USES. The hardy cyclamens are fine "woodland wildflower" plants for locations in light shade or filtered sun. Plant them in small groups or large drifts, or even as a ground cover beneath trees or shrubs.

In regions where outdoor culture is possible, florists' cyclamen can be used as a bedding plant along pathway borders and in the foreground of lightly shaded gardens. In pots or planters, it adds winter color to patios and decks.

GARDEN CULTURE. Grow the hardy species as follows: *C. coum* and *C. hederifolium* in Zones 3–9, 14–24, 32–34, 37; *C. cilicium* in Zones 3–9, 14–24, 32–34; *C. purpurascens* and *C. repandum* in Zones 4–9, 14–24, 32.

Hardy cyclamens need well-drained soil liberally amended with organic matter prior to planting in late summer or early fall. Space tubers 6 to 12 inches apart, covering them with ½ inch of soil. Plants need moisture all year, so water regularly during rainless periods. Each year, just after flowers finish, topdress the soil with about ½ inch of leaf mold or compost; this will provide enough nutrition for continued good performance the following year and keep soil in top condition for the plants' shallow roots.

Tubers grow a bit larger each year, producing more and more flowers and leaves as time goes on. They do not produce increases, but can multiply by self-sown seeds. If you need to transplant a cyclamen, do so during the brief summer dormant period.

In mild-winter Zones 15–24, *C. persicum* can be grown outdoors in the same manner as the hardy species. Don't cover tubers with soil, though: plant so that the upper one-third to one-half is above the soil surface.

CONTAINER CULTURE. Florists' cyclamen grows well in containers. Use one of the soil mixes described under "B" on page 207. Plant each tuber in a pot big enough to leave 2 inches of soil between all sides of the tuber and the container edges. As described above for in-ground planting of florists' cyclamen, the top part of the tuber should be exposed.

During the growing and blooming season, water plants regularly, but never let the container sit in a saucer of water. Once a month, apply a liquid fertilizer diluted to half strength. When you take plants indoors to escape freezing weather, give them a well-lit location (in a north- or east-facing window, for example) in a cool room—ideally about 50°F/10°C at night, no warmer than 65°F/18°C during the daytime.

Plants go nearly dormant in summer; at that time, place containers in a cool, shaded spot and water infrequently. Topdress containers annually with a light application of soil mix with complete fertilizer added, being careful not to cover the top of the tuber with the mix.

Scarborough lily looks much like a more delicate version of its close relative the Dutch hybrid amaryllis *(Hippeastrum)*. In summer and early fall, each thick flower stalk is topped with a cluster of up to 10 broad, funnel-shaped blossoms; the typical color is orange red, but you'll sometimes find white- or pink-flowered forms. The glossy evergreen leaves, strap shaped and 1 to 2 feet long, are attractive throughout the year.

Where winters are very mild, this South African native can be planted in the ground. But most gardeners, even those living within the plant's hardiness range, prefer to grow Scarborough lily in containers.

USES. Garden plants make attractive accent clumps or ground covers for small areas. Use container-grown plants for accents indoors or on patio, deck, or terrace.

GARDEN CULTURE. Select a spot receiving plenty of bright, indirect light—in light shade under deciduous trees, for example (bulbs will almost always survive competition from tree roots). Except where summers are cool and overcast, don't plant in direct sun. In spring, plant bulbs in well-drained soil enriched with organic matter prior to planting, setting them 1 to 1½ feet apart and positioning the tips just beneath the soil surface. Water regularly during growth and bloom; give less water during the dormant period, but never let soil go completely dry.

Divide clumps infrequently, only when overcrowding causes a decline in vigor and bloom quality. Small bulbs will eventually form around the larger bulbs; to increase your planting, remove these in summer, before the bloom season begins, and plant them separately.

CONTAINER CULTURE. Plant bulbs in early summer, in a container large enough to leave 2 inches between all sides of the bulb and the container edges. Plant the bulb so its neck and top half are above the soil surface, using the potting mix recommended for "C" on page 207. Firm the mix thoroughly, then water well. Throughout growth and bloom, water regularly and apply liquid fertilizer monthly. During winter and spring, when bulbs are dormant, keep the soil mix just barely moist and do not fertilize at all. When the plant fills its container, repot just as growth begins, moving it into a larger pot with fresh soil mix.

Dahlias are among the most varied and variable of the summer-flowering bulbous plants. Heights range from 1 foot to over 7 feet, flower diameters from about 2 to 12 inches. Colors include all but blue and true green, and many varieties are patterned or shaded with a second color. And though dahlias are native to Mexico, they are amazingly adaptable: they grow from coast to coast and in a great latitudinal range, encompassing both short- and long-summer climates.

Listing continues >

CYRTANTHUS elatus
(C. purpureus, Vallota speciosa)
SCARBOROUGH LILY
Amaryllidaceae
TRUE BULB

▲ 2 FEET

☼ LIGHT SHADE, EXCEPT AS NOTED

◖ NEEDS SUMMER MOISTURE

✂ ZONES 16, 17, 23–27

Cyrtanthus elatus

DAHLIA
Asteraceae
TUBEROUS ROOT

▲ 1 TO 7 FEET

☼ ◖ FULL SUN; PART SHADE WHERE SUMMERS ARE HOT

◖ NEEDS SUMMER MOISTURE

✂ ALL ZONES (SEE "GARDEN CULTURE")

The American Dahlia Society has divided flower types into 12 groups (formal decorative, anemone, and cactus, for example), each including plants of varying heights. Specialists use these classifications in describing available varieties—but the general nursery trade may not do so, nor do we use them in the discussion here.

USES. Plant dahlias in separate beds or in combination with other plants. Use smaller types as low borders, short accents, or container plants; taller ones make striking accents or temporary screens and hedges.

GARDEN CULTURE. Dahlias can be grown in all zones. Though the roots can be left in the ground where winter temperatures remain above 20°F/−7°C, gardeners in most areas prefer to dig them annually.

Plant dahlias in spring, after air and soil have warmed. The easiest gauge is this: when the time is right to plant tomatoes, corn, and potatoes, it's right for dahlias. Except where summers are hot, choose a location in full sun; in hot-summer regions, plants need light shade during the hottest part of the day. Also keep in mind that flowers face the source of light.

Dahlias grow best in well-drained soil liberally enriched with organic matter. Space roots of larger dahlias (over 4 feet tall) 4 to 5 feet apart, those of smaller types 1 to 2 feet apart. For each root, dig a 1-foot-deep planting hole—about 1½ feet across for larger dahlias, 9 to 12 inches across for smaller ones. (This deep-planting method gives the plant more stability as it grows taller.) Incorporate about ¼ cup of granular low-nitrogen fertilizer into the soil at the bottom of the hole. Then add a layer of pulverized native soil—about 4 inches if the soil is on the sandy side, about 6 inches if it's more claylike.

If you're planting a tall variety, drive a 5- to 6-foot stake into the hole just off center; place the root horizontally in bottom of hole, 2 inches from the stake and with the growth bud pointing toward it. Cover the root with 3 inches of soil and water well. Unless weather is dry and soil loses its moisture, don't water again until growth begins.

As the shoots grow, gradually fill in the hole with soil. For tall-growing varieties, thin out shoots when they're about 6 inches tall, leaving only the strongest one or two. When these shoots have three pairs of leaves, pinch out the growing tip just above the upper set of leaves to encourage bushy growth. Varieties with small flowers need just one pinching, but if you're growing large-flowered dahlias, pinch again after subsequent growth has produced three pairs of leaves.

Dahlias grow rapidly, so they need a steady supply of water after shoots emerge; be sure to moisten the soil to a depth of at least 1 foot each time you water. Mulch soil to conserve moisture. Properly prepared soil should contain enough nutrients to last plants through the season. But if your soil is light or if roots remained in the ground the previous year, apply a granular low-nitrogen fertilizer when the first flower buds show. During growth and bloom, watch for mildew on foliage.

In fall, after plants turn yellow or have been frosted (whichever comes first), cut stalks down to 6 inches. Where dahlias can overwinter in the ground, you can leave the roots undisturbed through a second and sometimes even a third bloom season before you dig and separate. To lift dahlias, carefully dig a 2-foot-wide circle around each plant and gently pry up the clump with a spading fork. Shake off loose soil, being careful not to break roots apart; then let the clump dry in the sun for several hours.

At this point, you have two choices. You can divide roots immediately; or you can store clumps intact, then divide them several weeks before planting in spring. Fall division is simpler, since growth buds are easier to recognize and separated roots are easier to store. However, fall-separated roots are more likely to shrivel in storage and are also more susceptible to rot. To divide clumps, cut them apart with a sharp knife, making

TOP: *Dahlia* 'Apache'
BOTTOM: *Dahlia* 'Prince Valiant'

sure that each separate root is attached to a portion of stalk with a visible growth bud (see page 205). Dust each cut with sulfur to prevent rot during storage.

To store divided roots (or intact clumps) over winter, place them in a single layer and cover with dry sand, sawdust, peat moss, vermiculite, or perlite. Keep in a dark, dry, cool place (40° to 45°F/4° to 7°C) until spring. Check occasionally for signs of shriveling; lightly moisten the storage material if necessary.

About 2 to 4 weeks before planting time, separate intact clumps, cutting them apart as directed above. Then place all roots—whether fall-divided or spring-divided—in moist sand to plump them up and encourage sprouting.

CONTAINER CULTURE. Smaller types are best for containers, since they don't require pinching or staking. Use one of the soil mixes described under "B" on page 207. Plant one tuberous root or cluster to a 10-inch pot, three to a 15-inch pot. When plants die down, knock them from pots; cut off tops and store clumps as directed above, then divide and repot in fresh soil mix at planting time. Or store plants in their pots over winter; then knock from pots, divide, and repot in fresh soil mix at planting time.

Dahlia flower forms, clockwise from top left: ball, anemone, formal decorative

DICHELOSTEMMA.
See BRODIAEA

DIETES
AFRICAN IRIS, FORTNIGHT LILY
Iridaceae
RHIZOME

- ▲ 1½ TO 3 FEET
- ☼ ◑ FULL SUN OR LIGHT SHADE
- ◐ NEEDS SOME SUMMER MOISTURE
- ⧄ ZONES 8, 9, 12–28

These South African natives are irislike in both foliage and blossom. The narrow, flat, evergreen leaves are arranged in fans; the branching stems carry flattish, six-segmented blossoms that could pass for beardless irises. Though each flower lasts for only one day, each blossom stalk carries a seemingly inexhaustible supply of buds. Flowering comes in bursts through spring, summer, and fall—and even in winter, in very mild climates. To prolong bloom and prevent self-sowing, break off any seedpods that develop.

For many years, these plants were grouped with *Moraea,* and some nurseries still offer them under their old names. *D. vegeta* (formerly known as *D. iridioides*) is the most widely grown species; it's also one of the tallest (2 to 3 feet) and largest flowered. Each 3-inch, waxy white blossom has an orange-and-brown blotch and some blue shading on the three outer segments. Variety 'Johnsonii' is larger and more robust. Flower stems are productive for several years. To groom plants, just break off developing seedpods; cut out stems only when they die.

The plant sold as *D. catenulata* is now considered merely a small-growing form of *D. vegeta.* Foliage and flowering stems reach 1½ to 2 feet; the stems frequently produce offsets that weigh them to the ground, where the offsets take root. This form is more sensitive to cold than the standard *D. vegeta,* its foliage suffering damage at 30°F/−1°C.

The blooms of *D. bicolor* are light yellow with dark brown blotches; they're slightly smaller and more rounded than those of *D. vegeta.* The 2- to 3-foot flower stems each last just 1 year.

Two white-flowered hybrids of *D. vegeta* and *D. bicolor* are occasionally sold. 'Orange Drops' has an orange spot on three of the six flower segments; 'Lemon Drops' has yellow spots. Both hybrids resemble *D. vegeta* in stem and foliage size, but have smaller, rounder blossoms more like those of *D. bicolor.*

USES. The thick clumps of narrow leaves, good looking all year, make effective accents; they're especially attractive in Japanese gardens and near water or rocks.

GARDEN CULTURE. Though all species and hybrids look their best with good soil and regular water, one of their virtues is toughness: once established, they'll turn in a satisfactory performance even in poor soil and with infrequent or erratic watering. Plant

Dietes vegeta

from containers (bare rhizomes are not sold) at any time of year. Choose a sunny or lightly shaded spot; set plants about 2 feet apart, at the depth they were growing in their pots.

Clumps can remain undisturbed for many years. If you need to divide or move them, do so in fall or winter.

CONTAINER CULTURE. The smaller plant sold as *D. catenulata* can be a conversation-piece hanging basket plant; plantlets will droop from its arching stems in the fashion of spider plant *(Chlorophytum)*. Follow directions "C" on page 207.

ENDYMION.
See HYACINTHOIDES

ERANTHIS HYEMALIS
WINTER ACONITE
Ranunculaceae
TUBER

▲ 2 TO 8 INCHES
☼ ◑ FULL SUN DURING BLOOM, PART SHADE DURING REST OF YEAR
◐ NEEDS SOME SUMMER MOISTURE
✂ ZONES 1–9, 14–17, 32–43

Eranthis hyemalis with *Crocus*

T his little European and Asian native is one of the harbingers of spring: blossoming stems often come up through snow, appearing before the leaves. Each stem bears its 1½-inch, buttercuplike yellow flower on a leafy collar. Rounded basal leaves, each divided into narrow lobes, emerge later.

USES. Rock gardens, pathway borders, and woodland plantings are all good settings for winter aconite. For an attractive mixed planting, combine it with other bulbs that bloom at around the same time.

GARDEN CULTURE. The best planting site is one receiving full sun during bloom time, part shade for the rest of the year. Set out tubers in late summer, as soon as they are available in nurseries; if they look dry or shriveled, plump them up in wet sand before planting. Set them about 3 inches deep and 4 inches apart, in good, well-drained soil enriched with organic matter. Throughout growth

Eranthis hyemalis

and bloom, keep soil moist but not saturated. Tubers will get by with less moisture during summer dormancy, but the soil should not dry out completely.

Divide clumps infrequently, since it takes plants a year or more to reestablish. Separate into smaller clumps rather than individual tubers.

EREMURUS
FOXTAIL LILY
Liliaceae
TUBEROUS ROOT

▲ 3 TO 9 FEET
☼ FULL SUN
◐ NEEDS SOME SUMMER MOISTURE
✂ ZONES 1–9, 14, 32–43; BEST WITH SUBFREEZING WINTER TEMPERATURES

N ative to western and central Asia, foxtail lily is an impressive plant. Its flowering stems reach 3 to 9 feet tall, rising from fountainlike rosettes of narrow, strap-shaped leaves in late spring or early summer. The upper one-third to one-half of each stem is packed with starlike blossoms ½ to 1 inch wide; buds open in sequence from the bottom of the stem, giving half-open spikes the look of a fox's tail. After bloom is over, the foliage yellows and dies back to the ground; new leaves don't emerge until early the following spring.

Specialty bulb growers offer various species as well as hybrid strains and selected named varieties. Among the species, pink-flowered *E. robustus* easily attains 8 to 9 feet when in bloom; white-flowered *E. himalaicus* is only 1 to 2 feet shorter. The runt of this group, at a mere 3 to 5 feet, is yellow-blossomed *E. stenophyllus* (formerly known as *E. bungei*).

Several hybrid strains—both long-established groups and newer ones—are now grouped under *E. × isabellinus*. The well-known Shelford Hybrids reach 4 to 5 feet, bearing flowers in pink, yellow, buff, orange, or white; the Highdown Hybrids, based on the Shelford work, include plants of shorter stature. The Ruiter Hybrids, developed in the Netherlands, feature bright, clear flower colors; some named selections are available, such as orange-and-red 'Cleopatra', chartreuse 'Obelisk', and salmon red 'Romance'.

USES. These imposing plants add vertical accents to the late-spring garden. Plant them where other perennials and annuals will fill in the blank spots left after the foliage dies down in summer.

GARDEN CULTURE. Plant in fall, in a sunny location with good, well-drained soil enriched with organic matter. Space the roots 2 to 4 feet apart. To plant each, dig a hole large enough to accommodate it easily; form a cone of soil and spread the roots over it and downwards, positioning the growing point about 1 inch below ground. Then cover with soil. Handle roots carefully: they are brittle and may rot if damaged.

Water regularly from the onset of growth until foliage has died back, then less often throughout late summer and fall. Roots will rot if soil is overly moist in winter, making well-drained soil especially critical in regions where winter rainfall is plentiful.

New growth can be harmed by freezing nights. To prevent damage, give winter protection (see page 205); remove after the danger of hard frosts is past.

Eremurus stenophyllus

M ost *Erythronium* species are woodland plants with lilylike spring flowers and broad, tongue-shaped, brown-mottled leaves. Because many are fairly exacting in their cultural requirements, they are generally sold only by bulb specialists—particularly those in western North America, where a number of species are native.

The various species have acquired a variety of common names, many of which describe the leaves. *E. americanum,* one of several species from eastern North America, is called trout lily or adder's tongue—the first name referring to leaves' mottled appearance, the second to their shape. Each 6-inch leaf is splotched with purplish brown and near-white; one nodding, yellow, 2-inch flower tops each 9- to 12-inch stem.

Dog-tooth violets take their name from the plants' fang-shaped corms. *E. dens-canis,* a European native, has 4- to 6-inch leaves mottled brown and white. Each 6- to 12-inch flower stem bears a single 1-inch blossom; the typical color is deep pink to purple, but specialists offer other choices, such as pure white 'Snowflake'. North American native *E. albidum,* another dog-tooth violet, has 6-inch leaves lightly mottled in silvery green; its foot-tall flower stems bear solitary yellow-centered white blossoms.

Western North America is home to a number of species, many of which are known as fawn lilies from the brown mottling on their leaves. All of these prefer little or no moisture from the time leaves yellow until autumn.

E. californicum sends up 6- to 10-inch stems from clumps of mottled, 6-inch leaves; each stem carries up to three white flowers, yellow at the base. *E. revolutum* is similar, but its foliage and flowers are larger and its stems can reach 16 inches. Its blossoms are usually lavender, but 'Rose Beauty' and 'White Beauty' are variants.

The brown-mottled, dark green leaves of *E. hendersonii* may grow to 8 inches long; each of its foot-tall stems bears one to four nodding lavender blossoms. *E. tuolumnense* has yellowish green, foot-long leaves and 12- to 15-inch stems, each carrying several starlike yellow blossoms.

Several named selections are available, variously listed as forms of *E. revolutum* or *E. tuolumnense,* or as hybrids of the two. 'Citronella' has lemon yellow blossoms; 'Kondo' and 'Pagoda' feature yellow flowers with brown centers. All are vigorous growers, better adapted to ordinary garden culture than the species.

Listing continues >

ERYTHRONIUM
Liliaceae
CORM

- ▲ 6 TO 16 INCHES
- ☼ FILTERED SUN OR LIGHT TO MODER-ATE SHADE, EXCEPT AS NOTED
- ●○ ALL BUT WESTERN NATIVES NEED SUMMER MOISTURE
- ✎ ZONES VARY BY SPECIES (SEE "GARDEN CULTURE")

Erythronium 'Kondo'

Erythronium hendersonii

USES. Plant clumps or drifts in woodland gardens, rock gardens, along pathways, or under deciduous trees and shrubs.

GARDEN CULTURE. Grow *E. albidum* in Zones 1–6, 32–43; *E. dens-canis* in Zones 1–7, 15–17, 31–43; *E. americanum* in Zones 1–7, 15–17, 28, 31–43; *E. californicum, E. hendersonii, E. revolutum* in Zones 2–7, 14–17, 33–41; *E. tuolumnense* and above-listed hybrids in Zones 2–7, 14–17, 32 (colder parts), 33–41.

With the exception of *E. dens-canis,* which needs only partial shade (preferably during the hot afternoon hours), all species do best in filtered sunlight or light to moderate shade. In fall, plant corms in well-drained soil liberally amended with organic matter; arrange them in clumps or drifts, setting them 2 to 3 inches deep and 4 to 5 inches apart. Withhold summer moisture from the western North American species and their hybrids (noted on previous page); all other species need moisture the year around. Divide plantings of all types infrequently—only when vigor and bloom quality decline.

EUCHARIS × grandiflora
AMAZON LILY
Amaryllidaceae
TRUE BULB

- ▲ 1½ TO 2 FEET
- ☼ LIGHT SHADE
- ● REGULATE WATER TO INDUCE FLOWERING (SEE "CONTAINER CULTURE")
- ✄ ZONE 25

Eucharis × grandiflora

Except in absolutely frost-free areas, this native of the South American tropics is strictly a container plant to be brought inside during cold weather (or kept indoors all year long). Its thin-textured, glossy, tongue-shaped leaves grow to 1 foot long, supported by equally long leafstalks. The 1½- to 2-foot flowering stems support clusters of up to six fragrant white blossoms, each resembling a 3-inch daffodil. It blooms primarily in winter, though it can flower periodically throughout the year under ideal conditions.

USES. Good-looking foliage and flowers make Amazon lily an excellent choice for a house plant. It's also attractive on patio, deck, or terrace in warm weather.

GARDEN CULTURE. To try Amazon lily in the garden, choose a spot where plants will receive as much light as possible without direct sun. Because dormancy is induced by withholding water (see "Container culture"), bulbs may be planted at any time of year. Set them 4 inches apart, tips even with the soil surface, in well-drained soil liberally amended with organic matter. Crowded clumps give the best performance.

CONTAINER CULTURE. Follow directions "C" on page 207. Water bulbs thoroughly just after potting, then sparingly until growth begins. Increase water as leaves grow, keeping soil moist; every other week, apply liquid fertilizer diluted to half strength.

After bloom finishes, stop fertilizing and cut back on water, giving just enough to keep leaves from wilting. When new growth begins, resume regular watering and fertilizing. This technique may induce plants to bloom several times in a year.

Repot or divide only when a plant crowds its container to capacity.

EUCOMIS
PINEAPPLE FLOWER
Liliaceae
TRUE BULB

- ▲ 1½ TO 3 FEET
- ☼ ◖ FULL SUN; FILTERED SUN OR LIGHT SHADE WHERE SUMMERS ARE HOT
- ● NEEDS SUMMER MOISTURE
- ✄ ZONES 4–29

As its common name suggests, this native of tropical southern Africa presents a convincing imitation of a pineapple fruit: the upper portion of each summer-flowering spike is topped with a tuft of leafy bracts and surrounded by a tight, cylindrical cluster of fragrant, starlike blossoms. Decorative purplish seed capsules follow the flowers.

E. bicolor has green blossoms with purple petal edges; flower spikes reach about 2 feet, rising from rosettes of broad, wavy-edged leaves. *E. comosa* (sometimes sold as *E. punctata*) grows to 3 feet tall, with leaves to 2 feet long; its greenish white blossoms are tinged with pink or purple. The shortest species, at 1½ feet, is *E. autumnalis;* it bears pale green flowers that fade to white.

USES. Pineapple flower is an attractive foliage plant at all times, and a conversation piece when in bloom. Grow it in containers or at the foreground of garden plantings.

GARDEN CULTURE. Choose a location in full sun (filtered sun or light shade where summers are hot) and enrich the soil with organic matter. Set out bulbs in fall, 4 to 6 inches deep and 1 foot apart. When growth begins in spring, apply a granular fertilizer. Water regularly during growth and bloom, but give little or no water during winter dormancy—plants can usually survive on rainfall. Divide plants infrequently, perhaps every 5 or 6 years.

CONTAINER CULTURE. Plant bulbs in spring, following directions "C" on page 207; set bulbs with tips just beneath the surface. For best results, repot yearly in fresh soil mix.

Eucomis autumnalis

T o people who know them, freesias and fragrance are synonymous. In spring, the wiry, 1- to 1½-foot-tall stems bear trumpet-shaped flowers that reach 2 inches long and flare to 2 inches across. Each stem bends at nearly a right angle just beneath the lowest bud, so a double rank of blossoms faces upward (or nearly so). Narrow, swordlike leaves to 1 foot tall grow in irislike fans.

The most widely available freesia in times past was creamy white, powerfully sweet-scented *F. alba,* from South Africa's Cape Province. In favorable climates, it naturalizes easily, both from offsets and self-sown seedlings. Today, though, the most popular freesias are hybrids offering larger blossoms (both single and double) in a color range that includes yellow, orange, red, pink, lavender, purple, and blue as well as the traditional white. Not all of these, however, are as fragrant as the old-fashioned favorite. Dutch and Tecolote hybrids represent the majority of the new kinds sold in the retail trade; you can buy mixed-color assortments as well as named varieties in specific colors.

USES. Try naturalizing freesias in clumps or drifts, or use them in borders of drought-tolerant plants.

GARDEN CULTURE. Freesias need well-drained soil and little or no water during their summer dormant period. Plant corms in fall, setting them 2 inches deep and about 2 inches apart. Close spacing—and planting in clumps or drifts—lets the somewhat floppy flowering stems prop each other up. Plants need moisture during growth and bloom, but you should cut back on watering when leaves start to yellow in late spring. In regions with dry summers and mild winters, you can leave corms in the ground if the soil can be kept fairly dry until autumn. In rainy-summer areas, it's best to dig corms when foliage yellows; store them over summer as for gladiolus (page 248), then replant in early fall.

Freesia corms increase rapidly. Dig and divide them for increase after several years, if you wish; or leave plantings in place until vigor and bloom quality decline. Unless you remove faded flowers, freesias tend to set seed and provide you with volunteer seedlings; many of these, however, will have white or creamy white flowers.

CONTAINER CULTURE. Plant corms 2 inches deep and 1 inch apart, following directions "B" (subgroup 2) on page 207. In cold-winter climates, you can grow freesias indoors in a cool room—60° to 65°F/16° to 18°C during the day, around 55°F/13°C at night. Bulb growers produce cold-treated corms that can be potted in spring to bloom in summer the first year. In subsequent years, these will bloom at the normal time in early spring.

FREESIA
Iridaceae
CORM

▲ 1 TO 1½ FEET
☼ ◑ FULL SUN OR PART SHADE
◌ WITHHOLD SUMMER MOISTURE
✎ ZONES 8, 9, 12–24, 28

Freesia hybrids

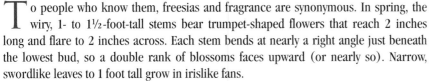

FRITILLARIA

FRITILLARY
Liliaceae
TRUE BULB

- ▲ 6 INCHES TO 4 FEET
- ☼ FILTERED SUN OR LIGHT SHADE,
  EXCEPT AS NOTED
- ● ◑ ◯ SUMMER MOISTURE NEEDS
  VARY BY SPECIES (SEE "GARDEN
  CULTURE")
- ✠ ZONES VARY BY SPECIES
  (SEE "GARDEN CULTURE");
  BEST WITH SUBFREEZING WINTER
  TEMPERATURES

Fritillaria imperialis

Native to temperate regions of the Northern Hemisphere, these spring bloomers are a contradictory group. Most have a wildflower charm, though the blossoms—in red, orange, yellow, maroon, purple shades, cream, and white—are often rather strangely and intricately marked.

The best-known species—*F. imperialis,* the crown imperial—is the exceptional individual and would hardly fit anyone's idea of a woodland wildflower. Its thick stems grow 3 to 4 feet tall, clothed for about half their height in whorls of lance-shaped 6-inch leaves. At the top of each stem is a circular cluster of drooping, bell-shaped flowers topped by a thick tuft of leaflike bracts. Blossoms are 2 to 3 inches long; the usual color is a clear and brilliant red, but orange and yellow forms are also available. Both bulb and plant have a musky odor that some people find objectionable.

The 2- to 3-foot stems of *F. persica* also are clothed in whorls of leaves over their lower half, but there the similarity to crown imperial ends. The upper portion of the stem is a spike of up to 30 pendent, 1-inch bells in a somber but alluring dark plum purple. *F. camschatcensis,* appropriately called black lily or chocolate lily, also has a leafy flowering stem; it reaches 1½ feet tall, with one to eight brownish maroon to black bells dangling from the top.

Most other fritillaries are more diminutive (though no less unusual or striking), bearing small, pendent bells atop slender, fairly short stems. Well-known European native *F. meleagris,* the checkered lily or snakeshead, produces stems to 15 inches high that rise above three or more narrow, 3- to 6-inch leaves. The nodding, bell-shaped 2-inch blooms, carried one to three per stem, are typically marked in an unusual checkerboard pattern. The most common color combination is light with dark maroon, but there are variations (pale gray with brownish purple, white with light violet) as well as solid colors of dark purple, lilac, and white. In *F. acmopetala,* one to three flowers nod from a 1½-foot stem; each green bell is brushed or striped purple on the outside. About the same size is *F. pallidiflora,* with one to six greenish yellow flowers per stem. *F. michailovskyi* is the shortest fritillary—just 6 inches high, with one to six flowers nodding from each stem. The blossoms are purple over the lower two-thirds, then yellow to the petal tips.

The western United States is home to several appealing fritillaries. Checker lily, *F. affinis,* has bell-like blossoms with a checkerboard pattern like that of *F. meleagris.* In *F. affinis,* however, the colors are brownish purple and yellow, while the stems, clothed in whorls of leaves on their lower part, reach 2½ feet. Scarlet fritillary, *F. recurva,* has the same general appearance as checker lily and grows about as tall, but its bell-shaped blossoms are bright red with yellow centers. Mission bells, *F. biflora,* produces 16-inch stems with leafy whorls, each bearing one to six purple-tinged brown blossoms; its selection 'Martha Roderick' has rusty orange bells centered in white.

Bulb specialists may offer other, less well-known species—some strikingly beautiful, some intriguing looking, and all worth growing.

USES. Naturalize fritillaries in grassland or meadow areas; the smaller species are also attractive in rock gardens and at the margins of woodland plantings. Crown imperial makes a striking and stately color accent in mixed perennial, bulb, and annual groupings.

GARDEN CULTURE. Grow *F. imperialis* in Zones 1–7, 14–17, 32–43; *F. camschatcensis* and *F. meleagris* in Zones 1–7, 15–17, 32–43; *F. pallidiflora* in Zones 1–7, 33–43; *F. michailovskyi* and *F. persica* in Zones 2–7, 14–17, 32 (colder parts), 33–41; *F. affinis, F. biflora,* and *F. recurva* in Zones 3–7, 14–17; *F. acmopetala* in Zones 7–9, 14–21. All fritillaries appreciate some winter chilling and tend to perform poorly where summers are hot and dry.

F. imperialis and *F. persica* can take full sun where summers are cool and overcast; elsewhere, locate them where they will get light shade in summer. The other species prefer filtered sunlight or light shade everywhere.

Fritillaries need good, well-drained soil enriched with organic matter. In fall, set the large bulbs of *F. imperialis* 4 to 5 inches deep, 8 to 12 inches apart; set those of the smaller species 3 to 4 inches deep, 6 inches apart. Give plants regular moisture during growth and bloom; cut back as foliage dies back in summer. After foliage is gone, withhold water entirely from the western natives *(F. affinis, F. biflora, F. recurva)* until fall. The other species prefer reduced summer moisture—except for *F. meleagris*, which requires regular to moderate watering during summer.

Established bulbs seldom need dividing; dig and separate only when you want to increase plantings.

Fritillaria meleagris

I n the cold-weather climates they prefer, snowdrops are among the first bulbs to bloom as winter draws to a close. Even if a snowfall catches plants in flower, the blossoming stems will pop back up again—as long as the snow melts quickly.

The various snowdrops are native to deciduous woodlands of Europe and Asia Minor. In all types, each bulb produces two or three slender leaves and one flower stem. Each stem bears one pendent, six-petaled white flower; the three inner petals are always shorter than the three outer ones, and are usually marked or infused with green.

Though all snowdrops need a climate in which at least some winter night temperatures drop below 32°F/0°C, the giant snowdrop, *G. elwesii*, is adapted to regions without too much winter chill. Its rather egg-shaped flowers are up to 1½ inches long, their inner petals heavily infused with green. Stems reach 1 foot tall, rising above two or three narrow 8-inch leaves.

Common snowdrop, *G. nivalis,* grows 6 to 9 inches tall; it has inch-long bell-shaped flowers, the inner petals marked at the tips with a precise green crescent. 'Flore Pleno' has double blooms; 'Viridapicis' is a vigorous form with green marks on all floral parts.

USES. Snowdrops find their niche in woodland landscapes and rock gardens. An ideal location is near deciduous trees or shrubs, where the planting area will be sunny during the bulbs' bloom period but lightly shaded later in the year.

GARDEN CULTURE. Plant in fall. Enrich the soil with organic matter; then set bulbs 3 to 4 inches deep and 3 inches apart. Snowdrops prefer moisture all year, so water periodically when rainfall doesn't do the job for you.

Snowdrop bulbs may stay in place for many years, naturalizing into large drifts. If you need to divide or move plants, do so in spring, just after flowers fade. Try to keep plenty of soil around bulbs; replant immediately and water regularly.

GALANTHUS
SNOWDROP
Amaryllidaceae
TRUE BULB

- ▲ 6 TO 12 INCHES
- ☀ ◐ FULL SUN DURING BLOOM, LIGHT SHADE DURING REST OF YEAR
- ◗ NEEDS SUMMER MOISTURE
- ✚ ZONES 1–9, 14–17, 31–45; BEST WITH SUBFREEZING WINTER TEMPERATURES

Galanthus nivalis

D espite its common name, this summer bloomer from southern Africa doesn't look much like the familiar spring-blooming hyacinth *(Hyacinthus)*. Each bulb produces a stout, erect stem that carries a spire of 20 or more sweet-scented, pendent white bells about 1½ inches long. The floppy, strap-shaped leaves reach a length of 2 to 3 feet.

USES. The white flower spikes add height and a welcome dash of coolness to the summer garden.

Listing continues >

GALTONIA candicans
SUMMER HYACINTH
Liliaceae
TRUE BULB

- ▲ 2 TO 4 FEET
- ☀ ◐ FULL SUN; LIGHT SHADE WHERE SUMMERS ARE HOT
- ◗ NEEDS SUMMER MOISTURE
- ✚ ZONES 4–32

Galtonia candicans

GLADIOLUS

Iridaceae

CORM

- ▲ 1½ TO 6 FEET
- ☼ FULL SUN
- ● NEEDS MOISTURE UNTIL LEAVES YELLOW
- ✎ ZONES VARY BY TYPE (SEE "GARDEN CULTURE")

Gladiolus tristis

GARDEN CULTURE. Summer hyacinth revels in rich soil and lots of water. Dig plenty of organic matter into the soil in advance of planting; choose a sunny spot if your summers are cool to moderate, a lightly shaded location in hot-summer regions. Plant bulbs 6 inches deep, 1 foot apart—in fall where winter lows won't fall below 10°F/−12°C, in spring in colder regions. Water plants regularly during growth and bloom; provide protection from slugs and snails.

Summer hyacinth gives the best display if allowed to remain undisturbed from one year to the next. Where winter lows range from 10° to −20°F/−12° to −29°C, protect the planting area with a mulch after foliage dies down. In colder regions, dig bulbs annually and store them over winter as for gladiolus (below).

If you need to divide or move plantings, do so at the best planting time for your climate.

The word "gladiolus" automatically brings to mind the large, tall, variously colored hybrids so familiar in summer gardens and as cut flowers. Derived from a number of species over a century of hybridization, these magnificent flowers are collectively known as grandiflora hybrids. Less well known, but no less lovely or desirable, are smaller hybrids and several species gladiolus. Whatever the size or flamboyance, all these plants conform to a general pattern. Funnel-shaped flowers are arranged alternately on either side of a slender blossom spike, all facing the same direction; the blooms open in sequence from the bottom to the top of the spike. The leaves are shaped like a sword blade (hence the name *gladiolus,* Latin for "little sword") and arranged in narrow, upright fans.

Grandiflora hybrids. Blooming in late spring and summer, these plants produce spikes that reach 3 to 6 feet tall, depending on the variety and growing conditions. The flowers (up to 30 per spike) are widely flaring and up to 8 inches across; colors include white, cream, yellow, orange, apricot, salmon, red, rose, lavender, purple, smoky shades, buff, and even green. Smaller selections from grandiflora breeding are grouped as small and miniature gladiolus; these grow 3 to 4 feet high and bear up to 18 flowers on each spike.

Primulinus and butterfly hybrids. These summer bloomers derive in part from *G. dalenii* (formerly *G. primulinus*), an African species with primrose yellow flowers that are hooded rather than funnel shaped. Named varieties grow 3 to 4 feet high, each spike bearing up to 18 blossoms spaced apart from one another; flowers are at least somewhat hooded, in a wide color range. The group known as butterfly gladiolus has 2- to 3-foot flowering stems, the blossoms more closely spaced; distinct throat markings or blotches of contrasting color give them the "butterfly" appearance.

Baby gladiolus. This group of hybrids derives in part from *G.* × *colvillei,* an early 19th-century hybrid that bore dark red blossoms on a spike a bit under 2 feet high; its pure white selection 'The Bride' is still available. Modern baby gladiolus are late spring bloomers with stems to 1½ feet tall and flaring flowers (like those of the large grandiflora types) to about 3 inches across; the color range is extensive, with some varieties showing throat blotches in a contrasting color. Plants listed under Nanus Hybrids are part of this group.

Species gladiolus. Several appealing gladiolus species are available from specialists. The tropical African native *G. callianthus* blooms in late summer and fall; it was classed as *Acidanthera bicolor* until recently, and some growers may still offer it under that name. Borne on 2- to 3-foot stems, its fragrant, creamy white blossoms are blotched with chocolate brown at the base; the elongated, pointed petals produce flowers of a more starlike shape than the blooms of other species. The selected variant 'Murielae' is taller, with crimson-blotched petals. Summer-blooming South African

G. tristis has 1½-foot stems bearing scented blossoms, typically in light yellow with purple veins. Byzantine gladiolus, *G. communis byzantinus,* is a southern European species; it blooms in summer, bearing flared maroon flowers on 2- to 3-foot stems that rise from clumps of distinctly narrow leaves.

USES. Many gardeners grow gladiolus for cut flowers, planting them in space-efficient rows. But clumps of gladiolus are much more pleasing to the eye: the plants' stiffness becomes an asset, providing a vertical accent in plantings of annuals and perennials.

GARDEN CULTURE. Grow grandiflora hybrids in Zones 4–9, 12–24, 29–33; primulinus and butterfly hybrids, *G. callianthus, G. communis byzantinus,* and *G. tristis* in Zones 4–9, 12–24, 29–31; baby gladiolus in Zones 4–9, 12–24 (baby glads sold as "winter-hardy" can also be grown in Zones 2, 3, 33–41).

Gladiolus × *colvillei* 'The Bride'

Plant baby gladiolus in fall or early spring for flowers in late spring. Plant corms of all others from midwinter (in the mildest regions) into spring, after soil has warmed. The showy grandiflora hybrids will flower about 100 days after planting; the smaller hybrids and species will bloom in about 80 days. If you plant corms at 1- to 2-week intervals over a period of 4 to 6 weeks, you can enjoy an extended flowering season.

During warm to hot summer weather, thrips can seriously disfigure gladiolus blossoms. Many growers prefer to plant corms as early as possible, so that bloom will be over before thrips can become a problem (systemic insecticides, however, can virtually eliminate a thrips problem). If you want gladiolus to flower before the onset of hottest weather, plant at these times: *mild West Coast:* January through March; *Pacific Northwest:* April through June; *Southwest low desert:* November through January; *Southeast:* April through June; *Midwest, Mid-Atlantic, and Northeast:* May and June.

For the best-looking plants and flowers, purchase corms that are high crowned for their width; broad, flat corms are older and less vigorous. Choose a bright, sunny planting area, preferably with sandy loam soil; then dig a generous amount of organic matter into the soil before you set out corms.

Planting depth varies according to soil type and corm size. Set corms deeper in light soils than in heavy ones; set thicker corms deeper than thinner ones. As a general rule, plant each corm about four times as deep as it is thick, making some adjustment for soil type. For example, you might set a 1-inch-thick corm 4 inches deep in its preferred sandy loam, only 2 to 3 inches deep in a heavy soil. Spacing depends on corm diameter; position broader corms about 6 inches apart, smaller ones about 4 inches apart.

Gladiolus, grandiflora hybrid

Water regularly from the time leaves emerge until bloom is over (this will entail providing moisture for some part of the summer, depending on when you planted). If you cut flowering stems for display indoors, leave at least four leaves on each plant; these will build up the corm for the next year's performance. Stems left to bloom out in the garden should be trimmed off beneath the lowest flower after blossoms fade. Uncut stems will set seeds, diverting energy from food storage in the corm.

Some time after flowering, leaves will begin to turn yellow. When this begins, withhold water and let foliage yellow completely. At this point, you face the question of digging or not digging. In zones beyond the stated hardiness, you must dig corms and store them over winter in a frost-free location. Within the stated hardiness zones, corms can remain in the ground over winter without risk. Nevertheless, many growers in these regions still prefer to dig corms each year, figuring that performance is better when corms are separated and replanted the next year in reworked or fresh soil. When you dig corms, shake off soil, then cut off stems and leaves just above each corm. Destroy cut-off tops to get rid of any thrips. (In rainy-summer areas, some growers dig plants before foliage yellows to prevent botrytis infection, which could ruin corms in storage.)

Listing continues >

Gladiolus callianthus

GLORIOSA rothschildiana

GLORY LILY, CLIMBING LILY

Liliaceae

TUBER

▲ 6 FEET (CLIMBING)

☼ ◑ FULL SUN; FILTERED SUN OR LIGHT
SHADE WHERE SUMMERS ARE HOT

◐ NEEDS SUMMER MOISTURE

✂ ZONES 24–27

⬦ ALL PARTS ARE POISONOUS
IF INGESTED

Gloriosa rothschildiana

HABRANTHUS

Amaryllidaceae

TRUE BULB

▲ 6 TO 12 INCHES

☼ ◑ FULL SUN OR PART SHADE

◐ NEEDS SUMMER MOISTURE

✂ ZONES 8, 9, 14–28

Place corms on a flat surface in a dark, dry area and let them dry for 2 to 3 weeks. Then examine corms carefully; discard those showing lesions, irregular blotches, or discoloration, all of which could indicate disease. Remove the old, spent base from each healthy corm. If you'd like to increase a particular variety, save the small offsets (cormels) for replanting; they should reach blooming size in 2 to 3 years.

Dust all corms and cormels with a powdered insecticide and keep them in a dry, cool place (40° to 50°F/4° to 10°C) until planting time. To store corms, place them in onion sacks or in discarded nylon stockings or pantyhose, then hang them up; or arrange them in a single layer on shallow trays. Stack the trays if necessary, placing spacers between them to allow for air circulation.

CONTAINER CULTURE. The smaller gladiolus make interesting container subjects. Use one of the soil mixes described under "B" on page 207. When plants die down, knock them from pots; cut off tops and store corms as directed above, then repot in fresh soil mix at planting time. Or store corms in their pots over winter; then knock from pots, separate, and repot in fresh soil mix at planting time.

A number of true lilies *(Lilium)* may reach 6 feet or more; this lily relative, native to tropical Africa and Asia, reaches that height in a distinctive manner. The tip of each lance-shaped, 5- to 7-inch leaf tapers to a tendril, which wraps around any handy support to stabilize the plant as it climbs. In summer, the top portion of the plant bears flashy 4-inch-wide blossoms, each with six recurved, wavy-edged segments in brightest red banded with yellow. This plant is now properly called *G. superba* 'Rothschildiana', but most catalogs still list it by its older, more familiar name, *G. rothschildiana.*

In completely frost-free regions, glory lily can survive outdoors all year—but even in these climates, it's best grown in containers. If you want the appearance of a permanent planting, just sink the containers into a garden flower bed, raised bed, or planter.

USES. Glory lily is a certain conversation piece for patio, terrace, or deck.

CONTAINER CULTURE. Plant tubers in a horizontal position, one to a container; set them 4 inches deep in the soil mix described in directions "A" on page 207. For the longest bloom season, start tubers indoors in late winter. After danger of frost is past, move containers to an outdoor spot in full sun (filtered sunlight or light shade in hot-summer regions). Be sure to provide the climbing stems with a support: a trellis, wires, strings, or even loose-growing shrubs or other vines.

During growth and bloom, water regularly and apply a liquid fertilizer every 3 weeks. Withhold water and fertilizer when foliage begins to yellow and die back in fall. After leaves are dry, sever dead stems and move containers to a dry, cool place (55° to 60°F/13° to 16°C) for the winter. In late winter, knock tubers out of containers; repot in fresh soil mix. Or dig tubers in fall and store as for dahlia (page 239) until planting time.

In their native habitats from Texas to Argentina, these plants sprout and flower almost immediately after the ground has been moistened by summer rainfall—hence one of their common names, "rain lily." The grassy foliage and trumpet-shaped to funnel-shaped blossoms are very similar to those of fairy lily *(Zephyranthes)*, a close relative; but while fairy lily has upward-facing flowers, those of rain lily are angled outward. Each stem usually bears just one blossom.

The best-known species, *H. tubispathus (H. andersonii)*, has 1½-inch-long yellow blossoms veined in red on the exterior of the petals; stems and leaves grow to about 6 inches high. The plant sold as *H. texanus* and known as "copper lily" in Texas is probably a naturally occurring variant of *H. tubispathus,* differing from it in having all-yellow flowers on slightly taller stems. Taller still (to about 9 inches) is *H. robustus.* Like the related belladonna lily *(Amaryllis belladonna),* this species blooms before its leaves emerge, bearing 3-inch flowers—sometimes two to a stem—in light pink with green throats and deeper pink veining. Stems of *H. brachyandrus* can reach a foot tall, each carrying a purple-throated pink flower that faces nearly upward.

USES. Tuck clumps in the foreground of mixed summer annuals and perennials, or plant in rock gardens.

GARDEN CULTURE. In spring, plant bulbs in well-drained soil, setting them with tops at soil level; space at least 3 inches apart. Water regularly throughout growth and bloom. If you live in a frost-free climate and can withhold moisture for about a month after flowers have finished, you may be able to initiate another bloom cycle in fall.

Plantings may be left undisturbed for many years; dig and divide only to increase plantings or when vigor and flower quality decline. Replant divided bulbs immediately.

CONTAINER CULTURE. Follow directions "C" on page 207.

Habranthus robustus

HAEMANTHUS KATHARINAE. See **SCADOXUS** MULTIFLORUS KATHARINAE

HEMEROCALLIS
DAYLILY
Liliaceae
TUBEROUS ROOT

- ▲ 1 TO 6 FEET
- ☀ ◑ FULL SUN; FILTERED SUN OR PART SHADE WHERE SUMMERS ARE HOT
- ◆ NEEDS SUMMER MOISTURE
- ✄ ALL ZONES, EXCEPT AS NOTED

I n recent years, the old orange and yellow daylilies from Europe and Asia—indestructible components of grandmother's garden—have undergone a dramatic transformation at the hands of hybridizers. Standard, miniature, and small-flowered types have all been improved, the most obvious change being a greatly expanded color range: the orange and yellow shades now include soft apricot and pale yellow as well as the familiar bright hues, and you'll also find purple, lavender, red, maroon, bronze, all shades of pink, deep to pale shades of cream (some almost white), and various multicolored combinations. Increased petal width and thickness are two other notable improvements. The only part that hasn't changed is the foliage, which gave the plant its old-fashioned name "corn lily": before bloom, daylilies still look like young corn plants. Some kinds are deciduous; others are evergreen or semievergreen.

Hemerocallis 'Metaphor'

Stems of standard-size daylilies generally grow 2½ to 4 feet tall, though some exceptional varieties reach heights of up to 6 feet. Miniature and small-flowered types grow just 1 to 2 feet tall. Since the flowering stems are branched along their upper portion, each one produces an abundance of blooms. The blossoms may be lily shaped or chalice shaped, from 3 to 8 inches across (1½ to 3 inches wide in the smaller varieties); some are fragrant. A typical flower is single, consisting of six petal-like segments—but double-flowered varieties with an indeterminate number of segments are also available, as are "spider" types with narrow, twisted segments. Each flower lasts just one day (hence the common name), but buds open on successive days to prolong the display. Some extended-bloom varieties feature blossoms that remain open into the evening and may even last until the following morning.

Bloom usually begins in midspring, but early and late bloomers are also sold; by planting all three types, you can extend the spring flowering period for a month or more. Scattered bloom may occur during summer, and reblooming types put on a second display in late summer to midautumn.

Hemerocallis 'Oodnadatta'

Listing continues >

TOP: *Hemerocallis* 'Stella de Oro'
BOTTOM: *Hemerocallis* 'Raging Tiger'

Most daylilies offered in retail and mail-order nurseries are named hybrids of complex ancestry, but you can find several species daylilies if you do some searching. All those described below are deciduous.

H. altissima. As the name suggests, this species is tall, with leaves to 5 feet long and stems to 6 feet high. Scented, 4-inch yellow flowers appear in late summer to early fall. 'Statuesque' is a 5-footer that flowers about a month earlier.

H. fulva, tawny daylily, long ago escaped from cultivation to become a familiar roadside "wildflower" in parts of eastern North America. It blooms in summer, its 3- to 5-foot stems topped with 5-inch blossoms in dull, tawny orange. 'Kwanso' ('Kwanso Flore Pleno') is double flowered; it also comes in a form with variegated leaves. 'Rosea', with rosy red blossoms, is the source of pink in modern hybrids. *H. fulva* and its forms all spread to make sizable clumps or colonies.

H. lilio-asphodelus (H. flava). Even among the glut of modern hybrids, this species—commonly called "lemon lily" or "lemon daylily"—deservedly remains a favorite. Rising above foliage clumps about 2 feet high, the 3-foot stems bear delightfully fragrant, 4-inch, pure yellow blossoms in mid- to late spring.

USES. By selecting varieties of different sizes, you can use daylilies as accents in the foreground, middle, or background of any border planting. They're good for drifts as well; for this use, space them about 2 feet apart. They can also function as a tall ground cover, even in some shade (they usually endure competition from tree roots).

GARDEN CULTURE. Grow *H. altissima* in Zones 3–10, 14–24, 26–34, 39. Other daylilies will grow in all zones, according to these guidelines. Where winters are very mild, deciduous types may not get enough chill to turn in a top performance; on the other hand, they are the hardiest without protection (to about −35°F/−38°C). Evergreen kinds are entirely at home in mild-winter regions, but they need protection (see page 205) to survive where lows dip below −20°F/−29°C. Semievergreen types are intermediate between the two in hardiness; some perform better than others in mild-winter areas.

Though daylilies have a reputation for toughness and adaptability, they more than repay the gardener who gives them extra attention. Where summers are dry and hot, plant in filtered sun or part shade; in cooler regions, give full sun. Set out bare-root plants in fall (in colder zones) or early spring; plant ½ to 1 inch deep, 2 to 2½ feet apart. Plant from containers at any time from early spring through midautumn (even in winter, in mild-winter regions). For best results, use well-drained soil amended with organic matter. Plants need regular moisture from spring through fall. Divide when clumps become crowded, usually after 3 to 6 years; do this in fall or early spring in hot-summer regions, in summer in cool-summer areas or where the growing season is short.

CONTAINER CULTURE. The smaller daylilies are suited to container life on sunny patios, terraces, and decks. Follow directions "C" on page 207.

HIPPEASTRUM

AMARYLLIS
Amaryllidaceae
TRUE BULB

▲ 2 FEET
☼ ☽ FULL SUN OR PART SHADE
◖ NEEDS SUMMER MOISTURE
❚ ZONES VARY BY SPECIES
　(SEE "GARDEN CULTURE")

The modern amaryllis sold as "Dutch hybrids" are the products of many European, American, and South African hybridizers, who developed them from various species native to Central and South America. In spring, each plant produces one or two thick stems, each bearing a cluster of three to six trumpet-shaped blossoms to 9 inches across. The broad, strap-shaped leaves usually appear after bloom; they may be nearly as long as the stems, but they're arching rather than upright. Flower colors range from pure white through blush and light pink to assertive, dramatic shades of crimson and orange scarlet; the lighter-colored blooms often have green throats. Many varieties are boldly veined—white veins on background colors of dark pink to red, reddish veins on white backgrounds. More recent developments include double-flowered varieties in white, creamy yellow, and pink, as well as miniature types with stems 12 to 15 inches high and flowers 3 to 5 inches across.

One Brazilian species, *H. papilio,* is also available; its 5-inch, greenish white trumpets are streaked with lavender to dark red. In parts of Texas and the lower South, *H. × johnsonii* is a reliable garden plant. A progenitor of the modern Dutch hybrids, it has stems to nearly 2 feet high and flowers with narrower petals than those of its hybrid descendants; the blossoms are bright red with white stripes.

USES. Pots of blooming amaryllis provide a focal point indoors or out. Where plants are hardy in the ground, you can set them out in large clumps or dramatic drifts.

GARDEN CULTURE. Grow *H. × johnsonii* in Zones 4–9, 14–29; *H. papilio* in Zones 8, 9, 14–28; Dutch hybrids in Zones 15–17, 21–28, and (with some shelter) in Zones 8, 9, 14, 18, 20.

In fall, set out bulbs 1 foot apart in well-drained soil enriched with organic matter; keep tops of bulb necks even with the soil surface. Water thoroughly, then keep soil just barely moist until leaves emerge. Increase watering after plants have sprouted, making sure that soil is moist at all times. Protect from slugs and snails.

After flowers have faded, cut off stalks. The leaves will grow through summer and disappear in fall if plants are dried off; otherwise, some foliage will remain. Divide infrequently—only when vigor and bloom quality decline or when you want to move or increase plantings. The best time to divide is early fall, just before growth begins.

CONTAINER CULTURE. Plant bulbs from midautumn through winter; the earlier you plant, the sooner flowers will appear (see also information on forcing, page 212). Select a container large enough to leave 2 inches between all sides of the bulb and the container edges. Use a soil mix described in "B" on page 207; plant bulb so its neck and top half are above the soil surface. Firm soil thoroughly and water well.

Move pots to a room receiving plenty of light (morning sun is fine, but not hot afternoon rays), with temperatures around 60° to 65°F/16° to 18°C at night, 70° to 75°F/21° to 24°C during the day. Keep soil mix just slightly moist until growth begins; then water regularly during growth and bloom. After blossoms fade, cut off flower stalks to prevent seed formation. Continue to water regularly and apply half-strength liquid fertilizer bimonthly until late summer. At that point, cut back on watering; when leaves are completely yellow, withhold water to give bulbs a dry dormant period. About 4 to 6 weeks before regular planting time, knock the plants out of their pots, scrape off part of the old soil mix, and replant in the same containers, using fresh mix (or, if bulbs have outgrown their original pots, replant in larger containers). Then resume watering as directed for newly planted bulbs.

TOP: *Hippeastrum,* Dutch hybrid
BOTTOM: *Hippeastrum papilio*

Homeria is a wispy, ephemeral plant, well adapted to the dry-summer, scant-rainfall region of South Africa from which it comes. Each corm produces a single lax, grasslike leaf, from which rises one slender, 1- to 1½-foot flowering stem in early to midspring. Each stem is topped with three or four flowers like those of ixia in warm pastel colors: soft orange, salmon to peach pink, or soft yellow. Soon after bloom, the foliage yellows and dies down, signalling the start of a long dormant period that lasts until late winter or early spring of the following year.

Listing continues >

HOMERIA collina

Iridaceae

CORM

▲ 1 TO 1½ FEET

☼ FULL SUN; PART SHADE WHERE SUMMERS ARE HOT

◖ ACCEPTS SUMMER MOISTURE BUT DOESN'T NEED ANY

✕ ZONES 4–29

Homeria collina

HYACINTHOIDES
(Endymion)
BLUEBELL
Liliaceae
TRUE BULB

- ▲ 12 TO 20 INCHES
- ☼ FILTERED SUN OR LIGHT SHADE
- ◖ NEEDS SOME SUMMER MOISTURE
- ✇ ZONES VARY BY SPECIES
  (SEE "GARDEN CULTURE")

Hyacinthoides hispanica

HYACINTHUS
HYACINTH
Liliaceae
TRUE BULB

- ▲ 6 TO 12 INCHES
- ☼ FULL SUN
- ◖ ACCEPTS SUMMER MOISTURE BUT
  DOESN'T NEED ANY
- ✇ ZONES VARY BY SPECIES (SEE "GAR-
  DEN CULTURE"); MOST NEED SUB-
  FREEZING WINTER TEMPERATURES

USES. In regions where soil does not freeze and corms can remain in the ground all year, homeria is a charming component of wildflower-type plantings. Plant corms in patches or drifts to gain color impact and compensate for the scant foliage.

GARDEN CULTURE. Where homeria is adapted, plant corms in a sunny location at any time from fall through winter, setting them 2 inches deep, 3 inches apart. Corms can remain in place for many years. In areas beyond the hardiness limits, set out corms in early spring for early summer bloom; dig them after leaves have died down and store over winter as for gladiolus (page 248). If corms are to accept moisture during their long dormancy, soil must be very well drained; if drainage is less than excellent and you can't keep the planting area dry, dig and store corms over summer or grow them in pots.

CONTAINER CULTURE. Follow directions "B" (subgroup 2) on page 207.

Both Spanish bluebell (*H. hispanica*) and English bluebell (*H. non-scripta*) are trouble-free spring-blooming bulbs. Botanists, however, have made them a bit troublesome by changing their names three times; before being given their current identity as *Hyacinthoides,* they were classed as *Scilla,* then moved to *Endymion.* Under any name, Spanish bluebell is the taller of the two, with straplike leaves and erect flower stems to 20 inches tall. Twelve or more ¾-inch, bell-shaped flowers hang from the upper part of each stem. English bluebell's flower stalks reach only about 1 foot and are gently arching rather than upright; the fragrant blossoms are slightly smaller and narrower than those of Spanish bluebell. Both species are available in blue, white, and pink forms. Wherever the two species grow near one another, hybrids are likely to appear, bearing appealing flowers intermediate in character between those of the two parents.

USES. Plant these bulbs in drifts or naturalize them at edges of woodland areas.

GARDEN CULTURE. Grow *H. hispanica* in Zones 1–11, 14–24, 28–43; plant *H. non-scripta* in Zones 3–6, 31–35, 37, 39–41. English bluebell is more climate specific, preferring cool to mild summer temperatures and definite winter chill. The more amenable Spanish bluebell is definitely the choice for hot-summer regions.

Choose a location in filtered sunlight or light shade. In fall, set bulbs 3 inches deep and 6 inches apart in clumps or drifts. Plants need regular moisture from planting time until foliage dies, and at least some moisture in summer. Divide infrequently, since the display grows in beauty as the plantings increase.

CONTAINER CULTURE. Follow directions "B" (subgroup 2) on page 207.

To most gardeners, a hyacinth is just one plant: the highly fragrant, fat-spiked Dutch hybrids of *H. orientalis,* a native of the eastern Mediterranean region. These grow to 1 foot tall, with straplike leaves that may be either erect or arching. The spikes of spring blossoms look like flowering drumsticks—they're tightly packed with small, outward-facing blooms shaped like flaring bells. Colors include pure white, cream, buff, yellow, pink, salmon, red, blue, and purple.

The largest bulbs (called exhibition size) produce the largest spikes; they're the best choice for container-grown and forced flowers. The next largest size is satisfactory for outdoor planting. The smallest bulbs produce smaller, looser flower clusters—the same results you'll get from larger bulbs left in the ground from year to year.

Native to the south of France, the Roman or French Roman hyacinth, *H. orientalis albulus,* is smaller than the *H. orientalis* hybrids and blooms earlier in the season. It thrives (and naturalizes easily) where winters offer little or no chill. Each bulb may produce several slender, foot-tall stems, each carrying loose spikes of white, pale blue, or pink flowers.

A third hyacinth is now classed as *Brimeura amethystina,* though most catalogs still list it as *H. amethystinus.* In bulb and leaf, it resembles the preceding species, but the 10-inch spikes of pendent bells that bloom in spring to early summer look just like those of bluebell *(Hyacinthoides).* Bright blue is the standard color, but a pure white form is also available.

USES. All but the Dutch hybrids are good for naturalizing or for informal drifts beneath deciduous trees and shrubs. The hybrids provide an impressive display when massed in beds or borders, but because of their rather stiff appearance, they look rigidly formal when planted in rows. All hyacinths can be grown in containers; the Dutch hybrids are the showiest.

GARDEN CULTURE. Grow *H. amethystinus (Brimeura amethystina)* in Zones 1–24, 29–43; grow *H. orientalis albulus* in Zones 4–24, 29–33. The Dutch hybrids can be grown in all zones, but bulbs left in the ground will persist only in regions where there is distinct winter cold. Where winters are mild, in-ground Dutch hybrid bulbs do not last long: if summers are dry, they soon dwindle and vanish for lack of winter chill; if summers are warm and moist, they are likely to rot during the first summer after flowering. In these regions, treat Dutch hybrid hyacinths as annuals.

Hyacinthus orientalis 'Gypsy Queen'

TOP: *Hyacinthus orientalis* in container
BOTTOM: *Hyacinthus orientalis albulus*

The Dutch hybrids and *H. orientalis albulus* must be planted early enough to establish vigorous roots before the ground freezes. Where winter temperatures drop below 20°F/−7°C, set bulbs out in earliest fall; in warmer regions, delay planting until mid- to late fall, when summerlike warmth is sure to be gone. Keep bulbs cool in the meantime; if you're planting only a few, store them in the vegetable crisper of your refrigerator.

Choose a sunny planting area with well-drained soil (preferably on the sandy side); dig plenty of organic matter into the soil prior to planting. Set the largest Dutch hybrid bulbs 4 to 5 inches deep, about 5 inches apart; the smaller hybrid bulbs and those of *H. orientalis albulus* should go about 3 inches deep and 4 to 5 inches apart.

Keep soil moist after planting so roots will become established; continue to water regularly from the time leaves emerge until the flowers fade. If bulbs are to remain in the ground for more than one flowering, apply a granular fertilizer just as blossoms fade; remove the spent flower spikes and continue to water regularly until foliage yellows. After foliage has died down, keep soil fairly dry during summer and into fall, until cool weather returns.

H. amethystinus (Brimeura amethystina) is more widely adapted than the other hyacinths. Plant bulbs in mid- to late fall (before ground freezes), 2 inches deep and 3 inches apart. In Zones 1, 2, and 41–43, mulch soil after the first hard frost. Give the same watering regime as for other hyacinths.

CONTAINER CULTURE. Follow directions "B" (subgroup 1) on page 207. For information on growing bulbs indoors in a hyacinth glass, see page 211.

HYMENOCALLIS

Amaryllidaceae

TRUE BULB

- ▲ 2 FEET
- ☼ ◑ FULL SUN; FILTERED SUN OR PART SHADE WHERE SUMMERS ARE HOT
- ◖ NEEDS SUMMER MOISTURE
- ✄ ZONES 5, 6, 8, 9, 14–31
- ⬦ BULBS ARE POISONOUS IF INGESTED

Hymenocallis 'Sulfur Queen'

I magine a fanciful hybrid between a belladonna lily *(Amaryllis belladonna)* and a daffodil, and you'll come close to visualizing this summer-blooming bulb. Like belladonna lily, it has strap-shaped leaves (usually about 2 feet long) and thick flower stems, each topped with several fragrant blossoms—though leaves and flowers appear simultaneously in hymenocallis. Like daffodils, the flowers have two sets of segments: the inner ones form a funnel, while the outer ones are longer, spidery, and recurved.

The most common species is *H. narcissiflora* (formerly known as *H. calathina* and *Ismene calathina*), the Peruvian daffodil. Its white flowers, striped green in the throat, are carried in clusters of two to five per stem. Its selected form 'Advance' has pure white flowers only faintly lined green in the throat. The hybrid 'Sulfur Queen' has a more circular cup surrounded by broader, less spidery segments; the color is soft primrose yellow, with green stripes in the throat. *H. × festalis* is at the more spidery end of the spectrum: its outer segments are like curled white ribbon, surrounding a broadly chalice-shaped inner cup with fringed lobes. Each stem bears about four flowers, held horizontally, over foliage like that of *H. narcissiflora*.

USES. Hymenocallis is attractive in border plantings of summer-flowering annuals and perennials. It's also a good choice for containers.

GARDEN CULTURE. Where bulbs are hardy in the ground, plant in fall or early winter. In colder regions, plant in spring, after all danger of frost is past; when foliage yellows and dies down after flowering, dig the bulbs and store them as for dahlia (page 239) until planting time the following spring.

Select a sunny location (filtered sun or part shade where summers are hot) with well-drained soil; dig a generous amount of organic matter into the soil before planting. Set tops of bulbs just beneath the soil surface, spacing bulbs about 1 foot apart. Plants need regular moisture during growth and bloom; leaves will remain green throughout summer if watering continues. At some point, leaves will start to turn yellow; at this point, withhold moisture and let them die down.

CONTAINER CULTURE. Follow directions "C" on page 207.

IPHEION uniflorum

SPRING STAR FLOWER

Liliaceae

TRUE BULB

- ▲ 6 TO 8 INCHES
- ☼ ◑ FULL SUN, PART SHADE, OR LIGHT SHADE
- ◖ ACCEPTS SUMMER MOISTURE BUT DOESN'T NEED ANY
- ✄ ZONES 3–24, 27–34

Ipheion uniflorum

T his rugged little spring bloomer from Argentina has an understated, wildflowerlike charm. Each bulb produces several slender stems, each bearing a ½-inch blossom with six overlapping petals arranged in star fashion. The usual color is white tinged with blue, but bulb specialists may offer selected variants such as white 'Album', bright blue 'Rolf Fiedler', and dark blue 'Wisley Blue'. All types have narrow, nearly flat bluish green leaves that give off an oniony odor when bruised.

USES. Plant spring star flower in borders or under deciduous shrubs. Or naturalize it in woodland areas or among low grasses.

GARDEN CULTURE. Though spring star flower prefers well-drained soil, it is not particular about the type; anything from light, sandy soil to clay is satisfactory. It is similarly unfussy about planting location, performing equally well in sun, part shade, and light shade.

Plant bulbs in early to midautumn, 2 inches deep and 2 inches apart. Water regularly during growth and bloom. The bulbs prefer dry conditions during their summer dormancy, but will accept moisture if drainage is good. Dig and divide infrequently, since plantings become more attractive over the years as bulbs multiply.

CONTAINER CULTURE. Follow directions "B" (subgroup 2) on page 207.

M ention iris, and most people will think of the showy tall bearded irises that are mainstays of the midspring flower display. But though these may be the most widely planted, they constitute only one part of a highly diverse group of plants.

Despite their considerable differences, all irises have the same basic flower structure. All blossoms have three true petals (the standards) and three petal-like sepals (the falls). Standards may be upright, arching, or flaring, while falls range from flaring to drooping. Flower types fit into two broad groups: *bearded,* with a caterpillarlike tuft of hairs on each fall; and *beardless,* without such hairs. In growth habit, irises are either *rhizomatous* or *bulbous.*

RHIZOMATOUS IRISES

Irises that grow from rhizomes may be bearded or beardless. Leaves are swordlike, overlapping each other to form a flat fan of foliage.

BEARDED IRISES

Bearded irises are available in a dazzling array of colors and color combinations. Irises of this type are divided into the four main classes outlined below: *tall, median, dwarf,* and *arils and arilbreds.* Except for the arils and arilbreds, which have special needs, all bearded irises require the same basic care (see "Bearded iris culture," page 258).

TALL BEARDED IRISES. Plants bloom in midspring, bearing large, broad-petaled blossoms on branching stems that grow 2½ to 4 feet tall. Reblooming (remontant) types will flower again in summer, fall, or winter (depending on the variety) if grown in a favorable climate and given cultural encouragement.

MEDIAN AND DWARF IRISES. Blossoms resemble those of tall beardeds, but on a smaller scale; stems and foliage are smaller as well. Median is a collective term for the first four types listed below.

Border bearded irises. These are segregates from tall bearded breeding with 15- to 28-inch stems and proportionately sized flowers and foliage. The bloom period is the same as for tall bearded irises.

Miniature tall bearded irises. Height range is the same as for border beardeds (15 to 28 inches), but miniature tall beardeds have pencil-slim stems, rather narrow and short leaves, and relatively tiny flowers—only 2 to 3 inches wide. The bloom time is the same as for tall beardeds; the color range is more limited. Members of this group usually have more stems per clump than the average tall bearded.

Intermediate bearded irises. Modern intermediates are hybrids of tall beardeds and standard dwarfs. Flowers are 3 to 5 inches wide, carried on 15- to 28-inch stems. Plants come into bloom 1 to 3 weeks before tall beardeds; some varieties bloom a second time in fall. In addition to modern types, this group includes the old, familiar "common purple" and "graveyard white" irises that flower in early spring.

Standard dwarf bearded irises. Most modern members of this group were developed from crosses of tall bearded varieties with a miniature dwarf species from central Europe. Standard dwarfs bloom even earlier than intermediates, producing a great profusion of 2- to 3-inch-wide flowers on stems 8 to 15 inches tall. There's a wide range of available colors and patterns.

Miniature dwarf bearded irises. These are the shortest and earliest blooming of the bearded irises, reaching just 2 to 8 inches high. They bear a wealth of flowers in a great variety of colors; blooms are often a bit large in proportion to the rest of the plant. Established, well-grown plants can form cushions of bloom—attractive in rock gardens, borders, and foreground plantings.

Listing continues >

IRIS
Iridaceae
RHIZOME; TRUE BULB

- ▲ 2 INCHES TO 7 FEET
- ☼ ☼ FULL SUN, FILTERED SUN, LIGHT SHADE, OR PART SHADE, DEPENDING ON TYPE AND CLIMATE
- ● ◐ ○ SUMMER MOISTURE NEEDS VARY (SEE DESCRIPTIONS)
- ✎ ZONES VARY BY TYPE (SEE DESCRIPTIONS)

TOP: Standard dwarf bearded iris 'Sarah Taylor'
BOTTOM: Tall bearded iris 'Cinderella's Coach'

ARIL AND ARILBRED IRISES. The word "exotic" might have been coined especially for the aril species, which take their name from the collarlike white cap (the aril) on their seeds. These irises comprise two groups, Oncocyclus and Regelia; both are native to arid regions of the Near East and central Asia. Hybrids between the two groups are called Oncogelias. For all, bloom comes during midspring.

Oncocyclus species typically feature 4- to 7-inch-wide, domed or globe-shaped blooms with a base color of gray, silver, lavender, gold, or maroon. In many types, the petals are intricately veined and dotted with darker hues. Flower stems are fairly short, usually reaching only about 1 foot; leaves are narrow, lightly ribbed, and typically sickle shaped.

Regelias have smaller and more vertical blossoms than the Oncocyclus types; both base colors and contrasting veining are in brighter shades (though *I. hoogiana* is pure blue), often with a lustrous sheen. Flower stems reach 1½ to 2½ feet, depending on care. The narrow, ribbed leaves are usually straight rather than curving.

All the aril species have strict cultural needs: perfect drainage (no standing water), alkaline soil, and a hot, dry summer dormant period. Oncocyclus species are the fussiest; Regelias and Oncogelias are more adaptable. All three are hardy in the ground to about −20°F/−29°C.

Arilbred iris 'Jeweled Veil'

Arilbred irises are hybrids of aril types and tall or median bearded irises; a number of named varieties are sold, with varying percentages of aril "blood." In general, those with more aril in their ancestry have a more exotic look. Many arilbreds are nearly as easy to grow as tall beardeds, or require only the addition of lime to the soil and a little extra attention to drainage.

BEARDED IRIS CULTURE. These irises are grown in Zones 1–24, 30–45; where winter temperatures are likely to drop below −20°F/−29°C, many gardeners give plantings winter protection (see page 205) just after the ground freezes. Bearded irises demand good drainage; as long as rhizomes don't sit in saturated soil, they'll do well in anything from light sand to clay. If you're growing irises in heavy soil, plant them in a raised bed or raised planting area to promote drainage.

In cool-summer climates, plants must have full sun from spring through fall. Where summers are hot, however, they may appreciate afternoon filtered sunlight or high shade—but too much shade will greatly decrease bloom production and interfere with the necessary summer ripening of rhizomes.

Plant rhizomes between July 1 and October 21 (limit planting to July or August in cold-winter climates, September or October where summer temperatures are high). Space rhizomes 1 to 2 feet apart; set them with tops just beneath the soil surface, spreading roots well. Growth proceeds from the leafy end of the rhizome, so point that end in the direction in which you want growth to occur initially. If the weather turns hot, shade newly planted rhizomes to prevent sunscald and subsequent rot.

After planting rhizomes, water the planting area to settle the soil and start root growth; thereafter, water judiciously until new growth appears, signalling that plants have taken hold. Water regularly unless rain does it for you or freezing weather arrives. From the time growth starts in late winter or early spring, water regularly until about 6 weeks after flowers fade (increases and buds for the following year are formed during the post-bloom period). During summer, plants can get by with less frequent watering—every other week in warm climates, once a month where summers are cool.

Apply a granular fertilizer as plants begin growth in late winter or early spring, then again right after the blooming season ends.

Clumps become overcrowded after 3 or 4 years, producing fewer flower stalks and blooms of poorer quality. When this occurs, dig clumps at the best planting time for your climate and separate old, woody rhizomes from healthy ones with good fans of leaves. Then trim leaves and roots to 6 to 8 inches and replant. If you're replanting in the same plot, dig plenty of organic matter into the soil before you plant.

BEARDLESS IRISES

Only two main characteristics are common to all irises in this category: the lack of a beard on the falls, and roots that are generally fibrous rather than fleshy. The most widely sold beardless irises are the four hybrid groups (the first four listings) described below.

JAPANESE IRISES. Zones 1–10, 14–24, 32–45. Derived from *I. ensata* (formerly *I. kaempferi*), these irises are graceful, moisture-loving plants which, when grown under ideal conditions, bear the largest flowers of all irises. The narrow, upright leaves, each with a distinct midrib, are reminiscent of rushes. Above the foliage clumps, 4- to 12-inch flowers float on stems up to 4 feet tall. Blossoms are fairly flat, either single (standards small and distinct in appearance from falls) or double (standards and falls of about equal size, shape, and markings). Colors include white and all shades of purple, violet, blue, and pink; light-colored blooms are often intricately marked, veined, or striped. Flowering begins in late spring.

Japanese irises must have rich soil and copious nonalkaline moisture from the time growth begins until the blooming season ends. Grow them at pond edges, or plant them in boxes, pots, or buckets of soil sunk halfway to the rim in the water of a pond or pool. If you water them very faithfully, they can also succeed in heavy garden soil. Where summers are cool, plant in full sun; in warm-summer regions, choose a spot receiving high shade or dappled afternoon sun.

Set out rhizomes in fall or spring, 2 inches deep and 1½ feet apart, pointing the leafy ends in the direction you want growth to take. (Or plant up to three rhizomes per 12-inch-wide container.) Divide crowded clumps in late summer or early fall, then replant as quickly as possible.

Tall bearded iris 'Mother Earth'

LOUISIANA IRISES. Zones 3–24, 26–43. The progenitors of this group are three or more species native to swamps and moist lowlands, primarily along the Gulf Coast. Leaves are long, linear, and unribbed; graceful, flattish blossoms are carried on 2- to 5-foot stems in spring. The range of flower colors and patterns is nearly as extensive as that of the tall beardeds.

Though the species come from milder climates, some varieties have succeeded as far north as South Dakota. Plants thrive in rich, well-watered garden soil as well as at pond margins; both soil and water should be neutral to acid. Full sun is best in cool- and mild-summer areas, but where heat is intense, choose a spot receiving light afternoon shade. Plant in late summer; set rhizomes 1 inch deep, 1½ to 2 feet apart. Where ground freezes in winter, give plants winter protection (page 205).

Japanese iris

Louisiana iris 'Inner Beauty'

Listing continues >

Siberian iris

Spuria iris 'Barbara's Kiss'

SIBERIAN IRISES. Zones 1–10, 14–23, 32–45. The most widely sold members of this group are named hybrids derived from *I. sibirica* and *I. sanguinea*. All have narrow, almost grasslike deciduous foliage and slender flower stems. Depending on the variety, leaf length ranges from 1 to 3 feet, stem height from about 14 inches to nearly 4 feet. In midspring, each stem bears two to five blossoms with upright standards and flaring to drooping falls. Colors include white and every shade of violet, purple, lavender, wine, pink, and blue; several recent hybrids are light yellow.

Plant Siberian irises in early spring or late summer in cold-winter regions, in fall where summers are hot and winters mild to moderate. Plant in sun (light shade where summers are hot) in good, neutral to acid soil; set rhizomes 1 to 2 inches deep, 1 to 2 feet apart. Water generously from the time growth begins until the bloom period is over. Divide infrequently; plants look most attractive in well-established clumps. Dig and divide (in late summer or early fall) only when old clumps begin to show hollow centers.

SPURIA IRISES. Zones 2–24, 28–43. In general flower form, Spurias are almost identical to florists' Dutch irises. The older members of this group have yellow or white-and-yellow flowers, but modern hybrids show a greatly expanded range of colors: blue, lavender, gray, orchid, tan, bronze, brown, purple, earthy red, and near black, often with a prominent yellow spot on the falls. Plants come into bloom a little later than tall bearded irises, their blossoms held closely against 3- to 6-foot flower stems. The narrow dark green leaves grow upright to 3 to 4 feet.

Plant these irises in late summer or early fall, in a full-sun location with good soil. Set rhizomes 1 inch deep, 1½ to 2 feet apart; water regularly from the time growth begins until flowering is over. Most Spurias need very little water during summer. Give plants winter protection (see page 205) where temperatures drop below −20°F/−29°C.

Divide plantings infrequently—only when they become overcrowded. Dig and replant rhizomes in late summer or early fall.

ADDITIONAL BEARDLESS SPECIES. Several beardless iris species that do not fit into the previous categories are good garden plants offered by specialty growers. The following three will grow in shallow water as well as in moist to boggy, acid garden soil. Plant all in late summer, setting them 1 inch deep and 2 feet apart.

I. laevigata grows in Zones 1–10, 14–24, 32–45. Handsome clumps of evergreen, glossy leaves grow to 2½ feet high; flower stems reach about the same height. Typical blossoms are blue violet, with upright standards and drooping falls with a yellow blaze. Named variants offer flowers in white, magenta, and combinations of purple and white, and those in which standards have the shape and carriage of falls, giving the effect of a double flower. The bloom period comes after that of tall bearded irises.

I. pseudacorus, yellow flag, succeeds in Zones 1–24, 28–45. Impressive foliage, deciduous in winter, may reach 5 feet tall under ideal conditions, with flower stems attaining 4 to 7 feet. The bloom period coincides with the latter part of the tall bearded season. Blossoms are bright yellow, though there are selected forms with flowers in ivory and light yellow; other forms include those with double petals, shorter or taller leaves, and creamy yellow young foliage.

I. versicolor, blue flag, grows in Zones 1–9, 14–17, 28–45. This familiar North American native grows wild in bogs and swamps in the Great Lakes region, the Ohio River Valley, and the Northeast. Narrow deciduous leaves grow 1½ to 4 feet high; leaves of shorter types are upright, while those of taller kinds recurve gracefully. Light violet blue is the typical color, but darker and lighter forms are available; 'Kermesina' is wine red, while 'Rosea' and 'Vernal' have pink flowers. Flowers of all appear during the latter part of the tall bearded season.

BULBOUS IRISES

Like bearded irises, all bulbous irises have foliage that grows in flattened fans, but the leaves tend to be more grasslike and rounder in cross section. In summer, the foliage dies back and the bulbs enter dormancy. At this time, they can be dug and stored until planting time in fall.

GARDEN CULTURE. For details on growing bulbous irises in the ground, see the individual listings below and on page 262.

CONTAINER CULTURE. All bulbous irises are appealing, easy-to-grow container subjects. See directions "B" (subgroup 1) on page 207.

DUTCH AND SPANISH IRISES

Bulb growers in Holland developed the Dutch hybrids from several Mediterranean species. All have stiff, 1½- to 2-foot stems bearing sturdy, rather stiff, 3- to 4-inch-wide blossoms with erect standards and down-curving falls. Colors include white and various bright, clear shades of blue, purple, mauve, bronze, yellow, and orange; some types have bicolored blooms. In warm-winter climates, flowering comes in March and April; where winters are colder, blossoms appear in May and June.

Dutch irises grow in Zones 3–24, 30–34. Choose a sunny planting area with well-drained soil, preferably in a part of the garden that can remain unwatered over the summer. Plant bulbs in October or November, 4 inches deep and 3 to 4 inches apart. Give plenty of water from the time leaves emerge until about a month after flowers finish; then withhold water and let foliage die.

Where summers are dry (and the planting area won't be watered in summer), you can leave bulbs in the ground for several years. Dig and divide when plants show a decline in vigor and bloom quality. But where there is summer watering or rainfall, dig bulbs after leaves die back and hold until planting time in fall.

Though it is usually sold as a Dutch iris and needs the same care, the variety 'Wedgwood' is larger, taller, and earlier blooming by about 2 weeks (at 'King Alfred' daffodil time). It succeeds only where winter temperatures remain above 10°F/−12°C.

Spanish irises are derived from species native to Spain. They grow in the same zones Dutch irises do (Zones 3–24, 30–34) and have the same cultural needs and general appearance, but the plants tend to be smaller flowered, shorter, and slimmer. Spanish irises come into bloom about 2 weeks later than the Dutch types.

ENGLISH IRISES

All the available named varieties and color variations of English irises are derived solely from *I. xiphioides* (sometimes sold as *I. latifolia*). This species gained the name "English iris" because it was first grown as an ornamental plant in England; its true home, though, is in the moist meadows of northeastern Spain and the Pyrenees Mountains.

Flower stems may reach 1½ feet tall. In early summer, each bears two velvety-textured blooms of white, mauve, maroon, bluish purple, or blue (bulb specialists may list varieties in specific colors). Flower form is similar to that of Dutch irises, but blossoms are a bit larger, with much broader falls.

Grow English irises in Zones 3–6, 15–17, 21–24, 32, 34, 39. They perform best in a climate with cool to moderate summers. Plant bulbs as soon as they arrive in nurseries (usually October or November); choose a location in full sun (or in part shade, where summers are warm to hot), with cool, moist, acid soil. General cultural requirements are the same as for Dutch irises, but English irises don't need complete dryness after flowering.

Listing continues >

Iris versicolor

Dutch iris hybrids

Reticulata iris

IXIA

IXIA, AFRICAN CORN LILY

Iridaceae

CORM

▲ 16 TO 24 INCHES

☼ FULL SUN

◊ WITHHOLD SUMMER MOISTURE

✄ ZONES 7–9, 12–24

Ixia

RETICULATA IRISES

The several species and varieties belonging to the Reticulata section are characterized by a netted outer covering on the bulb. They are small, slim plants (most no taller than 8 inches), classic choices for rock gardens and pathway border plantings.

Depending on the severity of the winter, flowering time varies from midwinter to early spring. Blossoms are 2 to 3 inches across. Slender, sometimes spikelike leaves may emerge simultaneously with the flowers or appear just after bloom ceases.

The group's best known member is *I. reticulata*, with flowers of pale to violet blue, red violet, or white. Blossoms of *I. histrioides* and its variety *I. h. major* are light to medium blue, with darker blue spots on the falls. Bright yellow *I. danfordiae* differs from the others in both flower color and form—the standards are almost nonexistent. Bulb specialists may offer other species and varieties.

Grow reticulata irises in Zones 3–24, 30–34; bulbs are hardy in the ground to about −10°F/−23°C, but do need some subfreezing winter temperatures to thrive. Reticulata irises appreciate a full-sun location with well-drained soil. Set out bulbs in fall, 3 to 4 inches deep and as far apart. Plants need regular water from fall through spring, but soil should be kept dry during the bulbs' summer dormant period. Dig and divide only when vigor and flower quality deteriorate.

Reticulata iris

I xia's clumps of narrow, almost grasslike leaves give rise to wiry stems topped by short spikes of bright, cheery, 2-inch flowers in late spring. Each six-petaled blossom opens out nearly flat in full sun, but remains cup shaped or closed on overcast days.

Most of the ixias available at nurseries are hybrids involving the South African *I. maculata*; the color range is extensive, including cream, yellow, red, orange, and pink, typically with dark centers. A lovely curiosity is *I. viridiflora*, with purple-centered bluish green flowers.

USES. Ixia offers a bright wildflower charm in the foreground of mixed plantings or naturalized in sunny drifts where summers are dry.

GARDEN CULTURE. Plant *I. maculata* and *I. viridiflora* in a sunny spot with light, well-drained soil (*I. viridiflora* in particular demands good drainage). In regions where winter lows usually remain above 20°F/−7°C, plant corms in early fall, setting them about 2 inches deep and 3 inches apart. Where temperatures may dip to 10°F/−12°C, plant after November 1; set corms 4 inches deep, then cover the planting area with a mulch (see page 200). The later planting time, greater planting depth, and mulch keep corms from sending up leaves that would be damaged by cold. Where temperatures fall below 10°F/−12°C, plant corms in spring for flowers in early summer.

Water plants regularly during growth and bloom, then let soil go dry when foliage yellows. If corms are planted among drought-tolerant plants or by themselves, you can leave them undisturbed in dry-summer areas where they are hardy in the ground. After several years, or when the planting becomes crowded and flower quality decreases, dig corms in summer and store as for gladiolus (page 248) until planting time in fall.

Where there is summer watering or summer rainfall, and in regions where corms are not hardy in the ground, dig them after foliage dies back and store as for gladiolus (page 248) until the best planting time for your climate.

CONTAINER CULTURE. Plant corms close together and about 1 inch deep in a deep container. Follow directions "B" (subgroup 2) on page 207.

Native to the steppes of central Asia, these floral star sapphires bejewel the garden in late spring. Wiry, 12- to 16-inch stems rise above narrow gray-green leaves, bearing loose clusters of 1½-inch, blue-violet blossoms, each with six narrow petals highlighted by a darker central line. Foliage dies down at some point during summer, not to reappear until the following spring.

USES. In clumps and drifts, these plants provide an effective blue front-of-border accent among other spring-flowering bulbs and perennials.

GARDEN CULTURE. Where ixiolirion is native, its bulbs receive a good baking over a long, dry summer, then get moderate moisture from fall through spring. In the garden, they need good, well-drained soil—especially where winter rain is plentiful or where they'll receive supplemental water after the foliage disappears. In Zones 3, 32 (colder parts), and 33, choose a planting spot where emerging foliage will be sheltered from late spring frosts. Plant in fall, setting bulbs 3 inches deep and about 3 inches apart; plantings can remain in place for many years before they need division. To grow ixiolirion in zones beyond its adaptability, set out bulbs in early spring; dig in fall and give covered storage (see page 205) until planting time the following spring.

CONTAINER CULTURE. Follow directions "B" (subgroup 2) on page 207.

IXIOLIRION tataricum
Amaryllidaceae
TRUE BULB

▲ 12 TO 16 INCHES

☼ FULL SUN

◐ ACCEPTS SUMMER MOISTURE BUT DOESN'T NEED ANY

✄ ZONES 3–11, 14–21, 29–33

Ixiolirion tataricum

Mild-winter gardeners searching for a hyacinthlike plant that persists from year to year find just what they want in this South African native. Each bulb usually produces just two broad, succulent, strap-shaped leaves (spotted with brown, in some kinds). Spikes of pendent, tubular blossoms appear at the tips of thick flowering stems in late winter or early spring.

The most common cape cowslip is *L. aloides* (formerly *L. tricolor*), with inch-wide leaves and 10- to 12-inch stems displaying yellow flowers tipped in red and green. Several named selections offer color variations. 'Aurea' has bright orange-yellow blossoms; flowers of 'Nelsonii' are bright yellow tinged green; 'Pearsonii' has yellow-orange blooms with red-orange bases on slightly taller stems.

Larger overall—with stems to 15 inches high, flowers 1½ inches long, and leaves 2 inches wide—is *L. bulbiferum* (formerly *L. pendula*). Its coral red and yellow blossoms are tipped in purple; blooms of 'Superba' are orange red. *L. contaminata* is reminiscent of grape hyacinth *(Muscari)*: its flowers (in white tipped red to brown) are nearly spherical, bell shaped, and carried in tight spikes. Both the stems and the narrow, upright leaves reach about 9 inches high. Growers specializing in tender bulbs may offer a number of other species.

USES. Plants are at home in rock gardens and border plantings, as well as in containers.

GARDEN CULTURE. Plant in late summer or early fall. Where summers are cool or mild, choose a sunny spot; in hot-summer climates, pick an area in part or light shade. Set bulbs in well-drained soil, 3 inches apart and 1 to 1½ inches deep. Water sparingly until growth starts, then give regular moisture until foliage yellows after bloom. Then gradually let soil dry out and keep as dry as possible until the next fall. Protect plants from slugs and snails.

CONTAINER CULTURE. Plant bulbs 2 to 3 inches apart, with tips just beneath the soil surface, in the soil mix described under "A" on page 207. Potted plants can grow outdoors all year in the dry-summer zones listed above right. They can also be grown outdoors in Zones 25–27, but must be protected from summer rain. Elsewhere, grow

LACHENALIA
CAPE COWSLIP
Liliaceae
TRUE BULB

▲ 9 TO 15 INCHES

☼ ◐ FULL SUN; PART OR LIGHT SHADE WHERE SUMMERS ARE HOT

◐ WITHHOLD SUMMER MOISTURE

✄ ZONES 16, 17, 23, 24

Lachenalia aloides

as a house or greenhouse plant. Outdoors, follow the watering regime described in "Garden culture." After planting for indoor bloom, water thoroughly and keep cool and dark until leaves appear, then bring into a light room with cool night temperatures (50°F/10°C). Apply a dilute liquid fertilizer every 2 weeks throughout the period of active growth. Store bulbs dry in pots over summer.

LEUCOJUM
SNOWFLAKE
Amaryllidaceae
TRUE BULB

- ▲ 6 TO 18 INCHES
- ☼ ◑ FULL SUN; FILTERED SUN OR LIGHT SHADE AFTER BLOOM WHERE SUMMERS ARE HOT
- ◖ NEEDS SOME SUMMER MOISTURE, EXCEPT AS NOTED
- ✎ ZONES VARY BY SPECIES (SEE "GARDEN CULTURE")

Leucojum aestivum
'Gravetye Giant'

Dainty appearance and delicate fragrance belie a tough constitution: where adapted, these natives of Europe and the western Mediterranean region are among the most tolerant of bulbs.

Of the two commonly grown species, the more widely adapted is *L. aestivum*. It's commonly called "summer snowflake," but the name is misleading: in warmer parts of the West and Southwest, flowering begins in late November and continues into winter. In cold-winter regions, blossoms appear in midspring. Narrow, strap-shaped leaves grow 1 to 1½ feet long; flower stems are equally long (or longer), each carrying three to five pendent, six-segmented white bells. The pointed tip of each blossom segment is marked with green. 'Gravetye Giant' is a bit taller and larger flowered than the species.

Spring snowflake, *L. vernum*, blooms in midwinter to earliest spring, depending on climate. Unlike *L. aestivum*, this species thrives only where it receives definite winter cold: 20°F/−7°C or lower. The blooms are similar to those of summer snowflake, but each foot-tall stem bears just one blossom.

Less widely grown than the preceding two species is *L. autumnale*. In late summer or fall, its 6-inch stems rise from bare earth, each carrying one to four pink-tinted white blossoms; grasslike leaves emerge after the flowers fade.

USES. Naturalize snowflakes under deciduous trees or shrubs; use clumps along lightly shaded pathways.

GARDEN CULTURE. Grow *L. aestivum* in Zones 1–24, 29–43; *L. vernum* in Zones 1–6, 30–43; *L. autumnale* in Zones 4–9, 14–34, 30–32.

In fall, set bulbs in well-drained soil, 3 to 4 inches deep and about 4 inches apart. Water regularly from planting time until foliage yellows and dies down in late spring of the next year. Less water is needed during the summer dormant period; *L. aestivum* can even get by without summer moisture as long as the soil is shaded.

Leave clumps undisturbed until diminished growth and flower quality indicate overcrowding. Dig and separate in summer; replant immediately.

CONTAINER CULTURE. These bulbs are best suited to garden culture, but they can be forced for early bloom (see pages 210–211). Use one of the soil mixes described under "B" on page 207.

LIATRIS
GAYFEATHER
Asteraceae
TUBEROUS ROOT

- ▲ 2 TO 5 FEET
- ☼ FULL SUN
- ◖ NEEDS SUMMER MOISTURE
- ✎ ZONES 1–10, 14–24, 26, 28–45

Although these summer-blooming eastern and central U.S. natives belong to the daisy family, their appearance is decidedly undaisylike. Clumps of narrow, almost grassy leaves send up leafy stems topped by foxtail-like spikes of small flowers with prominent stamens. Bloom proceeds from the top of the spike down, with the upper flowers opening before the lower ones—an unusual feature, since most blossoms borne in spikes open from the bottom of the spike up. All species and selections are similar in general build; the chief differences are in color and height.

The most widely available species, light purple–flowered *L. spicata* (sometimes sold as *L. callilepis*), grows to about 4 feet high; rosy lilac 'Kobold' (the best-known selection) and white-flowered 'Alba' top out at about 2 feet. 'Silvertips' has shimmering silvery lilac flowers on 3-foot stems.

Two species can send spikes up to 5 feet. *L. ligulistylis* typically has dark red buds and reddish purple flowers. Kansas gayfeather, *L. pycnostachya*, is purplish pink in the standard form, but its selection 'Alba' has white flowers.

The reddish purple flowers of 2½-foot *L. scariosa* differ from those of other gayfeathers in two ways: they're set more loosely on the spike, and they open nearly simultaneously all over the spike. 'September Glory' is a taller-growing selection; 'White Spire' is similar, but with white blossoms.

USES. All gayfeathers are trouble-free assets to the summer perennial border, where they look especially good alongside flowers of white, cream, light yellow, or blue.

GARDEN CULTURE. Gayfeathers need moderately fertile, well-drained soil; they are especially sensitive to soggy soil during their winter dormant period. Set out tuberous roots in early spring, placing them about 2 inches deep and 6 inches apart in clumps or drifts. Although plants tolerate drought, they look better if the soil is kept regularly moist (but not saturated) throughout growth and bloom. After a number of years, when performance declines, divide and reset overcrowded clumps in early spring.

Liatris spicata 'Kobold'

The word "aristocratic" has been aptly used to describe lilies. From foot-tall species in the wild to 9-foot modern hybrids in the summer flower border, all possess a highborn polish and elegance.

Wild lily species have been garden favorites for centuries in many parts of the world. But the lilies most widely grown today were developed only in this century, when growers and hybridizers embarked on intensive breeding programs. By selectively combining species, hybridizers produced varieties and strains with greater health and vigor than their species parents, new flower forms, and new colors: the lily palette now includes yellow, orange, red, maroon, pink, cream, white, lilac, purple, pale green, and multicolors. As the plants themselves were improved, so were the techniques used to grow them. The net result was a great gain for home gardeners: the new, more robust lilies were much easier to grow.

TYPES OF LILIES. Specialists' catalogs list a potentially bewildering assortment of hybrids (and sometimes species) that bloom in spring, summer, and fall. However, the International Lily Register's classification of hybrids and species into nine divisions establishes a logical order. The first eight divisions are reasonably cohesive hybrid categories; the ninth consists of lily species.

The nine divisions are listed below, along with the approximate hardiness of the plants in each group. For fuller descriptions of each division, consult a lily or bulb specialist catalog.

Division 1. Asiatic Hybrids. Hardy to about −30°F/−34°C.
Division 2. Martagon Hybrids. Hardy to about −30°F/−34°C.
Division 3. Candidum Hybrids. Hardy to about −20°F/−29°C.
Division 4. Hybrids of North American species. Hardiness varies, according to parent species, from −10° to −30°F/−23° to −34°C.
Division 5. Longiflorum Hybrids. Hardiness varies; most survive to about −20°F/−29°C.
Division 6. Aurelian Hybrids. Hardy to about −30°F/−34°C.
Division 7. Oriental Hybrids. Hardy to about −20°F/−29°C.

Listing continues >

LILIUM

LILY
Liliaceae
TRUE BULB

▲ 1 TO 9 FEET
☼ ◑ EXPOSURE NEEDS DEPEND ON CLIMATE (SEE "GARDEN CULTURE")
◗ NEEDS SUMMER MOISTURE, EXCEPT AS NOTED
✎ ZONES VARY BY TYPE AND SPECIES (SEE DESCRIPTIONS)

Lilium 'Golden Splendor' (Aurelian Hybrid)

TOP: *Lilium* 'Black Dragon' (Aurelian Hybrid)
BOTTOM: *Lilium martagon*

Division 8. Miscellaneous hybrids. Hardiness varies.

Division 9. Species lilies. Hardiness varies.

The majority of lilies available nowadays are hybrids that fit into Divisions 1–8, but a limited number of species lilies are sold by bulb specialists. These include:

L. candidum. Madonna lily. Zones 4–9, 14–24, 30–33. In late spring to early summer, fragrant pure white trumpets appear atop 3- to 4-foot stems. The foliage dies down soon after bloom, not to reappear until fall. Plant dormant bulbs in August; since plants do not make stem roots, set tops of bulbs just 1 to 2 inches below the soil surface. Growth begins soon after planting, with each bulb producing a rosette of leaves that persists over winter and gives rise to a flower stem in spring. The seed-raised Cascade strain is free of viral diseases that may affect performance of imported bulbs.

L. henryi. Zones 2–10, 14–21, 32–41. In midsummer, each slender 8- to 9-foot stem carries 10 to 20 bright orange blossoms with sharply recurved segments. This species performs best in light shade in all regions.

L. lancifolium (L. tigrinum). Tiger lily. Zones 1–10, 14–22, 31–43. This easy-to-grow old favorite blooms late in summer, its 4-foot stems bearing pendulous orange flowers spotted in black. Newer kinds are available in white, cream, yellow, pink, and red, all with black spots.

L. longiflorum. Easter lily. Zones 6–9, 14–24, 26–29. Every year at Easter, these lilies are widely sold as potted plants forced into bloom for the occasion. Long, notably fragrant white trumpets are borne on short stems. Named selections include 'Ace', 'Croft', and 'Tetraploid', all in the 1- to 1½-foot range, and 3-foot 'Estate'. Easter lily hybrids also offer flowers in pink, red, and yellow. Enjoy potted plants indoors until flowers fade, then plant them in the garden. The stems will ripen, then die down; growth may resume to produce more blooms in fall. In subsequent years, the plant should acclimate to the outdoors and flower in its normal (unforced) midsummer season.

L. martagon. Turk's cap lily. Zones 2–10, 14–17, 32–41. Easy to grow but slow to establish, this lily will form ever-enlarging clumps that become more beautiful each year. In early summer, 3- to 5-foot stems bear up to 50 pendent flowers with sharply recurved segments. Blossoms are typically purplish pink with darker spots, but darker and pure white variants exist. Flowers are fragrant, but the scent is unpleasant.

L. regale. Regal lily. Zones 3–9, 14–24, 30–34, 39. Modern hybrid trumpet lilies may surpass this species in beauty, but it is a sentimental favorite that is easy to grow. Stems reach 6 feet high; in midsummer, each bears up to 25 funnel-shaped white blossoms that are carried horizontally.

USES. Lilies are splendid components in mixed plantings of annuals, perennials, and even shrubs. And thanks to their great height range, they can be used in the foreground, center, or background. When planted in clumps, many have the mass of a shrub.

Many of the smaller species lilies are excellent candidates for naturalizing; try setting them out in drifts under high shade of deciduous trees, along with smaller types of ferns and other low plants that will keep their roots cool.

GARDEN CULTURE. Lilies have three basic cultural needs: deep, loose, well-drained, fertile soil; ample moisture all year (except for *L. candidum* and the Candidum Hybrids of Division 3); and coolness and shade at their roots, but sun or filtered sun for blooming tops. Begin by choosing a planting area with the right kind of light. Don't plant in full sun except where summers are cool and overcast; filtered sun, light shade, or afternoon shade is preferred in most climates. Don't expose bases of plants to bright, direct sun for any length of time. In all climates, avoid planting in windy locations.

Before planting, prepare the soil well: dig it to a depth of about 1 foot and add plenty of organic matter. The simplest method is this: dig the soil, spread a 3- to 4-inch layer of organic matter on the surface, and scatter on a granular fertilizer (using the amount the package directs); then thoroughly dig the organic matter and fertilizer into the loosened soil.

Plant bulbs as soon as you can after you get them. If you must delay, store them in a cool place. Before planting, check bulbs carefully; if they look shriveled, place them in moist sand or peat moss until the scales plump up and roots start to form. Also cut off any injured portions and dust the cuts with sulfur.

All lily bulbs should be planted about 1 foot apart, but planting depth varies according to bulb size and rooting habit. Some lilies send out roots only from their bulbs, but many others produce roots from stems as well (the hybrids in Divisions 1, 2, 4, 5, 6, and 7, for example). Stem-rooting types need deeper planting than those that root from bulbs alone. A general rule for stem-rooting types is to cover smaller bulbs with 2 to 3 inches of soil, medium-size bulbs with 3 to 4 inches, and larger bulbs with 4 to 6 inches. *L. candidum* and its hybrids (Division 3 lilies) root from bulbs only; plant these just 1 to 2 inches deep. If you're uncertain about correct planting depth, set bulbs shallower rather than deeper—lilies have contractile roots that will gradually pull the bulbs down to the proper depth.

Gophers are fond of lily bulbs. If these pests are a problem in your area, see "Foiling the Spoilers" (page 198) for planting methods that will thwart them.

Water well after planting, then mulch the soil with 2 to 3 inches of organic matter to conserve moisture and keep soil cool. Since most lilies never really enter a dormant period, they need constant moisture all year; try to keep soil moist to a depth of at least 6 inches. You can taper off on watering a bit after tops turn yellow in fall, but never let roots go completely dry. The exceptions to the constant-watering rule are the Candidum Hybrids (Division 3 lilies), *L. candidum* itself, and certain other species native to dry-summer parts of southern Europe, western Asia, and western North America. Let these types go dry during mid- to late summer.

Avoid overhead watering if possible, since it can spread diseases and also topple tall types when they're in flower.

Remove faded flowers to prevent seed formation, but don't cut back stems until leaves have yellowed in fall.

During active growth and bloom, watch for and control aphids, which spread an incurable viral disease that evidences itself as mottling on the leaves and, in many cases, as stunted growth. If you discover any apparently infected plants, dig and destroy them to eliminate sources of potential future infection. Where summers are humid, be watchful for signs of botrytis. For more on these pests and diseases, see page 203.

When clumps become crowded and bloom quality declines, dig and divide them—either in early spring just before growth begins, or in fall after foliage has yellowed. (*L. candidum* and its hybrids in Division 3 are again an exception; dig and divide these during their leafless period in summer.) If you simply need to transplant a lily clump without dividing it, you can do so at any time, even when plants are in full bloom. Just be sure to dig very carefully and replant immediately.

CONTAINER CULTURE. Lily roots need plenty of room, so always use deep containers. Plant one bulb in a 5- to 7-inch pot, up to five in a 14- to 16-inch pot. Follow directions "B" (subgroup 2) on page 207; fill container one-third full of either of the soil mixes described, then set in bulbs, with roots spread out and pointing downward. Add enough additional soil mix to cover tops of bulbs by 1 inch; then water thoroughly and place in a cool, shady spot. Keep soil only moderately moist during the rooting period. When top growth appears, water more frequently; as stems elongate, gradually add more soil until containers are filled to 1 inch beneath the rim. Then move containers to

TOP: *Lilium* 'Casablanca' (Oriental Hybrid)
BOTTOM: *Lilium,* Asiatic Hybrids

a partly shaded location for the bloom period. Apply liquid fertilizer monthly during growth and bloom.

After flowers fade, cut back on water, but never let soil dry out (except for *L. candidum* and Division 3 lilies). Repot when bulbs crowd their containers.

LYCORIS
SPIDER LILY
Amaryllidaceae
TRUE BULB

- ▲ 1½ TO 2 FEET
- ☀ FULL SUN
- ◊ WITHHOLD SUMMER MOISTURE
- ✀ ZONES VARY BY SPECIES
  (SEE "GARDEN CULTURE")

Lycoris squamigera

Spider lily has much in common with its better-known relative belladonna lily *(Amaryllis belladonna)*. Narrow, strap-shaped leaves appear in fall (in mild-winter regions) or spring; they remain green until some point in summer, then die down completely. The smooth flower stalks emerge shortly afterward, each bearing a cluster of lilylike blossoms in late summer or early fall. The blossoms are funnel shaped or wide open, with narrow, pointed petal-like segments; most have long, projecting, spidery-looking stamens.

The best-known species is 1½-foot *L. radiata*, a showpiece in coral red with a golden sheen, with long, curved stamens protruding from its 1½- to 2-inch trumpets; 'Alba' is a white-flowered selection. *L. sanguinea* reaches 2 feet tall; its 2½-inch, bright red to orange-red blooms lack the prominent stamens of *L. radiata*.

Appearing on 2-foot stems, the 3-inch lilac pink trumpets of *L. squamigera* resemble those of belladonna lily *(Amaryllis belladonna)*—and in fact, the plant was once known as *Amaryllis hallii*. *L. sprengeri* is a similar species with slightly smaller blossoms in a more purple-tinted pink. Both bloom in late summer. Golden spider lily, *L. aurea (L. africana)*, shows off its 3-inch, bright yellow blossoms in early fall.

USES. Spider lily provides a colorful accent among other plants that tolerate dry soil in summer.

GARDEN CULTURE. Grow *L. squamigera* in Zones 3–24, 29–33; *L. sprengeri* in Zones 4–24, 29–33; *L. sanguinea* in Zones 4–24, 29–31; *L. radiata* in Zones 4–9, 12–24, 29–33; *L. aurea* in Zones 16, 17, 19–24, 26, 28.

Choose a sunny planting area that can remain dry during the summer dormant period. In late summer, set bulbs in well-drained soil about 1 foot apart. Keep tops of bulb necks at or just above the soil surface—except in the colder part of the range, where tops of necks should be set just under the surface. Water regularly while plants are growing and again when flower stalks emerge, but withhold water and let soil go dry when foliage begins to wither.

Dig and divide just after bloom, only when you want to move or increase plantings.

CONTAINER CULTURE. In regions beyond their hardiness limits, all species can be grown in containers and overwintered indoors in a brightly lit room or greenhouse where temperatures fall between 40° to 65°F/4° to 18°C. Follow directions "C" on page 207.

While leaves are growing in winter and spring, water regularly and apply

Lycoris radiata

liquid fertilizer monthly. Move containers outdoors when danger of frost is past. Follow watering directions described in "Garden culture." Repot every 3 to 5 years, when bulbs crowd their containers.

Though more modest in flower than its relative the true hyacinth *(Hyacinthus),* grape hyacinth makes up for the difference in its profusion of early spring blooms and ease of culture. Native to the Mediterranean and southwest Asia, it typically bears fragrant, urn-shaped blossoms carried in short, tight spikes atop short stems; in blue-flowered forms, the blossom clusters resemble bunches of grapes. The fleshy, grasslike leaves usually emerge in fall, but foliage is rarely damaged by low temperatures.

M. armeniacum and its varieties are the most widely available grape hyacinths. The species has floppy foliage and 8-inch stems bearing bright blue flowers; 'Early Giant' is deep blue, while 'Blue Spike' has light blue double blossoms. 'Cantab', another light blue variety, has shorter stems and neater foliage than the species.

Italian grape hyacinth, *M. botryoides,* bears medium blue flowers (white in 'Album') on stems to 1 foot tall. Eight-inch-tall *M. tubergenianum* takes its common name—"Oxford and Cambridge hyacinth"—from its two-tone flower spikes: blossoms are light blue (Cambridge) at the top of the spike, dark blue (Oxford) in the lower portion.

The largest and showiest of the grape hyacinths is *M. latifolium.* Each bulb produces just one leaf and a flowering stem to 1 foot tall; the lower flowers in the spike are deepest violet, the upper ones vivid indigo blue.

M. azureum offers something of a floral difference, as its previous classifications under *Hyacinthus* and *Hyacinthella* suggest: its sky blue blooms, borne on 8-inch stems, are bell shaped, like those of true hyacinth. In its leaves and the form of its blossom spikes, though, it resembles a standard grape hyacinth. Distinctive *M. comosum,* the fringe or tassel hyacinth, is a complete departure from the other species. Its flowers, carried in loose clusters on 1- to 1½-foot-tall stems, have an odd shredded appearance. In the species, blossoms are greenish brown on the lower part of the spike, bluish purple in the upper portion; 'Monstrosum' has petals resembling lilac-colored shredded coconut.

USES. Naturalizing is a natural for grape hyacinths. They'll readily produce a carpet of bloom under deciduous trees and shrubs, along paths, and in transitional areas between garden and meadow. They are also prime container candidates.

GARDEN CULTURE. Grow *M. botryoides* and *M. tubergenianum* in Zones 1–24, 30–45; *M. latifolium* in Zones 2–24, 32–43; *M. azureum* and *M. comosum* in Zones 2–24, 30–43; and *M. armeniacum* in Zones 2–24, 29–43. In early fall, set bulbs about 2 inches deep and 3 inches apart in well-drained soil. Water regularly during fall, winter, and spring; in summer, when leaves have died down and bulbs are dormant, give less water or even no water at all.

Bulbs increase fairly rapidly, and many species also spread by self-sown seeds. When clumps become so crowded that vigor and flower quality decline, dig and divide in early fall.

CONTAINER CULTURE. Follow directions "B" (sub-group 1) on page 207.

MUSCARI
GRAPE HYACINTH
Liliaceae
TRUE BULB

- ▲ 8 TO 18 INCHES
- ☼ ◐ FULL SUN OR LIGHT SHADE
- ◐ ACCEPTS SUMMER MOISTURE BUT DOESN'T NEED ANY
- ✹ ZONES VARY BY SPECIES (SEE "GARDEN CULTURE")

Muscari armeniacum
'Blue Spike'

NARCISSUS

DAFFODIL, NARCISSUS

Amaryllidaceae

TRUE BULB

- ▲ 3 TO 18 INCHES
- ☼ ◑ FULL SUN; PART OR LIGHT SHADE AFTER BLOOM WHERE SUMMERS ARE HOT
- ◑ ACCEPTS SUMMER MOISTURE BUT DOESN'T NEED ANY
- ✎ ZONES 1–24, 28–45, EXCEPT AS NOTED

ABOVE: *Narcissus* 'Ice Follies'

Of all the bulbs that bloom in late winter and early spring, daffodils and other members of *Narcissus* have been judged the most trouble-free by generations of gardeners. Given minimum care at planting time, these natives of Europe and North Africa grow, bloom, increase—in other words, thrive—with virtually no further attention. They do not require summer watering (but will take it), need only infrequent division (and will even survive without it), and are totally unappetizing to the rodents that find tulips, for example, such a treat. They have just two principal enemies: encroaching shade, which can adversely affect performance; and the narcissus bulb fly, which, if unchecked, can seriously erode the bulb population.

All plants variously called "daffodil," "narcissus," and "jonquil" are properly *Narcissus*. In gardener's terms, however, "daffodil" refers only to the large-flowered kinds, while "narcissus" denotes the small-flowered (and usually early-blooming) types that bear their blossoms in clusters of four or more per stem. "Jonquil" correctly refers only to *N. jonquilla* and its hybrids.

All have the same basic flower structure. Each bloom has six outer petal-like segments (the perianth) and a central petal-like structure (the corona), which is usually elongated and tubular or more shallow and cuplike. Color range is also fairly consistent: the perianth may be orange, yellow, cream, or white, while the corona is white, cream, yellow, orange, red, pink, or a light color bordered by yellow, pink, orange, or red.

TYPES OF DAFFODILS. Despite their general similarities, blossoms do vary from one species or hybrid type to another. Based on this variation and on botanical relationships, the Royal Horticultural Society of England has established 12 divisions.

Division 1. Trumpet daffodils. Corona as long or longer than the perianth segments; one flower to each stem. The best-known trumpet daffodil is yellow 'King Alfred', but the newer varieties 'Unsurpassable' and 'William the Silent' bear better flowers. White varieties include 'Mount Hood', 'Cantatrice', 'Empress of Ireland'. White perianth/yellow trumpet combinations are 'Las Vegas' and 'Peace Pipe'; reverse bicolors (yellow perianth/white trumpet) include 'Honeybird', 'Lunar Sea', and 'Spellbinder'.

Division 2. Large-cupped daffodils. Corona shorter than the perianth segments, but always more than one-third their length; one flower to each stem. 'Stainless' is white; 'Carleton' and 'Saint Keverne' are yellow. Varieties with a white perianth and a colored cup include 'Ice Follies' (yellow cup); 'Accent', 'Romance', and 'Salome' (pink cup); 'Johann Strauss', 'Professor Einstein' (orange cup). 'Ambergate', 'Ceylon', 'Fortissimo', and 'Paricutin' all have a yellow perianth and a cup of pink, orange, or red. Reverse bicolors (yellow perianth/white cup) include 'Daydream' and 'Impresario'.

Division 3. Small-cupped daffodils. Corona no more than one-third the length of the perianth segments; one flower to each stem. 'Audubon' (white perianth/pink cup) and 'Barrett Browning' (white/orange-red) are good.

Division 4. Double daffodils. Corona segments greatly multiplied, and separate rather than joined together. Blossom has a fluffy appearance and looks more like a peony than a typical daffodil. One flower to each stem. Examples are 'Christmas Valley' (white with pink), 'Tahiti' (yellow with red), and 'White Lion' (white with yellow). 'Cheerfulness' (white) and 'Yellow Cheerfulness' are like double-flowered tazettas (see Division 8).

Division 5. Triandrus Hybrids. Derivatives of *N. triandrus*. Corona at least two-thirds the length of the perianth segments; several flowers to each stem. White 'Thalia' is an old favorite. Others include 'Hawera' (lemon yellow) and 'Silver Chimes' (white/yellow).

Division 6. Cyclamineus Hybrids. Derivatives of *N. cyclamineus;* early-flowering forms carrying one flower on each stem. Perianth segments are strongly recurved (as though facing a stiff headwind); 'February Gold' is the best-known example. Yellow 'Peeping Tom' has an especially long trumpet; 'Jack Snipe' has a white perianth and a yellow trumpet.

Division 7. Jonquilla Hybrids. Derivatives of *N. jonquilla.* Each stem bears two to four small, fragrant flowers; foliage is often rushlike. A growing number of varieties offer most of the color combinations found in larger daffodils. Choices include 'Bell Song' (white perianth/pink corona); 'Pipit' (yellow/white); 'Suzy' (yellow/orange); 'Trevithian' (all yellow).

Division 8. Tazetta & Tazetta Hybrids. Derivatives of *N. tazetta.* Hardy to about 10°F/−12°C. This division includes all the early-blooming, cluster-flowering types popularly known as "narcissus." Each stem bears four to eight or more highly fragrant flowers with short coronas. Many types have a white perianth and a yellow corona, but there are other color combinations. *N. tazetta* 'Orientalis', the Chinese sacred lily, has a light yellow perianth and a darker yellow corona; 'Paper White' is pure white; 'Early Splendor' is white/orange; 'Grand Soleil d'Or' is yellow/orange. Newer varieties include 'Cragford' and 'Geranium' (white/orange) and 'Hoopoe' and 'Scarlet Gem' (yellow/orange).

Division 9. Poeticus narcissus. Derivatives of *N. poeticus.* Perianth segments are white; very short, broad corona is in a contrasting color, usually with red edges. 'Actaea' and 'Pheasant's Eye' are old favorites.

Division 10. Species, their naturally occurring forms, and wild hybrids. Included here are numerous miniature types popular with collectors and rock garden enthusiasts. Prominent among these are the following:

N. asturiensis (often sold as *N.* 'Miniature'). Pale yellow flowers, only 1 inch long, are miniature trumpet daffodils (see Division 1, facing page). Plants are just 3 inches tall.

N. bulbocodium. Hoop petticoat daffodil. Hardy to about −10°F/−23°C. Six-inch-tall stems bear small yellow flowers with flaring coronas and almost threadlike perianth segments. Foliage is grassy.

N. cyclamineus. Hardy to about −10°F/−23°C. Small flowers, one to each 6- to 12-inch stem, have strongly recurved perianth segments and tubular coronas.

N. jonquilla. Jonquil. Stems to 1 foot tall bear small, fragrant blossoms in clusters of two to six. The cuplike corona is short in relation to the perianth segments; foliage is rushlike.

N. triandrus. Angel's-tears. Plants have rushlike foliage and one to six small, white to pale yellow flowers per stem. Corona is at least half as long as the perianth segments. The tallest forms of this species reach 10 inches.

Division 11. Split-corona hybrids. The corona is split for at least one-third of its length into two or more segments. 'Casata' (white perianth/yellow corona) and 'Palmares' (white/pink) are two of the more readily available varieties in this small but growing class.

Division 12. Miscellaneous. This category contains all types that don't fit the other 11 divisions. 'Tête-à-tête' and 'Jumblie' (both yellow) have Division 6 flowers but are rock-garden dwarfs to about 6 inches tall.

USES. These are among the most versatile of bulbs. Plant them in mixed borders of annuals and perennials, under deciduous trees and shrubs, or even beneath ground covers that grow loosely enough to let plants come through. You can also naturalize bulbs in high shade beneath deciduous trees or in open, grassy meadowland. The small species make good long-term container plants.

Listing continues >

TOP: *Narcissus* 'Early Splendor'
CENTER: *Narcissus bulbocodium*
BOTTOM: *Narcissus* 'Tête-à-tête'

GARDEN CULTURE. When buying daffodil bulbs, look for solid, heavy bulbs with no injury to the basal plate. So-called double-nose bulbs will give you the most and largest flowers the first season after planting. In most regions, it's best to plant in late summer or early fall, as soon as bulbs become available. But in areas with a long, warm autumn and fairly mild winter, put off planting until soil has cooled in midautumn.

Select a planting area that will be in full sun while bulbs are blooming, keeping in mind that blossoms will face the source of light. One traditional and attractive location is under high-branching deciduous trees. After bloom has ended, part or light shade can actually be beneficial to plants, especially in hot-summer regions.

For all members of the genus, good drainage is the primary soil requirement. To improve drainage in heavy soils, dig plenty of organic matter into the soil prior to planting (this will also aid moisture retention in light soils).

Plant bulbs approximately twice as deep as they are tall; this measures out to 5 to 6 inches deep for large bulbs, 3 to 5 inches deep for smaller sizes. Space bulbs 6 to 8 inches apart, so they can increase for a number of years without crowding each other.

Water newly planted bulbs thoroughly to initiate root growth. In many regions, fall and winter will be wet (or snowy) enough to take care of bulbs' water requirements until flowering time or later. But if rainfall is inadequate, keep plantings well watered between rains: plants need plenty of moisture during growth and bloom, especially after foliage has broken through the ground. After flowers have faded, continue to water plants regularly until foliage begins to turn yellow. Then stop watering, let foliage die down, and keep soil dry (or fairly dry) until fall.

The most serious pest is the narcissus bulb fly. An adult fly resembles a small bumblebee. The female lays eggs on leaves and necks of bulbs; when the eggs hatch, the young grubs eat their way into the bulbs, opening the way for rot organisms. See page 203 for controls.

Established clumps need dividing only when flower production and bloom quality decline. It's easiest to dig and divide clumps (or transplant them to another location) just after foliage dies down, when you can still see where plants are. After digging bulbs for division, give them ventilated storage (see page 204) until the best planting time for your climate, as specified above.

CONTAINER CULTURE. Follow directions "B" on page 207. The small species can be permanent container residents. All other types belong to the first subgroup under "B" (page 207): they make attractive pot plants for just one season, after which their performance declines and they should be moved to the garden. To force bulbs for earlier bloom, see pages 210–211.

TOP: *Narcissus* 'Christmas Valley'
BOTTOM: *Narcissus* (Tazetta Hybrid)
in wall container

NERINE
Amaryllidaceae
TRUE BULB

▲ 1½ TO 2 FEET

☼ ◑ FULL SUN; PART SHADE WHERE SUMMERS ARE HOT

◐ WITHHOLD SUMMER MOISTURE

✄ ZONES 5, 8, 9, 13–28

These South African natives are relatives of spider lily *(Lycoris)*, which they closely resemble. All have strap-shaped leaves to about 1 foot long that complete their growth and die back well before the late-summer or early-fall bloom period, then reappear later in the year (typically around bloom time or shortly afterwards). The broad, funnel-shaped flowers appear in clusters atop smooth stems; each has six spreading segments, recurved at the tips.

Soft pink, 3-inch-long trumpets of *N. bowdenii* typically have a darker pink stripe down each segment; 8 to 12 of these blossoms are clustered atop 2-foot stems. Bulb specialists may offer named selections, such as larger, later-blooming 'Pink Triumph' or pink-blushed white 'Alba'. The inch-wide leaves reappear shortly before or during the bloom period. This is the best species to try in marginally cold regions, where temperatures may occasionally dip below 10°F/−12°C.

Guernsey lily, *N. sarniensis,* is similar to *N. bowdenii* in size and height. The species has flowers of iridescent crimson, but its forms and hybrids bear blossoms in a wider range of colors: pink, coral, orange, scarlet, and white, usually with a silvery or golden sheen. Leaves reappear after the bloom period ends.

Prominently extended stamens, as in spider lily, distinguish the gold-dusted scarlet blossoms of *N. curvifolia* 'Fothergillii Major'. The bloom clusters are carried on 1½-foot stems; leaves re-emerge after flowering finishes.

Blossoms with narrow, curved, crinkled segments are the signature of rose pink *N. undulata* (sometimes sold as *N. crispa* or *N. sarniensis* 'Crispa'). Its 1½-foot stems bear clusters of 8 to 12 flowers; leaves reappear at flowering time.

USES. Like spider lily, nerine provides a bright accent among perennials or shrubs that tolerate (or require) dry soil in summer. It's also an excellent container plant.

GARDEN CULTURE. Nerine needs well-drained, preferably sandy soil. Plant in full sun; where summers are hot and dry, choose a planting area in partial shade.

In late summer or early fall, set bulbs 1 foot apart. Keep tops of bulb necks at or just above soil surface except in the colder part of range, where tops of necks should be just below the surface. Water thoroughly after planting, but wait until growth begins before starting regular watering.

When foliage starts to yellow and die down in late spring, cut back on water; after foliage has died back completely, withhold all water and keep soil dry until flower stalks emerge. Then resume a regular watering routine. Leave established clumps undisturbed unless you need to increase or move plantings.

CONTAINER CULTURE. All types of nerine can be grown in climates beyond their hardiness limits if planted in containers and overwintered indoors. Follow directions "C" on page 207. Handle as for spider lily *(Lycoris).*

Nerine sarniensis

Ornithogalum dubium

Six species are generally available from bulb growers. All bear starlike blossoms in white or nearly white (with one exception), and two take their common name, "star of Bethlehem," from the flower shape. True to the name, these last two (along with *O. nutans*) are native to the southern and eastern Mediterranean region; the remaining species come from South Africa. All flower in spring; *O. dubium* may start in late winter, while bloom of *O. saundersiae* may extend into early summer.

The most widely grown species is *O. umbellatum,* one of the two commonly known as star of Bethlehem. It increases rapidly, which can be an asset or a liability: plants quickly spread to fill bare areas, but may naturalize to the point of becoming weedy. Foot-tall stems bear loose clusters of inch-wide white flowers; the back of each narrow petal is striped green. Grasslike leaves are about as long as the flower stems.

Fragrant *O. arabicum,* Arabian star of Bethlehem, has the most striking blooms: broad-petaled, 2-inch blossoms of solid white, each centered with a shiny, beadlike black eye. Blossom clusters are carried on 2-foot stems; bluish green, strap-shaped leaves may reach the same length as the stems, but they're usually floppy rather than upright. Plants perform best where summers are warm and dry. Giant chincherinchee, *O. saundersiae,* is essentially a larger version of *O. arabicum,* with flower stalks to 3 feet tall rising above upright leaves that grow to about 2 feet.

Listing continues >

ORNITHOGALUM
Liliaceae
TRUE BULB

- ▲ 8 INCHES TO 3 FEET
- ☀ ◐ FULL SUN OR PART SHADE
- ◐◐○ SUMMER MOISTURE NEEDS VARY BY SPECIES (SEE "GARDEN CULTURE")
- ✎ ZONES VARY BY SPECIES (SEE "GARDEN CULTURE")
- ◊ ALL PARTS ARE POISONOUS IF INGESTED

Ornithogalum umbellatum

OXALIS
Oxalidaceae
TRUE BULB

- ▲ 4 TO 20 INCHES
- ☼ ☽ FULL SUN; FILTERED SUN OR LIGHT SHADE WHERE SUMMERS ARE HOT
- ◖ SUMMER MOISTURE NEEDS VARY BY SPECIES (SEE "GARDEN CULTURE")
- ✄ ZONES VARY BY SPECIES (SEE "GARDEN CULTURE")

O. thyrsoides, commonly called chincherinchee, produces elongated clusters of 2-inch flowers with brownish green centers. Stems grow 1½ to 2 feet tall; upright, bright green, 2-inch-wide leaves are shorter than the stems (to just 1 foot) and usually start to die back while the plants are in bloom.

Charming *O. nutans,* sometimes called silver bells, bears nodding, starlike to nearly bell-shaped blossoms with a pronounced central cluster of stamens; up to 15 blooms are spaced along the upper portion of each 1½- to 2-foot flower stalk. In color, the flowers combine light green and white. The narrow leaves are rather floppy. Like *O. umbellatum,* this species spreads rapidly and may become weedy.

Flower color makes *O. dubium* easy to recognize: though the blooms resemble those of *O. arabicum* and appear in similar rounded clusters, the petals surrounding the beady black eye come in shades of yellow or orange. Stems grow just 8 to 12 inches high; leaves are lance-shaped, to about 4 inches long.

USES. *O. nutans* and *O. umbellatum* are ideal choices for naturalizing. The other four species make attractive accent clumps in foreground locations, though three of them— *O. arabicum, O. dubium,* and *O. thyrsoides*—die down over summer and need a relatively dry dormant period.

GARDEN CULTURE. Grow *O. umbellatum* and *O. nutans* in Zones 4–33; *O. saundersiae* in Zones 4–32; *O. thyrsoides* in Zones 4–24; *O. arabicum* in Zones 5–24; and *O. dubium* in Zones 8, 9, 14–24. Choose a planting area with well-drained soil; dig in plenty of organic matter prior to planting in early fall. Set bulbs 3 inches deep, 3 to 4 inches apart. *O. nutans, O. saundersiae,* and *O. umbellatum* can take moisture all year round. *O. arabicum, O. dubium,* and *O. thyrsoides* need moisture throughout growth and bloom, but once flowering has finished and leaves have died down, withhold moisture until new foliage begins to emerge.

Dig and divide plantings only when a decline in vigor and bloom quality tells you that clumps have become overcrowded.

CONTAINER CULTURE. In areas with summer rainfall, growing *O. arabicum, O. dubium,* and *O. thyrsoides* in pots is the best way to cater to the plants' needs for a dry dormant period. Follow directions "C" on page 207.

Gardeners familiar only with the weedy, invasive *Oxalis* species will find the following attractive, well-mannered bulbous kinds a pleasant surprise. (Other species may grow from rhizomes or tubers.) All those described below are native to South Africa or South America, and all have cloverlike leaves and five-petaled flowers with a broad funnel shape.

O. adenophylla forms a dense tuft of foliage just 4 inches tall. Each gray-green leaf is divided into 12 to 22 crinkly leaflets. In late spring, 4- to 6-inch-high stems appear, each bearing up to three 1-inch-wide, lavender pink blossoms centered and veined with deeper lavender.

Summer-blooming *O. bowiei* has downy, 2-inch green leaves and foot-tall stems topped with clusters of 3 to 12 pink to rosy purple, 2-inch flowers. Novel flowers and foliage distinguish *O. versicolor,* which blooms in late summer or fall. Compact plants to 6 inches tall bear the typical three-lobed leaves, but each lobe is deeply cleft into two narrow segments. Flowers are about 1 inch across, white with yellow throats and a (usually) purplish margin. 'Candy Cane', with red-edged petals, is the most widely sold form; it owes its name to the diagonal red stripes on its furled buds.

The flexible, branching stems of *O. hirta* eventually trail with the weight of their small gray-green leaves. Inch-wide rose pink flowers appear in late fall and winter.

Blooming at the same time is *O. purpurea*, with yellow-throated flowers of white, lavender, or rose pink carried just above 5-inch-tall clumps of large dark green leaves. For the largest flowers (up to 2 inches across), look for forms sold as 'Grand Duchess'.

O. tetraphylla (formerly *O. deppei*) is grown primarily as a foliage plant, though it does bear clusters of red or white flowers on 6- to 20-inch stems in spring. Each 2-inch-wide leaf looks like a four-leaf clover with maroon staining on the lower third of the leaflets.

USES. Plants are attractive in rock gardens and along partly shaded walkways; all types are good container subjects.

GARDEN CULTURE. Grow *O. adenophylla* in Zones 4–9, 12–24, 30–32; *O. bowiei* in Zones 4–9, 14–24, 29–31; *O. hirta, O. purpurea,* and *O. tetraphylla* in Zones 8, 9, 12–24, 29–31; *O. versicolor* in Zones 6–9, 14–24. Plant in late summer or fall. Set bulbs 1 inch deep, 6 inches apart, in good, well-drained soil amended with plenty of organic matter. Filtered sunlight or light shade is preferable in hot-summer regions, but plants appreciate full sun where summers are cool to mild (or overcast). Water all types regularly during growth and bloom (those blooming in summer will need regular moisture then, but others can get by with little summer water). After bloom finishes, water sparingly until new growth resumes several months later. Divide infrequently, only when you need to move or increase plantings.

CONTAINER CULTURE. Follow directions "A" on page 207, spacing bulbs 2 inches apart. If you're growing plants indoors, place them in a window that receives morning sunlight. Water as outlined for in-ground plantings. Apply a liquid fertilizer monthly during growth and bloom. Leave bulbs in containers during the dormant period.

Oxalis bowiei

You'd need a botanist to explain why this plant doesn't belong to the genus *Hymenocallis*—judging by appearances, that's exactly where it ought to be. Each powerfully fragrant, 3-inch white flower is built like a daffodil: a central cuplike structure is surrounded by six narrow petal-like segments. Plants bloom for several weeks during mid- to late summer, bearing clusters of up to eight blossoms atop stems 1½ to 2 feet tall. The arching evergreen leaves are strap shaped, grayish green, and about 2 feet long.

USES. Where winter temperatures are mild and soil is very well drained, sea daffodil makes an attractive accent clump in the foreground of a mixed planting of perennials and annuals. However, it's more often grown in containers, where its needs for sharp drainage and protection from winter cold can more easily be satisfied.

GARDEN CULTURE. In early fall, plant the large, pear-shaped, long-necked bulbs in well-drained, organically enriched soil in a sunny location. Cover the tops of bulb necks by about 2 inches. In nature, bulbs grow in sand or sandy soil on Mediterranean beaches; some growers put an inch-deep layer of sand in the bottom of the planting hole to keep bulb bases from ever becoming too damp.

Plants need regular moisture from the time new growth begins in spring until flowering is finished and foliage has ceased growing. From that point until new growth resumes the next year, reduce watering, but be sure to give enough to keep foliage from wilting. In all but frost-free zones, foliage may be damaged by winter cold; if there's any danger of the soil freezing, apply a mulch around the plants.

CONTAINER CULTURE. Follow directions "C" on page 207. Several bulbs in a large pot make the best display. Set tops of bulb necks just at soil level, and allow an inch or more between bulbs and between bulbs and the edge of the container.

PANCRATIUM maritimum
SEA DAFFODIL
Amaryllidaceae
TRUE BULB

▲ 2 FEET
☼ FULL SUN
● NEEDS SUMMER MOISTURE
✂ ZONES 7–9, 12–28

Pancratium maritimum

POLIANTHES tuberosa

TUBEROSE

Agavaceae

RHIZOME WITH BULBLIKE TOP AND
TUBEROUS ROOTS

- ▲ 2½ TO 3½ FEET
- ☼ FULL SUN
- ◆ NEEDS SUMMER MOISTURE
- ✄ ZONES 7–9, 14–29

Polianthes tuberosa

The intense fragrance of this Mexican native is legendary. Popular with home gardeners around the turn of the century, it is more commonly grown today for the cut flower and French perfume industries.

Each rhizome produces a fountain of narrow, grasslike leaves about 1½ feet tall. Flower spikes rise above the foliage, producing loose whorls of outward-facing white blossoms in summer or early fall. The tallest tuberose (to 3½ feet) is the form sometimes sold as 'Mexican Single', which bears trumpet-shaped single blooms about 2½ inches long. Most widely sold, however, is double-flowered, 2½-foot-tall 'The Pearl'.

USES. Though tuberoses are attractive in foliage and flower, they are primarily valued for fragrance. Locate plants where both looks and scent can be appreciated: in mixed border plantings near walkways or in containers on patio, terrace, or deck.

GARDEN CULTURE. For bloom year after year, tuberoses need a long (at least 4-month) warm season before flowering. Where this can be provided outdoors, you can plant rhizomes directly in the ground; elsewhere, grow them in containers, or start them indoors in pots and plant outside after soil warms.

Plant in spring, choosing a sunny spot and providing well-drained soil generously amended with organic matter. Check rhizomes to make sure they're healthy: they should show signs of green at the growing tips. Set rhizomes 2 inches deep and 4 to 6 inches apart, then water the planting area to moisten the soil thoroughly. As soon as leaves appear, begin regular watering; plants need plenty of moisture during growth and bloom. If soil or water is alkaline, apply an acid fertilizer when growth begins.

When foliage starts to yellow in fall, withhold water and let soil go dry. Rhizomes can be left in the ground where winter lows remain above 20°F/−7°C, but even in these areas, many gardeners store rhizomes indoors over winter—and in colder regions, of course, indoor storage is required. Dig plants after leaves have yellowed; cut off dead leaves, let rhizomes dry for 2 weeks, and store covered (see page 205).

CONTAINER CULTURE. In regions where the growing season is shorter than 4 months, start rhizomes in pots indoors, keeping them where the temperature remains above 60°F/16°C. Plant one or two rhizomes in an 8-inch container, using the soil mix described under "A" on page 207. Water thoroughly after planting, but wait until leaves emerge to begin regular watering. As soon as night temperatures reliably remain above 60°F/16°C, you can move growing plants outdoors; keep them in containers for portable display, or carefully transplant into garden beds. Give container-grown plants liquid fertilizer monthly until flowering begins.

PUSCHKINIA scilloides

Liliaceae

TRUE BULB

- ▲ 6 INCHES
- ☼ ◑ FULL SUN OR LIGHT SHADE
- ○ WITHHOLD SUMMER MOISTURE
- ✄ ZONES 1–11, 14, 29–43; NEEDS
  SOME SUBFREEZING WINTER
  TEMPERATURES

One herald of springtime is this stocky native of Asia Minor, a relative of glory-of-the-snow (*Chionodoxa*) and squill (*Scilla*). Each bulb produces two broad, strap-shaped, upright leaves that are a bit shorter than the 6-inch flower stem. The starlike, 1-inch blossoms—up to 15 per stem—are pale blue, with a greenish blue stripe down the center of each petal. Bulb growers usually carry *P. s. libanotica,* which conforms to the above description; a white-flowered variant is offered as *P. s.* 'Alba' or *P. s. libanotica alba.*

USES. Puschkinia is a good choice for naturalizing and for rock garden plantings. Naturalize bulbs in grassy patches or plant in drifts under deciduous trees, along pathways, or in front of shrub borders.

Puschkinia scilloides 'Alba'

GARDEN CULTURE. In late summer into fall, set bulbs 3 inches deep in well-drained soil; for a massed effect, space them about 3 inches apart. After planting, give bulbs one thorough watering to settle soil and initiate root growth. Keep soil just slightly moist until foliage appears; then water regularly until leaves start to yellow in early summer. During the summer dormant period, plants need very little water.

Established plantings seldom need dividing to relieve overcrowding. However, you can dig bulbs as needed to increase a planting or start new ones; do so in mid- to late summer and replant right away.

CONTAINER CULTURE. Follow directions "B" (subgroup 1) on page 207.

RANUNCULUS asiaticus
Ranunculaceae
TUBEROUS ROOT

▲ 8 INCHES TO 2 FEET
☼ FULL SUN
◊ WITHHOLD SUMMER MOISTURE
❀ ZONES 4–9, 12–31

It's surprising that this native of Asia Minor has never acquired the common name "magic flower"—the production of bright, showy spring blossoms from such a small, peculiar-looking root is the equal of any conjuring trick. The 3- to 5-inch-wide, semi-double to fully double flowers have been variously (and accurately) described as resembling small peonies, camellias, and artificial crepe-paper flowers. One to four blooms are carried on each 1½- to 2-foot stem. Plants are full foliaged, with dark green, finely divided leaves; when not yet in bloom, they look much like bunches of flat-leaf parsley.

Most widely sold is the Tecolote strain, with a color range including pink, red, orange, yellow, cream, white, and multicolors; the group also offers pastel blooms edged with darker hues. The Bloomingdale strain is a dwarf equivalent just 8 to 10 inches tall. Nurseries offer tuberous roots of various sizes; both small and large roots produce equally large blossoms, but the larger ones produce a greater number of flowers.

USES. Set out plants in solid beds, use them in drifts of single or mixed colors, or spot them as accent clumps in mixed plantings of annuals and perennials. Plants are also excellent container subjects, and in mild-winter areas, they're a good alternative to tulips.

GARDEN CULTURE. The sooner you set out roots, the earlier they'll bloom. Where tuberous roots are hardy in the ground, plant in fall. In regions too cold for the roots to overwinter outdoors, plant in spring for bloom from late spring into early summer (hot weather terminates flower production). If you live in a cold-winter region, you'll get the longest possible flowering season by starting roots indoors 4 to 6 weeks before the normal last-frost date. Plant them in pots or flats, using either of the soil mixes described in "B" on page 207.

Plants need well-drained soil liberally amended with organic matter. In clay and other heavy soils, plant in raised beds to promote good drainage and set roots no deeper than 1 inch. (In lighter soils, they can be planted about 2 inches deep.) Position roots with the prongs facing down, spacing them 6 to 8 inches apart. Water thoroughly after planting, then withhold water until the leaves emerge.

Birds are very fond of ranunculus shoots, so you may need to protect sprouting plants with netting or wire. Another solution is to start plants in pots or flats (see above), then set them out in the garden when they're 4 to 6 inches tall—too mature to appeal to birds.

While plants are flowering, remove faded blossoms to encourage bloom. As the weather grows warmer, flowering will cease and foliage will begin to yellow. At this point, stop watering and let foliage die back. Where tuberous roots are hardy in the ground, you may leave them undisturbed—provided that soil can be kept dry throughout the summer. However, most gardeners in all regions dig plants when foliage yellows, cut off the tops, let the roots dry for a week or two, and then give covered storage (see page 205) until planting time.

CONTAINER CULTURE. Follow directions "B" (subgroup 2) on page 207.

Ranunculus asiaticus

RHODOHYPOXIS baueri

Hypoxidaceae

RHIZOME WITH OTHER CHARACTERISTICS

- ▲ 6 INCHES
- ☼ ◑ FULL SUN; PART OR LIGHT SHADE WHERE SUMMERS ARE HOT
- ◖ NEEDS SUMMER MOISTURE
- ✂ ZONES 4–7, 14–24, 28–33

Rhodohypoxis baueri

This charming alpine plant covers itself in bloom over a long period in spring and summer, when the tufts of narrow, hairy leaves are nearly invisible beneath a profusion of inch-wide, six-petaled blossoms. The typical color range runs from pink shades to rosy red, but white-flowered varieties are available. In the wild, the plant grows in the high elevations of South Africa's Drakensberg Mountains. The bulblike structure is difficult to categorize; it is most like a rhizome, but has characteristics of a corm, tuber, and tuberous root as well.

USES. These are excellent rock garden and edge-of-border plants wherever their water requirements can be met. More often, though, they are grown as container plants, where their beauty can be appreciated at close range and their need for a dry winter period can be easily satisfied.

GARDEN CULTURE. In its native habitat, rhodohypoxis grows in organically rich soil that is moist in summer and dry in winter; the atmosphere is often cool and fog-bathed. In the garden, an ideal location is a sunny rock garden with nonalkaline, well-drained soil, where winter moisture can be kept to a minimum. In early spring, plant roots 1 inch deep and 3 to 5 inches apart. Give enough water to moisten the soil thoroughly; then, when foliage emerges, start watering regularly, keeping the soil moist (but not soggy) throughout the bloom period and until foliage yellows in fall. From that point, withhold water until new leaves emerge the following spring. Divide crowded plantings in early spring, just as growth begins.

CONTAINER CULTURE. Follow directions "B" (subgroup 2) on page 207. Move containers to a cool, dry location when foliage dies down in fall and keep them there until new growth emerges in early spring. Divide and repot when containers become crowded and performance declines.

SCADOXUS multiflorus katharinae
(Haemanthus katharinae)

BLOOD LILY

Amaryllidaceae

TRUE BULB

- ▲ 1 TO 2 FEET
- ◑ LIGHT SHADE
- ◖ NEEDS SUMMER MOISTURE
- ✂ ZONES 21–27

Scadoxus multiflorus katharinae

The red stains on its large white bulbs gave this South African native its common name. In late spring or summer, ball-shaped clusters (to 9 inches across) of narrow-petaled, salmon-colored blossoms are borne atop thick flower stems; myriad threadlike, bright red stamens protrude from each bloom, giving the clusters the look of spherical bottlebrushes. Glossy, bright green, wavy-edged leaves are 12 to 15 inches long, up to 6 inches wide.

USES. Good-looking foliage and splashy flowers make this a prime accent plant for patio, terrace, or deck.

GARDEN CULTURE. In frost-free regions, you can plant blood lily in the ground—but even in such favored climates, it is usually grown in containers. To give the appearance of permanent plantings, just sink containers to their rims in soil.

Bulbs planted directly in the ground prefer a lightly shaded spot with well-drained soil enriched with organic matter. Plant in late winter or early spring, setting bulbs about 2 feet apart and keeping tips even with the soil surface. Water sparingly until leaves appear (this will occur in about 8 weeks); then water regularly throughout growth and bloom. Put out bait for slugs and snails. Leave clumps undisturbed indefinitely.

CONTAINER CULTURE. For each bulb, select a container large enough to leave 2 inches between all sides of the bulb and the container edges; use a soil mix recommended in directions "B" on page 207. Place planted containers in a fairly warm spot (no cooler than 55°F/13°C at night, around 70°F/21°C during the day) receiving plenty of bright light but no direct sun. Follow the watering regimen described above and apply a liquid fertilizer monthly.

After bloom is finished, stop fertilizing and gradually cut back on water; by midautumn, plants should not be receiving any water at all. Store the potted bulbs over winter in a dry, cool spot (50° to 55°F/10° to 13°C). Near the end of winter (or in early spring), tip plants out of containers and scrape some of the old soil mix off the root ball. Then repot in the same containers, filling in around bulbs with fresh mix. Switch to larger pots only after several years, when bulbs fill containers almost completely.

Like gladiolus, this South African denizen has upright, swordlike leaves and a spike of closely set flowers—but the starlike, bright-colored, 2-inch blossoms recall those of another relative, watsonia. As the common name indicates, the basic species has crimson blooms, but specialists sell a number of named color variants, including white 'Alba', watermelon red 'Oregon Sunset', and several in pink shades: 'Mrs. Hegarty', 'Sunrise', and 'Viscountess Byng'. The plants are a standout in midautumn, a time of year when few other flowers put on a major display.

USES. Clumps of crimson flag are attractive vertical accents.

GARDEN CULTURE. In its native habitat, crimson flag grows in highly organic soil that is moist but well aerated. Plant in spring; dig generous amounts of peat moss and other organic matter into the planting area, then set rhizomes ½ to 1 inch deep and 1 foot apart. Water generously from planting time until the flowering period ends; then water sparingly until growth resumes the following spring. If clumps become crowded, dig in early spring, separate so that each division has at least five shoots, and replant.

CONTAINER CULTURE. Follow directions "B" (subgroup 2) on page 207. In climates where winter lows dip below 10°F/−12°C, bring pots of dormant bulbs indoors. Follow the watering regimen described above; apply a liquid fertilizer monthly.

Gardeners in cold-winter climates know squill as one of the harbingers of spring: some of the early-blooming types come into flower along with winter aconite (*Eranthis hyemalis*) and snowdrop (*Galanthus*). The first four species described below are native to colder regions of Europe and Asia; Peruvian scilla, despite its common name, is native to the milder Mediterranean region. All squills have bell-shaped or starlike flowers, borne on leafless stems that rise from clumps of strap-shaped leaves.

Among the earliest to flower is 8-inch-tall *S. bifolia*; as the botanical name implies, each bulb usually produces just two leaves. The starlike blossoms, carried three to eight to each flowering stem, are suspended by short, threadlike stalks. A vivid, almost turquoise blue is the most common color, but you may also find forms with flowers in white, violet blue, or light pink.

Siberian squill, *S. siberica*, has several blossoms shaped like flaring bells hanging from each 3- to 6-inch stem. The typical flower color is an intense medium blue, but selected varieties bloom in white, lilac pink, and light to dark shades of violet blue, often with darker stripes. 'Spring Beauty' has brilliant violet blue blooms that are larger than those of the species.

The 6-inch-tall stems of *S. mischtschenkoana* (formerly *S. tubergeniana*) bear nodding clusters of three or four starlike blossoms in pale blue with darker blue stripes.

Unlike the previous species, *S. litardieri* (formerly *S. pratensis*) does not bloom until mid- to late spring, when it sends up 6- to 8-inch stems with dense spikes of small, bell-shaped, bright violet blossoms; there may be up to 15 blooms in each spike.

Listing continues >

SCHIZOSTYLIS coccinea
CRIMSON FLAG, KAFFIR LILY
Iridaceae
RHIZOME

- ▲ 1½ TO 2 FEET
- ☼ ◑ FULL SUN OR LIGHT SHADE
- ◗ NEEDS SUMMER MOISTURE
- ✄ ZONES 5–9, 14–24, 26–29, 31

Schizostylis coccinea 'Oregon Sunset'

SCILLA
SQUILL, BLUEBELL
Liliaceae
TRUE BULB

- ▲ 3 TO 12 INCHES
- ☼ ◑ FULL SUN DURING BLOOM, PART SHADE DURING REST OF YEAR
- ◗ NEEDS SOME SUMMER MOISTURE, EXCEPT AS NOTED
- ✄ ZONES VARY BY SPECIES (SEE "GARDEN CULTURE"); NEEDS SUBFREEZING WINTER TEMPERATURES, EXCEPT AS NOTED
- ◆ ALL PARTS ARE POISONOUS IF INGESTED

TOP: *Scilla bifolia*
BOTTOM: *Scilla peruviana*

SINNINGIA speciosa
GLOXINIA
Gesneriaceae
TUBER

▲ 1 FOOT
☼ BRIGHT INDIRECT LIGHT
💧 NEEDS SUMMER MOISTURE

Sinningia speciosa

Peruvian scilla, *S. peruviana,* differs from the above four species both in its appearance and its ability to thrive with little or no winter chill. Its large bulbs produce numerous rather floppy leaves; 10- to 12-inch stems rise from the foliage clumps, each topped with a dome-shaped cluster of 50 or more starlike flowers in late spring. Most forms have bluish purple blooms, but a white-flowered variety is sometimes available.

USES. Naturalizing is the best use for the four cold-hardy species; try them in small patches or larger drifts. Peruvian scilla may also be naturalized, but it's a bit coarse textured for wildflower-style plantings. Try it in clumps along pathways, at edges of mixed plantings, or in containers.

GARDEN CULTURE. Grow *S. siberica* in Zones 1–7, 10, 33–45; *S. mischtschenkoana* in Zones 1–11, 14–21, 29–43; *S. bifolia* and *S. litardieri* in Zones 2–11, 14–21, 30–41; and *S. peruviana* in Zones 14–17, 19–24, 26–29.

In fall, plant all types in well-drained soil enriched with organic matter. Set bulbs of the four cold-hardy species 2 to 3 inches deep, about 4 inches apart; plant Peruvian scilla bulbs 3 to 4 inches deep, about 6 inches apart. Water all types regularly during their growth and bloom periods; decrease water when foliage yellows. The hardy species will tolerate less moisture during their summer dormancy, though soil should not dry out completely. Peruvian scilla will accept summer moisture, but it doesn't need any.

Divide plantings only when decreased vigor and poorer blossom quality indicate that clumps are overcrowded. Peruvian scilla enters a brief dormant period after its leaves wither in late spring or early summer; if needed, dig and replant soon after foliage has died back completely. Other species may be divided in late summer or early fall.

CONTAINER CULTURE. Peruvian scilla is the best container candidate. See directions "C" on page 207.

B old-looking plants with velvety leaves and flowers, these Brazilian natives are long-time favorite pot plants. Squat and full foliaged, they have broad, oval leaves with the look of quilted green velvet, each growing to 6 inches or longer. In summer, showy blossoms cluster near the top of the plant—velvety-sheened, ruffled bells to 4 inches across. Available colors include white, red, pink, blue, and light to dark shades of purple. Many types show combinations of several hues: you'll see blooms in solid colors with light or white edges, and dots or blotches of darker color on a lighter background.

USES. Because they need 24-hour warmth, gloxinias are usually grown in greenhouses or as house plants. They can be taken outdoors during warm weather.

CONTAINER CULTURE. Tubers are available for planting in winter and spring. For each tuber, choose a container large enough to leave 2 inches between all sides of the tuber and the container edges. Fill with a soil mix of equal parts peat moss, perlite, and leaf mold or compost; then set in tubers ½ inch deep.

Place containers in a warm location (about 72°F/22°C during the day, no cooler than 65°F/18°C at night) where they will receive plenty of bright light but no direct sun. Water sparingly until the first leaves appear, then increase watering as roots and leaves grow. Apply water to the soil only, or pour it into containers' drip saucers to be absorbed through the bottom of the pot; be sure to pour off any water left unabsorbed after an hour. From the time leaves emerge until flowers fade, apply a liquid fertilizer diluted to half strength every 2 weeks.

After flowering ceases, gradually withhold water and let foliage wither. When leaves have died down entirely, plants are completely dormant; at this point, move containers to a dark place where temperatures will remain around 60°F/16°C. Mist soil just often enough to keep tubers from shriveling.

When tubers show signs of resuming growth in midwinter, repot in fresh soil mix. If you see that roots have filled a container, move the tuber to a container that's 1 to 2 inches wider; leaf and flower size decrease when plants become potbound.

O ne look at its bright late-spring blossoms explains why this South African is commonly called "harlequin flower." Each bloom has a patchwork arrangement of colors: yellow in the chalicelike center, a dark shade surrounding this, and still another color—red, pink, orange, or purple—on the rest of the spreading petals. Flowers are up to 2 inches across, borne in loose spikes on slender stems that rise from fans of swordlike leaves.

USES. The effect is best when plants are grouped as accents in borders or along pathways. For a brilliant tapestrylike effect, naturalize corms in a sunny garden spot.

GARDEN CULTURE. Well-drained soil in a sunny location suits harlequin flower. Plant corms 2 inches deep, 3 to 4 inches apart—in fall where corms are hardy in the ground, in early spring in colder regions. Water regularly during active growth. Withhold water when leaves yellow; keep soil dry during summer.

In the zones noted at right, you can leave plantings undisturbed for a number of years. In other zones, dig corms in summer after foliage dies down and store as for gladiolus (page 248).

CONTAINER CULTURE. Follow directions "B" (subgroup 2) on page 207.

SPARAXIS tricolor
HARLEQUIN FLOWER
Iridaceae
CORM

▲ 12 TO 15 INCHES
☼ FULL SUN
◯ WITHHOLD SUMMER MOISTURE
▨ ZONES 9, 12–24

Sparaxis tricolor

Sprekelia formosissima

T he linear foliage of this Mexican native is reminiscent of daffodil leaves—but wait until you see the flowers! The irregularly shaped dark red blossoms have understandably been likened to orchids. Each stem bears one 6-inch flower; the display increases if plants are left undisturbed for several years and allowed to form large clumps. Bloom comes primarily in early summer. The foliage may be evergreen in mild climates.

USES. Aztec lily is a striking accent in the summer garden. Plant it in clumps at the foreground of mixed annual and perennial beds, or grow it in containers.

GARDEN CULTURE. Plant bulbs 3 to 4 inches deep and about 8 inches apart in good, well-drained soil—in fall where bulbs are hardy in the ground, in spring in colder regions. Water regularly from the time growth begins until bloom finishes. In climates with little or no frost, plants may bloom several times a year if you can give them a dry period after blossoming, then resume regular watering to trigger a new growth cycle.

Where bulbs can overwinter in the ground, you can leave them undisturbed for many years. When vigor and bloom quality decline, dig, separate, and replant in fall. In colder regions, dig bulbs in fall before the first frost; dry them with foliage attached, then give covered storage (see page 205) until planting time.

CONTAINER CULTURE. Follow the directions outlined for amaryllis *(Hippeastrum)*, but keep temperatures about five degrees lower during growth and bloom.

SPREKELIA formosissima
AZTEC LILY, JACOBEAN LILY, ST. JAMES LILY
Amaryllidaceae
TRUE BULB

▲ 1 TO 1½ FEET
☼ FULL SUN
● NEEDS SUMMER MOISTURE
▨ ZONES 9, 12–24, 26–30

STERNBERGIA lutea

Amaryllidaceae

TRUE BULB

- ▲ 4 TO 9 INCHES
- ☼ FULL SUN
- ◌ WITHHOLD SUMMER MOISTURE
- ⚲ ZONES 3, 7–10, 14–24, 26–33

An ideal choice for the impatient gardener, this plant from the western Mediterranean to central Asia offers almost instant gratification: bulbs planted in mid- to late summer burst into bloom in early fall. Each bulb produces a single flower about 1½ inches long that looks something like a bright yellow crocus—chalice shaped at first, then opening out to a wide star. Narrow, linear leaves appear at the same time as or just after the blossoms, eventually reaching about 1 foot long; they persist through winter, then die back in spring.

USES. Locate in rock gardens or pockets in paved patios, alongside pathways, or in containers.

Sternbergia lutea

GARDEN CULTURE. Plant bulbs as soon as they are available. Choose a sunny spot with well-drained soil, preferably in an area that receives little or no watering during summer. Plant bulbs 6 inches apart and 4 inches deep. To establish newly planted bulbs, water from planting time until the bloom period ends; then let winter and spring rain or snow carry plants through to the next dormant time. Once plants are established, water regularly during growth and bloom; withhold summer water.

Where winter temperatures drop to 20°F/−7°C or lower, give plantings winter protection as described on page 205. Clumps increase in beauty as bulbs multiply, so dig and separate (in August) only when vigor and flower quality decline.

CONTAINER CULTURE. Follow directions "B" (subgroup 2) on page 207.

TIGRIDIA pavonia

TIGER FLOWER, MEXICAN SHELL FLOWER

Iridaceae

TRUE BULB

- ▲ 1½ TO 2½ FEET
- ☼ ◑ FULL SUN; PART SHADE WHERE SUMMERS ARE HOT
- ◖ NEEDS SUMMER MOISTURE
- ⚲ ZONES 4–31

This Mexican native bears flashy summertime blooms to 6 inches across. The three large outer segments of each triangular flower are red, orange, pink, yellow, or white; the cuplike center and three small inner segments are usually boldly blotched with a contrasting hue. The Immaculata strain is unspotted.

An individual flower lasts just one day, but since each stem carries a number of buds, the blooming period lasts for several weeks. Upright, branching flower stems to 2½ feet tall rise from fans of narrow, swordlike, ribbed leaves that may reach 1½ feet long.

USES. Tiger flower adds a dominant splash of color wherever you use it: in clumps, in summer flower borders, or in containers.

GARDEN CULTURE. Plant bulbs in spring after weather warms up (night temperatures should not fall below 60°F/16°C). If summer heat is not intense, choose a spot in full sun; in hot-summer regions, plants appreciate afternoon shade. Set bulbs 2 to 4 inches deep, 4 to 8 inches apart, in well-drained soil. Water regularly throughout growth and bloom, but stop watering after bloom finishes and leaves turn yellow.

Tigridia pavonia

Where bulbs are hardy in the ground, you can leave plantings undisturbed for 3 or 4 years before dividing. Then dig bulbs after foliage dies back in fall and store over winter as for gladiolus (page 248); wait until spring planting time to separate bulbs.

Spider mites (detectable by the yellowish or whitish streaks they leave on foliage) are the principal pest. Begin applying controls (see page 203) when leaves are several inches high. Gophers are another pest; they're fond of the bulbs. See "Foiling the Spoilers" (page 198) for controls.

CONTAINER CULTURE. Follow directions "B" (subgroup 2) on page 207.

F ans of swordlike leaves and branched spikes of bright, broad, funnel-shaped flowers mark this South African as a close relative of ixia, montbretia *(Crocosmia)*, freesia, and harlequin flower *(Sparaxis)*. Tritonia starts growth in early spring and blooms in late spring; after bloom, the foliage turns yellow and dies down until the next year's growth cycle begins.

The most commonly sold species is *T. crocata*, often called "flame freesia." It bears broad-petaled, reddish orange blooms to 2 inches across, arranged alternately on either side of branching spikes to 1½ feet high. *T. c. miniata* has bright red flowers, while 'Princess Beatrix' is a stunning deep orange. Occasionally, you'll find other named varieties in white, yellow, and shades of pink.

T. hyalina, the other commonly sold species, grows to about 1 foot tall; its bright orange flowers have narrower petals than those of *T. crocata*, with a transparent area near the base of each petal.

USES. Grow in clumps or drifts, as a colorful accent in the foreground of plantings that require little watering during summer.

GARDEN CULTURE. Like its close relatives, tritonia needs well-drained soil in a sunny location, regular watering during growth and bloom, and fairly dry conditions after foliage starts to yellow. Set corms 2 to 3 inches deep and 3 inches apart; plant in fall where winter temperatures remain above 20°F/−7°C, but wait until spring in colder climates. Where corms are hardy and can be protected from summer moisture, they can stay in the ground until a decline in vigor lets you know that plantings are overcrowded; at that point, dig (during the dormant period) and divide. Elsewhere, dig and store as for gladiolus (page 248) after plants die down; or grow in pots.

CONTAINER CULTURE. Follow directions "B" (subgroup 2) on page 207.

TRITELEIA. See BRODIAEA

TRITONIA
Iridaceae
CORM

▲ 1 TO 1½ FEET
☼ FULL SUN
◊ WITHHOLD SUMMER MOISTURE
✉ ZONES 9, 13–24, 26, 28, 29

Tritonia crocata 'Isabella'

TULBAGHIA
Amaryllidaceae
RHIZOME

▲ 1 TO 2 FEET
☼ FULL SUN
◆ NEEDS SUMMER MOISTURE
✉ ZONES 13–24, 26–28

O ne general description covers both available species (both are native to South Africa): dense clumps of straight, narrow evergreen leaves send up slim, 1- to 2-foot stems topped by clusters of small, trumpet-shaped, pinkish lavender flowers.

T. violacea has very narrow blue-green leaves and bears 8 to 20 blossoms per cluster; bloom is heaviest in spring and summer. The common name is "society garlic," and for good reason: both the leaves and the flower stems give off an oniony or garlicky odor when bruised or crushed (you can even use the leaves in cooking). Several named varieties are available. 'Silver Lace'

Tulbaghia violacea

has white-margined leaves; 'Tricolor', another white-edged type, has foliage tinted pink in early spring; leaves of 'Variegata' have a broad white stripe down the center.

The leaves of *T. fragrans* are gray green and, at 1 inch wide, broader than those of *T. violacea*. Its lightly fragrant flowers, carried in clusters of 20 to 30, bloom in winter or early spring.

USES. Grow plants in the foreground of borders; they're also attractive in containers.

GARDEN CULTURE. Plants will grow in light or heavy soil, though they do best in well-drained soil liberally amended with organic matter before planting. Plant at any time of year, from containers or divisions, in a sunny spot; give regular watering for best performance. Divide clumps whenever you want to increase plantings or when foliage and flower quality decline. (Where summers are hot, early spring and early fall are the best times to divide.)

CONTAINER CULTURE. Follow directions "C" on page 207. Where winter temperatures fall below 20°F/−7°C, move potted plants indoors at the first signs of frost; overwinter in a sunny window in a cool room (maximum temperature of 60°F/16°C).

TULIPA
TULIP
Liliaceae
TRUE BULB

- ▲ 3 INCHES TO OVER 3 FEET
- ☀ ◐ FULL SUN OR LIGHT SHADE
- ◗ ACCEPTS SUMMER MOISTURE BUT DOESN'T NEED ANY
- ✎ 1–24, 28–45; BEST AND MOST PERMANENT IN AREAS WITH SUB-FREEZING WINTER TEMPERATURES

Fringed tulip 'Blue Heron'

To many people—especially those in cold-winter regions—tulips and daffodils signify spring. But while daffodils may be strewn about with naturalistic abandon, tulips are generally thought of as orderly flowers: neatly planted in garden beds, in serried ranks of even height. In fact, many types of tulips are rather rigidly formal, but as a group, these plants vary considerably in height, form, color, and general character. Some are quite unusual (the "broken" kinds and parrot varieties); some of the short types and many of the species look like wildflowers; and the double-flowered sorts resemble peonies.

Most of the tulips in modern gardens fit into the classifications established jointly by the Royal Dutch Bulb Growers and the Royal Horticultural Society of England. These groupings are based primarily on appearance rather than on strict botanical relationship: all the varieties in each division have the same general flower shape and height range.

Tulipa hybrids

LARGE HYBRID TULIPS

The following 17 divisions encompass the familiar garden hybrid types, listed in approximate order of bloom.

SINGLE EARLY TULIPS. Tulips in this class have large red, yellow, or white single flowers on 10- to 16-inch stems. Though they are favorites for growing or forcing indoors in pots, they can also be grown outside, where they bloom from March to mid-April (depending on climate and variety). They are not adapted to mild-winter climates.

DOUBLE EARLY TULIPS. Peonylike double flowers, often measuring 4 inches across, grow on 6- to 12-inch stems. Double Early tulips have the same color range as Single Early types and are often forced for early bloom in containers. They're also effective massed in borders for spring bloom outside.

MENDEL TULIPS. Derived from Darwin tulips, Mendel tulips bear blossoms of red, pink, orange, yellow, or white on stems up to 20 inches tall. They bloom later than Single Early and Double Early tulips, but earlier than the Darwins.

TRIUMPH TULIPS. Crosses between Single Early, Darwin, and Cottage types produced the midseason Triumph class: earlier blooming than the Darwins, with heavier, shorter stems (usually not over 20 inches tall). Red, white, yellow, and bicolored varieties are available.

DARWIN HYBRIDS. Huge, shining, brilliant flowers show the influence of the *T. fosteriana* parent (see page 286), while fairly tall stems (to 2 feet) recall the Darwin parent. Colors include red and orange; bloom time comes in midseason, after the early-blooming *T. fosteriana* but before the Darwins come into flower.

DARWIN TULIPS. These popular midseason tulips are graceful, stately plants with large oval or egg-shaped blooms carried on straight stems to 3 feet tall. Blossoms are square at the base, but flower segments are typically rounded at the tips. There's a remarkably extensive range of clear, beautiful colors: white, yellow, orange, pink, red, mauve, lilac, purple, and maroon.

LILY-FLOWERED TULIPS. Formerly included in the Cottage division, these late midseason tulips have graceful, lilylike blooms with recurved, pointed segments. Flowers are longer and narrower than those of the Darwins; colors include white and shades of yellow, pink, and red. Flower stems reach 20 to 26 inches high.

FRINGED TULIPS. Variations from Single Early, Double Early, and Darwin tulips, these are late midseason bloomers with flowering stems 16 to 24 inches high. Edges of flower segments are finely fringed.

BREEDER TULIPS. These carry large oval or globular flowers on stems to 40 inches tall late in the season. Colors are quite unusual, with orange, bronze, and purple predominating.

COTTAGE TULIPS. Late-blooming descendants of varieties found in old gardens in Great Britain, Belgium, and France, the Cottage tulips are slightly shorter than the Darwins; flowers are oval or egg shaped, often with pointed segments. Colors include red, purple, yellow, pink, orange, and white.

REMBRANDT TULIPS. These late bloomers originally were exclusively "broken" Darwin tulips, so called because the background flower color is "broken"—streaked or variegated throughout—with different colors. Today, however, the division has been expanded to include the following two (Bizarre and Bybloems) as well.

BIZARRE TULIPS. "Broken" Breeder or Cottage tulips constitute this late-blooming class. Flowers have a yellow background striped or marked with bronze, brown, maroon, or purple.

BYBLOEMS (BIJBLOEMENS). Like the Bizarre division, these late bloomers are "broken" Breeder or Cottage tulips, but they have a white background with lilac, rose, or purple markings.

PARROT TULIPS. This class of late tulips includes sports (mutations) of solid-colored varieties of regular form. Their large, long, deeply fringed and ruffled blooms atop 16- to 20-inch stems are striped, feathered, and flamed in various colors. Parrot tulips once had weak, floppy stems, but modern types are stouter and stand up well.

DOUBLE LATE TULIPS. As the name implies, this class of tulips—often referred to as "peony-flowered"—has double blossoms late in the season. The

Fringed tulip hybrid

Lily-flowered tulip hybrids

extremely large, heavy flowers on 14- to 20-inch stems come in orange, rose, yellow, and white.

VIRIDIFLORA TULIPS. Late blossoms are edged in green or colored in blends of green with other hues—white, yellow, rose, red, or buff. Stems grow 10 to 20 inches tall.

MULTIFLOWERED TULIPS. Members of this class bear three to six flowers on each stem late in the season; most selections grow 1½ to 2 feet tall. Colors include white, yellow, pink, and red.

For decades, nurseries have sold tulips based on the divisions just described. Recently, these 17 divisions have been reorganized and simplified, as presented below. More and more catalogs and nurseries will be offering bulbs in these groupings:

SINGLE EARLY AND DOUBLE EARLY TULIPS. The earliest-blooming, large-flowered types.

MIDSEASON TULIPS. Blooming after the early classes, this group includes Mendel, Triumph, and Darwin Hybrid tulips.

SINGLE LATE OR MAY-FLOWERING TULIPS. This group now includes the Darwin, Breeder, and Cottage classes.

DOUBLE LATE, LILY-FLOWERED, AND NOVELTY TULIPS. In this class are the Double Late and Lily-flowered tulips, as well as the novelty groups: Rembrandts (including Bizarre tulips and Bybloems) and Fringed, Parrot, Viridiflora, and Multiflowered tulips.

SPECIES AND SPECIES HYBRID TULIPS

In addition to the divisions just described, there are classes covering species and species hybrids. Three of these include varieties and hybrids of *T. kaufmanniana*, *T. fosteriana*, and *T. greigii*—all good plants for mild-winter areas.

KAUFMANNIANA TULIPS. A very early bloomer known by the common name "waterlily tulip," *T. kaufmanniana* features 3-inch, creamy yellow flowers (marked red on the petal backs) with dark yellow centers; the blossoms open flat in the sunshine. Stems reach 6 to 8 inches high. Hybrids encompass a variety of colors, usually with flower centers in a contrasting color; many have mottled leaves like the Greigii tulips.

FOSTERIANA TULIPS. The early-flowering *T. fosteriana* has the largest flowers—to 8 inches across—of any tulip, whether species or hybrid. These great red blossoms appear atop 8- to 20-inch stems. Hybrids include varieties with flowers of red, orange, yellow, pink, and white.

GREIGII TULIPS. Leaves heavily spotted and streaked with brown are one feature of midseason-flowering *T. greigii*. Short stems (to about 10 inches) bear 6-inch scarlet flowers. Hybrids offer flowers in white, pink, orange, and red; many feature several colors combined in a single blossom.

Tulipa linifolia

Tulipa fosteriana hybrids

SMALLER SPECIES TULIPS. These are sold chiefly by bulb specialists. They have a simpler, more wildflowerlike charm than their large hybrid relatives; most are native to Central Asia. Several species will persist from year to year in mild-winter regions.

Tulipa batalinii
'Yellow Jewel'

T. acuminata. This late-flowering species has 1½-foot stems bearing red and yellow flowers with long, twisted, spidery segments.

T. batalinii. Soft yellow flowers bloom on 6- to 10-inch stems in midseason. Leaves are linear.

T. clusiana, the lady or candy tulip, is a graceful plant with 9-inch stems bearing slender, medium-size midseason flowers colored rosy red on the outside, creamy white on the inside. It's a good permanent tulip for areas with little winter chill. *T. c. chrysantha* also blooms in midseason, its 6-inch-tall stems bearing blooms that are star shaped when open. Outside flower segments are pure rose carmine, turning to buff at the base; inside segments are pure butter yellow.

T. eichleri. A striking, sculptured-looking early tulip. The shining scarlet flowers have jet black centers outlined with yellow. Stems reach about 1 foot tall.

T. linifolia. A midseason bloomer, this species has 6-inch stems bearing bold scarlet flowers with black bases and yellow centers. It makes a striking companion for *T. batalinii,* which blooms at the same time.

T. praestans. Pure orange-scarlet midseason flowers, often two to four to each 10- to 12-inch stem, contrast beautifully with pale green leaves edged in dark red.

T. sylvestris. This late-flowering species is a good choice for warmer-winter zones. Its yellow, 2-inch flowers sometimes come two to each 1-foot stem.

T. tarda (T. dasystemon). An appealing little early tulip with clusters of as many as four flowers on each 3- to 5-inch stem. The star-shaped white blossoms are prominently marked with yellow in the center.

T. turkestanica. Very early in the season, each 1-foot stem offers as many as eight flowers. Slender buds open to star-shaped blooms that are gray green on the outside, off-white with yellow petal bases inside.

USES. Rows of tulips look stiff and artificial, as though plants and flowers were made of plastic. Large hybrid types really shine when planted in masses or drifts; they also make bright clumps among other spring-flowering plants, especially lower-growing annuals and perennials.

The small species tulips are good choices for rock gardens and mixed plantings, and also naturalize easily where climate permits.

GARDEN CULTURE. In their native lands, tulips are accustomed to cold winters (often long and severe), short springs, and hot summers. Except for certain species, most are short-lived in mild-winter regions, even if summers are hot: winter chill is critical for permanence. But even in cold-winter regions, there's no guarantee of a good performance after the first year. Tulip bulbs form offsets that need several years to reach blooming size, but as the offsets mature, they draw energy from the mother bulb. The result is a decline in flowering. For this reason, most tulips are best treated as short-lived perennials (some species and species hybrids excepted).

You can encourage repeat flowering by fertilizing with nitrogen before bloom and by allowing foliage to yellow and wither before removing it after bloom. In mild-winter areas, tulip bulbs should be prechilled in the refrigerator and the plants treated as annuals (in Zones 25–27, however, even prechilled bulbs usually fail to perform well).

Listing continues >

TOP: *Tulipa tarda*
BOTTOM: *Tulipa turkestanica*

Tulipa 'William and Mary' in container

In areas with warm, wet summer soil, bulbs are prone to rot and shouldn't be expected to bloom for more than a year or two.

Tulips need sunshine at least while they are in bloom; stems will lean toward the source of light if the planting area is partly shaded. It's fine to plant bulbs under deciduous trees if the trees won't leaf out until after the blooming season ends. Well-drained soil is another requirement, though the particular type is not important—both light and heavy soils are satisfactory. Be sure, though, to add plenty of organic matter prior to planting. Tulips do poorly if planted in soil where other tulips have been growing recently. Set out bulbs in new locations, or replace the existing soil with new soil to the proper planting depth.

Set bulbs three times as deep as they are wide (a little shallower in heavy soils); space them 4 to 8 inches apart, depending on the eventual size of the plant. Tulips need plenty of moisture during growth and bloom, but they can get by with less after foliage dies back. In regions where temperatures regularly dip below 32°F/0°C, plant bulbs in October or November, after soil has cooled from the heat of summer. In warmer regions, plant in December or January.

To protect tulip bulbs from gophers and other burrowing animals, plant in wire baskets; thwart pests that like to dig up bulbs by securing chicken wire over new plantings. See "Foiling the Spoilers" on page 198 and "Rodents" on page 203.

If tulips do persist in vigor from year to year, they will eventually need separating. Dig and divide clumps in late summer; replant at the best time for your area.

Species tulips, unlike most of the larger hybrid types, may be left undisturbed for many years. Dig and separate them (in late summer) whenever they become crowded, or when you need bulbs for planting elsewhere. Replant at the best time for your climate.

CONTAINER CULTURE. Follow directions "B" (subgroup 1) on page 207 for basic container culture. To force tulips for earlier bloom, see pages 210–211.

VALLOTA SPECIOSA.
See CYRTANTHUS ELATUS

VELTHEIMIA bracteata
Liliaceae
TRUE BULB

- ▲ 12 TO 15 INCHES
- ☼ FILTERED SUN, PART SHADE, OR LIGHT SHADE
- ◊ WITHHOLD SUMMER MOISTURE
- ✍ ZONES 13, 16–25, 26 (WARMER PARTS), 27

Handsome foliage is reason enough to grow this South African native. Each bulb puts out a fountainlike rosette of wavy-edged foliage—glossy green leaves to 1 foot long and 3 inches wide in the most common (and perhaps only available) species, *V. bracteata* (formerly *V. viridiflora*). In winter or early spring, brown-mottled flower stems rise to about 1 foot, each topped by an elongated cluster of pendent, tubular flowers of pinkish purple tipped in green. At some point toward late spring, leaves yellow and die back for the summer; new growth resumes in autumn.

Veltheimia bracteata

Most plants sold as *V. capensis* are actually *V. bracteata;* the true *V. capensis* is easily distinguished by its nonglossy blue-green leaves and green-tipped pale pink blossoms.

USES. Even in the mildest climates, most gardeners prefer to treat this as a container plant for house, greenhouse, deck, or patio.

GARDEN CULTURE. In virtually frost-free regions, you can grow the large bulbs in the ground. Plant them in autumn, in organically enriched, well-drained soil; set tops of bulb necks just above the soil surface. Water regularly during growth and bloom. When foliage begins to die down in mid- to late spring, reduce watering; keep soil dry during the leafless summer dormant period. Resume regular watering when new growth appears in fall. Dig and divide (in late summer) only when growth becomes crowded. Plants can remain outdoors over the winter only where temperatures remain above 25°F/−4°C; where light frosts are possible, give them overhead protection.

CONTAINER CULTURE. Plant in August or September. For each bulb, use a container large enough to allow about 3 inches between all sides of the bulb and the container edges. Plant in soil mix described in directions "A" on page 207. Place containers in a cool location and keep the soil just barely moist until growth begins. Then provide more light and higher temperatures (around 60°F/16°C); follow the watering regimen described above and apply a liquid fertilizer every 2 weeks during the growing season. Divide bulbs when containers become crowded.

This elegant South African combines stateliness and delicacy. The fans of swordlike foliage and upright spikes of double-ranked blossoms reveal a close relationship to gladiolus, but there are clear differences as well. Watsonia's leaves are less rigid; its flower spikes are taller and slimmer, and the fragrant blossoms are smaller and more trumpetlike. Two species (and their hybrids) are commonly available. Botanists have recently changed these plants' names, but the old names persist in the nursery trade and in literature. In the descriptions below, the new names are given in parentheses.

Evergreen *W. beatricis* (*W. pillansii*) blooms in midsummer, sending up slightly branched, 3½-foot flower spikes from fans of 2½-foot leaves. The 3-inch-long blossoms are bright reddish apricot; you'll also find hybrids in colors ranging from peach to nearly red.

The late spring flowers of *W. pyramidata* (*W. borbonica*) are borne on 4- to 6-foot spikes that rise above 2½-foot-long leaves; flower color is cool pink, rosy red, or white. Hybrid forms have pink, red, or lavender blooms. Foliage dies back after flowering, then reappears with the onset of cooler weather in late summer to early autumn.

USES. These plants make handsome accent clumps in the background of mixed annual and perennial plantings, and even among shrubbery.

GARDEN CULTURE. Grow *W. beatricis* in Zones 4–9, 12–24, 26, 28–31, warmer parts of 32; grow *W. pyramidata* in Zones 4–9, 12–24, 26, 28–30.
Choose a sunny location—preferably with well-drained soil, though watsonia will perform in a great range of soils, from sandy to clay. Plant in early fall, setting corms 4 inches deep and 6 inches apart. Both species need regular water during their growth and bloom periods. Evergreen *W. beatricis* can take less moisture in summer after its flowers are finished. Deciduous *W. pyramidata* is dormant in summer; it accepts (but does not need) regular moisture at that time if the soil is well drained.
Where corms are hardy in the ground, you can leave them undisturbed for a number of years. Dig and divide only when plant and flower quality decline. In zones beyond its hardiness limits, you can grow *W. pyramidata* as you would gladiolus: plant corms in spring for late spring and early summer bloom, then dig after foliage dies down and store until planting time the following spring. Because *W. beatricis* is evergreen, it cannot be dug and stored; it grows only within its hardiness zones.

WATSONIA
Iridaceae
CORM

- ▲ 3½ TO 6 FEET
- ☼ FULL SUN
- ◐◑ SUMMER MOISTURE NEEDS VARY BY SPECIES (SEE "GARDEN CULTURE")
- ✎ ZONES VARY BY SPECIES (SEE "GARDEN CULTURE")

Watsonia beatricis

ZANTEDESCHIA

CALLA, CALLA LILY

Araceae

RHIZOME

- ▲ 1 TO 4 FEET
- ☼ ◐ EXPOSURE NEEDS VARY BY SPECIES (SEE "GARDEN CULTURE")
- ◐ SUMMER MOISTURE NEEDS VARY BY SPECIES (SEE "GARDEN CULTURE")
- ⟋ ZONES 5, 6, 8, 9, 12–29

The simple, streamlined beauty of the white calla lily is familiar to many from formal bouquets. Admirers of Art Nouveau are also well acquainted with these blooms, since they were a popular motif in metal and glass pieces. The calla's "flower" is really a cornucopia-shaped bract (the spathe) surrounding a central yellow spike (the spadix); the tiny true flowers cluster around the base of the spadix. All species have glossy, arrow-shaped leaves on erect stalks, but foliage color varies—the common calla's leaves are solid green, but other species often have variegated or spotted foliage.

The largest, most familiar species is *Z. aethiopica,* the common calla. Foliage clumps reach 2 to 4 feet, with individual leaves to 10 inches wide, 1½ feet long. Beginning in spring (and sometimes continuing into summer), 8-inch spathes of pure or creamy white appear on stems just slightly taller than the foliage. 'Hercules' is larger than the species, with broad, recurving spathes that open nearly flat. 'Green Goddess', also a larger plant, has partially green spathes. Smaller varieties include 'Childsiana' (to just 1 foot) and 'Minor' (to 1½ feet, with 4-inch spathes).

Zantedeschia aethiopica

Summer-blooming *Z. elliottiana,* the golden calla, reaches 2 feet tall; its white-spotted bright green leaves reach 10 inches long and 6 inches wide. The 6-inch spathes are greenish yellow when they open, then change to a bright, rich golden yellow.

Z. albomaculata, the spotted calla, is about the same size as *Z. elliottiana* and has similar but slightly larger foliage. The spathes differ, though—they're creamy yellow or white, with a red-purple blotch at the base. The blooming season extends from spring into summer. A similar species, summer-blooming *Z. pentlandii,* features purple-throated deep yellow spathes rising above unspotted green leaves.

Shortest of the species—just 1½ to 2 feet tall—is *Z. rehmannii,* the pink (or red) calla. Its foot-long leaves, typically unspotted, are lance shaped rather than arrow shaped. The 4-inch pink to red spathes appear in midspring; 'Superba' is dark pink.

Hybrid callas flower in late spring and summer. They're usually about the size of *Z. rehmannii;* spathe colors include cream, buff, orange, pink, lavender, and purple.

USES. A clump of any calla is sure to be an accent, whether in mixed groupings of other flowering plants, amid foliage plants, or surrounded by a ground cover. For an even showier effect, plant callas in drifts among lower-growing plants.

GARDEN CULTURE. Common calla, *Z. aethiopica,* has different cultural needs from the other species. It tolerates a great range of soils but does best in an organically enriched, moisture-retentive type; it even thrives in the constantly moist soil at pond and stream margins. Where summers are hot, locate plants in light shade; in cool- or mild-summer areas, they'll grow in full sun or light shade. Plant rhizomes in autumn through early spring, setting them about 4 inches deep and 1 foot apart. Provide water all year. Clumps can remain in place for many years; dig and divide only when declining performance indicates overcrowding. Plants are evergreen to semievergreen and cannot be dug and stored over winter in cold climates. Grow them in the ground in the zones listed; in colder zones, container culture is the only option.

The other calla species and hybrids are deciduous: foliage dies down in fall, then reappears in spring. They need regular water during growth and bloom, less in the period between the end of bloom and foliage dieback. Within the listed hardiness zones, plant rhizomes in fall, setting them 2 inches deep and 8 to 12 inches apart, in soil that is organically enriched, well drained (good drainage is especially important during the winter rest period), and, ideally, slightly acid. Choose a sunny location, but if you live in a hot-summer region, try to select a spot receiving light shade during the heat of the day. As for common calla, dig and divide in fall when performance declines. In zones beyond their hardiness limits, plant these calla species in spring for summer bloom; when leaves die back in fall, dig and store over winter as for tuberous begonia (page 224), then replant the following spring.

CONTAINER CULTURE. All callas are good container plants. For the deciduous kinds, follow directions "B" (subgroup 2) on page 207; for common calla, follow directions "C."

Zantedeschia rehmannii

Slender stems, each bearing just one blossom, rise from clumps of grassy leaves. Flowers are typically funnel shaped, resembling crocus blossoms; a few species have distinctly lilylike flowers. In their native lands—from the southern United States to Argentina—flowers often appear after rains, hence the common name "rain lily." You may be able to initiate several blooming cycles by following the procedure described in "Garden culture" (below).

The most widely available species, *Z. candida*, has foot-long, glossy leaves and 2-inch white blossoms that are sometimes stained pink in the throats; plants bloom in late summer and early fall. *Z. citrina* is similar in appearance and bloom season, but its blossoms are bright yellow.

True to its name, *Z. grandiflora* produces flowers twice as large as those of the previous two species; the rose pink petals form a lily-shaped flower in the morning, become flat by midday, then close in late afternoon. Blossoms come in late spring or early summer; foliage dies back in fall, then reappears at bloom time the next year.

With some searching, you may find named hybrids in a range of appealing colors—yellow-flushed deep rose pink 'Alamo', pink-shaded yellow 'Apricot Queen', pale yellow 'Aquarius', peach-and-yellow 'Ellen Korsakoff', pink-suffused light yellow 'Prairie Sunset', and rich cerise pink 'Ruth Page'.

From the southeastern United States comes *Z. atamasco*, appropriately known as wild Easter lily. Pink-striped white buds open to pure white, fragrant 3-inch blossoms with a distinct lilylike appearance. Unlike the other species and hybrids, this one blooms in midspring and has semievergreen leaves. Even earlier blooming (by as much as a month) is Florida native *Z. treatiae*. Its red buds open to crocuslike pure white, 4-inch flowers, carried above gray-green, nearly rushlike leaves.

USES. These trouble-free plants are attractive in the foreground of mixed perennial and annual plantings, along pathways, in rock gardens—even naturalized in grassy meadows. Grow them as container plants in zones beyond their hardiness.

GARDEN CULTURE. Grow *Z. candida* in Zones 4–9, 12–32; *Z. atamasco* in Zones 4–9, 12–31, warmer parts of 32; hybrids in Zones 6–9, 12–31; *Z. citrina* and *Z. grandiflora* in Zones 7–9, 12–29; *Z. treatiae* in Zones 12, 13, 25–29.

Choose a sunny or partly shaded site with well-drained soil; set bulbs 1 to 2 inches deep and 3 inches apart. Water regularly from the time growth begins until bloom finishes. Where the growing season is long and winter is mild, plants may bloom several times a year if you give them a short dry period after bloom, then resume watering to initiate another growth cycle. Otherwise, give little or no water after foliage dies back.

Within their hardiness zones, bulbs of the various species and hybrids can remain in the ground for many years with no need for digging and dividing.

CONTAINER CULTURE. Follow directions "C" on page 207.

ZEPHYRANTHES
FAIRY LILY, RAIN LILY, ZEPHYR FLOWER
Amaryllidaceae
TRUE BULB

- ▲ 1 FOOT
- ☼ ◑ FULL SUN OR PART SHADE
- ◗ NEEDS SUMMER MOISTURE
- ✽ ZONES VARY BY SPECIES
  (SEE "GARDEN CULTURE")

Zephyranthes candida

Sunset

Roses

by Hazel White and the Editors of Sunset Books

Menlo Park, California

contents

Placing Roses in the Garden

A ROSE IS A ROSE? NOT REALLY. The "queen of flowers" has many guises. She doesn't only stand aloof and regal behind clipped boxwood hedges in rose beds cut into the lawn. She also holds her own in the back of the border with the brawniest flowering shrubs; scales walls and even the roof; forms a chorus line along a garden boundary; swings around pyramids and posts; jazzes up pots with bold companions; and spills innocently over the path like a soft perennial. ❧ *In this chapter, you'll see just how many places a rose can grow. On the practical side, you need a place that's the right size for the particular rose. Beyond that, it's a matter of playing with the aesthetic possibilities of a rose's color, flower form, and fragrance. Don't overlook the beauty of fall hips and changing foliage color. And keep in mind that under the prettiness, or voluptuousness, may lurk some beautiful thorns.*

'Penelope' (page 386) makes a fine hedge at the Antique Rose Emporium in Texas.

Getting to Know Roses

There are more than twelve thousand varieties of roses for sale in the world. Next time you stop to smell a few in a rose garden, take a look at the details of the blossoms and how the types of roses are placed.

FULL: *'Yves Piaget'.*

LOOKING AT THE BLOSSOMS

A detailed examination of rose blossoms reveals differences not just in color but also in petal count, petal shape, flower shape (when viewed from the side), and the way the blossoms are carried on the plant. The huge variety in the combination of these characteristics is one reason why roses are so adored.

SINGLE A single rose has 11 or fewer petals. *Rosa eglanteria* is a single rose. Its blossoms are flat in shape; they are usually borne in a small cluster, but sometimes they appear singly.

SINGLE: Rosa eglanteria.

SEMIDOUBLE A semidouble rose has between 12 and 16 petals. 'Delicata' is a semidouble rose. Its petals are ruffled; the blossoms are cupped in shape, and they appear in clusters.

DOUBLE A double rose has between 17 and 25 petals. 'Pascali' is a double rose. Its blossoms have a high center, typical of hybrid tea roses, and reflexed outer petals (they curve down). 'Abbaye de Cluny' blooms are deeply cupped in shape and borne singly on the bush.

FULL A full rose has between 26 and 40 petals. 'Yves Piaget' has full blossoms. The petals have a wavy edge; the blossoms are deeply cupped, almost globular, in shape, and they appear singly.

VERY FULL A very full rose has 41 petals or more. 'The Pilgrim' has 170 petals; it has a rosette

VERY FULL: *'The Pilgrim' (above), 'Mme. Hardy' (below).*

shape (many short petals, with a flat, low center), and its inner petals are "quartered" (folded into four distinct sections rather than around a cone). The very full blossoms of 'Mme. Hardy' are cupped when young but flatten as they age; the petals surround a green eye, or pip.

SEMIDOUBLE: *'Delicata'.*

DOUBLE: *'Pascali' (left), 'Abbaye de Cluny' (right).*

LOOKING AT THE PLANTS

Rose bushes are natural choices for flower beds and shrub borders; some also make fine hedges or container plants. The largest are the old garden roses, grandifloras, and shrub roses. Hybrid teas and floribundas generally grow with more restraint. Miniature roses are the smallest; some reach only 1 foot tall. For a little formality, consider a standard rose, a bush rose grown on a tall bare stem; a patio rose is a small standard.

Climbing roses grow on vertical surfaces or free-standing supports. The most vigorous ones, the ramblers, will cover a house roof or grow to the top of a large tree. More moderate climbers clothe arbors and tall walls. Small climbers, sometimes called pillar roses, are suitable for a pyramid or trellis. In addition to the roses that are classified as climbers, there are old garden roses and shrub roses that climb, and climbing miniature roses.

Ground cover roses make a low, mounding carpet of color up to 8 feet wide. They are most often massed on a slope or an area of the garden where other knee-high shrubs might be used. They also make good container plants. Look for them in the landscape roses section, pages 376–390.

More details about the characteristics of each rose type appear in chapter 4, "More than 390 Recommended Roses," on pages 363–410.

OLD GARDEN ROSE

RAMBLER

CLIMBER

SHRUB

GRANDIFLORA

HYBRID TEA

FLORIBUNDA

PILLAR

MINIATURES

STANDARD

GROUND COVERS

Small Gardens

Small gardens are often the most beautiful. Save space by raising your roses off the ground (see pages 304–305). Use miniature roses, grow roses in pots—there are many options in small spaces.

ABOVE: *Catmint (Nepeta) and pink and coral diascias make perfect pot companions for 'Sunset Celebration' (page 374). They tolerate the rose's regular irrigation and feeding, but they don't compete for them. Visually, the diascias play off the pretty pinks and apricots in the rose, and the cool catmint blue makes those warm colors even warmer.*

LEFT: *Light and cool colors recede, creating a sense of space, which is particularly useful in small areas. Yet white, the coolest color of all, isn't a background color, quite the contrary; it's fresh and bright and attracts the eye faster than red or orange. This white garden is composed of an 'Iceberg' rose (page 382), 'White Nancy' lamium, white Silene uniflora, and foliage plants with white-variegated leaves.*

INSET: *The multiple colors in some roses, such as this miniature 'Rainbow's End' (page 409), can help unify the elements in a garden. Here, from late spring until frost, the house and the plantings have become an eye-catching composition of pastel and hot pinks and yellows.*

ABOVE: *Pots of roses—shrubby or trailing, alone or in a line or mixed with pots of other plants—can make a bold statement on steps, pillars, along the tops of walls, or on the floor of a balcony or deck. Keep potted roses well watered and fertilized (see pages 329 and 331).*

LEFT: *'Hawkeye Belle', 'Wind Chimes', and 'Mme. Isaac Pereire' (page 394) weave along the fence, 'Sombreuil' (page 403) climbs the house wall, and 'Zéphirine Drouhin' (page 397) spills over the stair rail. They help to screen this little space, and their beauty and perfume storm the senses of everyone entering here. Design: Paula Manchester.*

Recommended for Containers

Miniature roses are obvious candidates for container plantings. But polyanthas, floribundas, and even shrub and old garden roses can also work successfully provided they are compact. The list below includes all types.

PINK ROSES

China Doll, p. 379
Cupcake, p. 405
Flower Carpet, p. 380
Rose de Rescht, p. 397
Sexy Rexy, p. 388
The Fairy, p. 390

YELLOW ROSES

Baby Love, p. 404

WHITE ROSES

French Lace, p. 381
Gourmet Popcorn, p. 406
Sea Foam, p. 388

OTHER ROSES

Marie Curie, p. 384
Regensburg, p. 387

ABOVE: *Because they are relatively small, miniature roses often get lost in mixed plantings. But here their delicacy is beautifully displayed among the contrasting shapes and colors of Japanese blood grass (Imperata), blue elymus grass, and iris.*

Cottage Gardens

Although they look haphazard and easy, successful cottage gardens result from careful planning and usually many experiments. If you need more ideas for introducing some visual order into a chaotic planting, turn to pages 302–303.

ABOVE: *In a cottage garden, plants tumble over and thread through one another. Two or more different climbing roses might romp together over an arch. Here, a 'Victoria' clematis twines itself around a 'William Baffin' rose (page 403). Design: Paula and Peter Manchester.*

LEFT: *A cool flower border of fragrant 'Iceberg' roses (page 382), catmint (Nepeta), and a species geranium is arranged with the tallest plant at the back and the smallest in the front. This layering creates an illusion of depth in a narrow bed.*

BOTTOM LEFT: *Planting climbing roses among the species geraniums, euphorbias, and stachys makes it possible to maintain a sense of fullness and depth to this flower border as it narrows at the steps. Pale and cool colors recede into the distance; the garden would seem shorter if the roses were red. Design: Margaret de Haas van Dorsser.*

BOTTOM RIGHT: *A successful cottage garden gives an impression of profusion and pleasing chaos. A glimpse of a contrasting firm line— a fence or an arbor post—accentuates the "wildness."*

LEFT: *Seemingly a riot of color, this garden succeeds because the colors are of a similar intensity. Mixing pastel flowers among the orange climbing 'Warm Welcome' rose (page 410), the blue Himalayan poppy* (Meconopsis), *and the chartreuse euphorbia would tip the composition into an irritating jumble of colors.*

Recommended Companion Plants

Most roses need generous amounts of fertilizer and water, so choose companion plants that have similar needs. Don't crowd your roses; plant companions at least 1½ feet away. Here are some of the best choices:

Artemisia 'Powis Castle'
Delphinium elatum, English delphinium
Gypsophila paniculata, baby's breath
Hemerocallis, daylily
Iris, especially Siberian iris
Lavandula angustifolia 'Hidcote' and 'Munstead', English lavender
Myosotis, forget-me-not
Nemesia
Nepeta × faassenii, catmint
Penstemon × gloxinioides, border penstemon

BELOW: *In this double garden border, the colors are hot and visually striking but also harmonious. The harmony derives from a restrained use of color—shades of red, pink, and yellow, with a little contrasting blue and fresh white as accents. Repeating the pink and red roses, astilbe, and lychnis along the borders also contributes to the sense of order and quietness.*

Formal Gardens

Repetition, symmetry, geometric lines and patterns, clipped hedges or topiary, an axis with a focal point: these formal elements lend grace and elegance to a rose garden.

LEFT: *Formal in its simplicity—brilliant red 'Trumpeter' floribunda roses, an emerald carpet of lawn, a dark, clipped hedge—this garden blooms from late spring into fall and is always a place of peace.*

RIGHT: *Reducing the variety of textures, colors, and shapes within a garden vignette allows garden guests to take in the details better. Note how the shape of the wall finial mimics the line of the clipped conifer and the curves of the rose buds.*

Boxwood (Buxus) hedges traditionally edge formal rose beds to hide the roses' bare ankles, but these bushy roses have plenty of low foliage of their own. The raised urn is a traditional focal point for the end of a garden axis.

ABOVE: *Because of the repetition of the pillars, a pergola looks more formal than an arch or an arbor. Here a balance between formal and informal has been established: the stucco columns tend toward the formal, but the variety in rose colors and the absence of a focal point or clipped shrubs undercut the formality. Design: Jack Chandler Associates.*

Recommended for Beautiful Form

Traditionally, formal rose gardens are planted with hybrid tea roses, the roses with the most elegant blossoms. Their long, slender buds slowly spiral open around a high center, making a tall triangle when you look at one from the side. The hybrid teas listed here have exquisite form.

PINK ROSES

Bride's Dream, p. 365
Classic Touch, p. 365
Tiffany, p. 374

RED ROSES

Dublin, p. 366
Ingrid Bergman, p. 368
Opening Night, p. 371
Uncle Joe, p. 375

YELLOW ROSES

Elina, p. 367

WHITE ROSES

Jardins de Bagatelle, p. 369
Moonstone, p. 370
Sheer Bliss, p. 373

OTHERS

Fragrant Cloud, p. 367
Gemini, p. 367
Sunset Celebration, p. 374
Touch of Class, p. 375
Vanilla Perfume, p. 375

In this rose garden, in Birmingham, Alabama, the fountain directs the eye to a wall ornament between a pair of lattice arches. Aligning the elements like this to create a strong sight line is one way to establish a sense of formality. Design: Norman Kent Johnson.

'Gertrude Jekyll', a large shrub rose, contributes antique charm and heady perfume to this Islamic knot garden ribboned with barberry (Berberis). To keep the rose low-growing and the pattern of the garden clear, the canes must be pegged (see pages 360–361).

Vertical Roses

Growing some roses vertically adds a third dimension of space to a garden and makes room for more plants below. It also brings the blossoms closer to eye level.

ABOVE: *'Cl. Cécile Brünner' (page 399) has a sweet rustic charm. From its small, beautifully formed, delicately fragrant, pink blossoms you'd never guess it is vigorous. Unless kept in check, it will climb off this fence and up into the neighboring trees. Design: Michael Bates.*

BELOW: *People can't help but pause on their way under this arch, clothed with the large-flowered climber 'America' (page 398). Each of its abundant flowers is a beautifully formed cup stuffed with petals; the blossoms appear all summer, and they are heavily perfumed.*

This pergola (or series of arches joined together) is purposefully missing a few beams. It's at the edge of a garden, where formality is giving way to nature and the process of time. The low wall offers a casual place to put up your feet and watch the sweetly scented white petals of 'Sombreuil', left (page 403), drift off in the breeze. Design: Jack Chandler Associates.

BELOW: *Upright roses with limber canes, like this 'Mme. Grégoire Staechelin', make fine climbers. They are easy to train, and the blossoms naturally sag through an arbor so you can get close to them. Climbing roses with a stiff habit, such as some sports of hybrid teas, tend to produce their blossoms high in the air if left to their own devices.*

Recommended Small Climbers

Climbing roses come in different sizes. Use rampant ones to cover large arbors or an unsightly shed. For small situations, grow modest climbers, such as the following:

PINK ROSES

Clair Matin, p. 399
Jeanne Lajoie, p. 407
Zéphirine Drouhin, p. 397

RED ROSES

Blaze, p. 398

WHITE ROSES

Sombreuil, p. 403

OTHERS

Fourth of July, p. 400
Garden Sun, p. 400
Handel, p. 401
Polka, p. 402
Shadow Dancer, p. 402
Warm Welcome, p. 410

LEFT: *'Dortmund' (page 400) decorates a blue pillar with a mauve finial in this garden of strong bright colors in Sagaponack, New York. Like many of the roses commonly described as pillar roses (or pillar-climbers), it can be just as easily used as a shrub. Design: Robert Dash.*

ABOVE: *This double red rose has just the right amount of elegance for this boundary fence. A single "wild" rose might look too rustic in relation to the house; a pale rose wouldn't attract attention; a multicolored rose might seem gaudy.*

Hedges and Ground Covers

New series of roses have been bred specifically for hedges and ground covers. They are designed to be low-maintenance, which is essential for mass plantings. Some older roses fit the bill, too.

Recommended for Hedges

For a tall hedge, 5 feet or higher, choose shrub roses or tall floribundas, and plant them about 3 feet apart. For a lower hedge, choose compact shrub roses or floribundas, and plant them about 1½ feet apart. Hybrid teas are generally too upright and bare at the base to make a good bushy hedge; if you use them, prune the canes to different heights so the leaves and flowers aren't all at the top. For a very low hedge, under 2½ feet tall, choose miniature roses (pages 404–410).

PINK ROSES

Bonica, p. 378
Conrad Ferdinand Meyer, p. 379
Pink Meidiland, p. 386
Simplicity, p. 388

RED ROSES

Hansa, p. 382
Knock Out, p. 383
Linda Campbell, p. 383
Robusta, p. 387

WHITE ROSES

Iceberg, p. 382
Sally Holmes, p. 387

OTHERS

Carefree Delight, p. 378
Carefree Wonder, p. 379
Escapade, p. 379

ABOVE: *Barrier hedges need to be dense and leafy from base to top, but hedges for screening, like this aerial hedge of 'Lamarque' (page 394), can be more open. A climbing rose, it provides a comfortable sense of enclosure when people are seated, without entirely blocking the pleasant view.*

ABOVE: *Rosa rugosa roses, the species (page 396) and the many hybrids (pages 376–390), make magnificent hedges. They are dense and leafy, disease resistant, and thorny (so impenetrable). They bloom over a long period, are fragrant, and produce beautiful tomato-shaped hips (see page 311) in summer and fall. Choose carefully: the species rose can grow 7 feet tall and wide, while 'Snow Owl' (page 389) stays about 3 feet by 3 feet. Design: Natureworks.*

BELOW: *Ground cover roses cover up the bare knobby ankles of this chorus line of 'Summer Fashion' standard roses. Use them in the same way in front of a climbing rose or hybrid tea roses that are bare at the base. If you choose a rose with thorns, be diligent about clearing the soil of weeds before you plant.*

LEFT: *'Iceberg' (page 382)
(above) and pink 'Bonica'
(page 378) (below) are two
popular hedging choices.
Both generally grow from
3 to 5 feet tall, but be
aware that size depends
very much on climate and
growing conditions: 'Iceberg'
can grow to 8 feet tall and
wide in mild climates if it's
well tended. 'Bonica' also
makes a fine ground cover.*

BELOW: *'Flower Carpet'
(page 380) produces a
stunning display of
blossoms all summer long
in this perennials garden.
Its companions are
stachys, catmint (Nepeta),
Artemisia 'Powis Castle',
phormium, and daylilies
(Hemerocallis). Design:
Freeland Tanner.*

Recommended for Ground Covers

Ground cover roses arch
or creep over the ground.
They have dense foliage, are
vigorous, and flower freely—
some bloom nonstop until
frost nips them. Plant the
small shrubby types 2 feet
apart; for large sprawling
varieties, leave up to 5 feet
between plants.

PINK ROSES

Flower Carpet, p. 380
Pink Meidiland, p. 386

RED ROSES

Gourmet Pheasant, p. 407
Red Cascade, p. 409
Red Ribbons, p. 387
Scarlet Meidiland, p. 387

YELLOW ROSES

Sun Runner, p. 389

WHITE ROSES

Sea Foam, p. 388
White Meidiland, p. 390

INSET: *Gardeners
used to plant vigorous,
lax ramblers, Bourbons,
and hybrid perpetuals
to cover large areas of
ground. This rambler,
Rosa banksiae 'Lutea'
(page 395), could
cover the entire bank
if allowed.*

Fragrance

Fragrance is as important as color to most gardeners selecting roses. Place a fragrant rose where people have a chance to catch its perfume, and keep it well watered, which will help the petals excrete those micro-droplets of scent.

ABOVE: *An opulently perfumed, naturally arching old garden rose, like this 'Ispahan' damask, is beautiful to come upon at the edge of the garden. 'Ispahan' blooms for up to 2 months in early summer. Damask roses are grown commercially in central Europe for the production of attar of roses.*

LEFT: *The scent of these welcoming blooms of 'Golden Showers' (page 401), like that of several other roses, varies. To some, it is a very sweet perfume; others report no fragrance. One rose bush may produce more fragrance than another of the same variety; people's experience of scent differs; and blossoms may smell strongly in the morning but not at all by afternoon.*

INSET: *A sweet scent can lead you on a memorable journey through even a very small garden. The fruity fragrance of the 'New Dawn' rose (page 402) may bring you close enough to notice the interesting form of the* Clematis florida sieboldii *blossoms—and then to study the way the color changes on the blossoms of both plants as they age.*

LEFT: *To enjoy the fragrance of roses, you need to be close to the petals. This easily moved, comfortable wicker chair invites you to enjoy the strong sweet scent of the nodding blossoms of 'La Ville de Bruxelles' (page 393). Design: Michael Bates.*

If you have a good nose, you can learn to tell the difference between myriad rose fragrances.
CLOCKWISE FROM TOP LEFT: *'Queen Elizabeth' (page 372) smells slightly of moss and ferns, 'Jardins de Bagatelle' (page 369) smells of classic old-world rose, 'Dublin' (page 366) smells of raspberry, 'Belle Story' (page 377) smells of anise or myrrh.*

Recommended for Fragrance

Until fairly recently, perfume was most often associated with old garden roses. Now, to meet demand, new English (David Austin), Generosa, and Romantica varieties often have bountiful fragrance. The following list contains old and new highly scented roses, plus hybrid teas, a group usually lacking much scent. Roses with an asterisk (★) have won the James Alexander-Gamble Fragrance Medal from the American Rose Society, for top-performing, intensely fragrant roses.

PINK ROSES

Conrad Ferdinand Meyer, p. 379
Crested Moss, p. 392
Dainty Bess, p. 366
Magna Charta, p. 395
Mme. Isaac Pereire, p. 394
Sarah Van Fleet, p. 388
★Tiffany, p. 374

RED ROSES

★Chrysler Imperial, p. 365
★Crimson Glory, p. 365
Dupuy Jamain, p. 392
Mister Lincoln, p. 370

YELLOW ROSES

★Sunsprite, p. 389

WHITE ROSES

Jardins de Bagatelle, p. 369
Kiftsgate, p. 401
Sheer Bliss, p. 373

OTHERS

Abraham Darby, p. 376
★Double Delight, p. 366
★Fragrant Cloud, p. 367
Intrigue, p. 383

Foliage, Thorns, Hips, and History

Many roses produce not only silky, scented blooms but also magnificent hips and leaves. Others are worth adding to the garden because of their monstrously large thorns—or because they are North American natives.

Decorative mossy glands on the sepals around the flower buds give moss roses their name. The moss feels soft on the centifolia mosses (such as 'Crested Moss', page 392, and 'William Lobb', page 397) and prickly on the damask mosses (such as 'Henri Martin', page 393). It sometimes has a pine scent.

ABOVE: *Rose hips come in many colors, sizes, and shapes—round and oblong, but also curved like flagons and bulging like tomatoes. Some are thick and waxy, some almost translucent.* TOP TO BOTTOM: *Hips of* Rosa rugosa *(page 396),* R. moyesii *(page 396), and* R. eglanteria *(page 395).*

ABOVE, LEFT: *The Green rose (Rosa chinensis viridiflora; page 393) doesn't flower like most roses; its sepals have taken the place of petals. Flower arrangers grow it for its novel green "blossoms," which appear all summer long.* RIGHT: *Curious prickles, reminiscent of spiny chestnut burrs, cover the buds and hips of the Chestnut rose (Rosa roxburghii; page 396).*

LEFT: Rosa sericea pteracantha *(page 396), growing here with 'Claridge Druce' geranium, has huge wedged thorns that march up the canes with scarcely a space between them. On new canes, the thorns are translucent and glow beautifully when backlit.*

BOTTOM LEFT: *The Cherokee rose (Rosa laevigata) is widely naturalized throughout the southeastern United States; it has been made the state flower of Georgia. Hidden beneath its abundant elegant blossoms and lacquered-looking leaves are plenty of hooked thorns.*

BOTTOM RIGHT: Rosa setigera, *the Prairie rose, is a North American native. Like several of the other native roses— including* R. virginiana, R. carolina, *and* R. arkansana—*it produces bountiful crops of red hips in fall. Its vigor is best directed vertically unless you have a large garden.*

Recommended for Striking Hips

Many old garden roses and some shrub roses, particularly the hybrid rugosas, produce a crop of showy hips. They develop from spent flowers, so you must remember not to deadhead the last flush of blossoms.

PINK ROSES

Buffalo Gal, p. 378
Kathleen, p. 382
Rosa eglanteria, p. 395
Rosa roxburghii, p. 396

RED ROSES

Dr. Jackson, p. 379
Hansa, p. 382
Knock Out, p. 383
Rosa moyesii, p. 396

WHITE ROSES

Snow Owl, p. 389

OTHERS

Moje Hammarberg, p. 385
Rosa rugosa, p. 396
Scabrosa, p. 389

CHAPTER TWO

Growing Healthy Roses

GROWING HEALTHY ROSES *isn't really as complicated as people used to think. Forget about becoming an expert on spraying pesticides and fungicides; the excitement about chemicals is waning. In truth, like every other plant, roses need sunshine and water. They are fussy to the extent that they like quite a lot of both, and they like good drainage—usually easily supplied by digging in lots of compost—and, if you want big bushes and an abundance of showy flowers, some nitrogen-rich fertilizer.* ∿ *The time people used to spend pumping and cleaning sprayers you can spend lazily walking by your roses, looking out for any pests and diseases and picking off the occasional bugs or chewed leaves. Now you are pretty much advised about the hard work required.* ∿ *This chapter covers all that plus how to shop for roses that grow well in your climate, how to plant, special care in winter, and tips for creating beautiful displays of roses indoors once your garden is bursting with them.*

The healthy, handsome foliage of species rose R. glauca.

Shopping for Roses

If you shop wisely for rose plants, you'll be well on your way to a successful rose garden. Strong, healthy, top-grade plants make the fastest start. Varieties well-suited to your climate will help ensure an easy-care garden for years to come.

WHERE TO SHOP

Mail-order catalogs offer the widest choice of roses; they are practically the only way to shop if you are looking for lesser-known roses. You'll also find roses for sale in local nurseries and garden centers, in home-improvement and hardware stores, and even in some supermarkets.

Although you can't examine plants you buy from a catalog until the package arrives, don't let that deter you. Good mail-order suppliers' reputations are based on providing quality plants and service. And don't be put off by the idea of receiving a dormant rose plant with no soil on its roots (the way mail-order houses typically send them to you). It doesn't harm the rose to be dug up and shipped like that, and bare-root plants have advantages over plants sold in containers; see the chart on the next page. For names and addresses of a number of mail-order suppliers, turn to page 415.

A good local nursery or garden center usually stocks roses that do especially well in your area. Large retail chains are more likely to carry the current national best-sellers. During winter and early spring, the roses in these outlets are usually sold as bare-root plants; later in the season, they sell the plants potted in containers.

You can start your rose garden with bare-root plants or plants grown in containers. Bare-root is usually the choice of experienced rose growers, but it's really a matter of what works better for you. The chart on the next page compares the two options.

Where the Plants You Buy Are Grown

Most rose plants are grown in fields in California's San Joaquin Valley—millions of them in rows that stretch as far as the eye can see. During fall, at the end of their second year, they are lifted out of the ground and the soil is shaken from the roots. They are quickly graded and placed in moist cold storage to prevent the roots from drying out. Then they are shipped "bare-root" all over the country—directly to gardeners, to retail outlets, or, in some cases, to wholesale growers who will pot them and grow them on for another year.

Most container-grown roses are potted by the retail outlet, either as soon as the bare-root plants arrive from the grower or else at the end of the bare-root season, when the plants must be either potted or planted in the ground.

WHEN TO SHOP

Container-grown roses are sold almost all year, but, for the widest possible choice of varieties, shop in winter or early spring, as soon as bare-root plants become available in your area. Their arrival should roughly coincide with your earliest planting time (see page 322).

A HEALTHY BARE-ROOT ROSE

A healthy bare-root rose has many thick, green canes (stems); a big cluster of sturdy, fibrous roots; and, if it is budded, a stout, undamaged "bud union" (the swollen, knobby-looking place where the rose was grafted onto the rootstock). Reject any bare-root rose with dried-out or squishy roots or with canes that are weak, shriveled, or beginning to leaf out.

If the plant is packaged in a tube, it may be impossible to inspect the roots before you unpack it. Return the plant to the seller if the roots turn out to be dry—dry roots, more than anything else, lead to trouble.

A HEALTHY CONTAINER-GROWN ROSE

A healthy container-grown rose has flower buds, strong new growth, healthy foliage, and a firm rootball of moist, fibrous roots (ask someone who works at the retail outlet to show the rootball to you). It should be in a large (3- or 5-gallon) container— if it's in a smaller one, the roots were probably cut back hard to fit the pot.

Avoid any plant with roots protruding from the bottom of the container or coiling around the rootball. Also avoid any plant with dieback or weak, straggly growth. These are all signs that the rose has been in the container too long, and this means that it may not establish well in your garden.

WHETHER TO BUY BARE-ROOT OR CONTAINER-GROWN ROSES

BARE-ROOT ROSES	CONTAINER-GROWN ROSES
Available only during winter and early spring	Available almost year-round
Generally less expensive than roses sold in containers	Foliage, flowers, fragrance, vigor on display
Easier to carry home	Easier to store before planting
Need to be planted before they break dormancy, in early spring	Can be planted at almost any time
May establish vigorous roots faster	Provide an instant rose garden

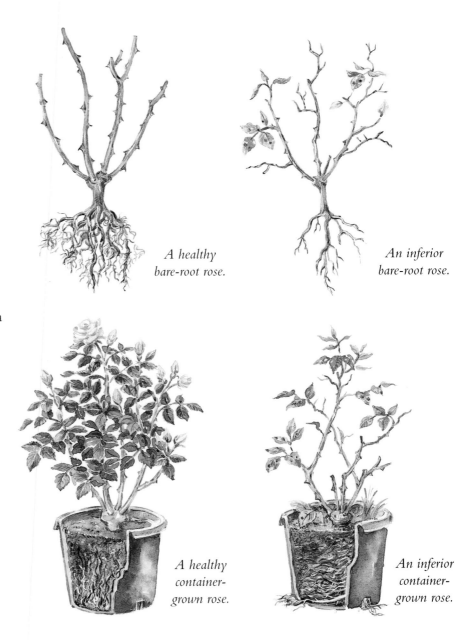

A healthy bare-root rose.

An inferior bare-root rose.

A healthy container-grown rose.

An inferior container-grown rose.

Budded and Own-Root Roses

Most modern roses are not grown on their own roots. To produce reliably vigorous plants, commercial growers raise a special variety, often 'Dr. Huey', for the rootstock, and then graft a bud of 'Peace' (or 'Queen Elizabeth', or any one of the hundreds of rose varieties they sell) into the cane bark of the rootstock plant. If the graft is successful, the bud swells, opens, and gives rise to a whole framework of 'Peace' canes, foliage, and flowers. The top of the rootstock plant is then cut back to the bud union, the place where the 'Peace' bud was inserted.

Many historic and shrub roses, in contrast, are grown on their own roots—as are miniatures.

WHICH GRADE TO BUY

Commercial growers must grade their budded roses according to the number and thickness of the canes. There are three grades: 1, 1½, and 2. Grade 1 roses are the best. They have the greatest number of thick, vigorous canes and are likely to grow into the best bushes. Grade 1½ roses have fewer and thinner canes. Grade 2 plants aren't worth buying even if they are heavily discounted, most gardeners believe.

Roses growing on their own roots are typically smaller to start with than budded roses. They may be graded 3X, 2X, and 1X; the best grade is 3X.

AARS AWARDS

Roses that win an AARS (All-America Rose Selections) award are vigorous plants that perform well in a wide range of climates. These roses have been grown for 2 years in test gardens throughout the United States by the AARS, a nonprofit research organization; of all the new varieties entered in the trials, they have received the most votes in secret-ballot elections.

However, the absence of an AARS award—only three or four are given each year—does not automatically brand a rose as inferior. First, not all new varieties are entered in the trials, so excellent roses can reach the market without AARS testing. And second, some roses, whether or not they have been entered in AARS trials, perform superbly in certain climates or regions but are outclassed by other roses elsewhere.

STORING ROSES

Plant bare-root roses as soon as possible, or the roots may dry out or start growing in the package. If you can't plant right away, because the ground is frozen or too wet, keep the packing around the roots moist, and set the plants in a cool area out of sunlight, such as a garage. In a warm, light place, the roots and shoots may start to grow.

You can store bare-root plants in this way for up to 2 weeks. If you still can't plant, remove the packaging, and place the roses in a dishpan or bucket of moist soil or compost, so that the roots and bud union (for budded roses) are covered. Pack the soil around the plants, and return them to a cool, dim place; keep the soil moist.

To store container-grown roses, place them in a sunny place sheltered from wind. Water them regularly (the soil should always be damp) until you can plant them.

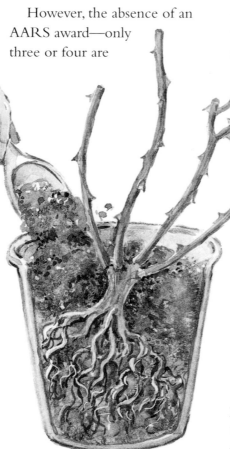

Storing a bare-root rose.

CLIMATE MATTERS

Try not to fall in love with any rose until you know how it does in your climate. Love can turn quickly to disillusionment and sorrow if you have to constantly nurse the poor rose just to keep it alive. Check the advice below and on the following pages to learn which roses suit your climate and which ones spell trouble. To be as sure as you can about whether a particular rose will thrive in your garden, contact someone at a local nursery or rose society who has grown that variety.

COLD-TOLERANT ROSES

Although any rose has a fighting chance of surviving anywhere if you give it enough winter protection (see "The Minnesota Tip," on page 341), you can make your life easier and reduce your disappointments by growing varieties that are hardy in your climate.

If you live where winter temperatures drop below –30°F/ –34°C, choose the most cold-tolerant varieties. The hardiest rose in this book is *Rosa rugosa*, page 396. The popular hybrid rugosa roses listed in "Landscape Roses," on pages 376–390, are just as hardy, or almost. Also consider the Iowa-bred Dr. Griffith Buck hybrids and the Explorer roses, bred to survive southern Canadian winters unprotected. In the descriptions of the recommended roses on pages 364–410, look for the words "good winter hardiness."

Choosing Flower Color

Often, a rose looks striking because the color of its flowers so beautifully suits the surroundings. When you're choosing a rose to plant near your house, make sure its flowers complement the colors of the walls and trim. In fact, consider the background wherever you plant a rose—whether next to a gate, against a fence, or in a multicolored shrub planting.

Any rose looks excellent with a quiet, neutral, or plain background such as a weathered wood fence, a stone wall, or a boxwood hedge. Soft pink roses are usually particularly pleasing with old brick (new brick often has a harsh color that's difficult to work with). Warm-colored pink, orange, red, and yellow roses can take the chill off a cold-looking gray or white wall.

On a hot patio, white and other pale-colored roses make the brightness seem cooler during the day, and they glow as night falls. Light-colored roses

A good match: soft apricot against painted brick.

are also easier to use than strong-hued ones in flower borders, since they are more likely to blend with what's there already. (For examples of superb mixed plantings, see pages 300–303.)

In regions where winter temperatures stay above –20°F/ –29°C, you can probably also grow the alba and gallica old garden roses without protection and any of the hybrid kordesii climbing roses. Bear in mind that hardiness is not a precise science— the pattern of cold snaps and thaws affects hardiness, for example.

Hybrid teas and grandifloras generally do not tolerate temperatures below 20°F/–6°C without protection. Shrubs are typically hardier. Listed in the chart on page 319 are modern roses that show unusual hardiness (but they still need protection in cold-winter climates). The list was composed from several sources.

Rose canes tied securely to supports for the winter in New York.

CLOCKWISE FROM TOP LEFT: *'Blaze' thriving in the dry heat of Santa Fe, New Mexico; good disease resistance makes 'Just Joey' a beautiful candidate for gardens in humid climates; vivid roses brighten a garden on a foggy afternoon; 'The Fairy' offers a profusion of small blossoms in a lightly shaded garden area.*

HEAT-TOLERANT ROSES

Heat can stress roses. The plants may stop growing, the production of flowers may slow down, the blossom colors may bleach or deepen, the flowers of varieties with few petals may "blow" (open too quickly), and the foliage may burn.

Where summers are hot, plant heat-sensitive roses in a spot that's lightly shaded in the afternoon. Keep your roses deeply watered so they continue to grow and bloom through the summer. Consider densely petaled roses such as the centifolias, which perform well only in warm climates. Or see the chart for a list of heat lovers, gathered from recommendations by Kathleen Brenzel in California and Russ Bowermaster in Florida.

HUMIDITY-TOLERANT ROSES

Humidity makes roses more susceptible to diseases, particularly black spot, powdery mildew, and rust (see pages 336–339). If you garden in a humid climate, be sure to select varieties that are not especially prone to these diseases, and plant them in sites with good air circulation (bear in mind that almost no rose is so disease resistant that it is never subject to disease). The list in the chart is composed of recommendations by Russ Bowermaster in Florida and Michael Ruggiero in New York City.

ROSES FOR COOL SUMMERS

Cool, moist air doesn't suit densely petaled roses such as the centifolias; the flowers ball up and fail to open. Either avoid those kinds or try one in the warmest spot of your garden, say against a south- or west-facing wall. Look for roses noted for their disease resistance, because fungal diseases such as black spot, powdery mildew, and rust (see pages 336–339) are common in cool-summer regions. Peggy Van Allen, in the Northwest, recommends all the rugosa roses and also her other favorites listed in the chart.

ROSES FOR SHADY PLACES

Most roses require 6 hours of sunshine a day to thrive. But you can enjoy roses in areas that are marginally shady (not fully shaded). Alba roses (see pages 391–397) do well in lightly shaded spots, as do the varieties listed in the chart.

Cold-Tolerant Roses*	Heat-Tolerant Roses	Humidity-Tolerant Roses	Roses for Cool Summers	Roses for Shady Places
PINK ROSES				
Betty Prior, p. 377 New Dawn, p. 402 Pink Peace, p. 372 Sexy Rexy, p. 388 The Fairy, p. 390	Cécile Brünner, p. 399 Flower Carpet, p. 380 Souvenir de la Malmaison, p. 397	Blossomtime, p. 399 Classic Touch, p. 365 Playgirl, p. 386 Rosarium Uetersen, p. 403 Sarah Van Fleet, p. 388 The Fairy, p. 390	Ballerina, p. 377	Betty Prior, p. 377 Kathleen, p. 382 New Dawn, p. 402 The Fairy, p. 390
RED ROSES				
Altissimo, p. 398 Knock Out, p. 383 Loving Memory, p. 369 Mister Lincoln, p. 370 Oklahoma, p. 371 Uncle Joe, p. 375	Blaze, p. 398 Europeana, p. 380 Miss Flippins, p. 408 Mister Lincoln, p. 370 Olympiad, p. 371 Proud Land, p. 372 Uncle Joe, p. 375	Hunter, p. 383 Knock Out, p. 383 Olympiad, p. 371 Robusta, p. 387 Roseraie de l'Hay, p. 387	Dortmund, p. 400 Ingrid Bergman, p. 368 Love, p. 369 Olympiad, p. 371 Opening Night, p. 371	Altissimo, p. 398 Knock Out, p. 383
YELLOW ROSES				
Arthur Bell, p. 379 Golden Wings, p. 381 Gold Medal, p. 367 Sunsprite, p. 389	Fairhope, p. 405 Midas Touch, p. 370 Morning Has Broken, p. 385 St. Patrick, p. 373	Golden Wings, p. 381 Maigold, p. 401 Molineux, p. 385	Mrs. Oakley Fisher, p. 370 Sunsprite, p. 389	Alberic Barbier, pp. 355, 359
WHITE ROSES				
Iceberg, p. 382 Snow Bride, p. 409	Green rose, p. 393 Iceberg, p. 382 Nicole, p. 385 Sombreuil, p. 403 White Flower Carpet, p. 380	Gourmet Popcorn, p. 406 Moonstone, p. 370 Sea Foam, p. 388 White Dawn, p. 403	Iceberg, p. 382 Sally Holmes, p. 387	Kiftsgate, p. 401 Prosperity, p. 387 Sally Holmes, p. 387
OTHERS				
Peace, p. 372 Playboy, p. 386 Tropicana, p. 375	Fourth of July, p. 400 Louise Estes, p. 369 Rosa rugosa, p. 396	Buff Beauty, p. 378 Cardinal de Richelieu, p. 391 Fourth of July, p. 400 Jean Kenneally, p. 407 Just Joey, p. 368 Rosa rugosa, p. 396 Tamora, p. 390	Intrigue, p. 383 Stephens' Big Purple, p. 373 Sunset Celebration, p. 374	Eugène de Beauharnais, p. 393 Kordes' Perfecta, p. 368

*Hardier roses are discussed on page 317.

Getting the Site Ready

Growing roses starts with good siting and good soil. Although roses aren't as fussy as people say, they do perform much better if you plant them in a sunny area and make an excellent home for their roots.

WHAT ROSES NEED

Roses need sunshine, little or no wind, and a fast-draining but moisture-retentive soil that's neither too acidic nor too alkaline.

SUNSHINE AND LITTLE WIND

Choose a planting place where your rose will receive at least 6 hours of sunshine daily. If your weather is consistently cool or overcast, choose a place that's open all day to any sun that might appear. If summer heat is intense, find a spot that receives filtered sunlight during the hottest afternoon hours. Some roses are able to thrive in partial shade (see page 319).

Avoid windy locations. Wind spoils the flowers and increases transpiration from the leaves, so that you need to water more often.

MOISTURE-RETENTIVE, FAST-DRAINING SOIL

To make your soil more moisture retentive, add organic matter. It acts as a sponge, slowing the passage of water and dissolved nutrients so that they are available to the rose roots longer.

To find out how fast your soil drains, do a simple test: Dig a hole about 1½ feet deep in the planting area, and fill it with water. If water remains in the hole after 8 hours, the soil drains poorly.

To remedy poor drainage, you have two options: plant your roses in raised beds, which is the plan surest to succeed; or dig the planting area deeply, and add lots of organic matter, which creates air spaces so that the water can penetrate more easily through the soil.

A MODERATE SOIL pH

Soils with a pH number less than 7 are acid; those with a pH of 7 are neutral; and those with a pH above 7 are alkaline. Roses grow well in soils that are moderately acid, from about 6.3 to 6.8.

The soil test kits sold at nurseries and garden centers will give you a reading accurate enough to tell whether your soil is extremely acidic or alkaline. You can amend highly acidic soils with lime, strongly alkaline ones with sulfur. Add these amendments as you prepare the soil, following the package instructions. (To be on the safe side, if you suspect you have a major imbalance, you may want to consult a soil lab or local agricultural extension; the experts there will be able to give you specific advice on your problem.)

Raised Beds—the Easy Solution

A stone raised bed adds elegance and height to this rose hedge.

There's a simple solution to dealing with soil that is too shallow or drains poorly: heap soil on top of it and grow your roses above grade. To form the sides of a raised bed, use landscape timbers, decay-resistant wood, brick, concrete block, or stone; or simply make a firm mound with sloping sides and a surrounding ditch. Plan to have the soil surface within the raised bed 1 foot or more above the normal grade outside.

Dig a 4-inch layer of organic material into the existing soil, going down a foot or more if you can. Then add topsoil (taken from another part of the garden or purchased), and dig it into the improved native soil, adding another 4-inch layer of organic matter at the same time. Water the bed deeply and let it settle before you plant it. If it sinks significantly, mix more topsoil into the bed.

HOW TO PREPARE THE SOIL

The big question as you set about preparing for planting is this: Must you dig up and add organic matter to the entire planting area, or can you just dig it into the soil in the planting hole. The answer depends on your soil type.

AMENDING A PLANTING AREA

If your soil drains poorly, work organic matter into the entire planting area, not just the planting hole. Otherwise, the soil in the hole will absorb water from the surrounding soil, and the area around the rose's roots will become waterlogged.

To amend a planting area, begin by digging or tilling the soil, ideally to a depth of 12 to 18 inches.

AMENDING SOIL IN A PLANTING HOLE

You can amend just the soil in the planting hole if your purpose is only to make the soil more moisture retentive (always a good idea, even if the soil isn't very sandy), but make the hole big, at least 2 feet wide and 1½ feet deep.

Remove the soil from the planting hole, and mix it with organic mate-rial—as much organic matter as you have soil if the soil is very sandy. Set the rose in the hole (see the next pages), and fill in around it with the improved soil.

IS YOUR SOIL GOOD ENOUGH?

If your garden soil is growing good vegetables (or crops of husky weeds), it will probably grow good roses just as it is.

TYPES OF ORGANIC MATTER

All types of organic material—homemade compost, sawdust, steer manure, leaf mold, shredded bark, and so on—are suitable for improving soil. If you are buying wood by-products such as saw-dust and bark, which are not decomposed, make sure nitrogen has been added; otherwise, they'll steal nitrogen from the soil as they decompose. Fresh animal manure will burn rose roots; if you use it, prepare the soil a few months ahead of planting, so the manure has time to decompose.

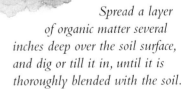

Spread a layer of organic matter several inches deep over the soil surface, and dig or till it in, until it is thoroughly blended with the soil.

Water the area, and then let the amended soil settle for at least a week before you plant.

Planting Your Roses

It's natural for roses to grow. Help them along by planting them at the right time and deep enough to survive the winter. Be sure to take care of the rose's roots—don't let them dry out.

WHEN TO PLANT

The best time to plant roses depends on your climate and whether you are starting with bare-root roses or container-grown plants.

SCHEDULE FOR BARE-ROOT ROSES

Plant bare-root roses at any time during the dormant season provided your soil is not frozen or waterlogged. January and February are the prime planting months in much of the South, Southwest, and West Coast, where winter temperatures seldom dip below 10°F/−12°C. In regions where subfreezing temperatures alternate with warm spells, and freezing weather can last for many months, late fall and early spring are the best planting times. In decidedly cold-winter regions, you need to plant in spring.

SCHEDULE FOR CONTAINER-GROWN

ROSES You can plant container-grown roses during much of the year—as soon as they are available in winter, provided the ground is not frozen, and on through to fall in mild regions. The best time is spring, when the plants have the longest growing season ahead in which to get established.

If you plant during hot weather, be sure to water your roses frequently.

PLANTING AT THE PROPER DEPTH

Planting a rose at the right depth is always important, but it's of special concern in cold-winter climates—especially if you're planting a budded rose.

BUDDED ROSES Some gardeners keep the bud union above ground; others bury it 1 or 2 inches or even more. The reasoning is this: Exposed to air and sunlight, the bud union tends to produce more canes, but in cold-winter climates an exposed bud union (even when well-protected) is more vulnerable to freezes.

In mild-winter regions where temperatures are unlikely to fall below 10°F/−12°C, you can safely plant your roses with the bud union at or slightly above soil level.

In colder-winter areas, however, choose one of the two options on the right.

OWN-ROOT ROSES If your rose is growing on its own roots (it has no bud union), planting depth is less critical. Where winters are mild, set the rose so the juncture of roots and canes is even with or slightly below the soil level. In cold-winter areas, set the juncture about 1 inch below the soil.

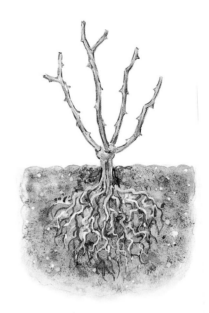

More Canes

Position the bud union just above soil level, and then protect the plants heavily during winter or tip and bury them under the soil (the Minnesota tip; see page 341).

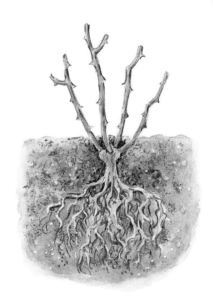

More Protected

Position the bud union 1 to 2 inches (some rosarians recommend as much as 4 inches) below soil level. This is a better guarantee of survival than the first option, but cane production may be less robust.

ALLOWING GENEROUS SPACE

Roses perform best, are less prone to disease, and are easier to maintain when they are not crowded.

Space hybrid teas and grandifloras 2 to 8 feet apart. Use the 2-foot spacing in very-cold-winter regions where the growing season lasts just 3 to 4 months and roses generally don't grow large. Space 3 feet apart in the warmer parts of the West, Southwest, and South; space 4 to 8 feet apart, depending on the variety, where there's little or no frost to enforce winter dormancy and roses grow prodigiously (much of Florida, the Gulf Coast, California, and parts of Arizona).

Space floribundas (which are usually smaller than hybrid teas and grandifloras) 1½ to 3 feet apart; plant small-growing miniatures from 1 to 1½ feet apart, and the larger-growing ones 2 to 3 feet apart. Use the closer spacing in colder regions, the widest one where winters are mild.

Rose species (wild roses), shrub roses, and old garden roses need the most room. Allow 5 to 6 feet between plants where winters are cold and long, and up to twice that distance in the mildest areas. In any climate, allow a bit more room for varieties with long, arching canes.

GOOD PLANTING WEATHER

A perfect planting day is calm and overcast, because strong breezes and bright sunlight dry out rose canes and roots.

PLANTING A BARE-ROOT ROSE

It's easy to plant a bare-root rose successfully. First, prepare the soil (see pages 320–321). Until you are ready to put the rose in the ground, keep the roots in water or cover them with a damp cloth so they don't dry out. To plant, follow these steps:

1 Soak the roots in a bucket of water for up to 24 hours before planting, to replenish any moisture they may have lost during transportation and storage. If the rose looks thoroughly dry and shriveled, you might try to plump it back to health by immersing the *entire plant* in water for 24 hours.

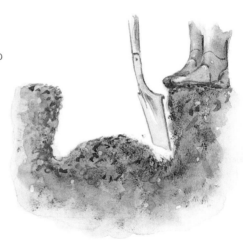

2 Dig a large planting hole with sides that slope outward from top to bottom (save the removed soil for step 3). The hole's sides should be rough, not smoothly sculpted. Leave a "plateau" of undug soil at the center of the hole to keep the rose from settling too low. Dig the edges deeper to help the roots penetrate into the soil.

3 Form a firm cone of soil over the plateau at the bottom of the hole. Trim any damaged roots or canes from the rose; then place it in the hole, spreading the roots over the soil cone. Put a stick across the hole to gauge the proper planting depth (see "Planting at the Proper Depth," on the opposite page). Fill in the hole with soil, and water well. If the plant settles, raise it gently, and fill in with more soil. Some gardeners mound mulch over the rose for a few weeks to prevent moisture loss from the canes.

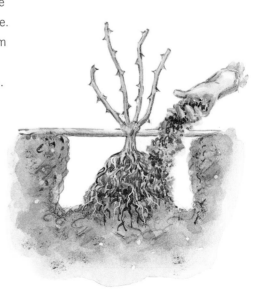

PLANTING A CONTAINER-GROWN ROSE

Container-grown roses are even easier to plant than bare-root ones. First, prepare the soil (see pages 320–321). Before planting, water the rose (still in its pot) thoroughly. To keep the roots moist, don't leave the rootball exposed during the planting process for any longer than necessary. To plant, follow these steps:

1 Dig a large planting hole with sides that slope outward from top to bottom (save the removed soil for step 3). The hole's sides should be rough, not smoothly sculpted. Leave a "plateau" of undug soil at the center of the hole to keep the rose from settling too low. Dig the edges deeper to help the roots penetrate into the soil.

2 Take the rose out of its container. If it doesn't slide out easily, lay the container on its side, and gently roll it from side to side to loosen the rose, or tap the pot's sides or bottom sharply, or run a knife around the inside edge. With your fingers, loosen the soil on the surface of the rootball, and uncoil any circling or twisted roots.

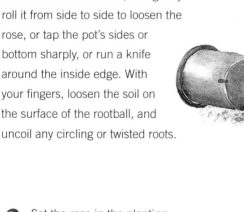

3 Set the rose in the planting hole on the soil plateau. Spread out the loosened roots. Add soil beneath the rootball, if needed, to adjust the planting depth (see "Planting at the Proper Depth," on page 322). Fill in the hole with soil, and water well. If the plant settles, raise it gently, and fill in with more soil.

PLANTING MINIATURE ROSES

Most miniatures are small-scale descendants of larger bush roses; they're virtually always grown on their own roots and sold in containers. Plant them as you would a regular container-grown rose, but set them slightly lower than they were in their nursery containers to encourage more roots to form. Because they have shallow root systems, you need to keep the soil constantly moist after planting.

The miniatures known as pot minis, tiny roses sold already flowering in 2½- or 4-inch pots, have spent their lives in green-houses. Before you plant them outdoors, get them used to out-door temperatures gradually, moving them out to a sheltered spot for a few hours every day for several days. Plant them in a container (at least 6 inches deep) or in the ground, as instructed above for regular minis. Water them more frequently though.

PLANTING AND STAKING STANDARD ROSES

Standard roses must be staked at planting time. Choose a sturdy stake that is 2 feet longer than the stem of the standard, measuring from just beneath the bud union at the top of the stem to the soil level in the nursery can—or, if your rose is bare-root, to the old soil level on the stem.

Follow the general planting instructions on pages 322–323, but install the stake before you place the plant in the hole.

Staking a standard.

Drive it 2 feet into the ground, just off the center of the hole, on the side of the prevailing wind—place your back to the prevailing wind as you face the hole, and set the stake on your side of center. This way, when the wind blows, the stem will lean away from the stake and not thrash against it.

After planting, check that the top of the stake sits just below the bud union. Because the bud union is vulnerable to damage, it should be clear of the stake.

Tie the stem to the stake in two places: once near the top of the stem, and again halfway up it. Use a figure 8 tie or any other kind of tie that will keep the stem from rubbing against the stake.

Planting a Climber

Check whether your plant is a rambler. If it is, you may prune it back low to the ground before planting it, thus encouraging it to produce strong new shoots from the base. If it's any other type of climber, however, don't prune it before planting.

Follow the general planting instructions on pages 322–323, but make these adjustments: Make your planting hole about 1½ feet away from the wall, arbor, or post. Set the plant at a 45° angle, so the canes lean toward the support. If you are planting against a wall, spread all the roots, as best you can, away from the wall.

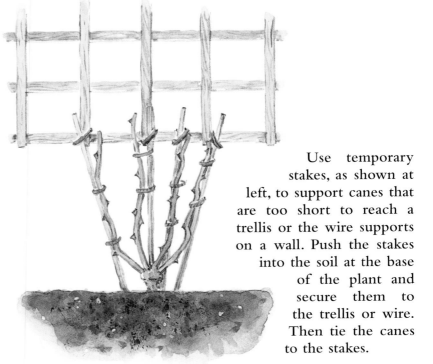

Use temporary stakes, as shown at left, to support canes that are too short to reach a trellis or the wire supports on a wall. Push the stakes into the soil at the base of the plant and secure them to the trellis or wire. Then tie the canes to the stakes.

Growing Roses in Containers

Roses thrive in containers. You just need to spend a little time choosing suitable roses and the right containers for them.

CHOOSING A ROSE

Roses with small or moderate growth habits grow more happily in containers than large roses do. Choose miniatures, polyanthas, floribundas, patio roses, or small shrub roses. You'll find a list of varieties recommended for containers on page 299.

CHOOSING A POT THAT'S BIG ENOUGH

Miniature roses thrive in containers as small as a 2-gallon nursery can. But regular-size bushes, standard roses, and climbers need large containers to give their roots room to develop well. A container roughly the size of a 5-gallon nursery can is the very smallest you should consider, and bigger ones are much better. Wooden half-barrels offer plenty of space—even enough room to plant annuals beneath the rose.

ALLOWING FOR GOOD DRAINAGE

Any container you choose must have drainage holes. Use an electric or hand drill to make holes in wood or plastic containers; for clay and concrete, use an electric drill with a masonry or carbide bit. One or two ½-inch holes are sufficient for a small container; for a half-barrel, drill four or five ¾-inch holes. To prevent cracking, drill with a small bit first, then increase the bit size until you have made the hole as big as you want.

Be sure there's space beneath your container for water to drain away. If necessary, raise it on small blocks of wood or sit it on pot "feet" that you can buy for this purpose. Keeping the container off the floor also helps prevent water stains on decks and patios. Saucers are even more effective at keeping water off a surface that might stain, but be sure to empty them so that the soil in the pot doesn't get soggy.

Choosing an Attractive Container

Choose a container that will look attractive when the rose you've chosen is planted and the pot is set in place—on the deck, atop a wall, gracing the front steps. If you are not adept at creating beautiful compositions with unusual pots, choose a simple container made of wood or glazed terra-cotta. The natural, earthy colors of these materials show off the beauty of any rose and fit well into most settings.

To be more playful, match the container to elements in its surroundings—steel to echo steel furniture or handrails, blue-glazed clay to match a blue door. Be wary about choosing a multicolored pot or one with a very decorative pattern; when the rose is blooming, the combination of pot and plant may look fussy.

Think twice before you buy a container with a narrow neck—you may have to break it when the rose needs repotting. In hot-summer climates, avoid black containers, which  absorb heat and scorch roots. Also steer clear of unglazed terra-cotta pots—they are porous, so you'll need to water more to compensate for moisture lost to evaporation.

BEST PLANTING TIME

The best time to plant a rose in a container is spring. Then the roots have a chance to become established before summer heat arrives.

PLANTING THE ROSE

You can plant either container-grown roses or bare-root roses in a container. For soil, buy a bagged potting mix from a local garden center or nursery. These mixes are guaranteed to retain moisture and also to drain well, which is important for roses.

A CONTAINER-GROWN ROSE

Water the rose thoroughly, and then remove it from its nursery container. If it doesn't slide out easily, lay the container on its side, and gently roll it from side to side to loosen the rose, or tap the pot's sides or bottom sharply, or run a knife around the inside edge. With your fingers, loosen the soil on the surface of the rootball, and uncoil any circling or twisted roots. Then follow the steps on the right.

1 Pour moist (but not soaking wet) potting mix into the container—enough to hold the top of the rootball about 2 inches below the container rim. Place the rose in the container, and fill in around it with more moist potting mix. Press the mix in firmly.

2 Gently water the newly planted rose until water runs out the drainage holes. If the rose settles more than 2 inches below the rim, grasp it just above the roots, and jiggle it upward to the proper height; then fill in with more soil. Water often to keep the soil moist. Fertilize regularly with a liquid or timed-release fertilizer (see page 331).

A BARE-ROOT ROSE

Soak the rose's roots in a bucket of water for up to 24 hours before planting, to replenish any moisture they may have lost. If the rose looks thoroughly dry and shriveled, you might try to plump it back to health by immersing the *entire plant* in water for 24 hours.

If the roots are a little too long to fit the container, bend them slightly to fit. If they are so long you must coil them to fit, cut them back just enough to eliminate the coiling. Then follow the steps on the right.

1 Pour moist (but not soaking wet) potting mix into the container so that it forms a firm cone—high enough to hold the bud union (or, if the rose is not budded, the juncture of roots and canes) about 2 inches below the container rim.

2 Spread the roots over the cone, and fill in around them with more moist potting mix. Fill the container to within 2 inches of the rim. Press the mix in firmly. Then follow step 2 for "A Container-Grown Rose," above.

Watering Your Roses

To perform well, roses need moisture all the way down through their root zone, all through the year. Water them deeply and consistently.

HOW MUCH TO WATER

A rose needs water to the full depth of its roots (assume 16 to 18 inches), in enough quantity to keep the soil constantly moist but not waterlogged. Grown without enough water, the plant will be smaller, the flowers will be smaller, and the blooming season will be shorter.

We can't tell you how many gallons to apply, because the amount varies enormously, according to whether the soil is sandy (needs more water) or mostly clay. To figure out how much water it takes to wet your soil, a day after you water dig a hole to see how far the moisture has penetrated.

The first sign of underwatering is wilting shoots at the top of the bush. Overwatering, without sufficient drainage, causes the lower leaves to turn yellow and drop.

HOW OFTEN TO WATER

Soil type also plays a role in how often roses need watering. During "average" spring weather, roses growing in sandy soil may need watering every 5 days, those in loam every 7 to 10 days, and those in clay every other week. Roses need less frequent watering if it rains or if you mulch (see the box on the left). They need more frequent watering if the weather is windy, hot, or sunny.

If you don't know your soil well, water deeply—in fact, always water deeply; light sprinkling does no good—so that the entire root zone is moist, and check the soil 4 or 5 days later: Dig a small hole with a trowel. If the soil is moist at a depth of 2 to 3 inches, don't water yet; if it's dry, turn on the water now.

Once you've checked your soil on a few occasions, you'll get a sense of how often to water. Remember to water in the dormant season, as necessary, for as long as the soil is not frozen.

Mulching Conserves Water

Placing an organic mulch around your roses keeps the soil cool and moist, so you don't have to water as often; it also suppresses weeds and provides nutrients to the soil as it decomposes. Mulching roses is altogether a very good idea.

Organic mulches include homemade compost, pine needles (although they acidify the soil), shredded leaves from hardwood trees (oak leaves, for instance), redwood bark, sawdust, rice hulls, ground corn cobs, well-rotted manure, and lawn clippings (as long as they are free of herbicide and grass and weed seeds). In windy spots, avoid lightweight mulches like straw. If you use corn cobs or undecomposed wood products such as bark or sawdust, sprinkle a high-nitrogen fertilizer over the soil surface to replace the nitrogen that the mulch will steal from the soil as it decays.

A straw mulch.

Spread the mulch in early spring. In cold-winter regions, wait until the soil has warmed; if you spread mulch too early it will delay soil warming and will slow growth. Make a layer 2 to 3 inches thick, extending it to within an inch of the base of the rose. Add more mulch when necessary to keep the layer thick.

Generally, it's best to water just the soil, not the rose foliage, because many fungal diseases that attack the leaves, like black spot, flourish in a damp environment. If you want to hose the leaves to remove dust, aphids, or mites, do it early on a sunny day so that the leaves won't stay damp for long.

HOW TO WATER

Most gardeners use some form of irrigation. Even when it rains in the summer, rainfall is not always sufficient to penetrate deep into the soil, where the rose roots are.

FLOOD BASINS Flood basins are the low-cost option. Around each bush, build an earthen dike 2 to 6 inches high and about 3 feet across. When it's time to irrigate, gently flood the basins, using a hose. If you dislike the look of the basins, spread a mulch in and between them, or, if the soil is level, forget the individual basins and instead surround the entire rose bed with a berm.

DRIP IRRIGATION Drip irrigation consists of lines of flexible black tubing and emitters that release water in drips or light sprays. It can be automated and is relatively inexpensive and simple to install. It is usually the best choice if you want to conserve water. To water a rose bed, lay the tubing in parallel rows to soak the whole bed. For widely spaced bushes, snake the tubing to and around the individual plants. Place mulch over the tubing to hide it.

PERMANENT SPRINKLERS A permanent sprinkler system supplied by underground pipes is the costliest option. It lets you automate the irrigation and avoid loops of tubing on the soil surface, but you may need professional help to install it. If roses in your area are prone to fungal diseases, choose bubbler or flat-spray sprinklers, so the foliage doesn't get wet.

Watering Roses in Containers

Roses growing in a container need more frequent watering than roses in the ground. Don't wait for them to wilt. Check the soil often, daily in hot or windy weather. If you find dry soil 2 inches below the surface, water the container immediately.

The rootball may shrink away from the sides of the container if it gets very dry. Plug the gaps with potting soil, and water the rootball slowly or pour water into the saucer and let the rootball absorb it that way.

Feeding Your Roses

Roses won't dwindle away and die without fertilizer, but virtually all modern roses and many of the old garden sorts need at least a little to perform well.

WHEN TO APPLY FERTILIZER

After planting your roses, generally wait until after the first flush of bloom before fertilizing them.

In subsequent years, apply fertilizer soon after you finish pruning, to give the roses a boost for putting out new growth when the growing season begins. Do a follow-up application after the first round of spring bloom. For old garden roses that flower only once, this is the only fertilizer you need apply. For repeat-flowering roses, continue to apply fertilizer through the summer.

HOW OFTEN TO FERTILIZE

How often to fertilize repeat-flowering roses depends mostly on the product you choose. Timed-release fertilizers last many months. Granular fertilizers last longer than liquid ones.

Soil type also affects the situation. Clay holds dissolved nutrients longest, so you can fertilize less frequently. If your soil is sandy, you may want to fertilize more often to compensate for faster leaching of the nutrients.

Heavy rainfall can flush fertilizer from the soil and leave roses short of necessary nutrients.

AN ORGANIC FERTILIZER PROGRAM

Organic fertilizers are derived from the remains of living organisms; examples include bone meal, alfalfa meal, cottonseed meal, blood meal, fish emulsion, and steer manure. Many gardeners prefer them because these materials occur naturally and sustain the natural life of the soil. They have a low percentage of nitrogen (with the exception of blood meal) and release their nutrients slowly, so they are unlikely to cause fertilizer burn or to leach large amounts of nitrates into the groundwater.

Start in spring by spreading an organic mulch rich in nutrients, such as compost or aged manure. Then incorporate alfalfa meal or cottonseed meal or a mix of the two into the soil (see "Dry Fertilizer," on the next page) after the first flowering and again in midsummer. Alternatively, after the mulch, use fish emulsion or seaweed extract regularly through the season; because these are in liquid form, they provide nutrients quickly to the rose's roots.

A SYNTHETIC FERTILIZER PROGRAM

Synthetic fertilizers are manufactured and have names like ammonium sulfate and potassium phosphate. These fertilizers are high in nutrients and can be very fast acting. But they are easily leached from the soil by rainfall or regular heavy irrigation.

The simplest program to follow is regular applications of synthetic "rose food," a complete fertilizer, containing phosphorus and potassium as well as nitrogen. Alternatively, to reduce the number of applications, apply a timed-release synthetic fertilizer in early spring and then just one or two applications of rose food or a plain nitrogen formula in late spring and summer.

EPSOM SALTS

Epsom salts (magnesium sulfate), an old home remedy for aches and pains, has become popular among rose growers, who say it encourages strong new canes to grow from the base of the bush. Apply it along with your other

How to Read a Fertilizer Label

The label on a bag of fertilizer shows the percentages of nutrients in the mix. The three numbers shown most prominently, called the N-P-K ratio, refer to the amounts of nitrogen (N), phosphorus (P), and potassium (K) in the bag. For example, an 8-4-4 fertilizer contains, by weight, 8 percent nitrogen, 4 percent phosphorus, and 4 percent potassium. Nitrogen is the most critical element. It promotes good foliage growth and flowers, and you need to add it to the soil to give roses enough.

fertilizer after pruning, using about ¾ cup for each plant. A second, slightly smaller application after the first flush of bloom may also be beneficial.

WHEN TO STOP FERTILIZING

In cold-winter areas, it's conventional to stop fertilizing for the year sometime during the summer, so that the roses have time to harden off and become properly resistant to cold before winter. The rule of thumb about when to stop is no later than 6 weeks before the expected first frost; that means stopping anywhere between August 1 and early September. (For the expected first-frost date in your area, ask your local nursery.)

In mild-winter areas, gardeners may stop fertilizing in October to encourage winter dormancy. They can then remove the leaves and spray the canes to help keep plants healthy (see page 336). Some gardeners fertilize year-round.

APPLYING FERTILIZER

Before applying fertilizer to the soil, be sure to water first. If you apply fertilizer to dry soil and then water it in, it can burn the rose's surface feeder roots. There are three basic types of fertilizer: dry, liquid, and foliar.

DRY FERTILIZER To apply dry fertilizer, first lightly scratch the soil surface (no more than 1½ inches deep) beneath your rose.

If you mulch, you'll have to move some of the mulch aside. Work as far out as the branches spread, but leave several inches around the base of the rose uncultivated. On the cultivated soil, scatter the amount of fertilizer recommended on the package label; then water again well.

LIQUID FERTILIZER To apply liquid fertilizer to individual roses, mix the fertilizer in a watering can, and apply the recommended amount to each bush.

For larger plantings, consider buying an injector device that lets

you run the fertilizer solution through your watering system. The simplest is a siphon attachment that draws liquid concentrate from a pail into your hose or watering line. Another sort is a small canister that attaches between the faucet and the hose (or drip irrigation line).

FOLIAR FERTILIZER To apply foliar fertilizer, spray the nutrient solution onto the undersides of the rose leaves, where it is quickly absorbed. Use any liquid fertilizer recommended for foliar application. Because foliar fertilizer can burn leaves in hot weather, don't use it when temperatures will reach 80°F/27°C or above.

FERTILIZING CONTAINERS

Roses growing in containers need more fertilizer than roses growing in the ground. Choose a liquid fertilizer or a dry fertilizer, and look for a complete fertilizer with nitrogen, phosphorus, and potassium, plus micronutrients. Apply the fertilizer every 2 weeks, reducing the strength of the solution if necessary to match the recommendations on the package.

Fixing Cultural Problems

Roses grow luxuriantly in most soils, especially if you supply some nitrogen. Occasionally, they suffer from nutrient deficiencies or extreme weather conditions or a lack of proper care or even too much of a good thing. Use the information here to identify and correct the most common cultural problems.

NOT ENOUGH WATER
Stems and leaves droop, starting at the top of the bush. Soak the soil to a depth of 18 inches, and water again, deeply, whenever the soil is dry 2 to 3 inches beneath the surface.

BALLING
Buds fail to open fully; petals turn brown; common among roses with thin petals growing in damp climates. Choose rose varieties carefully (see pages 317–319). Plant in full sun, so moisture doesn't linger in the buds. May also be caused by a heavy infestation of aphids or thrips (see pages 338–339).

NOT ENOUGH IRON
Large yellow areas on leaves (veins stay green); new growth is most affected. Apply an iron chelate fertilizer for fastest results. Most likely caused by a high pH soil (see page 320).

FERTILIZER BURN
Leaf edges or whole leaves turn brown and crisp; growth slows. Water heavily to flush some of the fertilizer out of the soil. Remove burned foliage. Follow the directions on the fertilizer package to determine the correct dose. Always water the soil before applying fertilizer.

NOT ENOUGH PHOSPHORUS
Dark green leaves with purple tints on undersides; leaves drop early. Apply a high-phosphorus fertilizer to the root zone; if you are planting new bushes, mix it into the backfill soil. Check the soil pH (see page 320), which may be the cause of the problem.

NOT ENOUGH NITROGEN
Light green or yellow-green leaves, with some red spots; leaves drop pre-maturely; slow overall growth; symptoms appear first at base of bush. Apply a nitrogen fertilizer regularly (see pages 330–331). A high-nitrogen foliar fertilizer, sprayed onto the undersides of the leaves, will give the fastest results.

HERBICIDE DAMAGE

Leaves twist and die; new growth is stunted and deformed; the plant may die if the dose was heavy. Should you accidentally spray an herbicide on your bush, hose it off immediately. Once the herbicide is absorbed, the damage is done, and all you can do is cut off the affected growth. Use herbicides only on still, cool mornings, and read the label carefully. Wait at least 2 months before mulching with grass clippings or manure that may contain traces of herbicide. Don't use your watering can to mix or apply herbicides.

SUNBURN

Blackened areas on canes; leaf burn, especially on south and west sides of bush. Excessive heat is the cause. Cut off affected growth. Move the rose away from a reflective surface, such as white masonry or a white rock mulch. To reduce the chances of sunburn, don't let the soil dry out or the bush become defoliated because of pest problems.

NOT ENOUGH MAGNESIUM

Yellowing and dead tissue at the center of leaves; old leaves are most affected. Apply a fertilizer that contains a high level of magnesium or Epsom salts (see page 330).

NOT ENOUGH MANGANESE

Bands of yellow between the leaf veins. Apply a fertilizer that contains chelated micronutrients, including manganese. Check the soil pH (see page 320); if it's above 7.0, that may be the cause of the problem.

TOO MUCH WATER

Leaves turn yellow (first the veins and leaf center) and fall off, starting at the base of the bush. Water only when the soil is dry 2 to 3 inches beneath the surface and only to moisten the dry layer. Check drainage.

NOT ENOUGH POTASSIUM

Brown, brittle edges to old leaves; small flowers. Apply a fertilizer high in potassium, such as potassium nitrate. Check the soil pH (see page 320), which may have caused the problem.

Cutting Roses for Indoors

After working in your garden, bring at least one or two roses indoors with you. If you care for them a little, they'll last long enough to brighten someone's spirits—and inspire you to grow more roses so you can bring dozens inside.

LONG-LASTING BOUQUETS

How long your roses last indoors depends on the rose varieties you are growing (see the box below) and how careful you are with the cutting.

CAREFUL CUTS For the longest-living bouquets, cut your roses early in the morning or in late afternoon to early evening. Choose stems with flower buds that are no more than half open. Make cuts just above a leaf, which will encourage a new stem to grow. Check that the portion of stem you are leaving behind has at least two sets of leaves—cutting too long a stem may weaken your plants.

Carry a bucket of water with you into the garden, and put the cut stems into it immediately. Once you've finished cutting, take the bucket out of the sunlight into a cool place, and fill it with warm water until most of the leaves are submerged and the flowers are just above the water surface. To enhance their freshness, leave the roses immersed like this for about an hour.

Before placing your cut roses in a vase, recut the stems under water, making slanting cuts. Underwater cutting helps prevent air from getting into the stems, which causes bent necks. Remove any foliage that will be underwater in the vase, so it doesn't rot and spoil the water.

AFTERCARE Recut the stems under water every other day, removing about ½ inch of stem each time. To extend the life of the flowers and keep the water looking fresh, use floral preservatives.

Roses for Cutting

Any rose is beautiful indoors. But the most popular roses for cutting—because they have long, strong stems and large flowers and they are easy to maintain in a bouquet—are hybrid teas and grandifloras. The best of those have thick petals (which don't wilt quickly) and blooms that open slowly. Here are a number of proven choices, listed by flower color.

PINK
Bewitched
Bride's Dream
Fame!
Queen Elizabeth

RED
Mister Lincoln
Olympiad
Uncle Joe

ORANGE/WARM BLENDS
Brandy
Fragrant Cloud
Just Joey
Touch of Class

YELLOW/CREAM
Elina
Gold Medal
St. Patrick

LAVENDER
Lagerfeld
Paradise

WHITE
Crystalline
Honor
Pascali

MULTICOLOR
Double Delight
Peace

Cut at a 45° angle just above a leaf with five leaflets, preferably one pointing toward the outside of the plant.

How to Display Roses Beautifully

You can show off a single exquisite rose alone, fill a vase with dozens of the same variety, make a duo of roses and one other flower, or include your roses in a bouquet of many different flowers. Try them all, if you have enough roses.

RIGHT: A perfect rose can be an effective arrangement all by itself. Displaying it this way encourages people to discover every detail of its beauty and complexity. Place it where it can be appreciated at close range—beside a sink or on a bedside table, for example.

ABOVE: A mixed bouquet that's predominantly one color is the easiest kind to make. These roses, columbine, and Jupiter's beard are lovely together because they combine a range of pinks, from deep to very light. Green foliage pulls the colors together. White flowers add sparkle and freshness.

ABOVE: This all-of-a-kind 'Pat Austin' rose bouquet looks particularly lavish because it contains more than two dozen roses. For a natural look, flowers in various stages of development have been included. A few geranium leaves soften the rim of the vase and hide the ¼-inch grid of floral tape, which is holding the roses in place.

BELOW: Fluffy white hydrangeas form a bed of clouds for these sweet pink roses. The rose stems are cut fairly short and inserted one by one among the hydrangea heads, which hold them in place without the need for a frog or floral foam. The silver bowl makes a bright, elegant container.

Pests and Diseases

Many sprays kill the good bugs as well as the bad ones. It's often best to tolerate a little damage in order to keep your garden naturally healthy.

CLOCKWISE FROM TOP LEFT:
Black spot, caterpillar, mite damage, cane borer damage, aphids.

STEP ONE: PREVENT

Well-tended, healthy roses are less likely to fall prey to damaging pest infestations or diseases. Here are eight ways to reduce the risk of trouble:

- Choose roses that are suitable for your climate (see pages 317–319) and that have a natural resistance to disease (check the listings on pages 364–410). Be aware that disease resistance is more common among old roses and shrub roses than among hybrid teas.
- Get your roses off to a good start: choose a sunny, well-drained site, amend the soil, plant at the recommended spacing, and water sufficiently (see pages 320–329).
- Fertilize appropriately, not too little but also not too much—bugs love lush new leaves (see pages 330–331).
- Start the year with a garden cleanup: After pruning, clear the ground of prunings, leaves, and old mulch. Then, before the plants leaf out, spray them and the soil to kill any insect eggs and disease spores (especially black spot); use a combination of horticultural oil and lime-sulfur fungicide. After this preventive spraying, no other sprays may be necessary.
- Encourage beneficial insects (see "Step Three") to make their home in your garden, to feed on aphids and other rose pests.
- Prune your roses to improve air circulation around the foliage, which helps prevent disease.
- Avoid overhead watering and spray heads that splash water from the soil onto the leaves, because water droplets can spread disease spores. If you need to hose off pests, do it early in the day, so the leaves dry quickly; wet leaves are an invitation to black spot and other fungal diseases.
- Inspect your roses frequently, to catch problems early.

STEP TWO: PICK, HOSE, CLEAN UP

A very effective way to control pests on your roses is to pick them off and drop them in a bucket of soapy water. If the bugs are tiny, hose them off with a strong jet of water. The number one rose pest—aphids—can be controlled this way. And it's a sensible, effective first line of defense against spider mites, beetles, cane borers, rose scale, leafhoppers, rose slugs, and caterpillars.

To combat many of the rose diseases, think first of simply picking and disposing of the affected leaves or flowers and cleaning up any fallen leaves or flowers, which may harbor eggs or disease spores.

STEP THREE: SUPPORT THEIR ENEMIES

Many rose pests, including aphids, rose slugs, rose scale, spider mites, grasshoppers, and thrips, have natural enemies that prey on them, such as ladybugs (lady beetles), lacewings, beetles, flies, spiders, birds, and wasps.

Support these predators by finding a place in your garden for their favorite plants, such as fennel, Queen Anne's lace, and yarrow. Avoid broad-spectrum pesticides, which kill the predators as well as the pests. If a spray may be harmful to predators, spray

---

LOCK THEM UP

Young children love to play with liquids and containers, so store *all* of your garden pesticides—even some of the "natural" ones are toxic to humans—out of their reach, preferably under lock and key.

Controlling Pests and Diseases the Natural Way

Here are the most common "natural" products:

INSECTICIDAL SOAP SPRAYS Made from potassium salts of fatty acids, these control soft-bodied pests, such as aphids, in their immature nymph stages.

HORTICULTURAL OILS These refined oils from plants or petroleum smother insects, eggs, and disease spores. Depending on type, they can be used during the growing season or as a dormant spray. Oils may burn leaves, so do not use them if the temperature is expected to exceed 80°F/27°C.

SODIUM BICARBONATE (BAKING SODA) Mixed in water, this is a home remedy for powdery mildew and black spot (see pages 338–339). Keep it out of fish ponds. Also consider commercial products containing potassium bicarbonate.

NEEM A botanical insecticide derived from the bark of a tree native to India, neem repels pests and causes them to stop feeding. It also inhibits black spot and powdery mildew. May be less effective in hot weather.

PYRETHRUM Derived from a chrysanthemum species, this and its more concentrated form, pyrethrin, are highly toxic to insects. Note that the more common pyrethroid products are made from a synthetic chemical; they are more toxic and stay in the environment longer than pyrethrum and pyrethrin.

late in the day when they are not active.

Some predators, also known as *beneficial insects* or *biological controls,* can be purchased and released into the rose garden. Ladybugs eat aphids; lacewings attack thrips. Bt *(Bacillus thuringiensis)* is a bacterium that kills caterpillars; milky spore, another bacterium, kills the larvae of Japanese beetles.

CLOCKWISE FROM TOP LEFT: *Thrips damage, grasshopper, powdery mildew, downy mildew.*

It is important to release predators at an appropriate time—for example, not before the pests are present, or the predators will have no food; and only during the pest's larval stage if the predator doesn't touch the adults. You may need to make more than one release. Ask your local nursery or mail-order supplier for advice on timing.

STEP FOUR: USE NATURAL POISONS

Many naturally occurring substances are lethal to pests and diseases. It makes sense to use these before resorting to synthetic poisons, because natural remedies have less impact on the environment. But be sure to read the labels, for these controls are not harmless; many kill beneficial insects and can harm fish. Apply them only if you already have an infestation or have good reason to fear one.

STEP FIVE: CONSIDER SYNTHETIC CHEMICALS

Think of synthetic pesticides as the last resort. Many common ones are toxic to humans, animals, and the beneficial predators in your garden; they may also be approved for use only on ornamental crops, not edible crops, so be extremely careful if you have a vegetable garden near your roses.

If you need to spray with a synthetic chemical to save a rose, look for a substance targeted to the specific pest or disease. Combination products and broad-spectrum sprays that kill everything are avoided by gardeners who treasure the diversity of natural life in their gardens.

Synthetic products can be safe and highly effective when they are used properly. Read the label carefully, wear protective gear as advised, and use the product only as directed—it's against the law to do otherwise.

Controlling Pests and Diseases

Respond quickly to pests and diseases but don't overreact. Once you've identified the problem, using these pages, choose the control least likely to harm the environment and beneficial insects. These controls are listed first.

APHIDS (GREENFLIES)
These soft bodied, ⅛-inch-long insects may also be red, brown, or black. They cluster on new growth and suck out the sap, which causes damage only if they are present in very high numbers. Hose off with water; purchase and release ladybugs (their natural enemy); spray with insecticidal soap, neem oil, or pyrethrum products if the plant is truly infested.

BEETLES
Several kinds. The Japanese beetle, with bronze body and metallic head, is a serious pest in eastern states. Many other beetles do little damage; some eat holes in buds, petals, and leaves. Handpick; treat the soil and lawn with milky spore (this works for Japanese beetles but not all others); spray with neem oil or a suitable insecticide.

DOWNY MILDEW
Purplish red leaf spots with smudged edges; leaves turn yellow and drop; canes can also become infected. Spores spread in water, overwinter in cane lesions and on old leaves. Warm weather, above 80°F/27°C, kills spores, so you may not need to spray with fungicide. Remove prunings and old leaves. Avoid overhead watering, unless done early in day.

BLACK SPOT
Circular black spots on leaves, sometimes with yellowing around spots. Disease thrives in warmth and is spread by water (rainfall, sprinklers). If left unchecked, it can defoliate a plant. Canes can also become infected. Remove affected leaves and debris; spray with a combination of baking soda and summer-weight horticultural oil (2 teaspoons of each per gallon of water), or neem oil, or a suitable fungicide. Avoid overhead watering. Since spores overwinter, do careful winter cleanup, and apply a preventive spray (see page 336).

RUST
Small orange spots on leaf undersides enlarge to form thick, powdery masses of orange spores; yellow blotches appear on leaf surfaces. If severe, rust can defoliate a plant. Remove affected leaves, clean up debris, avoid overhead watering; spray with a suitable fungicide.

Save the Leafcutter Bee

Leafcutter bees cut semicircular holes in rose leaves and use the material to line their nests. Don't take action against these bees; they are important pollinators in the garden.

THRIPS

These nearly invisible insects deform and discolor flower petals by rasping and puncturing the tissue. White and pastel flowers are their favorites. Plants in dry soil are more likely to be attacked, so water properly. Remove affected buds; release lacewings; spray with insecticidal soap, neem oil, or a suitable insecticide.

SPIDER MITES

These tiny spider relatives suck juices from the leaf surface, causing dry-looking, russeted leaves; in heavy infestations, undersides of leaves show silvery webbing. Mites increase rapidly in hot, dry weather. Hose off leaf surfaces and undersides with water regularly during an infestation; spray with horticultural oil (summer weight), insecticidal soap, or neem oil.

SCALE INSECTS

Small, round to oval, grayish crusty scales on canes are unsightly and stunt growth. Scrape off with a nail file; spray with insecticidal soap; spray with horticultural oil in winter (see pages 336–337).

MOSAIC VIRUS

Yellow zigzag, vein clearing, or splotching pattern on leaves; reduced plant vigor and flower production. The virus is transmitted through the budding process, at the commercial grower's nursery. No treatment or cure.

ROSE MIDGES

Tiny fly larvae rasp the tender tips of new growth, causing them to shrivel and blacken. Stop the larvae from pupating in the soil by laying sheets of black plastic under the plants. Remove affected shoots. Clear away leaf litter, weeds, and debris. Try insecticidal soap on the foliage, or spray plants and soil with a suitable insecticide.

POWDERY MILDEW

A fungal disease producing gray to white, furry to powdery coating on new leaves, stems, and flower buds. Leaves become crumpled and distorted. Is encouraged by crowding (poor air circulation), shade, and fog. Spray with a combination of baking soda and horticultural oil (2 teaspoons of each per gallon of water), or neem oil, or a suitable fungicide.

CATERPILLARS AND WORMS

Larvae of various flying insects skeletonize or chew holes in leaves (look for leafroller caterpillars inside a rolled leaf). Handpick; spray with Bt.

CANE BORERS

These worms bore into new shoots or pruned canes and consume the stem's pith. New growth tips wilt and collapse. Handpick by cutting off infected stems and crushing them. Prune canes until you find healthy pith.

Winter Protection

In mild regions, all roses are safe from the risk of winter freeze damage. In much of the country, however, preparing the plants for winter is part of routine rose-garden maintenance.

IS PROTECTION NECESSARY?

Generally speaking, modern hybrid teas, grandifloras, miniatures, and climbers run little risk of damage in areas where winter lows seldom dip below 10°F/ −12°C. Some floribundas and many miniature, shrub, and old garden roses can remain unprotected where 0°F/−18°C is a standard low temperature, and a few species and species hybrids are even tougher. Be sure to check the listings on pages 364–410 for information on specific varieties.

Occasional temperatures colder than those minimums may or may not hurt exposed canes. Dry or very cold winds greatly increase the risk of damage. Plants are also more susceptible to winter injury if temperatures fluctuate and the soil freezes, thaws, and refreezes.

SURVIVAL TIPS

The best insurance against winter losses is to buy roses that are hardy in your region (see pages 317 and 319). It makes sense to mound your roses, as additional insurance, if you live in a very-cold-winter climate; you must do it if you are experimenting with marginally hardy roses. You can also minimize the effect of winter cold on your roses in these ways:

- Plant them against a sheltered wall or on the lee side of windbreak shrubs; avoid the most exposed and the lowest-lying spots in the garden, which are the coldest.
- Plant budded roses so that the bud union is protected below ground (see page 322).
- Provide good care to your roses during the growing season;

roses defoliated by pests or diseases are not so well equipped to survive a hard winter.

- Stop deadheading and stop fertilizing 6 weeks before first frosts are expected in your area, so no new growth is produced. Your plants then have a chance to produce hips and go into a protective deep dormancy.
- Be sure to continue watering until the ground freezes. If the roots are well watered, the plants can better resist the desiccating effects of wind.

MOUNDING AND TIPPING

Don't rush to cover or tip your roses too soon. Begin with a thorough cleanup in early or midautumn, clearing away all old leaves and spent flowers, and removing all debris and mulch from around the base of each plant. Then strip away and discard any leaves remaining on the canes, and cut back any dead or diseased canes.

MOUNDING

Cut the canes back to 3 feet, and tie them together; then mound soil at least 1 foot high over the base of the bush. After the soil mound freezes, cover it with an insulating mound of straw, hay, cut conifer boughs, or other noncom-pacting organic material. To hold the mound in place, surround the bush with a wire mesh cylinder. If you use a rose cone instead of wire mesh, be sure it has ventilation, and weight it down with a brick.

OWN-ROOTS MAY COME BACK

Own-root roses are favorites in very cold climates, because, if the canes die during winter, the roots often send up new replacement canes in spring. Budded roses do the same, but the canes from the roots are of the rootstock variety not the glorious budded variety growing before.

If you are tipping your roses (the most thorough form of protection and usually used only for nonhardy roses in really cold-winter areas), do it before the soil freezes, around midautumn. If you are mounding your plants, you can mound the bases of the plants in early to midautumn, but wait until the soil freezes to apply mulch over the mounds. Just before you expect the soil to freeze, give the roses a deep soaking.

REMOVING PROTECTION

Resist the urge to remove protection at the first sign of spring; temperatures may drop suddenly many times before spring truly arrives. In general, the best time to uncover the plants is the time best for dormant-season pruning in your area (see page 348).

PROTECTING POTTED ROSES

The soil in containers gets much colder in winter than ground soil. If you live in a region where temperatures fall more than a few degrees below freezing, move your pots into an unheated garage or shed (the temperature mustn't fall below 10°F/−12°C). Let the plants go into dormancy, remove any remaining leaves, and water only occasionally. In spring, when all danger of frost is past, take them back outdoors, prune lightly, and start fertilizing them again.

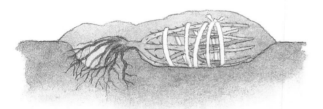

THE MINNESOTA TIP
Make a trench to one side of the rose. Loosen the roots on the side of the plant away from the trench, and bend the plant over into the trench, being careful to bend the roots—not the trunk or it may snap. Cover the roots and the plant with soil.

To tip a standard, loosen the roots on the side opposite the bud union at the base of the trunk. Then bend the plant over the bud union into the trench, being careful to bend the roots—not the trunk or it may snap. Pin the trunk in place, and cover both trunk and canes with soil.

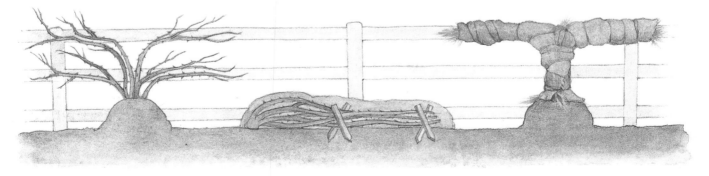

NONHARDY CLIMBERS
Where winter lows range from 5° to 15°F/−15° to −9°C, protect nonhardy climbing roses with soil mounds (left). Where lows will drop below −10°F/−23°C, remove the climbing canes from the supports, pin them, and cover them with soil (center). Where low temperatures fall in the 5° to −10°F/−15° to −23°C range, you can leave the climbing canes in place if you insulate them with straw and then cover the insulated canes with burlap (right).

Propagating Your Roses

With so many roses available for sale, why bother starting your own? Simply the pleasure it brings, is the usual answer: imagine being able to point out a beautiful rose that you nurtured from seed or a piece of stem one spring.

TAKING CUTTINGS

A simple way to propagate roses is to take cuttings during the blooming season. (Using suckers and layering, described on the next page, are even simpler methods but not possible with all roses.) If you haven't already set your heart on propagating a particular variety, take your cuttings from the most vigorous rose you can find, because those have the best chance for success. But remember that it's against the law to propagate a patented rose by cuttings. Most new roses are patented; look for the symbol on the label.

Once you've selected a rose, follow these steps:

1 Choose a strong young shoot that has just flowered. Take an 8-inch-long portion of the stem, cutting just above a leaf at the flower end of the stem and just beneath a leaf at the bottom end. Use very sharp pruners, and make slanting cuts, as shown.

2 Remove the lowest leaves. Dip the bottom end of the stem in rooting hormone. Fill a pot with perlite, and place the stem into it. Water the pot well.

3 Insert a stake into the pot, put the pot into a plastic bag, and tie the top of the bag (the stake keeps the bag upright). Place the pot in a shaded but well-lit spot outdoors. Water only if the cutting wilts; it probably won't need watering until step 4.

4 When new growth shows that the cutting has rooted (within 1 to 2 months), remove the bag gradually, over 7 to 10 days, opening the top just a little to start, and water just enough to keep the leaves from wilting. Place the new plant in the garden during the next planting season.

SOWING SEEDS

Roses grown from seed are rarely as lovely as the parent plant, but it's fun to harvest the rose hips and see what comes up in the seedling tray. You can expect seedlings of bush hybrid teas, grandifloras, floribundas, and miniatures to flower as soon as 6 weeks after germination. Climbing roses and some shrub and old garden roses may not bloom for 2 to 3 years.

Follow these steps:

1 Pick rose hips when they turn from green to red, orange, yellow, or brown; don't wait until they shrivel. Place them in a plastic bag; cover them with damp peat moss or sand; and place them in the vegetable crisper of your refrigerator.

2 After 6 to 8 weeks, the hips will be black and partially decomposed. Take them out of the bag and remove the seeds. To test the seeds for viability, put them in water; sow the ones that sink.

3 Fill individual pots (at least 3 inches deep) with moist seed-starting mix. Sow the seeds ⅜ to ½ inch deep and 2 inches apart. Lightly firm the surface. Germination may start within 6 weeks and continue for 2 months or over a year.

4 In mild-winter regions, you can place the pots outdoors, away from wind and direct sunlight. In cold-winter regions, place the pots in a greenhouse, or indoors on a sunny windowsill or under artificial lights. As soon as the danger of frost is past, take them into a sheltered place outdoors. After a year, you can plant the new roses in the garden, at planting time.

USING SUCKERS AND LAYERS

Some roses growing on their own roots produce *suckers* at the base of the plant. The suckers have roots of their own, so you can dig them up in early spring (keeping plenty of soil around the roots) and plant them elsewhere just as you would a new rose.

Layers are almost as easy as suckers, but you need a rose that produces long, flexible canes. In spring, select a mature cane growing close to the ground, and bend it to touch the soil. Loosen the soil there, and work in a shovelful of compost.

Long, flexible canes make layering this 'Mme. Isaac Pereire' rose easy.

With a sharp knife, slice along the underside of the cane where it will touch the ground; make the cut about 3 inches long and no deeper than halfway through the cane. Dust the cut with rooting hormone, and insert a pebble to hold it open.

Bury the cut section, and hold it down with a piece of wire. Firm the soil around it, keep the soil moist, and, when you are sure roots have formed (a few months to a year), cut the new plant free from the parent plant. Dig it up, keeping plenty of soil around the roots, and plant it in its new location.

A Rose Gardening Calendar

Roses thrive on attention, at least a little in every season. If you care for them at the proper time, you'll be rewarded—they'll grow strong and healthy, and you'll be able to sit down and enjoy them.

SPRING

- Finish planting new bare-root roses; plant new container-grown roses (see pages 322–325).
- Plant roses into display pots (see pages 326–327).
- Start a new rose by digging up and replanting a sucker from an own-root rose, or by layering a long, flexible cane (see page 343).
- Apply fertilizer to give roses a boost for the coming growing season (see pages 330–331).
- Spread an organic mulch around roses; in cold-winter climates wait until the soil has warmed (see page 328).
- Check the soil for moisture (see page 328); if necessary, begin watering deeply to keep the root zone moist.
- Start inspecting your roses frequently for pests and diseases (see pages 336–339); aphids are common on new spring growth.

- Remove and discard suckers from budded roses (see page 350).
- To propagate, take rose cuttings from shoots that have just flowered (see page 342).
- Fertilize roses after the first round of spring bloom (see pages 330–331).
- After they have flowered, prune climbing roses, ramblers, shrub roses, and species roses that flower only in spring (see pages 348–355).

SUMMER

- Check the soil for moisture (see page 328); if necessary, water more often to keep the root zone moist. Check roses in pots daily in hot or windy weather (see page 329).
- Check the mulch; replenish it if necessary, to keep the layer 2 to 3 inches thick.
- Remove weeds as they appear. Try not to disturb the mulch.

- Train and tie in the long new shoots of climbers.
- Deadhead repeat-flowering roses to encourage the next cycle of blooms.
- Prune away weak, broken, or diseased stems.

- Disbud grandifloras and floribundas to make a more impressive flower display.
- Continue applying fertilizer to repeat-flowering roses through the summer; in cold-winter climates, stop fertilizing 6 weeks before the expected frost date (see page 331).
- Keep the rose garden clean: remove fallen leaves, petals, and debris.
- Continue to watch for pests and diseases.
- Visit rose gardens and rose nurseries to study new varieties and plant combinations.

FALL

- Check soil moisture (see page 328); reduce the amount of irrigation or the number of applications if appropriate, but keep the entire root zone moist as plants prepare for dormancy.
- In cold-winter regions, drain underground sprinkler irrigation systems before the first freeze; drain above-ground drip lines,

Controlling Weeds

Spreading a thick layer of mulch (see page 328) around your roses in spring and keeping it topped up throughout the season are good strategies for controlling weeds. Laying landscape fabric is another option, but you'll need to put mulch on top of it so it doesn't show.

Pull weeds as they appear. If you like to use a hoe, hoe shallowly or you may damage the rose roots. Herbicides must be used with extreme caution around roses; if spray touches the rose foliage, it will kill the leaves and possibly the whole plant (see page 333).

and consider taking them up and storing them indoors until spring.

- To grow new roses from seed (see page 343), collect hips when they change color; don't wait until they shrivel.

- Assess the performance of your roses this year. Decide which, if any, need to be replaced. Place your rose order early.
- If you are planning to plant new roses, check the soil pH and drainage, and get the ground ready (see pages 320–321). In most climates, it's best to delay planting until early spring (see page 322).
- In cold-winter climates, protect roses against winter freeze damage (see pages 340–341).

WINTER

- Check soil moisture (see page 328); continue watering while the soil is not frozen.

DISBUDDING CLUSTER ROSES

Many roses, particularly grandifloras and floribundas, produce flowers in clusters or sprays, the central flower opening first, followed by the others. To get a bigger, better, and neater display, pinch out the central bud, so it doesn't hold back the opening of the others.

Deadheading

Deadheading your roses—cutting off the flowers when they fade—keeps the garden looking fresh and attractive. If you have repeat-flowering roses, it will also give you more and bigger flowers during the next bloom cycle.

Cut the dead flower, or spray of flowers, back to a healthy leaf with five leaflets, on the outside of the bush, two or three leaves down from the flower if the bush is mature and vigorous (remove less stem on a new or struggling bush). A new shoot will grow from the leaf axil.

If you have lots of free-flowering roses and little time for deadheading, you can shear the bushes instead, but they may take longer to bloom again.

- Clean tools, sharpen pruners, check the expiration dates of pesticides.

- Plan any new rose beds, checking color combinations and planting distances (see pages 317 and 323).
- In cold-winter regions, if plants start to heave out of the soil, pack soil around them as best you can.
- For best selection of new rose plants, order from mail-order catalogs or watch for the arrival of bare-root plants in local nurseries (see page 314).

- In mild-winter regions, plant new bare-root roses in January and February (see pages 322–325).
- In cold-winter regions, remove winter protection from roses only at the end of the dormant season, just before pruning (see page 341).
- As growth buds along the canes begin to swell, prune hybrid teas, miniatures, and varieties of climbers and shrub roses that repeat-bloom (see pages 348–355).
- After pruning, do a careful winter cleanup, removing prunings, dropped leaves, and old mulch. Then spray plants and soil with horticultural oil and lime-sulfur fungicide to kill any insect eggs and disease spores (see page 336).

CHAPTER THREE

Pruning and Training

ONCE YOU FALL IN LOVE *with your roses, it's irrelevant that roses have grown wild and been beautiful for thousands of years without pruning or training. You want to prune them so that they have a chance to rejuvenate every year and produce a more lovely show. From there, you go on to dreaming how a rose might look trained over a window, its cupped blossoms sagging into view from inside the house. Or perhaps you'd like to try a pillar of roses with the flowers aloft and gay against the sky, or to set a rose loose into a tree so you can witness it making its own wild way through the foliage into the sun.* ❧ *Pruning and training are fairly simple. Most roses, as you'll find out in this chapter, don't need much pruning. And training can be as easy as pegging a few canes into the ground or tying them to the beams of an arbor.*

'Coral Dawn' climbing a rustic log arbor.

Pruning Roses

All roses benefit from annual pruning. You may enjoy pruning each cane with precision pruning shears, or perhaps your instinct is to lop off the top of the bush with hedge shears; sometimes it matters which you do, and sometimes it doesn't. Here's what you should know about pruning different types of roses.

WHY PRUNE?

Pruning allows you to shape your rose bush, and it's good for the plant. With careful pruning, you can make your rose pleasingly symmetrical, or direct it toward an arch or a window, or reduce its size if it has grown out of bounds. Pruning also encourages new growth, promotes large flowers, and keeps a rose healthy.

The benefits of pruning outweigh any consequences of the few mistakes you might make as you learn to prune. So relax, if you are pruning for the first time; you'll be a confident pruner by next year and able to correct any errors.

WHEN TO PRUNE

For *repeat-flowering roses,* the best time to prune is toward the end of the dormant season, when the buds along the canes begin to swell. In mild-winter regions, this can be as early as January; in the coldest-winter areas, April may offer the first opportunity.

In the many areas where chilly, wintry days alternate with more springlike spells during March and April, it's hard to know when to prune. Gardeners in those areas often use one of two indicators: either they prune when forsythia comes into bloom, or they prune about 30 days before the area's last expected killing frost (your local nursery will know when that is).

For *roses that flower only in spring* (mostly old garden roses), pruning at the end of the dormant season cuts away some of that spring's potential flowers. For the most abundant bloom, therefore, delay your major pruning until just after these roses flower. But remove any dead or old, unproductive canes while the plants are dormant and leafless, because it's easier to see what you are doing then.

PRUNING TOOLS

To prune roses well, you need at least two basic tools: sharp pruning shears and a small pruning saw.

The shears can do most of the work, but a pruning saw helps you remove large-diameter old canes and dead wood. Buy hook-and-blade (bypass) shears, the type with two curved blades that cut like scissors, rather than the anvil type, which has one curved and one flat blade that make a snap cut. The hook-and-blade design makes cleaner, closer cuts and is less likely to crush stems than the anvil type.

Two other tools may also be useful, if you have certain types

CLOCKWISE FROM TOP LEFT: *Hook-and-blade pruning shears, pruning saw, hook-and-blade loppers, hedge shears with extra-long handles.*

THINNING, CUTTING BACK

There are two forms of pruning: thinning and cutting back. It's important to know the difference, because they produce quite different results.

THINNING Thinning is removing an entire shoot or cane back to its point of origin. For example, you might cut a spindly shoot back to a strong cane or cut an unproductive old cane back to the base of the plant. These thinning cuts don't stimulate new growth the way cutting back does (see below). Thin to remove dead wood and damaged, diseased, or weak canes; to reduce the size of a bush; and to open up the center of a bush.

CUTTING BACK Cutting back is removing just part of a cane, not all of it as you do in thinning. You cut back to just above a bud, which stimulates buds just below the cut to grow. The immediate result of cutting back is a smaller, more compact bush—but it does not stay that way for long. The cut-back canes soon put out vigorous new growth and produce large flowers. Cutting back is also useful to direct growth: if you want a strong cane to grow over a window or away from the center of the bush, cut it back to just above a bud that is facing in the desired direction.

Shearing is a quick, imprecise form of cutting back. It's particularly suitable for hedges and ground covers.

Slip-on protective sleeves.

of roses. Loppers are helpful for pruning the interiors of large bushes, which may be too congested and thorny to reach comfortably with regular pruning shears. Their long handles also give you more leverage to make clean cuts in thicker canes. Again, choose a hook-and-blade design.

Hedge shears are the best tool for pruning a lot of landscape roses (shrubs, hedges, or ground covers). Consider buying ones with extra-long handles to extend your reach.

Before you start to prune, put on a pair of protective heavy gloves that thorns can't puncture. You might also like to equip yourself with protective arm wear.

Thinning cuts are shown in gray, cutting-back cuts in red.

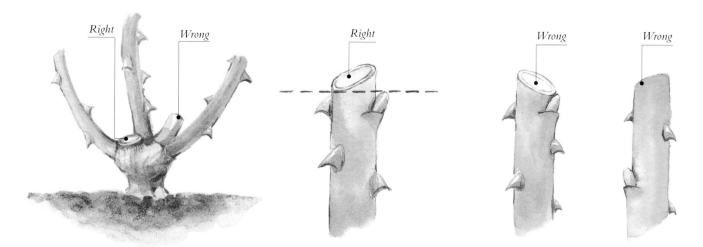

Right   *Wrong*   *Right*   *Wrong*   *Wrong*

When you're removing an entire cane (thinning), cut it flush with the bud union or growth from which it sprang. Don't leave a stub, or it will die back, allowing entry to disease.

When you're cutting back a cane, make a slanting cut at approximately a 45° angle. The lowest point should be opposite and slightly higher than the bud; the upper point should be ⅛ to ¼ inch above the bud. If you angle the cut down toward the bud, water will drain into it and might damage it; if you cut too high, the stem may die back and become diseased.

GOOD CUTS

Pruning cuts do no harm if you make them cleanly and in the correct places. However, if you leave behind stubs and crushed or ripped canes, you create new havens for pests and diseases.

Before you start cutting, be sure your tools are sharp and up to the job: pruning shears can usually easily cut canes up to ½ inch thick; for thicker canes, switch to loppers or a saw.

Start the cut in the correct place, not too high and not too low.

CUTS AFTER FROST DAMAGE

In cold-winter climates, frosts may kill part or all of each cane. Cut back past the blackened areas as far as necessary until you reach healthy tissue. You'll know when you get there because the pith, at the center of the cane, will be white, not brown.

WHAT TO DO WITH SUCKERS

On budded plants, a shoot called a *sucker* may grow from below the bud union. Cutting it off won't solve the problem; you'll get new suckers before long. Instead, grasp the sucker and pull it *down* and off the plant. If it originates from below ground, gently remove the soil, track the sucker back to the roots, and pull it off from there.

DON'T PRUNE TOO HARD

Pruning removes some of the reserves of nutrients that are stored in the canes for the next season's growth. When you have the option (when the canes haven't been killed back too far by frost), prune your rose lightly or moderately.

Removing a sucker.

PRUNING HYBRID TEAS, GRANDIFLORAS, FLORIBUNDAS, AND POLYANTHAS

Regardless of where you live, you can follow the two steps below to prune these popular modern roses. Almost all are repeat-flowering, so you prune them at the end of the dormant season, when the buds begin to swell. Before you start, spend a minute studying your bush; notice that the canes are of varying thicknesses, ages, and health.

1 *Thin* the bush: Entirely remove old canes that produced only spindly growth last year. Also remove weak, twiggy branches. Now open up the bush by removing branches that cross through the center. This will give you a vase-shaped plant—slender or fat, depending on your rose's natural habit—without a central tangle of twigs and leaves that can harbor insects and diseases. (Gardeners in very hot climates often just shorten these central branches, rather than removing them, so they will produce leaves to shade the canes.)

2 *Cut back* the remaining stems. In mild-winter regions, reduce the length of the remaining healthy stems by about one third (a little less than that for floribundas and polyanthas). In cold-winter regions, where the canes may be killed back to their protecting mound, you have to cut back more heavily—until you reach white healthy pith. Make slanting cuts (see the previous page) to outward-facing buds, which will help keep the center of the bush open. (If you want to encourage a spreading bush to grow more upright, cut to inward-facing buds.)

Remove the Prunings

When you have finished pruning—either deadheading in summer or the annual pruning during winter or spring—rake up the prunings, and dispose of them. Left in place, they may become a breeding ground for pests and diseases that overwinter in debris. Composting the prunings isn't recommended, because it may not kill the insect eggs and fungal spores. Once you have raked the garden clean after winter pruning, before the plants leaf out, spray your roses with a preventive mix of horticultural oil and lime sulfur.

Raking up debris.

Mystery Bushes

What should you do if you don't know what kind of bush rose you have? Prune it lightly, removing only dead, damaged, diseased, or crossing stems. During the bloom season, compare the flowers to the photographs on pages 364–410, take a bouquet

of flowers to a local rose society meeting, or contact the American Rose Society (see page 415). Once the rose is identified, you can prune it properly when the following pruning season comes around.

Pruning dead wood.

canes (many of the hybrid perpetuals, for example) can be trained in the manner of climbers and pruned the same way as climbers (see pages 354–355). The floribunda shrub roses can be pruned hard, like regular floribundas (see page 351).

Some of the old garden roses—most gallicas, albas, damasks, centifolias, and moss roses—flower only once, in spring, so they should be pruned after flowering. Most of the modern shrub roses and the other old garden roses—most bourbon, china, portland, hybrid musk, and rugosa roses—are repeat-flowering and are pruned at the end of the dormant season, just before new growth begins.

To prune old garden and shrub roses, follow the two steps below.

PRUNING OLD GARDEN ROSES AND SHRUB ROSES

Most old garden roses and shrub roses need only a light annual pruning—provided you've allowed these typically vigorous roses sufficient space. They are most graceful if you let them grow naturally, with a little shaping as necessary and thinning to take out the old wood.

The roses in these groups that produce long, arching

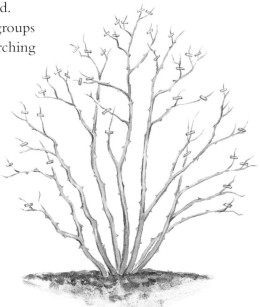

1 *Thin* the bush. Cut out a few old, woody stems at the base of the bush if the center of the bush is dense and overcrowded. To keep the bush healthy, remove any dead, damaged, or weak canes and any canes rubbing against or crossing one another.

2 *Cut back* the remaining canes lightly, pruning just the tips. If the center of the bush is crowded, shorten the side shoots to outward-facing buds.

PRUNING GROUND COVERS

Ground cover roses need little pruning. Prune the shrubby types the same way you prune shrub roses: remove any dead, damaged, or diseased canes; and open up the center, if it is too dense, by removing woody canes, shortening the laterals, and pruning the tips of the canes.

Keep rambler types in check by cutting back any wayward, overlong stems. To spread the roses over a larger area, peg down the shoots (see pages 360–361) instead of cutting them back.

PRUNING MINIATURE ROSES

The quick way to prune miniature bush-type roses is to take a pair of hedge shears to them, and trim them into a pleasing dome shape. The more precise, finicky method is to prune them as you would hybrid teas and floribundas (see page 351); the bushes will look nicer up close if you prune them carefully like this.

A rangy miniature bush rose before pruning.

After careful pruning it is compact and ready to grow vigorously.

Prune lightly if the bushes are growing and flowering well; if they are rangy—miniatures grown in pots sometimes are— reduce the length of the canes by half or even three-quarters, to encourage bushy, compact, new growth.

Prune miniature ground covers, standards, and climbers as you would their full-size counterparts.

Pruning Rose Hedges

Prune hedges as you would the individual roses in them. Cut back any shoots that depart from the general lines of the hedge, but don't try to force the bush into a formal shape; by nature a rose hedge is informal. To encourage new canes to grow from the bases of the bushes remove some of the old woody canes and apply Epsom salts (see page 330).

'Complicata' hedge.

PRUNING CLIMBING ROSES

A variety of roses climb: true climbers, climbing varieties of bush roses, ramblers, and some shrub roses that get carried away in mild climates. What they all have in common is long, flexible canes that produce most of their flowers along the length of the cane.

The best way to prune a climber depends on whether it repeat-blooms through the summer—most popular climbers do—or blooms only once, in spring. (To prune a rambler, see the next page.) After pruning, train the remaining canes into position (see pages 356–361).

REPEAT-BLOOMING CLIMBERS

After planting, let the rose grow unpruned for 2 to 3 years, which will give it time to become established and build up strength to put out good climbing canes. Remove only dead, damaged, or diseased

> ### GLUE FOR BORERS
>
> It's unnecessary to treat small pruning cuts, but you can seal them with dabs of white glue if you have had cane borers (see page 339). Very large pruning cuts may heal more quickly if you treat them with pruning paint.

shoots during this time. In subsequent years, just before growth begins in spring, follow the steps as shown below.

1 Remove the old and obviously unproductive canes—the ones that produced no strong growth the previous year.

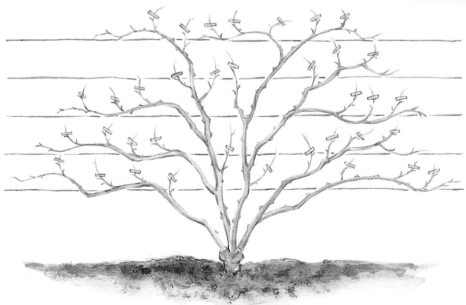

2 On the remaining canes, cut back to two or three buds all the side branches (called *laterals*) that flowered during the last year; this will encourage spectacular new blooms all along the canes.

SPRING-BLOOMING CLIMBERS

Prune just after flowering. To replace old canes with vigorous new ones, thin out the oldest and least vigorous canes. The plant will put out new canes and laterals on the remaining canes to carry next spring's flowers.

PRUNING RAMBLERS

Prune ramblers after they have finished flowering and when new growth has begun. Completely remove canes that have just flowered and show no sign of producing any long, vigorous new shoots. On canes that have flowered and are starting to send out some strong new growth, cut back to the new growth.

PRUNING STANDARD ROSES

Prune standard bush roses as you would a regular bush rose of that type (many are hybrid teas; see page 351), but pay particular attention to shaping the head so that it looks symmetrical and is open at the center. During the growing season, check for and remove any shoots that grow from the trunk.

Weeping standards, which may be created with a rambler or a climbing or ground cover rose, shouldn't be pruned as hard as hybrid teas. For 2 years after planting, simply remove any dead, damaged, or diseased wood, and cut back any weak shoots. In following years, remove some of the old canes—

Pruning Roses in Trees

A fairly restrained climber growing in a small tree may be reachable from a ladder when it's time for deadheading and pruning. A rampant rambler planted beneath a tall tree, however, may quickly escape way over your head to the treetop—and from there to another treetop or your neighbor's roof. If you need to keep it within bounds, remove most of the old canes every year.

Rambler 'Alberic Barbier'.

just one or two each year if the rose is only moderately vigorous; as many as you like if the rose is supervigorous. To complete the pruning, follow the pruning guidelines for the individual rose type.

Shape the head symmetrically.

Pinch off shoots from the trunk.

Training Roses

Roses don't climb naturally, the way ivy and honeysuckle do. You must train them—tie their stems to something—if you want them to grow up a wall or archway or other structure. Perhaps you'd like them to grow along the ground or to form neat, unusual shapes—well, you can train them those ways too.

BENDING CANES FOR MORE FLOWERS

Left to their own devices, the long canes of most climbing roses grow upward, and the buds along the canes don't develop. Most of the leaves and flowers are then at the top of the plant.

To bring the flowers closer to eye level, and increase the number of flowers, train the canes horizontally, or as close to horizontal as they'll go. This encourages the many buds along the canes to grow; a few will develop as *growth laterals,* but most will become *flowering laterals* profuse with blooms.

Some short, stiff-caned climbers (called *pillar-climbers* or *pillar roses*) grow upright and still produce flowering laterals. They are more like narrow shrubs than actual climbers, and the canes don't require bending.

ROSES ON FENCES AND WALLS

For a low fence, select a modest-growing climber or lax shrub rose; a rampant climber is suitable only for a very large wall. You can tie the rose canes directly to a rail fence. On solid fences and walls, you need to install supporting wires or a trellis.

WIRES Screw eyebolts into the fence posts or wall; space them about 4 feet apart. Place the lowest wire 18 inches off the ground and the wires above it 15 inches apart. Leave as much space as you can between the wires and the fence or wall to improve air circulation around the rose and reduce the risk of pests and diseases, such as mildew.

If your surface is stone, concrete, or brick, drill holes for the eyebolts, insert expanding anchors (preferably lead) into the holes, and screw the eyebolts into the anchors.

Thread 14-gauge galvanized wires between the eyebolts, and twist the wires to secure them in place. Tie the rose canes to the wires; don't weave the canes around them.

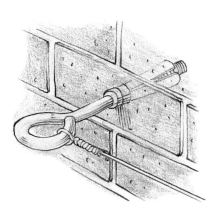

Attaching wires to masonry.

TRELLIS A trellis with an 8- to 12-inch grid is a suitable support for climbing roses. Use wood spacer blocks to keep the trellis at least 4 inches away from the fence or wall, for good air circulation. Because the trellis will be heavy, attach it to the wall framing or to posts, not just to thin siding or fence boards. Use lag screws; on a masonry wall, insert expanding anchors. In very-cold-winter climates, if you plan to tip your climber to protect it (see pages 340–341), avoid weaving the canes through or around the trellis, because they'll be difficult to remove.

Good air circulation.

TRAINING After pruning in spring, allow any new young canes to grow upward; make no attempt to train them. Take the mature canes, last year's growth, bend them from the vertical, and tie them in place.

If the canes are fairly limber, you can angle them outward into horizontal positions; if they are a bit stiffer, you may have to settle for spreading them into a vase outline. In either case, tie the canes into place with their tips pointing downward.

Training a climber.

Follow the same procedure with the mature growth laterals, which will encourage them to produce flowering laterals.

TIPS ON TIES

Avoid using wire or nylon twine to tie rose canes to supports, because it will cut into the canes as they grow. Plastic tape is soft and stretches. You can also use raffia or twine, but you must remember to loosen those ties periodically.

Tie the tape or twine around the support first, and then tie it once again, loosely, around the rose cane.

Tie twice.

Classic Partners: Rose and Clematis

Choose a clematis that flowers at the same time as your rose and that you can prune in the same season. (Clematis are divided into three groups: group 1 clematis are pruned after flowering, at the same time as roses that bloom only once a year; groups 2 and 3 are pruned in early spring, before flowering, the same time as repeat-blooming roses.) Choose a clematis variety with a modest growth habit, not a rampant plant that will overwhelm and perhaps pull down the rose.

Let the rose grow for 2 years to build a framework for the clematis to climb on. Plant the clematis at least 1 foot from the rose, preferably in a place where its roots will be shaded. It will support itself by twining its leaf stalks around the rose stems.

Clematis 'Elsa Spath' (group 2) has a modest growth habit.

ROSES ON ARCHES, ARBORS, AND PERGOLAS

It's easy to grow a rose over an arch, an arbor, or a pergola. First, choose a variety that will grow to a height appropriate for your structure (some climbing hybrid teas reach only 7 feet; some ramblers grow to 30 feet). Plant one rose at the foot of each post, about 15 inches away from it, to allow room for the rose's roots. Then train the roses as follows:

ROSES IN TREES

A climbing rose can support itself in a tree once its long canes, with their hooked thorns, have threaded through the branches. But you'll need to help it scale the trunk.

Plant the rose a few feet from the tree trunk, so it has room to spread its roots. And place it on the side of the tree that faces the prevailing wind, so that the wind will blow the rose stems against and into the tree, instead of away from it. As you plant, tip the rose toward the tree, as you would if you were planting a climbing rose next to a wall (see page 325).

If the rose canes do not reach the tree trunk, place stakes, as

1 Guide the rose canes up the posts. Spiral them around the posts—separately, not as a bunch—to encourage flowering laterals to develop along the canes. Tie the canes to the posts with bands of plastic tape or twine.

2 When the canes reach the tops of the posts, bend them over the structure. For a full effect, train stems along each piece of an arbor or a pergola, the diagonal braces as well as the horizontal beams. Wrapping the canes around the beams, or the top of the arch, also makes the roses fuller. Tie the canes in place regularly during the growing season.

RAMBLERS VERSUS CLIMBERS

Ramblers grow fast and are easy to train, because they have lax, pliable stems. But nearly all of them bloom only once, in spring, and they need heavy annual pruning. Climbers generally repeat-bloom through the summer, but they have stiffer canes, which are harder to train.

shown, to guide the rose canes to the tree. Secure the stakes to a band of twine or tape looped around the tree.

As the rose grows, loop twine or plastic tape around the trunk, as shown, to secure the canes. Check at least twice a year that the ties are not cutting into the rose canes or the tree trunk. To increase flowering, spiral the canes around the trunk.

As soon as the rose gets a hold among the tree branches, you can remove the climbing aids.

Guide stakes.

Trunk ties.

Rose Swags for Paths and Boundaries

To make a swag, attach a rope—the thick nautical type—or chain to hang loosely between the tops of two posts. Plant a rose at the base of each post, and train the canes up the posts, securing them to the posts with plastic tape. Then train the canes along the swag to meet midway.

The rose shown here is a wichuraiana hybrid rambler, 'Alberic Barbier'. Wichuraiana hybrids are ideal for swags because they have long, flexible canes and heavy bloom clusters. But usually they flower only once, in spring, and they need retraining every year: At the end of the growing season, untwine the canes, and cut away all but two or three of the strongest new ones on each rose. Train those up the posts, and wind them around the rope or chain, tying them at intervals with tape.

Any climber with fairly limber canes can be grown on a swag. Follow the pruning instructions on page 354, and then train the canes along the swag and tie them in place.

Swags make a beautiful boundary for a rose garden: Install a series of posts, and train the roses in just one direction, toward the next post, except for the rose at the last post, which has to be trained back toward its neighbor. If you don't need to walk under the swag, perhaps loop it a little lower than shown here, so you can smell the roses.

A swag of 'Alberic Barbier'.

ROSES ON TRIPODS AND PYRAMIDS

An open, spreading shrub or small climber, such as a hybrid musk, bourbon, or kordesii climber, is easy to train on a pyramid or tripod. Plant the rose in the center of the structure; if your pyramid or tripod is extra-large, plant a rose inside each corner. Attach the most vigorous canes to the corners. Weave the canes around the structure as they grow, tying in the new growth while it is flexible. Use new canes that grow from the base of the plant to plug any large gaps.

A rose on a tripod.

PEGGING DOWN ROSES

The flexible canes of vigorous shrub, rambler, and hybrid perpetual roses can be bent down and pegged to the ground, for various effects. Make pegs from lengths of wire, forked twigs, or notched or crossed wood stakes.

GROUND COVER ROSES You can peg down the long arching stems of ground cover roses if you want to spread the plants over a larger area, keep them looking prostrate, or increase flowering. Simply bend the stems, lay them along the ground, and peg them in place. (The stems may root where they touch the ground; see page 343 if you'd like to propagate more plants this way.)

Pegged-down ground cover.

Roses on Pillars and Posts

Choose a climbing rose that grows only 8 to 10 feet tall (small shrub climbers, called *pillar roses* are ideal). Plant it about 15 inches away from the foot of the pillar, to allow room for the rose's roots. Wind the canes in a spiral around the pillar; you can run all of them in the same direction or braid them—half clockwise, half counterclockwise—for an attractive pattern.

Consider the best way to tie the canes to the pillar. If your pillar is like the one shown, you can use simple tape ties around its horizontal extensions. If the pillar is a smooth column, you might attach eye hooks to it and tie the canes to those, or you might loop soft green or clear plastic tape around the column to secure the canes. For an elegant pillar or one that is easily damaged, consider installing a slim trellis against one side of it or running wires from the top of the pillar to the ground and attaching the canes to those.

A rose braided on a pole.

Creating a Cascade of Flowers

To encourage a climber to produce a cascade of flowers down to the ground, rather than a cluster all at the top, prune the canes to different heights. Train the mature canes to climb to the tallest point, such as a balcony or the peak of an arbor. Cut back a couple of younger canes to the halfway point, and cut back the very youngest canes to within 2 or 3 feet of the ground.

'Joseph's Coat' in bloom
from top to bottom.

SHRUBS AND CLIMBERS Pegging down some of the long stems of vigorous shrub and climbing roses will encourage them to produce more flowers along the stems. It also helps to keep vigorous roses within bounds. Bend the stems carefully, so they don't snap. Ask someone to hold the stem as you peg it; it may hurt you if it flies loose.

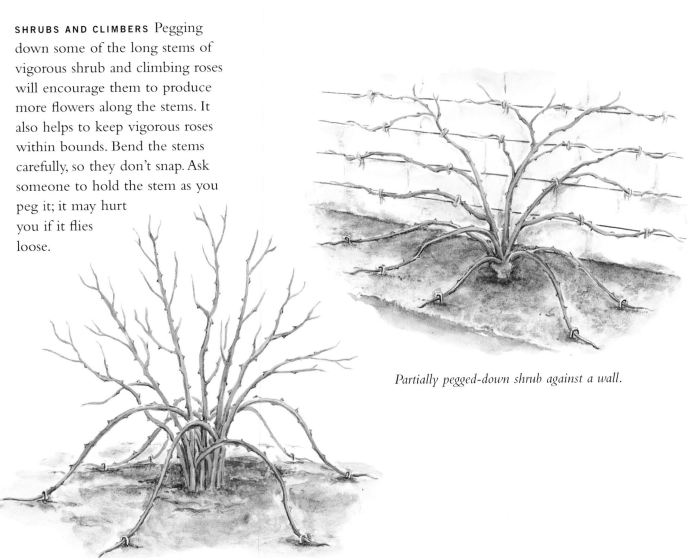

Partially pegged-down shrub against a wall.

Partially pegged-down shrub freestanding.

CHAPTER FOUR

More than 390 Recommended Roses

YOUR DREAM ROSE might be an opulent cup of a hundred damask-scented petals delicately tucked and quartered, or a long, elegant hybrid tea bud unfurling to a high-centered blossom. Perhaps it's a sturdy shrub that blooms brightly all summer, resists diseases, and weathers hard winters, or a fragrant wild climbing rose, with hips among the flowers, that reminds you of an old country garden. ✺ All those and more are here, recommended by six rose experts from different regions who have each grown hundreds. They've listed their favorites in every color and rose category, and then each selected a handful to recommend above the others. ✺ Browse this chapter, seeking all the roses in the color you have set your heart on. Or check the varieties listed by the rose expert in your region on pages 411–414. Or just let the images and descriptions here steer you to something new.

Rose blossoms vary not only in color but also in the number and arrangement of their petals and in their scent.

Hybrid Teas and Grandifloras

Hybrid teas and grandifloras are the classic, aristocratic roses with long, stylish pointed buds that spiral open to large blossoms with high centers. Hybrid teas typically carry one blossom at the end of each flowering stem, bloom profusely in spring, and then continue to produce blossoms—either in flushes or continuously—until frosty weather. Their strong, long stems are good for cutting and bringing indoors. Grandifloras are much like hybrid teas but produce small clusters of blossoms as well as individual blooms.

Hybrid teas and grandifloras tend to have an upright, narrow, almost stiff habit. Group three or more together to create a generous, bushy look, unless you choose plants described as bushy. Consider underplanting them with perennials or placing them behind a low hedge to hide their bare ankles—the bases of the canes are usually sparse in foliage. Both types need good conditions and good care. They are not as hardy in cold-winter climates as most shrub roses and species roses, and are generally more susceptible to pests and diseases. Those described as short (or low-growing) are under 3 feet high. Medium are around 4 feet. Tall reach 5 feet or more.

In the listings, AARS means the rose has received the All-America Rose Selections award (see page 316). For some roses, an alternative name is noted in parentheses. For an explanation of plant and flower form terms, see pages 296–297.

Artistry
Hybrid tea; 1998 / From the plump, pointed buds to the broad-petaled open blossoms, the color remains largely unchanged. Mild fragrance. Plenty of large, glossy leaves. Husky, medium tall. AARS.

Abbaye de Cluny
Hybrid tea; 1996 / This Romantica rose, not obviously a hybrid tea, is much admired by Larry Parton, in Spokane, Washington. "My personal favorite of all my 600 roses, this 3-foot variety has huge apricot blooms of old form with a wonderful fragrance. I pick a flower and carry it around with me sometimes." For a list of Parton's recommendations, see page 413.

Bewitched
Hybrid tea; 1967 / Long, stylish-looking buds on long, strong stems open slowly to fragrant "show-rose" flowers with pale petal backs. Good for cutting. Gray-green leaves. Compact plant. Tall. AARS.

Brandy
Hybrid tea; 1981 / From burnt-orange buds, the large, broad-petaled, prettily formed flowers open well in all kinds of weather. Mildly fragrant. Bronzy new leaves. Medium tall. Poor winter hardiness in cold climates. AARS.

Brigadoon

Hybrid tea; 1991 / From bud to open flower, the delicious combination of strawberry and cream constantly changes: pink-blushed, pointed buds unfold to camellia-like, warm dark pink blossoms with creamy recesses. Fragrant. Good disease resistance. Slightly spreading bush. Tall. AARS.

Candelabra

Grandiflora; 1999 / Long, pointed buds in small clusters open to finely formed coral-orange blossoms. Fragrance is slight. Bushy. Medium tall. AARS.

Caribbean

Grandiflora; 1992 / Full, pointed buds in a blend of tangerine and gold spiral open to softer-toned flowers with pointed petal tips. Moderate fragrance. Long stems. Bright green leaves. Vigorous. Medium height. AARS.

Cary Grant

Hybrid tea; 1987 / The name lets you know this rose has class. Long, tapered buds are a vivid reddish orange, washed yellow at the bases. They open to large, full, well-shaped, intensely fragrant flowers. Medium tall.

Chrysler Imperial

Hybrid tea; 1952 / This classic rose has shapely buds, full blossoms, and a rich fragrance. Petals turn purplish red as they age. Excellent cut flower. Bushy. Medium height. Needs a warm-summer climate. AARS. ARS James Alexander Gamble Rose Fragrance Medal.

Crimson Bouquet

Grandiflora; 1999 / Large, pointed maroon buds open to dark garnet-red blossoms with glossy red petal backs. Good for cutting, although only lightly scented. Glossy leaves. Medium tall. AARS.

Crimson Glory

Hybrid tea; 1935 / Large, velvety deep red flowers, powerfully perfumed, open from pointed ultra-dark red buds. Vigorous, bushy, spreading habit. ARS James Alexander Gamble Rose Fragrance Medal.

Also Recommended

Bride's Dream

Hybrid tea; 1985 / Large, very pale pink, full flowers with a pleasing form open from long, pointed, oval buds. The blossoms are borne singly and are slightly fragrant. Matte medium green leaves. Tall.

Chris Evert

Hybrid tea; 1996 / Finely formed orange-yellow blossoms are finished with red at the tips and have a lighter red blush on the petal backs. Moderately fragrant. Medium height.

Classic Touch

Hybrid tea; 1991 / Large light pink flowers are beautifully formed and slightly fragrant. A sport of 'Touch of Class' (page 375). Tolerates humidity well. Tall.

Dainty Bess

Hybrid tea; 1925 / Russ Bowermaster, from Florida, recommends this rose highly for its "marvelous, spicy aroma. Prune it lightly, and it will keep producing blooms all year; unlike many other singles, it does not seem to mind the heat of Florida's west coast." Also tolerates cool summers well. Medium tall. For a list of Bowermaster's recommendations, see page 412.

Crystalline

Hybrid tea; 1987 / Once a greenhouse rose grown for cut flowers, this variety has "escaped" to the garden, where it provides long-stemmed, fragrant flowers with the elegance of fine crystal. Tapered, pointed buds open to full, shapely flowers. Tall.

Desert Peace

Hybrid tea; 1992 / This is a descendant of 'Peace' (page 372) with intensified color. Buds are more slender and pointed than those of 'Peace', and flowers are not as full. Light fragrance. Glossy leaves. Medium tall.

Double Delight

Hybrid tea; 1977 / These blooms have a delightful fragrance. The red edges increase with heat and the petal's age. Glossy leaves; susceptible to mildew. Medium height. Poor winter hardiness in cold climates. AARS. ARS James Alexander Gamble Rose Fragrance Medal. World Rose Hall of Fame.

Dublin

Hybrid tea; 1982 / The large, classic hybrid tea blooms are borne mostly singly on long, strong stems, which are great for cutting. Performs best in warm climates. Notable raspberry scent. Medium height.

Earth Song

Grandiflora; 1975 / Another popular Buck hybrid (see 'Aunt Honey', page 376), this rose produces long, urn-shaped buds that open to large, cupped, moderately fragrant flowers, which turn a lighter pink as they age. Good disease resistance and winter hardiness. Bushy. Medium tall.

Fame!

Grandiflora; 1998 / Small clusters of large, oval buds open to slightly fragrant, camellia-like blossoms of a dark electric pink, a color impossible to ignore. Extremely robust; tall. AARS.

Elina
Hybrid tea; 1984 / Renowned for its color, elegance, bushy habit, and success in virtually all rose-growing regions, this medium-tall rose is one of Peter Schneider's favorites: "Elina is the greatest hybrid tea I have found for growing in Ohio. Its large, perfect, lemon-yellow blooms appear in profusion all year long on top of a vigorous, trouble-free bush." Light fragrance. For a list of Schneider's recommendations, see page 412.

Fragrant Cloud
Hybrid tea; 1967 / Scarlet-orange buds unfurl to paler flowers with a delightful form and fragrance. Profusely flowering. Glossy leaves. Bushy. Medium height. ARS James Alexander Gamble Rose Fragrance Medal. World Rose Hall of Fame. Peggy Van Allen, in the Northwest, recommends it highly: "'Fragrant Cloud' has always been my favorite. It has intense fragrance and color." For a list of Van Allen's recommendations, see page 413.

Folklore
Hybrid tea; 1977 / A child of 'Fragrant Cloud' (above on this page), this rose has a beautiful form and is intensely fragrant. Vigorous. Tall. Can be grown as a climber.

Glowing Peace
Grandiflora; 2001 / This recent, award-winning grandchild of 'Peace' (page 372) bears golden yellow blossoms suffused with orange. The blooms appear in small clusters and are lightly fragrant. Glossy leaves; burgundy fall color. Bushy. Medium height. AARS.

Gold Medal
Grandiflora; 1982 / Great vigor and good health are among this rose's winning traits. Small clusters of long, oval, golden yellow buds—sometimes tinged with pink or orange—unfurl to large, full, lightly fragrant blossoms. Very tall.

Also Recommended

Gemini
Hybrid tea; 2000 / Oval, pointed, creamy buds tinged with coral-pink open to large, perfectly formed, lightly fragrant flowers, with pink petal edges. As the flowers age, the pink spreads through the petals. Glossy leaves. Tall. AARS.

Heart O' Gold
Grandiflora; 1997 / Large, well-formed yellow flowers have gold centers and cerise-pink edges. The pink spreads over the petals as they age. Carried in large clusters. Strong fragrance. Vigorous. Tall.

Heirloom

Hybrid tea; 1972 / Oval, long, pointed, deep lilac to purple buds open to full, deliciously fragrant flowers in a rare color. Vigorous. Medium tall.

Honor

Hybrid tea; 1980 / Satiny white buds slowly unfurl to really large, long-lasting blossoms. The flowers are lightly scented and only moderately full. Leathery, olive-green leaves; good disease resistance. Tall. AARS.

Ingrid Bergman

Hybrid tea; 1984 / From the shapely, oval buds to the wonderfully formed open flowers, the color remains: a solid rich red with no fading or bluing. Slight fragrance. Good disease resistance. Tolerates cool summers well. Bushy. Medium height or a bit shorter. World Rose Hall of Fame.

John F. Kennedy

Hybrid tea; 1965 / Long, classically tapered buds (often tinged with green) slowly spiral open to form full, notably fragrant, pristine flowers of great size. Flowers have the best form in warm regions. Medium tall.

Joyfulness

Hybrid tea; 1984 / The classic shapeliness of the large blossoms is much admired, as is the changing blend of colors. Mild fragrance. Good for cutting. Bushy. Medium height.

Just Joey

Hybrid tea; 1972 / Here's a pleasing medley of soft warm tones. From attractive buff-orange buds come moderately full, highly fragrant, ruffled flowers that soften to apricot shades. Bushy. Medium height. Good disease resistance. Tolerates humidity well. World Rose Hall of Fame.

King's Ransom

Hybrid tea; 1961 / Long buds of classic hybrid tea shape open to large, full flowers with an unfading chrome-yellow color and a pronounced sweet scent. Glossy leaves. Medium tall. AARS.

Kordes' Perfecta

Hybrid tea; 1957 / Pointed buds of pink-edged cream are huge and flawless; when conditions are right, they spiral open to breathtaking fully double, intensely fragrant flowers. Does best with a little shade (especially in hot-summer regions). Leaves are bronzy when new. Vigorous. Tall.

Louise Estes
Hybrid tea; 1991 / Pointed buds open to nicely formed, moderately fragrant pink blossoms with white petal backs. Tolerates heat well. Medium tall.

Love
Grandiflora; 1980 / Brilliant red petals with silvery white backs unfold from beautifully pointed buds. Half-open blooms show red and white, while fully open ones look entirely red. Light scent. Tolerates cool summers well. Somewhat spreading habit. Medium height. AARS.

Jardins de Bagatelle
Hybrid tea; 1986 / A favorite of Michael Ruggiero's, at the New York Botanical Garden: "It produces a multitude of blooms with over 40 petals, over a long season, above distinctive blue-green, disease-resistant foliage. The strong perfume is reminiscent of the old garden roses. Exceptionally winter hardy (with protection) for a hybrid tea rose." Medium height. For a list of Ruggiero's recommendations, see page 411.

Love and Peace
Hybrid tea; 2001 / Another award-winning child of 'Peace' (page 372), this soft yellow rose blushed with pink has a perfect high-centered, spiral form. Blossoms are large, but only mildly fragrant. Glossy leaves. Bushy. Medium tall. AARS.

Marco Polo
Hybrid tea; 1994 / Moderately fragrant, unfading yellow blossoms are carried mostly singly on a vigorous bush. Long stems, good for cutting. Tall.

Also Recommended

Lady X
Hybrid tea; 1965 / Large, double, lavender-pink flowers have only a mild fragrance but are greatly admired for their perfect form. Vigorous. Tall.

Lagerfeld
Grandiflora; 1986 / Medium-size, pointed buds of classic hybrid tea shape swirl open to form small clusters of subtly elegant silvery lavender blooms. Intensely fragrant. Long stems, good for cutting. Matte, medium green leaves; susceptible to mildew. Vigorous, tall.

Lasting Peace
Grandiflora; 1997 / This variety has orange-red buds that unfurl into coral-orange blooms. Mild fragrance. Glossy leaves. Medium tall.

Leonidas
Hybrid tea; 1995 / Blossoms are a striking color for a rose: cinnamon-orange, from ochre buds. Lightly fragrant. Medium height.

Loving Memory
Hybrid tea; 1983 / Attractive buds open slowly to large red blossoms with a slight fragrance. Good disease resistance and surprising winter hardiness for a hybrid tea. Medium tall.

Marijke Koopman
Hybrid tea; 1979 / Lightly fragrant, shapely blossoms in a deep, satiny pink, open from long, pointed buds, usually in small clusters. Vigorous. Medium-tall.

Michelangelo
Hybrid tea; 1997 / This richly colored and perfumed, antique-looking rose is one of the Romantica roses from France. Grows vigorously and quite tall, like a shrub, which is how it is sometimes classified.

Midas Touch
Hybrid tea; 1992 / The blooms glow like beacons in the garden. Pointed buds open to moderately full flowers with jauntily waved petal edges; the blossoms hold their color until the petals fall. Moderate fragrance. Bushy. Tolerates heat well. Medium height. AARS.

Mister Lincoln
Hybrid tea; 1964 / Long, lovely buds open to very full, long-stemmed flowers in a completely satisfying rich red. Powerful fragrance. Glossy leaves, somewhat susceptible to mildew. Good for cutting. Tolerates heat well, and has good winter hardiness for a hybrid tea. Tall. AARS.

Mon Cheri
Hybrid tea; 1981 / The combination of vivid pink and glowing red is almost too bright to look at. Soft pink buds open to very full, lightly fragrant blossoms that turn velvety red wherever sun strikes the petals. Medium height. AARS.

Moonstone
Hybrid tea; 1998 / Very large, beautifully formed ivory-white blossoms are edged delicately with pink. Slight scent. Long stems, good for cutting. Tolerates humidity well. Medium height.

Mrs. Oakley Fisher
Hybrid tea; 1921 / This dainty single rose with bright stamens ranges in color from pale yellow to almost orange (the color is richest in cool weather). Fragrance also varies, from light to strong, so select a plant in flower. Bronzy green glossy foliage. Medium height.

Mt. Hood
Hybrid tea; 1998 / Clusters of pointed buds open to full-petaled, fragrant blossoms. Flowers almost continuously. Glossy leaves. Medium tall. AARS.

Natasha Monet
Hybrid tea; 1993 / The pale lilac beautifully formed blossoms have the most color during cool weather; in hot climates, they may fade to white. Little if any fragrance. Good for cutting. Bushy. Tall.

New Zealand
Hybrid tea; 1989 / Large, wonderfully formed, soft-colored blossoms release a strong honeysuckle scent. Blooms best in cool climates. Good for cutting. Medium height.

Octoberfest
Grandiflora; 1998 / A blend of red, pink, orange, and yellow, this rose has a pleasing flower shape and a slight scent. Glossy leaves; reddish when young. Tall.

Oklahoma
Hybrid tea; 1964 / Inky black buds open to very large, rather globular, dusky red flowers that remain beautiful when fully open; an intense perfume adds to their appeal. Flowers are not at their best in cool, foggy regions. Winter hardiness is good for a hybrid tea. Vigorous. Bushy. Tall.

Olympiad
Hybrid tea; 1982 / From long buds emerge large, long-lasting, lightly scented flowers that hold their color without turning bluish. Long stems. Grayish green leaves. Good disease resistance. Tolerates both heat and cool summers well. Tall. AARS.

Opening Night
Hybrid tea; 1998 / This offspring of 'Olympiad' (left) has inherited the parent's vigor, long stems, and perfect form (from bud to open blossom)—but the blooms have an even richer color. Slight fragrance. Good disease resistance. Tolerates cool summers well. Medium tall. AARS.

Also Recommended

Mellow Yellow
Hybrid tea; 2001 / Mellow and pale in color it is, but it doesn't fade. Flowers are lightly fragrant, large, plentiful, and borne on long stems. Good for cutting. Medium tall.

Mikado
Hybrid tea; 1987 / A touch of yellow at each petal base enhances the bright cherry color. Urn-shaped, flat-topped buds unfold to full, unfading blossoms with a light fragrance. Glossy leaves. Medium height. AARS.

Moon Shadow
Hybrid tea; 1998 / The full, shapely, intensely fragrant flowers are a rare lavender color and usually grow in small clusters. Glossy leaves. Vigorous. Medium height.

Paradise
Hybrid tea; 1978 / A distinctive and changing color combination: ruby red at first edges the young silvery lavender petals and then spreads over more of the petal surfaces as the flowers age. Shapely buds. Moderate fragrance. Good for cutting. Medium height. AARS.

Piccadilly
Hybrid tea; 1960 / Gold petal bases and reverses flash brilliantly with the scarlet surfaces of the petals. Faintly scented. Glossy leaves. Vigorous. Medium height.

Paris de Yves St. Laurent

Hybrid tea; 1995 / Large, attractively formed flowers release a slight fragrance. Good for cutting. Glossy leaves; disease resistant. Medium height.

Pascali

Hybrid tea; 1963 / This is perhaps the finest white rose for dependable production of good-quality flowers in all climates. Tapered, pointed buds unfold to full, perfectly formed, lightly perfumed flowers. Blooms almost continuously. Tall. AARS. World Rose Hall of Fame.

Peace

Hybrid tea; 1945 / Buds of yellow touched with pink or red unfold into extra-large blossoms with pink-rimmed yellow petals (colors vary depending on the amount of heat and sun). Light scent. Glossy leaves; somewhat susceptible to black spot. Medium height. AARS. World Rose Hall of Fame.

Pink Peace

Hybrid tea; 1959 / Numerous plump oval buds open to large, full, shapely blossoms with a heady fragrance. Susceptible to rust. Good winter hardiness for a hybrid tea. Medium height.

Pristine

Hybrid tea; 1978 / This delicate confection of a blossom comes on a plant that is anything but delicate: it's medium tall and spreading, with oversized leaves. Buds are long, oval, pink blushed; they open quickly to full, long-lasting, lightly fragrant flowers.

Proud Land

Hybrid tea; 1969 / Full-petaled, velvety bright blossoms offer a heavy, pervasive perfume. The buds are long, pointed, and produced almost continuously on long stems. Tolerates heat well. Medium height.

Queen Elizabeth

Grandiflora; 1954 / Small clusters of medium-size, radiant pink blooms develop from attractive, pointed buds. Fragrance is mild. Glossy leaves. Tolerates cool summers well. Extremely vigorous and tall; can be used for hedges and background planting. AARS. World Rose Hall of Fame.

Rio Samba

Hybrid tea; 1991 / Pointed buds and moderately full open flowers are a little small for a hybrid tea, but the color makes up for the size. Blooms come both singly and in small clusters. Colors are best in cool climates. Slight fragrance. Bushy. Medium height. AARS.

Secret

Hybrid tea; 1992 / The secret is a sweet-spicy perfume. Lovely pointed, oval buds are a pastel medley of cream, white, and pink; they unfurl to full, shapely blossoms in which the darkest pink tones are brushed on the petal margins. Plum-brown new leaves. Good for cutting. Medium height. AARS.

Signature

Hybrid tea; 1996 / Elegant red buds open to reveal satiny pink petals with pointed tips and brushes of cream on their lower parts. Moderately fragrant. Vigorous. Medium tall.

Sheer Bliss

Hybrid tea; 1985 / Kathleen Brenzel, in California, thinks it is well named: "Elegant pointed buds open to such beautifully formed blooms that they look as though crafted from fine porcelain—angular and refined. The creamy blossoms have the pink blush of an English schoolgirl's cheeks in winter—pure perfection." Fragrant flowers. Glossy leaves. Medium height. AARS. For a list of Brenzel's recommendations, see page 414.

Solitude

Grandiflora; 1991 / Despite a somber-sounding name, this is a bright, vibrant rose. Fully double, large blooms with lightly scalloped petal margins open from small clusters of plump buds that show golden highlights on the petal backs. Lightly fragrant. Vigorous. Medium tall. AARS.

St. Patrick

Hybrid tea; 1996 / Shapely buds slowly spiral open to golden yellow blooms in cool weather, lovely yellow-green ones (hence the name) only when it's hot. Slight fragrance. Gray-green leaves. Poor winter hardiness in cold climates. Medium height. AARS.

Also Recommended

Portrait

Hybrid tea; 1971 / Very shapely blossoms blend two shades: light pink on the petal edges, dark pink in the center. Very fragrant. Glossy leaves. Medium tall. AARS.

Precious Platinum

Hybrid tea; 1974 / Admired for brilliant red color that doesn't fade, vigorous growth, and good disease resistance, this rose lacks only one quality—lots of fragrance. Medium tall.

Rouge Royal

Hybrid tea; 2002 / A recently introduced Romantica rose, with the old-fashioned character and sweet fragrance the Romanticas are known for. The large, quartered blossoms are bright raspberry red. To 4 feet tall.

Stainless Steel

Hybrid tea; 1991 / An improved descendant of 'Sterling Silver' and as classy as its predecessor. Elegantly tapered silvery lavender buds unfold to large, moderately full flowers with a noteworthy perfume. Vigorous. Tall.

Stephens' Big Purple

Hybrid tea; 1985 / Large, intensely perfumed flowers of deepest, darkest purple make this a winner. The buds open slowly. Tolerates cool summers well. Tall.

Tequila Sunrise
Hybrid tea; 1988 / Oval buds open slowly to lightly fragrant cupped blossoms of dazzling yellow petals edged with scarlet. Borne singly and in clusters. Bushy. Medium height.

The McCartney Rose
Hybrid tea; 1995 / Large, long buds open to big, full, high-centered blossoms that become cupped as they age. Named after the ex-Beatle. Very fragrant. Bushy. Medium height.

Sunset Celebration
Hybrid tea; 1998 / This festival of sunset tones celebrates the centennial of *Sunset* magazine. The shapely, full flowers open from long, tapered buds. Moderately fragrant. Tolerates cool summers well. Medium height. AARS. Peggy Van Allen, in the Northwest, recommends it highly: "This rose is always in bloom; as soon as the old blooms fall, new buds are forming." For a list of Van Allen's recommendations, see page 413.

Tiffany
Hybrid tea; 1954 / Large, long buds, as perfect as finely cut jewels, open to moderately full flowers with an intense, fruity fragrance. Susceptible to powdery mildew. Tall. AARS. ARS James Alexander Gamble Rose Fragrance Medal.

Timeless
Hybrid tea; 1997 / Long, tapered buds open slowly to large, moderately full blossoms, which are long-lasting and hold their vibrant, even color from start to finish. Mild fragrance. Good disease resistance. Somewhat spreading habit. Medium height. AARS.

Toulouse-Lautrec
Hybrid tea; 1994 / Delicate tucked and ruffled petals give this rose an antique look, but it's a contemporary Romantica introduction from France. Tapered buds open into flowers that are almost flat; as the blooms age, the outer petals turn a lighter yellow. Fragrance varies. Medium height.

Tournament of Roses
Grandiflora; 1988 / Both the oval buds and the symmetrical, camellia-like open flowers display two shades of pink: dark coral on the petal backs, warm light pink on the upper surfaces. Blooms profusely. Mild fragrance. Glossy leaves; good disease resistance. Vigorous. Medium height. AARS.

Tropicana
Hybrid tea; 1960 / Pointed buds unfold into full, rather cupped flowers with a sweet fragrance. Matte green leaves; susceptible to mildew. Good for cutting. Vigorous, somewhat spreading plant. Tall. AARS.

Uncle Joe (Toro)
Hybrid tea; 1972 / Big is the word for this rose. Long, pointed, oval buds on long stems open slowly to large, full, shapely, moderately fragrant blossoms. Flowers open best where nights are warm. Good winter hardiness for a hybrid tea. Tall.

Touch of Class
Hybrid tea; 1984 / Elegant tapered buds open to large, moderately full, beautifully formed flowers, which are good for cutting. Russ Bowermaster, of Florida, highly recommends this rose: "There is little fragrance, but the foliage is attractive and it resists black spot, which is a distinct advantage in this climate." Bushy. Tall. AARS. For a list of Bowermaster's recommendations, see page 412.

Voodoo
Hybrid tea; 1984 / Dark buds open to large, heavily perfumed flowers that soften in color to yellow and peach shades, then finally fade to pink. Glossy, dark, bronze-green leaves. Tall. AARS.

White Lightnin'
Grandiflora; 1980 / Ruffled petals give the full, intensely citrus-scented blossoms a distinct personality. Glossy bright green leaves. Flowers almost continuously. Bushy. Medium height. AARS.

Yves Piaget
Hybrid tea; 1985 / Fat, pointed buds unfold to deeply cupped, peony-like blossoms with frilly petals and a rich fragrance. Flowers are very large, up to 6 inches across, and produced in abundance. A Romantica rose. To 5 feet tall.

Also Recommended

Traviata
Hybrid tea; 1998 / This dark red Romantica rose has about 100 petals tucked and quartered into each very full bloom. Fragrance is only light. Good for cutting. Disease resistant. Medium height.

Vanilla Perfume
Hybrid tea; 1999 / Smelling sweetly of vanilla, the large, perfectly formed, light cream and apricot blossoms appear singly or in small clusters. Tall.

Veterans' Honor
Hybrid tea; 1999 / Large, shapely, velvety, dark red blossoms give off a light to moderate raspberry scent. Most grow singly on long stems. Part of the proceeds from this rose go to the Department of Veterans Affairs. Medium tall.

Landscape Roses

Landscape roses are flowering shrubs used in borders, as hedges and ground covers, and as background plantings. These roses can be quite trouble-free, and many are hardy in cold-winter climates. New hybridizing programs have produced notably lovely shrubs with striking or sumptuous colors; some are very fragrant. The roses listed here are repeat-flowering (unless otherwise noted).

Landscape roses are commonly divided into the following classes: *English roses,* produced by David Austin, combine the character of old European roses with modern colors and repeat-bloom; many can be grown as small climbers in mild-winter areas, where they reach maximum size. Most *hybrid rugosa roses* are as tough as the *Rosa rugosa* parent (see page 396), with excellent disease resistance and cold tolerance. They have distinctive rugosa foliage, and many form large, round hips. The original *floribunda roses* were as bushy, vigorous, and profuse in bloom as polyanthas, with the color range and flower form of hybrid teas. Today's floribundas range from 2½ to 4 feet tall, and some bear large clusters of rather informal flowers. *Ground cover roses* are low-growing; their canes spread to about three times the plant's height, making an undulating carpet of color. *Hybrid musk roses* typically are vigorous, lax shrubs, with clusters of blossoms; the larger ones can be grown as small climbers in mild climates. This group is notably disease resistant. Most perform well in partial shade as well as full sun. *Polyantha roses* are short and bushy, with large clusters of small blossoms. *Shrub roses,* as an official class, contains English roses, ground cover roses, and roses that fit into no other class. The new Generosa roses and Romantica roses are classified mostly as shrubs; a few are hybrid teas (featured on pages 364–375). The Buck hybrids are bred for cold-winter areas.

In the listings, AARS means that the rose has received the All-America Rose Selections award (see page 316). For some roses, an alternative name is noted in parentheses. For an explanation of plant and flower form terms, see pages 296–297.

Abraham Darby
English rose; 1985 / Apricot, peach, gold, and cream mingle in an always lovely combination in these large, extremely full, cupped, fragrant blossoms. Flowers are abundant and carried in small clusters. A spreading, arching shrub (to about 10 feet) or a modest climber. Large thorns.

All That Jazz
Shrub; 1991 / This vigorous, stiff, bushy shrub grows to about 5 feet tall and has the look of an oversized floribunda. Large clusters of moderately scented blossoms. Plentiful, high-gloss, disease-resistant foliage. AARS.

Aunt Honey
Shrub; 1984 / Larry Parton, in Spokane, Washington, says: "I love many of the Dr. Griffith Buck roses because they are hardy in USDA zone 5 (−20°F/−29°C) and have interesting colors. 'Aunt Honey' and 'Earth Song' [page 366] are prolific and awesome. For gardeners who want reliable, easy-care beauty, these roses are the best." Moderately fragrant. Bushy, to 5 feet tall. For a list of Parton's recommendations, see page 413.

Angel Face
Floribunda; 1968 / Rose
and red tints enliven these
ruffled, very full, very fragrant lavender blossoms,
borne in clusters on a
low, spreading plant that
blooms heavily. Bronze-
tinted leaves. The climb-
ing sport grows to about
10 feet. AARS.

Anthony Meilland
Floribunda; 1994 / Large,
lightly fragrant blossoms
are held in small clusters.
Bush flowers almost con-
tinuously. Has a rounded
habit, reaching about
5 feet tall.

Apricot Nectar
Floribunda; 1965 / In-
tensely fragrant, large
flowers blushed delicately
with apricot, pink, and
yellow make this a
favorite floribunda.
Flowers appear in tight
clusters and are long-
lasting. To 4 feet tall.
AARS.

Autumn Sunset
Shrub; 1986 / Large clus-
ters of pointed buds open
to loosely cupped apricot
blooms with touches of
orange, gold, and peach.
Color is best in cool
weather. Strongly fra-
grant. Orange hips in fall.
A tall shrub or a moder-
ate climber (to about
12 feet).

Ballerina
Hybrid musk; 1937 /
Single, small flowers with
the airy charm of dog-
wood or apple blossoms
are carried in giant,
domed clusters. Only
lightly fragrant. Dense,
glossy foliage. Tiny
orange-red hips. Tolerates
cool summers well.
Rounded shrub, to about
5 feet tall.

Belle Story
English rose; 1984 / Shell-
like petals unfold around
a central tuft of stamens,
giving each large bloom
the look of a peony.
Borne in small clusters,
the blossoms appear
throughout the growing
season and have an
unusual fragrance: some
say anise; others myrrh.
Vigorous, to 4 feet tall.

Betty Boop
Floribunda; 1999 / These
bold cherry-red, white,
and yellow blossoms, with
gold stamens at the cen-
ter, begin as ivory buds
tinged with red. Flowers
almost continuously.
Moderate fragrance.
Glossy leaves are reddish
when new. Bushy, to
about 4 feet tall and
wide. AARS.

Betty Prior
Floribunda; 1935 / Here is
all the charm of a wild
rose and much of the
vigor as well. Red buds
open to blossoms that
resemble dogwood
blooms in size and shape.
Lightly fragrant. Blooms
almost continuously.
Tough, disease resistant,
and cold tolerant. To
6 feet tall and wide.

Blanc Double de Coubert

Hybrid rugosa; 1892 / Pointed buds surrounded by elongated sepals flare open to highly fragrant, fairly full but loose blossoms. Leathery, disease-resistant rugosa foliage colors well in fall. Orange hips. Spreads by suckers. Good winter hardiness. Vigorous. Reaches about 6 feet tall.

Blueberry Hill

Floribunda; 1999 / Plump, pointed, dark lilac buds open to large, fragrant, clear lilac flowers with a center of golden stamens. Flowers are carried in small clusters. Glossy leaves. Good disease resistance. Rounded bush, to 4 feet tall and wide.

Buffalo Gal

Hybrid rugosa; 1989 / Michael Ruggiero, at the New York Botanical Garden, chose this as one of his five favorite roses: "It has larger flowers than other rugosas. Its clean rugosa leaves, great fragrance, large red hips, rebloom, and disease resistance make this an easy-to-grow and fabulous rose." To 4 feet tall. For a list of Ruggiero's recommendations, see page 411.

Bonica

Shrub; 1985 / Arching canes form a mounding, spreading shrub to about 5 feet high, decked out in dark, glossy leaves and large flower clusters. Good disease resistance. Faint fragrance. Bright orange hips. Makes a nice hedge. AARS.

Buff Beauty

Hybrid musk; 1939 / Small clusters of very full, shapely, fragrant flowers open a glowing golden apricot, then fade to creamy buff. New foliage is a plum-bronze color. An arching, 6- to 8-foot shrub or small climber. Tolerates humidity well.

Cardinal Hume

Shrub; 1984 / Pointed buds unfurl to antique-looking cupped flowers with a moderate fragrance. Spreading form, to 5 feet tall and a little wider.

Carefree Delight

Shrub; 1993 / This mounding, spreading plant is densely covered in small, dark leaves and reaches about 4 feet high. From spring to autumn, it's covered in a froth of clustered single blossoms. Little or no fragrance. Excellent disease resistance. Makes a good hedge. AARS.

Carefree Wonder
Shrub; 1990 / There's a lively look to these clustered flowers: the carmine-pink petals are backed in creamy white, with a bit of white infusing the margins as well. Fragrance is slight. Upright (to about 5 feet) and bushy. Excellent disease resistance. Makes a good hedge. AARS.

Champlain
Shrub; 1982 / Informally double blossoms come in floribunda-like clusters on a bushy 3- to 4-foot plant with glossy leaves. Lightly fragrant. One of the Canadian Explorer series, bred to survive southern Canadian winters unprotected.

China Doll
Polyantha; 1946 / Rounded clusters of very full, small flowers may appear in such abundance that the glossy, bright green leaves are almost obscured. Slightly fragrant. Low-growing (reaching just 1½ feet) and nearly thornless. Good disease resistance. Nice for containers.

Country Dancer
Shrub; 1973 / Easy is a common description of this Buck hybrid. It's disease resistant, it flowers almost continuously, its petals drop cleanly when they are done, and it has good winter hardiness. The blossoms fade to light pink with age. Moderate fragrance. About 4 feet tall and wide.

Delicata
Hybrid rugosa; 1898 / The cool pink of the scented, silky-petaled blossoms contrasts well with the dense rugosa foliage. After the flowers fade, you'll get a good crop of bright orange hips. Small for a rugosa, about 3 feet high. Good winter hardiness.

Distant Drums
Shrub; 1985 / This rose has a distinct fragrance and unique colors. Oval, pointed purple buds unfurl to large, slightly ruffled flowers that are peachy bronze in the center and light rosy purple at the petal tips. Upright and bushy, to about 4 feet.

Escapade
Floribunda; 1967 / As charming as wild roses, these delicately colored blossoms appear in profusion in large clusters among glossy leaves. Slight fragrance. Bushy, to 5 feet tall. Makes a fine hedge.

Also Recommended

Arthur Bell
Floribunda; 1965 / The creamy yellow flowers have a strong perfume. Vigorous. Good winter hardiness. To about 4 feet tall.

Charlotte
English rose; 1994 / Cupped, fragrant, soft lemon-and-butter-yellow blooms fade to cream on the outer petals. They are borne in small clusters. To 5 feet tall.

Conrad Ferdinand Meyer
Hybrid rugosa; 1899 / Large, cupped, intensely fragrant silvery pink blossoms. Vigorous and tall (to 10 feet); makes a fine pillar rose, small climber, or tall hedge.

Dr. Jackson
English rose; 1992 / Brilliant scarlet single rose with a tuft of golden stamens. No fragrance. Showy hips. To about 4 feet tall and wide.

Easy Going

Floribunda; 1999 / Larry Parton, in Spokane, Washington, ranks this rose among his favorites: "It really stands out from the crowd because of its productivity and gorgeous form. The foliage is beautiful, too, and the plants take on a nice shape. Even if it didn't bloom, it would be a good landscape bush." Glossy leaves. To about 4 feet tall. For a list of Parton's recommendations, see page 413.

Europeana

Floribunda; 1963 / This lightly fragrant rose is a favorite of Russ Bowermaster's, in Florida: "A dark red floribunda with very attractive foliage and large clusters of flowers. It repeat-blooms quite well and resists most diseases. Ideal for use as a landscape plant." Tolerates heat well. To 3 feet tall. AARS. For a list of Bowermaster's recommendations, see page 412.

Fair Bianca

English rose; 1982 / Its floral perfection elicits comparisons to the damask 'Mme. Hardy' (page 394): the blossoms are flat and circular, their petals packed around a green central eye, their strong myrrh fragrance a delight to the nose. To about 3 feet tall, an English rose for a small space.

First Light

Shrub; 1998 / The parents are 'Ballerina' (page 377) and 'Bonica' (page 378), so it's no wonder the child is outstanding. It produces large clusters of nearly circular, single, fragrant flowers with dark red stamens. The dense, rounded, glossy-leaved bush reaches about 3 feet high and wide. AARS.

Flower Carpet and White Flower Carpet

Ground cover; 1989 / floribunda; 1991 / Low (to about 2 feet) and spreading, these lightly fragrant roses are suited to mass plantings as ground covers but also serve nicely as container plants or border plantings. Foliage is dense and glossy. Both tolerate heat well.

380

French Lace

Floribunda; 1980 / Strongly recommended by Kathleen Brenzel, in California: "I've grown it in an 18-inch-diameter pot on my patio for years. On bright May days, the blooms look as refreshing as dollops of ice cream." Bushy, about 4 feet tall. Tender; not recommended for cold-winter climates, unless grown as an annual. AARS. For a list of Brenzel's recommendations, see page 414.

Florence Delattre

Shrub; 1997 / This Generosa rose has a fine, old-fashioned form and a rich perfume. Vigorous, with long arching canes, to about 5 feet tall. Makes a fine pillar rose.

Flutterbye

Shrub; 1996 / Pointed, red-tinged yellow buds open to ruffled, fragrant, single yellow flowers that change to creamy buff, pink, and coral—often within a single cluster. Very glossy, disease-resistant leaves. A fountain-like 6- to 10-foot shrub or small climber in mild climates, a more compact (but still large) shrub elsewhere.

Glamis Castle

English rose; 1994 / A cross between 'Graham Thomas' (page 382) and 'Mary Rose' (page 384), this rose has cupped, ruffled blossoms with a strong sweet scent. It's small for an English rose, reaching less than 4 feet.

Golden Celebration

English rose; 1993 / Fat yellow buds touched with red open to large flowers that are cupped at the center but open at the edges. Intensely scented, notched petals. Rounded shrub, grows to 5 feet tall.

Golden Wings

Shrub; 1956 / Large soft-colored petals surround a cluster of bright orange-red stamens. Moderately fragrant flowers are borne in small clusters. Tolerates humidity well. Somewhat rounded, to about 5 feet tall and 4 feet wide.

Also Recommended

Fire Meidiland

Ground cover; 1999 / Fire-truck-red flowers open in small clusters on a fast-growing, sprawling plant (to about 2 feet tall and 4 or 5 feet wide). Glossy, bright leaves. Good disease resistance.

Gingersnap

Floribunda; 1978 / Ruffled, slightly scented, glowing orange petals are packed into very full flowers. Rounded, bushy plant, to about 3 feet tall. New leaves are a deep bronze-purple.

Guy de Maupassant

Floribunda; 1996 / This Romantica rose has old-fashioned form and intense perfume. Pretty pink flowers, each reputedly having about 100 petals. Glossy leaves with good disease resistance. Height varies from 3 to 8 feet.

Graham Thomas

English rose; 1983 / Modest clusters of plump, red-tinted yellow buds open to cupped blossoms of brightest butter-yellow. Moderate to strong fragrance. Canes may reach 10 feet or more in length. Can be grown as a climber in mild-winter climates; elsewhere, it's a slender, tall shrub.

Heidelberg

Shrub; 1959 / Clusters of deep red buds open to large, lightly scented crimson flowers with lighter petal backs. Vigorous; can be grown as an upright, bushy shrub, to about 6 feet tall, or as a small climber, to about 8 feet tall. Glossy leaves. Good disease resistance.

Hansa

Hybrid rugosa; 1905 / Peggy Van Allen, in the Northwest, says: "It's my favorite rugosa rose. It has a great fragrance and color, and you can find buds, blooms, and hips all at the same time on the bush." Reaches about 6 feet high and wide; makes a superlative hedge. Yellow fall foliage. Orange-red hips. Good disease resistance and winter hardiness. For a list of Van Allen's recommendations, see page 413.

Iceberg

Floribunda; 1958 / Kathleen Brenzel, in California, advises, "If there ever was a rose to use in a big way—for example, as a hedge along a picket fence or as rose trees lining an entry walk—this is it. Blooms come almost continuously on a disease-resistant plant." To 6 feet tall. Sweet scent. Takes both heat and cool summers. Dense glossy foliage. World Rose Hall of Fame. For a list of Brenzel's recommendations, see page 414.

Kaleidoscope

Shrub; 1998 / These ruffled blossoms with a mild sweet fragrance move through a series of interesting colors. The buds are orange-pink; the petals open tan and mauve. Glossy leaves. To 4 feet tall.

Kathleen

Hybrid musk; 1922 / Reminiscent of apple blossoms, the single flowers appear in airy, lightly fragrant clusters that become sprays of bright orange hips in fall. Gray-green leaves. Vigorous, arching bush to about 6 feet tall; can be trained as a small climber.

Intrigue

Floribunda; 1982 / Another Kathleen Brenzel favorite: "I can never pass this red-purple beauty without stopping to sniff its heady floral perfume. Its color is rich, too—sumptuous, like a velvet robe." In overall appearance, much like a small hybrid tea. Tolerates cool summers well. Rounded, bushy, to about 3 feet tall. AARS. For a list of Brenzel's recommendations, see page 414.

Knock Out

Shrub; 2000 / This stunningly bright rose is also a hit because of its excellent disease resistance, tolerance of humidity and shade, abundance of flowers into fall, reddish purple fall foliage, and orange-red hips. Mild fragrance. Bushy, to about 3 feet tall and wide. Makes a fine low hedge. AARS.

L. D. Braithwaite

English rose; 1988 / The rich flower color comes from its parent 'The Squire' (page 390); blossom shape and plant quality derive from the other parent, 'Mary Rose' (page 384). The large, fragrant flowers retain their red color without bluing. Prickly canes and stems. Upright to slightly spreading bush, about 5 feet high.

Lilli Marleen

Floribunda; 1959 / Moderately fragrant, intensely red flowers are finely formed. Vigorous. Reaches about 5 feet tall.

Livin' Easy

Floribunda; 1992 / Plentiful, high-gloss foliage would make this an attractive shrub even if it didn't bloom. Add the glowing blossoms and you have a garden beacon throughout the growing season. Rounded bush, about 3 feet tall; good for foreground planting and border hedges. AARS.

Also Recommended

Hunter

Hybrid rugosa; 1961 / Here's a rugosa hybrid with some floribunda genes, hence the crimson-red double blossoms and the handsome leaves without wrinkles. Moderate fragrance. Vigorous. Tolerates humidity well. To about 5 feet tall.

Johann Strauss

Floribunda; 1994 / The large clusters of very full, pink, antique-looking Romantica flowers have a mild lemon verbena scent. Bronze-tinted, disease-resistant leaves. Bushy, 2 to 4 feet tall.

Linda Campbell

Hybrid rugosa; 1990 / The foliage is less textured than that of most rugosa hybrids, and the velvety blossoms are the purest red. Large clusters of blooms. Arching; to 8 feet tall; makes a fine tall hedge.

Love Potion

Floribunda; 1993 / A strong raspberry scent wafts from the large, deep lavender blossoms borne in small clusters. Leaves are shiny. To 5 feet tall.

Magic Blanket

Ground cover; 1999 / From scores of tiny peach-colored buds emerge small white flowers with light yellow centers and gold stamens, which cover the bushes all summer. After flowering, petals drop naturally. To 3 feet tall and 6 feet wide. Light fragrance.

Madison

Shrub; 1998 / One of the Towne and Country landscape roses, 'Madison' produces large clusters of small blossoms on a rounded, compact shrub 2 feet high and wide. Petals drop cleanly, so they don't need deadheading. Usually massed or used as an edging. Slight fragrance.

Margaret Merril

Floribunda; 1977 / This is a child of the superlative white hybrid tea 'Pascali' (page 372), and it has the same admirable form. Small clusters of pointed, off-white buds open to pure white blooms with ruffled petals and a strong perfume blending citrus and spice. Bushy. To 5 feet tall.

Margo Koster

Polyantha; 1931 / Nearly round buds composed of many shell-like petals unfurl to small, cupped flowers resembling ranunculus blossoms. Blooms come in large clusters. Little if any fragrance. Glossy light green leaves. Twiggy plant, 1½ to 2 feet tall.

Marie Curie

Floribunda; 1996 / This small Romantica rose puts out lots of trusses of lightly scented, ruffled shrimp-pink blossoms. Compact in habit, to about 3 feet tall, it's a handsome old-fashioned-looking variety for a small garden or a container.

Marmalade Skies

Floribunda; 2001 / The blossom clusters appear in abundance all summer. They are good for cutting, but only lightly fragrant. Rounded, bushy habit, to about 3 feet tall and wide. AARS.

Martine Guillot

Shrub; 1996 / A light gardenia scent wafts from these sprays of finely formed, creamy blossoms blushed with soft apricot. They are long-lasting and good for cutting. A Generosa rose. To 6 feet tall and a little wider.

Mary Rose

English rose; 1983 / The broadly cup-shaped, lightly fragrant blossoms have outer petals that reflex to form a circular frame. Flowers almost continuously. Bushy, with prickly stems. Susceptible to powdery mildew. Grows 4 to 6 feet high and wide.

Mme. Plantier

Hybrid alba; 1835 / This graceful, tall, arching plant blooms once, in spring, bearing exquisite, fragrant, 2-inch blossoms that capture the essence of old rose beauty. Plump, red-tinted ivory buds. Nearly thornless. As a shrub it grows to 8 feet tall, but it can also be trained as a small climber.

Molineux

English rose; 1994 / 'Molineux' is smaller than 'Golden Celebration' (page 381), 'Graham Thomas' (page 382), and 'The Pilgrim' (page 390), the other yellow English roses listed. It's nicely delicate in color, too. Strong fragrance. Good disease resistance. Tolerates humidity well. To 4 feet tall.

Morning Has Broken

Shrub; 1996 / A child of 'Graham Thomas' (page 382), this rich yellow rose with gold stamens fades slowly to soft yellow as it ages. Blossoms are carried in small clusters. Little if any fragrance. Smaller than its famous parent— to about 4 feet tall and wide. Tolerates heat well.

Outta the Blue

Shrub; 2001 / Larry Parton, of Spokane, Washington, recommends this rose highly: "It was incredible in my garden last year. The bush itself is wonderful, but the blooms are really eye-catching. The colors are very striking—yet under control." Flowers almost continuously. Fragrant. Varies from 3 to 6 feet tall. For a list of Parton's recommendations, see page 413.

Napa Valley

Shrub; 1995 / This small, mounding shrub in the Towne and Country landscape roses series produces bright red, slightly fragrant blossoms in clusters. Small, glossy leaves; disease resistant. To about 2 feet tall and wide.

Nicole

Floribunda; 1985 / The white petals unfurl from the buds with intense cerise-red on the petal edges; the red may then fade in strong sunlight. Light fragrance. Glossy leaves; good disease resistance. Tolerates heat well. Vigorous, to 5 feet tall or taller.

Oranges 'n' Lemons

Shrub; 1994 / Arching canes form a fountain of dazzling yellow blossoms splashed with orange, from 4 to 10 feet tall. It blooms and holds color best in cool weather. Mild to moderate scent. Red new growth. Good disease resistance. Can be grown as a climber or pillar rose in mild climates.

Also Recommended

Moje Hammarberg

Hybrid rugosa; 1931 / Large, intensely fragrant, reddish violet blossoms are crowned with gold stamens. Showy red hips in fall. Dense, crinkled rugosa leaves. To 5 feet tall and wide.

Mountain Music

Shrub; 1984 / These bright pink-yellow blossoms are speckled sometimes with pink, sometimes with yellow. They appear in large clusters. Moderately fragrant. To 3 feet tall and wide.

Nevada

Shrub/hybrid moyesii; 1927 / Early in spring and again in fall, the canes carry white blossoms all along their length. Little or no scent. Somewhat susceptible to black spot. Spreading habit; reaches about 8 feet tall.

Paul Bocuse

Shrub; 1997 / Kathleen Brenzel, of California, says: "I love the colors of the sky at sunset and the cupped, many-petaled form of old roses. This Generosa shrub combines them. Rich apricot blooms open in clusters—as many as nine blooms, with several buds fattening between them. The plant is disease resistant, too." Light to moderate fragrance. To about 5 feet tall. For a list of Brenzel's recommendations, see page 414.

Penelope

Hybrid musk; 1924 / Coral-orange buds in medium-size clusters open to fluffy blossoms that vary from creamy pink or apricot to buff-cream, according to weather and season. Sweet scent. Coral-pink hips. Dense and shrubby, to about 6 feet tall.

Pink Meidiland

Shrub; 1984 / Compared to 'Scarlet Meidiland' (page 387), 'White Meidiland' (page 390), and the others of this group, 'Pink Meidiland' is more of a bushy, upright plant. Little if any fragrance. Somewhat susceptible to black spot. To about 4 feet, with ample foliage; makes a fine hedge.

Playboy

Floribunda; 1976 / These clustered blossoms bring fiery color into the garden. The yellow centers blend out to orange, and the petals are brushed and infused with red toward the margins. Seductive fragrance. Glossy, disease-resistant leaves. Good winter hardiness. To about 3 feet high.

Playgirl

Floribunda; 1986 / Sprays of single, hot-pink blossoms with pretty yellow stamens are produced abundantly through summer into fall. Fragrance is slight. Tolerates humidity well. Bushy and quite compact, to 4 feet tall at most.

Prairie Sunset

Shrub; 1984 / A Buck rose, bred in Iowa for winter hardiness, 'Prairie Sunset' has large blossoms that blend yellow, pink, and orange. Moderately fragrant. To 4 feet tall.

Prospero

English rose; 1983 / It looks, and is perfumed, like a lovely old gallica rose, but it repeat-blooms like the modern rose it is, and it's small enough to be grown in a container. Fat buds. Ruffled rosettes age to an old-fashioned deep purple. Susceptible to powdery mildew and rust. To 4 feet tall.

Red Ribbons

Ground cover; 1990 / Bright yellow stamens grace the centers of lipstick-red flowers that come in clusters. Slightly scented. Plentiful dark green foliage. Low, spreading plant, to 2 feet tall and 5 feet wide.

Regensburg

Floribunda; 1979 / The pinkish ivory buds give no hint of the blooms to come: striking strawberry-pink flowers with white centers, brushings of white on the petal edges, and nearly white petal backs. Sweet scent. Glossy, disease-resistant leaves. To 2 feet tall. Suitable for a container.

Sally Holmes

Shrub; 1976 / Peggy Van Allen, in the Northwest, lists this rose as a favorite: "This is a beautiful vigorous shrub in our area. It has huge flower heads, some as much as 12 inches in diameter. As the outside blooms fade, the inside buds emerge, so it has a long bloom period." Light fragrance. To 8 feet high; in warm regions, can be trained as a climber. Tolerates light shade. For a list of Van Allen's recommendations, see page 413.

Roseraie de l'Hay

Hybrid rugosa; 1901 / Tapered buds unfold into blowsy, pleasantly spice-scented blossoms that become increasingly purple with age. Densely clothed in apple-green leaves that turn to bronzy yellow in fall. Good disease resistance. Tolerates humidity well. Few hips. To 6 feet tall and wide.

Scarlet Meidiland

Shrub; 1987 / Small, ruffled blossoms in unfading scarlet come in great clusters that can weigh down the branches. Little if any fragrance. Glossy leaves. Grows into a husky, arching mound to about 4 feet high and 6 feet across. Good as a tall ground cover, barrier, or informal hedge.

Also Recommended

Peter Mayle

Shrub; 2001 / A rich old-rose fragrance is released from the large, brilliant fuchsia-pink blossoms. To 6 feet tall.

Prairie Harvest

Shrub; 1985 / A Buck rose with large straw-yellow flowers that are sweetly fragrant. Blooms until frost. Glossy leaves. To 5 feet tall.

Prosperity

Hybrid musk; 1919 / Large clusters of elegant buds flushed with pink open to sweetly fragrant creamy white blossoms with a hint of pink in cool weather or light shade. Glossy leaves. Vigorous. To 5 feet tall and wider. Can be grown as a small climber or pillar rose.

Queen Bee

Shrub; 1984 / Velvety dark red blossoms are large, well-formed, beautifully fragrant, and carried in clusters. A Buck hybrid. To 4 feet tall.

Robusta

Shrub; 1979 / Sturdy and fast-growing, with slightly crinkled leaves, this scarlet rose flowers abundantly into fall. Fragrance varies. Disease resistant. Tolerates humidity well. Makes a fine hedge. To 6 feet tall and wide.

Rugosa Magnifica

Hybrid rugosa; 1905 / Almost-flat, magenta-red blossoms with crowns of gold stamens appear until frost. Strong, spicy fragrance. Orange-red hips. Disease resistant. To 5 feet tall and wide.

Sarah Van Fleet

Hybrid rugosa; 1926 / Michael Ruggiero, at the New York Botanical Garden, says: "Most catalogs list it as growing to 8 feet, but 'Sarah Van Fleet' grows to 10 or 11 feet in my garden and is wider than high. Its double rose-pink flowers are highly perfumed and repeat-flower from late spring until frost. Like most rugosa hybrids, it is very disease resistant." For a list of Ruggiero's recommendations, see page 411.

Scentimental

Floribunda; 1997 / Instantly recognizable, the variably striped and marbled blossoms combine rich red and chalk white. Flower shape—from the plump buds to the open flowers—is attractive as well, and the fragrance is, of course, notable. Rounded habit, to about 3½ feet tall. AARS.

Sea Foam

Shrub; 1964 / A creamy foam of clustered, full, rosette-shaped blossoms billows on a sea of glossy leaves. Faint scent. Lax and spreading, to about 3 feet high and twice as wide; makes fine ground cover or container plant, and can also be grown as a small climber.

Sexy Rexy

Floribunda; 1984 / Peggy Van Allen, in the Northwest, describes this as "A very valiant rose; a flower spray is a bouquet by itself." Peter Schneider, in Ohio, says it "provides as stunning an impact as any floribunda in this climate. Its huge pink trusses will completely hide its foliage in June." Mild fragrance. From 3 to 5 feet tall and wide. For a list of Schneider's and Van Allen's recommendations, see pages 412 and 413.

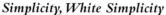

Simplicity, White Simplicity

Floribundas; 1978, 1991 / Classed as a floribunda but promoted as a shrub, 'Simplicity' is a bushy, 4- to 5-foot plant that is easily maintained as an ever-blooming hedge. Slender, pointed buds in small clusters open to cupped blossoms. Little scent. 'Purple Simplicity', 'Red Simplicity', 'White Simplicity', and 'Yellow Simplicity' are in the same mold as the original pink version.

Sevilliana

Shrub; 1976 / Not to be confused with 'Sevillana' (or 'La Sevillana'), a fiery red floribunda, this rose is a Buck hybrid with fragrant, freckled pink petals around a cluster of golden stamens. To 4 feet tall.

Singin' in the Rain

Floribunda; 1994 / The changeable color is hard to nail down: the blooms have been called golden apricot and russet-orange, often with a brownish cast described as cinnamon. The small clusters of blooms have a sweet scent. Glossy leaves; good disease resistance. To about 5 feet. AARS.

Sunsprite

Floribunda; 1977 / Larry Parton, of Spokane, Washington, thinks highly of this rose: "It is still the best yellow rose in my garden. The deep yellow petals hold their color until they drop." Rich fragrance. Flowers almost continuously. Good winter hardiness and tolerates cool summers well. To about 3 feet tall. ARS James Alexander Gamble Rose Fragrance Medal. For a list of Parton's recommendations, see page 413.

Sir Thomas Lipton

Hybrid rugosa; 1900 / Bushy and bulky (to 8 feet high and wide), this one has plenty of leathery foliage to serve as a backdrop for the well-shaped, highly scented blossoms it bears both individually and in small clusters.

Starry Night

Shrub; 2002 / One of two winners of the prestigious ARS All-America Rose Selections award in 2002, this rose blooms profusely. Large clusters of single bright white blossoms almost cover the bush all summer. No fragrance though. From 3 to 6 feet tall and wide. AARS.

Also Recommended

Scabrosa

Hybrid rugosa; 1950 / Fragrant, slightly crinkly, mauve-pink blossoms are up to 5 inches across. Glossy leaves turn color in fall. Large red hips. Good winter hardiness. To 6 feet tall and can be as wide.

Snow Owl (White Pavement)

Hybrid rugosa; 1989 / Fragrant, cupped, white blossoms are centered with showy bright yellow stamens. Impressive hips. Just 3 to 4 feet tall.

Sun Runner

Ground cover; 1992 / Clusters of little buttercup-yellow blossoms with creamy white edges drop cleanly. Small, bronze-tinted, shiny leaves. Light fragrance.

Sunny June

Shrub; 1952 / Rich yellow, single blossoms with amber stamens open in large clusters into late fall. Light scent. Vigorous. To 8 feet in mild climates; can be a small climber or a pillar rose.

Sweet Inspiration

Floribunda; 1991 / Pink blooms with creamy centers appear almost continuously all summer. Little or no fragrance. To 4 feet tall.

The Dark Lady

English rose; 1994 / This lady, alas, is dark red only in cool temperatures; she fades quickly in the heat. Heady old-rose fragrance. Very full blossoms that may nod. To 5 feet tall and a little wider.

Tamora

English rose; 1992 / Michael Ruggiero, at the New York Botanical Garden, says: "Tamora's flowers are made up of over 40 silky petals in a wonderful mixture of apricot, peach, and orange. It's highly fragrant and low-growing, to about 3½ feet tall and wide, and I've had great success using it as a mass planting but could also see it as a low hedge or ground cover." For a list of Ruggiero's recommendations, see page 411.

Sun Flare

Floribunda; 1981 / Bushy plants, to about 2½ feet high, produce great quantities of shapely, fragrant blossoms. The luminous lemon color is beautifully displayed against the bright green, extra-glossy foliage. The climbing sport is sold as 'Yellow Blaze'; it grows to 14 feet. AARS.

The Fairy

Polyantha; 1932 / The small, full-petaled flowers appear in great profusion into autumn. The elongated, pyramidal clusters cover the bush in a pale pink cloak. No fragrance. Glossy, diseaseproof leaves. Spreading, to about 3 feet tall; recommended for containers. Tolerates light shade and humidity.

The Pilgrim

English rose; 1991 / The rosettes are a delicate mass of soft, folded petals—reputedly there are 170 per blossom. The center petals are a rich yellow, fading to pale yellow or white petals at the outside. Strong, spicy scent. To 6 feet tall, more in warm climates.

The Squire

English rose; 1976 / Imbued with heady perfume second to none, the blossoms are large, velvety, and black-tinged, with a petal complexity like that of the Bourbon 'Souvenir de la Malmaison' (page 397). To about 4 feet tall. Stiff, upright habit. Susceptible to mildew.

White Meidiland

Ground cover; 1986 / The combination of dark, glossy foliage and pure white flowers gives this rose a fresh, clean look. Elongated, airy sprays of blossoms (twice the size of those of its white stablemate 'Alba Meidiland'). Faint scent. Low and spreading, to about 2 feet high and 6 feet wide.

White Pet (Little White Pet)

Polyantha; 1879 / Clouds of little pompon blossoms appear through summer and into fall. The tiny buds are pink, and in cool weather a tint of pink may grace the open petals. Moderate to strong fragrance. Good disease resistance. To 3 feet tall, but often much smaller.

Old Garden Roses

Strictly speaking, old garden roses, also called *antique roses,* are those that existed in 1867. But many old garden rose catalogs and the listings in this section also include roses closely related to them. These wonderfully fragrant roses vary in size from giant climbers to bushes suitable for containers. Some bloom only once a year; others flower repeatedly, flush after flush, from spring until frost. (All roses listed here repeat-bloom unless noted otherwise.) Disease resistance varies among old garden roses, as does hardiness. *Rosa rugosa* is the hardiest, surviving to −35°F/−37°C or below without much protection. Most others are hardy to at least −20°F/−29°C, but China and centifolia roses generally need the same sort of winter protection hybrid teas require. Noisette and tea roses are relatively tender and best used in regions where temperatures fall no lower than about 10°F/−12°C.

In the listings, AARS means the rose has received the All-America Rose Selections award (see page 316). Alternative rose names are noted in parentheses. For an explanation of plant and flower form terms, see pages 296–297.

Alba Semi-Plena
Alba; before 1867 / The powerfully scented blossoms, each consisting of several rows of pure white petals surrounding a central clump of golden stamens, are scattered like a light snowfall over an arching, 6-foot shrub. Doesn't repeat-bloom. Red hips.

Baronne Prévost
Hybrid perpetual; 1842 / Cupped to flat, the full, bright blossoms usually have a central buttonlike eye. Heavy fragrance. Thorny stems and somewhat coarse leaves. Upright, to 6 feet tall.

Boule de Neige
Bourbon; 1867 / More than 100 richly scented, creamy white petals make up each blossom. The buds are flushed with pink, and tinges of scarlet may linger on the rounded, open blossoms. Upright form, to 5 feet.

Camaieux
Hybrid gallica; 1830 / A striking patchwork quilt of harmonious colors: white to pale pink petals show crimson and pink stripes that change to lavender and grayed purple as the flowers age. Delicious scent. Upright to arching; may reach 4 feet. Only one flush of bloom per season.

Cardinal de Richelieu
Hybrid gallica; 1847 / Round buds in small clusters open to sweetly scented, rosy violet flowers that become almost ball-shaped at maturity—by then, the shell-like petals are smoky purple with silvery reverses. Nearly thornless. Dense bush, to about 4 feet high. Tolerates humidity well. Only one burst of bloom per season.

Céline Forestier

Noisette; 1858 / The pale yellow deepens in the center, around the green button eye, and fades to cream as the blossoms age. Strongly scented. Blooms appear all summer and into fall. To 8 feet; can also be grown as a climber.

Comte de Chambord

Portland; 1860 / Upright, 3-foot plants with light green leaves produce petal-crammed, very fragrant blooms in a luscious rich pink; the flowers start out cupped, then open flat, even quartered, to reveal a button eye. Susceptible to black spot.

Crépuscule

Noisette; 1904 / The name means "twilight" in French—but this is the sun's final blaze, not the end-of-day purple shadows. Clusters of small orange buds open to sweetly fragrant blooms of bright saffron-salmon, fading to buff. Blooms all summer. A shrubby climber, to 12 feet.

Crested Moss (Cristata)

Moss; 1827 / The elaborately fringed calyx, so visible in unopened buds, accounts for the name. From this rococo cocoon emerges a typical full, cupped, spicily fragrant centifolia blossom in silvery pink. Blooms only in spring. Light green foliage. Upright, to 6 feet tall.

Dupuy Jamain

Hybrid perpetual; 1868 / Larry Parton, in Spokane, Washington, lists this rose as a favorite: "Its large, vibrant red-pink blooms are very fragrant and showy, but it doesn't get as huge as other hybrid perpetuals in my garden." To 5 feet. Good winter hardiness. For a list of Parton's recommendations, see page 413.

Ferdinand Pichard

Hybrid perpetual; 1921 / These small, striped, fragrant blossoms change color as they mature, starting pink with scarlet stripes and aging to white with purple stripes. They are usually borne in tight clusters among light green, pointed leaves. Good winter hardiness. To 6 feet tall.

Frau Karl Druschki

Hybrid perpetual; 1901 / Long, pointed buds, sometimes tinged pink, open completely even in damp regions. Lacks fragrance. Extremely vigorous, to 7 feet tall. Can be trained as a restrained climber, to about 10 feet, though a truly climbing sport is also available. Susceptible to mildew.

Great Maiden's Blush
Alba; before 1738 / This lovely, delicately scented antique has been known by various names, including *Rosa alba incarnata* and the more suggestive 'La Séduisante' and 'Cuisse de Nymphe'. Clustered, full, milky blush-pink blossoms. Plentiful foliage. To 7 feet tall and arching. Blooms once, in spring.

Henri Martin
Moss; 1862 / Lightly mossed blooms are a fragrant, rich, clear crimson, turning deep rose-pink with age. They are borne in great profusion on a 5-foot, arching plant with wiry stems and fresh green leaves. Blooms only in spring.

Henry Nevard
Hybrid perpetual; 1924 / Glowing deep crimson blossoms—large, cupped, and strongly fragrant—are perfectly complemented by ample dark foliage on a husky, upright bush, to about 5 feet tall.

Honorine de Brabant
Bourbon; date unknown / The petals are irregularly striped in purplish pink to violet, but the effect is harmonious rather than garish. Full, cupped, very fragrant blossoms are borne on a fairly tall plant, to about 6 feet, with thick foliage and few thorns. Good disease resistance.

La Ville de Bruxelles
Damask; 1849 / A prickly bush with elongated leaves bears large blooms of superb fragrance and form. Each one holds countless elaborately folded petals around a button eye. Blooms once, in spring. Upright, to about 5 feet, becoming rather spreading when freighted with blossoms.

Lady Hillingdon
Tea; 1910 / Decorative plum-purple new growth harmonizes well with the large, fragrant saffron-yellow blossoms that open from long, pointed buds. The upright, spreading bush is tall, to 6 feet, and rather open—less dense than most other teas. Often grown as a climber, to 15 feet.

Also Recommended

Anna de Diesbach (Gloire de Paris)
Hybrid perpetual; 1858 / Long, pointed buds unfurl to large, cupped clear pink blossoms that are highly fragrant. Vigorous, bushy habit; to 6 feet or taller.

Ducher
Hybrid China; 1869 / Lovely buds open to somewhat cupped, fragrant blossoms in pure white. Bronzy new leaves. To about 4 feet. Less angular than many Chinas.

Eugène de Beauharnais
Hybrid China; 1838 / Very fragrant, velvety, deep crimson blossoms appear into fall. Compact, thorny bush. Can be planted in sun or light shade. To around 3 feet tall.

Green rose (Rosa chinensis viridiflora)
Hybrid China; before 1856 / The "blossoms" are bright green sepals, not petals (see page 311). Flower arrangers are its main fans; it "flowers" through the growing season. Disease resistant. Tolerates heat. To 4 feet tall.

La Reine
Hybrid perpetual; 1842 / Very full, cupped, pink, fragrant flowers are produced in abundance on a bushy plant, to about 3 feet high.

Léda (Painted Damask)
Damask; before 1867 / Crimson markings tip the countless blush-to-white petals. Very fragrant. Blooms once, in late spring. To about 4 feet.

Lamarque

Noisette; 1830 / Plenty of pointed, medium green leaves clothe this vigorous climber. Bloom time brings a lavish display of blossoms with a powerful, sweet scent: small clusters of medium-size flowers in creamy white to palest lemon, opening from shapely buds. To 20 feet or more.

Mme. Alfred Carrière

Noisette; 1879 / It's big and vigorous, with plentiful gray-green foliage; you can use it as a climber (to 20 feet) or maintain it as a large, arching shrub (around 10 feet). The blush-white to lightest salmon-pink flowers are moderately large, full, and sweetly fragrant.

Marchesa Boccella (Marquise Boçella; Jacques Cartier)

Hybrid perpetual; 1842 / Peter Schneider, in Ohio, recommends this rose highly: "If you want to grow only one old garden rose, I recommend this one. It has all of the charm and fragrance we expect from a heritage rose without any of the drawbacks. It maintains a perfect habit, repeats continuously, has good disease resistance, and doesn't mind winter." To 4 feet tall. For a list of Schneider's recommendations, see page 412.

Mme. Hardy

Damask; 1832 / Its special beauty is in its open flowers: cupped to flat, each packed with symmetrically arranged, pristine white petals around a green center. Clusters of these fragrant blossoms decorate a moderately tall plant (to 6 feet). Blooms once, in spring.

Mme. Isaac Pereire

Bourbon; 1881 / Everything about this rose says "big"—including its intoxicating fragrance. Full-petaled blossoms of an intense purplish pink are backed by large leaves on a plant so vigorous it is better used as a small climber. Grows to 8 feet, taller as a climber. Susceptible to black spot.

Mutabilis

Hybrid China; before 1894 / Peggy Van Allen, in the Northwest, says: "My bush is four years old but not yet 3 feet tall because of winter die-back. Still, it blooms from early summer to late fall, and I love the different colors all at the same time. On the slender canes, the flowers bounce, nod, and flutter like butterflies." To 10 feet tall in warm climates; can be trained as a climber. For a list of Van Allen's recommendations, see page 413.

Reine des Violettes

Hybrid perpetual; 1860 / Intensely perfumed, full, flat flowers with a central button eye start out carmine-red, then quickly fade to shades of magenta, violet, and lavender. Nearly thornless, with gray-green leaves. To 8 feet tall.

Rêve d'Or

Noisette; 1869 / The foliage is among the best you'll see on any climbing rose—thick, semi-glossy, bronzed green. Shapely, fragrant blossoms vary from buff-apricot to gold to nearly orange, depending on the weather. Vigorous, to 18 feet; can also be grown as a very large shrub.

Rosa banksiae (Banksia rose)

Species / Where winter temperatures remain above 0°F/−18°C, these rampant climbers are smothered in pendent clusters of small blossoms in early spring. *R. b.* 'Lutea' (Lady Banks' rose) has yellow, unscented blossoms; *R. b. banksiae* (usually sold as 'Alba Plena' or 'White Banksia') has white blossoms that smell of violets. Both flower only once a season. Stems are thornless in the double forms (the single-flowered forms are rarely available). Disease-resistant foliage. Virtually evergreen in all but the coldest areas of the plant's range. Tolerates heat and humidity. Reaches 30 feet.

Rosa eglanteria (R. rubiginosa) (Sweet Brier, Eglantine)

Species / Both the flowers and the dense foliage have a green-apple scent (most pronounced in damp weather). Blooms once, in spring. Oval red to orange hips. Reaches 8 to 12 feet. Given an annual trimming, can be used as a hedge.

Rosa foetida bicolor (Austrian Copper)

Species / Few spring bloomers put on a brighter show than this rose with its blaze of coppery orange petals backed with yellow. Fragrance is strong, but some think it unpleasant. Susceptible to several foliage diseases. No repeat-bloom. From 5 to 10 feet tall.

Rosa gallica officinalis (Apothecary's Rose)

Gallica; ancient / This rose was cultivated by medieval herbalists—hence the popular name 'Apothecary's Rose'. The intensely fragrant blooms adorn a bushy, 3- to 4-foot plant with few thorns. Forms thick colonies if grown on its own roots. Doesn't repeat-bloom.

Also Recommended

Magna Charta
Hybrid perpetual; 1876 / The bright pink, cupped blossoms with hints of red are abundant, large, and fragrant. Glossy foliage. Susceptible to black spot and mildew. To 5 feet.

Maréchal Niel
Noisette; 1864 / The fragrant, soft yellow blossoms face downward. Needs a warm climate and good care. Grows 8 to 12 feet tall.

Roger Lambelin
Hybrid perpetual; 1890 / The velvety, dark, purplish red petals are precisely margined in white. Heavy fragrance. Needs regular feeding and watering. To 5 feet.

Rose du Roi à Fleurs Pourpres
Portland; 1819 / Fragrant dark red flowers have a strong infusion of purple. Bushy, to 3 feet.

Rosa gallica versicolor (Rosa mundi)

Gallica; ancient / A sport of *Rosa gallica officinalis* (page 395) and identical to it in all respects save the flowers, which are irregularly striped, dashed, and flecked pink and red on a background of white.

Rosa hugonis (R. xan-thina bugonis) (Father Hugo's Rose; Golden Rose of China)

Species / In mid- to late spring, every branch is a garland of 2-inch, bright yellow blossoms with a light scent. Flowers only in spring. Pea-sized, brownish red to maroon hips. Good disease resistance. To about 8 feet tall.

Rosa moyesii

Species / A profusion of brilliant red flowers to 2½ inches across makes an arresting show. Blooms once, in spring, but in autumn bottle-shaped hips of blazing orange-red dangle from the spreading branches. Large, loose, and rather sparse; to 10 feet or so. 'Geranium' (with red flowers) and 'Sealing Wax' (with pink blooms) are shorter and more compact than the species. For areas where low temperatures in winter remain above −10°F/−23°C. Little if any scent.

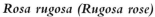

Rosa rugosa (Rugosa rose)

Species / A hybridizer could hardly have designed a rose with more virtues. Silky-petaled, fragrant flowers appear in spring, summer, and autumn. The glossy leaves have a distinctive heavy veining that gives them a crinkled appearance—and, best of all, they are nearly diseaseproof. Large "tomato" hips. From 3 to 8 feet high, spreading into colonies if grown on its own roots. Extremely tough and cold-hardy, enduring hard freezes, aridity, wind, and salt spray. Tolerant of cool summers, humidity, and heat. Excellent hedge plant. *R. r. alba* (left) has white blossoms. *R. rugosa* and *R. r. rubra* (right) have magenta-purple ones.

Rosa roxburghii (Chestnut rose, Chinquapin rose)

Species / The bud emerges from a bristly calyx that gives this disease-resistant rose its common names. Blooms once, in spring. Fragrance varies. Peeling cinnamon-colored bark on older stems. Prickly hips. To 10 feet or taller and 15 feet across. Tolerates heat and humidity.

Rosa sericea pteracantha

Species / The broad, red-brown thorns that march up the canes (see page 311) make this rose instantly recognizable. The flowers have just four petals and little or no scent; they appear once, in spring. Leaves consist of up to 19 small leaflets. Vigorous and arching, to around 10 feet.

Rose de Rescht
Portland; date unknown / These little pompons pack a powerful fragrance. Borne in clusters, they bloom continuously on a bushy, upright, 3-foot plant densely clothed in leaves. A good rose for containers.

Soleil d'Or
Hybrid foetida; 1900 / Long pointed buds unfurl to large, dusky gold, cupped blossoms that are spicy in scent. Small leaves; susceptible to black spot. To 4 feet tall.

Souvenir de la Malmaison
Bourbon; 1843 / Russ Bowermaster, in Florida, says of this rose: "It blooms early and late, with aromatic, large flowers, repeating very reliably, and it continues to bloom all winter in our climate. This is probably the most desired old garden rose for most rosarians." Reaches 4 feet. 'Kronprinzessin Viktoria' (1887) is a creamy white sport; a dark pink to rosy red sport is 'Red Souvenir de la Malmaison' (1845). For a list of Bowermaster's recommendations, see page 412.

Tuscany Superb (Superb Tuscan)
Hybrid gallica; before 1837 / Wavy petals that look as if cut from maroon velvet form a perfumed blossom with a cluster of gold stamens in the center. Few thorns. Upright, to around 4 feet. Only one flush of bloom per season.

Variegata di Bologna
Bourbon; 1909 / Cupped blossoms, in small clusters, flaunt a peppermint-stick combination of white petals striped purplish red. Fragrant. Repeat-bloom is spotty. Tall and vigorous; can be trained on a pillar or simply allowed to become a 6-foot fountain of canes. Susceptible to black spot.

Zéphirine Drouhin
Bourbon; 1868 / Richly fragrant flowers adorn the plant like a flight of butterflies. Naturally a restrained climber, from 8 to 12 feet—but treat it as a large shrub if a climber would be too large for your available space. Almost thornless. Susceptible to black spot and mildew.

Also Recommended

Souvenir du Docteur Jamain
Hybrid perpetual; 1865 / Fragrant, black-shaded petals the color of port wine compose a cupped, ruffled-looking flower. Reaches 7 feet, or 12 feet as a climber.

William Lobb (Old Velvet Moss)
Moss; 1855 / Magenta, crimson, purple, and lilac are richly mixed in the heavily mossed, strongly scented blossoms. Tall and rangy, to around 8 feet, it does best if given support or treated as a climber. No repeat-bloom.

York and Lancaster
Damask; before 1867 / The fragrant blossoms may be pinkish white, light to medium pink, or a pink-and-white combination; all variations may appear in a flower cluster. Blooms once, in late spring. Thorny. To 7 feet.

Climbing Roses

Climbing roses produce long, strong canes that will grow upright on a vertical surface or freestanding structure—provided you train and tie them. They vary in size from 6 feet to 30 feet. The largest are often the ramblers; they produce massive floral displays, usually in one big flush in spring. The smallest are the pillar roses, which are just barely climbers; their canes have the desirable habit of flowering well when grown completely upright. You'll also find here climbing sports of bush roses that have long and more-or-less pliable canes. The *large-flowered climbers* (LCLs) and Kordesii climbers are natural climbers with no bush counterparts. For cold-winter regions, look for the Canadian Explorer series. All roses listed here repeat-bloom unless noted otherwise.

Choose your climbers carefully. Climbing roses take several years to reach a desirable height, and a poor choice might mean that you have to start over with a different selection.

In the listings, AARS means the rose has received the All-America Rose Selections award (see page 316). For some roses, an alternative name is noted in parentheses. For an explanation of plant and flower form terms, see pages 296–297.

Alchymist
Hybrid eglanteria; 1956 / The open blossoms have the flat, swirled and quartered form of some old garden roses and are an ever-changing mélange of gold, yellow, apricot, and pink. Glossy, bronzy green leaves. Can be a restrained climber, to 8 feet, or large shrub. Blooms only once; lovely fragrance.

Altissimo
LCL; 1966 / Clusters of small buds open to spectacular single flowers of velvety bright red with showy yellow stamens and a light, clovelike scent. Glossy leaves add to the brilliance. Train as a small climber or pillar rose to 12 feet; or maintain as a tall shrub.

America
LCL; 1976 / This repeat-bloomer has lovely, shapely buds and large, full, highly fragrant flowers of the best hybrid tea form. Vigorous, to about 15 feet; can also be trained as a pillar rose. Susceptible to black spot. Poor winter hardiness in cold climates. AARS.

Berries 'n' Cream
LCL; 1998 / A pleasing, fruity fragrance enhances the extravagant clusters of blooms splashed with rosy pink and cream, which call to mind the ancient *Rosa gallica versicolor* (page 396). Strong 10- to 12-foot canes. Few thorns.

Blaze
LCL; 1932 / Clusters of scarlet 2- to 3-inch flowers cover the plant over a long spring bloom season. Tolerates heat well. Vigorous but not huge; ideal for fences, walls, and pillars. Slight fragrance. Susceptible to black spot and mildew. 'Blaze Improved' is reputed to repeat-flower more reliably.

Cl. Iceberg

Climbing floribunda; 1968 / This is often rated the finest climbing white rose; some even call it the finest climber, period. Profuse flowering and good repeat-bloom come on a vigorous plant that reaches 15 feet. Susceptible to mildew.

Cl. Sutter's Gold

Climbing hybrid tea; 1950 / Elegant, elongated buds in classic form open to large, glowing yellow flowers, with petals warmed by a red flush. Train the 8- to 12-foot canes on a pillar or trellis. Very fragrant (the bush form won an ARS James Alexander Gamble Fragrance Medal).

Cl. Cécile Brünner (Cl. Mlle. Cécile Brünner)

Climbing polyantha; 1904 / Kathleen Brenzel, in California, says: "This climber is the star attraction in my garden, spread across three trellises to form a leafy tunnel. When its sweetheart buds open, it looks like a pink cumulus cloud." Tolerates heat. To 20 feet. Sweet scent. Healthy. May bloom till fall. The bush 'Cécile Brünner' grows to 5 feet. Not hardy in cold climates. For a list of Brenzel's recommendations, see page 414.

Clair Matin

LCL; 1960 / Red-tinted, pointed buds open to blossoms with a cluster of gold stamens among petals of palest pink, blushing to a soft salmon hue with time. Fragrant. Consistent rebloom. Reaches 8 to 12 feet high; can also be grown as a shrub.

Compassion

LCL; 1972 / A beautiful fragrance emanates from these high-centered blooms, awash in shades of apricot, pink, and peach. Lavish rebloomer. Vigorous; climbs 9 to 15 feet; can also be kept as a shrub.

Constance Spry

Shrub/LCL; 1961 / The large, full, cupped, fragrant blossoms resemble the old European roses—and, like them, it flowers profusely in spring only. Vigorous; to 15 feet if trained as a climber but can be pruned to remain a large shrub. Disease resistant.

Also Recommended

All Ablaze

LCL; 1999 / Ruffled candy-apple-red blossoms are carried in clusters. Flowers freely through the growing season. A hint of fragrance. To 12 feet.

Blossomtime

LCL; 1951 / 'New Dawn' (page 402) is parent to this alluring climber (to 10 feet) with shell-pink blossoms that have reverses of deeper pink. Fragrant. Good bloomer. Tolerates humidity well. A shrub, or pillar rose.

Cl. Angel Face

Climbing floribunda; 1981 / Everything that makes the bush form (see page 377) so popular is available in a climber that grows to about 10 feet. Lemony scent. Poor winter hardiness in cold climates.

Don Juan

LCL; 1958 / Velvety red buds of the best hybrid tea form and size come singly or in small clusters on long stems and open well in all climates; flowers are very fragrant. A moderate climber, to about 10 feet; suitable as a pillar rose. Poor winter hardiness in cold climates.

Dortmund

Hybrid kordesii; 1955 / This rose radiates health and vigor. The blossoms are displayed against excellent foliage—holly-like and virtually disease-proof. Light to strong scent. Tolerates cool summers well. To 12 feet; much taller in warm climates. A climber, a shrub, or even a ground cover.

Dublin Bay

LCL; 1974 / This medium-size climber or pillar rose (to about 10 feet) glows with health. Velvety bright red flowers come in waves from spring into autumn. Moderate to fleeting fragrance. Foliage is plentiful and disease resistant.

Gloire de Dijon

Climbing tea; 1853 / Very full and rather flat flowers, shaped like those of its Bourbon parent, 'Souvenir de la Malmaison' (see page 397), are sweetly scented and keep coming. Susceptible to mildew, black spot, and balling. To 12 feet, but often becomes established slowly.

Fourth of July

LCL; 1999 / Kathleen Brenzel, in California, says: "Beautiful blooms in various combinations of red and white unfurl along the length of its canes, not just at the tips. Some blossoms are striped like peppermint; others are splashed or spotted with red. All have prominent yellow stamens. The effect is clean, crisp, bold." Mild scent. Tolerates heat and humidity well. To 14 feet. AARS. For a list of Brenzel's recommendations, see page 414.

Garden Sun

LCL; 1998 / This is another of Kathleen Brenzel's favorites: "In our test garden at Sunset, this lovely rose drapes over a split rail fence, bearing clusters of rich yellow blooms, with apricot blush, against deep green foliage. The fragrance is only mild, but the blooms are as cheerful as a sunny day. A neat, tailored climber with a sunny disposition." Grows 10 to 12 feet high. For a list of Brenzel's recommendations, see page 414.

Golden Showers
LCL; 1956 / Pointed buds of butter-yellow open to rather ruffled, fragrant, lighter blossoms with showy red-orange stamens. Blooms early, with an excellent fall flush. A pillar rose, but grows to 15 feet in mild climates. Susceptible to mildew. Poor winter hardiness in cold climates. AARS.

Handel
LCL; 1965 / Throughout the growing season, great numbers of shapely, hybrid tea–style buds swirl open to moderately full, creamy white flowers edged with strawberry-pink. Little fragrance. Fine bloom in fall. Susceptible to black spot. Reaches 10 to 15 feet.

Illusion
Hybrid kordesii; 1961 / Generous clusters of large, silky blossoms open scarlet-red and then turn dusky vermilion and maroon. Moderately fragrant. Blooms through the summer. Healthy foliage. Vigorous, but not big: use it on a trellis or to dress up a wall or fence.

John Cabot
Hybrid kordesii; 1978 / Clusters of fragrant flowers are borne profusely in spring, then sporadically. One of the Canadian Explorer roses, developed to withstand southern Canadian winters without protection, it makes a modest climber or a large arching shrub. Excellent disease resistance.

Joseph's Coat
LCL; 1969 / As the yellow buds expand, the color intensifies to orange; then, with exposure to sunlight, the petals flush with red, until the entire flower is crimson. To 12 feet; a climber, pillar rose, shrub, or hedge. Slight scent. Repeats now and then. Susceptible to black spot and mildew.

Lace Cascade
LCL; 1992 / From late spring onward, shapely buds open to full, ice-white flowers with a slight fragrance. Train the 10- to 12-foot canes on a pillar or trellis; or prune to a 5- to 7-foot shrub. Repeats well. Good disease resistance.

Maigold (Maygold)
Shrub; 1953 / Intensely fragrant, richly colored blooms of a bronze-gold hue appear early in the season; no rebloom. Very thorny. Tolerates humidity well. Not a large climber; encourage it to scale a pillar or spread out over a trellis; or grow it as a 5-foot shrub.

Also Recommended

Cl. Souvenir de la Malmaison
Climbing Bourbon; 1893 / Like the bush form (see page 397), but reaches 15 feet, more in mild climates. Spotty repeat-bloom. Rain may cause balling. Poor winter hardiness in cold climates.

Dynamite
LCL; 1992 / Explosions of dark red, hybrid tea–style blossoms repeat from spring into autumn on an upright pillar rose, to about 10 feet. Lightly scented. Glossy, disease-resistant foliage.

Kiftsgate
Species; 1954 / For a few weeks each summer, this giant climber (20 feet or more) glows with creamy white blossoms accented by yellow stamens. Delicious fragrance. Tolerates some shade.

Paprika
LCL; 1997 / The bright flowers of this Romantica climber-cum-shrub open in clusters, from pointed buds. Reblooms well. Slight scent. Large glossy leaves. To 10 feet.

Pierre de Ronsard (Eden)
LCL; 1987 / The plump, creamy buds and cupped, pink-blushed flowers with row upon row of petals on this Romantica rose have the style of old European roses, but they appear throughout the growing season. Slight scent. Glossy, healthy foliage. From 8 to 10 feet; a climber or pillar rose.

New Dawn
LCL; 1930 / Peter Schneider, in Ohio, says: "What repeat-blooming climber will cover an arbor in Zone 5? I know of three: 'New Dawn', 'Quadra', and 'William Baffin' [both on the next page]. But nothing beats 'New Dawn' for beauty and reliability." Bewitching scent. To about 15 feet; can be used as a pillar rose or shrub. World Rose Hall of Fame. For a list of Schneider's recommendations, see page 412.

Piñata
LCL; 1978 / Glossy foliage sets off floribunda-style, golden yellow flowers edged and washed in orange-red. An almost nonstop show of blooms. Slightly fragrant. Restrained, 8 to 10 feet, and somewhat shrubby; best used as a pillar rose or shrub.

Polka
LCL; 1996 / From plump orange buds, petals un-fold and expand into large, full, fragrant, grace-fully waved blossoms of golden, peachy apricot. A Romantica rose. Good for cutting. Glossy, light green leaves. To 12 feet high, or use as a shrub.

Royal Sunset
LCL; 1960 / Shapely buds of hybrid tea elegance are predominantly orange; as the flowers open, sunset tones take over, leading to buff-apricot or creamy peach with age. Fruity scent. Dark bronzy green, glossy leaves. Poor winter hardiness in cold climates. To 10 feet; a modest climber or large shrub.

Shadow Dancer
LCL; 1999 / This child of 'Dortmund' (page 400) has the same handsome, glossy, dark leaves as its parent but bigger, fancier, and more plentiful blos-soms. Fragrance is only slight, but flowers appear all summer. Reaches about 8 feet, taller in mild climates.

Rosarium Uetersen

LCL; 1977 / Russ Bowermaster, in Florida, says this about his favorite climber: "A quite large climber, with huge clusters of blooms. The first blush of bloom in the spring, following pruning, stops the traffic on the street where we live. Quite disease resistant, and repeat-blooms when spent flowers are properly pruned." Fragrant. To around 12 feet. For a list of Bowermaster's recommendations, see page 412.

Sombreuil

Climbing tea; 1850 / Plump buds open to flat, circular, creamy white flowers intricately packed with petals that are sometimes flushed pink and fade to white in sun. Beautifully fragrant. Reblooms sporadically. Heat tolerant. Poor winter hardiness in cold climates. To 15 feet; a climber or pillar rose.

Spectacular (Danse du Feu)

LCL; 1953 / Glossy, bronze foliage sets off bountiful clusters of cupped blooms shaded orange and scarlet. Fragrant. Good vigor. Grows 8 to 10 feet tall.

Veilchenblau

Hybrid multiflora; 1909 / The most widely available of several "blue ramblers" (others are 'Violette', on this page, and 'Bleu Magenta'). Small flowers open a deep violet, sometimes streaked with white, then fade to nearly gray. Moderately fragrant. No rebloom. Grows 8 to 15 feet high.

White Dawn

LCL; 1949 / This child of 'New Dawn' (page 402) features ruffled blossoms with the scent of gardenias. Lavish spring display, moderate bloom in summer, and another big burst in fall. Good disease resistance. Tolerates humidity well. Vigorous, to about 12 feet; can be used as a climber or shrub.

William Baffin

Hybrid kordesii; 1983 / Slightly fragrant carmine-pink blossoms appear in large clusters throughout the growing season on a plant with disease-resistant foliage. One of the extra-hardy Canadian Explorer roses, it can be grown as a modest climber (to 12 feet) or a large, arching shrub.

Also Recommended

Kiss of Desire (Harlekin)
LCL; 1986 / Cherry-red edges the creamy white blooms. A light wild-rose scent. Repeats sporadically. Grows to 12 feet.

Quadra (J. F. Quadra)
Hybrid kordesii; 1981 / Pink to dark red blossoms have little if any scent. To 6 feet, more in mild climates. Hardy. Can also be used as a shrub.

Ramira (Agatha Christie)
LCL; 1988 / Fragrant, strawberry-pink blossoms have hybrid tea form. Reblooms well. To 12 feet, or grow as a large shrub.

Violette
Hybrid multiflora; 1921 / A "blue rambler" (see also 'Veilchenblau', left) with small, fragrant, reddish violet blooms, fading to soft mauve. Blooms once. To 15 feet.

Miniature Roses

Miniature roses are scaled-down versions of larger roses, with small leaves and smallish flowers. Most are dainty bushes—diminutive hybrid tea, shrub, or old garden roses—but some are 7-foot climbers or ground covers. Typically, miniatures bloom abundantly and almost continuously (unless otherwise stated, all the miniatures described here are repeat-bloomers). Although many are short on fragrance, there are notable exceptions. Plant them in containers or the fronts of flower beds, or use them to edge a path. They are tough plants, in the main, but, to keep them bushy and thriving, provide winter protection in regions where temperatures fall below 10°F/−12°C. Those described as short are about 1 foot high. Medium are 1 to 2 feet. Tall are over 2 feet.

In the listings, AARS means the rose has received the All-America Rose Selections award (see page 316). AoE means the rose has received the Award of Excellence from the American Rose Society, based on trials conducted for 2 years in test gardens throughout the United States. For some roses, an alternative name is noted in parentheses. For an explanation of plant and flower form terms, see pages 296–297.

Adam's Smile
1987 / Elegant, pointed buds unfurl to full blossoms with petals that roll back at the edges to create pointed petal tips. Deep pink flowers are infused with yellow on the petal backs. No scent. Glossy leaves. Medium height.

Amy Grant
1998 / Light pink, double blossoms with high centers like a hybrid tea appear singly among dark, glossy foliage. Slight fragrance. Good for cutting. Medium height.

Beauty Secret
1965 / One of the oldest miniatures and still popular, this rose produces lovely long, pointed buds that open to semidouble, cherry-red blossoms with pointed petal tips. Fragrant. Upright and bushy, to medium height. ARS Miniature Rose Hall of Fame. AoE.

Baby Love
1992 / Peter Schneider, in Ohio, says: "This is the ideal accent rose. Its neat, rounded habit makes it perfect for a container and easy to tuck into any garden space. Covered with flowers all summer long, it is one of only two roses ('Flower Carpet' [page 380] being the other) that won't black spot in my garden." Slight fragrance. Good disease resistance. Tall. For a list of Schneider's recommendations, see page 412.

Black Jade
1985 / Dusky deep red—almost black—buds of the best hybrid tea form open to full, fairly large blossoms of velvety dark red. The flowers come singly and in clusters. Little or no scent. Medium height. AoE.

Cal Poly
1991 / Brilliant color and easy care are the selling points of this rose. Against a dense backdrop of leaves, the pointed buds open to double flowers. Faint scent if any. Good disease resistance. Medium height. A climbing form (to about 8 feet) is also available. AoE.

Child's Play
1991 / The child who could color these elegant hybrid tea–style blooms would have to wield the crayons carefully: each broad white petal has a precise edging of delicate pink. Fragrant. Blooms freely. Good disease resistance. Medium height. AARS. AoE.

Crackling Fire
1999 / Coppery orange petals have deep red-orange backs. Blossoms appear in small clusters. No fragrance. Compact bush of medium height.

Cupcake
1981 / The buds and very full mature blossoms, both in a clear, cotton-candy pink, show the finest hybrid tea style. Plenty of glossy foliage completes the picture. No fragrance. Medium height. AoE.

Figurine
1991 / Borne on long stems, the long, pointed buds and full open blossoms have the smooth delicacy of fine porcelain. The petals are ivory, washed in softest pink. Fragrant. Medium height. AoE.

Also Recommended

Carnival Glass
1979 / The slightly ruffled blossoms, a blend of warm yellow, apricot, and orange, are magnificent against the glossy, bronze-tinted leaves. Bushy, medium height, spreading wider than it is tall. Good for hanging baskets.

Dreamer
1990 / Oval buds, borne either in sprays or one per stem, open to 3-inch cupped, dusty pink blossoms. Fragrance varies. Bushy, upright plant; tall.

Fairhope
1989 / The light yellow flowers, almost white on occasion, have elegant high centers and open from slender, tapered buds carried singly on long stems. Slightly fragrant. Heat tolerant. Medium height.

Giggles

1987 / An elegant combination of pinks: the deep pink buds open to blossoms of light pink with darker pink on the petal backs, and then, with age, become creamy pink. High-centered hybrid tea form. Slightly fragrant. Matte green leaves. Medium height.

Green Ice

1971 / Pink-tinted white buds open to ruffled blossoms that mature into soft pale green, sometimes with pink tinges. Little or no scent. Mounding and spreading habit. Good for hanging baskets. Medium height.

Gourmet Popcorn

1986 / Michael Ruggiero, at the New York Botanical Garden, says: "In all my 27 years of rose growing, I have not grown a better miniature rose. It produces copious numbers of 1-inch white-petaled flowers that have distinct golden stamens—the 'butter' for the popcorn. It flowers all season long until frost, whether it is deadheaded or not." Tall. For a list of Ruggiero's recommendations, see page 411.

Herbie

1987 / Rich mauve blossoms are flushed with deeper mauve at the petal edges. Shapely, like hybrid tea blossoms, they appear singly and in clusters. Slight fragrance. Bushy, to medium height.

Hot Tamale

1993 / As the shapely yellow buds unfold, the petal surfaces show a blend of orange and pink, while the undersides remain largely yellow. Blossoms are carried in small clusters. Little or no fragrance. Good disease resistance. Tall. AoE.

Irresistible

1989 / Long-stemmed, long-budded blossoms suggest a small version of the hybrid tea 'Pristine' (page 372): they are a satiny ivory-white, tinged ever so slightly with pink and centered with blush pink. Blooms profusely. Moderately fragrant. Tall.

Jean Kenneally

1984 / Elegant, pointed buds open slowly to semidouble, slightly scented flowers that are always shapely. Vigorous; blooms freely. Tolerates humidity well. Tall. AoE.

Jeanne Lajoie

1975 / This popular climbing miniature produces bountiful clusters of very double, lightly scented blossoms. Train it as a climber, from 6 to 10 feet tall; use it as a hedge; or let it develop as an arching shrub. Good disease resistance. AoE.

Lemon Gems

2000 / Deep yellow, cupped blossoms are 2½ inches across, which is large for a miniature rose. They appear mostly one per stem. Fragrance is slight. Glossy leaves. Medium height. AoE.

Lavender Jewel

1978 / The plump hybrid tea–style buds and full, fragrant 1-inch blossoms are soft lavender, tinged with magenta on the petal edges. Bushy and compact habit. Medium height.

Little Jackie

1982 / Glossy foliage provides a pleasing background for the bright combination of sherbet-orange petal surfaces and yellow petal backs. The buds are shapely, the blossoms fragrant. Medium height. AoE.

Loving Touch

1983 / Bountiful urn-shaped, apricot buds open to 3-inch, moderately double blossoms of a smooth, creamy apricot. Lightly fragrant. Spreading form. Tall. AoE.

Magic Carrousel

1972 / From bud to open bloom, you can clearly see the precise cherry-red edges to the white petals. Flowers come singly and in clusters. Little if any scent. Vigorous and free-flowering. Tall. ARS Miniature Rose Hall of Fame. AoE.

Also Recommended

Giselle

1991 / Deep pink, semidouble blossoms with paler centers are wonderfully formed and open from pointed buds. Glossy leaves. Short.

Gourmet Pheasant

1995 / Massive clusters of deep cherry-pink-to-red blossoms with golden stamens cover this fast-growing ground cover. Little scent. Glossy leaves. Medium height, to 8 feet wide.

Irish Heartbreaker

1990 / This child of 'Rise 'n' Shine', page 409, is a climber, to 5 feet tall, with Chinese-red, 2-inch, full blossoms. Slight scent.

Minilights

1987 / Abundant small yellow flowers open in clusters among glossy leaves. Spreading habit, medium height. Slight fragrance. Good disease resistance.

Minnie Pearl

1982 / Long, shapely buds of a soft ivory-infused coral-pink swirl open to full blossoms that darken a little in sunshine. Mild fragrance at best. Medium height.

Miss Flippins

1997 / Wonderfully formed, bright red blossoms with pink petal backs unfurl from long, pointed buds. The long-lasting blossoms are borne mostly singly and are good for cutting. Tolerates heat well. No fragrance. Susceptible to mildew. Tall.

Old Glory

1988 / A perfect, red, hybrid tea blossom reduced to 2½ inches across—that's 'Old Glory'. Plenty of these richly colored blossoms appear on a vigorous bush with disease-resistant foliage. Medium height. AoE.

Petite Perfection

1999 / Classy red hybrid tea–style blossoms with high centers are flushed with deep yellow at the bases of the petals and on the petal backs. Fragrance is slight, at best. Medium height.

Pierrine

1988 / Elegant pink blossoms take on apricot hues in cool weather. Most are borne one per stem; they last well and are popular for small bouquets. Mild fragrance if any. Little orange-red hips in fall. Medium height.

Popcorn

1973 / Like a popper full of corn, the full, bushy plant bursts with bloom, bearing clusters of small, globular buds and dime-sized white flowers with butter-yellow stamens. Mild fragrance. Good disease resistance. Medium height.

Pride 'n' Joy

1991 / Fat buds open to moderately full, vivid blossoms in bright orange with yellow shading on the petal backs. Fruity fragrance. Vigorous. Matte green, disease-resistant leaves. Tall. AARS.

Red Cascade
1976 / The name describes the effect it gives when grown in a hanging basket, but this 5-foot, lax-caned plant, with its clusters of bright red, 1-inch blossoms, can be grown as a climber, too (it's classified as a climber), or as a ground cover. AoE.

Rise 'n' Shine (Golden Sunblaze)
1977 / Beautifully shaped buds and full flowers glow like early morning sunshine on a vigorous, free-flowering bush with excellent foliage. Little or no scent. Medium height. ARS Miniature Rose Hall of Fame. AoE.

Rainbow's End
1984 / Shapely yellow buds are touched with red on the petal tips; as the full blossoms unfold, the red appears at the petal edges (more so in sunshine, much less in shade and when skies are overcast). Little or no fragrance. Glossy leaves. Medium height. A climbing form is available; it grows from 6 to 10 feet. AoE.

Robin Red Breast
1983 / This mini-flora (a new class of roses not quite as mini as miniatures) is an eye-catcher. The dark red, single blossoms have a white eye, and they appear among glossy, dark leaves. No fragrance. Spreading habit, medium height.

Scentsational
1995 / The first in the Scentsation series of heavily perfumed miniature roses, this mauve-pink rose has creamy pink petal backs. Good for cutting. Tall. Also in the series are 'Seattle Scentsation', a deep mauve-pink, and 'Overnight Scentsation', a medium pink.

Also Recommended

Orchid Jubilee
1992 / This climbing miniature has clusters of fluffy, pinkish lavender blossoms slightly more than an inch across. No scent. Vigorous. Let it climb, to about 6 feet, or use it as an arching shrub.

Pink Symphony (Sweet Sunblaze)
1987 / One of the Sunblaze series of miniature roses, this is a slightly fragrant, light pink double, with a center of showy yellow stamens. Leaves are dark and glossy. 'Cherry Sunblaze' is also recommended. Medium height.

Scarlet Moss
1988 / A child of 'Dortmund' (page 400) and a moss rose, this has predictably bright scarlet-red blossoms with mossy sepals. The blossoms are semidouble and borne in small sprays. Tall.

Snow Bride
1982 / Creamy buds of perfect hybrid tea form, carried both individually and in small clusters on long stems, open to pure white, moderately full, lightly fragrant blossoms. Susceptible to mildew. Medium height. AoE.

Starina

1965 / This is a popular classic, its glossy, dark leaves framing faultless buds and blossoms that truly are hybrid teas in miniature. A little fragrance. Good disease resistance. Medium height. ARS Miniature Rose Hall of Fame.

Texas

1984 / Sunny, hybrid tea–style blooms come singly and in small clusters, borne above glossy leaves on an upright plant. Slight fragrance. Tall.

Sun Sprinkles

2001 / Deep yellow, high-centered blossoms, quite large for a miniature, are borne singly or in small clusters among glossy foliage. Light, spicy fragrance. Good disease resistance. Medium to tall. AARS. AoE.

Warm Welcome

1992 / This relative of 'Cl. Sutter's Gold', page 399, is a climber, too, to 7 feet tall. The fragrant blossoms appear in small clusters. Orange-vermilion petals have yellow backs.

Winsome

1984 / Adorning a large, vigorous, dark-foliaged plant are perfect hybrid tea–form blossoms in blended tones of lilac, magenta, and purple. Slight fragrance. Tall. AoE.

Y2K

2000 / A child of 'Cal Poly', page 405, this buttery yellow hybrid tea–style rose picks up touches of red in full sun. Blossoms are slightly fragrant and borne mostly singly. Glossy leaves. Medium height.

Also Recommended

Sweet Chariot

1984 / Low and spreading when planted in the ground, it cascades gracefully when grown in a container or hanging basket. Clusters of tiny, full, grape-purple blossoms have a strong, sweet perfume. Good disease resistance. Medium height.

Top Marks

1992 / This vibrant vermilion rose has won many top European rose awards. Slightly fragrant blossoms are produced in abundance. Medium height.

Work of Art

1989 / Coral, orange, and yellow mingle in the finely formed blossoms of this climbing miniature. Slight fragrance. Stems long enough for cutting. To about 6 feet.

Regional Recommendations

Six connoisseurs of roses from different regions of the country compiled the list of roses from which we built this chapter. Here we present their recommendations by region. Michael Ruggiero made the recommendations for the Northeast; he's the senior curator of the Peggy Rockefeller Rose Garden at the New York Botanical Garden. The list for the South was drawn up by Russ Bowermaster, in Florida; he's been a rose hobbyist for 37 years and served as the American Rose Society's national chairman of judges for 6 years. Peter Schneider, who grows more than a thousand roses in Ohio and compiles the annual Combined Rose List (see page 415), made the recommendations for the Midwest. The list for the Mountain States was the work of Larry Parton, of Northland Rosarium in Spokane, Washington. Peggy Van Allen, a consulting rosarian and Skagit County, Washington, master gardener, put together the list for the Pacific Northwest. Our rose expert for California was Kathleen Brenzel, senior garden editor of *Sunset Magazine* and editor of the *Sunset Western Garden Book*.

THE NORTHEAST

PINK ROSES
Ballerina, p. 377
Betty Prior, p. 377
Buffalo Gal, p. 378
Clair Matin, p. 399
Cupcake, p. 405
Flower Carpet, p. 380
Giselle, p. 407
Jeanne Lajoie, p. 407
La Ville de Bruxelles, p. 393
Marchesa Boccella, p. 394
Mary Rose, p. 384
Mme. Isaac Pereire, p. 394
New Dawn, p. 402
Paris de Yves St. Laurent, p. 372
Pink Symphony, p. 409
Portrait, p. 373
Queen Elizabeth, p. 372
Rosarium Uetersen, p. 403
Sarah Van Fleet, p. 388
The Fairy, p. 390
Tiffany, p. 374
William Baffin, p. 403
Zéphirine Drouhin, p. 397

RED ROSES
Altissimo, p. 398
Black Jade, p. 405
Chrysler Imperial, p. 365
Europeana, p. 380
Hunter, p. 383
Illusion, p. 401
Ingrid Bergman, p. 368
Knock Out, p. 383
L. D. Braithwaite, p. 383
Lilli Marleen, p. 383
Mister Lincoln, p. 370
Olympiad, p. 371
Opening Night, p. 371
Precious Platinum, p. 373
Robusta, p. 387
Rosa moyesii, p. 396
Roseraie de l'Hay, p. 387

ORANGE OR WARM-BLEND ROSES
Abraham Darby, p. 376
Apricot Nectar, p. 377
Brandy, p. 364
Buff Beauty, p. 378
Caribbean, p. 365
Cary Grant, p. 365
Cl. Sutter's Gold, p. 399
Gloire de Dijon, p. 400

Livin' Easy

Glowing Peace, p. 367
Just Joey, p. 368
Livin' Easy, p. 383
Loving Touch, p. 407
Marmalade Skies, p. 384
Rêve d'Or, p. 395
Rosa foetida bicolor, p. 395
Singin' in the Rain, p. 389
Starina, p. 410
Sunset Celebration, p. 374
Tamora, p. 390

YELLOW OR CREAM ROSES
Anthony Meilland, p. 377
Cal Poly, p. 405
Gold Medal, p. 367
Golden Showers, p. 401
Golden Wings, p. 381
Graham Thomas, p. 382
Maigold, p. 401
Marco Polo, p. 369
Midas Touch, p. 370
Molineux, p. 385
Rise 'n' Shine, p. 409
Rosa banksiae 'Lutea', p. 395
Rosa hugonis, p. 396
Sunsprite, p. 389
Texas, p. 410
The Pilgrim, p. 390
Toulouse-Lautrec, p. 374

WHITE ROSES
Alba Semi-Plena, p. 391
Ducher, p. 393
Glamis Castle, p. 381
Gourmet Popcorn, p. 406
Iceberg, p. 382
Jardins de Bagatelle, p. 369
John F. Kennedy, p. 368
Mme. Alfred Carrière, p. 394
Mme. Hardy, p. 394
Pascali, p. 372
Popcorn, p. 408
Sea Foam, p. 388
Sir Thomas Lipton, p. 389
Snow Bride, p. 409
Sombreuil, p. 403
Starry Night, p. 389
White Dawn, p. 403
White Lightnin', p. 375

LAVENDER OR MAUVE ROSES
Angel Face, p. 376
Blueberry Hill, p. 378
Camaieux, p. 391
Cardinal de Richelieu, p. 391
Escapade, p. 379
Intrigue, p. 383
Lagerfeld, p. 369
Orchid Jubilee, p. 409
Paradise, p. 371
Reine des Violettes, p. 395
Rosa rugosa, p. 396
Rosa rugosa rubra, p. 396
Stainless Steel, p. 373
Tuscany Superb, p. 397
Veilchenblau, p. 403
William Lobb, p. 397
Winsome, p. 410

St. Patrick

THE MOUNTAIN STATES

Sexy Rexy

THE PACIFIC NORTHWEST

Double Delight

Resources and Suppliers

Petite Perfection

INFORMATION RESOURCES

American Rose Society
P.O. Box 30,000
Shreveport, LA 71130-0030
(318) 938-5402
www.ars.org
The ARS offers rose gardeners an extensive array of information and services, including regional evaluations of rose varieties and advice from local ARS experts. Contact the society to learn about membership.

The Combined Rose List
Peter Schneider
P.O. Box 677
Mantua, OH 44255
www.combined roselist.com
The ultimate shopping guide, updated annually, this booklet provides an index of all roses commercially available.

MAIL-ORDER SUPPLIERS

The widest variety of roses is available by mail order.

MODERN ROSES

Edmunds' Roses
6235 S.W. Kahle Road
Wilsonville, OR 97070-9727
(503) 682-1476
(888) 481-7673
www.edmundsroses.com

Jackson & Perkins Company
One Rose Lane
Medford, OR 97501
(800) 292-4769
www.jacksonandperkins.com

Tate Nursery
10306 FM Road 2767
Tyler, TX 75708-9239
(903) 593-1020
www.tyler-roses.com

MODERN AND OLD GARDEN ROSES

The Antique Rose
Emporium
9300 Lueckemeyer Road
Brenham, TX 77833-6453
(800) 441-0002
www.weAREroses.com

Arena Roses
525 Pine Street
P.O. Box 3570
Paso Robles, CA 93447
(805) 238-3742
(888) 466-7434
www.arenaroses.com

Heirloom Roses
24062 Riverside Drive N.E.
St. Paul, OR 97137
(503) 538-1576
www.heirloomroses.com

Heritage Roses of
Tanglewood Farm
16831 Mitchell Creek Drive
Fort Bragg, CA 95437-8727
(707) 964-3748

High Country Roses
P.O. Box 148
Jensen, UT 84035
(800) 552-2082
www.highcountryroses.com

Hortico, Inc.
723 Robson Road R.R. 1
Waterdown, Ontario
L0R 2H1
Canada
(905) 689-6984
www.hortico.com

Mt. Hood

Martin & Kraus
1191 Centre Road
P.O. Box 12
Carlisle, Ontario L0R 1H0
Canada
(905) 689-0230
www.gardenrose.com

Mendocino Heirloom Roses
P.O. Box 904
Redwood Valley, CA 95470
(707) 485-6219
www.heritageroses.com

Muncy's Rose Emporium
11207 Celestine Pass
Sarasota, FL 34240
(941) 377-6156
www.muncyrose.com

Northland Rosarium
9405 S. Williams Lane
Spokane, WA 99224
(509) 448-4968
www.northlandrosarium.com

Petaluma Rose Company
P.O. Box 750953
Petaluma, CA 94975
(707) 769-8862
www.petrose.com

Pickering Nurseries, Inc.
670 Kingston Road
Pickering, Ontario L1V 1A6
Canada
(905) 839-2111
www.pickeringnurseries.com

Regan Nursery
4268 Decoto Road
Fremont, CA 94555
(510) 797-3222
(800) 249-4680
www. regannursery.com

Spring Valley Roses
P.O. Box 7
Spring Valley, WI 54767
(715) 778-4481
www.springvalleyroses.com

Vintage Gardens
2833 Old Gravenstein
Highway South
Sebastopol, CA 95472
(707) 829-2035
www.vintagegardens.com

Wayside Gardens
1 Garden Lane
Hodges, SC 29695-0001
(800) 845-1124
www.waysidegardens.com

MINIATURE ROSES

Justice Miniature Roses
5947 S.W. Kahle Road
Wilsonville, OR 97070
(866) 836-8840
www.justiceminiature
roses.com

Michigan Miniature Roses
45951 Hull Road
Belleville, MI 48111
(734) 699-6698
www.michiganmini
roses.com

Nor'East Miniature Roses
P.O. Box 307
Rowley, MA 01969
(800) 426-6485
www.noreast-miniroses.com

Tiny Petals Nursery
2880 Ramsey Cut-Off
Silver Springs, NV 89429
(775) 577-4474
www.tinypetalsnursery.com

container
Gardening

By Vicki Webster and the Editors of Sunset Books, Menlo Park, California

contents

CHAPTER ONE

The Basics

THE PRACTICE OF GROWING PLANTS in pots is almost as old as human civilization. But in the past decade or so, container gardening has soared to new heights of popularity. The reasons are many. Gardening has become the country's number one leisure pastime, and potting up a few geraniums or petunias gives novices an easy and inexpensive way to test the waters. Interest in outdoor decor is on the rise, and beautiful plants paired with carefully chosen pots enhance any setting. ❧ *Then there are simple demographics: For more and more Americans, the only "land" they have to call their own is a balcony, a rooftop, or a courtyard with a few square feet of planting beds. The popularity of container gardening has given rise to countless books that explain the techniques of choosing, planting, and tending plants in pots. This book goes one step beyond and shows you how to design, grow, and care for a garden that just happens to be in containers.*

Tall, simple terra-cotta pots are a perfect match for these dramatic-looking— and unthirsty—succulents.

Choosing Containers

Whether you garden on a rooftop high above a big city or tend a few pots on the porch of a country cottage, the key to beautiful, thriving container plants is simple: plenty of tender loving care. Plants growing in containers are in an artificial environment, with a finite amount of soil from which to draw water and nutrients and little to protect their roots from drying winds, scorching sun, or freezing cold.

FIRST STEPS

That concept may sound daunting, but the reality needn't be. It simply means that to ensure success, you'll want to give your plants the best possible growing conditions right from the beginning. The process starts with choosing containers that suit your plants and your site.

In one sense, when it comes to selecting containers for your garden, the only limits are your taste and imagination. After all, a plant will send out roots in anything that holds soil, from a custom-crafted alabaster urn to a cast-off bathtub. From a practical standpoint, though, your choice of containers is more than a matter of style; it can determine how well your garden will grow and how much time and attention you will have to give it.

SIZE AND SHAPE

When selecting a container, keep in mind the mature size, growth rate, and root structure of the plants you intend to put in it. It's crucial that a pot be neither too

ABOVE: *This softly mounded planting of verbena and rose vervain* (Verbena canadensis) *complements its rounded pot.* RIGHT: *Any plant would make a strong statement in this classically inspired pot.*

A garden of lavender and a table for two lend Mediterranean flair to this tiny balcony.

big nor too small. Without ample room to spread, a plant's roots quickly exhaust the nutrients and oxygen in the soil.

On the other hand, in a container that is too large, rapid growers may put out too much leaf growth, which delays and can even prevent flowering and fruiting. When slowly growing plants are put in quarters that are too big, the roots cannot fully permeate the soil, which—except perhaps in a very warm climate—stays cold and wet. Eventually the soil turns sour, inviting fungus, diseases, and other root problems.

Shape, too, is important for plants' health as well as simple aesthetics. For example, spring crocuses, with their shallow roots and short top growth, will look good and perform well in a pot that's only a few inches high. On the other hand, dill, with its tall foliage and long taproots, needs a container that's deep enough to accommodate the roots without their bending and also visually balance the upper portion.

How does "big enough" translate into specific measurements? That's where growth rate comes into play. Often a rampant grower such as mint will fill a seemingly too-large container very quickly. As a general rule, though, plants perform their best when you allow about 1 inch of space all the way around the root ball.

421

MATERIALS

Although improvised containers can be made of anything under the sun, the pots most commonly available commercially are made of terra-cotta, wood, or plastic. Each type has advantages and disadvantages. Which one will work best in your garden depends on your climate, the style of your house, and the time and inclination you have for garden maintenance.

TERRA-COTTA IS ...

Porous. That keeps soil from getting soggy—a very useful feature in cool, rainy, or humid climates—but it does necessitate frequent watering. Salts and minerals are wicked outward and collect on the pot, not in the soil. That's good for plants' health but does cause white stains on pots.

Heavy. That provides for stability—a big plus for trees and tall shrubs, or any plants in a windy location. On the downside, a large pot filled with soil is difficult to move and may be too heavy to use on a rooftop or balcony.

Fragile. Top-quality, high-fired pots are more durable than their mass-produced, low-fired counterparts, but all terra-cotta can chip, crack, and break. Except in very mild climates, clay containers need winter protection. Where winter weather is severe, pots are safest indoors.

WOOD IS ...

Porous (maybe). Untreated wood is somewhat breathable, but wooden containers that have been treated with waterproof paint or other sealer become nonporous.

Naturally insulating. Potting mix remains at a fairly even temperature in a wooden container, as long as the walls are at least ⅞ inch thick.

Durable. Wooden containers can be remarkably long-lived if they're made of rot-resistant redwood, cedar, or cypress. Other woods can be treated to last a long time. Wood rarely breaks, cracks, or chips, and it's not greatly affected by changes in the weather.

These ornamental cabbages, in their terra-cotta pot, will need plenty of water.

Plastic pots (above) come in shapes that echo those of stone containers (left).

PLASTIC IS ...

Nonporous. Water remains in the soil longer—a big plus if you live in a hot, dry climate or want to grow plants that love moisture. In a wet climate, however, or in the case of plants that need drier soil, plastic can be a big drawback.

Noninsulating. Plastic provides little protection from heat or cold. To keep plants safe from temperature extremes, it's best to set plastic pots inside other insulating containers.

Lightweight. On the plus side, that means plastic will work where other materials might be too heavy. But it also means that in a windy or exposed location, plastic pots need to be anchored to the ground or set inside heavier containers.

Durable (maybe). Better-quality plastics are not prone to weather damage, but less expensive versions tend to crack after a few years in the sun and become brittle in the cold.

Salvia and rosemary prefer soil on the dry side, so these unsealed wooden planters are ideal for them.

Not-So-Ordinary Containers

Some of the best containers were never designed to hold plants at all. Take these, for instance: part of an old stone pillar (top), a venerable chimney pot (middle), and a shiny new horse trough (bottom). For these and other winners, check antiques and thrift stores, architectural salvage yards, and farm-supply dealers.

Drainage

Waterlogged soil is the most common cause of death for container plants. The simplest way to avoid the problem is to use free-draining planting mix and make sure that each pot has at least one opening in the bottom to expel excess water. If you fall in love with a container that has no drainage hole, don't despair—you do have options.

DRILL A HOLE

Use either a hand or electric drill for wood, plastic, or fiberglass. For stone, terra-cotta, or concrete, use an electric drill with a masonry or carbide bit. (To avoid cracking the pot, drill a small hole first and increase the bit size to a larger one.) Heavy lead or iron containers

You can use an electric drill with either a carbide or masonry bit to make drainage holes in terra-cotta, stone, or concrete pots.

require the use of a metal bit, but for lighter ones, such as buckets or decorative tins, you can easily punch holes with a hammer and large nail. A single ½- to 1-inch hole will suffice for small- to medium-size containers. For larger ones, such as half-barrels, drill four or five 1-inch holes.

DOUBLE-POT

If drilling is not an option, plant in a smaller container that has drainage holes and set it inside the solid one. Just be sure to raise the inner pot on bricks or pebbles so that it never sits in water. Size permitting, it's also a good idea to remove the inner pot from time to time and empty any water that has accumulated at the bottom of the outer container.

Before you plant, test your double-pot combo for size. Set the inner, draining pot on bricks or pebbles so that it reaches just below the rim of the outer container.

SAY NO TO SHARDS

At planting time, ignore the traditional advice to cover your containers' drainage holes with pot shards. New studies show that rather than improving drainage, they can actually hinder it. Instead, put a small square of window screening over each opening in the bottom. It will keep soil in the pot but still allow water to drain out.

Nurseries and garden shops sell terra-cotta pots in countless styles, sizes, and price ranges. Most come equipped with drainage holes, which will spare you drilling time and effort.

Set Them Up

One way to promote good drainage and increase air circulation—as well as prevent water stains on decks and patios—is to lift containers off the ground. You can buy pot "feet" for just that purpose (the lions in the photo at right are one example), but wood blocks, bricks, or small overturned flower pots work just as well. Other ways and means: nail cleats to the bottoms of wooden containers, or look for pots with built-in risers.

Potting Mixes

It might seem that good topsoil, straight from the garden, should work fine in your pots. Not so. Even the best loam is too dense to use by itself in containers. It's possible to combine garden soil with other additives to get the right combination of fast drainage and rich nutrition that container plants need. But there's no reason to bother when many high-quality mixes are available.

HOW MUCH POTTING MIX?

Whether you're potting a basket of petunias for the summer or planting a container garden filled with long-lived trees, shrubs, and perennials, there are ready-made mixes to suit your needs (and those of your plants).

While potting mix is generally sold by the cubic foot, standard containers are usually labeled by inches. Listed below are some helpful translations.

A 2-cubic-foot bag of potting mix is enough to fill

- eight to ten standard 10- to 12-inch pots;
- two pots 12 inches in diameter and 15 inches deep;
- one window box or planter that measures 36 by 8 by 10 inches.

SOIL OR SOILLESS?

Most garden centers carry a bewildering array of potting mixes, but they all fall into one of two broad categories: soil-based or soilless. As the name implies, soil-based mixes contain real, garden-variety loam (steril-ized, of course) along with varying amounts of plant food and additives such as peat, sand, bark chips, vermiculite, or per-lite. Soil-based mixes are heavier than soilless versions, and they tend to be messier to use. On the plus side, they retain water and nutrients better and provide greater stability for plants. They are by far the better choice for plants that will stay in the same pots for more than a year or so.

Soilless mixes are based on peat or a peat substitute such as coir, which is made from shred-ded and composted coconut husks. Depending on the form-ulation, these mixes contain the same kinds of additives you'll find in the soil-based types. Soilless mixes dry out and lose nutrients fairly rapidly, but their light weight and ease of handling make them ideal for hanging baskets and annual plantings of all kinds.

GETTING SPECIFIC

For most plants a general-purpose potting mix, either soil-based or soilless, will work just fine. For others, you'll want to use a spe-cial formulation. When in doubt, don't guess about which kind to use; consult with the nursery staff when you purchase your plants, and be sure to mention any requirements specific to your site, such as lightweight or good

Standard potting mix, either peat- or soil-based, works fine for most plants.

water retention. Here are some of the most common specialty potting mixes.

AQUATIC PLANT MIX A heavy, viscous, soil-based mix designed to stay in place when pots are submerged in water.

CACTI AND SUCCULENT MIX A mixture of soil, sand, and peat or peat substitute, with gravel or other grit added to ensure excel-lent drainage.

ERICACEOUS MIX A must for acid-loving plants such as azaleas, camellias, and rhododendrons. Most brands are peat-based, with no lime added to neutralize the peat's natural acid.

CONTAINER AND HANGING-BASKET MIXES Peat-based formulas with both water-retaining gel crystals and slow-release fertilizer gran-

Planting with Polymers

Water-retaining gel crystals absorb hundreds of times their weight in water, making them a real boon to container gardeners. Mixed into the soil, these superabsorbent polymers hold on to both water and dissolved nutrients, keeping them readily available to plant roots. That's a particular advantage for hanging baskets or for pots in hot climates or exposed sites where containers dry out quickly. You can buy commercial potting mixes with gel already added, but mixing it yourself is simple. Just remember that no matter how dry or windy your garden site, more is not better; follow package instructions precisely. An overdose of gel will keep the soil too wet, which could kill your plants.

1

Sprinkle the dry crystals into water and stir until they swell up to form a thick gel. The package will tell you the correct proportion of crystals to water.

2

Pour your potting mix into a wheelbarrow or other large container and add the bloated crystals to the potting mix.

3

Using gloved hands or a trowel, combine the crystals with your potting mix. Again, follow the package directions for the ratio of crystals to soil.

4

Once you've thoroughly combined the potting mix and crystals, put the gel-laced soil in your pots and plant in the normal way.

ules added. These mixes save time and labor, but they are expensive. If you have more than a few containers to fill and your budget is a factor, you'll be better off buying crystals and fertilizer separately and adding them to a standard potting mix. (See "Planting with Polymers" above.)

In order to thrive, any container plant needs regular supplies of water and fertilizer. Even potting mixes with food added have to be replenished eventually. Read the bag carefully so that you'll know when to start supplementary feedings.

CHAPTER TWO

Entryways

ANY BEAUTIFUL ENTRANCE GARDEN offers a festive greeting to guests, delights passersby, and welcomes you home in style after a long, hard day—or even a short, easy one. An entry garden in containers does more than that: it provides the makings of an ever-changing "welcome mat," letting you create a new floral greeting with each passing season or whim. The display needn't be large or elaborate to be effective. A simple window box or a hanging basket beside a doorway will catch eyes, lift spirits, and enhance your home's architecture. Of course, along with the joy of creating a work of living art for all the world (or at least all your neighborhood) to see comes a challenge: keeping that showplace looking good throughout the year.

Containers of nasturtiums (Tropaeolum), *foxgloves* (Digitalis purpurea), *and geraniums usher guests up these stairs in colorful style.*

Year-Round Appeal

In places where mild weather reigns throughout the year, keeping your entry garden in top form is pretty straightforward. Simply find plants that please you and suit your growing conditions; give them good, basic care (see pages 517–539); and replace them when they outgrow their pots or when you want a change of scene. In most parts of the country, though, it helps to have a few tricks up your sleeve.

KEEP IT SIMPLE

It can be tempting to deck your entryway with the beautiful, multiplant creations you see in magazines and in this book. It is a satisfying way to let your creative juices flow, especially if an entryway is the only planting space you have.

But remember that the more complex a planting is, the more care and attention you will have to give it, and the greater are the chances that something will go awry and spoil the arrangement. (After all, plants are living organisms, not decorative objects.) For the ultimate in easy good looks, plant one or, at most, two varieties per container. Then, for instance, when your tulips pass their prime, black spot befalls your miniature roses, or a heat wave flattens your pansies, it takes only minutes to whisk the victims out of sight and bring in healthier replacements.

BELOW LEFT: *'Blue Delft' hyacinths and tiny 'Tête-à-Tête' narcissus march up a stairway. This no-fuss-no-muss display is easy to care for and a snap to change with the seasons.*

BELOW: *An ivy geranium* (Pelargonium peltatum) *forms a fluffy pink cloud on an entry ledge.*

LEFT: *The lush foliage of scented geraniums, ornamental grasses, and succulents keep this entry looking fresh and inviting. From a distance, the arrangement looks more like an in-ground bed than a cluster of pots.*

BELOW LEFT: *The ultimate in simple welcomes: a basket of variegated English ivy* (Hedera helix) *hung on a door. To achieve a similar visual effect with an aromatic bonus, you could substitute a trailing herb such as creeping thyme* (Thymus serpyllum) *or Corsican mint* (Mentha requienii).

BELOW: *Pots of golden-leafed hosta glow like beacons, pointing the way through a hidden garden to the entrance of the house.*

FOCUS ON FOLIAGE

Foliage plants supply structure, form, and long-lasting good looks. Choose plants that pack a dramatic, leafy punch on their own, such as coleus, ornamental grasses, and hostas. Or use more subtle foliage like that of ferns, boxwood, and ivy as a backdrop for colorful flowers. For a display that pleases the nose as well as the eye, add herbs with aromatic foliage such as mint, scented geraniums, basil, and artemisia. Bear in mind, though, that your climate will determine whether even the hardiest plants can grace your entry all year long.

A Matter of Style

The most successful container gardens bring out the best features of the houses they accompany. And though it may sound overly dramatic, the effect achieved at the entrance can make or break the scheme. After all, that is where people get their first glimpse of your home, and in the words of countless mothers and high school guidance counselors, you get only one chance to make a good first impression.

HARMONY OR HISTORY?

There are two basic approaches to blending house and garden. Some gardeners strive to replicate period gardens that are authentic to the tiniest detail. If you live in a historic or architecturally significant house and have a penchant for the past, you may want to pick up a book on the subject. Like container gardening, period gardening is growing in popularity throughout the country. If you're like most gardeners, though, chances are you just want to create beautiful surroundings that harmonize with the house. Whichever of these camps you fall into, containers add one more element to your design palette.

TOP: *A rustic stuccoed house with a Mediterranean feel meets its match in this low-key yet sophisticated planting. A tall terra-cotta jar, with a palm in the center, echoes the strong vertical lines of the doorway.*

LEFT: *Color and structure make this entry garden a standout. The architectural shapes of succulents complement the simple lines of the house, while the red tones of coleus play off its adobe-colored walls.*

ABOVE: *An entryway that is as unpretentious as this one calls for an equally down-home planting scheme. Simple terra-cotta pots of geraniums, petunias, pansies, and nasturtiums fill the bill perfectly. Note that the pots are set as close as possible to the stair rail, allowing free passage up and down the steps. (For more tips on stairway container gardens, see page 436.)*

LEFT: *The pale shingled wall of an old-fashioned porch forms the perfect backdrop for a pair of blue ceramic pots filled with equally old-fashioned blooms. Given basic care, these trouble-free performers will strut their stuff all summer long. The cast includes geraniums, petunias, sweet alyssum* (Lobularia maritima), *common heliotrope* (Heliotropium arborescens), *and daisies.*

ABOVE: *In the entry to this contemporary Asian-influenced house, pots of ornamental grasses and huge specimen hostas hold their own against the striking architecture.*

LEFT: *To accent the stylish door, a single well-designed container features curly straw-colored sedge, along with the hot tones and multiple layers of zinnias, strawflowers (Helichrysum bracteatum), petunias, and geraniums.*

FACING PAGE, TOP: *'Barbara Karst' bougainvillea, Russian sage (Perovskia atriplicifolia), and woolly thyme (Thymus pseudolanuginosus) help pull off this entryway's Mediterranean theme.*

FACING PAGE, BOTTOM: *A lead planter echoes the symmetrical lines of a formal doorway. Red geraniums, purple violas, and blue lobelia add a splash of color.*

Think "Bones"

Attractive containers and accessories can do for a potted garden what well-shaped trees and shrubs do for an in-ground landscape: provide lasting interest (what garden designers call "bones") long after flowers and leaves have fallen.

To put that principle to work in your entryway, top a stunning container with an equally eye-catching support system and plant a flowering vine at its base. Foliage and flowers will cloak the support throughout the growing season. When the plant dies back, the architectural framework will remain. At that time you can choose to leave it bare or deck it with trimmings of your choice, such as evergreen boughs and twinkling lights.

435

Stairs and Walkways

A container garden can turn a ho-hum sidewalk or set of stairs into a magical passageway, luring you onward with color and scent. As with any garden, the first key to success is choosing plants that thrive in your climate and setting, and giving them good care. The second lies in remembering one major fact: this garden will not simply be looked at, it will be walked through—possibly run, skipped, and romped through—on a regular basis.

CLOSE QUARTERS

A designer's rule of thumb says that the ideal walk or stairway leading to a house measures at least 4 feet wide, the minimum space needed to give two or three people room to stroll comfortably. But in real life, many of us are not blessed with that much room. That doesn't mean you have to abandon your dreams of a verdant passageway; just allow as much space as possible and take a few basic precautions to ensure the safety of people, pets, and plants. Some, or all, of the following measures will help.

AVOID FRAGILE CONTAINERS

Setting a terra-cotta pot beside a narrow path or on a steep set of stairs is asking for trouble. Instead, look for attractive containers made of unbreakable materials such as wood, metal, or sturdy plastic. And steer clear of narrow, top-heavy shapes that can tip over.

KEEP PLANTS LOW When space is tight, use compact, low-growing plants. They are far less likely to be damaged or to fall over than trees, shrubs, and trellised plants.

DON'T GO LIGHT The heavier a pot is, the less likely it will be to topple if someone, or some lawn tool, bumps into it. Choose the biggest, weightiest containers your space and budget will allow. Then, to both increase stability and conserve potting mix, use a variation of the pot-lightening technique described on page 492. Once you've placed your containers at their final sites, fill the bottom 8 inches or so with rocks. (Use this trick only with annuals and shallow-rooted perennials, not for trees and shrubs; the latter two plantings need all the root room they can get.)

CLAMP DOWN If your garden rests on a wooden stairway or board-walk, fasten containers to the surface. Whenever possible, attach planters to railings so that they hang outside of the walking area.

ABOVE LEFT: *The lesson to be learned from this delightful stairway garden: if you've got it, flaunt it. Here, galvanized-metal pails, kettles, pots, and watering cans keep culinary herbs within easy clipping distance—and provide a welcome that no guest is likely to forget.*

LEFT: *An urban entrance provides a textbook example of savvy stairway design. Narcissus-filled pots all but shout "Happy Spring!" now, but when their glory has faded, they'll be easy to whisk away and replace with summer annuals. Their location, outside the stair rails, puts them beyond reach of hurrying feet. As further insurance, the pots are plastic—unlikely to break in the event of a fall.*

BELOW: *Narrow stairs could spell disaster for a freestanding pot, especially one made of fragile ceramic or terracotta. So instead, the owner of this house opted for the ultimate in safety from a plant's perspective: a built-in wooden box. This container holds colorful butterfly flower* (Schizanthus pinnatus).

ABOVE: *Large, heavy pots deliver visual substance and are unlikely to topple if a guest or a pet bumps into them. The plants, which include common yarrow* (Achillea millefolium), *purple coneflower* (Echinacea purpurea), Coreopsis grandiflora, *and Mexican bush sage* (Salvia leucantha), *hold their own against the adobe wall.*

LEFT: *When you set containers along a busy walkway, keep the center of gravity low. These stout pots, filled with mounding petunias and twinspur* (Diascia), *are more stable than they would be filled with taller plants.*

A Fragrant Welcome

Research has shown that of the five senses, smell is the one fully developed at birth. It is also the one most closely tied to memory—which explains why the faintest whiff of lilacs might send your mind racing back to your grandmother's garden. So why not tap into the power of scent to create a container garden that will linger in your guests' minds for years to come?

BEFORE

Fragrant red miniature roses flank an eye-stopping pot of dahlias and blanket flower (Gaillardia × grandiflora 'Burgundy'). The scent of hedge lavender (Lavandula × intermedia 'Provence') wafts from the background.

On the stairs, a one-two punch of geraniums: salmon-pink common geraniums (Pelargonium × hortorum) in front, backed up by lemon-scented P. 'Atomic Snowflake'.

BEAUTIFUL BECOMES BETTER

Even unadorned, this stunning entryway offered a gracious welcome to guests and to the family that lives here. Now it makes every arrival both festive and memorable, thanks to a container garden that focuses on color, form, texture, and fragrance.

FACING PAGE, BOTTOM: *To the right of the doorway a cluster of pots captivate the eye and nose alike. The intensely fragrant standard rose 'Charisma' stands tall, underplanted with red miniature roses. A mixed planting of lantana, yarrow, and kangaroo paw (Anigozanthos) complements a bowl-shaped terra-cotta pot. The container on the top step emits the blended aromas of pineapple sage and lavender. To the left of the doorway, the lavender and rose scents repeat, joined by the smells of a dwarf citrus tree and lemon-scented geraniums on the steps.*

Fragrance Is Back

For a while, fragrant flowers all but disappeared from the nursery trade as hybridizers focused on bigger, showier blossoms and a wider color range. Unfortunately, most often that visual drama came at the expense of scent. But in recent years, fragrant gardens have gained favor. As a result, nurseries and catalogs offer an increasing number of aromatic plants every year. The list below offers some good choices.

Angel's trumpet (*Brugmansia*)
Chocolate cosmos (*Cosmos atrosanguineus*)
Common heliotrope (*Heliotropium arborescens*)
English lavender (*Lavandula angustifolia*)
Freesia
Hosta plantaginea **'Aphrodite'**
Mint (*Mentha*)
Oriental lily (*Lilium* Oriental hybrids such as 'Rosy Dawn', 'Lush Life', 'Stargazer', or 'Black Beauty')
Petunia × *hybrida* **(Not all petunias are fragrant, so sniff before you buy!)**
Pineapple sage (*Salvia elegans* or *S. elegans* 'Honey Melon Sage')
Pink (*Dianthus*)
Scented geranium (*Pelargonium*)
Shining jasmine (*Jasminum laurifolium nitidum*)
Stock (*Matthiola incana*)
Sweet alyssum (*Lobularia maritima*)
Sweet azalea (*Rhododendron arborescens*)
Sweet olive (*Osmanthus fragrans*)
Sweet pea (*Lathyrus odoratus*)

CHAPTER THREE

Decks and Porches

A WELL-DESIGNED DECK OR PORCH can add character and charm to any home. But these structures are far more than simply architectural appendages. Physically and psychologically, decks and porches bridge the space between indoors and out. And they perform that task much more smoothly with the help of plants in containers. ∾ Whether that means perching a few window boxes on the railings, adding colorful pots to tables, or installing a potted herbaceous border around the perimeter depends on your taste and how you plan to use the space. For instance, will your portable garden serve as a warm-weather living room, a play area for active children, or simply a quiet place to sit, sip, and watch the world go by? However you want your outdoor room to function, a well-planned container garden will enrich the hours you spend there.

Bright red Adirondack chairs, arranged for easy conversation, and big color-filled pots transform this deck into an outdoor room. A strawberry jar puts pick-your-own treats just a short reach away.

A Gallery of Decks and Porches

Regardless of its style or purpose, a deck or porch really comes into its own when you add a container garden. It is important, however, that the container plantings complement the structure, thrive in your climate zone, and suit both your taste and your inclination for plant tending. In the gallery of photographs that follows, you'll find plenty of inspiration to start you on the road to satisfying these various criteria.

FACING PAGE, TOP: *A bare-bones deck gets a lift from a prairie-style arrangement of ornamental grasses and meadow flowers, including gloriosa daisy* (Rudbeckia hirta) *and—spilling over the edge—black-eyed Susan vine* (Thunbergia alata).

RIGHT: *This upper-deck container garden features resilient plants that can handle sea breezes and salt spray, such as blanket flower* (Gaillardia × grandiflora) *and Santa Barbara daisy* (Erigeron karvinskianus).

ABOVE: *A brick-paved porch becomes one with the backyard beyond, thanks to careful plant selection. Standard roses and pots of bright annuals echo the tones of the plantings in the rest of the yard.*

LEFT: *A lush container garden brings life to the sedate tones of a second-story deck. Flowers contrast with the monotone gray of house, deck, and railing, but the space retains a peaceful and relaxed feeling. The secret is a well-planned color scheme of mostly green and white, with splashes of yellow and hot pink.*

ABOVE: *Symmetry is the name of the game here. A quartet of identical containers has been painted to match the gray color of the house and deck. Inside the pots, look-alike plantings with flowers in tones of yellow and pink add sparkle without altering the low-key mood.*

LEFT: *When it comes to playing up water views with container plants, there are two schools of thought. One favors cool, aqueous shades of blue, mauve, and lavender that all but melt into the scenery. The other votes for vibrant contrast. This lakeside deck near Seattle clearly falls into the latter category. The eye-popping arrangement includes red geraniums, white marguerites (Chrysanthemum frutescens), yellow Euryops, purple and white petunias, feathery green parrot beak (Clianthus puniceus), deep blue lobelia, ivy, and gray dusty miller.*

RIGHT: *An elegant porch greets spring with a pink, white, and yellow chorus line. When the tulips, daffodils, and primroses (Primula) have gone by the wayside, summer-blooming bulbs and annuals will take their places. Likely candidates are pastel and white lilies against the railing, with lower-growing impatiens and violas below.*

BELOW: *Neatly trained spiral box-wood topiaries, paired with a teak table and chairs, lend a formal air to this dining alcove. If you're tempted to copy the look, be forewarned: you'll have to spend time snipping and clipping to keep the topiaries shipshape.*

RIGHT: *Bordered by columns and bountiful pots of flowers, a long and narrow porch overlooks a Florida canal. This waterside retreat boasts furniture worthy of an indoor living room.*

BELOW: *On a tiny deck in the woods, massed pots of tulips are about to burst into bloom. They'll be white, like the blooms of surrounding trees. Even the cushioned bistro chairs carry out the soothing green and white scheme.*

LEFT: *Here's the ultimate in innovative containers: concrete drainage pipes planted with red impatiens and lit with neon rings. Across the walkway from this offbeat lineup, orange cannas repeat the earth-and-fire-toned theme. Aside from a successful use of color, there's another design lesson to be learned from this container garden: you never know where you'll find a fabulous container—so keep your eyes open and your imagination working overtime.*

RIGHT: *Like many old-time flowers, cannas have enjoyed a resurgence of popularity. They are a perfect choice for sleek blue planters beside an ultra-modern chaise. Also in the planter are coleus, sweet potato vine* (Ipomoea batatas), *and ornamental grasses.*

447

On the Long and Narrow

When you build a deck or porch from scratch or expand an existing one, you can easily tailor the design to suit your needs and tastes. Often, the much tougher challenge is to define appealing outdoor living areas when the spaces can't be tailored. This is particularly true when a patio or deck is long and narrow, as is often the case. It's then that plants and containers come into their own as architectural elements, helping to delineate space and even fooling the eye.

DIVIDE AND CONQUER

One way to deal with an awkwardly proportioned structure is simply to break it up into smaller areas with more pleasing measurements. By clever arrangement of plants, furniture, and accent pieces, you can create as many separate alcoves as your space will allow. You can establish permanent areas for activities such as entertaining, family dining, solo relaxation, or even down-and-dirty gardening chores. Or choose lightweight furnishings, keep your plants in wheeled containers, and redesign the scene to suit the occasion.

GO WITH THE FLOW

Some porches and decks are so narrow that any attempt to disguise the fact would be a losing battle. In that case, just accept your structure's limitations as a chance to let your creativity run riot. It matters little whether the style of your container garden is sophisticated, whimsical, or cottage-garden quaint; if the display is eye-catching enough, no one will notice the proportions of the venue.

A purposeful arrangement of containers disguises this deck's narrow, rectangular shape. By themselves, the pots and hanging baskets in the far corners would emphasize the structure's length. But with the addition of a curving border of containers along one wall, the space becomes a well-proportioned dining nook.

Planter boxes, mounted to the outside of the wall, draw the eye upward and outward, thereby visually broadening a deck that's little wider than a ship's passageway.

A simple collection of white tulips blurs the corner and far edge of this deck, leading the eye diagonally across the surface. The result is that the deck doesn't seem narrow at all.

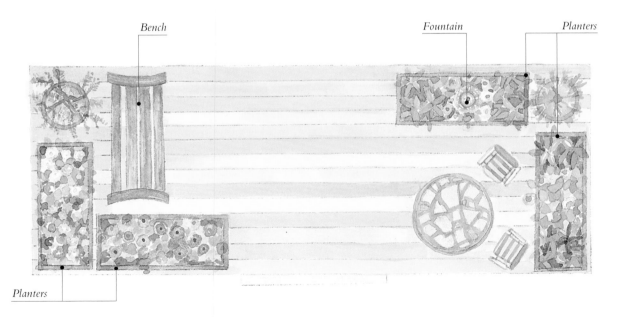

Bench

Fountain *Planters*

Planters

FOCUS ON FORM

You may not be able to change the shape of your deck or porch, but a few simple tricks will make it appear more expansive than it really is. L-shaped planter arrangements at both ends lead the eye across the space in a diagonal direction, creating the illusion of a larger area. The bench and fountain, used as focal points, further draw attention away from the deck's short front-to-back dimension.

Personality Plus

The problem: the house you've just purchased comes equipped with a deck that has as much charm as a lump of clay. The solution: use container plants to transform the space from ho-hum to heavenly. You'll be reaching into the same bag of tricks that garden designers use to add visual interest to a dull plot of ground. These styling techniques work just as much magic when the plants are firmly rooted in containers.

BUILD A BORDER

When you want to pack a sophisticated punch, no garden feature beats a lush, flower-filled border. On an in-ground site, that pizzazz can take a lot of time and effort to achieve. On a deck, though, it's a quick cure for the common blahs. Aside from choosing plants and containers that suit your taste and architecture, though, it pays to remember a few other important keys to success.

REPETITION A good design contains elements that repeat. They may be specific plants, or merely color, texture, or shape, or all of the above. And bear in mind that the importance of repetition applies to containers as well as their contents.

SCALE While it is true that plantings look best when they're in keeping with the size of the garden, it's rare that a container plant is too large for its site. It's far more common to err on the side of puniness. When in doubt, think big. A few big containers (the largest size your space can hold) filled with substantial plants will pack a more impressive punch than a jumble of small to midsize pots of fluffy annuals.

STAYING POWER The best borders look good throughout the year. With a border of container plants, you have a couple of options for achieving that goal. You can simply move plants in and out of the spotlight as their moments of glory come and go. Or, your climate permitting, you can assemble combinations of plants that have something to offer season after season— whether flowers, foliage, berries, seedheads, or distinctive branching patterns.

ABOVE LEFT: *Cobalt blue planter boxes of yellow 'Sunburst' coreopsis line up in front of a matching fence.*

LEFT: *The tones of yellow and orange repeat in this potted border, spiked by the icy greenish white colors of 'Envy' zinnias.*

VARY THE TERRAIN

Arranging containers at different heights adds visual punch to any setting, and a banal deck or porch is no exception. Pedestals, baker's racks, and tables allow you to raise the level of a planting scheme without launching a building project. (For more on planting in the vertical dimension, see page 478.) But many decks come already equipped with varied topography—a stairway. Whether tall and steep or low and broad, those wooden treads, and sometimes their handrails, offer a place to display plants on multiple levels.

RIGHT: *Thanks to the owner's collection of weathered metal pots, sap buckets, and watering cans, the stairs of this backdoor porch have personality to spare.*

BELOW: *Terra-cotta pots, filled primarily with herbs and ferns, march up the stairs and across the deck, breaking up a long stretch of board. The containers also fill in the empty space below the railing.*

REFOCUS THE EYE

It's one of the oldest design tricks in the world: when you want to disguise a bland scene (in this case, a boring deck) you simply add new elements that capture attention and refocus the eye. And with plants and containers, the sky's the limit.

Installing a dramatic focal point is an obvious option. A piece of sculpture, a fountain, an outdoor fireplace, or a beautiful furniture grouping will camouflage a less than stellar backdrop. But a successful focal point can be as simple as a corner filled with plants. In fact, it's a symbiotic relationship: flowers and foliage soften the sharp angles of the structure, while the sheltered nook keeps both flora and pots safe from foot traffic.

BELOW: *The pastel tones of striking Asiatic lilies draw all eyes to a corner.*

ABOVE: *Colorful standards never fail to draw attention, especially when they're grouped in eye-catching pots like these white ceramic models. This trio of standards consists of Solanum, Asclepias, and pomegranate (Punica granatum). Red candles floating in a blue opaline glass bowl add more color to the scene.*

ABOVE: *A pair of sleek chaises and a terra-cotta bowl brimming with succulents turn a plain square of decking into a showplace.*

ABOVE RIGHT: *This grouping refocuses eyes—and fools them, too. The tall pillar candlestick looks like a found architectural fragment, but it's actually a ceramic look-alike. The ceramic containers are masquerading as well-traveled metal boxes.*

RIGHT: *Often the most effective focal points are the simplest. A case in point is this trio of terra-cotta pots filled with ornamental grasses that are different in color but similar in shape and texture.*

453

Tying It All Together

Aside from enhancing the appearance and usefulness of a porch or deck, container plants perform another important role: linking the structure to the broader landscape, both visually and psychologically.

THE ECHO EFFECT

Whether what lies beyond your porch or deck is your own tiny backyard or a vast stretch of wilderness, there is a simple way to blur the distinction: fill your containers with plants that echo the colors, forms, and textures that appear in the broader arena. That doesn't mean duplicating the varieties of plants themselves. In fact, this trick works even if there are no plants to be seen. For instance, if your deck overlooks a broad body of water and you want your view to flow seamlessly, choose fine-textured foliage in the gray-blue range and flower colors in soft, watery tones of mauve, blue, lavender, and white.

BY CONTRAST

But what if you want to make the viewer's eye leap across the boundary of your deck and into the distant scenery? In that case, at the farthest edge of your structure, place a container planting that contrasts sharply in color and texture with the landscape beyond.

FAR LEFT: *A container of soft pinks and grays blurs the border between the deck and the lawn, leading the eye into the broader picture.*

LEFT: *Staged for a garden show, this setting carries the tying-together concept to the level of an art form. Stainless steel containers on the deck mimic the walls of raised beds and even pathway risers in the garden beyond. Likewise, the colors and rounded shapes of the plants remain consistent throughout the scene.*

ABOVE: *In a garden filled with rich green foliage and clouds of white tulips, it's all but impossible to tell where the container-filled deck ends and the rest of the garden begins.*

LEFT: *Plantings, in containers or otherwise, don't come more dramatic than these floral "bonfires" marking the edge of a deck that's also a dock. At sunset, the flowers cast their own red glow on the water, blending with the tones from the sky.*

Save That Surface

Container gardening is certainly not a hazardous pastime, but it can be risky for your bank account if your garden sits atop a wooden deck or porch. Even pressure-treated and rot-resistant woods will deteriorate under the steady onslaught of water runoff and fertilizer salts. Tile and masonry surfaces are more durable, but even they can suffer from the by-products of plant care. Although the damage may take a long time to materialize, water and fertilizers can create ugly stains on pricey hardscape. Some protective measures are in order.

PAINT ON PROTECTION

It's crucial to coat all wooden surfaces with a high-quality, water-repellent sealer every two or three years. Adding exterior stain or paint over the sealer will give you longer-term protection. Commercial coatings are available to protect brick, tile, and concrete—and to remove stains that are already in place. A couple of other simple measures can help, too.

CATCH THE DRIPS Either use nonporous saucers or set draining pots inside other containers without holes. To waterproof untreated terra-cotta, simply paint the interior with clear acrylic enamel. Besides ending drips, you'll also cut back on water lost to evaporation through the container's sides.

DIRECT THE DRIPS Whenever possible, position hanging baskets and window boxes so that they drain onto open ground, not onto the porch or deck surface.

LEFT: *Wheeled plant trolleys catch water before it drips to the decking below. They also make it easy to push plants to shelter when cold—or steamy—weather spells trouble.*

FACING PAGE, BOTTOM: *The ultimate in deck protection: a built-in, bottomless planter that drains directly to the soil. If your deck doesn't have one of these designs, you can achieve the same effect by constructing planters on the ground along the structure's edges.*

RIGHT: *Stainless steel trays, tailor-made to fit their painted wooden containers, keep drips from touching this deck's surface. In the boxes: hostas, ferns, and bamboo.*

BELOW: *These railing-mounted planters of scarlet geraniums drain mostly on the deck; if the planters were mounted outside the railing, they would drain directly on the ground.*

Havens for Butterflies and Hummingbirds

Even the smallest container garden can offer a warm welcome for these jewels on the wing. Your best floral choices for attracting nectar-sippers depend on your area of the country, but you'll find good starter lists of plants on these pages.

Plants to Lure Butterflies

The sipping tastes of butterflies are more wide-ranging than those of hummingbirds. Their favorites, though, are daisy-type blooms and any plant with small flowers arranged in clusters or spikes. Butterflies love all colors, but purple tops the list.

Blanket flower, annual *(Gaillardia pulchella)*

Butterfly weed *(Asclepias tuberosa)*

Common heliotrope *(Heliotropium arborescens)*

Cosmos

Dahlia

Four o'clock *(Mirabilis jalapa)*

Mexican sunflower *(Tithonia rotundifolia)*

Pink *(Dianthus)*

Sweet alyssum *(Lobularia maritima)*

RIGHT: *A trio of pots provides food for butterfly larvae and nectar for adults. The pot on the left features purple Mexican bush sage* (Salvia leucantha), *pale yellow lantana,* Coreopsis verticillata *'Zagreb', and pale purple aster. The front pot combines purple heliotrope, 'Early Sunrise' coreopsis, and yellow lantana. The tallest pot contains orange lion's tail* (Leonotis leonurus), *blood flower* (Asclepias curassavica), *and pale yellow lantana. The shallow stone bowl holds water for both butterflies and larvae.*

Plants to Lure Hummingbirds

Hummingbirds favor flowers that are tubular in shape, with blossoms arranged around stems so that tubes point outward, and without leaves or branches to get in the way of their whirring wings. Red and orange colors draw these tiny birds like magnets; however, they are also fond of blue flowers.

Canna
Coral bells *(Heuchera)*
Cypress vine *(Ipomoea quamoclit)*
Daylily *(Hemerocallis)*
Fuchsia
Lily *(Lilium)*
Lobelia *(Lobelia erinus)*
Parrot's beak *(Lotus berthelotii)*
Petunia × hybrida
Sage *(Salvia)*

ABOVE: *Although red and reddish orange blooms are famed as hummingbird drawing cards, the tiny wingers are also fond of blue flowers like these 'Heavenly Blue' morning glories. Their appeal lies in the tubular-shaped blossoms, which stand out from the foliage, thereby allowing the birds' wings to flap unimpeded as their beaks probe deeply for nectar.*

Old-Fashioned Charmer

All across the country, old-time porches are staging a big-time comeback. For many home owners, the reason is aesthetic: some types of houses simply look better with porches. Others want to recapture the spirit of a time when everyone gathered on porches, lemonade in hand, to visit with neighbors, greet passersby, and watch children play. Regardless of the purpose a porch serves in your life, it is the perfect setting for simple, old-fashioned flowers.

BEFORE

A wicker loveseat nestles between pots while cushions of flowers soften the porch's straight-edged design. Among the blooms are Oriental lilies (Lilium), *white 'Palace' miniature roses, white marguerites, yellow strawflowers* (Bracteantha bracteata), *and a pink hydrangea.*

A caladium (Caladium bicolor) *and an ornamental asparagus fern* (Asparagus densiflorus) *form a billowy mound in the corner. Pink miniature roses punch up the foreground.*

COME SIT A SPELL

What do you do when your beautiful old house sports a porch that complements its architecture perfectly—but the space is a bare, uninviting rectangle? The answer is easy: just gather up some attractive pots and fill them with simple old-time plants. Add comfortable wicker furniture, and you've got the perfect spot to put up your feet and shift your mind into low gear.

FACING PAGE, BOTTOM: *At the far end of the porch, geraniums climb up bamboo supports. Pink hydrangeas flank the front door, and pink and white petunias tumble from boxes on the porch railing. Terra-cotta pots spill over with lilies, daisies, and miniature roses by the dozens.*

Longtime Favorites

All of these simple annuals and tender perennials (usually treated as annuals) perform well in containers and look perfectly at home on a classic porch. What's more, many of them are deliciously fragrant.

American marigold (*Tagetes erecta***)**
Baby's breath (*Gypsophila paniculata***)**
Bachelor's button (*Centaurea cyanus***)**
Common heliotrope (*Heliotropium arborescens***)**
Cosmos
Dame's rocket (*Hesperis matronalis***)**
Evening scented stock (*Matthiola longipetala bicornis***)**
Flowering tobacco (*Nicotiana alata* and *N. sylvestris* for flowers and fragrance)**
Four o'clock (*Mirabilis jalapa***)**
Garden nasturtium (*Tropaeolum majus***)**
Love-in-a-mist (*Nigella damascena***)**
Mignonette (*Reseda odorata***)**
Morning glory (*Ipomoea tricolor***)**
Pincushion flower (*Scabiosa caucasica***)**
Primrose (*Primula***)**
Snapdragon (*Antirrhinum majus***)**
Stock (*Matthiola incana***)**
Sweet alyssum (*Lobularia maritima***)**
Sweet pea (*Lathyrus odoratus***)**

CHAPTER FOUR

Patios, Courtyards, and Terraces

IN THE PAST DECADE OR SO, people all across the country have discovered what dwellers in balmy climates have always known—that patios (and their alter egos, courtyards and terraces) can function as real outdoor rooms, not simply places to park a barbecue grill. The interest in container gardening has risen hand in hand with the popularity of open-air living. After all, well-chosen plants in attractive pots not only decorate outdoor spaces, but they can also divide them, letting you carve out separate nooks for entertaining, family dining, solo lounging, or even working with your laptop computer. Furthermore, if you choose your living "room dividers" with portability in mind, you can easily move them from place to place to suit the activity of the day or the weather of the season.

A padded bench and attractive container plantings turn a courtyard into a lush garden hideaway.

Possibilities Aplenty

How do you design a container garden that will turn your paved piece of real estate into outdoor living quarters? Start by studying the photographs on the following pages. As you peruse these photos, note what colors, textures, and styles appeal to you in plants, pots, and accessories. If you are drawn to a garden filled with plants that would never work in your climate, remember that you can achieve the same feeling with plants better suited to your area.

ABOVE LEFT: *Huge terra-cotta pots filled with greenery set the tone on this elegant wraparound terrace.*

LEFT: *Boxwood balls in tall pots mark the entrance to an urban patio. Italian limestone paves the floor and tops the table.*

ABOVE: *In Mexico and Spain, gardeners brighten courtyards by filling them with colorful annuals in a multitude of pots. In this adobe-walled retreat in Phoenix, petunias reign in vibrant shades of red and pink, accented by splashes of purple and white.*

RIGHT: *A water garden surrounded by containers of foliage plants forms the centerpiece of this venerable, tranquil courtyard.*

RIGHT: *Standards like these "lolli-pop" bays add a formal touch to any garden. The braided trunks are actually the result of training two shoots around a supporting stake. Growing a bay "tree" this size takes several years, so if you want formality fast, buy finished models at the nursery. (For more on standards, see page 527.)*

BELOW: *Wisteria-covered walls, pots spilling over with white petunias, and subdued lighting beckon evening swimmers to this lap pool. (For more on gardens that shine after dark, see pages 482–483.)*

FACING PAGE, TOP: *Jolts of cobalt blue make a strong statement on this terrace carved out of a hillside. Plants include hostas, cannas, and phormiums. A palm in a huge urn takes center stage, while blue ceramic wedges surrounding the pot provide extra seating.*

FACING PAGE, BOTTOM LEFT: *Pots of violas add spots of color to a neutral-toned patio that functions as an outdoor living room.*

FACING PAGE, BOTTOM RIGHT: *It took relatively few plants to turn a small, bare space into a verdant niche. This size of this tiny courtyard also allowed the owner to splurge on intricate stone paving.*

FACING PAGE, TOP LEFT: *Striking pots, ornamental grasses, and succulents give this high-walled courtyard an architectural feel.*

FACING PAGE, TOP RIGHT: *For a courtyard garden that's used mostly at night, the owners chose white walls and raised beds, clipped boxwood, and standard photinias. Uplights and candles on the planter edges supply even more drama.*

FACING PAGE, BOTTOM: *Cool blue flowers and rich greenery underscore the billowy forms and earthy hues of ornamental grasses. Featured here are fountain grass (*Pennisetum setaceum *'Rubrum'), Sinaloa sage (*Salvia sinaloensis*), and Japanese silver grass (*Miscanthus sinensis *'Yaku Jima').*

ABOVE: *Completely surrounded by high building walls, this courtyard has what nearly every urbanite craves—privacy and quiet. Thanks to painted lattice and a light-colored stone floor, enough light reaches the scene to please the calla lilies and the houseplants spending their summer outdoors.*

LEFT: *With distinctive patterns on house walls and terrace floors, this container garden benefits from a simple color palette. Purple flowers accent the green and white scene supplied by foliage plants and calla lilies.*

Living in the Light

Like all garden sites, patios have their challenges. Two of the biggest can be either too little or too much sun. A cool, shady courtyard is a treat for people, but it limits choices for container plants. At the other extreme, an enclosed patio can trap and hold the sun's rays. Without deep layers of cool soil to protect their roots, container plants are especially vulnerable to blistering heat. Fortunately, you have some excellent coping mechanisms at your disposal for either situation.

TOO MUCH OF A GOOD THING

Depending on where you live, you might have as much trouble grasping the concept of "too much sunlight" as a five-year-old would have imagining a birthday party with "too many toys." But for container gardeners in many parts of the country, sheltering plants from the sun's harsh rays can be a major undertaking. If your patio has less protection from the sun than you would like, call on the following strategies for help.

MAKE INSTANT SHADE Place free-standing screens or panels of lath or canvas where they'll block the most intense sunlight. You can construct your own or purchase ready-made protectors that are either permanent or retractable, in styles ranging from rustic to elegant.

GROW SHADE Position containers holding rough and rugged trees, shrubs, or vines where they will cast shade on more sensitive plants. The best choices will depend on your particular situation, but it's wise to look for plants native to your region that prefer full, intense sun.

BELOW: *Potted climbing roses thrive in full sun on the outside pillars of a pergola. But under its roof, people can dine in shady comfort.*

Glass windows intensify the light and heat that reach this patio. Dahlias cheerfully soak up the sun, while a fence and umbrella shield the owners from its rays.

PLAY AROUND

When you're shopping for container plants, don't simply take the sun/shade recommendations in books and catalogs at face value. A plant that prefers full sun in one region may thrive in far lower light someplace else. For instance, in northern latitudes the long hours of daylight in the summer can compensate for a lack of direct sunshine. And in the South and Southwest, or at high altitudes anywhere, even the most sun-loving plants benefit from some midday shade. So how do you know what to put where? Experiment. (Remember that transportability is one of the great beauties of container gardening!) Move your plants around until you find the light level that suits them best, and give them shelter when needed.

MIND THE BACKGROUND Keep container plants away from sources of reflected light. Mirrors, glass doors, windows, and light-colored masonry walls reflect and intensify both sunlight and heat. At best, these conditions will give your plants a thirst that won't quit; at worst, they will cook your plants' roots.

AVOID BLACK CONTAINERS Whether hand-thrown ceramic creations or plastic nursery pots, black containers capture and retain heat. That can be a real plus in a cool climate, but in a warm climate with hot temperatures it can spell disaster for your container plants.

KEEP THEM MOVING An advantage of container gardening is that you can move pots around to suit changing light levels. If your site demands a periodic game of hide-and-seek with the sun, keep sensitive plants on wheeled dollies or grouped on a decorative cart. You need only roll them from sun to shade or vice versa.

RIGHT: *Lady's-mantle* (Alchemilla), *lamb's ears* (Stachys byzantina), *and bacopa* (Sutera cordata) *bask in the light shade under trees.*

In a hot climate or at high altitudes, sunlight is more intense. Translation: these cannas, nasturtiums (Tropaeolum), and blanket flowers (Gaillardia × grandiflora), and other plants commonly described as needing full sun, can thrive on less.

MORE LIGHT, PLEASE

You may not be able to increase the amount of sun that reaches your site, but there are ways you can increase the potency of the light you have. For instance, mirrors hung on or propped against walls or fences will catch and magnify any light that reaches them. Water performs the same feat. A small fountain, a potted water garden, or even a birdbath will make your garden lighter. Likewise, white or very pale walls and floor surfaces reflect light onto nearby plants—and make your garden appear more spacious at the same time.

ABOVE: *Sunlight bounces off the white walls of this courtyard, providing all the illumination necessary for shade lovers such as ferns, violets, variegated ivy* (Hedera), *and Corsican mint* (Mentha requienii).

FACING PAGE, BOTTOM: *Even heavily shaded gardens like this one can be delightfully lush, as long as you're happy with plenty of foliage and few flowers. Ivies in particular perform well in low-light settings; even plants that prefer some sun will flourish but may bloom sparsely.*

ABOVE: *Here's a textbook example of improving the hand you've been dealt. The designers of this passage have pulled out all the stops to increase the light level, including painting the walls white and installing a white-tiled floor and borders around the planting beds.*

Shades of Difference

Shade is not an absolute like the numbers on a thermometer. In gardening terms, light—or the lack thereof—is broken down into six basic categories:

■ FULL SUN means 6 or more hours of direct sunlight a day. This is what most vegetables need to perform their best.

■ PART SUN or PART SHADE means that the site receives anywhere from 2 to 5 hours of sun a day. The effect of sunlight on plants depends not only on how long it lasts but also on how intense it is, and that varies enormously depending on time of day, time of year, and even altitude and latitude. (See "Play Around" on page 471.)

■ FILTERED LIGHT comes through the small leaves of trees like willows or birches, the openings in a trellis or arbor, or a translucent canopy. When a book or catalog says a plant performs well in shade, more often than not it really means filtered light. Many excellent container plants fall into this category, including hosta, astilbe, and dead nettle *(Lamium)*.

■ DAPPLED SHADE is cast by large-leafed trees, like oaks, maples, and hickories. Though foliage blocks the sun, light still comes through. Impatiens, early-blooming bulbs, and violas perform well in dappled shade.

■ BRIGHT LIGHT is a common condition in city gardens and other densely built areas. It means that no direct sun reaches the site but nothing blocks the sky. Azaleas, rhododendrons, and camellias do beautifully in bright light.

■ DENSE SHADE is cast by tall, north-facing walls or the low, dense branches of evergreen trees. Many ivies thrive in dense shade, but few flowering plants can survive for long.

A Design Primer

Even when a patio lacks enclosing walls, it can easily function as an outdoor room. And no matter the style of your decor—from cutting-edge trendy to down-home country—designing with portable plantings can help create exactly the mood and look you want.

TRICKS OF THE TRADE

You don't have to be a design professional to turn an empty patio into your favorite spot to entertain or relax. With a few plants in pots and the simple design ideas on the following pages, you can create a movable garden that transforms your space, from serene to dramatic and from cozy to grand.

KEEP IT SIMPLE A garden with a palette of one or two colors (especially white or pastels) plus green, in similar or identical containers, looks more spacious than one with a crazy-quilt mixture of shades in a jumble of pots.

Perfectly trimmed boxwood balls marching up a set of stairs lend an air of sleek uniformity to this scene.

To make a small space seem bigger, opt for a limited color palette like the green and pink color scheme on this patio.

474

Don't confuse "just green" with "simple." Here, a bronzey Cordyline fans out above golden 'Garden Party' and 'So Dainty' dahlias.

The brilliant reds of cannas, dahlias, and Crocosmia dance against a blue-framed window.

ABOVE: An orange wall is a dramatic backdrop for a simple but striking quartet of white lilies.

DO IT WITH MIRRORS Besides increasing the light level in a garden, mirrors hung in strategic places deceive the eye, creating an illusion of space and multiplying the plantings. Just make sure you place the mirrors where they won't reflect the viewer, thereby giving the game away.

USE PERSPECTIVE As we all learned in grade-school art class, distant objects appear smaller than those close at hand. One simple way to make this principle work in your garden is to find two potted plants that are identical in everything but size. (Boxwood balls or ivy on topiary frames would be perfect.) Set the larger one in the foreground and the smaller one at the farthest point possible. Your eye will perceive the small plant—and therefore your boundary—as being farther away than it really is. If your garden has room for several sizes of plants, that's even better.

DON'T CROWD Do use distinctive containers to highlight entry points, play up architectural features, and delineate walkways. But leave plenty of room for people and pets to move around in comfort. How much space you need depends on how you use the area. For instance, the rule of thumb for dining is to allow 3 feet on all sides of the table when the chairs are pulled back. (If you can only dream about having that much room, just do the best you can!)

TOP: *With just two big pots, this small pool patio has ample room for swimmers to move about in comfort.*

ABOVE: *In this restrained garden, tall, trim planters line the walkway; one marks the entrance to a tiny dining area—leaving plenty of room for a bistro table and chairs.*

SPOTLIGHT A SUBJECT The world is full of beautiful plants, pots, and garden accessories. But too many of them in one place add up to clutter. To make a tiny garden look and "live" bigger, opt for a few choice plants in simple pots and one dramatic focal point. A fountain or a sculpture will do the trick. So will a found treasure, such as a big, quirky piece of driftwood or a massive boulder.

ABOVE: *If you have limited space and a limited container budget, focus on a fabulous find. One-of-a-kind planters are worthy of a splurge.*

TOP RIGHT: *A sundial is a classic attention-getter, especially when it's surrounded by billows of potted geraniums. Two standards in pots flank the garden gate.*

RIGHT: *Nothing adds drama like a fountain—even one without water. Here, a cascade of white bacopa gushes forth. Under the cherub's toes is a froth of bellflowers (Campanula) and strawberries.*

477

The Vertical Dimension

Like other prime container-gardening venues, patios are often less than capacious. Whether your quarters are tight or you always seem to need room for just one more pot (well, maybe two), these tricks will help you make the most of every inch of growing space.

ABOVE: *An urban gardener has taken full advantage of every planting space in this tiny courtyard.*

RIGHT: *In a no-soil situation, big pots of scarlet cypress vine (Ipomoea quamoclit) bring vibrant color to a narrow patio.*

ABOVE: *Terra-cotta pots, both natural and painted blue, adorn a patio wall in Cordoba, Spain.*

FROM THE GROUND UP Vines grown in containers will scramble up trellises and posts as lustily as their in-ground relatives. What's more, rampant growers and self-seeders such as morning glory, anemone clematis *(C. montana),* and some honeysuckles are easier to keep within bounds when their roots are in pots.

HANG IT Wall-mounted planters and baskets cloak walls and fences in greenery and free up valuable floor space at the same time. Stick with one style for a more sophisticated look, or go all out with a mixture of designs and materials.

STACK THEM Baker's racks, étagères, and even stepladders give you vertical planting space without the need for additional wall attachments.

Trellises and hanging baskets aren't the only means of adding vertical planting space. A simple stepladder can hold multiple pots—with no hardware needed.

LEFT: *Built-in risers lift this herb garden out of the ordinary.*

RIGHT: *Flames of orange lantana leap from a retired fire bucket; icy gray leaves of licorice plant (Helichrysum petiolare) lower the heat.*

A savvy use of repetition—in this case of both color and plants—makes this gray, stone terrace a winner. Red geraniums in pots and planting beds are echoed in the window box and hanging baskets.

A simple baker's rack can increase planting space by many times its small footprint. In this garden, there's room for a birdhouse and the owner's collection of culinary herbs and edible flowers, including sage, thyme, rosemary, and nasturtiums.

Espalier

Espalier, the art of training a tree or shrub to grow more or less flat against a wall or fence, is a classic space-saver. It's also a surprisingly simple way to add a touch of sophistication to any container garden. Potted, dwarf fruit trees make excellent candidates for formal shaping. Simply fasten a trellis or wires to a fence or wall and set the tree in its pot 8 to 12 inches away. As the tree grows, prune off any branches that stick out, and tie those remaining to the trellis or wires to form either a series of horizontal branches or a fan pattern. (Apple and pear trees take well to horizontal espaliers; cherries are most often fan-trained.)

For a more free-form espalier, set a potted tree or shrub in front of a wall, fence, or trellis and allow it to branch naturally. As the plant grows, clip off anything that juts out. The key to success is consistency: check the plant every few weeks during the growing season.

1 Choose two strong branches to form the first tier; remove all other shoots and cut back the leader (the main trunk) to just above the bottom wire. Bend the branches at a 45-degree angle and secure them to the wire with soft cloth or plastic ties.

2 During the first growing season, gradually tighten the ties so that by the end of the season the branches are horizontal. When the newly sprouted leader is long enough, hold it erect and tie it to the second wire.

3 During the first dormant season, cut back the leader to the second wire. Choose two branches for the second tier and remove competing shoots. Cut lateral growth on the lower branches back to three buds.

4 During the second growing season, gradually bring the second-tier branches to a horizontal position, as described above in step 2. Keep the leader upright and tie it to the third wire.

5 Repeat the process for a fourth wire, if desired. When the leader reaches the top wire, cut it back to just above the top branch. Keep horizontal branches in bounds by pruning back the ends to downward-facing side branches in late spring and summer.

Creating an informal espalier is a simpler process. As the tree or shrub grows, clip off shoots that jut out too far from the wall or fence. Plants with a naturally horizontal branching pattern, such as cotoneaster (depicted above), work well for informal training.

Some Enchanted Evenings

If you're like many busy people, chances are you seldom even see your garden during the daylight hours, much less have a chance to relax and enjoy it. So why not design a container garden that comes into its own at dusk—just when you're free to settle in and soak up its charms?

BEFORE

White pots and flowers alike glow in candlelight. The large container holds calla lilies (Zantedeschia) and Clematis 'Garland'. To the right, an autumn fern (Dryopteris erythrosora) cloaks the "feet" of a moth orchid (Phalaenopsis). An azalea spills over the pot in the foreground.

The white-margined leaves of Hosta fortunei 'Green Gold' take center stage here. In the pots surrounding them are (clockwise from top right) moth orchids, an autumn fern, New Guinea impatiens 'Pearl White', and pansy orchids (Miltoniopsis).

INTO THE NIGHT

This covered patio had all the makings of a charming outdoor sitting room, but no one ever used it. Now it's become the family's favorite after-work gathering spot. The key to a garden that beckons at night can be summed up in one word: white. Plants with white flowers or white-margined leaves hold their own at dusk and beyond, long after even pastel tones have vanished into the darkness.

FACING PAGE, BOTTOM: *White flowers, white pots, and glowing candles set the stage for relaxing evenings in this container garden.*

Plants for an Evening Garden

The plants listed here are annuals and tender perennials that are grown as annuals in most parts of the country.

Aster (any dwarf white variety)
Baby's breath (Gypsophila paniculata)
Common sunflower (Helianthus annuus 'Italian White')
Cosmos (Cosmos bipinnatus 'Sonata White')
Evergreen candytuft (Iberis sempervirens)
Flowering tobacco (Nicotiana alata or N. sylvestris for evening fragrance; not the Nicki or Domino strains often sold at garden centers)
Four o'clock (Mirabilis jalapa)
Gardenia (Gardenia augusta)
Impatiens (any white variety; the Fiesta series has an attractive double type)
Iris (any white variety)
Love-in-a-mist (Nigella damascena 'Miss Jekyll Alba')
Moonflower (Ipomoea alba)
Poet's jasmine (Jasminum officinale)
Snow-in-summer (Cerastium tomentosum)
Spider flower (Cleome hasslerana 'Helen Campbell')
Tuberose (Polianthes tuberosa)
Tuberous begonia (any white variety)
Tulip (Tulipa, any white variety)

CHAPTER FIVE

Roof Gardens and Balconies

ANY GARDEN CAN BE *a place of beauty and repose, but a garden perched on a balcony or a rooftop is more than that. For many city dwellers, and for increasing numbers of suburbanites, it's a cherished, private slice of the great outdoors. Whether it's a sprawling rooftop oasis or a balcony scarcely big enough to stand on, a garden-on-high is like a verdant magic carpet, soaring above a world of noise and hard-edged technology.* ❧ *That's the human viewpoint. From a plant's perspective, that elevated Eden is hostile territory. Because sun and wind become more intense as distance from the ground increases, both top growth and potted roots are far more vulnerable to weather than they are at ground level. Without proper protection, even the hardiest vegetation can suffer. The good news is that by choosing your plants carefully and taking some simple precautions, you can enjoy a beautiful and thriving green scene, even high above terra firma.*

A verdant roof garden seems light-years away from the busy street below.

Coping with the Elements

On a small, shady balcony that normally gets only light, balmy breezes, your plants may need no added protection at all. But be prepared to cover them or whisk them indoors if the weather turns blustery. On a wide-open rooftop, both plants and people benefit from structures that filter sun and block wind. And if you live where strong gusts are commonplace, you'll probably want to construct built-in planters or anchor containers to the floor or walls.

LEFT: *Vine-covered trellises and adjoining buildings shield this rooftop sitting area from wind and harsh sun.*

ABOVE: *It may be wide open to the big-city sky, but with its sheltering walls and comfortable furniture, this penthouse garden has all the charm of a country living room.*

RIGHT: *This elevated garden features tempered glass panels to block wind, a heavy and all-but-indestructible rail- way sleeper bench, and firmly anchored planters. Inside the planters are Phormium tenax 'Rainbow Queen' and P. 'Platts Black'—rugged New Zealand natives that can take all the sun and wind that come their way.*

HOLD IT RIGHT THERE!

On a rooftop or high balcony, strong winds can topple both plants and furniture or even send them sailing—sometimes with disastrous results. When you garden in the air, you'll need to consider some factors aside from design and horticulture.

WEIGHTY MATTERS While it is true that lightweight pots filled with ultralight planting mix will put the least strain on structural supports, they're also easy to knock over, especially when they hold large plants. The same weight considerations apply to furniture and decorative objects. Anything made of plastic, tubular metal, or lightweight wood is too flimsy to stay in place for long. You may need to experiment to find containers and furnishings that strike the ideal balance between too heavy and too light.

ABOVE: *These wooden planters with attached, camellia-covered trellises soften the walls much more effectively than a collection of pots could. What's more, the structures are sturdy enough to stay firmly rooted in place through all but the fiercest gales.*

LEFT: *Built-in wooden planters keep pots of herbs securely in place on this tiny riverfront balcony.*

TIES THAT BIND At truly lofty heights or in extremely windy areas, it pays to anchor even heavy containers and furnishings (including barbecue grills) to floors or walls. Better yet, opt for built-in planters and furniture.

WORST-CASE SCENARIO Ask your insurance agent whether your home-owner's or renter's policy covers damage inflicted by objects falling from your balcony or roof. If the answer is no, it might be wise to add coverage.

A low railing with tempered-glass inserts provides all the protection this Washington, D.C., roof garden needs and leaves a clear view of the Potomac meandering below. Ceramic pots and a lightweight metal table and chaises are easily stored for the winter.

HOLD IT DOWN

On a rooftop, high balcony, or other exposed location, it's wise to anchor trees and tall shrubs so that they won't topple and break in gusty winds. It's a simple task in a wooden planter. Screw sturdy eye-hooks into the sides of the container (one anchor per major limb). Then run support wire from the limbs to the hooks. Use adjustable hardware so that you can lengthen the lines as the tree grows. Prevent damage to the bark by wrapping the wire in rubber or plastic tubing. If your trees are growing in stone or concrete planters, use screw-in hooks designed for masonry.

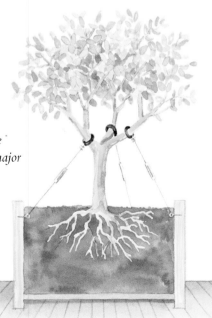

Standing Fast

While any plant can fall victim to strong gusts, the following trees and shrubs tolerate more wind than most.

Bayberry *(Myrica pensylvanica)*
Birch *(Betula)*
Cinquefoil *(Potentilla)*
Common privet *(Ligustrum vulgare)*
Cotoneaster
Flowering crabapple *(Malus)*
Juniper *(Juniperus)*
Pussy willow *(Salix discolor)*
Russian olive *(Elaeagnus angustifolia)*
Yew *(Taxus)*

489

Weight and Drainage

Even more than weather, two factors are crucial to the success of a rooftop or balcony garden: safe weight distribution and efficient water drainage.

WEIGHT

How elaborate your weight investigation must be depends on the size of your intended garden and the type, age, and condition of your building.

If you live in a recently built house, condominium, or apartment building, the contractor, home-owners' association, or landlord should be able to advise you about safe weight limits, as

well as any design restrictions or local building codes.

In the case of an older structure—or if your plans call for anything more elaborate than a few lightweight pots—get a structural survey. For a modest sum, a structural engineer can tell you the weight tolerances of every part of your roof or balcony, as well as the condition of any walls, fences, and railings. If possible, get a personal recommendation from an architect or builder whose judgment you trust; failing that, look under "Engineers—Structural" in the yellow pages. Use a licensed engineer and make sure you are provided with a detailed written report. Avoid low-cost "semi-pros" who employ such tactics as jumping up and down on a roof to test its strength.

ABOVE: *The owners of this roof terrace came up with a clever drainage plan: a gravel border extending around the perimeter of the floor. Large containers are strategically positioned over structural beams.*

LEFT: *Symmetry serves a double purpose in this elegant roof garden. The corner placement of cotoneaster and boxwood topiaries in stone containers lends a formal air to the urban sanctuary and, more important, spreads the weight around. With the heavy planters resting on secure supports, the decking can easily handle the hefty load of the cast-iron furniture.*

HOW HEAVY IS IT?

The load-bearing capacity of your structure will affect your choices of floors, containers, and furnishings. Here are the weights of common building and garden materials.

MATERIAL	POUNDS PER CUBIC FOOT	KILOGRAMS PER CUBIC METER
Brickwork (average)	115	1,865
Cast iron	450	7,297
Concrete: Lightweight	80–100	1,298–1,622
Precast	130	2,108
Reinforced	150	2,433
Granite	170	2,757
Gravel	120	1,946
Limestone	155	2,514
Marble	170	2,757
Pebbles	120	1,946
Sandstone	145	2,352
Slate	160–180	2,595–2,919
Tile and setting bed	15–73 lbs./sq. ft.	73–353 kg/sq. m
Timber: Hardwood (average)	45	730
Softwood (average)	35	568
Water	62.428	1,013

Source: Reprinted by permission of The McGraw-Hill Companies, from Charles W. Harris and Nicholas Dines, eds., *Time Saver Standards for Landscape Architecture,* 2nd edition (New York: McGraw-Hill, 1997).

LIGHTEN THE LOAD

Attractive, high-tech container materials and ultralight potting mixes give aboveground gardeners many options for reducing weight without having to sacrifice aesthetics.

The simplest way to lighten the load on your building is to fill your planters with a commercial seed-germinating mix, which weighs less than regular potting soils. If you use self-watering pots, a seed starter has another advantage over more conventional mixes—its coarse texture allows moisture to rise much more readily from the reservoir on the bottom. One note of caution: Because a seed starter contains no nutrients, you'll need to be very diligent

A layer of overturned plastic nursery pots and foam peanuts can make heavy containers suitable for use on roof gardens and balconies.

about fertilizing. Use a slow-release granular fertilizer at the recommended rate; it should last about four months.

REDUCE THE VOLUME

Very large containers are heavy even when they're filled with lightweight mixes. To reduce both weight and the amount of planting mix you'll have to buy, fill the pot about one-third to one-half with light, bulky material, such as beer or soda cans, plastic pots, or chunks of plastic foam, before you add soil. (If you use packing "peanuts," make sure they're not made from cornstarch, which will soon dissolve.) This technique works well for annuals and shallow-rooted perennials grown in large pots, but don't use it for trees or shrubs, which need all the root room they can get.

Lightweight Potting Mix

If you prefer to make your own lightweight soil, here's a simple recipe:

- 5 gallons of ground sphagnum moss or coir fiber
- 5 gallons of vermiculite or perlite
- 2 gallons of compost
- 1 cup of granular, slow-release fertilizer

The end product weighs about the same as a seed-starting mix and has two sizable advantages: The compost supplies trace nutrients and, according to recent evidence, inhibits the growth of disease-causing fungi and bacteria. The scoop holds a mix of compost, perlite, sphagnum moss, and slow-release fertilizer (clockwise from top).

492

DRAINAGE

Even if your garden consists of only a few featherweight containers, you need to know one crucial piece of information: where the water goes when it leaves the pots. The same engineer who determines your structure's load-bearing capacity can investigate your roof and walls for potential leaks. If there are flaws, no matter how minor, have them attended to before you lay down any flooring or arrange your plants. Make sure the floor surface (new or existing) slopes gently toward drains. Keep container weight as light as possible, given wind conditions, and use platforms or decks to distribute heavy loads over a broader area.

AN OUNCE OF PREVENTION To prevent drainage trouble in the future, keep a watchful eye out. In particular:

- Keep drains and downspouts free of debris and unobstructed by containers, furniture, or flooring materials.
- Check your plants' roots periodically, and when you find them poking through drainage holes, trim them back or move the plants to bigger quarters. Otherwise, they could grow into floor joints or wall crevices in search of water.

UP AND AWAY
Water and fertilizer salts can spell trouble for both floor surfaces and roof structures. To avoid stains and leaks, keep saucers under pots and arrange containers, furniture, and accessories so that all drains remain clear.

Flooring Choices

In large part, your garden-surface options depend on the weight-bearing capacity of your roof or balcony (see page 490). The strongest roofs can handle the same kinds of paving you might use in a conventional garden. You can even spread soil and plant a lawn, if you want to.

OPTIONS UNDERFOOT

There are other factors to consider, though, including climate, budget, whether you own or rent your home, and how long you intend to be there. For example, if you live in a rental apartment and plan to move in a year or two, you may want to install a floor you can pick up and take with you. The style of your garden, as well as its purpose, will also influence your choices. Will you use it as an outdoor living area or simply as display space for plants?

Varied as they are, flooring materials break down into three basic categories:

PAVING On the upside, paving sets a tone of sophistication and permanence. With a virtually limitless range of tiles, bricks, concrete slabs, and natural stone to choose from, it's easy to find one that suits your taste, style, and budget.

On the downside, paving is heavy, some materials are affected by freezing temperatures, and aboveground installation requires extra care to allow for drainage. You can either set pavers on battens or pads to lift them clear of the roof, or spread a layer of free-draining gravel over the roof and set tiles into it, leaving the joints open.

ABOVE: *Concrete pavers, some set in river stones, provide a smooth and sophisticated floor for this roof garden. If the owner decides to move, both pavers and stones can be transported to a new garden.*

LEFT: *Quarry tile makes a fine floor in a mild climate like that of London, the home of this thriving roof garden.*

FACING PAGE, BOTTOM LEFT: *Gravel provides excellent drainage for a roof garden; slate tiles make for easier walking and plant tending.*

GRAVEL AND STONE CHIPS They are inexpensive, easy to install, and available in a range of colors and sizes. Their uneven surface makes them less than ideal for sitting and dining areas, but you can set stepping-stones into them to make walking easier.

DECKING It has some distinct advantages over other materials. For one thing, you can easily suspend it above the roof surface, which allows for free drainage. Installation can be permanent or temporary, and you can make or buy modular sections that are simple to lift for maintenance— or for loading into a moving van. Traditional wood decking requires periodic cleaning and sealing, but new versions made from composite lumber or recycled plastic lumber need no upkeep beyond an occasional hosing. What's more, these new lumbers are slip-resistant when wet and splinter-free.

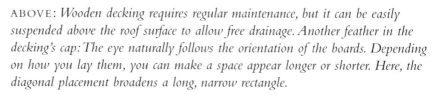

ABOVE: *Wooden decking requires regular maintenance, but it can be easily suspended above the roof surface to allow free drainage. Another feather in the decking's cap: The eye naturally follows the orientation of the boards. Depending on how you lay them, you can make a space appear longer or shorter. Here, the diagonal placement broadens a long, narrow rectangle.*

Safe and Sound

Protective railings are a crucial part of any balcony or roof garden. Not only do they keep people, pets, and plants from going overboard, but they can also block unpleasant views or play up good ones, help muffle noise, and provide vertical planting space.

ABOVE LEFT: *An open-mesh steel and wire railing, a bistro table and chairs, and a collection of container plants make a private nook for two, complete with ocean view.*

LEFT: *Window boxes stretch along the railing of this backdoor landing, and pots cluster in corners. Plants include million bells (Calibrachoa), purple-leafed basil (Ocimum basilicum), coral bells (Heuchera 'Santa Ana Cardinal'), and verbena.*

ABOVE: *At the height of summer, a lush green and white garden blocks a view of the busy street below and fills this balcony with serenity and scent. Plants include roses, geraniums, boxwood, and lilies.*

RIGHT: *Sometimes a railing is the star of the show. This curvaceous gem, spilling over with red geraniums and silvery licorice plant (Helichrysum petiolare), would catch eyes in any neighborhood.*

A Pint-Size Kitchen Garden

Even the tiniest balcony can produce bumper crops of vegetables, fruits, and herbs. And because many edible plants look as good as they taste, your miniplot can be as beautiful as any ornamental garden. To make the most of the small space, choose compact varieties that are well suited to your growing conditions and climate.

BEFORE

A crazy-quilt mixture of colors enlivens the formerly bland space. Careful arrangement of pots allows just enough space for a chair and tiny table, so the gardener can survey her domain from indoors or out. African daisies (Arctotis 'Safari Pink') brighten up the railing.

A console table makes a clever focal point at one end. Herbs crowd the drawers and top, while pots planted with Spanish lavender (Lavandula stoechas 'Otto Quast') afford much-needed privacy. Tomatoes, peppers, and a dwarf citrus, 'Lisbon Lemon', stand ready for picking.

BARE TO BOUNTIFUL

This tiny, bare-bones balcony reflected the plight of many apartment and condo dwellers: no privacy, no character, and no ground whatsoever. Now, though, what was nothing but an elevated concrete slab has become a lush garden brimming with fruits, vegetables, herbs, and cutting flowers. What's more, this small garden puts dinner makings only steps away from the kitchen and screens the view of, and from, neighboring units.

FACING PAGE, BOTTOM: *A small stepladder has been retrofitted with boards on the bottom treads to make room for 'Bright Lights' Swiss chard. Herbs and flowers soften the corner and blur the distinction between the balcony and the wooded landscape beyond.*

Container Winners

When growing space is limited, look for vegetables that have eye appeal as well as great flavor. Here's a small sampling.

- EGGPLANT 'Bambino' (1-inch dark purple fruit), 'Applegreen' (small, oval, light green), and 'Tango' (white, cylindrical, 7 inches long) are all good choices.

- PEPPERS Choose a novel color such as 'Purple Beauty' or 'Sweet Chocolate', or go with miniature red 'Baby Belle' or 'Jingle Bells'. On the hot side, try 'Super Cayenne' or 'Hungarian Yellow Wax Hot'.

- POTATOES All potatoes have attractive foliage, but 'All Blue' also gives you blue flowers—plus tubers that are blue inside and out, with a rich, nutlike flavor. Other winners include 'All Red' (red inside and out), 'Donna' (red skin with yellow flesh), and 'Huckleberry' (beet-colored skin with red and white marbled flesh).

- TOMATOES 'Patio' and 'Tiny Tim' are perfect for containers; 'Tumbler' is especially bred for hanging baskets.

- SWISS CHARD Plant 'Bright Lights'. Aside from delicate flavor and crunchy texture, it has bright green leaves and a mixture of stem colors: red, white, pink, yellow, and bright orange.

CHAPTER SIX

Container Plant Projects

SOME OF THE MOST EFFECTIVE PLANTINGS are the simplest—single, beautiful plants in exactly the right containers. Certainly those are the easiest design schemes to pull off successfully. But once the container-gardening bug bites, you may find the artist within clamoring for a bigger say in the goings-on. When that happens, there's only one thing to do: give in. ◆ Every artist needs inspiration, though, and that's where this chapter comes in. In these pages you'll find ideas and simple directions for container projects large and small. Follow them to a T if you like, develop variations on the themes, or merely use them as a springboard for your own improvisations. ◆ If you're just starting out in the game of artful combining, there's one thing to keep in mind. When you start with cell-pack seedlings, visualizing the end product can be difficult. So instead, go for instant lushness by using plants that are mature enough to fill out the container right from the start.

Cast-concrete boxes, custom-tinted to resemble limestone, make an elegant addition to a travertine stone patio (see page 508 for plant information).

Front and Center

Looking for a centerpiece that goes beyond cut flowers and candles? Try one of these all-but-instant projects.

SHAPING UP

This one-dimensional "topiary" heart could declare your love of gardening, or it could represent a valentine—one in a series of holiday-themed creations. To make it, first order an undivided flat of baby's tears *(Soleirolia soleirolii)* from your local nursery. Make an outline with string or set a heart-shaped stencil or cake pan on top, and then use a sharp knife to cut around the form, removing excess plants outside it as you go. Very carefully lift the heart from the flat and press it into a container filled with potting mix fortified with slow-release fertilizer. When your topiary is not performing at the dinner table, keep it in a shady spot. As the baby's tears grow beyond the outline, trim them back.

Design: Jill Slater

QUILTING CLASS

Whether on a table, wall, or bed, a patchwork quilt is a classic show-stopper. Here is one that actually grows. The only "makings" are a flat, square container 3 to 5 inches high, potting mix, and cell packs of three different low-growing ground covers. This container features *Dichondra micrantha* (upper right and lower left in the container) and Irish moss *(Sagina subulata)* for the square patches, and *Dymondia margaretae* for the center strip. Simply spread enough potting mix on the bottom of the container to ensure that the plants' crowns will be just below the top edge. Then remove the plants from their cells and press them into place inside the container.

Design: Kathleen N. Brenzel

PARTY THYME

Next time you're invited to a potluck, take along some deep-dish lemon-lime thyme. To fill a bowl that's 13 inches wide by 4½ inches deep, you'll need two 4-inch pots each of lemon and lime thyme (*Thymus × citriodorus, T. × c.* 'Lime'), and a six-pack or two of common thyme (*T. vulgaris*). Before planting, set a terra-cotta candle holder with a hurricane shade (not shown here) in the center of the bowl. Add potting mix and plants. The finishing touch is a candle with a light citrus scent.

Design: Kathleen N. Brenzel

A TABLE TO GO

When plants on the tabletop won't pack the visual punch you want, try this project. Fill an old wheelbarrow to within 3 inches of the rim with potting mix, position a few ceramic or glass tiles on the surface, and plant your choice of greenery around them. Irish moss is shown at left, but any low-growing, spreading plant would work, such as Corsican mint (*Mentha requienii*) or pennyroyal (*M. pulegium*). For after-dark interest, tuck in a few white flowers, such as the geraniums (*Pelargonium* 'Alba') shown at left; white sweet alyssum (*Lobularia maritima*) would add aromatic interest.

Design: Jill Slater

Carefree Combinations

If you're timid about combining varied shapes, textures, and sizes in a pot, study the groupings on these pages and note what makes them work. Then copy the combinations if you like, or aim for similar results with different plant material.

1 ANNUAL MALLOW
(*Lavatera trimestris* 'Mont Blanc')

2 PURPLE SWAN RIVER DAISY
(*Brachyscome*)

3 PINK
(*Dianthus*)

4 WHITE-EDGED PURPLE PANSY
(*Viola*)

5 LICORICE PLANT
(*Helichrysum petiolare*)

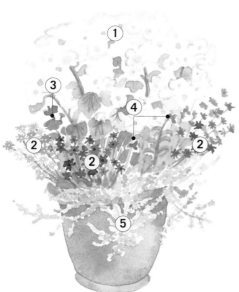

THE MAGIC OF COLOR

This pot holds five different kinds of plants, yet the effect is simple and serene. The secret is a limited color palette. Annual mallow spreads a white cloud over a band of purple with just a tiny jolt of hot pink. Silvery licorice plant softens the composition as it tumbles over the edge.

Design: Teena Garay

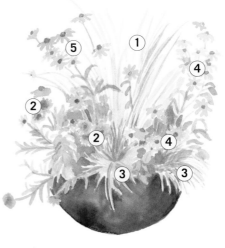

1 MEXICAN FEATHER GRASS
(*Nassella tenuissima*)

2 BLANKET FLOWER
(*Gaillardia × grandiflora*)

3 COMMON BLUE FESCUE
(*Festuca glauca*)

4 GLORIOSA DAISY
(*Rudbeckia hirta*)

5 PURPLE CONEFLOWER
(*Echinacea purpurea*)

A NATURAL BEAUTY

When in doubt about assembling a winning combination, look to nature. Here, prairie grasses and wildflowers team up in a stone bowl 18 inches wide by 9 inches deep. Another key to the success of this composition is the bowl's dark color, which intensifies the jewel-like tones of the plants.

Design: Kathleen N. Brenzel

KEEP IT COOL

In the ground or in a pot, a green and white garden flaunts a cool sophistication. Spires of white foxglove (*Digitalis purpurea* 'Foxy') stand tall above calla lilies (*Zantedeschia rehmanii* 'Crystal Blush'), variegated English ivy (*Hedera helix*), and variegated licorice plant (*Helichrysum petiolare* 'Variegatum'). And here's proof that you can combine practicality with elegant good looks: what appears to be a stunning terra-cotta pot is actually a plastic replica, complete with "water" and "fertilizer" marks.

Design: Jill Slater

Containers
Multiplied

One well-designed container combination is exactly that. Gather three or more compatible combinations together, though, and you have a garden that happens to be in containers. Here's a trio of excellent and varied examples.

1 HEN AND CHICKS
   (Echeveria elegans)
2 *E.* 'Morning Light'
3 *E. moranii*
4 *E.* 'Violet Queen'
5 *E. lilacina*
6 *E.* 'Colorata'
7 × *Graptoveria* 'Fred Ives'
8 STONECROP
   (Sedum dasyphyllum)

MADE TO ORDER

These succulents, including a half-dozen *Echeveria* species, are as well suited to their broad, shallow bowl as they are to the climate and the architecture of this southwestern patio. The massing of identical containers around a focal-point tree makes this garden a design standout.

ALL IN THE WASH

A wash of identical color unifies a trio of containers. The subdued tones of the plantings help, too. The pedestal pot holds a boxwood topiary (*Buxus microphylla japonica* 'Green Beauty') underplanted with white petunias. A clump of pink border penstemon (*Penstemon* × *gloxinioides* 'Apple Blossom') performs solo in the urn. Sharing honors in the rectangular planter are a pastel peony *(Paeonia)* and a pink-flowered indigo bush *(Indigofera incarnata)* underplanted with variegated English ivy *(Hedera helix)*.
Design: Jill Slater

RIGHT IN STEP

The color scheme is cool and soothing; the pots classic, clean-lined terra-cotta; and the plants old-time favorites—fuchsias and petunias—as well as bacopa (*Sutera cordata*). The resulting container garden is the perfect complement to the time-worn stone stairs on which it sits.

507

Window Dressing

When you want to add pizzazz to a house quickly, nothing beats a window box brimming with lush plants. But that trick is not limited to windows. Window boxes work their charms just as well when they're hung on railings or lined up along the edge of a patio.

1 CARDINAL FLOWER
   (Lobelia cardinalis)

2 *Cosmos bipinnatus*

3 *Zinnia elegans* 'Envy',
   'Peter Pan Princess'

4 PETUNIA

5 SWEET POTATO VINE
   (Ipomoea batatas 'Blackie')

6 BACOPA
   (Sutera cordata)

7 SWAN RIVER DAISY
   (Brachyscome)

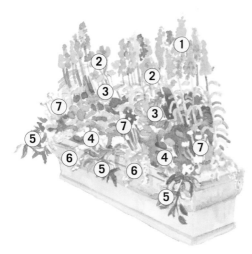

AN ALL-STAR CAST

Window boxes that are stars in themselves, such as these expansive cast-concrete models, call for dramatic plantings. Placed beneath room-height windows, these selections put on a colorful show all summer long in shades of rosy red, deep pink, lime green, and white.

Designs: Jill Slater (plants), Lynn Hollyn (concrete containers)

1 SAGE
  (*Salvia × sylvestris*)

2 PETUNIA

3 SWAN RIVER DAISY
  (*Brachyscome*)

4 GARDEN VERBENA

5 VARIEGATED LICORICE
  PLANT
  (*Helichrysum petiolare*
  'Variegatum')

6 SPIDER PLANT
  (*Chlorophytum comosum*)

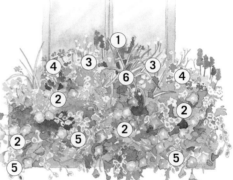

OUTSIDE THE BOX

Flowers and foliage in watery shades of gray-green, lavender-blue, purple, and white tumble from a window box—all but hiding the container in the process. The contents are simple and easy to grow.

WHAT WINDOW?

Who says window boxes are for windows only? This one, filled with a collection of pungent herbs, offers nourishment for all the senses. Shown in the photo from left to right: curry plant (*Helichrysum italicum*), sage (*Salvia officinalis*), variegated sage, and curly-leafed French parsley (*Petroselinum crispum*).

Potting Up Strawberries

No edible plants look more beautiful or grow better in containers than strawberries. Here are two ways to pot up a crop of this classic summertime treat.

STRAWBERRY JAR

Start with a pot that is at least 16 inches high (anything smaller will dry out too quickly). Choose a berry variety that performs well in your area (ask for recommendations at a good local nursery). You'll also need potting mix fortified with slow-release fertilizer, a piece of 1- to 2-inch-diameter PVC pipe to make a watering tube, and a cap to cover one end of the tube. Then follow these simple steps:

1 Cut the PVC pipe so that one end will be even with the pot's rim when it is placed vertically inside. Cap it on one end. Drill ½-inch-diameter holes about 1 inch apart along alternate sides of the pipe.

2 Partially fill the pot with soil, and insert the watering tube, capped end down, near the center. Add more potting mix, loosely filling the jar to the rim.

3 Working from the bottom up, tuck a strawberry plant into each pocket, adding soil around the roots as needed, and soaking the soil well.

4 Keep the plants in as much sun as they'll tolerate without drying out too rapidly, especially when berries are ripening. Feed once a month with a liquid organic fertilizer, and water whenever the top inch of soil feels dry—once a day in hot weather. To irrigate evenly, slip a funnel into the top of the PVC pipe and pour water into it; the holes will distribute moisture throughout the pot.

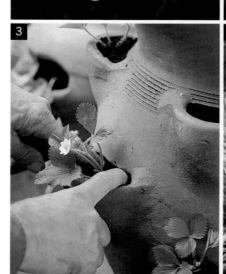

Strawberries 101

There are dozens of varieties of strawberries, but they all fall into one of three types.

- June bearers form buds in the fall, then produce a single crop of fruit over a period of about six weeks beginning in late spring. In northern parts of the country, that's usually June; in warm climates, it's earlier. 'Honeoye', 'Surecrop', and 'Earliglow' are all flavorful, hardy, and resistant to the diseases that most commonly plague strawberry plants.

- Day-neutrals bloom and bear fruit pretty much continuously from spring to fall, as long as temperatures remain between 35 and 85°F/2 and 29°C. 'Tristar' produces a cascade of fruit and foliage that make it ideal for hanging baskets. 'Tribute' offers excellent disease resistance and big crops of plump, flavorful fruit.

- Everbearers, contrary to their name, do not bear fruit all season long. Rather, they produce one crop in late spring (June in most places) and another in fall. 'Ogallala' and 'Fort Laramie' perform well anywhere, but they are especially good choices in cold or dry climates.

- Regardless of type, the best strawberries to grow are the ones that taste best to you. Sample different varieties at neighbors' homes, local farmers' markets, and pick-your-own berry farms.

FILL SOME BASKETS

To put your crop at eye level—and beyond the reach of snails and slugs—grow your strawberries in hanging baskets. To make one like this, you'll need about 24 strawberry plants, potting mix enriched with slow-release fertilizer, a 16-inch wire basket, and a liner. You can purchase a green polyester-and-plastic version, or use either coir fiber or damp sphagnum moss.

Set 18 plants into the basket's sides, inserting them through the moss or through 3-inch slits in the liner. Add enough fertilizer-enriched potting mix to reach just below the rim and set in the remaining six plants. Follow the same care guidelines described for the strawberry pot.

Hanging Baskets

In private and public spaces alike, hanging baskets are a classic part of the summertime scene. Here are some new takes on the theme.

STACK 'EM UP

When planting space is at a premium—or you simply want to pack a lot of color into one small spot—try this moss-lined triple decker. You can buy ready-made triads, but if you can't find one, simply purchase small, medium, and large wire baskets. Then plant each one in the normal way (see the instructions for planting a hanging basket on page 511) and connect them with rust-proof chain.

Design: Bud Stuckey

1 PINK POLKA-DOT PLANT (*Hypoestes phyllostachya*)

2 SILVER FERN (*Pityrogramma calomelanos*)

3 WHITE SWEET ALYSSUM (*Lobularia maritima*)

4 *Pilea depressa* 'Tigers Eyes'

5 AUTUMN FERN (*Dryopteris erythrosora*)

6 PURPLE-LEAF OXALIS

7 *Microlepia splendens*

8 DWARF CUP FLOWER (*Nierembergia caerulea* 'Purple Robe')

9 PURPLE SWEET ALYSSUM (*Lobularia maritima*)

10 IMPATIENS, NEW GUINEA HYBRIDS

11 BABY'S TEARS (*Soleirolia soleirolii*)

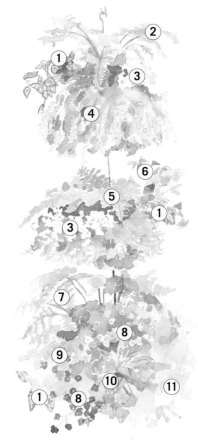

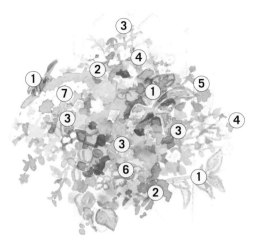

1 COLEUS

2 FLOSS FLOWER
(*Ageratum houstonianum*)

3 AMETHYST FLOWER
(*Browallia speciosa*
'Blue Bells Improved')

4 WHITE FIBROUS BEGONIA

5 MAGENTA IMPATIENS

6 DEAD NETTLE
(*Lamium maculatum*)

7 WHITE IMPATIENS

HOLD ON

Hanging baskets don't have to dangle from above.
They look just as stunning mounted on walls or,
like this colorful number, on a lattice-trimmed pillar.
To make your own, start with a wire-mesh basket
that's flat on one side, fit it with a liner, and insert
your plants.
Design: Hilda Schwerin

A REAL COOL TRIO

This seldom-seen combo adds a cool touch to a late-
summer day—and it can sail right through the winter
in a very mild climate. The stars: white ornamental
cabbage 'Northern Lights', Scotch heather *(Calluna
vulgaris),* and variegated English ivy *(Hedera helix).*
Design: John Glover

Water Gardens

Water works magic in a garden, reflecting light, intensifying any aromas, and—even in a tiny container—relaxing both body and spirit.

A MINI LILY POND

Pink and white miniature water lilies (*Nymphaea* 'James Brydon' and *N.* 'Marliacea Albida') share this "pond" with water lettuce (*Pistia stratiotes*), variegated yellow flag iris (*Iris pseudacorus* 'Variegata'), water canna (*Canna glauca*), and soft rush (*Juncus effusus*). This garden needs full sun to perform its best; in less light, the water lily plants will still thrive, but the flowers will not open fully.

HOW SWEET IT IS

Convinced that you don't have a wet green thumb? Try this time-honored trick from Lafayette, Louisiana, where sugar mills—and sugar-kettle water gardens like this one—salted the landscape. Just fill a large glazed ceramic or metal pot with water, and then add a few pots of water plants. The ones shown here are water hyacinth (*Eichhornia crassipes*), Louisiana iris, and cast-iron plant (*Aspidistra elatior*). Set the pots on bricks or pebbles so that they rest at the proper water level (see the instructions on the facing page).

Design: Scott Daigre

MAKE YOUR OWN WATER GARDEN

To make your own water garden, all you need are a nonporous container (such as the ceramic bowl at right), clean rocks and pebbles, and naturally small plants that thrive in wet soil or an aquatic environment. Garden centers and water-garden nurseries can recommend both plants and equipment suited to your climate and your site.

Design: Jill Slater

1 Set the container in its intended site and fill the bottom with rocks.

2 Place the plants, in their pots, on the rocks. For a decorative twist, the yellow-eyed grass *(Sisyrinchium californicum)* is in its own ceramic container (see step 3 for a list of the plants in this water garden). Add or remove pebbles as needed so that the plants will stand in water of the depth they need (consult the instructions that come with the plants when you purchase them).

3 Fill the container with water almost to the rim. To prevent too-rapid evaporation, try to keep your water garden out of direct sun. This water garden features (clockwise from the top): yellow-eyed grass, *Houttuynia cordata* 'Variegata', parrot feather *(Myriophyllum aquaticum),* and water hyacinth.

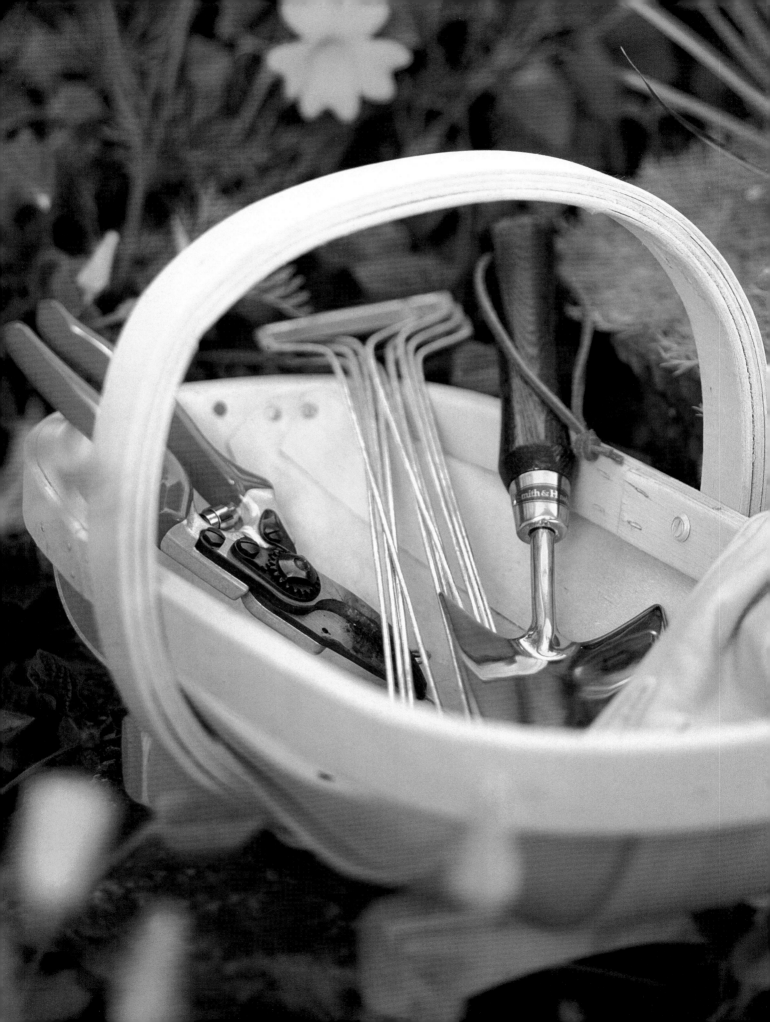

CHAPTER SEVEN

Care and Maintenance

DESIGNING THE CONTAINER GARDEN *of your dreams, and then shopping for exactly the right plants, pots, and accessories, can be a lot of fun. So can modestly accepting the "oohs" and "aahs" of admiring visitors. But no garden will remain praiseworthy for long without care and attention, and it's a fact of horticultural life that plants in containers need more TLC than identical versions planted in the ground. They need more feeding, watering, and pruning. They need more coddling during heat waves, cold snaps, high winds, and whatever else Mother Nature tosses our way.* ❧ *That's the bad news. The good news is that the burgeoning interest in container gardening has led to a multitude of products that make potted-plant tending easier than ever before. That includes everything from dwarf trees that are bred to thrive in close confines to slow-release fertilizers that feed your plants on demand to watering systems that deliver exactly the right amount of water, whether you're around or not.*

High-quality tools can make container-gardening chores easier and faster.

Watering

Watering is the single most important job in caring for your container garden. Because plants in containers have a limited amount of soil from which to draw moisture, they dry out much faster than their in-ground counterparts.

WHEN TO WATER

How do you know when your plants need moisture? This easy trick works in most cases: poke your finger into the top inch of soil; if it feels dry, the plant needs watering. But that's not a universal guideline. Some plants need soil that stays evenly moist, while others fare better in drier conditions. Ask about the needs of specific plants at the nursery where you purchase them, or consult a gardening book.

Plant preferences aside, there are a few general rules. For instance, light-weight potting mixes dry out faster than heavier ones. Plants in hanging baskets dry out faster than potted versions on the ground. Porous containers lose moisture more quickly than nonporous ones, and small pots, regardless of material, require more frequent watering than large ones.

Weather plays a part, too. Plants nearly always need extra watering in hot, dry, or windy conditions. In very hot weather, you may need to water two or three times a day.

HOW TO WATER

When you water, fully saturate the soil; don't just moisten the top few inches. You've done the job right when water runs freely from the drainage hole. When watering a container without a drain, add water equal to about one-quarter the volume of soil.

When a saucer under a container is full, empty it right away if you can. If that's not possible, at least drain it within 24 hours; water that's allowed to stand much longer will keep the soil soggy. (Use a bulb-type baster to remove water from saucers under big containers.)

BELOW: *Watering plants with an old-fashioned can is a relaxing pastime with a practical advantage: when you look at each plant close-up every day, you can spot small problems before they become big ones.*

LEFT: *A watering wand on the end of a hose lets you reach hanging baskets easily.* RIGHT: *Submersing pots in a tub of water for a 30-minute soak can be a lifesaver in hot weather.*

WAYS AND MEANS

There are numerous ways to deliver needed moisture to your plants. The best method for you depends on the size and location of your container garden and on your own routine. No matter what watering equipment you choose, always apply the water in a gentle stream, drip, or spray; a strong flow can displace soil and damage plant roots.

WATERING CAN Watering each pot as needed may be your choice if you have a small garden or if you simply enjoy puttering. If so, use a can that has a "rose"—a sprinkler head that fits onto the spout.

GARDEN HOSE Attach a flow head that will deliver a gentle trickle to the soil surface or, bet-ter yet, use a watering wand with a rose like the ones made for watering cans. One caution: water from a hose that's been baking in the sun can be hot enough to damage plants; before watering, let the hose run until the water is fairly cool.

SUBMERSION For hanging baskets and small pots, watering by submersion is a real time-saver. A good soak in the morning can keep soil moist all day or revive plants when their potting soil has become dangerously dry. Simply lower the pot into a tub of water (covering the pot rim but not the plant itself) and keep it there for about half an hour. A periodic dunk is also good for terra-cotta pots, which tend to dry out even in mild weather.

Drainage Solutions

Getting water into and out of a container to ensure well-drained soil is always a concern. Below are two easy fixes.

WHEN WATER DOESN'T DRAIN ... chances are the drainage hole is blocked. Turn the pot on its side (or as far over as you can get it) and push a pointed stick or large nail into the opening to clear the blockage in the hole.

WHEN WATER DRAINS TOO FAST ... the potting mix has probably dried out so much that it has shrunk away from the container walls. If the pot is small enough, submerge it in a tub of water for about half an hour. Otherwise, set a hose on the soil surface near the base of the plant and adjust the flow to a trickle. Let the water run until the soil in the container is fully saturated.

SELF-WATERING POTS

Catalogs and garden centers sell containers with built-in reservoirs that deliver consistent moisture to the soil. You still need to fill the reservoir, of course, but depending on the weather and the size of the container, you can go for many weeks between refills. If you don't care for the look of plastic, you can put these pots inside other, more elegant containers, as long as you leave room to reach the holes to fill them.

DRIP IRRIGATION

A drip system delivers water to individual containers through a network of thin tubes and emitters. You customize the layout according to your needs, and the water goes directly into each plant's root zone with little moisture loss to evaporation or runoff, and no harmful fluctuations in soil moisture. A simple automated system can make watering effortless, reduce your water bill, and help your plants grow lush and full.

INSTALLING A BASIC DRIP SYSTEM

If you already have an automatic watering system for your lawn, it's usually a simple matter to add another valve for your container system. Failing that, you need only connect the system to an existing hose bibb, using a Y attachment so that you can still connect a standard garden hose. You can add an automatic timer or operate the system manually. If you choose the former approach, look for a controller that lets you run the system several times a day; that's a big plus in hot, dry, or windy weather.

The main line. Use either ⅜- or ½-inch-diameter black polyethylene tubing to take water from the valve to your container garden, and conceal it any way you can. Don't take it too far, though, or you'll risk uneven water distribution. A ⅜-inch line should extend less than 100 feet; a ½-inch line can safely go to just under 200 feet.

Into the pots. Run ¼-inch vinyl minitubing from the main line into each container. For containers that you seldom move, you can run the tubing up through the drainage hole; otherwise, take it up the side and over the lip. For hanging baskets, run the microtubing up the wall or a post and across to the basket's hanger wire. To prevent backflow on hanging baskets, put an atmospheric breaker on the line 6 inches above the highest emitter, or simply keep all emitters 2 inches away from the foliage or soil.

Running the system. You'll need to experiment to find the optimum running time for your garden. Start by turning it on for 5 minutes, and then check the results. A container is properly watered when the soil is wet and some water is coming from the drainage holes. If water streams out, it means you've run the system too long. If no water emerges and the soil is not thoroughly wet, you need to let the water flow longer or replace your emitters with larger ones.

This hanging-basket emitter is actually a 2- to 4-gallon-per-hour mister that sprays both soil and foliage. Bonsai wire holds the tubing in place and keeps the mister head aimed in the right direction.

A basic drip system consists of a backflow prevention device—in this case, an automatic antisiphon valve (A)—a filter (B), a pressure regulator (C), and a compression fitting (D). The automatic controller (E) operates the system, and a T fitting above the shutoff valve (F) accommodates a hose bibb.

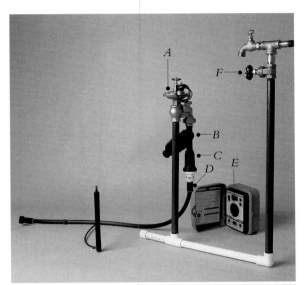

Whether water is in short supply where you live or you simply want to spend less time watering, you can take some simple steps to reduce your plants' thirst:

- Mulch the soil surface with pebbles, bark, or compost.
- Put one container inside of another; fill the space between with damp peat moss or coir fiber, and cover the whole surface with small pebbles.
- Group pots closely together so that they shelter and provide shade for one another.
- In a hot climate or when a heat wave strikes, provide a source of shade during the hottest part of the day.
- Use the largest possible containers that are appropriate for your plants; the more soil a pot contains, the more slowly it will dry out.
- Select unthirsty plants. In particular, look for plants that are native to dry climates.
- When you plant or replant, use soil polymers in your potting mix. They hold on to both water and dissolved nutrients, keeping them readily available to plant roots. You can buy commercial potting mixes with gel already added or mix it in yourself. (If you mix it, use the manufacturer's recommended proportions; see page 427 for more information.)

A pot up to 10 inches wide needs only a single emitter. Here, an elbow fitting takes the tubing over the pot edge at a 90-degree angle; a U stake holds tubing and emitter in place.

Two emitters will suffice for pots that measure 10 to 15 inches across. Above, a notched stake holds the tubing in place, and the emitters are attached to a T fitting.

Large pots can be handled in a couple of ways. Here, tubing with factory-installed emitters encircles a plant. U stakes hold the emitter line in place.

Another good option for big pots is a multi-outlet emitter, sometimes called a "bubbler." The head can be adjusted to change the spray.

Feeding

Plants in the ground can send their roots deep into the soil in search of nutrients. But potted plants depend on you to supply nourishment. If you're a novice gardener, that chore can seem daunting when you first glimpse a garden center's bewildering array of fertilizers. Fortunately, keeping your plants well fed is much simpler than it may appear.

TYPES OF FERTILIZER

Fertilizers come in two basic types: inorganic/chemical and organic/natural. Both types are available in all-purpose plant foods as well as specialty formulas for plants such as roses, citrus trees, and acid-loving shrubs.

INORGANIC/CHEMICAL FERTILIZERS

These fertilizers are made from synthetic substances that contain highly concentrated amounts of specific nutrients—primarily nitrogen, phosphorus, and potassium. When you apply an inorganic fertilizer, you see almost instant results because the nutrients are immediately available to your plants. This quick fix is perfect for times when you want to make a big impact in a hurry, such as for temporary displays of flowering annuals, or for giving perennials a fast start.

ORGANIC/NATURAL FERTILIZERS

These fertilizers don't feed your plants directly. Rather, they add essential nutrients, major and minor, to the soil, where they become available to the plants' roots. Organic fertilizers are made from the remains or by-products of living or once-living organisms. Manure, fish emulsion, bonemeal, and kelp meal are all examples of organic fertilizers that can be used alone or in various combinations.

In addition to providing essential nutrients, organic fertilizers improve the structure of the soil, thereby allowing water and oxygen to move freely.

Organic fertilizers tend to work more slowly than inorganics, but they're longer lasting. This soil-building staying power makes them ideal for use with trees, shrubs, and long-lived perennials—or for large planters in which you keep the same soil from year to year.

Edible plants, too, benefit from organic fertilizers. Many gardeners swear that vegetables grown with organic fertilizers taste better than their chemically grown counterparts. And university studies have shown that the organically grown versions do contain more nutrients.

DIETARY TROUBLESHOOTING

Often, the first signs of a nutrient deficiency—major or minor—appear in a plant's leaves. Here are some symptoms to watch for. In each case, your local nursery can recommend a foliar spray (see "Liquid Fertilizers" on page 523) to solve the immediate problem and a fertilizer supplement for long-term care.

LEAF SYMPTOMS	DEFICIENCY
Yellow and smaller than normal; on some plants they may turn red or purple. Overall growth is stunted or dwarfed.	Nitrogen
Small, with edges scorched, purplish, or blue-green in color. May fall early. Overall growth is reduced and weakened; flower and fruit production diminished.	Phosphorus
Tips and edges are yellow and scorched-looking, with brownish-purple spotting underneath.	Potassium
Turn dark from the base outward and die.	Calcium
Yellow between the veins; veins remain green or slightly yellow.	Iron
Leaf centers are reddish or yellow; dead spots appear between the veins.	Magnesium
Upper leaves are yellow in the center, between the veins, with no sign of red.	Manganese
Veins are lighter in color than the tissue in between.	Sulfur

Both chemical and organic fertilizers come in liquid and dry forms to meet a variety of plants' nutritional needs.

FORMS OF FERTILIZER

You'll find both organic and inorganic fertilizers in two basic forms: dry and liquid. Whichever kind you choose, follow the package directions and don't be tempted to toss in a little extra "for good measure." Too much fertilizer all at once—especially the potent chemical kinds—can do harm to your plants.

DRY FERTILIZERS Dry varieties come in both traditional powders and granules and the newer timed/controlled-release capsules. The latter are a real boon to container gardeners. You mix the fertilizer into the potting mix at planting time, and a small amount of nutrients diffuses into the soil with each watering. When necessary throughout the growing season, you can scratch more capsules into the surface. They remain active for varying lengths of time, usually from about 3 to 8 months.

LIQUID FERTILIZERS Choose from crystals, granules, or liquid concentrates that you mix with water, and apply with a hose, watering can, or spray bottle.

The spray types, known as "foliar feeds," are generally used to deliver instant supplies of specific nutrients, either on a routine basis or to correct deficiencies.

PLANT NUTRITION

All plants require the same basic "big three" nutrients—nitrogen, phosphorous, and potassium—as well as various secondary minerals and trace elements. But how often they need them, and in what proportions, can vary. Most plants need regular feedings from spring through summer or early autumn, when they're actively growing, and none from mid- to late autumn through winter, when they are dormant. Containers filled with multiple plants may need extra fertilizer.

DOING THE NUMBERS The three-number formulas on fertilizer labels represent the percentage by weight of nitrogen (N), phosphorus (P), and potassium (K). For instance, 5–10–5 fertilizer contains 5 percent nitrogen, 10 percent phosphorous, and 5 percent potassium. Each element is essential for a different aspect of growth. Nitrogen supplies the power for leaf and stem growth. That's why too much of it can make plants overly lush and leafy. Phosphorus promotes strong, vigorous roots and the formation of flowers, fruits, and seeds. Potassium supports all phases of growth and helps plants control aphids.

Trees, Shrubs, and Perennials

Annuals are quick-change artists, allowing you to play with color, form, and texture as your mood decrees (as you have seen in earlier chapters). But for structure and a sense of permanence in a garden—even one with all its roots in containers—look to trees, shrubs, and hardy perennials. With proper care these long-lived plants can thrive in pots for years.

TREES

The best trees for containers are small, slow-growing, and tidy in habit, with compact root systems. Steer clear of varieties that drop large quantities of leaves, seed heads, or messy fruits throughout the growing season. On the other hand, do look for trees with year-round charms such as fragrant spring blooms, colorful autumn foliage, bird-enticing berries, and distinctive branching patterns that hold their appeal even after leaves have dropped. And, of course, choose a variety that's suited to your climate and the growing conditions in your garden.

Like any other plants, trees vary in their shade tolerance and their ability to withstand such common hazards as high winds, air pollution, and salt spray. Some of the best candidates are too tender to remain outdoors year-round except in mild climates. And if you live where winters get very cold, you will have to move any contained tree to protected territory (see page 538).

Use a container with plenty of room for root growth and for staking a young tree, if that's a temporary necessity. In general, 18 to 20 inches across and 16 to 24 inches deep is the minimum size you'll need to start. (Keep in mind that you always want to have about 1 to 2 inches of open soil on all sides of the root ball.) As the tree grows, you can either trim its roots and refresh the soil, or move up to a larger pot.

In most parts of the country, spring is the best time for tree planting (in containers or otherwise). Where winters are mild, you can do the job any time from early autumn to midwinter. Apply a balanced fertilizer once in spring and again in summer. Withhold fertilizer as autumn approaches; it will spur tender new growth that is vulnerable to killing frosts.

A trio of dwarf Alberta spruce trees coexists happily in a planter with English ivy (Hedera helix).

Good Container Trees

CONIFERS

Dwarf Alberta spruce (*Picea glauca albertiana* 'Conica')
Japanese red pine (*Pinus densiflora* 'Umbraculifera')
Nordmann fir (*Abies nordmanniana*)
Norfolk Island pine (*Araucaria heterophylla*)
Scotch pine (*Pinus sylvestris* 'French Blue')
Weeping Atlantic cedar (*Cedrus atlantica* 'Glauca Pendula')

BROAD-LEAFED EVERGREENS

American holly (*Ilex opaca*)
English holly (*Ilex aquifolium*)
Evergreen pear (*Pyrus kawakamii*)
Strawberry tree (*Arbutus unedo*)
Sweet bay (*Laurus nobilis*)
Sweet olive (*Osmanthus fragrans*)

DECIDUOUS TREES

Eastern redbud (*Cercis canadensis*)
Flowering cherry, flowering plum (*Prunus*)
Japanese maple (*Acer palmatum*)
Japanese snowdrop tree (*Styrax japonicus*)
Star magnolia (*Magnolia stellata*)
Vine maple (*Acer circinatum*)

CLOCKWISE FROM TOP LEFT: *Japanese maple, strawberry tree, star magnolia, vine maple, English holly*

POTTED FRUIT TREES

Many fruit trees, as well as fruit-bearing shrubs and vines, can prosper in containers. For the most part, these plants require the same basic care as their strictly ornamental counterparts. As always, though, learn as much as you can about the specific needs of your choices before you offer them a home in a pot.

Nearly all standard fruit trees come in dwarf forms that produce full-size crops, including apple, apricot, cherry, nectarine, peach, pear, and plum. Bear in mind, though, that in many cases you will need two different varieties to ensure pollination. The nursery staff or catalog can advise you on which varieties make the best combinations.

Dwarf citrus trees, including orange, lemon, lime, kumquat, and calamondin (a kumquat–mandarin orange hybrid), are excellent candidates for container growing. In northern gardens they thrive outdoors all summer and then sail right through the winter in a sunny window.

Trees are not your only fruit options, though. If you choose your varieties carefully, you can grow blueberries, raspberries, guavas, and even grapes in pots. And potted kiwi vines—both tender (*Actinidia deliciosa*) and hardy (*A. kolomikta* and *A. arguta*)—actually bloom and bear fruit faster than most of their in-ground counterparts.

SHRUBS

As with trees, the best shrubs for containers are compact, slow-growing varieties. Many popular shrubs come in dwarf versions, which often have the word "nana" in their botanical names. Plant in spring in cold-weather regions, early autumn to midwinter in warmer climates. Some shrubs need a lightweight potting mix; others perform better in heavier soil. And acid lovers, such as camellias and rhododendrons, need a special potting mix.

In general, potted shrubs perform best with a monthly application of balanced fertilizer from spring through summer. If you plant in spring or summer, wait 2 weeks before the first feeding, and don't fertilize autumn- or winter-planted shrubs until spring.

When your shrubs outgrow their pots, you have the same choices you have with trees: either move them to bigger containers or trim the roots (see page 533 for root-pruning pointers).

Favorite Container Shrubs

CONIFERS

English yew (*Taxus baccata*)
Juniperus **(Especially good choices include**
    J. conferta **'Emerald Sea',** *J. horizontalis*
    'Bar Harbor', and *J. procumbens* **'Nana')**
Mugho pine (*Pinus mugo mugo*)
Umbrella pine (*Sciadopitys verticillata*)
**Weeping Norway spruce (*Picea abies*
    'Pendula')**

BROAD-LEAFED EVERGREENS

Angel's trumpet (*Brugmansia*)
Boxwood (*Buxus*)
Camellia
Flowering maple (*Abutilon* hybrids)
Japanese aucuba (*Aucuba japonica*)
Oleander (*Nerium oleander*)
Oregon grape (*Mahonia aquifolium*)
Rhododendron

DECIDUOUS SHRUBS

Bigleaf hydrangea (*Hydrangea macrophylla*)
**Butterfly bush, summer lilac (*Buddleja
    davidii*)**
Daphne
Fuchsia
Japanese barberry (*Berberis thunbergii*)
Rose (*Rosa*)
Slender deutzia (*Deutzia gracilis*)
Tree peony (*Paeonia*)

CLOCKWISE FROM TOP LEFT: *Angel's trumpet, rhododendron, English yew, Japanese barberry, fuchsia, bigleaf hydrangea, Oregon grape, tree peony*

STANDARD TIME

If you want the look of a tree without the size, opt for a "standard"—a shrub or vine trained to grow on a single, upright trunk. You can buy pretrained standards or grow your own.

STAKING Choose a plant with a strong, straight main stem. Set it in a pot, along with a stake that's almost as high as the plant. Tie the stem to the stake in several places, using soft fabric strips. (No wire!)

TRIMMING Remove all side shoots up to the point where you want the foliage to start, about 3 feet above the base for most shrubs and vines. Turn the plant regularly to keep it from growing toward the sun.

PINCHING When the plant reaches the desired height, pinch off the growing tip to stop upward growth and encourage side branching. You may want to trim the crown into a rounded ball, the style that gives standards

the nickname "lollipop trees." If your standard is a vine or a climbing rose, let its stems cascade down naturally. To keep the plant from reverting to its shrubby form, remove any suckers that emerge along the trunk.

TRAINING A STANDARD

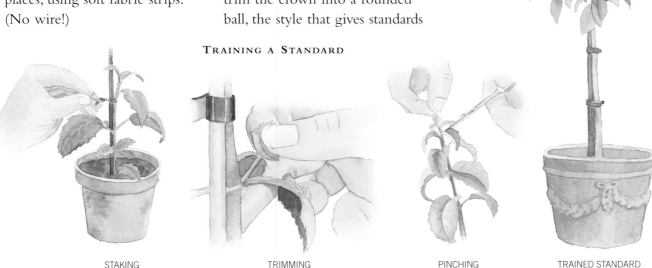

| STAKING | TRIMMING | PINCHING | TRAINED STANDARD |

Some Favorite Standards

Bottlebrush *(Callistemon)*
Bougainvillea
Camellia
Common heliotrope *(Heliotropium arborescens)*
Flowering maple *(Abutilon* **hybrids)**
Fuchsia
Hibiscus
Holly *(Ilex)*
Lantana
Rose *(Rosa)*
Rosemary *(Rosmarinus officinalis)*
Wisteria

CLOCKWISE FROM TOP LEFT: *Rosemary, hibiscus, camellia*

SPRING TUNE-UP

In the spring, perennials that are less than two years old, or that have been divided the previous year, benefit from a light perk-me-up. Using a screwdriver or dibble, poke three 1-inch holes about 6 to 8 inches deep in the soil (keep holes about 2 inches from the plant crowns to avoid damaging roots). Drop about a teaspoon of slow-release fertilizer into each hole and cover with soil. Then lightly scratch the soil surface (an ordinary table fork works well for this procedure) and add about 1 inch of compost.

Unlike most perennials, herbaceous peonies, such as 'Mrs. Franklin D. Roosevelt', should not be divided. When a plant outgrows its pot, ease it out gently and move it to bigger quarters.

PERENNIALS

Perennials can be stunning as the basis of a more or less permanent container garden, but unless you have the space to conceal "off-duty" plants, choose your stock carefully. Unlike annuals, which generally put out nonstop color from spring to fall, most perennials bloom in a single flush, with perhaps a second, smaller wave later on. For the biggest impact, look for varieties that have a longer-than-normal blooming period or foliage that's eye-catching even without flowers attached.

Don't cramp your perennials; most will quickly outgrow a small container long before the end of the season. If one or two newly planted specimens look lonely in a pot, surround them with lower-growing annuals to add some temporary color. Generally, an 18-inch-wide container will hold two 1-gallon plants, and a 20- to 24-inch container will hold four to five 1-gallon plants.

Perennials differ in their moisture requirements, but most need regular watering during spring and summer growth periods, and less frequent applications during the fall and the winter dormant season. Food needs, too, can vary, but as a general rule, apply a balanced fertilizer monthly during the growing season.

Perennial Pleasers

Astilbe *(Astilbe × arendsii)*
Basket-of-gold *(Aurinia saxatilis)*
Bellflower *(Campanula)*
Carnation *(Dianthus caryophyllus)*
Daylily *(Hemerocallis)*

Dead nettle, spotted nettle *(Lamium maculatum)*
Evergreen candytuft *(Iberis sempervirens)*
Fringed bleeding heart *(Dicentra eximia)*
Hosta
Pink *(Dianthus 'Allwoodii')*
Yarrow *(Achillea)*

CLOCKWISE FROM TOP LEFT: *Evergreen candytuft, daylily, yarrow, hosta, carnation*

Pruning

The reasons for pruning container plants are the same as for pruning those in the ground: to maintain the health of the plants, to increase the production of flowers or fruit, to direct growth where you want it to go, or simply to keep growth within the desired bounds.

PRUNING FOR HEALTH

The golden rule of garden health is to remove diseased, damaged, or odd-looking growth the minute you spot it, regardless of the time of year. That applies to all plants, from venerable trees to new seedlings, in the ground or in containers. Cut all the way back into healthy tissue, and unless you know the plant part is healthy (for instance, if you're pruning off a storm-damaged branch), destroy it or send it off with the trash; don't put it in the compost bin. In the case of shrubs and trees, prune out crossing or crowded branches to provide good air circulation as well as pleasing form.

PRUNING FOR PRODUCTION

A few simple procedures will ensure that your container garden puts on the longest, most prolific show possible.

ANNUALS There's a one-word secret to making annuals put on a spectacular show all summer long: deadhead. Pluck or clip off all flowers as soon as they've passed their peak—and definitely before seed heads appear. The more you pluck, the more blooms the plant will produce. The reason is simple. In biological terms, the purpose of any organism is to reproduce itself. In the case of an annual, that means when its flowers have set seed for the next generation, the plant's work is finished.

PERENNIALS Some plants produce a primary show of flowers, followed by a second, less profuse display later on. For these, cut or shear back the plants by one-half or more after the initial bloom period to encourage the best "second wave." For perennials that bloom only once, clip off spent flowers as they appear, and then at the end of the growing season cut the plant back. This will encourage compact growth and abundant bloom the following year.

To keep annuals like these petunias blooming abundantly all summer long, clip or pinch off all flowers before they set seed.

FRUIT Trees, shrubs, and vines that produce fruit vary greatly in their pruning requirements. Ask for specific guidelines at the nursery where you purchase your plants, or consult a pruning manual or fruit-growing book.

PRUNING FOR SHAPE AND SIZE

Clipping early and often encourages plants to grow in the desired direction, stay small enough to thrive in a pot, and continue to look their best year after year.

INITIAL PRUNING After planting, prune young shrubs and perennial vines to a few strong shoots, leaving two or three buds on each one. This will increase fullness and strength, and encourage the plant to grow in the desired direction. As stems get long enough, which may not be until the following season, you can tie them to their supports and begin any formal shaping (see guidelines for creating an espalier on page 481).

CONTAINMENT PRUNING Tree growth is best controlled by root pruning (see "Major Tune-Up" on page 532), but you can easily clip shrubs to keep them to a manageable size (provided you've chosen wisely to begin with). Because shrubs tend to grow vertically, with most growth occurring close to the stem tip, all you need to do is cut the

The Right Cut

Whether you're clipping spent blooms from annuals or pruning a tree limb, you always want a clean, precise cut. A ragged cut or torn stem provides easy entry for diseases and insect pests. Use sharp, good-quality pruning shears (or scissors for flower stems and thin shoots). When you're working with diseased plants, dip your shears in a 10 percent bleach and water solution after each cut to avoid spreading the problem to healthy tissue.

The angle of your cut is determined by the bud pattern of the plant.

When a plant's buds occur alternately along the shoot, cut on the diagonal just above an outward-facing bud.

For a plant with buds opposite each other, make a straight cut directly above both buds.

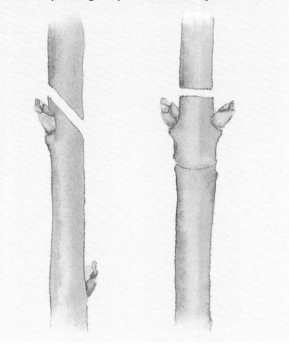

growing tips back to the appropriate length. Just be sure to leave a couple of pairs of buds on each shoot, and make your cut just above an outward-facing bud (see "The Right Cut" above).

REMEDIAL PRUNING In addition to cutting out diseased, damaged, or dead wood, it's important to remove crossing, crowded, or misshapen shoots from shrubs and trees both. Not only does this process improve your plants' appearance, but it also opens up the branch structure to permit

good air circulation—and that's essential for good health.

From time to time you may notice shoots with leaves that look different in color or shape from those on the rest of the plant. For instance, the new leaves may be solid green, when the others are variegated. Clip them off immediately. It may be that your cultivar is reverting to the color of the species it was bred from. Or perhaps the plant's stem has been grafted to the roots of an entirely different plant (normal practice with roses and fruit trees in particular).

The Show Must Go On

In a container garden, especially a small one, you want your plants to look their best throughout the growing season. Many perennials perform that task naturally; all you need to do is keep them fed and watered, and spent blooms clipped, just as you would with annuals (see "Pruning for Production" on page 530). Daylilies *(Hemerocallis)*, yarrow *(Achillea)*, false sunflowers *(Heliopsis)*, balloon flower *(Platycodon)*, hostas, and astilbes (along with numerous others) fall into this category. Some perennials, though, require a little more help to keep their youthful good looks. For these perennials, two simple techniques—shaping and shearing—can work wonders.

Perennials that bloom in a single flush, such as blue false indigo *(Baptisia australis)*, *Euphorbia polychroma*, and catmint *(Nepeta × faassenii)*, benefit from shaping. After the flowers fade, cut the foliage back by about a third to form a pleasing shape that blends well with other plants in your garden. Hedge clippers work best for this job.

Some perennials, including cranesbill *(Geranium)*, lungwort *(Pulmonaria)*, and lady's-mantle *(Alchemilla)*, can get lanky and leggy as the summer progresses. When this happens, shear the plants all the way back to the ground. Scratch a little fertilizer into the potting soil, mulch with compost, and keep the plants well watered. Within a couple of weeks, you'll have an attractive mound of new, compact foliage. And sometimes you'll be rewarded with a second flush of blossoms.

Shaping

Shearing

MOVING ON UP

If a container plant looks crowded even after being trimmed, or if a plant simply looks too big for its container, move it to a larger pot. A plant that just seems to be growing poorly, with no signs of pests or disease, is also a candidate for larger quarters (most likely it's become pot-bound). In most cases, one pot size larger is best, but fast-growing plants can go up two sizes. If the container you choose has been used before, scrub it according to the instructions on page 533 before moving in the new plant.

MAJOR TUNE-UP

After a plant has been in a container for about three years, or starts to look less than stellar, it's time to refresh it by trimming or (in the case of perennials only!) dividing the roots.

EXAMINE THE ROOT BALL If the roots of a tree or shrub are twisted and wound around the soil clump, they need to be trimmed. First, pull out and untangle large roots (soil will fall away from the root ball as you do this), then use shears or a pruning saw to cut the big roots back by a third to a half. Divide crowded perennials by slicing through the crown or, in the case of tuberous-rooted plants like daylilies or irises, through the fleshy roots.

REPOT First, clean the pot using a stiff brush and a solution of 4 parts water to 1 part household bleach; rinse the pot with clear water, and replace the drainage-hole cover with a fresh one. If you found any sign of disease or pest damage on the roots, add all-new soil. Otherwise, it's fine to combine part of the old soil with fresh mix and a healthy helping of compost. Set the plant back in the pot. Add soil to cover the roots, scratch in some slow-release fertilizer, and you should be in good shape for another three years.

BIG-TIME ROOT PRUNING

If you're faced with a tree that's too large to wrestle out of its pot, try this method in early spring. Using a narrow, very sharp shovel or spade, dig as far as you can reach into the pot along one side. Cut off clumps of old roots and remove each section from the pot. Continue until you've pruned off at least half a dozen good-size root sections from mature or pot-bound trees. Take fewer from less crowded or immature plants.

Fill the empty spaces with fresh potting mix and compost. Repeat the procedure on the opposite side of the container; leave the other two sides intact until the following spring.

Perennials need to be divided about every three years, or when they start thinning in the center or looking crowded in their pots. The procedure is simple (if somewhat messy): Start by easing the plant out of its container (1). Using a knife or sharp spade, slice through the crown (2). Pull the sections apart, keeping vigorous outer growth and discarding portions that are weak, woody, shriveled, or diseased (3). Rub some old soil off the root ball to make room for fresh potting mix, and replant the divisions in fresh containers (4).

Pests and Diseases

Diseases and pests can pay visits to any garden, even one with all its roots in containers. Fortunately, though, there is much you can do to protect your plants—without launching a spraying campaign, which would be likely to cause more harm than any pest or disease ever could.

PREVENTION

As with most problems in life, garden pests and diseases are far easier to avoid than to deal with after they've struck. Nothing can guarantee a trouble-free garden, but these tactics go a long way toward safeguarding your plants.

KEEP IT CLEAN Always use clean containers and sterile potting mix. Pull weeds, and pick up fallen fruit and dead flowers and leaves as soon as you spot them. Disease organisms and many insect pests breed or overwinter in weeds and plant litter.

KNOW YOUR PLANTS Learn what each plant needs in the way of food, water, light, winter protection, and other environmental factors. By providing optimum growing conditions, you'll keep plants healthy and better able to fend off pests and diseases.

KNOW WHEN TO SAY NO You may fall in love with a plant that would require extra care to thrive in your locale. Unless you're sure you can—and will—provide the conditions it needs, leave it at the nursery. At best, it will suffer undue stress, and stressed plants (like stressed people) tend to attract more than their share of physical problems.

PROVIDE HEALTHY SURROUNDINGS Raise your containers off the ground to provide good drainage and make them less attractive to crawling pests. Maintain enough distance between plants to allow good air circulation and adequate light. Erect or plant barriers to protect plants from harsh, drying winds. Provide adequate shelter from cold winter weather (see page 538).

KNOW YOUR ENEMY Learn how to recognize both disease symptoms and "bad bugs"; don't panic when you see either one. Many diseases are easy to remedy if caught in the early stages, and most pests cause little harm in small numbers.

In a garden that's free of pesticides, beneficial insects and other predators can usually keep bad bug populations well under control. Shown here, clockwise from top left, are four of the hardest-charging good guys: lacewing, ladybug, tachinid fly, soldier beetle.

ENCOURAGE ALLIES Beneficial insects and other garden residents, such as birds, toads, bats, and lizards, consume many times their weight in destructive, disease-carrying pests. The most effective way to draw helpful predators to your garden is simply to not use pesticides, which kill the "good guys" along with the bad ones.

CONTROL

Usually, the most effective way to deal with larger insect pests, such as slugs, snails, caterpillars, beetles, and weevils, is to hand-pick them and drown them in a bucket of water laced with soap or alcohol. If you find that chore less than appealing, put a price on the pests' heads and hire a "posse" of young bounty hunters; most children love nothing better than insect search-and-destroy missions. To get rid of aphids, thrips, white-flies, and other small insects, simply blast them from your plants with a strong spray from a garden hose.

In the event of severe infestations, homemade sprays generally provide all the fire power you need. For instance, a spray made by mixing 2 tablespoons of dishwashing liquid in 1 gallon of warm water will kill soft-bodied insects on contact. To penetrate the hard, waxy shells of beetles and weevils, add 2 teaspoons of citrus oil or peppermint extract to the mix. Add a tablespoon or two of baking soda to the soap solution, and the spray will kill fungi as well as insects. Sprays made from garlic, hot pepper, and coffee are also potent pest killers. If homemade remedies are not your style, you can buy similar products at most nurseries and through many catalogs.

Two warnings, though: First, these sprays will kill beneficial insects along with the "bad" ones, so when you use them, make sure you've got the right target, and aim carefully. Second, even though a pesticide may be lethal only to insects, ingesting it could harm humans or other animals. Make sure you keep all pest-control products away from children and pets—preferably under lock and key.

Three for the Road

Plant diseases are caused by three types of organisms: fungi, bacteria, and viruses. Unfortunately, if the disease has progressed very far, your only option may be to destroy the plant and replace it with a new one. In the early stages, though, there is often hope. (See page 536 for some options, and for more detail on diseases and treatments, consult your Cooperative Extension Office.)

FUNGAL DISEASES are the most common by far and usually take the form of molds and mildews. Any part of a plant may be affected, and common symptoms include wilt, rot, and leaf spots. Fungal spores multiply rampantly on warm, wet leaves or stems. They overwinter in soil or in plant debris and come to life when spring rains begin. The one good thing about fungi is that they tend to spread slowly, so if you respond quickly, you stand a very good chance of saving your plants.

BACTERIA are nearly all harmless, and many are beneficial—even necessary to life. But the few disease-causing types move fast and cause serious problems, usually in the form of wilt or rot. Because most of the bacteria that attack plants can't survive in frozen soil, they cause the most damage in mild-winter climates. Unfortunately, a few destructive bacteria overwinter in the bodies of insects, which transmit the diseases to plants the following spring.

VIRUSES seldom cause serious damage, but the few real killers cause plants to suddenly wilt and die. If your plants' leaves become twisted, crinkled, or mottled, the likely cause is a virus. The tiny organisms overwinter in wild plants, and they're transmitted by insects such as aphids, whiteflies, thrips, and leafhoppers.

MINIMIZING PESTS AND DISEASES

Even with the best preventive maintenance, pests and diseases can strike your garden. The key to minimizing damage: identify the cause and act fast. But don't overreact—you could cause more problems than you had to begin with. These pages illustrate the problems that most often plague container plants, along with your best coping mechanisms.

DOWNY MILDEW

Downy mildew rarely kills, but it can turn plants unsightly, stunted, and unproductive. Symptoms vary but often include a powdery whitish, gray, or light brown mold on the undersides of leaves. Remove and destroy infected plant parts, or entire plants if the condition has progressed far. Prevent future outbreaks by practicing good garden hygiene: clean up debris, provide good air circulation for plants, and water early in the day so that foliage dries before nightfall.

SPIDER MITES

These tiny spider relatives suck juices from leaves, stems, and flower buds. Early symptoms include stippled, spotted, bleached, or deformed tissue. One sure clue that mites are present: soft, white webbing on buds or between stems and leaf petioles. A good hosing down usually gets rid of mites. Do the job regularly in hot, dry weather, and make sure you get the undersides of leaves. Or spray with a solution of 1 teaspoon of nondetergent dishwashing liquid and 3 teaspoons of ammonia per 2½ gallons of water.

MOSAIC VIRUS

Symptoms include splotched, mottled, or puckered leaves and stunted growth. Remove and destroy affected tissue or the whole plant. Sterilize tools and wash your hands before touching healthy plants; plant resistant cultivars; control sap-sucking insects, especially aphids, which spread viruses.

BEETLES, WEEVILS, AND BUGS

A multitude of these hard-bodied insects chew holes in leaves, stems, buds, petals, or fruits, sometimes transmitting diseases in the process. Handpick and drop the pests into a bucket of hot, soapy water. Alternatively, buy commercial traps or spray with soap and peppermint (see page 535). If you know the culprits are Japanese beetles, destroy the next generation (white grubs) by treating your lawn with milky spore disease, an otherwise harmless bacteria that kills several types of beetle grubs.

RUST

Usually appears first as small orange or dark brown spots on undersides of leaves. The spots enlarge and spread rapidly, especially in damp or humid weather. Remove affected leaves, clean up debris, and spray once a week with this fungicide: in 1 gallon of water, combine 3 teaspoons of baking soda and either 1 teaspoon of nondetergent dishwashing liquid or 1 teaspoon of canola oil (but not both).

SLUGS AND SNAILS

Slugs and snails chew large, ragged holes in stems, flowers, and foliage—and leave behind their telltale silvery trails of slime. They're especially fond of citrus trees, hostas, and lettuce, but there are few plants they won't devour. Handpick them, and fasten a 1-inch band of copper around each container, just below the rim. Or sprinkle diatomaceous earth, wood ashes, sharp sand, or eggshells on the soil surface.

THRIPS

These all-but-invisible insects (about 1/10 inch long) suck the juices from leaves, buds, flowers, and new growth tips. Affected leaf surfaces often look bronze or silvery with a pattern of dots where the chlorophyll has been siphoned off. Cut off and destroy infested plant parts (or toss the whole plant in the case of a badly damaged annual); release lacewings or entice wild ones; as a last resort, spray with insecticidal soap spray, either commercial or homemade (see page 535).

POWDERY MILDEW

Round white fungal spots appear on upper leaf surfaces, then expand until they merge into a gray or white powder on foliage and flowers (but not on woody parts). It is encouraged by poor air circulation, shade, and fog. Remove affected plant tissue; improve growing conditions; spray with a solution of 2 teaspoons each of baking soda and horticultural oil per gallon of water.

LEAF SPOTS

Many fungi and bacteria cause dark spots to develop on leaves. In most cases the damage is primarily cosmetic. Remove affected foliage immediately, keep containers and their surroundings free of plant debris, water early in the day, and avoid overhead watering.

MEALYBUGS

Sap-sucking insects leave white, fluffy wax and sticky honeydew; leaves spotted, distorted, or yellowed. Spray with a hose, and wash plants with soapy water (see "Scale").

APHIDS (GREENFLIES)

These 1/8-inch-long soft-bodied insects cluster primarily on new growth and suck out the sap, causing real damage only if they are present in great numbers. In most instances, a blast from a garden hose will solve the problem; in the case of severe infestation, use insecticidal soap or the soap and water spray on page 535. Ladybugs, the aphids' natural predator, provide long-term control.

SCALE

Scale appears as a bubbly, fuzzy, or crusty growth on leaves, stems, branches, and bark. Inside that crust, insects suck out plant juices, usually causing only cosmetic damage, with tissue looking sticky, rough, or spotted. Gently scrape off scale with a nail file; wash the plant with a solution of 2 teaspoons of nondetergent dishwashing liquid per gallon of water.

CATERPILLARS AND WORMS

The larvae of numerous flying insects skeletonize leaves or chew holes in flowers, foliage, and fruit. Handpick; cover vegetable plants in spring to deter egg-laying adults (but remove covers when blossoms appear); spray with Bt.

Winterizing Your Garden

Unless you live in one of the country's warmest regions, your container plants will need protection from winter's chill. Some years, even in areas where potted plants can generally breeze through winter without missing a beat, Mother Nature might throw you a curve ball.

CHILLY WEATHER

At the first hint of a chill in the air—or when the weather forecast predicts dipping temperatures—move your pots to a protected place. Set them under a tree, carry them onto a covered porch, or haul them into the garage. In other words, do whatever you need to do to protect them from the open sky. If the containers are too heavy to move, use one or (better yet) all of the following tactics:

COVER THE PLANT Pound stakes in the ground or around the edges of the pot, and cover them with burlap, heavy plastic, a sheet or blanket, or (for smaller plants) a trash bag or cardboard box. If you use a box, cut off the bottom and slip the box over the plant; open the top flaps during the day to let in sunlight, and then close them at night.

INSULATE THE POT Wrap burlap sacks, blankets, or plastic bubble wrap around a container and tie it on with twine.

MULCH THE SOIL If you expect only a mild frost, a thick layer of straw, wood chips, or pine needles should give the roots all the protection they need.

CIRCLE THE WAGONS Draw pots close together for mutual protection and insulation.

Horticultural fleece (below left) and plastic bubble wrap (below right) provide excellent insulation from cold temperatures.

Protecting Pots

Containers, as well as plants, take a beating from freezing and thawing cycles. If possible, move your pots to shelter. Terra-cotta is particularly susceptible to damage, but even plastic can become brittle and crack when exposed to freezing temperatures (below).

If you have clay pots that you simply can't move indoors, try this: After digging up the plants, sink a 2-inch-wide shaft of plastic foam (from a hardware or craft store) down the center of the pot through the soil. When moisture in the soil freezes and expands, the foam will be compressed, taking pressure off the container walls.

REAL WINTER

In parts of the country where winter brings steady hard freezes, an outdoor container garden is a spring-to-fall pleasure only. Even the hardiest plant can't survive with its roots above ground in constant freezing or frequent below-zero temperatures. In these areas, if you want to grow anything but annuals, you have two choices:

MOVING INDOORS Tropical plants, with their year-round growing season, can carry on business as usual in a sunny south- or west-facing window. Plants that go dormant in winter can stay in a well-lighted garage or basement that doesn't freeze, or in an unheated room of the house. Deciduous plants can tolerate abrupt moves to a warmer area, but give evergreens some time in

a transition zone, such as a protected porch, a spot below a deck, or a temporary shelter.

STAYING OUTDOORS Some hardy deciduous trees and shrubs, such as Japanese maples, hydrangeas, and roses, can be overwintered in their containers using a variant of the "Minnesota tip" method of protecting in-ground roses (presuming, of course, that you have soil to tip into). Once the plant has dropped all its leaves, dig a 10- to 12-inch-deep trench, and tip both container and plant over on their sides. Then cover both pot and plant with an 18- to 24-inch layer of leaves or straw, and top it off with a sheet of heavy plastic.

ABOVE: *Many herbs, as well as other plants, will winter cheerfully on a sunny windowsill. Shown here are parsley, sage, and golden marjoram.*

BELOW: *In places where winter is serious business, a gardener's best friend is a greenhouse. Catalogs and nurseries sell attractive versions that are small enough for many container-garden sites.*

GARDEN
DESIGNS

BY PHILIP EDINGER AND THE EDITORS OF SUNSET BOOKS

SUNSET BOOKS · MENLO PARK, CALIFORNIA

CONTENTS

Why do some gardens "work," while others simply look jumbled, boring, or undistinguished? The answer is "advance planning"—but that can be hard to believe, since so many appealing gardens have a natural look that seems to deny the existence of an underlying plan.

GARDENING BY
DESIGN

In this book, you'll discover that planning is indeed the secret of a successful garden, but that not all plans are obvious or rigid. You'll also come to realize that advance planning doesn't have to dictate hours at the drawing board with T square and triangle. Some of our designs are precisely laid out, but others are unabashedly free-form. Some deal with total outdoor space where that space is small, but most illustrate planting schemes that fit within a larger garden framework, addressing typical landscape problems and situations—and garden wish lists, too.

Regardless of size or style, all our plans aim to show you how to develop pleasing designs through effective plant combination. And all are adaptable, too. You can use them as blueprints or as points of departure: replicate them exactly for guaranteed enjoyable plantings and gardens, or just let them suggest lovely combinations you can adjust to your particular needs.

Foliage in a range of sizes, shapes, textures, and colors brings three-season interest to this lightly shaded garden. Design by Dan Heims.

A robust planting of favorite perennials forms a multicolored mosaic of flowers and leaves in a sunny entry garden.

WHAT DO YOU WANT?

No two homes present exactly the same garden-design challenges, and not all gardeners see the same solution to similar problems. Thus, no two gardens are alike, not even if one was originally intended to be an exact replica of the other.

With this firmly in mind, we have assembled 88 attractive and imaginative plans to address familiar garden situations, typical problems, and popular gardening themes (seasonal color, rose gardens, and many more). Many designs suit a wide range of climate zones; others focus on particular regions with special gardening advantages or limitations. To learn where your area fits into *Sunset*'s climate zone scheme, see pages 644–648.

The plans are divided into two groups. The first covers common garden situations, while the second involves plantings with a theme or a special purpose.

COMMON GARDEN SITUATIONS

On pages 550–595, you'll find plans designed to handle landscaping challenges common to virtually all homes. "First Impressions" (pages 550–565) tackles the transition area between sidewalk and front door, a space often overlooked as a potential beauty spot. "Filling in the Blanks" (pages 566–581) shows a variety of ways to approach planting along fences and house walls, in shady patches and hot spots, and in open expanses of lawn or bare ground. "Thinking Small" (pages 582–595) offers beautiful gardens just right for the ever-shrinking suburban yard (including those yards that are entirely deck or patio) and also covers two traditional limited-space problem spots—narrow side yards and parking strips.

SPECIALTY PLANTINGS

In this collection are designs for gardens with a theme or a purpose—herb plots, cut-flower gardens, lovely shrub borders, and numerous others. Many of these fit neatly into a larger framework: you can install an herb nook near the back door, for example, and still have plenty of garden left to devote to another design (or designs).

"Themes and Variations" (pages 598–615) presents plans highlighting seasonal flowers, schemes for cottage-style gardens and rose gardens, and plantings to enhance a backyard pool or pond. The gardens in "Designed for a Purpose" (pages 616–631) have a theme, too, but it's one with a functional element: these plans provide more than beauty. Some give flowers for cutting, others attract birds and butterflies; you'll also find plantings supplying scented flowers and foliage, five herb gardens, and a traditional kitchen garden. "Color Gardens" (pages 632–643) focuses strictly on color and color combinations. Look here for hot-color, cool-color, mixed-color, and all-white plantings; gardens of gray or silver foliage with white or pastel blossoms; and plantings in which foliage provides almost all the color.

COMBINING PLANTS EFFECTIVELY

Cottage gardens (see pages 604–606) seem to prove that planting without a plan can succeed brilliantly: they look casual, almost haphazard, their beauty derived from almost limitless variety. We now realize, however, that many of the original cottagers' apparently random plans were governed by an innate sense of design. In modern parlance, this design sense is known as *effective plant combination.*

Though they address myriad specific situations, the plans presented on pages 550–643 all rely on effective plant combination. All follow the same basic tenets, making each plant choice on the basis of color, texture, shape, and size. We review these basics below; you'll find them invaluable guidelines when you adapt or modify plans.

Contrast lends vitality to a planting. Here, foliage and blossoms offer equal interest.

(those opposite each other on the color wheel) such as blue and orange or yellow and violet.

Size matters. A soft yellow hollyhock can command more attention than a brilliant gold French marigold simply because there is more of it to draw the eye.

Petal texture or sheen also affects a color's projection: a shiny-petaled red flower, for example, will stand out more than one of the same shade with matte, nonreflective petals.

COLOR

For most of us, the word "garden" is virtually synonymous with "color" (vegetable gardens excepted, of course!). Visit any garden center or plant outlet, and you're tempted by ranks of colorful flowers ready for spur-of-the-moment purchase and immediate planting. But not all colors assort well or compete equally, and the planting assembled on impulse may end up the floral equivalent of an out-of-tune brass choir.

The subject of color is complex enough to warrant entire books of its own. Nonetheless, it's possible to make a few simple, general statements.

Light colors advance, dark ones retreat. Warm colors usually combine well with warm colors, cool ones with other cool colors and white. Pastel shades generally look good together but may lack "punch." Combined bright colors, on the other hand, can pack too much punch—they can be attractive in combination, but their tendency to vie with each other for attention can give a planting a rather strident look. In bright-plus-pastel plantings, the brights tend to dominate, even if they're in the minority.

In combining dissimilar colors, you can achieve good contrasts with primary colors (yellow, red, blue) and with complementary colors

TEXTURE

Whether you are working with flowers or focusing on foliage, texture is probably the most frequently overlooked design element. In simple terms, textural contrast arises from mixing various sizes (large to small) and different shapes (broad to narrow).

Sometimes you can achieve a stunning textural mix by using variations of just one plant. Hosta cultivars, for example, include plants with great paddlelike leaves as well as those with tiny spoonlike or dagger-shaped foliage, and there are countless leaf sizes and shapes in between. More often, though, textural interest derives from joining radically different plants: think, for example, of filmy common yarrow in combination with fountainlike eulalia grass and the broad, sandpapery leaves of purple coneflower.

Among flowers alone, the variations are seemingly limitless. Just consider the tiny blossoms of baby's breath, borne in airy sprays; lush, large, many-petaled roses; daisylike flowers, from simple asters to mammoth dahlias; the bell-shaped blossoms of the various campanulas; and the chalicelike blooms of daylilies. Manner of floral presentation offers yet another textural variation. Spikes of flowers—as in delphinium, hollyhock, and snapdragon—can provide vertical contrast to the flattened heads of yarrow or sedum blossoms or the starburst drumsticks of lily-of-the-nile and ornamental allium.

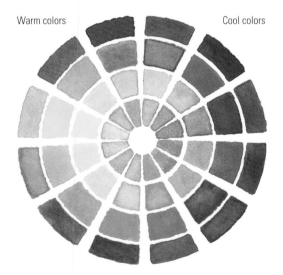

Warm colors   Cool colors

The primary colors (red, blue, yellow) are spaced equally around the color wheel; transitional colors connect them. Warm colors appear on the left side of the wheel, cool colors on the right.

READING THE PLANS

For each design in this book, a watercolor illustration depicts the planting in its peak season. Accompanying the illustration is a plot plan that shows the entire planted area. Within the plan, the area occupied by each kind of plant is shaded in the basic color of its foliage or flowers and labeled with a letter. These letters correspond to those in the accompanying plant list, where the plants used are listed by botanical name and common name (if there is one). The total number of each plant needed for the plan is indicated in parentheses (for certain ground-cover plants typically sold by the flat, we do not give a number, but simply indicate the appropriate plant spacing). To see where a plant fits into the design, check for its letter on the plan.

The example below (taken from page 567) shows how to read the plans on pages 550–643.

PLAN ILLUSTRATION AND DESCRIPTION

BEAUTIFUL BOUNDARY

Some fences are quite open in structure, marking boundaries without creating visual barriers—as here, where a post-and-rail fence defines the edge of a cultivated garden while allowing a clear view into the wild meadow beyond. Given regular moisture and a full-sun location, this varied floral assortment delivers a summer's worth of color. The plants are all herbaceous perennials, dying back to the ground or to low tufts of foliage when the growing season ends. A quick cleanup in late winter readies the planting for spring growth. This plan is especially well suited to Zones 32–41 but will also succeed in Zones 2–9, 14–21.

_____ Botanical name

PLANT LIST

A. **Hibiscus moscheutos 'Blue River'.** Perennial hibiscus (1)

B. **Echinacea purpurea 'Magnus'.** Purple coneflower (4) ⟶ Common name

C. **Liatris spicata 'Kobold'.** Gayfeather (2)

D. **Geranium psilostemon** (2)

E. **Hemerocallis 'Black-eyed Stella'.** Daylily (2)

F. **Coreopsis grandiflora 'Early Sunrise'** (4+) ⟶ Cultivar name

G. **Salvia × superba 'May Night'** (7+)

Number of plants used in plan

Letter corresponds to plant location in plot plan

PLOT PLAN

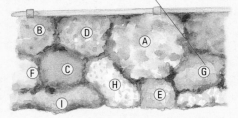

Planting area: 22' x 6'

Dimensions of planting

Climate zones suitable for planting (see pages 644–648)

SHAPE

One reason a planting of just one kind of flower often looks monotonous is that all the plants are built alike. There's no variation in overall appearance. The most interesting gardens assort plants of varied outlines: upright, rounded, spreading, fountain-like, and so forth. Factor texture into this equation, and the combinations are virtually endless. Upright shapes alone, for example, include all sorts of outlines, from the spirelike blossom stems of hollyhock and mullein to swordlike iris foliage and pencil-like conifers to bushy but upward-thrusting lupine. Some spreading plants, such as lamb's ears, are essentially low growing but produce upright flower stems at bloom time.

SIZE AND DENSITY

The time-honored rule of "tall in back, short in front" is still good advice: you wouldn't plant a husky viburnum at the front of a bed and diminutive forget-me-nots behind it. Still, the rule does allow exceptions for the sake of contrast. You can effectively accent some taller and/or bulkier plants by giving them a more forward position and surrounding them with shorter plants that provide a setting. In such cases, density also can come into play. A larger plant with some see-through quality—witch hazel and some kinds of mahonias, for example—can be showcased closer to the front of a border. Consider size and texture together, too; you'll find that a bulky, small-leafed plant at the rear of a planting will seem to be located farther back than will a bulky plant with large leaves.

PUTTING THE PLANTS IN PLACE

For the most part, the plants called for in these plans are not unusual or hard to find. Many are sold in local nurseries, garden centers, and even in the garden departments of hardware and home-improvement emporia. Established mail-order nurseries likewise stock most of these plants, and they often carry numerous less-common types as well.

Timing is important when setting out plants. As a general rule of thumb, plant when roots can begin growing in cool, moist soil and when new growth can unfold in cool to mild weather. Given these conditions, plants establish more rapidly and perform better in their first season.

Where winters are fairly mild (Zones 4–9, 12–31), trees, shrubs, and most perennials are best planted from midautumn through winter; where summers are cool, planting time can extend into spring. In colder regions (Zones 1–3, 10, 11, 32–45), most plants are best set out in late winter or early spring, though fall planting is also possible if the plants are given winter freeze protection.

Mail-order nurseries try to ship each plant at the preferred planting time; retail nurseries are usually well stocked at optimum planting times.

Varied shapes, textures, and colors combine in a garden that highlights the individual beauty of each plant, yet presents an harmonious overall picture.

Container-grown plants are available everywhere for planting throughout the growing season, and it's hard to resist the odd impulse purchase in spring and summer. Be aware, though, that plants set out during the warmer months will need close attention to watering and may require some shelter from wind and sun. Their relatively small, unestablished root systems are more subject to drying than are roots of established plants and may have trouble drawing enough moisture from the soil to replace that lost through transpiration in hot, windy weather.

Plotting a planting bed is easier if you outline the bed (and even the planting areas within it) in powdered chalk, flour, or a common soil amendment such as gypsum or lime.

COMMON GARDEN
SITUATIONS

Old or new, cutting-edge contemporary or frankly old-fashioned, brick or clapboard, grand or modest—there's no counting the ways in which one house can differ from another. Still, despite their endless variety, all houses share certain outdoor features that often present challenges for garden design. In this chapter, we offer solutions for many such situations.

We lead off with the approach to the front door: the transition from public to private domain. Suggestions range from dressing up a walkway with beds or borders to converting the entire front yard to garden. Next, we turn to ideas for coping with blank spots: fences and house walls, completely shaded areas beneath trees, unrelieved stretches of lawn or even gravel that cry out for the adornment of a colorful "island."

Creating beauty in limited spaces is a challenge most gardeners face at one time or another. If you have a small backyard, you can turn the whole space into a garden, perhaps keeping just a postage-stamp plot of lawn. If your back (or front!) yard is nothing more than a deck or patio, don't despair—four plans will help you turn these areas from stark to stunning. You'll also find dazzling designs for two familiar problem spots: narrow side yards and parking strips.

A densely planted bed of roses and durable spring- and summer-blooming perennials fills a long, narrow space between sidewalk and fence. Design by Lauren Springer.

FIRST IMPRESSIONS

The short trip from public space to private front door offers guests their first glimpse of your domain. At its most basic, the path is an unadorned concrete ribbon that takes dead aim from sidewalk to door, bisecting a lawn on the way—or, where there's an attached garage, making a dogleg progression from driveway to entrance. Such bald pedestrian efficiency is neither inspiring to your guests nor uplifting for you—so why not chart a more imaginative course? The designs on these 16 pages present a variety of appealing entry plantings; all can be adapted to existing situations or created from scratch if you're remodeling a landscape or starting on a new home.

FORMAL ENTRY IN TWO STYLES

The arrow-straight entry walk is inherently formal—a characteristic you can choose to accentuate or to soften. The treatments shown here illustrate both approaches, with the striking difference in appearance achieved strictly through choice of plants.

The rigidly formal scheme at lower left (Style A) gains its effect from manicured plants in an obviously symmetrical arrangement. This simple design can succeed in Zones 3–9, 14–24, 32–34 (warmest part). The plan shown above (Style B) has the same regular plant placement and repetition as the first, but soft contours and fluffy, irregular edges lend it an almost informal feeling. These plants will grow in mild-winter climate Zones 8, 9, 12–28.

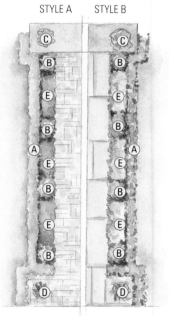

Entry walk: 27' long

PLANT LIST
STYLE A

A. **Buxus microphylla japonica 'Green Beauty'.** Japanese boxwood (44)
B. **Platycladus orientalis 'Bonita'.** Oriental arborvitae (8)
C. **Taxus baccata 'Stricta'.** Irish yew (2)
D. **Liriope muscari 'Silvery Sunproof'.** Big blue lily turf (2)
E. **Vinca minor 'Ralph Shugert'.** Dwarf periwinkle (18)

PLANT LIST
STYLE B

A. **Lavandula angustifolia 'Hidcote'** or **'Twickel Purple'.** English lavender (44)
B. **Punica granatum 'Chico'.** Dwarf pomegranate (8)
C. **Nerium oleander 'Petite Salmon'.** Oleander (2)
D. **Phormium 'Bronze Baby'.** New Zealand flax (2)
E. **Gazania hybrids in pink, salmon, cream, white** (18)

CURVED WALK WITH FREE-FORM PLANTING

Surprising though it may seem, the natural walking path between two unobstructed points is not a straight line but a gently sinuous curve. Establishing such a route from sidewalk to front door gives the approach the feel of a relaxed amble rather than a no-time-to-spare rush—and offers ample opportunity for plantings that will delight even the casual passerby.

The plant assortment shown here features color from both blossoms and foliage, providing interest over at least three seasons. The plan works best where it gets just a touch of shade (as from high, open trees) during the afternoon. It's most successful in Zones 4–6, 32, 34, 37, and 39, but you can also enjoy it in Zones 3, 35, 36, 38, 40, and 41 by using *Rhododendron* (azalea) 'Orchid Lights' in place of *R. mucronulatum* 'Cornell Pink' (B in the list below) and replacing *R.* 'Boule de Neige' (C) with *Hydrangea arborescens* 'Annabelle'.

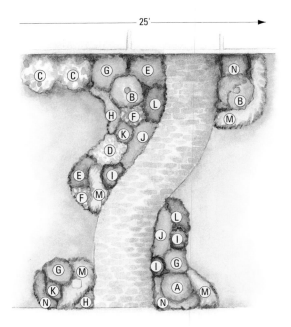

PLANT LIST

A. Acer palmatum 'Ornatum'.
Red laceleaf Japanese maple (1)

B. Rhododendron mucronulatum
'Cornell Pink' (2)

C. Rhododendron 'Boule de Neige' (2+)

D. Daphne × burkwoodii 'Carol Mackie' (1)

E. Helleborus niger. Christmas rose (6)

F. Astrantia major. Masterwort (3)

G. Alchemilla mollis. Lady's-mantle (7)

H. Heuchera 'Palace Purple' (7)

I. Bergenia 'Bressingham Ruby' (5)

J. Astilbe simplicifolia 'Sprite' (9)

K. Hosta 'Krossa Regal' (2)

L. Hosta tardiflora (9)

M. Hakonechloa macra 'Aureola'.
Japanese forest grass (16)

N. Ajuga reptans. Carpet bugle (18+)

PLANT LIST

A. Hamamelis × intermedia 'Ruby Glow'.
Witch hazel (1)

B. Magnolia 'Betty' (1)

C. Enkianthus campanulatus (1)

D. Pinus mugo mugo. Mugho pine (1)

E. Rhododendron yakushimanum
'Koichiro Wada' (2)

F. Erica darleyensis 'Silberschmelze'.
Heath (5)

G. Erica 'Dawn'. Heath (7)

H. Calluna vulgaris 'Nana'.
Heather (6)

I. Viburnum davidii (2)

J. Juniperus conferta.
Shore juniper (3)

K. Epimedium × versicolor 'Sulphureum'.
Bishop's hat (11)

L. Helleborus orientalis.
Lenten rose (9)

M. Heuchera 'Palace Purple' (16)

N. Imperata cylindrica 'Red Baron' ('Rubra').
Japanese blood grass (10)

O. Campanula portenschlagiana
(C. muralis). Dalmatian bellflower (9)

P. Sagina subulata 'Aurea'.
Scotch moss (eighteen to twenty 3-inch
squares, spaced 6 inches apart)

Q. Ajuga reptans. Carpet bugle (15)

R. Rhododendron (azalea) 'Coral Bells' (2)

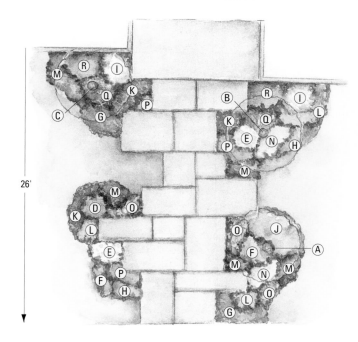

26'

DIVERSIONARY TACTIC

Deliberate asymmetry disguises the fact that this entry path actually moves directly from sidewalk to front door. Rectangular pavers of different sizes are laid out in a staggered pattern, their edges softened with irregularly shaped planting beds—and the eye sees meandering twists and turns, not a straight line.

Suitable for Pacific Northwest Zones 4–6 and coastal California Zones 15–17, this scheme offers year-round visual interest. There's no mass color display; blossoms on shrubs and perennials come and go from midwinter through fall, while the foliage of various perennials and low shrubs offers more sustained color. In winter, the bare limbs of deciduous shrubs serve as living sculpture.

DIRECT ACCESS

No doubt about it: this path gets you to the front door in a straight line. Yet the walkway is also part of a larger design comprising the three rectangular beds that flank and intersect it.

Suited to mild-winter California and the arid Southwest (Zones 8, 9, 12–24), the planting appears lush, but all its mem- bers require just moderate watering. The pebble-aggregate path reflects the stoniness of a natural landscape; Spanish tile insets echo one of the region's favorite architectural inspirations. Floral color is at its height in spring, before the inevitable heat in many of the zones noted above slows or stops growth for the summer.

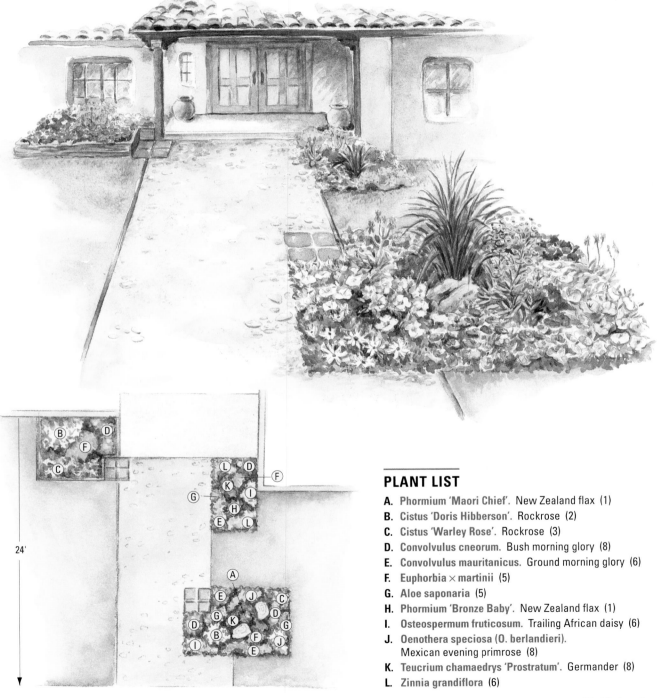

PLANT LIST

A. Phormium 'Maori Chief'. New Zealand flax (1)

B. Cistus 'Doris Hibberson'. Rockrose (2)

C. Cistus 'Warley Rose'. Rockrose (3)

D. Convolvulus cneorum. Bush morning glory (8)

E. Convolvulus mauritanicus. Ground morning glory (6)

F. Euphorbia × martinii (5)

G. Aloe saponaria (5)

H. Phormium 'Bronze Baby'. New Zealand flax (1)

I. Osteospermum fruticosum. Trailing African daisy (6)

J. Oenothera speciosa (O. berlandieri).
Mexican evening primrose (8)

K. Teucrium chamaedrys 'Prostratum'. Germander (8)

L. Zinnia grandiflora (6)

FRANKLY MODERN

An essentially straight entry path and angular planting beds reinforce the stripped-down, no-frills "modern" architecture of the 1950s. Yet the beds also relieve rigidity: because they impinge on either side of the walk, the journey to the front door describes a gentle curve.

Many of the plants are mounding or billowy, softening the straight lines of walk and bed edges—but the fortnight lily, New Zealand flax, and daylily offer spiky and fountain-like foliage clumps as well. Flowering starts in spring, with most perennials continuing through summer. Use this plan in full sun, in Zones 8, 9, 14–24.

TOP: *Cerastium tomentosum*
BOTTOM: *Limonium latifolium*

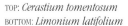

PLANT LIST

A. **Nandina domestica.** Heavenly bamboo (1)

B. **Rhaphiolepis (Raphiolepis) indica 'Indian Princess'.** India hawthorn (5+)

C. **Berberis thunbergii 'Crimson Pygmy'.** Japanese barberry (2)

D. **Phormium 'Apricot Queen'.** New Zealand flax (1)

E. **Dietes bicolor.** Fortnight lily (1)

F. **Hemerocallis 'Stella de Oro'.** Daylily (2)

G. **Salvia officinalis 'Berggarten'.** Common sage (3)

H. **Achillea millefolium, Galaxy strain.** Common yarrow (4)

I. **Limonium latifolium.** Sea lavender (7)

J. **Iberis sempervirens 'Snowflake'.** Evergreen candytuft (6)

K. **Verbena tenuisecta 'Tapien Purple'.** Moss verbena (8)

L. **Teucrium chamaedrys 'Prostratum'.** Germander (10)

M. **Cerastium tomentosum.** Snow-in-summer (6)

FRAMED BY IRREGULAR BEDS

Even if a perfectly straight entry walk is the best choice for your landscape, it doesn't have to look like a package ribbon tied across the yard. Here, curving beds hold relaxed plantings of shrubs and perennials, arranged in outward-sweeping drifts that de-emphasize the underlying severity. Leaf shapes vary, but all the plants are mounding, billowing, or spreading, offering a soft contrast to the straight walk. Warm flower colors play against cooler hues of white, silver, blue, and violet.

This plan is suited to Zones 3–6, 31, 32, 34, 35, 37, 39. To extend it to Zones 2, 40, and 41, replace A, B, C, and E in the list below with (respectively): beauty bush *(Kolkwitzia amabilis)*; *Weigela florida* 'Variegata'; *Spiraea* × *bumalda* 'Goldmound'; and variegated purple moor grass *(Molinia caerulea* 'Variegata').

PLANT LIST

A. **Buddleia davidii 'Black Knight'.** Butterfly bush (1)

B. **Buddleia 'Lochinch'.** Butterfly bush (1)

C. **Phlomis russeliana** (4+)

D. **Miscanthus sinensis 'Purpurascens'.** Eulalia grass (1)

E. **Pennisetum alopecuroides 'Hameln'.** Fountain grass (2)

F. **Achillea 'Fireland'** (2)

G. **Achillea filipendulina 'Coronation Gold.'** Fernleaf yarrow (4)

H. **Achillea 'Moonshine'** (10)

I. **Hemerocallis 'Happy Returns' or other short yellow.** Daylily (5)

J. **Sedum 'Autumn Joy' (Hylotelephium 'Autumn Joy')** (9)

K. **Salvia × superba 'May Night'** (11)

L. **Chrysanthemum weyrichii 'White Bomb' (Dendranthema weyrichii 'White Bomb')** (10)

M. **Artemisia stellerana 'Silver Brocade'.** Beach wormwood (17)

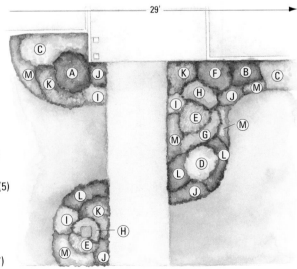

A FRONT YARD "SECRET GARDEN"

Why devote the front yard to grass or ground cover if you can instead enjoy an ever-changing tapestry of foliage and flowers? Especially if your lot is small, you can quite easily develop the plot bounded by sidewalk, driveway, and entry walk—a space usually given over to lawn and seldom walked upon.

In this design, a post-and-rail fence is a subtle foil for the plantings that flank and flow through it. Flower color starts in late winter with redbud and flowering quince, then continues with honeysuckle, daylily, and other plants until fall; foliage color adds interest for three or even all four seasons. All the plants thrive in Zones 4–9, 14–24.

Achillea, Galaxy strain

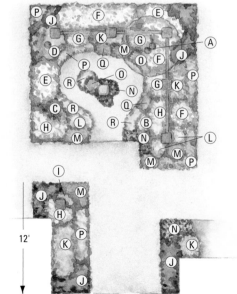

PLANT LIST

A. Cercis occidentalis.
Western redbud (1)

B. Calamagrostis × acutiflora 'Karl Foerster' ('Stricta').
Feather reed grass (1)

C. Chaenomeles 'Enchantress'.
Flowering quince (1)

D. Rhamnus alaternus 'Variegata'.
Italian buckthorn (1)

E. Teucrium fruticans.
Bush germander (5)

F. Abelia 'Edward Goucher'
(A. × grandiflora 'Edward Goucher') (5)

G. Lavandula angustifolia.
English lavender (3)

H. Achillea millefolium, Galaxy strain.
Common yarrow (10)

I. Lonicera × heckrottii.
Gold flame honeysuckle (1)

J. Mahonia aquifolium 'Compacta'.
Oregon grape (16)

K. Spiraea × bumalda 'Goldflame' (8)

L. Euphorbia characias wulfenii (3)

M. Salvia officinalis 'Berggarten'.
Common sage (8)

N. Verbena tenuisecta 'Tapien Purple'.
Moss verbena (12)

O. Hemerocallis, apricot pink cultivar.
Daylily (4)

P. Liriope spicata. Creeping lily turf (22)

Q. Sedum 'Autumn Joy'
(Hylotelephium 'Autumn Joy') (4)

R. Coreopsis verticillata 'Moonbeam'.
Threadleaf coreopsis (8)

NORTHWEST SECRET GARDEN

Aside from a few minor alterations in plant placement, our second "secret garden" is a replica of the design on the facing page. The most conspicuous difference is in the plants: this scheme is tailored for Pacific Northwest Zones 4–6, where coolness and moisture provide the ideal environment for a rich palette of choice plants.

Like the previous plan, this one offers a variety of foliage textures and colors for interest through all four seasons. Flower color, however, is concentrated more in the first half of the year. Lenten rose starts the floral procession in winter; the other flowering plants bloom throughout spring and into summer. An amelanchier in one corner gives small-tree height without density or gloom, and its leafless branches are attractive in winter.

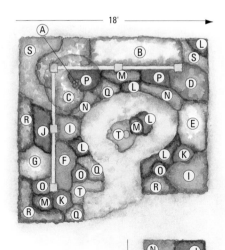

PLANT LIST

A. Amelanchier canadensis (1)

B. Rhododendron yakushimanum 'Ken Janeck' or 'Mist Maiden' (3)

C. Rhododendron (azalea) 'Gumpo' (3)

D. Paeonia suffruticosa. Tree peony (1)

E. Kalmia latifolia 'Elf'. Mountain laurel (2)

F. Spiraea × bumalda 'Goldflame' (2)

G. Pieris japonica 'Variegata'. Lily-of-the-valley shrub (3)

H. Clematis 'Hagley Hybrid' (1)

I. Geranium pratense. Meadow cranesbill (5)

J. Helleborus orientalis. Lenten rose (11)

K. Iris, Siberian, 'Flight of Butterflies' (2)

L. Iris, Pacific Coast native (16)

M. Hosta 'Krossa Regal' (6)

N. Hosta 'Gold Edger' (12)

O. Adenophora confusa. Lady bells (3)

P. Dicentra spectabilis. Common bleeding heart (2)

Q. Heuchera 'Pewter Veil' (4)

R. Alchemilla glaucescens (A. pubescens) (13)

S. Campanula portenschlagiana (C. muralis). Dalmatian bellflower (8)

T. Sagina subulata 'Aurea'. Scotch moss (twelve 3-inch squares, set 6 inches apart)

A FLOWERY WELCOME

Whether your front yard is spacious or small, you can dazzle your visitors and satisfy your gardening soul with plantings full of flowers.

If a driveway extends past the house to a garage farther back (as shown on this page), an entry walk can link drive and front door; the challenge here is to craft a planting striking enough to draw attention away from so much bare pavement. In the plan below—especially fine in Zones 3–6, 32–41—a gently winding path is flanked by irregular beds that give three-season color from flowers and foliage, including some fall leaf color.

If your front yard is shallow, planting it with lawn alone may make the space seem over-exposed to the street. Add the illusion of depth by converting the entire yard to garden (as shown on the facing page), with converging paths from drive and sidewalk leading through a three-season flower fête. This scheme suits California Zones 8, 9, 14–24, where new homes are being built on ever smaller lots.

PLANT LIST

A. **Acer palmatum 'Sango Kaku'.**
Japanese maple (1)

B. **Juniperus conferta.**
Shore juniper (4+)

C. **Berberis thunbergii 'Crimson Pygmy'.**
Japanese barberry (6)

D. **Clematis 'The President'** (1)

E. **Rosa 'White Dawn'** (1)

F. **Clethra alnifolia.** Summersweet (1)

G. **Viburnum opulus 'Compactum'.**
European cranberry bush (2)

H. **Spiraea × bumalda 'Goldflame'** (2)

I. **Chrysanthemum pacificum (Dendranthema pacificum).** Gold and silver chrysanthemum (4)

J. **Molinia caerulea 'Variegata'.**
Variegated purple moor grass (2)

K. **Achillea 'Fireland'** (4)

L. **Iris, Siberian, 'Fourfold White'** (4)

M. **Hemerocallis 'Happy Returns' or other short yellow.** Daylily (9)

N. **Rudbeckia fulgida sullivantii 'Goldsturm'.**
Black-eyed Susan (3)

O. **Salvia × superba 'May Night'** (16)

P. **Sedum 'Autumn Joy' (Hylotelephium 'Autumn Joy')** (7)

Q. **Prunella grandiflora.** Self-heal (28)

PLANT LIST

A. Lagerstroemia 'Natchez' (multitrunked). Crape myrtle (1)

B. Rosa, such as 'First Light', 'Iceberg', 'Scentimental' (4)

C. Rosa 'The Fairy', as standard (1)

D. Coleonema album (Diosma alba, D. reevesii). White breath of heaven (3)

E. Escallonia × langleyensis 'Apple Blossom' (1)

F. Artemisia 'Powis Castle' (6)

G. Erigeron karvinskianus.
Mexican daisy, Santa Barbara daisy (7)

H. Penstemon × gloxinioides 'Firebird'.
Border penstemon (4)

I. Nepeta × faassenii. Catmint (6)

J. Erysimum 'Bowles Mauve' (7)

K. Achillea millefolium 'Appleblossom'.
Common yarrow (3)

L. Calamagrostis × acutiflora 'Karl Foerster' ('Stricta').
Feather reed grass (2)

M. Thymus praecox arcticus (T. serpyllum).
Mother-of-thyme, creeping thyme (17)

N. Stachys byzantina 'Silver Carpet'. Lamb's ears (9)

O. Geranium sanguineum. Bloody cranesbill (3)

P. Festuca ovina 'Glauca'. Sheep fescue (21)

Q. Liriope muscari 'Silvery Sunproof'. Big blue lily turf (12)

R. Potentilla neumanniana (P. tabernaemontanii, P. verna 'Nana'). Cinquefoil (40)

S. Mahonia aquifolium 'Compacta'. Oregon grape (12)

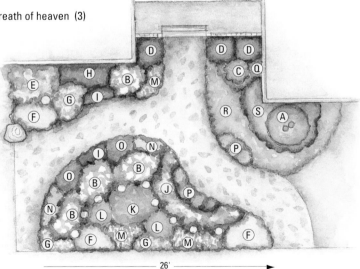

26'

GRAND ENTRANCE

In bygone days, a curving drive was a standard feature of wealthy homes, typically sweeping under a porte-cochere where elegant carriages paused to discharge their occupants. Today, such drives usually lack the imposing overhead and are likely to serve only ordinary vehicles—and, perhaps, the occasional stretch limousine! Still, this design retains a bit of yesteryear's formality.

Color appears in all seasons, but aside from the striking display provided by azaleas and India hawthorn, the amount at any given moment is restrained. The sweet olive's blossoms, in fact, offer no particular show; instead, they proclaim their presence by their penetrating fragrance. All the plants are evergreen, appropriate for Western and Southeastern Zones 14–24, 28–31.

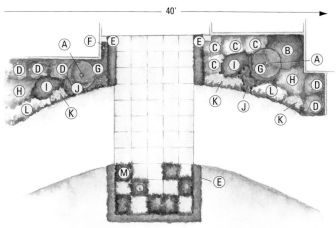

PLANT LIST

A. **Osmanthus fragrans.** Sweet olive (2)

B. **Rhaphiolepis (Raphiolepis) indica 'Springtime'.** India hawthorn (1)

C. **Rhododendron (azalea) 'Gumpo'** (4)

D. **Rhododendron (azalea) 'Gumpo Pink'** (5+)

E. **Buxus microphylla koreana 'Tide Hill'.** Korean boxwood (33)

F. **Camellia sasanqua 'Mine-No-Yuki' ('White Doves')** (1)

G. **Liriope muscari 'Silvery Sunproof'.** Big blue lily turf (18)

H. **Nandina domestica 'Harbour Dwarf'.** Heavenly bamboo (7)

I. **Aspidistra elatior.** Cast-iron plant (8)

J. **Ajuga reptans.** Carpet bugle (16)

K. **Hemerocallis 'Stella de Oro'.** Daylily (5)

L. **Iberis sempervirens 'Snowflake'.** Evergreen candytuft (11)

M. **Ophiopogon japonicus.** Mondo grass (24)

GRAND ENTRANCE, COUNTRY STYLE

In country-suburban properties, where land is more plentiful, the crescent drive offers an efficient entry for both cars and people. By running it through a garden, you make it interesting as well as practical. In this plan, the front yard could be shallow—with the fence set back several feet from a sidewalk—or quite deep, with the planted area located in a large expanse of lawn or ground cover. In either case, the low, open fence defines the planting while still letting parts of it flow through to the "outside."

Gardeners in chilly Zones 2–6, 32–41 will appreciate the hardiness of these plants: in fact, you may occasionally need to curb the spread of the yellowroot, loosestrife, and sweet woodruff. Flowers come and go during spring and summer; woody plants give good fall leaf color and some showy fruits.

PLANT LIST

A. Crataegus phaenopyrum. Washington thorn (2)

B. Cornus alba 'Elegantissima'. Tatarian dogwood (1)

C. Xanthorhiza simplicissima. Yellowroot (3)

D. Rosa 'Frau Dagmar Hartopp' ('Fru Dagmar Hastrup') (3)

E. Cotoneaster adpressus. Creeping cotoneaster (7)

F. Berberis thunbergii 'Atropurpurea'. Red-leaf Japanese barberry (2)

G. Lysimachia clethroides. Gooseneck loosestrife (3)

H. Astilbe × arendsii 'Bridal Veil' (8)

I. Athyrium filix-femina. Lady fern (7)

J. Iris, Siberian, light blue cultivar (2)

K. Hemerocallis, cream to light yellow cultivar. Daylily (4)

L. Epimedium × versicolor 'Sulphureum'. Bishop's hat (9)

M. Bergenia 'Abendglut' ('Evening Glow') or 'Bressingham Ruby' (3)

N. Hosta 'Gold Edger' (9)

O. Galium odoratum. Sweet woodruff (7)

P. Thymus praecox arcticus 'Coccineus' (T. serpyllum 'Coccineus'). Mother-of-thyme, creeping thyme (20)

Q. Sagina subulata 'Aurea'. Scotch moss (fifteen 3-inch squares, set 6 inches apart)

R. Chamaemelum nobile. Chamomile (9)

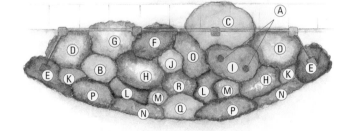

Planting area: 40' x 12'

Weigela florida 'Variegata'

CONTEMPORARY GATED ENTRANCE

Where privacy or noise abatement is a priority, a substantial wall with an entry gate will give the desired result. With the wall set back from the street, the challenge is to come up with an attractive streetside planting that is uncluttered and easy to maintain. The focus is on the wall's public face. The overall design is formal—but the plants are largely informal, tied together by a tightly trimmed boxwood hedge. Foliage variegation and seasonal flowers on hydrangea and weigela, as well as blossoms on the magnolias, keep the planting looking interesting. This plan suits Zones 3–9, 14–17, 32–34, 39. To use it in Zones 2, 35–38, and 41, substitute Korean boxwood *(Buxus microphylla koreana)* and *Hydrangea arborescens* 'Annabelle' for the boxwood and hydrangea selections noted under A and B in the list below.

PLANT LIST

A. **Buxus microphylla japonica 'Green Beauty'.** Japanese boxwood (46+)

B. **Hydrangea macrophylla 'Tricolor'.** Bigleaf hydrangea (2)

C. **Magnolia kobus 'Wada's Memory'.** Kobus magnolia (2)

D. **Weigela florida 'Variegata'** (4+)

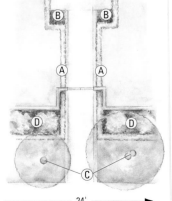

24'

A ROMANTIC PORTAL

What could be more romantic than a picket-fenced garden with an entry arbor bedecked in a tangle of roses and clematis? From a distance, its colorful extravagance proclaims "Welcome!" (if not also "Surrender!")—and once through the arbor, you're greeted by a cottage-garden array of flowering perennials.

Blossoms beguile you from spring through summer (and on into fall, in warmer zones). The color scheme is pastel—white,

pink, yellow—with the purple of the clematis and salvia for accent. Except for the lavandin, these plants will grow in Zones 2–9, 14–21, 32–41; the roses need winter protection in Zones 2, 3, 33–41. The lavandin (K in the list below) grows in Zones 4–24, 30–34, 39. In its place, use blue mist *(Caryopteris × clandonensis)* in Zones 3, 40, 41; use common wormwood *(Artemisia absinthium)* in Zones 2, 35–38.

PLANT LIST

A. Rosa 'Climbing Iceberg' (1)

B. Clematis 'Etoile Violette' (1)

C. Rosa 'Awakening' (2)

D. Gypsophila paniculata 'Bristol Fairy'. Baby's breath (3)

E. Chrysanthemum × superbum 'Becky' (Leucanthemum maximum 'Becky'). Shasta daisy (7)

F. Nepeta × faassenii 'Six Hills Giant'. Catmint (5)

G. Digitalis × mertonensis. Foxglove (7)

H. Salvia × superba 'May Night' (7)

I. Potentilla nepalensis 'Miss Willmott' ('Willmottiae'). Cinquefoil (11)

J. Hemerocallis 'Stella de Oro'. Daylily (7)

K. Lavandula × intermedia 'Provence'. Lavandin (16+)

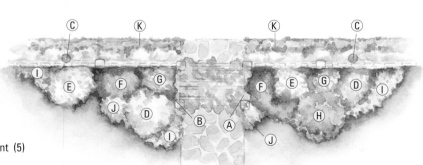

Planting area: 34' x 9'

SURROUND THE WALL WITH GARDEN

Concrete paving and a stucco wall clearly mark this as a contemporary design, yet its roots are in Mediterranean antiquity, where concrete and plaster originated. These are hard, bright surfaces that look stark without the softening influence of plants—and the assortment shown here rises beautifully to the task. Mounded, irregular, loose, grassy, or frothy, they smooth sharp corners and gently blur straight edges.

Summer is the prime flowering season. The prevailing colors are blue, violet, yellow, and orange, with highlights of white and red. All the plants will succeed in Zones 3–7, 14–17, 32–34, 39. In Zones 35–38, 40, 41, you can substitute *Spiraea × bumalda* 'Goldmound' for phlomis (C in the list below), *Verbena canadensis* 'Homestead Purple' for moss verbena (G), and catmint (*Nepeta × faassenii*) for germander (I).

PLANT LIST

A. Lonicera sempervirens.
Trumpet honeysuckle (2)

B. Caryopteris × clandonensis. Blue mist (2)

C. Phlomis russeliana (4+)

D. Panicum virgatum 'Heavy Metal'.
Switch grass (3)

E. Rudbeckia fulgida sullivantii 'Goldsturm'.
Black-eyed Susan (8)

F. Limonium latifolium. Sea lavender (12+)

G. Verbena tenuisecta 'Tapien Purple'.
Moss verbena (18)

H. Cerastium tomentosum.
Snow-in-summer (16+)

I. Teucrium chamaedrys 'Prostratum'.
Germander (4)

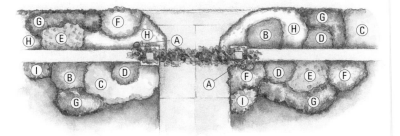

Planting area: 40' x 11'

UNDERSTATED ELEGANCE

A brick wall is the image of formality and restraint: when it separates public sidewalk from private yard, it clearly states "no trespassing." Nonetheless, its looks are often warm, not concrete-cold, conveying a welcome to those who are expected.

In keeping with this reserved yet friendly mood, the plants in the scheme shown here are elegant without being formally stiff. Contrasts in foliage texture make a three-season statement; flower color is at its peak in late spring, with the hydrangea carrying on into summer. The lightest afternoon shade suits all these plants, which perform best in Zones 3–9, 14–17, 32–34, 37–39. To suit the plan to Zones 40 and 41, substitute *Hydrangea arborescens* 'Annabelle' and *Rhododendron* (azalea) 'Orchid Lights' for the hydrangea and rhododendron suggested at right under C and D.

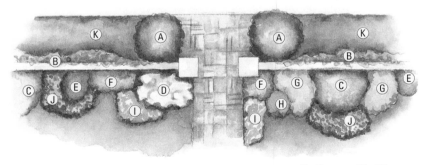

Planting area: 40' x 13'

PLANT LIST

A. Berberis thunbergii 'Cherry Bomb'. Japanese barberry (2)

B. Parthenocissus quinquefolia. Virginia creeper (2)

C. Hydrangea serrata 'Preziosa' (2)

D. Rhododendron yakushimanum (2)

E. Iris, Siberian, 'Caesar's Brother' (4)

F. Astrantia major. Masterwort (6)

G. Alchemilla mollis. Lady's-mantle (6)

H. Bergenia 'Bressingham Ruby' (1)

I. Hosta 'Gold Edger' (9)

J. Epimedium alpinum. Bishop's hat (7)

K. Pachysandra terminalis. Japanese spurge (20+)

FILLING IN THE BLANKS

In every suburban and rural home, gardeners face the same planting challenges: how to dress up a bare fence, a stark house wall, the empty ground beneath a tree, or a blank expanse of lawn or earth. The following 16 plans present a variety of schemes to address these often-difficult situations, with attention to the ever-present variables of sun, shade, rainfall patterns, and overall climate, be it mild or harsh.

FLORIFEROUS FENCEROW

Boundary fences are a fact of suburban life—but to the gardener's eye, even the most attractive fence can look a bit stark without some sort of horticultural costuming. In the plan shown below, a weathered wooden fence is a backdrop for a lush-looking planting that needs only moderate water, yet provides good color from spring into fall. This scheme is intended for a sunny location in California's Zones 14–24, where winters are mild, summers are warm to hot, and water is at a premium. It's a relatively low-maintenance planting: one round of cleanup and discretionary pruning in winter will prepare it for a return engagement the next year.

PLANT LIST

A. **Anisodontea capensis.** Cape mallow (1)

B. **Erysimum 'Bowles Mauve'** (1)

C. **Verbena bonariensis** (1)

D. **Penstemon × gloxinioides 'Sour Grapes'.** Border penstemon (3)

E. **Agapanthus orientalis 'Albus'.** Lily-of-the-Nile (1)

F. **Erigeron karvinskianus.** Mexican daisy, Santa Barbara daisy (4+)

G. **Helichrysum italicum (H. angustifolium).** Curry plant (2)

H. **Aloe saponaria** (2)

I. **Osteospermum fruticosum.** Trailing African daisy (4+)

J. **Scaevola 'Mauve Clusters'** (2)

K. **Convolvulus mauritanicus.** Ground morning glory (2)

L. **Stachys byzantina 'Silver Carpet'.** Lamb's ears (5+)

Planting area: 22' x 6'

BEAUTIFUL BOUNDARY

Some fences are quite open in structure, marking boundaries without creating visual barriers—as here, where a post-and-rail fence defines the edge of a cultivated garden while allowing a clear view into the wild meadow beyond. Given regular moisture and a full-sun location, this varied floral assortment delivers a summer's worth of color. The plants are all herbaceous perennials, dying back to the ground or to low tufts of foliage when the growing season ends. A quick cleanup in late winter readies the planting for spring growth. This plan is especially well suited to Zones 32–41 but will also succeed in Zones 2–9, 14–21.

PLANT LIST

A. **Hibiscus moscheutos 'Blue River'.**
   Perennial hibiscus (1)

B. **Echinacea purpurea 'Magnus'.**
   Purple coneflower (4+)

C. **Liatris spicata 'Kobold'.** Gayfeather (2)

D. **Geranium psilostemon** (2+)

E. **Hemerocallis 'Black-eyed Stella'.**
   Daylily (2)

F. **Coreopsis grandiflora 'Early Sunrise'** (4+)

G. **Salvia × superba 'May Night'** (7+)

H. **Chrysanthemum × superbum 'Snow Lady'**
   (Leucanthemum maximum 'Snow Lady').
   Shasta daisy (3)

I. **Nepeta × faassenii.** Catmint (6+)

J. **Iberis sempervirens.**
   Evergreen candytuft (5)

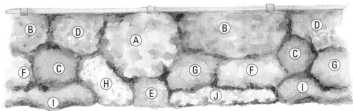

Planting area: 22' x 6'

TOP: *Nepeta × faassenii*
BOTTOM: *Liatris spicata* 'Kobold'

Campanula poscharskyana

SHADED FENCE FOR THE SUNBELT

Over much of California's Zones 14–24 and throughout the Southeast's Zones 31 and 32, summers are warm to hot. In these areas, summer shade is a welcome relief for people, but it may not always suit plants. The assortment suggested here, though, is perfectly at home in very light shade all day, or with a little morning sun followed by light shade in the afternoon. There's no peak season for flower color, but you do enjoy it in all seasons, from winter's camellia through fall's Japanese anemone and the last of the impatiens. Heuchera, lily turf, and Japanese forest grass provide subtle but steady foliage color throughout the growing season.

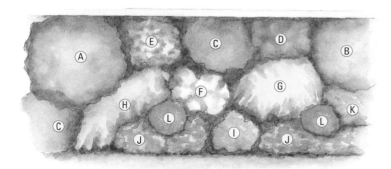

Planting area: 20' x 8'

PLANT LIST

A. **Camellia japonica 'Nuccio's Pearl'** (1)

B. **Rhododendron (azalea) 'George Lindley Taber'** (1)

C. **Rhododendron (azalea) 'Hinodegiri'** (2)

D. **Anemone × hybrida.** Japanese anemone (3)

E. **Digitalis × mertonensis.** Foxglove (4)

F. **Helleborus argutifolius (H. lividus corsicus).** Corsican hellebore (2)

G. **Hakonechloa macra 'Aureola'.** Japanese forest grass (3)

H. **Liriope muscari 'Variegata'.** Big blue lily turf (5)

I. **Heuchera 'Palace Purple'** (2)

J. **Ajuga reptans.** Carpet bugle (14+)

K. **Campanula poscharskyana.** Serbian bellflower (3+)

L. **Impatiens wallerana** (annuals, in pots)

SHADED FENCE
FOR COLDER REGIONS

Where houses are fairly close together, shade is sure to affect plantings along a fence or wall—and those areas will be even dimmer and cooler (and for more hours of the day) if the houses are tall and mature trees grow nearby. Nonetheless, you can still enjoy a visually interesting planting punctuated by floral color. The scheme shown here works well in Zones 3–6, 32–41, where the plants will thrive in light to moderate shade all day if given regular watering. Summer is the most colorful season: the foliage of bergenia and hosta is at its most striking, and the meadow rue, masterwort, astilbe, and summersweet are all in bloom.

Convallaria majalis

PLANT LIST

A. **Clethra alnifolia.** Summersweet (1)
B. **Rhododendron 'PJM'** (2)
C. **Thalictrum rochebrunianum.** Meadow rue (6)
D. **Astrantia major.** Masterwort (5+)
E. **Polystichum acrostichoides.** Christmas fern (4)
F. **Hosta sieboldiana 'Elegans'** (2)
G. **Astilbe simplicifolia 'Sprite'** (5)
H. **Bergenia 'Bressingham Ruby'** (2)
I. **× Heucherella tiarelloides 'Pink Frost'** (4)
J. **Convallaria majalis.** Lily-of-the-valley (8+)

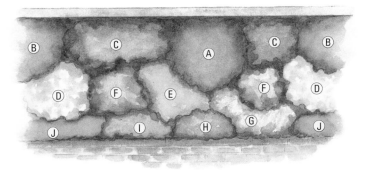

Planting area: 20' x 8'

Sedum 'Autumn Joy'

PICTURE PERFECT

Plantings along a house have a softening effect on the landscape, creating a transition from manmade structure to natural environment. Where these foundation plantings are easily seen from a window, you'll want to create an especially eye-pleasing scheme. One such "picture window" design is shown here, offering colorful flowers and foliage from earliest spring into autumn. This assortment prefers regular moisture but will forgive occasional lapses. It may be satisfied by natural rainfall in Zones 32–39, but you'll surely need to provide some water in Zones 3–9, 14–16, 18–21. Substitute *Geranium* 'Ann Folkard' for *G.* × *magnificum* (E in the list below) and the plan can also be enjoyed in Zones 2, 40, and 41.

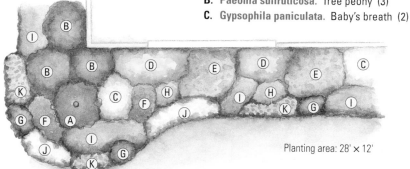

Planting area: 28' × 12'

PLANT LIST

A. **Prunus × cistena.**
Purple-leaf sand cherry (1)
B. **Paeonia suffruticosa.** Tree peony (3)
C. **Gypsophila paniculata.** Baby's breath (2)
D. **Hemerocallis, yellow cultivar.** Daylily (8)
E. **Geranium × magnificum** (4)
F. **Geranium himalayense (G. grandiflorum)**
'Birch Double' ('Plenum') (3)
G. **Heuchera 'Palace Purple'** (3)
H. **Sedum 'Autumn Joy'**
(Hylotelephium 'Autumn Joy') (2)
I. **Salvia × superba 'May Night'** (10+)
J. **Dianthus × allwoodii 'Aqua'.** Pink (8)
K. **Potentilla nepalensis 'Miss Willmott'**
('Willmottiae'). Cinquefoil (8)

VIEW FROM A WINDOW

In regions where water is scant or expensive, the gardener's challenge is to create plantings with limited thirst. In California's Zones 8, 9, 14–24, rainfall may take care of winter water needs, but the warm months are typically too dry to support a varied garden without some assistance from the hose. The scheme shown here follows the same plot plan as "Picture Perfect" (facing page), but it uses plants that will prosper with less than regular watering. Consistent color comes from a variety of plants with gray, yellow, and purplish foliage. Flower color is present from spring into fall, but it crests in the summer display depicted above.

PLANT LIST

A. **Buddleia davidii 'Dark Knight'.** Butterfly bush (1)

B. **Phlomis fruticosa.** Jerusalem sage (3)

C. **Lavandula × intermedia 'Provence'.** Lavandin (2)

D. **Pennisetum setaceum 'Rubrum'.** Fountain grass (5)

E. **Coleonema pulchrum 'Sunset Gold' (Diosma pulchra 'Sunset Gold').** Pink breath of heaven (2)

F. **Achillea taygetea** (5)

G. **Convolvulus cneorum.** Bush morning glory (3)

H. **Kniphofia uvaria 'Little Maid'.** Red-hot poker (2)

I. **Erigeron karvinskianus.** Mexican daisy, Santa Barbara daisy (6+)

J. **Verbena tenuisecta 'Tapien Purple'.** Moss verbena (7)

K. **Gazania 'Burgundy'** (10)

Gazania 'Burgundy'

Brunnera macrophylla

SHADEMASTERS

One or more sides of your house are bound to be shady. The eastern and western faces may have half-day shade, but the northern exposures (as well as any walls shaded by trees or buildings) will be at least partly in shadow all day long. And if a shaded wall jags in and out rather than proceeding in an unbroken line, the shadows will be especially deep and cool in the nooks thus created. Fortunately, you needn't consign these darker regions to ivy and moss. The grouping illustrated below offers both subtle foliage color and periodic floral color. The birdbath rises from a "pool" of blue scaevola blossoms, but you can certainly construct a real pond if you prefer. With regular watering, this planting will thrive in all-day light shade in Zones 8, 9, 14–24; by substituting bishop's hat (*Epimedium × rubrum* 'Snow Queen') for vancouveria (J in the list below) and carpet bugle *(Ajuga reptans)* for scaevola (K), you can achieve virtually the same effect in Zones 4–7, 32, and 33.

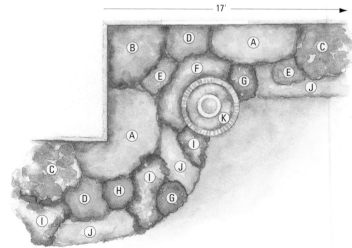

PLANT LIST

A. Rhododendron (azalea) 'Gumpo' (4)

B. Aucuba japonica. Japanese aucuba (1)

C. Hydrangea macrophylla 'Tricolor'. Bigleaf hydrangea (2)

D. Brunnera macrophylla (2)

E. Adenophora confusa. Lady bells (4)

F. Liriope muscari 'Variegata'. Big blue lily turf (6)

G. Bergenia 'Bressingham Ruby' (2)

H. Iris foetidissima. Gladwin iris (1)

I. × Heucherella tiarelloides 'Pink Frost' (7+)

J. Vancouveria hexandra (7+)

K. Scaevola 'Mauve Clusters' (3)

HOT SPOTS

Spend a bit of time in the sun near a south-facing house wall, and soon you're gasping for breath. But while the environment may be too hot for most people to handle comfortably, a variety of good-looking plants thrive in just these spots. This gathering features natives of regions where blistering summers are the norm; given the same conditions in your garden, they'll feel right at home. (Flowering is at its peak in summer, too.) Try this plan in desert Zones 12 and 13, as well as in Zones 14, 18–21.

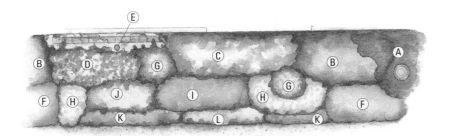

Planting area: 37' x 8'

PLANT LIST

A. Lagerstroemia 'Zuni'. Crape myrtle (1)

B. Teucrium fruticans. Bush germander (3)

C. Nerium oleander 'Petite Salmon'. Oleander (3)

D. Punica granatum 'Nana'. Dwarf pomegranate (3)

E. Tecomaria capensis 'Aurea' (Tecoma capensis 'Aurea'). Cape honeysuckle (1)

F. Pittosporum tobira 'Wheeler's Dwarf'. Tobira (3+)

G. Dietes vegeta. Fortnight lily (2)

H. Erigeron karvinskianus. Mexican daisy, Santa Barbara daisy (5)

I. Santolina chamaecyparissus. Lavender cotton (2)

J. Achillea taygetea (3)

K. Teucrium chamaedrys 'Prostratum'. Germander (8)

L. Oenothera speciosa (O. berlandieri). Mexican evening primrose (3)

Helleborus orientalis

VENERABLE SHELTER

Though a mature deciduous tree is a treasure to be cherished, it often sits squarely in a spot where you'd also like to establish an ornamental planting. Some trees (such as sweet gum, *Liquidambar*) have aggressive surface root systems that will ultimately defeat your efforts. But given a reasonably deep-rooted tree like the scarlet oak (*Quercus coccinea*) shown here, you can literally have it all. The limbs extend to shelter a potpourri of shade-tolerant plants that reach a crescendo of color in summer, brightening the garden with both flowers and non-green foliage. These plants will succeed in Zones 3–6, 32–41.

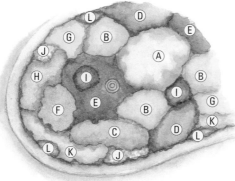

Planting area: 20' x 16'

PLANT LIST

A. **Aruncus dioicus (A. sylvester).** Goat's beard (2)

B. **Alchemilla mollis.** Lady's-mantle (8+)

C. **Hakonechloa macra 'Aureola'.** Japanese forest grass (4)

D. **Helleborus orientalis.** Lenten rose (6+)

E. **Brunnera macrophylla** (8+)

F. **Thalictrum aquilegifolium.** Meadow rue (3)

G. **Corydalis lutea** (6+)

H. **Astilbe simplicifolia 'Sprite'** (5)

I. **Athyrium filix-femina.** Lady fern (2)

J. **Galax urceolata** (4)

K. **Hosta 'Gold Edger'** (10+)

L. **Endymion non-scriptus (Scilla non-scripta).** English bluebell (16)

DRY-SHADE DENIZENS

Shade and dryness characterize the conditions of many a forest floor, where the typical flora features plenty of greenery and few or no blossoms. The same basic scheme holds true in dry, low-light garden spots: you can choose a variety of green shades and variegations to create a subtle tapestry, but any color will serve as an exclamation point. The planting shown above adorns the ground beneath a Japanese scholar tree *(Sophora japonica)*.

The variegated leaves of Japanese aucuba, osmanthus, and lily turf add light to the composition; red tints in the foliage of heavenly bamboo and bishop's hat contribute a touch of color. Notable flower color comes just from lily turf, bishop's hat, and cinquefoil. Use this grouping in Zones 4–9, 14–17, 32, and 33. Gardeners in Zones 10, 18–21 can substitute dwarf periwinkle *(Vinca minor)* for bishop's hat (G in the list below).

PLANT LIST

A. **Aucuba japonica 'Picturata'** **('Aureo-maculata').** Japanese aucuba (2)

B. **Osmanthus heterophyllus 'Variegatus'.** Holly-leaf osmanthus (3)

C. **Mahonia aquifolium 'Compacta'.** Oregon grape (12)

D. **Nandina domestica 'Harbour Dwarf'.** Heavenly bamboo (9+)

E. **Iris foetidissima.** Gladwin iris (5)

F. **Liriope muscari 'Silvery Sunproof'.** Big blue lily turf (7)

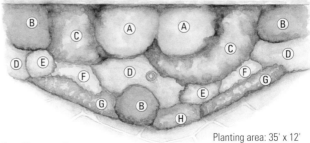

Planting area: 35' x 12'

G. **Epimedium × rubrum.** Bishop's hat (10)

H. **Potentilla recta 'Macrantha' (P. recta 'Warrenii', P. warrenii).** Cinquefoil (4)

BENEATH A COAST LIVE OAK

California gardeners in Zones 7–9, 14–24 treasure mature specimens of the coast live oak *(Quercus agrifolia)*, the signature tree of the state's oak-dotted hillsides. With the spread of housing into their native territory, many of these trees now find themselves in gardens, where they often receive watering during their accustomed summer-dry period—a situation that ultimately proves fatal for them. To garden successfully with a mature (and for-

merly wild) coast live oak, you must keep off-season water away from its roots as much as possible. The plan shown here maintains a 10-foot buffer zone of gravel between tree trunk and planting, and it concentrates on unthirsty plants that can be given the occasional summer drink via a drip-irrigation system that largely bypasses the oak. There's no mass color display, but flowers dot the planting in winter and spring.

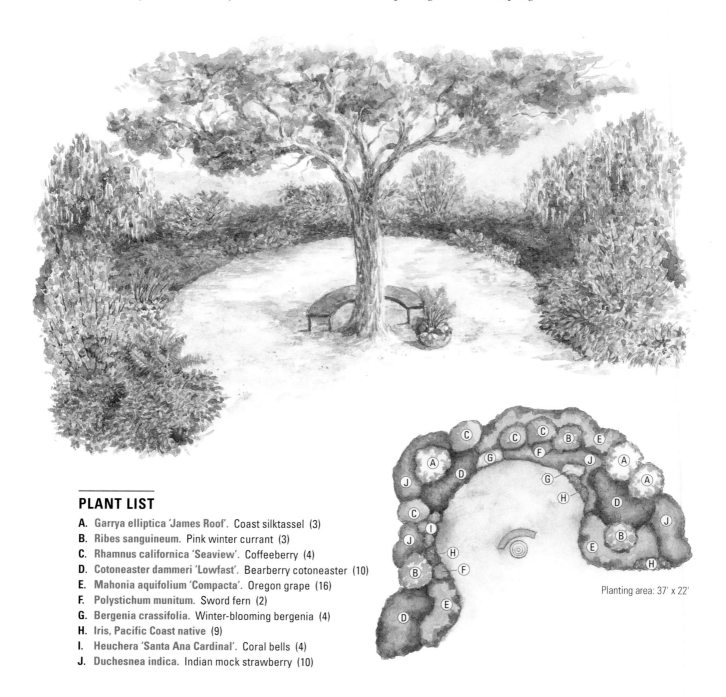

Planting area: 37' x 22'

PLANT LIST

A. **Garrya elliptica 'James Roof'.** Coast silktassel (3)

B. **Ribes sanguineum.** Pink winter currant (3)

C. **Rhamnus californica 'Seaview'.** Coffeeberry (4)

D. **Cotoneaster dammeri 'Lowfast'.** Bearberry cotoneaster (10)

E. **Mahonia aquifolium 'Compacta'.** Oregon grape (16)

F. **Polystichum munitum.** Sword fern (2)

G. **Bergenia crassifolia.** Winter-blooming bergenia (4)

H. **Iris, Pacific Coast native** (9)

I. **Heuchera 'Santa Ana Cardinal'.** Coral bells (4)

J. **Duchesnea indica.** Indian mock strawberry (10)

A CANOPY BED

Where two or more trees join forces to shelter an area, you can craft a fairly ambitious garden of shade-loving plants. Here, two garden-compatible trees—a locust and a dogwood—spread their limbs above a good-sized plot, casting mottled shadows over a diverse planting that sports variegated or colored foliage throughout the growing season and provides bursts of flower color from spring through fall. Both the plants and the two trees perform best with regular water, in Zones 4–9, 14, 15, 32.

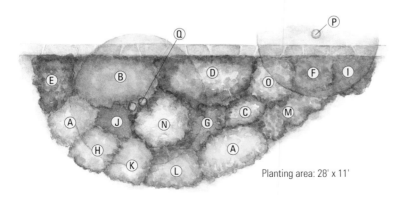

Planting area: 28' x 11'

PLANT LIST

A. Alchemilla mollis. Lady's-mantle (3)

B. Anemone × hybrida 'Honorine Jobert'.
Japanese anemone (5)

C. Molinia caerulea 'Variegata'.
Variegated purple moor grass (1)

D. Berberis thunbergii 'Atropurpurea'.
Red-leaf Japanese barberry (2)

E. Bergenia crassifolia.
Winter-blooming bergenia (3)

F. Digitalis purpurea. Common foxglove (4)

G. Helleborus argutifolius (H. lividus corsicus).
Corsican hellebore (3)

H. Hosta 'Chinese Sunrise' (3)

I. Hosta sieboldiana 'Elegans' (1)

J. Iris foetidissima. Gladwin iris (2)

K. Lamium maculatum 'White Nancy'.
Dead nettle (3)

L. Liriope muscari. Big blue lily turf (3)

M. Liriope muscari 'Variegata'. Big blue lily turf (4)

N. Thalictrum aquilegifolium. Meadow rue (3)

O. Thalictrum rochebrunianum 'Lavender Mist'.
Meadow rue (3)

P. Cornus × rutgersensis 'Aurora'.
Stellar dogwood (1)

Q. Robinia pseudoacacia 'Frisia'. Black locust (1)

Santolina chamaecyparissus

DESERT ISLAND

As originally conceived, the "island bed" was a sizable plant grouping afloat in a sea of turf. But in semiarid regions (where seas of turf are a troublesome extravagance), there's no reason an island can't be an oasis of flowers and foliage in an otherwise dry expanse. This grouping gets its vivid color from both blossoms and an abundance of non-green foliage; the display is at its showiest from midspring to midsummer. The plants coexist swimmingly in California's dry-summer Zones 14–24. In the coastal zones, they may sail through the growing season with no supplemental water; in hotter inland zones, they'll probably need an occasional summer drink from the hose.

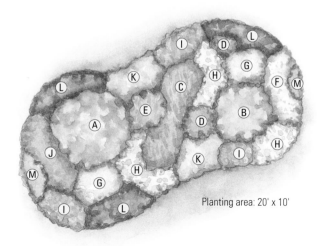

Planting area: 20' x 10'

PLANT LIST

A. **Cistus ladanifer.** Crimson-spot rockrose (1)

B. **Phlomis fruticosa.** Jerusalem sage (1)

C. **Lavandula × intermedia 'Provence'.** Lavandin (2)

D. **Euphorbia characias wulfenii** (2)

E. **Phormium 'Yellow Wave'.** New Zealand flax (1)

F. **Convolvulus cneorum.** Bush morning glory (3)

G. **Centranthus ruber 'Albus'.** Jupiter's beard (4)

H. **Erigeron karvinskianus.** Mexican daisy, Santa Barbara daisy (8)

I. **Oenothera speciosa (O. berlandieri).** Mexican evening primrose (8)

J. **Penstemon 'Garnet'** (4)

K. **Santolina chamaecyparissus.** Lavender cotton (4)

L. **Verbena tenuisecta 'Tapien Purple'.** Moss verbena (11)

M. **Aloe saponaria** (3)

WATER-THRIFTY ISLAND

Though it follows the same plan as our "Desert Island" (facing page), this water-thrifty grouping is intended especially for Zones 32–41, where gardens receive some summer rainfall but not always enough to sustain plants needing regular moisture. Flower color begins in late spring with the false indigo, then continues on into summer (peaking in July and August) and maintains a good display well into the autumn, weather permitting.

Given periodic watering during summer, this planting will also succeed in Zones 3–7, 14–17.

Asclepias tuberosa

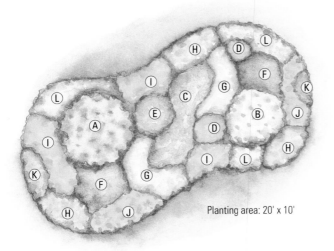

Planting area: 20' x 10'

PLANT LIST

A. Echinacea purpurea 'Magnus'. Purple coneflower (7)

B. Echinacea purpurea 'White Swan' (5)

C. Baptisia australis. Blue false indigo (2)

D. Asclepias tuberosa. Butterfly weed (2)

E. Panicum virgatum 'Heavy Metal'. Switch grass (1)

F. Caryopteris × clandonensis. Blue mist (2)

G. Achillea ptarmica 'The Pearl' (7)

H. Achillea tomentosa 'King George'. Woolly yarrow (9)

I. Coreopsis grandiflora 'Early Sunrise' (9)

J. Gaillardia × grandiflora 'Goblin'. Blanket flower (7)

K. Sedum 'Autumn Joy' (Hylotelephium 'Autumn Joy') (5)

L. Cerastium tomentosum. Snow-in-summer (9)

Aster × frikartii 'Mönch'

COOL ISLAND

From spring through summer, this soothing oasis presents an ever-changing array of flowers in tones of blue, purple, white, and pink—the perfect cooling antidote for the midsummer blahs. When flowering wanes, colored and variegated foliage keeps the planting interesting. All the plants will succeed with regular (but not lavish) watering in Zones 3–9, 32, and 33. Gardeners in Zones 14–21 can enjoy the plan as well if *Dictamnus albus* 'Albiflorus' and *D. a.* 'Purpureus' are replaced with *Liatris spicata* 'Alba' and *L. s.* 'Kobold'.

PLANT LIST

A. Achillea millefolium 'White Beauty'. Yarrow (4)

B. Ajuga reptans 'Purpurea'. Carpet bugle (8)

C. Aster × frikartii 'Mönch' (4)

D. Cerastium tomentosum. Snow-in-summer (3)

E. Dictamnus albus 'Albiflorus'. Gas plant (1)

F. Dictamnus albus 'Purpureus'. Gas plant (1)

G. Gaura lindheimeri (2)

H. Hemerocallis 'Little Grapette'. Daylily (5)

I. Heuchera 'Palace Purple' (4)

J. Hibiscus syriacus 'Diana'. Rose of Sharon (1)

K. Iberis sempervirens 'Snowflake'. Evergreen candytuft (8)

L. Iris, tall bearded, 'Pallida Variegata' ('Zebra') (4)

M. Iris, tall bearded, 'Titan's Glory' (4)

N. Iris, tall bearded, 'Stepping Out' (3)

O. Limonium latifolium. Sea lavender (6)

P. Liriope muscari 'Silvery Sunproof'. Big blue lily turf (8)

Q. Nepeta × faassenii. Catmint (3)

R. Salvia × superba 'East Friesland' (13)

S. Scabiosa caucasica. Pincushion flower (4)

T. Stachys byzantina 'Silver Carpet'. Lamb's ears (11)

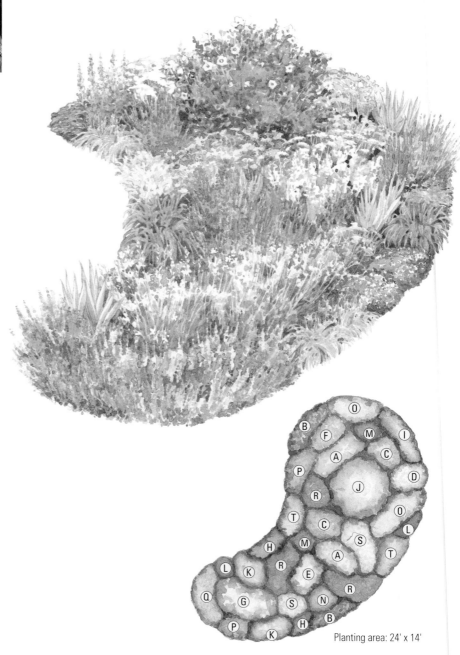

Planting area: 24' x 14'

Echinacea purpurea

GRAND ISLAND

Where space is not an issue, set this island into your lawn for a Really Big Show. It's centered with a sinuous "spine" of shrubs in varying sizes; plantings on either side of this backbone flow outward to the perimeter. The effect is grand indeed, with flowers and foliage offering interest from early spring clear into fall. Due to its width, the island is a bit awkward to maintain—you have no choice but to wade into it to reach the interior plants. When you see it in its glory, though, you'll know the extra work is worth the effort! All the plants need routine summer moisture and are well suited to summer-rainfall Zones 32–35, 37, and 39; they'll also thrive (with watering from you) in Zones 3–9, 14–17. To extend the planting into Zones 2, 36, 38, 40, and 41, replace the butterfly bush (C in the list at right) with blue false indigo *(Baptisia australis)* or lead plant *(Amorpha canescens)*.

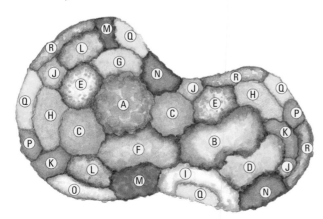

Planting area: 35' x 22'

PLANT LIST

A. Hibiscus syriacus 'Aphrodite'. Rose of Sharon (1)

B. Weigela florida 'Variegata' (2)

C. Buddleia davidii 'Nanho Purple'. Butterfly bush (2)

D. Spiraea × bumalda 'Goldflame' (2)

E. Malva moschata 'Alba'. Musk mallow (2)

F. Helictotrichon sempervirens (Avena sempervirens). Blue oat grass (5)

G. Liatris scariosa 'White Spire'. Gayfeather (3)

H. Achillea millefolium, pink cultivar (e.g. 'Appleblossom', 'Heidi'). Common yarrow (7)

I. Achillea ptarmica 'The Pearl' (6)

J. Hemerocallis 'Hyperion'. Daylily (6)

K. Liatris spicata 'Kobold'. Gayfeather (7)

L. Echinacea purpurea 'Magnus'. Purple coneflower (10)

M. Aster × frikartii 'Mönch' (6)

N. Salvia × superba 'May Night' (11)

O. Salvia × sylvestris 'Schneehügel' ('Snowhill') (6)

P. Sedum 'Autumn Joy' (Hylotelephium 'Autumn Joy') (5)

Q. Coreopsis auriculata 'Nana' (17)

R. Nepeta × faassenii. Catmint (13)

THINKING SMALL

Many homeowners think of the ideal garden as a big one, planted with a little bit of everything. Reality, however, often compels urban and suburban gardeners to scale down that dream to suit the constraints of limited space. And the results are often wonderful: smaller spaces can be soul-satisfying realms of beauty and variety, a sort of painting with small brush strokes. On these 14 pages, you'll find ideas for postage-stamp backyards, patio plantings, narrow side yards, parking strips, and the ultimate in small gardens: the deck.

SPLIT-LEVEL GARDEN

This group of three interlocking beds is adaptable to many a small yard. The "island" design can enliven a lawn or patio or form an oasis in an expanse of bare earth or gravel, and the two raised sections make it easy to tailor the planting scheme to suit your taste. In the plan we show, the raised-bed parts hold flowering perennials (suited to Zones 3–10, 14–24, 33), but they could just as well feature vegetables or herbs, leaving the ground-level bed free for seasonal color. Reverse the arrangement and you could have edible row crops at ground level, a cut-flower garden in the raised parts. This planting gives you color from late spring into fall, with a peak in early summer. To extend the plan into Zones 32, 34, and 35, use *Oenothera fruticosa* in place of the two Mexican evening primroses suggested under L and M in the list below.

PLANT LIST

A. **Gaura lindheimeri** (2)

B. **Hemerocallis, yellow cultivar.** Daylily (3)

C. **Perovskia atriplicifolia.** Russian sage (2)

D. **Achillea millefolium, Galaxy strain.** Common yarrow (2)

E. **Achillea 'Moonshine'** (1)

F. **Achillea tomentosa.** Woolly yarrow (1)

G. **Sedum 'Autumn Joy' (Hylotelephium 'Autumn Joy')** (3)

H. **Limonium latifolium.** Sea lavender (2)

I. **Salvia officinalis 'Purpurascens'.** Common sage (2)

J. **Coreopsis lanceolata 'Goldfink'** (3)

K. **Nepeta × faassenii.** Catmint (7)

L. **Oenothera speciosa 'Siskiyou' (O. berlandieri 'Siskiyou').** Mexican evening primrose (3)

M. **Oenothera speciosa 'Woodside White' (O. berlandieri 'Woodside White').** Mexican evening primrose (3).

N. **Santolina chamaecyparissus.** Lavender cotton (3)

O. **Stachys byzantina 'Silver Carpet'.** Lamb's ears (12)

P. **Ceratostigma plumbaginoides.** Dwarf plumbago (1)

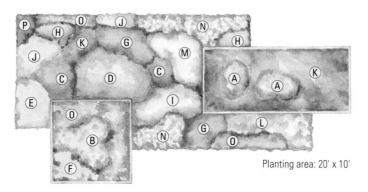

Planting area: 20' x 10'

BACKYARD EDEN

Though this space is only 30 feet deep and 40 feet wide, it offers the amenities of a large yard. There's an ample deck for lounging and entertaining, and enough lawn to provide play space for children and pets (and the occasional round of croquet). An orange or lemon tree satisfies that urge for home-grown produce; a compact rose garden promises plenty of flowers to enjoy both indoors and out. Finally, the view from the house is framed by plantings that remain attractive all year. The garden is at its showiest in mid- to late spring, but you will enjoy color throughout the warmer times of year. The citrus tree identifies this plan as one for mild-winter regions: Zones 8, 9, 14–24.

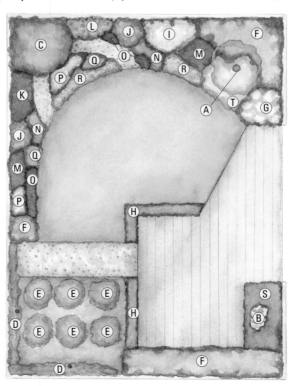

Planting area: 40' x 30'

ALL THE GARDEN A PATIO

If the thought of mowing even a small lawn is anathema to you, consider transforming your 30- by 40-foot yard into a patio garden. In this design, the entire space is visible from the house, drawing you outdoors to experience the plantings close up. The 5-foot-square pavers are arranged to form several intimate nooks, where benches or chaises longues invite you to linger and enjoy the blossoms of bougainvillea and bright perennials (color is at its height in early summer). Beneath the shade of a Brazilian butterfly tree, a tranquil pool offers a soothing note—and a home for gleaming koi, if you're so inclined. Use this planting scheme in Zones 12, 13, 15–17, 19, 22–28.

Acanthus mollis

PLANT LIST

A. Bougainvillea 'California Gold' ('Sunset') (2)

B. Bougainvillea 'Tahitian Dawn' (2)

C. × Fatshedera lizei (1)

D. Bauhinia forficata (B. corniculata, B. candicans). Brazilian butterfly tree (1)

E. Yucca gloriosa. Spanish dagger (1)

F. Osmanthus fragrans. Sweet olive (3)

G. Feijoa sellowiana. Pineapple guava (3)

H. Pittosporum tobira 'Wheeler's Dwarf'. Tobira (11)

I. Punica granatum 'Nana'. Dwarf pomegranate (7)

J. Abelia 'Edward Goucher' (Abelia × grandiflora 'Edward Goucher') (3)

K. Rhaphiolepis (Raphiolepis) indica 'Clara'. India hawthorn (2)

L. Dietes bicolor. Fortnight lily (3)

M. Agapanthus orientalis. Lily-of-the-Nile (3)

N. Agapanthus 'Peter Pan'. Lily-of-the-Nile (10)

O. Hemerocallis, large yellow cultivar. Daylily (6)

P. Hemerocallis 'Black-eyed Stella'. Daylily (5)

Q. Liriope muscari 'Silvery Sunproof'. Big blue lily turf (9)

R. Ophiopogon japonicus. Mondo grass (24)

S. Acanthus mollis. Bear's breech (4)

T. Erigeron karvinskianus. Mexican daisy, Santa Barbara daisy (15)

U. Achillea tomentosa 'King George'. Woolly yarrow (14)

V. Verbena rigida 'Flame' (7)

W. Verbena tenuisecta 'Tapien Purple'. Moss verbena (20)

X. Ajuga reptans. Carpet bugle (24)

Y. Teucrium chamaedrys 'Prostratum'. Germander (22)

Z. Hedera helix 'Glacier'. English ivy (12 starts)

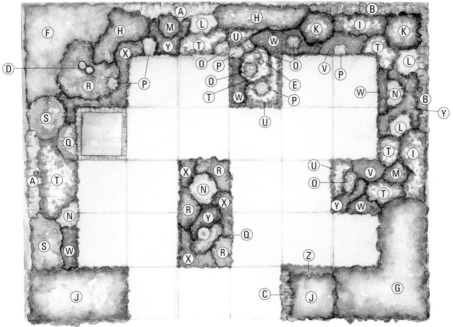

Planting area: 40' x 30'

KEEP IT SIMPLE

Though this design calls for nineteen different plants, it doesn't have a busy look: it gives the impression of unity and simplicity. Shrubs are its mainstay, and the mass planting of just a few sorts helps draw the garden together. Thanks to the profusion of rhododendrons and azaleas, the flower show is most striking in late spring, but bloom begins earlier on, with late winter's flowering quince and the redbud's flashy pink early-spring display. Even when flowers are not present, the garden has a subtle sparkle from colorful and variegated foliage on redbud, heather, iris, lily-of-the-valley shrub, and several other plants. Zones 4–6, 14–17 are best for this plan, but it will also succeed in Zones 34, 37, and 39 if you make a few changes: substitute locally successful rhododendrons and azaleas for those suggested under E through I in the list below, use carpet bugle *(Ajuga reptans)* in place of blue star creeper (R), and eliminate the gladwin iris (O).

PLANT LIST

A. **Acer palmatum 'Sango Kaku'.** Japanese maple (1)

B. **Cercis canadensis 'Forest Pansy'.** Eastern redbud (2)

C. **Chaenomeles 'Toyo Nishiki'.** Flowering quince (1)

D. **Clematis 'Henryi'** (2)

E. **Rhododendron 'Lem's Monarch' ('Pink Walloper')** (1)

F. **Rhododendron 'Unique'** (1)

G. **Rhododendron 'Moonstone'** (1)

H. **Rhododendron 'PJM'** (6)

I. **Rhododendron (azalea) 'Gumpo'** (4)

J. **Euonymus fortunei 'Emerald Gaiety'** (8)

K. **Pieris japonica 'Variegata'.** Lily-of-the-valley shrub (3)

L. **Calluna vulgaris 'Blazeaway'.** Heather (5)

M. **Hosta 'Frances Williams'** (3)

N. **Hosta 'Hadspen Blue'** (4)

O. **Iris foetidissima 'Variegata'.** Gladwin iris (2)

P. **Helleborus orientalis.** Lenten rose (5)

Q. **Sagina subulata 'Aurea'.** Scotch moss (3-inch squares, set 6 inches apart)

R. **Pratia pedunculata (Laurentia fluviatilis, Isotoma fluviatilis).** Blue star creeper (twelve 3-inch squares, set 6 inches apart)

S. **Equisetum hyemale.** Horsetail (1, in pot in pool)

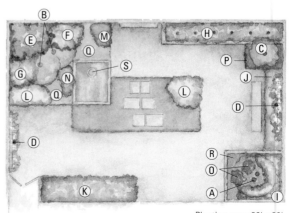

Planting area: 30' x 20'

SUMMER SHOWPIECE

Jam packed with color, this jewel-like planting is a mere 20 feet deep and 30 feet wide. Stroll along the path that leads throughout the garden, pausing to admire each plant; or, for prolonged contemplation, take advantage of a sheltered gazebo or *plein air* bench. The planting is designed for chilly-winter Zones 3–6, 32–41, where summer is the prime season for floral splendor and outdoor living. The flowering year, though, begins in spring, with the early show of serviceberry, wisteria, sand cherry, and lily-of-the-valley followed by the later spring blossoms of cranberry bush, mountain laurel, and Siberian iris.

PLANT LIST

A. Amelanchier × grandiflora. Apple serviceberry (1)

B. Wisteria sinensis. Chinese wisteria (1)

C. Prunus × cistena. Purple-leaf sand cherry (2)

D. Viburnum opulus 'Compactum'. European cranberry bush (2)

E. Kalmia latifolia. Mountain laurel (2)

F. Kalmia latifolia 'Elf'. Mountain laurel (2)

G. Spiraea × bumalda 'Goldflame' (4)

H. Spiraea japonica 'Shirobana' ('Shibori') (3)

I. Berberis thunbergii. Japanese barberry (4)

J. Berberis thunbergii 'Crimson Pygmy'. Japanese barberry (1)

K. Potentilla fruticosa 'Abbotswood'. Cinquefoil (3)

L. Calamagrostis × acutiflora 'Karl Foerster' ('Stricta'). Feather reed grass (1)

M. Gypsophila paniculata 'Bristol Fairy'. Baby's breath (3)

N. Geranium himalayense (G. grandiflorum) 'Birch Double' ('Plenum') (8)

O. Coreopsis verticillata 'Moonbeam'. Threadleaf coreopsis (4)

P. Penstemon digitalis 'Husker Red' (4)

Q. Iris, Siberian, blue cultivar (e.g. 'Orville Fay') (4)

R. Heuchera 'Palace Purple' (7)

S. Nepeta × faassenii. Catmint (4)

T. Prunella grandiflora. Self-heal (16)

U. Campanula portenschlagiana (C. muralis). Dalmatian bellflower (5)

V. Thymus praecox arcticus 'Coccineum' (T. serpyllum 'Coccineum'). Mother-of-thyme, creeping thyme (8)

W. Convallaria majalis. Lily-of-the-valley (12)

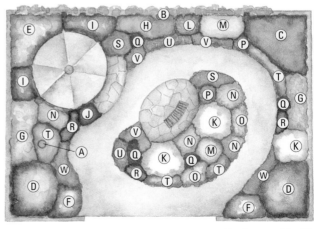

Planting area: 30' x 20'

Pacific Coast native iris

A SECRET-GARDEN PATIO

From inside the house, you see a bit of paving, a stunning actinidia vine on a trellis, and just a hint of something beyond. Venturing outside, you discover a leafy, secluded retreat screened from the house yet still linked to it by the flow of paving and plantings. The look is serene, not flashy: color comes and goes with the seasons, sparking the garden here and there. Varied foliage textures and colors sustain interest for most of the year. The plan is especially well suited to Zones 4–6, 15–17; it also thrives in Zones 7–9 if you substitute locally successful rhododendrons for those listed under E and F on the facing page. To enjoy this patio in Zone 32 as well, again choose rhododendrons that thrive in your climate, and replace the Pacific Coast iris (P) with iris 'Paltec'.

PLANT LIST

A. **Cercis canadensis 'Forest Pansy'.** Eastern redbud (1)

B. **Corylus avellana 'Contorta'.**
Harry Lauder's walking stick (1)

C. **Chimonanthus praecox (C. fragrans).** Wintersweet (1)

D. **Acer palmatum 'Ever Red' ('Dissectum Atropurpureum').** Japanese maple (2)

E. **Rhododendron 'Trude Webster'** (2)

F. **Rhododendron 'Unique'** (1)

G. **Pieris japonica 'Mountain Fire'.**
Lily-of-the-valley shrub (4)

H. **Pieris japonica 'Variegata'.** Lily-of-the-valley shrub (2)

I. **Rhododendron (azalea) 'Gumpo'** (4)

J. **Mahonia bealei.** Leatherleaf mahonia (2)

K. **Skimmia reevesiana (S. fortunei)** (18)

L. **Actinidia kolomikta** (2)

M. **Clematis 'Henryi'** (2)

N. **Hakonechloa macra 'Aureola'.**
Japanese forest grass (8)

O. **Hosta 'Sum and Substance'** (2)

P. **Iris, Pacific Coast native** (5)

Q. **Alchemilla mollis.** Lady's-mantle (6)

R. **Helleborus orientalis.** Lenten rose (10)

S. **Epimedium grandiflorum 'White Queen'.**
Bishop's hat (22)

T. **Sagina subulata 'Aurea'.** Scotch moss
(3-inch squares, set 6 inches apart)

U. **Pachysandra terminalis 'Silver Edge' ('Variegata').**
Japanese spurge (sprigs, set 1 foot apart)

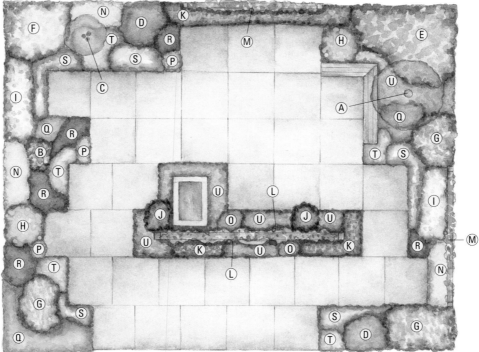

Planting area: 40' x 30'

ALL DECKED OUT

Ready for a long, warm summer, this deck brims with inviting color and enticing fragrances. Its anchor points are the two citrus trees that frame the trellises and provide a leafy, scented backdrop for the seating. In Zones 14–24, where these plants succeed (provided the angel's trumpet is protected from freezes in Zones 14 and 15), bloom begins in midspring and continues into fall. Long-flowering perennials are featured, and assorted annuals intensify the color. Further color notes come from non-green foliage on New Zealand flax, lily turf, heuchera, begonia, licorice plant, dusty miller, 'Crystal Palace' lobelia, and assorted succulents.

PLANT LIST

A. Citrus (lemon or orange) (2)
AS UNDERPLANTING: **Lobularia maritima, white** (sweet alyssum)

B. Brugmansia candida.
Angel's trumpet (1)
AS UNDERPLANTING: **Gazania hybrid, cream; Helichrysum petiolare 'Limelight'** (licorice plant)

C. Abutilon megapotamicum.
Flowering maple (2, on trellises)
AS UNDERPLANTING: **Begonia** (bedding type, bronze leaves); **Liriope muscari 'Silvery Sunproof'** (big blue lily turf); **Campanula poscharskyana** (Serbian bellflower)

D. Buxus microphylla japonica.
Japanese boxwood (15)

E. Phormium 'Maori Maiden'.
New Zealand flax (1)
AS UNDERPLANTING: **Petunia × hybrida, pink; Centaurea cineraria** (dusty miller); **Helichrysum petiolare** (licorice plant)

F. Heliotropium arborescens (H. peruvianum).
Common heliotrope (3)
AS UNDERPLANTING: **Brachycome multifida** (Swan River daisy); **Verbena × hybrida, white**

G. Agapanthus 'Peter Pan'.
Lily-of-the-Nile (1)
AS UNDERPLANTING: **Nierembergia hippomanica violacea 'Mont Blanc'** (dwarf cup flower); **Lobelia erinus 'Crystal Palace'**

H. Hemerocallis 'Stella de Oro'.
Daylily (2)
AS UNDERPLANTING: **Lobelia erinus, white**

I. Heuchera 'Palace Purple' (4)

J. Echeveria imbricata (hen and chicks) (1); **Sedum sieboldii (Hylotelephium sieboldii)** (1); **Sempervivum, bronze cultivar** (houseleek) (2)

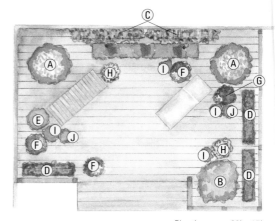

Planting area: 20' x 15'

A SHADY RETREAT

Cool and leafy, this deck is a serene oasis, a perfect place for just relaxing. Thanks to shade from house walls and off-deck trees, it's ideal for deckscaping with favorite shade plants. Unlike the sunny, mass-of-color plan shown opposite, this one gives you flower color in individual bursts off and on from winter through summer. But colorful and variegated foliage does offer a display throughout the growing season: coleus in a rainbow of hues, non-green foliage on hosta, dead nettle, bishop's weed, and heuchera. Try this plan in Zones 4–9, 14–21, being sure to move the potted fuchsia to a sheltered, frost-free spot during winter.

Planting area: 22' x 16'

PLANT LIST

A. Acer palmatum 'Bloodgood'. Japanese maple (1)
AS UNDERPLANTING: **Lamium maculatum 'White Nancy'** (dead nettle)

B. Camellia japonica 'Nuccio's Pearl' (1)
AS UNDERPLANTING: **Campanula poscharskyana** (Serbian bellflower)

C. Hydrangea macrophylla, French hybrid. Bigleaf hydrangea (1)

D. Rhododendron (azalea) 'Sherwood Pink' (1)

E. Aegopodium podagraria. Bishop's weed (4)

F. Impatiens wallerana (9)

G. Hosta 'Gold Edger' (4)

H. Fuchsia 'Gartenmeister Bonstedt' (1)

I. Heuchera 'Pewter Veil' (1)

J. Hosta sieboldiana 'Elegans' (2)

K. Coleus × hybridus (6)

L. All pots on slat bench are bonsai specimens

PLANT LIST

A. **Lonicera × heckrottii.**
   Gold flame honeysuckle (4)

B. **Ribes sanguineum.** Pink winter currant (1)

C. **Digitalis × mertonensis.** Foxglove (7)

D. **Iris foetidissima.** Gladwin iris (3)

E. **Liriope muscari 'Silvery Sunproof'.**
   Big blue lily turf (6)

F. **Polystichum polyblepharum.**
   Japanese lace fern (2)

G. **Bergenia cordifolia.**
   Heartleaf bergenia (5)

H. **× Heucherella tiarelloides
   'Bridget Bloom'** (6)

I. **Corydalis lutea** (6)

J. **Lamium maculatum 'White Nancy'.**
   Dead nettle (8)

K. **Campanula poscharskyana.**
   Serbian bellflower (7+)

L. **Ajuga reptans.** Carpet bugle (8)

M. **Sagina subulata 'Aurea'.**
   Scotch moss (about twenty-two
   3-inch squares, set 6 inches apart)

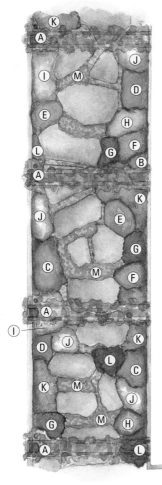

Planting area: 8' x 30'

DOWN THE GARDEN PATH

All too often, the narrow strip between side house wall and property line is ignored, left to serve as a drab conduit between front and back yards. But if you choose your plants carefully, there's no reason you can't include this no-man's-land in the grander scheme of your garden. Here, a stone path leads through an inviting bower. Fragrant honeysuckle on the overheads gives a sense of enclosure, while various low-growing plants and ground covers provide a patchwork carpet of leaf and flower color, punctuated here and there by the vertical accents of foxglove and gladwin iris. Zones 4–9, 14–24, and 32 are congenial climates for this plan; color reaches its peak in spring.

PASSAGEWAY GARDEN

Even a formal, essentially straight path offers an opportunity to transform a forgotten side yard into a passageway garden, with plantings that give you a reason to slow down and admire the view. The lively assortment shown here thrives in day-long dappled sun or light shade, or in a situation where sunny mornings are followed by light shade in the afternoon. Summer bloom time brings the brightest display, but you'll also enjoy more subtle color throughout the growing season from variegated and non-green foliage. This plan does best in Zones 3–6, 32–35, 37, 39–41.

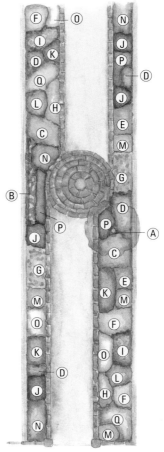

Planting area: 8' x 35'

PLANT LIST

A. **Amelanchier × grandiflora.** Apple serviceberry (1)

B. **Clematis 'Hagley Hybrid'** (1)

C. **Alchemilla mollis.** Lady's-mantle (4)

D. **Polygonatum odoratum 'Variegatum'.** Solomon's seal (6)

E. **Astrantia major.** Masterwort (3)

F. **Astilbe × arendsii 'Peach Blossom'** (4+)

G. **Astilbe simplicifolia 'Sprite'** (6)

H. **Athyrium nipponicum 'Pictum' (A. goeringianum 'Pictum').** Japanese painted fern (5)

I. **Brunnera macrophylla 'Variegata'** (4)

J. **Heuchera 'Pewter Veil'** (4)

K. **Corydalis flexuosa 'Blue Panda'** (6)

L. **Hosta 'Frances Williams'** (2)

M. **Hosta 'Shade Fanfare'** (4)

N. **Hosta 'Hadspen Blue'** (9+)

O. **Pulmonaria saccharata 'Mrs. Moon'.** Bethlehem sage (6+)

P. **Campanula portenschlagiana (C. muralis).** Dalmatian bellflower (6)

Q. **Hakonechloa macra 'Aureola'.** Japanese forest grass (4)

Agapanthus orientalis

ROADSIDE RIOT

In many suburbs, city planners incorporate parking strips into street design—and indeed, these zones between street and sidewalk offer a great gardening opportunity that homeowners too often waste on lawn. Despite their narrowness (widths vary from 3 to about 6 feet), the plots can pack in a dazzling variety of colorful plants, affording both you and passersby great pleasure. What you need are tough plants and, in much of the country, a rudimentary watering system: sandwiched between strips of pavement, these areas can dry out rapidly. In the planting shown here (ideal for Zones 14–24), a kaleidoscope of California favorites sizzles with color from spring through summer.

PLANT LIST

A. Agapanthus orientalis.
Lily-of-the-Nile (4)

B. Phormium 'Yellow Wave'.
New Zealand flax (1)

C. Hemerocallis, cream cultivar.
Daylily (4)

D. Pennisetum setaceum
'Burgundy Blaze' ('Rubrum Dwarf').
Fountain grass (3)

E. Erigeron karvinskianus.
Mexican daisy,
Santa Barbara daisy (2)

F. Convolvulus cneorum.
Bush morning glory (2)

G. Aloe saponaria (4)

H. Echeveria imbricata.
Hen and chicks (5)

I. Osteospermum fruticosum.
Trailing African daisy (6)

J. Oenothera speciosa
(O. berlandieri).
Mexican evening primrose (5)

K. Verbena tenuisecta 'Tapien Purple'.
Moss verbena (8)

L. Teucrium gussonei (T. cossonii,
T. majoricum). Germander (4)

M. Cerastium tomentosum.
Snow-in-summer (11)

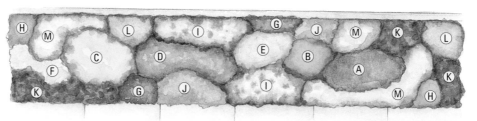

Planting area: 30' x 5½'

TRAFFIC STOPPER

Knockout color guaranteed! Blazing in hot hues (with a tempering touch of cool blue and purple), these plants are rugged customers, well suited to life on the street. They're impressively tolerant of varied climates too, thriving in Zones 3–9, 14–17, and 29–41—areas that encompass virtually the entire spectrum of summer and winter conditions. From late spring until autumn, you can count on an arresting show of colorful flowers, with the lamb's ears and fescue providing colored foliage as well. Aside from the shrubby blue mist, all the plants are perennials that need just an annual cleanup (in late fall or early spring, depending on climate) to stay tidy.

TOP: *Gaillardia* × *grandiflora* 'Goblin'
BOTTOM: *Hemerocallis* 'Stella de Oro'

PLANT LIST

A. **Caryopteris** × **clandonensis.** Blue mist (2)

B. **Asclepias tuberosa.** Butterfly weed (1)

C. **Liatris spicata 'Kobold'.** Gayfeather (4)

D. **Sedum 'Autumn Joy' (Hylotelephium 'Autumn Joy')** (2)

E. **Festuca 'Elijah Blue'.** Blue fescue (9)

F. **Gaillardia** × **grandiflora 'Goblin'.** Blanket flower (10)

G. **Hemerocallis 'Stella de Oro'.** Daylily (7)

H. **Achillea tomentosa.** Woolly yarrow (10)

I. **Salvia** × **superba 'May Night'** (14)

J. **Iberis sempervirens 'Snowflake'.** Evergreen candytuft (5)

K. **Stachys byzantina 'Silver Carpet'.** Lamb's ears (7)

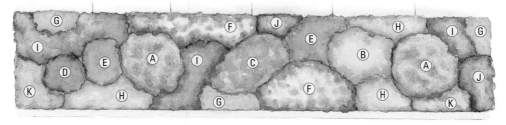

Planting area: 30' x 5½'

SPECIALTY PLANTINGS

Have you ever promised yourself a rose garden? Perhaps you've been yearning for a flower bed that can fill the house with summer bouquets, or for a garden all in white. This chapter can help you bring those dreams—and many more—to life. We start with "theme" ideas, from plans that showcase the beauties of one season to riotous cottage gardens to designs centered on pools (whether natural or made by the gardener). You'll find a trio of rose gardens, too: one modest, one grand, and one featuring heritage roses.

The next 15 designs are plantings with a purpose. Some are intended to provide flowers for cutting, others herbs for the kitchen; still others are filled with plants chosen for their fragrances. And gardeners who feel that no planting is complete without frequent attention from birds and butterflies won't be disappointed: we've designed five plans to attract just these visitors.

Finally, you'll find color-focused plantings—sizzling-hot combinations, vibrant or muted mixed colors, gray and cool-color plantings, white gardens, and two designs that derive color from foliage alone.

In riotous bloom from spring through summer, this assortment of cottage-garden perennials is a living outdoor bouquet that provides plenty of flowers for cutting, too. Design by Dariel Alexander.

THEMES AND VARIATIONS

Often, we design our gardens with a particular vision in mind: a glorious sweep of spring flowers, a rose plot lush with color and scent, a collection of water lovers to enhance a still backyard pool. If you have only a small space at your disposal, you know you'll have to be very selective in your choices; if your property is larger, you can let yourself go, adopting the motto "nothing succeeds like excess"! The plans on these 18 pages, varying in scale from modest to grand, address a number of themes: seasonal flowers, rose beds, cottage and mixed plantings, water gardens, and—for the ultimate in permanence—shrub collections.

SPRING SYMPHONY

As winter's drear slowly gives way to brighter days, nothing is more heartening than flowers. They first appear in scattered bursts, but as the season progresses, the garden is flooded in waves of bloom. The cheerful assortment of perennials shown here captures all the color and bounty of spring in one compact planting. Some of these plants continue their show into summer or at least offer briefer moments of color later in the year. You'll have the best results with this plan in climates offering some winter chill (Zones 3–9, 14–16, 33, and 34). However, you can also employ it in Zones 2, 35–41 if you make a few substitutions: in place of red-hot poker (A in the list below), use three plants of foxtail lily (*Eremurus,* Shelford hybrids); for gaura (K), substitute three *Penstemon digitalis* 'Husker Red'; for *Geranium* 'Johnson's Blue' (L), use *G. pratense.*

PLANT LIST

A. Kniphofia uvaria, yellow cultivar. Red-hot poker (1)

B. Baptisia australis. Blue false indigo (1)

C. Paeonia 'Festiva Maxima'. Peony (2)

D. Centranthus ruber 'Albus'. Jupiter's beard (4)

E. Penstemon barbatus 'Pink Beauty' (3)

F. Aster × frikartii 'Mönch' (4)

G. Chrysanthemum coccineum (Tanacetum coccineum, Pyrethrum roseum). Pyrethrum, painted daisy (3)

H. Iris, Siberian, 'Caesar's Brother' (1)

I. Hemerocallis, cream cultivar. Daylily (2)

J. Hemerocallis 'Stella de Oro'. Daylily (4)

K. Gaura lindheimeri 'Siskiyou Pink' (1)

L. Geranium 'Johnson's Blue' (4)

M. Papaver orientale, pink cultivar. Oriental poppy (1)

N. Geum chiloense 'Lady Stratheden' (2)

O. Heuchera 'Palace Purple' (6)

P. Iberis sempervirens 'Snowflake'. Evergreen candytuft (2)

Q. Campanula portenschlagiana (C. muralis). Dalmatian bellflower (2)

R. Aurinia saxatilis (Alyssum saxatile). Basket-of-gold (3)

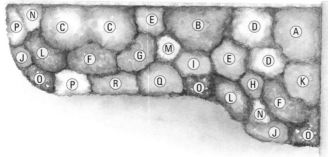

Planting area: 20' x 8'

SUMMER SPLENDOR

Spring may usher in the flowering year, but summer's show is no less dazzling. In fact, many summer-blooming perennials mount a longer-lasting display than spring bloomers do, staying showy throughout the summer and even into autumn. In keeping with the season's temperatures, many of these perennials offer distinctly warm colors. In the plan illustrated here, summery hues of yellow and rosy red are balanced with plenty of white and blue, cool shades that offer welcome (if only psychological!) relief on scorching days. These plants are suited to a wide range of climates: Zones 2–9, 14–17, 32–43.

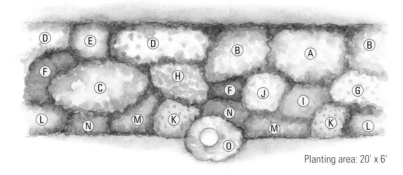

Planting area: 20' x 6'

Rudbeckia fulgida sullivantii 'Goldsturm'

A BACKYARD PRAIRIE

You don't have to live in the Midwest to enjoy a view of the prairie out your window: this backyard planting evokes the spirit of the plains, of sweeps of tall grass dotted with native daisies. It's less uniform in appearance than a true prairie, though, with a variety of grasses and perennial flowers set out in discrete drifts—it's a garden, not a recreated meadow. Flower color reaches its peak in summer. Count on these plants for toughness and relatively trouble-free performance in Zones 4–9, 14–17, 32–34. If you replace the feather grass (C in the list below) with purple moor grass (*Molinia caerulea arundinacea* 'Skyracer'), the plan will also succeed in Zones 3, 35, 37, and 39.

PLANT LIST

A. **Miscanthus sinensis 'Morning Light'**. Eulalia grass (1)

B. **Calamagrostis × acutiflora 'Karl Foerster' ('Stricta')**.
Feather reed grass (1)

C. **Stipa gigantea**. Feather grass (2)

D. **Molinia caerulea**. Purple moor grass (2)

E. **Helictotrichon sempervirens (Avena sempervirens)**.
Blue oat grass (5)

F. **Pennisetum alopecuroides 'Hameln'**.
Fountain grass (5)

G. **Festuca 'Elijah Blue'**.
Blue fescue (8)

H. **Perovskia atriplicifolia**. Russian sage (1)

I. **Rudbeckia fulgida sullivantii 'Goldsturm'**.
Black-eyed Susan (5)

J. **Echinacea purpurea 'White Swan'** (3)

K. **Liatris spicata 'Silvertips'**. Gayfeather (3)

L. **Achillea filipendulina 'Coronation Gold'**.
Fernleaf yarrow (4)

M. **Achillea millefolium, Galaxy strain**.
Common yarrow (5)

N. **Achillea 'Moonshine'** (5)

O. **Gaillardia × grandiflora 'Goblin'**. Blanket flower (6)

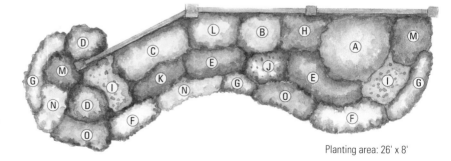

Planting area: 26' x 8'

HARVEST BOUNTY

Autumn clearly signals the close of the gardening year—but it's a terrific last act, brimming with color. Most of the flowering plants in this plan hold their fire through spring and summer, bursting into bloom only when the shorter, crisper days of fall arrive and deciduous trees and shrubs, too, display their year-end finery. The ornamental grasses vary their looks with the seasons, presenting here their last change of costume for the year. Try this plan as an autumn pick-me-up in Zones 3–21, 31–35, 37, 39. To enjoy it in Zones 2, 36, 38, 40, and 41 as well, substitute purple moor grass *(Molinia caerulea)* for the fountain grass (B in the list below).

Heliopsis helianthoides

PLANT LIST

A. Calamagrostis × acutiflora 'Karl Foerster' ('Stricta'). Feather reed grass (3)

B. Pennisetum alopecuroides. Fountain grass (2)

C. Helictotrichon sempervirens (Avena sempervirens). Blue oat grass (2)

D. Boltonia asteroides 'Snowbank' (4)

E. Heliopsis helianthoides 'Golden Plume' (H. scabra 'Golden Plume'). Ox-eye (4)

F. Solidago virgaurea 'Goldenmosa'. Goldenrod (3)

G. Aster novi-belgii 'Audrey'. New York aster (2)

H. Aster novi-belgii 'Marie Ballard'. New York aster (2)

I. Helenium autumnale 'Brilliant'. Common sneezeweed (2)

J. Hemerocallis 'Parian China'. Daylily (2)

K. Sedum 'Autumn Joy' (Hylotelephium 'Autumn Joy') (5)

L. Chrysanthemum pacificum (Dendranthema pacificum). Gold and silver chrysanthemum (2)

M. Chrysanthemum arcticum (Arctanthemum arcticum) (3)

N. Chrysanthemum × morifolium (Dendranthema grandiflorum), cream or light yellow cushion type. Florists' chrysanthemum (7)

Planting area: 20' x 7'

Planting area: 7' x 24'

THREE-SEASON MIXED GARDEN

From spring through fall, this garden's wrought-iron bench offers a prime vantage point for admiring the shifting colors of perennials, shrubs, and graceful crape myrtle. The illustration shows the planting in its early-summer dress, when the rockcress, daylily, cottage pink, and iris have already finished their bloom and the sedum and crape myrtle have yet to flower. Throughout the three growing seasons, you'll enjoy consistent non-green foliage color from the barberry, 'Moonshine' yarrow, lavender, sedum, 'Lime-mound' spiraea, and lamb's ears. This pleasant potpourri is available to gardeners in Zones 7–9, 14, 31.

PLANT LIST

A. Achillea millefolium, Galaxy strain, pink selection. Common yarrow (2)

B. Achillea 'Moonshine' (2)

C. Arabis caucasica (A. albida). Wall rockcress (1)

D. Berberis thunbergii 'Atropurpurea'. Red-leaf Japanese barberry (1)

E. Buxus microphylla koreana. Korean boxwood (8)

F. Clematis 'Henryi' (2)

G. Dianthus plumarius. Cottage pink (3)

H. Baptisia alba. White false indigo (1)

I. Echinacea purpurea. Purple coneflower (9)

J. Hemerocallis 'Little Grapette'. Daylily (5)

K. Iris, Siberian, 'Caesar's Brother' (6)

L. Lagerstroemia indica, pink cultivar. Crape myrtle (1)

M. Lavandula angustifolia. English lavender (3)

N. Liatris spicata 'Kobold'. Gayfeather (4)

O. Nepeta × faassenii. Catmint (5)

P. Rosa 'Heritage' (1)

Q. Rosa 'White Pet' (1)

R. Rosa 'New Dawn' (1)

S. Salvia × superba 'May Night' (4)

T. Sedum 'Autumn Joy' (Hylotelephium 'Autumn Joy') (7)

U. Spiraea × bumalda 'Limemound' (1)

V. Spiraea japonica 'Little Princess' (1)

W. Stachys byzantina 'Silver Carpet'. Lamb's ears (4)

LOW-MAINTENANCE MIXED PLANTING

Unique to this three-season planting is its composition: all the plants are shrubby, from shrubby perennials through true shrubs to a magnolia that blurs the boundary between shrub and tree. The flowering year begins with the magnolia's waxy purple-and-white blossoms, then carries on with the springtime assortment of bloom shown here. Roses, cinquefoil, butterfly bush, blue mist, and dwarf plumbago sustain the show through summer and into early fall. And throughout the seasons, you'll have constant foliage interest from leaves in shades of yellow, bronze, and soft gray. Try this combination in Zones 4–6, 14–17, 32, 34.

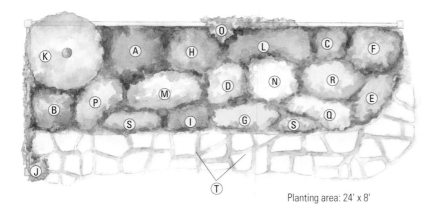

Planting area: 24' x 8'

PLANT LIST

A. **Abelia × grandiflora 'Sherwoodii'.** Glossy abelia (1)

B. **Berberis thunbergii 'Cherry Bomb'.** Japanese barberry (1)

C. **Buddleia davidii 'Black Knight'.** Butterfly bush (1)

D. **Caryopteris × clandonensis 'Worcester Gold'.** Blue mist (1)

E. **Ceratostigma plumbaginoides.** Dwarf plumbago (3)

F. **Erysimum 'Bowles Mauve'** (1)

G. **Genista lydia.** Broom (2)

H. **Lavandula angustifolia.** English lavender (3)

I. **Lavandula angustifolia 'Munstead'.** English lavender (2)

J. **Lonicera × heckrottii.** Gold flame honeysuckle (1)

K. **Magnolia 'Randy'** (1)

L. **Nandina domestica 'Woods Dwarf'.** Heavenly bamboo (3)

M. **Potentilla 'Katherine Dykes'.** Cinquefoil (2)

N. **Rosa 'Fair Bianca'** (1)

O. **Rosa 'New Dawn'** (1)

P. **Salvia officinalis 'Berggarten'.** Common sage (2)

Q. **Santolina chamaecyparissus 'Nana'.** Lavender cotton (3)

R. **Spiraea × bumalda 'Limemound'** (2)

S. **Teucrium chamaedrys 'Prostratum'.** Germander (5)

T. **Thymus pseudolanuginosus (T. lanuginosus).** Woolly thyme (between paving stones)

COMPLEAT COTTAGE GARDEN

Even if you don't have a 19th-century cottage, you can still have the garden that would go with it! The essence of such gardens is informality and apparent lack of plan; they give the impression of growing not by design, but simply according to the gardener's changing whims. The original cottage gardens contained just one representative of many different plants, and cottagers even mixed flowers with vegetables to create plantings that were practical as well as aesthetically pleasing. This contemporary homage to the cottage garden (best suited to Zones 4–7, 14, 34, 39) excludes the edibles, but it has all the other traditional characteristics: color, immense variety, and seemingly haphazard design. To adapt the plan to Zones 3, 35–38, 40, and 41, simply replace the lavender (F in the list below) with blue mist (*Caryopteris* × *clandonensis* 'Dark Knight' or 'Longwood Blue').

PLANT LIST

A. Rosa 'Cornelia' (1)

B. Rosa 'Ballerina' (1)

C. Rosa 'Iceberg' (1)

D. Syringa vulgaris 'President Lincoln'. Common lilac (1)

E. Spiraea × bumalda 'Anthony Waterer' (2)

F. Lavandula angustifolia. English lavender (4)

G. Paeonia 'Festiva Maxima'. Peony (3)

H. Gypsophila paniculata 'Perfecta'. Baby's breath (3)

I. Foeniculum vulgare 'Purpurascens' ('Smokey'). Bronze fennel (1)

J. Alcea rosea (Althaea rosea), Chater's Double strain. Hollyhock (3)

K. Delphinium elatum 'Summer Skies'. Candle delphinium (7)

L. Lupinus, Russell Hybrids. Russell lupine (3)

M. Achillea filipendulina 'Coronation Gold'. Fernleaf yarrow (5)

N. Chrysanthemum × superbum 'Alaska' (Leucanthemum maximum 'Alaska'). Shasta daisy (6)

O. Campanula persicifolia 'Telham Beauty'. Peach-leafed bluebell (5)

P. Aster × frikartii 'Mönch' (6)

Q. Iris, tall bearded, light yellow cultivar (7)

R. Geranium × oxonianum 'Claridge Druce' (4)

S. Scabiosa caucasica. Pincushion flower (6)

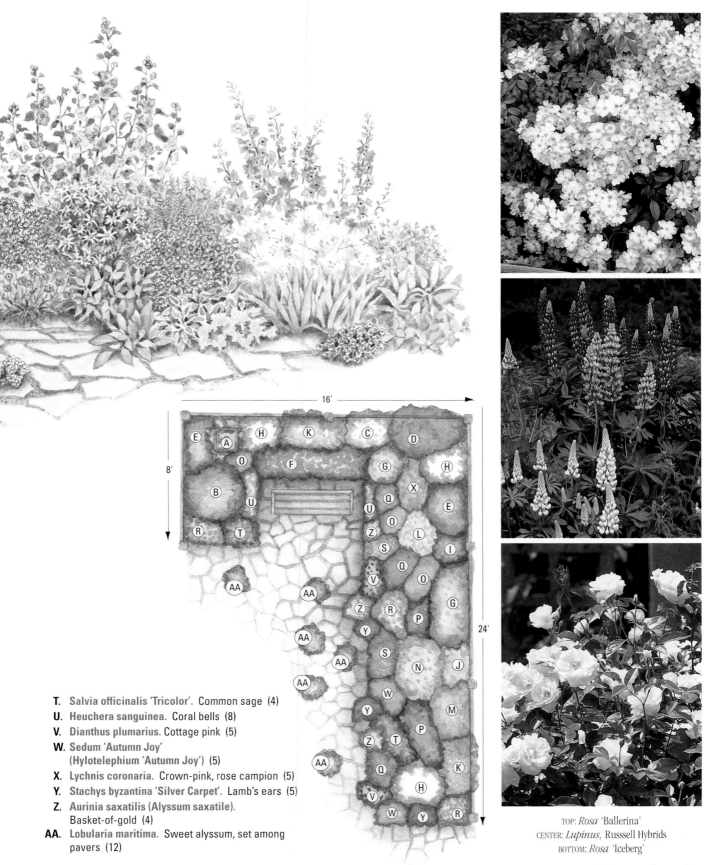

T. **Salvia officinalis 'Tricolor'.** Common sage (4)

U. **Heuchera sanguinea.** Coral bells (8)

V. **Dianthus plumarius.** Cottage pink (5)

W. **Sedum 'Autumn Joy'**
(Hylotelephium 'Autumn Joy') (5)

X. **Lychnis coronaria.** Crown-pink, rose campion (5)

Y. **Stachys byzantina 'Silver Carpet'.** Lamb's ears (5)

Z. **Aurinia saxatilis (Alyssum saxatile).**
Basket-of-gold (4)

AA. **Lobularia maritima.** Sweet alyssum, set among
pavers (12)

TOP: *Rosa* 'Ballerina'
CENTER: *Lupinus,* Russsell Hybrids
BOTTOM: *Rosa* 'Iceberg'

COTTAGE CORNER

Soft, fragrant, and colored in whites, creams, pinks, and blues—this is a cottage garden for fairy tales and romances. Many of the plants are frothy, billowy, and filmy, spilling into one another and onto the pavement, but the spikes of delphinium, foxglove, and campanula provide sharp vertical punctuation. Late spring and early summer find the garden at the zenith of its bloom, but the climbing rose, yarrow, delphinium, queen of the prairie, baby's breath, and bee balm continue to provide color later into the year. Zones 4–9, 14–16, and 32 suit all the plants listed; the plan will also succeed in Zones 34 and 39 if you substitute deep pink *Rosa* 'William Baffin' for 'Climbing Cécile Brunner' (M in the list at left).

PLANT LIST

A. **Achillea ptarmica 'The Pearl'** (9)

B. **Campanula glomerata, Alba strain** (6)

C. **Convallaria majalis.** Lily-of-the-valley (12)

D. **Delphinium elatum 'Summer Skies' and 'Galahad'.** Candle delphinium (9)

E. **Digitalis purpurea, Excelsior strain.** Common foxglove (7)

F. **Filipendula rubra 'Venusta'.** Queen of the prairie (5)

G. **Gypsophila paniculata 'Bristol Fairy'.** Baby's breath (5)

H. **Lavandula angustifolia 'Hidcote'.** English lavender (6)

I. **Linum perenne.** Perennial blue flax (14)

J. **Monarda didyma 'Croftway Pink'.** Bee balm (4)

K. **Nigella damascena 'Persian Jewels'.** Love-in-a-mist (19)

L. **Rosa gallica 'Versicolor' ('Rosa Mundi')** (2)

M. **Rosa 'Climbing Cécile Brunner'** (2)

N. **Viola wittrockiana, Imperial Antique Shades strain.** Pansy (20)

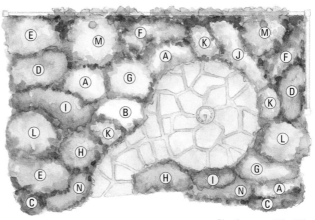

Planting area: 16' x 10'

A GATHERING OF SHRUBS

If you think of shrubs as nothing more than leafy green lumps, useful only for marking property lines, this planting will alter your perception. Leafy they are, but not all are green; and many have showy flowers, while some even bear decorative fruits. The assortment shown here (suited to Zones 3–9, 15–17, 32–35, 37, 39) features flower color off and on from midspring to late summer. Only the arborvitae and juniper are flowerless, but they make up for the lack with year-round color from non-green foliage. The entire scheme works as an island bed, but you can also use it as a boundary planting along a property margin or fence by eliminating the 'Minuet' weigela and the deutzia (L and M in the list at right).

For a planting suited to Zones 36, 38, 40, and 41 as well, replace *Viburnum* 'Eskimo' (B) with either *V. opulus* 'Compactum' or *V. trilobum* 'Compactum'.

PLANT LIST

A. **Viburnum prunifolium.** Black haw (1)

B. **Viburnum 'Eskimo'** (1)

C. **Hydrangea quercifolia 'Snow Queen'.** Oakleaf hydrangea (1)

D. **Philadelphus virginalis 'Glacier'.** Mock orange (1)

E. **Weigela florida 'Variegata'** (3)

F. **Berberis thunbergii 'Atropurpurea'.** Red-leaf Japanese barberry (1)

G. **Thuja occidentalis 'Yellow Ribbon'.** American arborvitae (1)

H. **Spiraea × bumalda 'Anthony Waterer'** (2)

I. **Caryopteris × clandonensis 'Worcester Gold'.** Blue mist (2)

J. **Juniperus sabina 'Blue Danube'.** Savin juniper (2)

K. **Cotoneaster adpressus praecox** (2)

L. **Weigela florida 'Minuet'** (3)

M. **Deutzia gracilis 'Nikko'.** Slender deutzia (2)

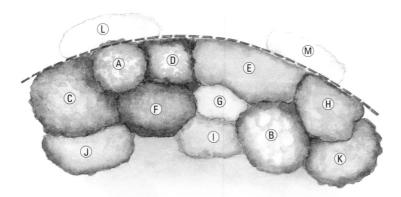

Planting area: 40' x 12' (excluding L and M)

CALIFORNIA COLLAGE

Cistus salviifolius

Abundant sunshine and relatively mild winters make California's Zones 14–24 an ideal climate for an amazing array of plants from around the globe. Those that do best here are also agreeable to one other California characteristic—a long dry period covering most of the growing season. This shrub border is an appropriately unthirsty array; all are flowering plants that reach a crescendo of color in late spring. Another trait they share is foliage in gray to grayish green, a leaf color typical of plants that hail from the world's drier places.

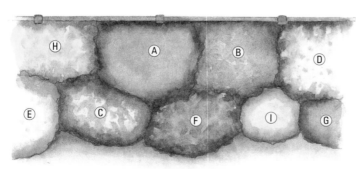

Planting area: 20' x 8'

PLANT LIST

A. **Anisodontea hypomandarum.** Cape mallow (1)

B. **Teucrium fruticans 'Azurea'.** Bush germander (1)

C. **Convolvulus cneorum.** Bush morning glory (2)

D. **Cistus ladanifer.** Crimson-spot rockrose (1+)

E. **Cistus salviifolius.** Sageleaf rockrose (1+)

F. **Cistus 'Warley Rose'.** Rockrose (1)

G. **Lavandula stoechas 'Otto Quast'.** Spanish lavender (1+)

H. **Phlomis fruticosa.** Jerusalem sage (1)

I. **Phlomis lanata** (1)

NOTABLY NORTHWESTERN

In western Washington and Oregon, gardeners consider the plants in this plan virtually foolproof: you plant them, they thrive. Assembled as a shrub border, they present a fetching array of foliage texture and color, as well as striking bursts of flower color from earliest spring well into summer. The Northwest's misty, overcast Zones 4–6 are ideal for these plants, and in these regions they'll take full sun all day. With a bit more attention, they'll succeed in Zones 16, 17, 34, and 37; here, the rhododendrons, lily-of-the-valley shrub, and hydrangea are likely to prefer a little afternoon shade in summer. For a plan suited to Zone 39, replace *Rhododendron* 'Christmas Cheer' (C in the list at right) with *R.* 'Vernus' and substitute *Daphne* × *burkwoodii* 'Carol Mackie' for lily-of-the-valley shrub (E).

PLANT LIST

A. **Magnolia liliiflora (M. quinquepeta).** Lily magnolia (1)

B. **Hydrangea serrata 'Preziosa'** (1)

C. **Rhododendron 'Christmas Cheer'** (1)

D. **Rhododendron (deciduous azalea) 'Irene Koster'** (2)

E. **Pieris japonica 'Variegata'.** Lily-of-the-valley shrub (1)

F. **Kalmia latifolia 'Elf'.** Mountain laurel (1)

G. **Spiraea japonica 'Shirobana' ('Shibori')** (1)

H. **Erica ciliaris 'Stoborough'.** Dorset heath (1+)

I. **Erica vagans 'Lyonesse'.** Cornish heath (1+)

J. **Calluna vulgaris 'Silver King'.** Heather (2)

K. **Calluna vulgaris 'Mrs. Pat'.** Heather (2)

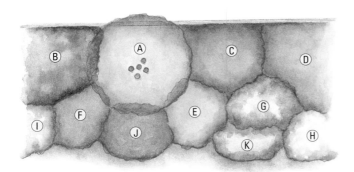

Planting area: 20' x 9'

A ROSY CORNER

So many choices, so little space! For many gardeners, that's the annual lament at bare-root planting time, when nurseries are flooded with roses of all sorts, from brand-new hybrid teas to old-fashioned heritage types. If you have only a modest plot available, make the most of it with this design. Including just 12 different roses, it nonetheless offers the full spectrum of colors in varieties of proven performance and popularity. An assortment of perennials fronts the bed, serving as a colorful, informal transition between the rather stiff rose bushes and the surrounding paving. Zones 4–9, 12–24, and 32 are best for this plan, but you can also use it in Zones 33, 34, and 39 if you give the roses winter protection.

PLANT LIST

A. **Rosa 'Climbing Iceberg'** (1)
B. **Rosa 'Altissimo'** (1)
C. **Rosa 'Queen Elizabeth'** (1)
D. **Rosa 'Peace'** (1)
E. **Rosa 'Fragrant Cloud'** (1)
F. **Rosa 'Mister Lincoln'** (1)
G. **Rosa 'Double Delight'** (1)
H. **Rosa 'Pascali'** (1)
I. **Rosa 'Perfume Delight'** (1)
J. **Rosa 'Amber Queen'** (1)
K. **Rosa 'Europeana'** (1)
L. **Rosa 'Angel Face'** (1)
M. **Lavandula angustifolia 'Munstead'.** English lavender (5)
N. **Geranium himalayense (G. grandiflorum) 'Birch Double' ('Plenum')** (2)
O. **Geranium cinereum 'Ballerina'** (4)
P. **Potentilla nepalensis 'Miss Willmott' ('Willmottiae').** Cinquefoil (4)
Q. **Dianthus plumarius.** Cottage pink (9)
R. **Stachys byzantina.** Lamb's ears (9)
S. **Cerastium tomentosum.** Snow-in-summer (6)

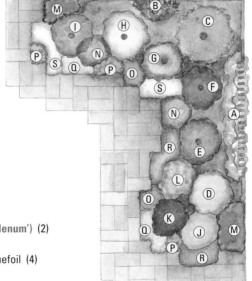

Planting area: 16' x 21'

ROSES IN THE GRAND MANNER

If rosemania strikes and you have the space to indulge it to the full, succumb to your desires with this formal design. It accommodates 51 plants, ranging from climbers to miniatures. The geometric layout, trelliswork, brick paving, and comfortable seating recall estate and park plantings of days gone by—old-fashioned in style, perhaps, but still providing effective display for a sizable rose collection. In maintenance terms, Zones 4–9, 12–24, 30, 32 are best for this planting, but it will also work in Zones 11, 33, 34, and 39 with winter protection for the roses (in Zones 34 and 39, you'll also need to overwinter the potted lily turf in a frost-sheltered spot).

Planting area: 34' x 28'

All plants in island are G except as noted.

PLANT LIST

A. Rosa 'New Dawn' (1)

B. Rosa 'Abraham Darby' (1)

C. Rosa 'Graham Thomas' (1)

D. Rosa 'The Fairy', as standard (2)

E. Rosa, hybrid tea (assorted) (26)

F. Rosa, floribunda cultivar (2)

G. Rosa, miniature (assorted) (18)

H. Lavandula × intermedia 'Grosso'. Lavandin (6)

I. Lavandula angustifolia 'Hidcote'. English lavender (8)

J. Artemisia stellerana 'Silver Brocade'. Beach wormwood (14)

K. Liriope muscari 'Majestic'. Big blue lily turf (in urn) (1)

ROSES FROM THE PAST

The roses of yesterday are not outmoded or obsolete. Quite to the contrary, they're being rediscovered, retrieved, and cherished by thousands of gardeners enchanted by the styles and histories of old or "heritage" roses. Unlike most modern hybrid teas, grandifloras, and floribundas, many heritage sorts are informal to lax shrubs that should not be planted in stiff, precisely spaced ranks. Give them room to mound, sprawl, or droop, then enjoy the resulting floral resplendence. This plan features eight old rose types—gallica, damask, alba, moss, China, tea, Noisette, and polyantha—in colors ranging from white and soft yellow to pink shades and deep red. Accompanying the roses are assorted perennials, many of them also suitably antique. Zones 4–9, 14–24 yield the best results; with winter protection of the climbers, Zone 32 is also possible.

Rosa 'Marie Louise'

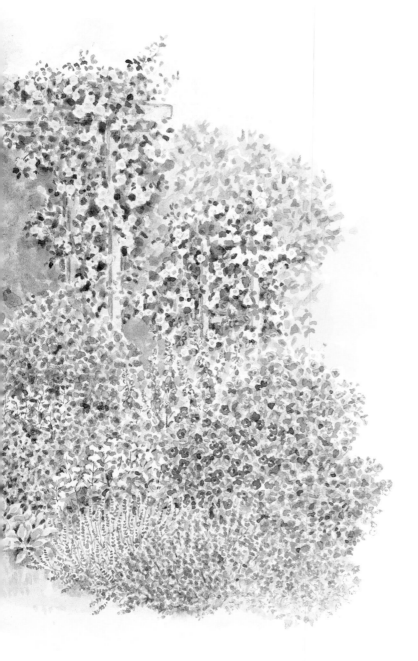

PLANT LIST

A. Rosa 'Awakening' (1)
B. Rosa 'Sombreuil' (1)
C. Rosa 'Alister Stella Gray' (1)
D. Rosa 'Alba Maxima' (1)
E. Rosa 'Great Maiden's Blush' (1)
F. Rosa 'Mme. Lambard' ('Mme. Lombard') (1)
G. Rosa 'Duchesse de Brabant' (1)
H. Rosa 'Marie Louise' (1)
I. Rosa 'Paul Ricault' (1)
J. Rosa 'Alfred de Dalmas' (1)
K. Rosa 'Empress Josephine' (1)
L. Rosa 'Perle d'Or' (1)
M. Rosa 'Hermosa' (1)
N. Rosa 'Comte de Chambord' (1)
O. Rosa 'Superb Tuscan' ('Tuscany Superb') (1)
P. Rosa 'Grüss an Aachen' (1)
Q. Rosa 'Pink Grüss an Aachen' (1)
R. Ilex cornuta 'Dazzler'. Chinese holly (6+)
S. Juniperus chinensis 'Hetz's Columnaris'.
     Chinese juniper (5)
T. Digitalis purpurea. Common foxglove (10)
U. Lavandula × intermedia 'Provence'.
     Lavandin (6)
V. Centranthus ruber 'Albus'.
     Jupiter's beard (7)
W. Geranium pratense. Meadow cranesbill (4)
X. Geranium sanguineum. Bloody cranesbill (4)
Y. Nepeta × faassenii. Catmint (7)
Z. Dianthus plumarius. Cottage pink (8)
AA. Iberis sempervirens 'Snowflake'.
     Evergreen candytuft (4)
BB. Aurinia saxatilis (Alyssum saxatile) 'Citrina'
     ('Lutea'). Basket-of-gold (5)
CC. Stachys byzantina 'Silver Carpet'.
     Lamb's ears (7)

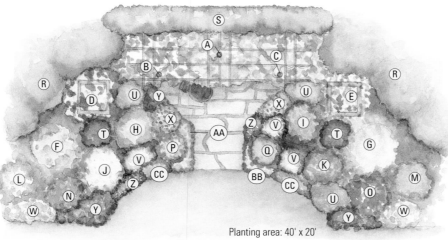

Planting area: 40' x 20'

A SHADED POOL

Soothing shade and tranquil water are sure to ease stress and restore the spirit. No strident colors assault the eye, demanding attention; instead, chartreuse and silvery leaves offer a counterpoint to basic green, while a smattering of pastel blossoms assort with the foliage in subtly attractive combinations. Bloom is most noticeable (though never overwhelming) in spring and summer. This serenity can be yours if you garden in Zones 4–9, 14–17, 32, and 34.

THE PLANTS

A. **Mahonia bealei.** Leatherleaf mahonia (1)

B. **Rhododendron 'Moonstone'** (1)

C. **Alchemilla mollis.** Lady's-mantle (3)

D. **Milium effusum 'Aureum'.** Bowles' golden grass (3)

E. **Hosta 'Gold Edger'** (16)

F. **Lamium maculatum 'White Nancy'.** Dead nettle (18)

G. **× Heucherella tiarelloides 'Pink Frost'** (5)

H. **Athyrium nipponicum 'Pictum' (A. goeringianum 'Pictum').** Japanese painted fern (5)

I. **Sagina subulata.** Irish moss (about sixteen 3-inch squares, set 6 inches apart)

J. **Nymphaea, hardy hybrid.** Water lily (optional) (1)

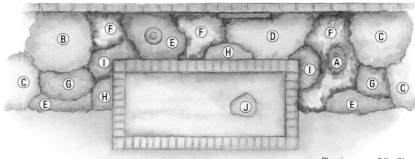

Planting area: 24' x 6'

GONE FISHIN'

You'd almost expect to find fish biting in this naturalistic pond. With luck, you'll have a suitable natural pond to adorn with these moisture-loving plants—but with a little contrivance, you can create your own pool and take the plan from there. Noteworthy is the assortment of foliage types: grasslike in rush and sedge, swordlike in irises and acorus, finely cut and fernlike in goat's beard and astilbe, huge and paddlelike in the ligularia. Flowering runs from spring through early fall, beginning with irises and marsh marigold and finishing with turtlehead, hardy ageratum, and astilbe. Try this plan in Zones 3–7, 15–17, 32, 34, 36–41.

Planting area: 19' x 11'

THE PLANTS

A. **Iris virginica.** Southern blue flag (3)

B. **Iris pseudacorus.** Yellow flag (3)

C. **Carex morrowii expallida (C. m. 'Variegata').** Variegated Japanese sedge (5)

D. **Juncus effusus.** Soft rush (1)

E. **Acorus gramineus 'Variegatus'** (2)

F. **Chelone obliqua.** Turtlehead (3)

G. **Caltha palustris.** Marsh marigold (2)

H. **Aruncus dioicus (A. sylvester).** Goat's beard (1)

I. **Filipendula ulmaria.** Meadow sweet (1)

J. **Eupatorium coelestinum 'Cori'.** Hardy ageratum (4)

K. **Astilbe chinensis taquetii 'Purple Lance'** (3)

L. **Astilbe simplicifolia 'Sprite'** (6)

M. **Ligularia stenocephala 'The Rocket'** (3)

DESIGNED FOR A PURPOSE

Anyone who plans and plants a garden wants the result to be beautiful. But sometimes the objectives go beyond mere prettiness to include a particular purpose. In the following pages, you'll find plans that focus on some of the "extras" gardeners most often want. For those who love fragrance, there are designs emphasizing scented flowers and foliage. A duo of cut-flower plantings will please those who like to take the garden indoors; a half-dozen plans for herb and kitchen gardens will delight cooks and history buffs alike. And for backyard naturalists, we've devised bird and butterfly gardens certain to deliver abundant seasonal entertainment.

SUMMER ANNUALS FOR CUTTING

Nothing equals annual flowers for abundance and duration of bloom. This flashy patch brings together some of the best cut-flower sorts, along with a single non-annual addition: a clump of shrubby perennial dahlias. A planting of this kind must be taken out when the growing season ends and started from scratch the next year; even the dahlias, though technically perennial tubers, should be lifted and stored over winter. Such yearly replanting does, of course, entail a fair amount of early-season labor—but your work will be rewarded with the garden's later luxuriance, as shown below. In addition, starting fresh each year lets you try out new arrangements, new color schemes, and new plant varieties as the mood strikes. And annuals offer one other undeniable advantage: they'll succeed in all zones.

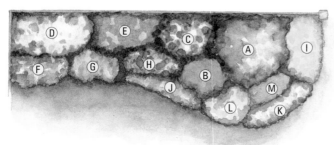

Planting area: 18' x 7'

PLANT LIST

A. Dahlia (2)

B. Moluccella laevis. Bells-of-Ireland (3)

C. Scabiosa atropurpurea. Pincushion flower (4)

D. Cosmos bipinnatus, Sensation strain (6)

E. Consolida ambigua, Steeplechase strain. Larkspur (3)

F. Centaurea cyanus. Cornflower, bachelor's button (6)

G. Antirrhinum majus. Snapdragon (6)

H. Helichrysum bracteatum. Strawflower (6)

I. Tagetes erecta, Sundance strain or other mid-height yellow. African marigold (8)

J. Tagetes patula. French marigold (6)

K. Limonium sinuatum. Sea lavender (6)

L. Zinnia elegans (6)

M. Celosia 'Plumosa'. Plume cockscomb (4)

A PERMANENT CUTTING GARDEN

Annuals don't have a lock on the cut-flower category. Many perennials, too, bloom lavishly enough to be enjoyed indoors as well as in their garden beds. This simple rectangle, measuring just 6 feet across, contains some of the best, most widely adapted cut-flower perennials, all suited to Zones 1–9, 14, 18–21, 32–43. Bloom reaches a peak in summer—but the first flowers appear in spring, and the show doesn't completely close until fall.

Tucked in among the perennial throng is one indispensable "outsider": the hybrid tea rose 'Mister Lincoln'. What is the classic cut flower, after all, if not a long-stemmed red rose?

Because the planting is bounded on three sides by lawn and pavement, access for maintenance is simple. In Zones 1–3, 32–43, this maintenance will include some degree of winter protection for 'Mister Lincoln'.

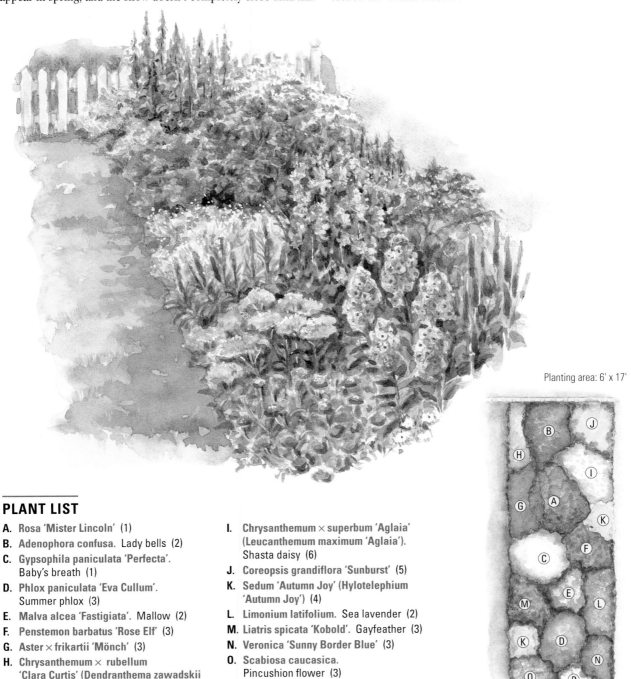

Planting area: 6' x 17'

PLANT LIST

A. Rosa 'Mister Lincoln' (1)

B. Adenophora confusa. Lady bells (2)

C. Gypsophila paniculata 'Perfecta'. Baby's breath (1)

D. Phlox paniculata 'Eva Cullum'. Summer phlox (3)

E. Malva alcea 'Fastigiata'. Mallow (2)

F. Penstemon barbatus 'Rose Elf' (3)

G. Aster × frikartii 'Mönch' (3)

H. Chrysanthemum × rubellum 'Clara Curtis' (Dendranthema zawadskii 'Clara Curtis') (3)

I. Chrysanthemum × superbum 'Aglaia' (Leucanthemum maximum 'Aglaia'). Shasta daisy (6)

J. Coreopsis grandiflora 'Sunburst' (5)

K. Sedum 'Autumn Joy' (Hylotelephium 'Autumn Joy') (4)

L. Limonium latifolium. Sea lavender (2)

M. Liatris spicata 'Kobold'. Gayfeather (3)

N. Veronica 'Sunny Border Blue' (3)

O. Scabiosa caucasica. Pincushion flower (3)

P. Dianthus × allwoodii 'Aqua'. Pink (3)

BREATHE DEEPLY

Viola odorata varieties

Step into the garden, take a seat on the strategically placed bench, and inhale! This planting combines over a dozen famously fragrant perennials and shrubs—but you won't have to risk olfactory overload by trying to take in their varied perfumes all at once. Flowering starts with sweet violets in early spring, then progresses to lily-of-the-valley, lilac, mock orange, viburnum, and peony as the season advances. The remaining plants begin their bloom in late spring or early summer; in milder regions, rose and heliotrope will linger into autumn. All these plants should thrive in Zones 2–6, 32–41, though the potted heliotrope will need winter shelter in a frost-free location.

PLANT LIST

A. Syringa vulgaris 'President Lincoln'. Common lilac (1)

B. Viburnum carlesii. Korean spice viburnum (1)

C. Clethra alnifolia. Summersweet (2)

D. Philadelphus virginalis 'Dwarf Minnesota Snowflake'. Mock orange (1)

E. Rosa 'Rotes Meer' ('Purple Pavement') (2)

F. Paeonia 'Edulis Superba'. Peony (2)

G. Dictamnus albus. Gas plant (2)

H. Phlox paniculata 'Eva Cullum'. Summer phlox (4)

I. Hemerocallis lilio-asphodelus (H. flava). Lemon daylily (5)

J. Convallaria majalis. Lily-of-the-valley (7)

K. Viola odorata. Sweet violet (7)

L. Reseda odorata. Mignonette (12)

M. Heliotropium arborescens (H. peruvianum). Common heliotrope (1, in pot)

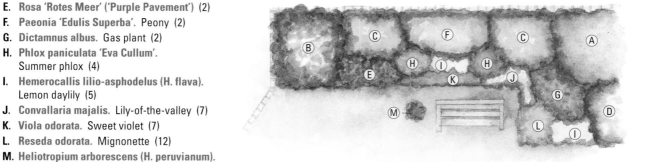

Planting area: 24' x 9'

A SCENTED RETREAT

In milder-winter Zones 9, 14–24, this plan gives gardeners even more to savor than fabulously fragrant flowers. Fully a third of the garden's occupants have leaves that reward a casual pinch or crush with a puff of perfume—lemon, pineapple, anise, mint, and that fragrance in a class of its own: lavender. Shrubs form the backbone of the garden; perennials and one bulb (soft pink, headily sweet amarcrinum) fill out the design. Pockets of two blooming annuals—flowering tobacco and sweet alyssum—complete the bouquet. Vining woodbine adds a double dose of color: its blooms are followed by shiny red berries.

PLANT LIST

A. Lonicera periclymenum 'Serotina'. Woodbine (1)

B. Buddleia davidii 'Black Knight'. Butterfly bush (1)

C. Rosa 'Frau Dagmar Hartopp' ('Fru Dagmar Hastrup') (2)

D. Aloysia triphylla (Lippia citriodora). Lemon verbena (1)

E. Lavandula angustifolia. English lavender (2)

F. Lavandula × intermedia 'Grosso'. Lavandin (7)

G. Agastache foeniculum. Anise hyssop (2)

H. Salvia elegans. Pineapple sage (2)

I. Iris, tall bearded, purple cultivar (2)

J. × Amarcrinum memoria-corsii (× A. 'Howardii', × Crinodonna memoria-corsii) (1)

K. Calamintha nepetoides. Calamint (3)

L. Dianthus plumarius. Cottage pink (6)

M. Teucrium gussonei (T. cossonii, T. majoricum). Germander (3)

N. Nicotiana alata. Flowering tobacco (4)

O. Nicotiana alata, Domino strain. Flowering tobacco (6)

P. Lobularia maritima. Sweet alyssum (16)

Q. Gardenia jasminoides 'White Gem' (1, in container)

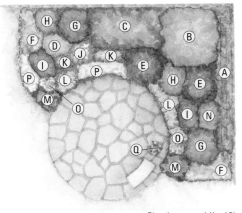

Planting area: 14' x 18'

Chives *(Allium schoenoprasum)*

POCKET-SIZE HERB SAMPLER

Just 48 square feet is space enough for a diverse assortment of scented herbs plus a compatible fragrant rose. Seven of the nine herbs have culinary uses, making this planting especially appealing to cooks (particularly if it's located near a kitchen door). The two nonculinary choices—lavender cotton and catmint—add to the plot's beauty with their soft textures and equally soft gray-green to gray-white leaf color. In fact, much of this garden's charm derives from its varied foliage colors and textures; conspicuous flowers appear chiefly on the chives, catmint, lavender cotton, rosemary, and rose. All the plants will grow in Zones 4–24, 30, 32. In Zone 33, choose the hardy rosemary cultivar 'Arp' for G in the list below.

PLANT LIST

A. **Allium schoenoprasum.** Chives (3)

B. **Artemisia dracunculus.** French tarragon (4)

C. **Nepeta × faassenii.** Catmint (3)

D. **Origanum majorana (Majorana hortensis).** Sweet marjoram (1)

E. **Origanum vulgare.** Oregano (2)

F. **Rosa 'Sunsprite'** (1)

G. **Rosmarinus officinalis.** Rosemary (1)

H. **Salvia officinalis 'Icterina'.** Common sage (1)

I. **Santolina chamaecyparissus 'Nana'.** Lavender cotton (3)

J. **Thymus × citriodorus 'Aureus'.** Lemon thyme (1)

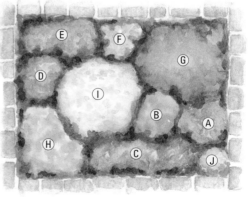

Planting area: 8' x 6'

LINGER AWHILE WITH HERBS

The soothing magic of flowers, fragrance, and appealingly varied foliage textures will lure you to this garden again and again. Offering a potpourri of relaxing, restrained blossom and leaf colors, the herbs in the design include selections used (now or in the past) in medicine and perfumery as well as those of culinary value. The illustration shows the garden in early summer, but bloom time covers a long season, starting in early to midspring and concluding at summer's end. The scented geranium must spend the winter in a sheltered, frost-free location; the other plants succeed outdoors year-round in Zones 4–24, 30, 32–34, 39. To enjoy the plan in Zones 3, 36–38, 40, and 41, replace the two lavenders (B and C in the list below) with anise hyssop (*Agastache foeniculum*) and *Hyssopus officinalis,* respectively.

Achillea 'Moonshine'

PLANT LIST

A. Rosa gallica 'Officinalis'.
Apothecary's rose (2)

B. Lavandula angustifolia. English lavender (2)

C. Lavandula angustifolia 'Hidcote'.
English lavender (2)

D. Artemisia absinthium 'Lambrook Silver'.
Common wormwood (2)

E. Ruta graveolens. Rue (2)

F. Salvia officinalis 'Purpurascens'.
Common sage (1)

G. Salvia officinalis 'Tricolor'. Common sage (1)

H. Achillea 'Moonshine' (4)

I. Foeniculum vulgare 'Purpurascens'
('Smokey'). Bronze fennel (1)

J. Echinacea purpurea. Purple coneflower (9)

K. Iris, tall bearded, 'Pallida Variegata'
('Zebra') (2)

L. Chrysanthemum parthenium 'Aureum'
(C. p. 'Golden Feather', Tanacetum parthenium
'Aureum'). Feverfew (3)

M. Dianthus plumarius. Cottage pink (6)

N. Nepeta × faassenii. Catmint (2)

O. Viola odorata. Sweet violet (2)

P. Prunella grandiflora. Self-heal (2)

Q. Thymus × citriodorus. Lemon thyme (1)

R. Stachys byzantina. Lamb's ears (6)

S. Pelargonium odoratissimum.
Apple geranium (1)

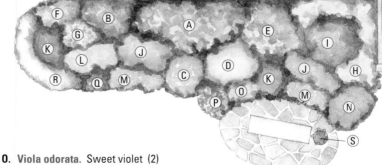

Planting area: 20' x 12'

TIED UP IN KNOTS

Gardeners have enjoyed intricate knot plantings for hundreds of years, delighting in their fanciful yet formal designs. Shown here is the *closed* knot, composed of two or more kinds of plants set out to form an interweaving pattern; the short, dense evergreen herbs historically used for such knots are still ideal for the purpose today. Traditional patterns are many and varied, but the typical knot garden fits within a 12-foot square—as does the planting illustrated directly below, though the circle and arcs of its design obscure the underlying square frame. Gravel fills the gray areas between the clipped arcs, forming part of the design and also offering easy access to the planting's interior for frequent trimming. The alternate plan at lower left is more obviously square and uses just one more plant, a green-and-gold sage. Try both garden whimsies in Zones 4–24, 29, 30, 32. To extend the plans into Zones 3, 33, 34, and 39, replace *Santolina rosmarinifolia* (B in the list below) with *Hyssopus officinalis*.

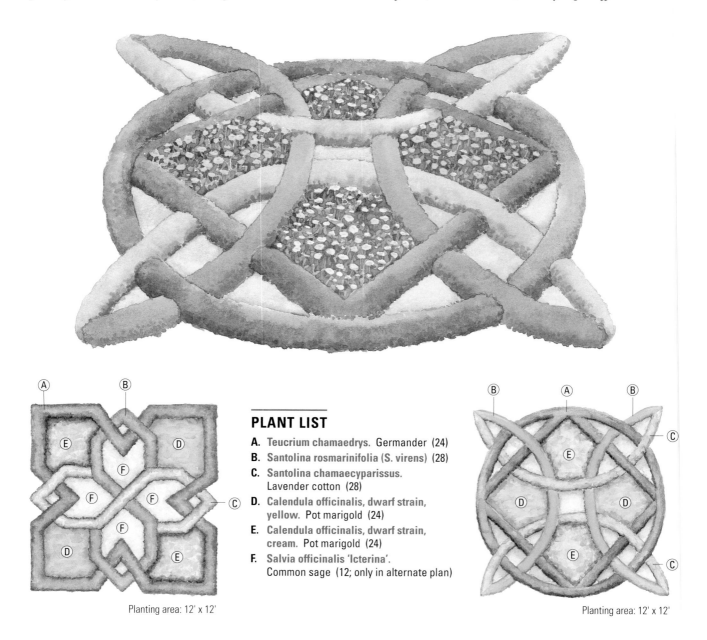

PLANT LIST

A. Teucrium chamaedrys. Germander (24)

B. Santolina rosmarinifolia (S. virens) (28)

C. Santolina chamaecyparissus. Lavender cotton (28)

D. Calendula officinalis, dwarf strain, yellow. Pot marigold (24)

E. Calendula officinalis, dwarf strain, cream. Pot marigold (24)

F. Salvia officinalis 'Icterina'. Common sage (12; only in alternate plan)

Planting area: 12' x 12'

Planting area: 12' x 12'

FORMALITY WITH FLOWERS AND HERBS

The boxwood hedge, symmetrical beds, and sundial recall a formal English garden, but in its choice of plants, this double-bed plan is really a cottage garden with herbs. Oregano, thyme, and sage are the culinary selections; more prominently featured are various herbs traditionally used in medicine and perfumery, interspersed with favorite perennials (peony, daylily, coral bells) and small shrubs (the spiraeas). The plan can shrink or expand: either bed can stand alone, or you can repeat each one to make a square garden divided by intersecting pathways. You'll have the best success with this planting in Zones 4–9, 14–16, 32–34, 39. To enjoy it in Zones 2, 3, 35–38, 40, and 41 as well, replace C, J, and Y in the list below with (respectively) blue mist *(Caryopteris × clandonensis),* garden burnet *(Sanguisorba minor),* and Korean boxwood *(Buxus microphylla koreana).*

PLANT LIST

A. Rosa gallica 'Officinalis'. Apothecary's rose (2)

B. Spiraea × bumalda 'Limemound' (1)

C. Lavandula angustifolia. English lavender (3)

D. Ruta graveolens. Rue (4)

E. Artemisia absinthium. Common wormwood (4)

F. Hyssopus officinalis. Hyssop (3)

G. Salvia officinalis 'Purpurascens'. Common sage (3)

H. Spiraea × bumalda 'Anthony Waterer' (2)

I. Echinacea purpurea. Purple coneflower (10)

J. Teucrium chamaedrys. Germander (7)

K. Alchemilla mollis. Lady's-mantle (2)

L. Thymus × citriodorus 'Argenteus'. Silver thyme (2)

M. Thymus × citriodorus 'Aureus'. Lemon thyme (2)

N. Dianthus plumarius. Cottage pink (4)

O. Paeonia 'Festiva Maxima'. Peony (2)

P. Hemerocallis, pink cultivar. Daylily (4)

Q. Hemerocallis 'Stella de Oro'. Daylily (1)

R. Sedum 'Autumn Joy' (Hylotelephium 'Autumn Joy') (6)

S. Chrysanthemum parthenium 'Aureum' (C. p. 'Golden Feather', Tanacetum parthenium 'Aureum'). Feverfew (5)

T. Iris pallida (1)

U. Nepeta × faassenii. Catmint (3)

V. Origanum vulgare 'Aureum'. Oregano (2)

W. Stachys byzantina 'Silver Carpet'. Lamb's ears (5)

X. Heuchera sanguinea. Coral bells (6)

Y. Buxus microphylla japonica. Japanese boxwood (48)

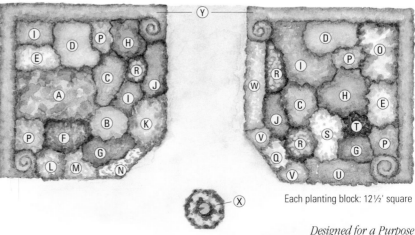

Each planting block: 12½' square

Rhubarb *(Rheum × cultorum)*

MIXED KITCHEN GARDEN

Here's a garden of edibles covering a wide culinary spectrum, from fruits to vegetables to savory herbs. The focal point of the design is the living fence of espaliered dwarf apple trees; brick paths allow easy access for harvest and pruning. The nasturtiums, basil, sweet peppers, and pot marigolds are annuals and must be planted anew each year; the remaining fruits and vegetables are permanent-resident perennials or shrubs that need only some annual maintenance or cleanup. Zones 4–6, 17, 32, 34–41 are favorable regions for this planting; to adapt it to Zones 14–16, 30, 31, and 33, replace the blueberry (C in the list below) with genetic dwarf peach 'Bonanza II'. In Zones 15–17, select an apple cultivar that needs little winter chill.

PLANT LIST

A. **Malus pumila, dwarfed cultivar.** Apple (2)

B. **Asparagus officinalis.** Asparagus (4)

C. **Vaccinium corymbosum.** Blueberry (2)

D. **Calendula officinalis.** Pot marigold (8)

E. **Allium schoenoprasum.** Chives (6)

F. **Monarda didyma 'Cambridge Scarlet'.** Bee balm (2)

G. **Capsicum annuum annuum.** Sweet pepper (5)

H. **Rheum × cultorum.** Rhubarb (2)

I. **Origanum vulgare.** Oregano (2)

J. **Salvia officinalis 'Icterina'.** Common sage (1)

K. **Salvia officinalis 'Purpurascens'.** Common sage (1)

L. **Salvia officinalis 'Tricolor'.** Common sage (1)

M. **Ocimum basilicum 'Dark Opal'.** Sweet basil (6)

N. **Thymus × citriodorus 'Aureus'.** Lemon thyme (4)

O. **Tropaeolum majus.** Garden nasturtium (4)

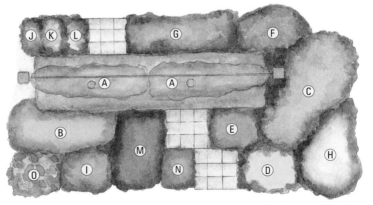

Planting area: 30' x 15'

KITCHEN GARDEN OF HERBS

When a modest cornucopia of culinary herbs grows just a few steps away from the kitchen, it's a simple matter to pop outside and snip a few sprigs to add to the dishes simmering indoors. Besides enhancing your cooking, frequent clipping helps keep the shrubby herbs compact and bushy. In this plan, two favorites get special planting treatment. Spearmint is confined to a large container to keep its invasive tendencies in check. The bay tree, too, is displayed in its own terra-cotta pot, since it needs winter protection in some areas. It's suited to year-round outdoor culture only in Zones 5–9, 14–24; in the other regions to which this scheme is adapted (Zones 4, 10, 11, 30–32), it must overwinter in a frost-free shelter. Gardeners in Zone 33 can also use this plan if they choose the rosemary cultivar 'Arp' for I in the list below. Sweet marjoram (G) will be an annual in Zones 32 and 33; sweet basil (B) is an annual in all zones.

PLANT LIST

- **A. Petroselinum crispum.** Parsley (2)
- **B. Ocimum basilicum.** Sweet basil (6)
- **C. Allium schoenoprasum.** Chives (8)
- **D. Salvia officinalis.** Common sage (2)
- **E. Origanum vulgare.** Oregano (2)
- **F. Artemisia dracunculus.** French tarragon (2)
- **G. Origanum majorana (Majorana hortensis).** Sweet marjoram (1)
- **H. Satureja montana.** Winter savory (2)
- **I. Rosmarinus officinalis.** Rosemary (1)
- **J. Thymus vulgaris.** Common thyme (1)
- **K. Thymus × citriodorus 'Aureus'.** Lemon thyme (1)
- **L. Mentha spicata.** Spearmint (2)
- **M. Laurus nobilis.** Sweet bay (1)

Planting area: 11' x 6'

TOP: *Echinacea purpurea* with female American goldfinch

CENTER: *Cotoneaster apiculatus*

BOTTOM: *Crataegus phaenopyrum* with male cardinal

CALLING ALL BIRDS

Keep a variety of birds happy throughout the year with this expansive planting. Its varied shrubs and trees offer sites for shelter and nesting—and even a measure of protection, thanks to the thorny stems of barberry and Washington thorn. The food supply is ample, too: many of the plants produce berries from late summer through winter, while the birches, perennials, and moor grass bear an abundance of tasty seeds. Aphids (a bane to gardeners, a favored snack for many birds) are likely to be found on the birches and viburnums. An elevated pool provides a safe place for a drink or a dip.

This plan is suited to larger properties, where it would serve nicely as transition from maintained yard to open field or woods. The plants all need at least some winter chill and do best in Zones 3–6, 31–35, 37, 39. In Zones 36, 38, 40, and 41, replace the doublefile viburnum (D in the plant list) with either *Viburnum opulus* or *V. sargentii*.

PLANT LIST

A. **Betula nigra 'Heritage'.** River birch (3+)

B. **Crataegus phaenopyrum.**
Washington thorn (3)

C. **Juniperus chinensis 'Hetz's Columnaris'.**
Chinese juniper (1)

D. **Viburnum plicatum tomentosum 'Shasta'.**
Doublefile viburnum (1)

E. **Euonymus alata.** Winged euonymus (1)

F. **Amelanchier alnifolia.** Saskatoon (1)

G. **Viburnum opulus 'Compactum'.**
European cranberry bush (1)

H. **Berberis thunbergii 'Atropurpurea'.**
Red-leaf Japanese barberry (2)

I. **Aronia arbutifolia.** Red chokeberry (2)

J. **Cotoneaster adpressus praecox** (3)

K. **Cotoneaster apiculatus.**
Cranberry cotoneaster (2)

L. **Cotoneaster dammeri.**
Bearberry cotoneaster (3)

M. **Echinacea purpurea.**
Purple coneflower (12)

N. **Coreopsis grandiflora 'Sunburst'** (12)

O. **Molinia caerulea.** Purple moor grass (4)

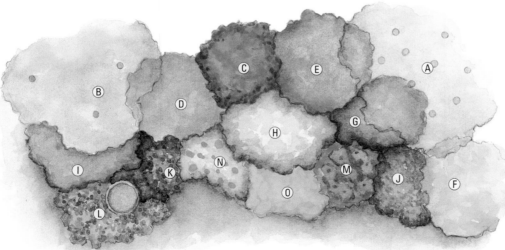

Planting area: 60' x 27'

WESTERN BIRDSCAPE

Smaller than the extensive plan for colder regions shown on pages 626–627, this scaled-down design is suited to mild-winter Zones 8, 9, 12–24. Though it lacks trees and a watering hole, it otherwise offers the same inducements as the larger plan: berries, seeds, and shelter. The irresistible lure—as legions of gardeners have come to know—is the yearly crop of firethorn berries, but the garden's feathered patrons will also feast on the fruits of lantana, heavenly bamboo, cotoneaster, and elaeagnus. Seed-eaters will appreciate the bounty of coreopsis, blanket flower, black-eyed Susan, and fountain grass. The shrubs all afford ample shelter, with the firethorn's forbidding spines providing some protection as well.

PLANT LIST

A. Elaeagnus × ebbingei (1)

B. Pyracantha coccinea 'Kasan'. Firethorn (1)

C. Lantana 'Radiation' (3+)

D. Nandina domestica. Heavenly bamboo (2)

E. Cotoneaster salicifolius 'Emerald Carpet'. Willowleaf cotoneaster (2+)

F. Rudbeckia fulgida sullivantii 'Goldsturm'. Black-eyed Susan (11)

G. Pennisetum setaceum. Fountain grass (6)

H. Gaillardia × grandiflora. Blanket flower (5)

I. Coreopsis grandiflora 'Sunburst' (4)

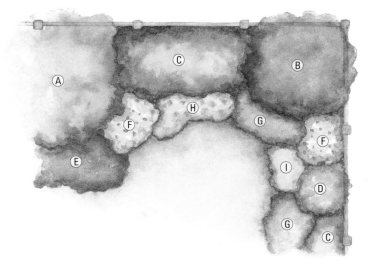

Planting area: 25' x 18'

HUMMINGBIRD CORNER

This colorful garden nook offers long-lasting floral bounty: a feast for the gardener's eyes, a literal banquet for hummingbirds. The blossoms feature the birds' favorite vivid reds and blues, and all provide plentiful, readily available nectar that makes any flight worth the effort. The tantalizing tableau lures hummers over a prolonged period, beginning in mid- or late spring and continu-

ing through summer (and even into fall, in mild-winter areas). The plants listed here will thrive over much of good hummingbird territory: Zones 2–9, 14–17, 32–41. Note that the three annuals—flowering tobacco, scarlet sage, and petunia—will require replanting each year.

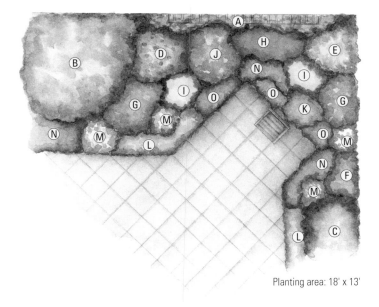

Planting area: 18' x 13'

PLANT LIST

A. Lonicera periclymenum 'Serotina'. Woodbine (1)

B. Weigela florida 'Bristol Ruby' (1)

C. Weigela florida 'Minuet' (1)

D. Monarda didyma 'Jacob Cline'. Bee balm (6)

E. Alcea rosea (Althaea rosea). Hollyhock (7)

F. Digitalis × mertonensis. Foxglove (4)

G. Agastache foeniculum. Anise hyssop (9)

H. Penstemon barbatus 'Prairie Fire' (4)

I. Asclepias tuberosa, yellow cultivar. Butterfly weed (3)

J. Salvia × superba 'Blue Hill' (6)

K. Lychnis chalcedonica. Maltese cross (4)

L. Heuchera sanguinea. Coral bells (9+)

M. Nicotiana alata, Nicki strain, mixed colors. Flowering tobacco (12)

N. Salvia splendens, dwarf red strain. Scarlet sage (16)

O. Petunia × hybrida, blue or purple (8)

WESTERN BUTTERFLY OASIS

Rich in nectar, the plants shown here will attract a variety of butterflies in Zones 8, 9, 12–24. Butterfly bush is, of course, the nonpareil of lures, and as the largest member of the planting it advertises the garden's attractions from afar with its wands of fragrant blue-violet blossoms. But once they arrive, butterflies are likely to linger, moving from one treat to another and yet another.

Bloom is at its most vivid in the first half of summer, but you'll enjoy flowers from midspring until early autumn, long enough to satisfy all the annual butterfly battalions. Sweet alyssum is an annual in all zones, but it produces plenty of volunteer seedlings to carry on from year to year. In Zones 8, 9, 12, and 13, the salvia is also an annual and will need to be replaced each year.

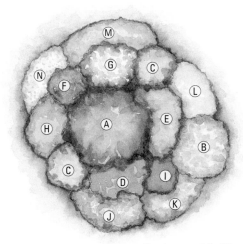

Planting area: 14' x 16'

PLANT LIST

A. Buddleia davidii 'Empire Blue'. Butterfly bush (1)

B. Lantana 'Irene' (1)

C. Agapanthus orientalis. Lily-of-the-Nile (2)

D. Penstemon × gloxinioides 'Garnet'. Border penstemon (3)

E. Centranthus ruber. Jupiter's beard (4)

F. Lavandula × intermedia 'Provence'. Lavandin (1)

G. Chrysanthemum × superbum 'Alaska' (Leucanthemum maximum 'Alaska'). Shasta daisy (6)

H. Salvia coccinea (5)

I. Verbena bonariensis (1)

J. Dianthus gratianopolitanus 'Bath's Pink' (D. caesius 'Bath's Pink'). Cheddar pink (5)

K. Scabiosa columbaria. Pincushion flower (3)

L. Iberis sempervirens 'Snowflake'. Evergreen candytuft (2)

M. Coreopsis grandiflora 'Early Sunrise' (4)

N. Lobularia maritima. Sweet alyssum (5)

BUTTERFLY ISLAND

This could be the perfect butterfly vacation spot: an all-you-can-drink nectar bar. And rising as it does from a sea of lawn, it's both a floral focal point in the landscape and a beacon for butterflies throughout the feeding period. All the plants are suited to Zones 3–9, 14–17, 32–41, regions where, due to the typically long winters, adult butterflies often emerge fairly late in the season. Appropriate to their customers' schedules, these plants begin flowering in late spring (the catmint), then continue through the summer and as far into autumn as climate and the particular year will allow.

PLANT LIST

A. Vernonia noveboracencis. Ironweed (3)

B. Caryopteris × clandonensis. Blue mist (1)

C. Spiraea × bumalda 'Anthony Waterer' (2)

D. Asclepias tuberosa. Butterfly weed (3)

E. Liatris spicata. Gayfeather (4)

F. Echinacea purpurea 'Magnus'. Purple coneflower (5)

G. Aster × frikartii 'Mönch' (5)

H. Agastache foeniculum. Anise hyssop (1)

I. Solidago virgaurea 'Goldenmosa'. Goldenrod (2)

J. Nepeta × faassenii. Catmint (5)

K. Achillea taygetea (7)

L. Sedum spectabile 'Meteor' (Hylotelephium spectabile 'Meteor') (8)

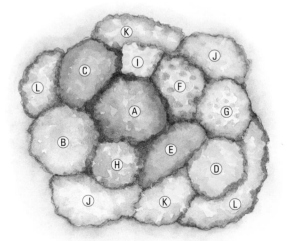

Planting area: 17' x 15'

COLOR GARDENS

Hot or cool, loud or muted, flowery or leafy—whatever your preferences in garden color, there's a plan to satisfy you in these pages. The hot-color plantings are bright enough to make you reach for your sunglasses; the white, cool, and gray schemes, in contrast, suggest sweaters and foggy skies. For those who prefer variety to exclusivity, four mixed-color gardens offer inspiration for all climates. And finally—who says foliage alone can't make a colorful planting?

SUMMERTIME BLUES

If a big part of your summer involves trying to escape the heat, this cool collection should bring you at least the illusion of relief. From late spring through a midsummer crescendo until the last aster fades in fall, you'll be soothed by a continuous procession of blossoms in blue, purple, lavender, and white. Anchoring the island garden is a secluded seating area where you can receive your blue therapy at close range. Given regular moisture, all the plants will thrive in Zones 1–7, 32–43. An annual cleanup of the previous year's growth in late winter or early spring will ready the planting for a repeat performance.

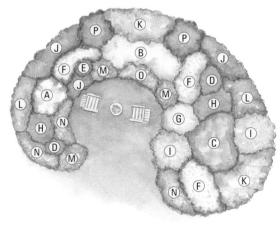

Planting area: 17' x 15'

PLANT LIST

A. Paeonia, white cultivar. Peony (1)

B. Dictamnus albus 'Albiflorus'. Gas plant (3)

C. Baptisia australis. Blue false indigo (3)

D. Iris, Siberian, 'Caesar's Brother' (3)

E. Allium christophii (A. albopilosum). Star of Persia (4)

F. Chrysanthemum × superbum 'Snowbank' or 'Snow Lady' (Leucanthemum maximum 'Snowbank' or 'Snow Lady'). Shasta daisy (14)

G. Gypsophila paniculata 'Perfecta'. Baby's breath (1)

H. Eupatorium coelestinum 'Cori'. Hardy ageratum (4)

I. Geranium 'Johnson's Blue' (2)

J. Geranium himalayense (G. grandiflorum) 'Birch Double' ('Plenum') (5)

K. Nepeta × faassenii. Catmint (5)

L. Aster amellus 'Violet Queen'. Italian aster (7)

M. Veronica 'Goodness Grows' (7)

N. Prunella grandiflora 'Purple Loveliness'. Self-heal (6)

O. Dianthus × allwoodii 'Aqua'. Pink (5)

P. Hosta 'Francee' (6)

SILVER SETTING

Cool, elegant, and restrained, this assemblage of gray, silver, white, ivory, lavender, and pink has an aura of refinement, a sophisticated shimmer that suggests the daytime equivalent of moonlight. Despite the quiet blend of colors, there's no lack of variety here; you'll note a range of plant shapes, leaf sizes, and foliage textures. Iris and allium bloom in spring, but most of the flowering plants put on their show in summer. This patrician pastiche is available to gardeners in much of the country: Zones 2–9, 14–24, 32–41.

Stachys byzantina 'Silver Carpet'

PLANT LIST

A. **Salvia officinalis 'Berggarten'.** Common sage (1)

B. **Malva moschata 'Rosea'.** Musk mallow (2)

C. **Centranthus ruber 'Albus'.** Jupiter's beard (3)

D. **Artemisia absinthium.** Common wormwood (2)

E. **Lysimachia clethroides.** Gooseneck loosestrife (1)

F. **Nepeta × faassenii.** Catmint (3)

G. **Ruta graveolens 'Jackman's Blue'.** Rue (1)

H. **Limonium latifolium.** Sea lavender (3)

I. **Liatris spicata 'Kobold'.** Gayfeather (3)

J. **Verbascum chaixii 'Album'.** Mullein (5)

K. **Helictotrichon sempervirens (Avena sempervirens).** Blue oat grass (2)

L. **Iris, tall bearded, 'Silverado'** (2)

M. **Hemerocallis, cream cultivar.** Daylily (1)

N. **Allium aflatunense** (3)

O. **Achillea clavennae.** Silvery yarrow (7)

P. **Dianthus × allwoodii 'Aqua'.** Pink (6)

Q. **Cerastium tomentosum.** Snow-in-summer (5)

R. **Artemisia stellerana 'Silver Brocade'.** Beach wormwood (3+)

S. **Stachys byzantina 'Silver Carpet'.** Lamb's ears (7)

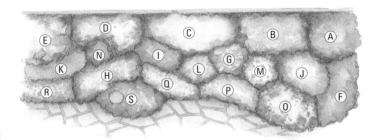

Planting area: 20' x 7'

PLANT LIST

A. Buddleia davidii 'White Ball'.
Butterfly bush (1)

B. Rosa 'Iceberg' (2)

C. Euonymus fortunei 'Emerald Gaiety' (22)

D. Paeonia, white cultivar. Peony (2)

E. Liatris scariosa 'White Spire'.
Gayfeather (5)

F. Gypsophila paniculata 'Perfecta'.
Baby's breath (3)

G. Chrysanthemum × superbum 'Aglaia'
(Leucanthemum maximum 'Aglaia').
Shasta daisy (9)

H. Achillea ptarmica 'The Pearl' (3)

I. Centranthus ruber 'Albus'.
Jupiter's beard (5)

J. Phlox maculata (P. carolina,
P. suffruticosa) 'Miss Lingard'.
Thick-leaf phlox (5)

K. Iris, Siberian, 'Fourfold White' (3)

L. Scabiosa caucasica 'Alba'.
Pincushion flower (3)

M. Campanula persicifolia, white cultivar.
Peach-leafed bluebell (4)

N. Arrhenatherum elatius bulbosum
'Variegatum'. Bulbous oat grass (4)

O. Dianthus × allwoodii 'Aqua'. Pink (4)

P. Prunella grandiflora 'White Loveliness'.
Self-heal (7)

Q. Potentilla alba. Cinquefoil (5)

PEARLS AND JADE

Plant habits and foliage textures are so varied you may not immediately realize that this plan includes just two colors: white and green. The combination makes for a refreshing, tranquil garden, a perfect spot for taking a breather from the day's activities. Iris, peony, and 'Iceberg' rose bloom in mid- to late spring (depending on zone), with the other plants following close behind; the rose continues right through summer. The plants suggested here all succeed in Zones 3–7, 32–34, 37, and 39. To extend the plan into Zones 35, 36, 38, 40, and 41, use a white cultivar of common lilac *(Syringa vulgaris)* in place of butterfly bush (A in the list at left). In Zones 8, 9, 10, and 14, replace oat grass (N) with lily turf *(Liriope muscari* 'Monroe White'; the lily turf may outperform oat grass in Zones 7, 32, and 33, as well).

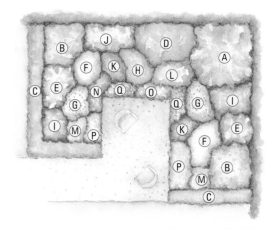

Planting area: 19' x 15'

WHITEWASH

Because many of the plants native to dry-summer, semiarid regions are gray foliaged, a white garden designed for such areas naturally becomes a symphony in white and silver. Carrying the silver banner in this planting are bush morning glory, artemisia, ballota, silvery yarrow, and lamb's ears. Blossoms—all of them in white, of course—begin in midspring with the bearded iris and continue through summer. This scheme flourishes in Zones 8, 9, 14, 18–21; with the simple substitution of *Nerium oleander* 'Morocco' for crape myrtle (A in the plant list), it will also succeed in Zones 15, 16, 22–24.

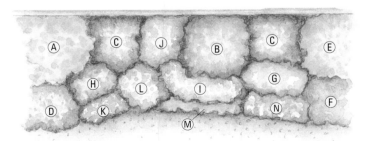

Planting area: 20' x 7½'

PLANT LIST

A. **Lagerstroemia indica 'Petite Snow'.** Crape myrtle (1)

B. **Lantana 'Dwarf White'** (1)

C. **Lavandula × intermedia 'White Spike'.** Lavandin (2)

D. **Convolvulus cneorum.** Bush morning glory (1)

E. **Artemisia arborescens** (1)

F. **Ballota pseudodictamnus** (1)

G. **Agapanthus 'Rancho White' ('Dwarf White', 'Rancho', 'Peter Pan Albus').** Lily-of-the-Nile (4)

H. **Iris, tall bearded, 'Skating Party' or other white cultivar** (3)

I. **Penstemon × gloxinioides 'Holly White'.** Border penstemon (5)

J. **Centranthus ruber 'Albus'.** Jupiter's beard (2)

K. **Gazania, white cultivar** (4)

L. **Achillea clavennae.** Silvery yarrow (4)

M. **Stachys byzantina 'Silver Carpet'.** Lamb's ears (5)

N. **Verbena tenuisecta 'Alba'.** Moss verbena (3)

NORTH STAR

The long, cold winters of higher latitudes and altitudes do limit the variety of plants you can grow, but they put no limits on garden beauty. The planting shown here provides a confettilike cascade of harmonious flower colors from late spring through summer. Foliage is only slightly less varied, featuring leaves in gray as well as green, with an assortment of textures. The 'Jens Munk' rose is heroically hardy, needing just a modicum of cold protection (which can come from snow cover alone, if the winter provides it). The full design is an island, but you can split it into two plans for use against a fence or walk; divide it along the dotted line. The planting is suitable for the coldest zones as well as more temperate regions, succeeding in Zones 1–9, 14–16, 32–45.

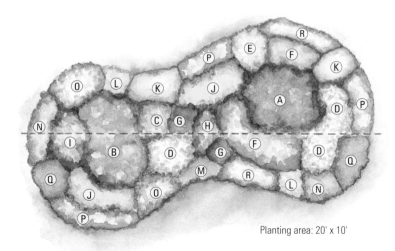

Planting area: 20' x 10'

PLANT LIST

A. Rosa 'Jens Munk' (1)

B. Paeonia, pink cultivar. Peony (2)

C. Campanula persicifolia. Peach-leafed bluebell (2)

D. Gypsophila paniculata 'Perfecta'. Baby's breath (3)

E. Gypsophila paniculata 'Viette's Dwarf' or 'Compacta Plena'. Baby's breath (2)

F. Achillea 'Moonshine' (6)

G. Iris, Siberian, 'Caesar's Brother' (3)

H. Liatris spicata. Gayfeather (3)

I. Liatris spicata 'Kobold'. Gayfeather (4)

J. Hemerocallis 'Happy Returns'. Daylily (7)

K. Oenothera fruticosa (O. tetragona) 'Fireworks' ('Feuerwerkeri', 'Fyrverkeri'). Sundrops (5)

L. Euphorbia epithymoides (E. polychroma) (2)

M. Heuchera × brizoides, pink cultivar. Coral bells (4)

N. Heuchera sanguinea. Coral bells (10)

O. Iberis sempervirens 'Snowflake'. Evergreen candytuft (3)

P. Dianthus × allwoodii, pink cultivar. Pink (12)

Q. Phlox subulata, lavender cultivar. Moss pink (3)

R. Artemisia schmidtiana 'Silver Mound'. Angel's hair (7)

EAST MEETS WEST

Step into this garden, and you could be in Portland or San Jose, Philadelphia or Cleveland. That's the beauty of the plants collected here: adaptability. Their tolerant and flexible nature does not mean they're undistinguished "weeds," though—far from it! From late spring through summer, they provide a knockout, full-palette flower show, given routine watering and little else. As a bonus, a number of the blossoms are good for cutting. Take your ease in this colorful company if you garden in Zones 3–9, 14–21, 32–35, 37, or 39.

PLANT LIST

- **A.** Rosa 'Bonica' (1)
- **B.** Buddleia davidii 'Nanho Purple'. Butterfly bush (1)
- **C.** Panicum virgatum 'Heavy Metal'. Switch grass (1)
- **D.** Nepeta × faassenii 'Six Hills Giant'. Catmint (1)
- **E.** Achillea 'Salmon Beauty'
  (A. millefolium 'Salmon Beauty') (2)
- **F.** Achillea 'Moonshine' (3)
- **G.** Chrysanthemum × superbum 'Aglaia'
  (Leucanthemum maximum 'Aglaia'). Shasta daisy (7)
- **H.** Penstemon barbatus 'Prairie Fire' (4)
- **I.** Geranium 'Johnson's Blue' (3)
- **J.** Geranium 'Ann Folkard' (2)
- **K.** Coreopsis verticillata 'Zagreb'. Threadleaf coreopsis (1)
- **L.** Scabiosa caucasica. Pincushion flower (3)
- **M.** Hemerocallis 'Stella de Oro'. Daylily (4)
- **N.** Dianthus deltoides 'Zing'. Maiden pink (4)
- **O.** Prunella grandiflora 'Purple Loveliness'. Self-heal (6+)
- **P.** Cerastium tomentosum. Snow-in-summer (7)

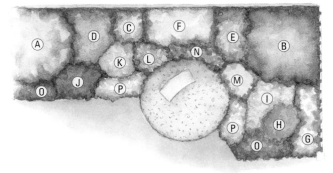

Planting area: 20' x 10'

PLANT LIST

A. **Rhaphiolepis (Raphiolepis) 'Majestic Beauty' (multitrunked).** India hawthorn (1)

B. **Leucophyllum frutescens.** Texas ranger (1)

C. **Nerium oleander 'Petite Salmon'.** Oleander (2)

D. **Lavandula × intermedia 'Provence'.** Lavandin (2)

E. **Salvia leucantha.** Mexican sage (2)

F. **Gaura lindheimeri** (2)

G. **Artemisia 'Powis Castle'** (2)

H. **Penstemon × gloxinioides 'Firebird'.** Border penstemon (4)

I. **Penstemon × gloxinioides 'Appleblossom'.** Border penstemon (4)

J. **Agapanthus 'Queen Anne'.** Lily-of-the-Nile (4)

K. **Dietes vegeta.** Fortnight lily (1)

L. **Santolina chamaecyparissus.** Lavender cotton (1)

M. **Convolvulus cneorum.** Bush morning glory (1)

N. **Convolvulus mauritanicus.** Ground morning glory (2)

O. **Verbena peruviana (V. chamaedryfolia)** (4)

P. **Gaillardia × grandiflora 'Goblin Yellow'.** Blanket flower (3)

Q. **Gazania, mixed colors** (8)

R. **Cistus 'Victor Reiter'.** Rockrose (1)

S. **Cistus laurifolius.** Rockrose (1)

T. **Cistus 'Doris Hibberson'.** Rockrose (1)

U. **Cistus salviifolius.** Sageleaf rockrose (2)

V. **Cistus 'Sunset'.** Rockrose (2)

W. **Cistus 'Warley Rose'.** Rockrose (1)

STRICTLY SOUTHWEST

One of the advantages of gardening in Southwestern Zones 12–24 is the mild winter, which favors a great variety of plants. On the down side, though, are the dry conditions that prevail over much of the territory for much of the year. Except for a few desert areas where showers come in summer, winter is the rainy season—and that means that you, not nature, will be providing the garden with water from spring through summer and into autumn. No wonder, then, that plantings thriving on just moderate moisture are highly favored in these zones. When you choose the plan shown here, you can trade hauling the hose for reclining on the chaise to soak up some sun. The most concentrated color display runs from midspring into the first half of summer, though in milder-summer regions the show will continue unabated until early autumn, when vibrant purple Mexican sage provides the garden's grand finale.

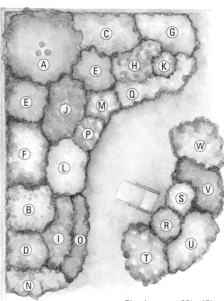

Planting area: 20' x 15'

Bi-coastal tropics

You're not in Kansas anymore. This is Honolulu…or Miami…or San Diego, where frost is a stranger and tropical luxuriance is the norm. The plant assortment shown here, while tender, is still tough enough to weather the occasional slight frost, making it suitable not only to Zone 25 but also to Zones 24, 26, and 27. Prominent are several signature plants of tropic climes: kahili ginger, colorful Chinese hibiscus, and that epitome of jungle foliage, elephant's ear. When bloom is at its peak in summer, you'll also be treated to intoxicating fragrances from the angel's trumpet, ginger, and gardenia. Most of these plants are permanent shrubs and perennials; the coleus, New Guinea hybrid impatiens, and star clusters may live into a second year, but the display is usually better if plants are replaced annually.

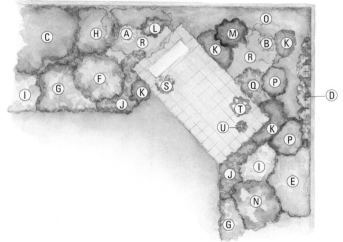

Planting area: 20' x 16'

PLANT LIST

A. Brugmansia candida. Angel's trumpet (1)

B. Tibouchina urvilleana. Princess flower (1)

C. Hibiscus rosa-sinensis 'Fiesta' or 'Ross Estey'. Chinese hibiscus (1)

D. Mandevilla 'Alice du Pont' (1)

E. Brunfelsia pauciflora 'Macrantha'. Yesterday-today-and-tomorrow (1)

F. Justicia brandegeana (Beloperone guttata). Shrimp plant (2)

G. Cuphea ignea. Cigar plant (5)

H. Phygelius × rectus 'African Queen'. Cape fuchsia (2)

I. Hemerocallis (evergreen), yellow cultivar. Daylily (6+)

J. Liriope muscari 'Silvery Sunproof'. Big blue lily turf (14)

K. Clivia miniata. Kaffir lily (9)

L. Zantedeschia aethiopica. Common calla (2)

M. Colocasia esculenta 'Black Magic'. Elephant's ear, taro (2)

N. Hedychium gardneranum. Kahili ginger (3)

O. Chlorophytum comosum 'Variegatum' or 'Vittatum'. Spider plant (12)

P. Pentas lanceolata. Star clusters (4)

Q. Impatiens, New Guinea hybrid, 'Tango' (3)

R. Zoysia tenuifolia. Korean grass (sprigs or plugs, set 6 inches apart)

S. Gardenia jasminoides 'White Gem' (1)

T. Caladium bicolor 'White Queen'. Fancy-leafed caladium (3)

U. Coleus × hybridus (3)

TROPIC TEMPO

Neon-brilliant reds, oranges, and yellows are tempered with splashes of dark blue and purple in a tropical tapestry so vivid it virtually vibrates. Even the dominant foliage plants—canna and New Zealand flax—carry out the bright, hot theme. The planting is long and fairly narrow, suitable for a spot at the front of a garden or along a walkway, where it's certain to grab any passerby's attention. At its blazing best from late spring through summer, this assortment thrives in Zones 14–24.

PLANT LIST

A. Phormium 'Maori Chief'.
New Zealand flax (1)

B. Rosa 'Charisma' (1)

C. Canna 'Phasion' ('Tropicanna')
or 'Pretoria' (3)

D. Felicia amelloides 'San Gabriel'
or 'San Luis'. Blue marguerite (1)

E. Penstemon × gloxinioides 'Firebird'.
Border penstemon (3)

F. Ratibida columnifera. Mexican hat (4)

G. Hemerocallis, red cultivar. Daylily (3)

H. Hemerocallis, orange cultivar. Daylily (4)

I. Hemerocallis 'Stella de Oro'. Daylily (3)

J. Agapanthus 'Storm Cloud'.
Lily-of-the-Nile (2)

K. Coreopsis grandiflora 'Early Sunrise' (7)

L. Coreopsis verticillata 'Zagreb'.
Threadleaf coreopsis (2)

M. Gaillardia × grandiflora 'Goblin'.
Blanket flower (7)

N. Osteospermum fruticosum 'African Queen'
or 'Burgundy'. Trailing African daisy (3)

O. Verbena tenuisecta 'Tapien Purple'.
Moss verbena (8)

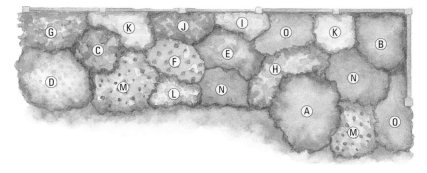

Planting area: 20' x 7'

HEAT WAVE

Unabashedly hot, this lava-bright combination of perennials and two annuals puts on a summer-long show in Zones 1–9, 14–21, 31–43. The dominant plant is the annual Mexican sunflower, which zooms up and out like Jack's beanstalk, quickly reaching shrublike proportions. The other annual is that old favorite,

French marigold—much lower than the sunflower, but almost as striking when massed in a tight circle to form a pool of glowing color. You can use this design as an island; it's especially stunning when set in a green lawn. Or modify it to form a curving bed along a fence: divide it along the dotted line, then plant the larger half.

PLANT LIST

A. Rudbeckia fulgida sullivantii 'Goldsturm'. Black-eyed Susan (3)

B. Achillea 'Fireland' (2)

C. Achillea 'Moonshine' (7)

D. Asclepias tuberosa, Gay Butterflies strain. Butterfly weed (3)

E. Hemerocallis, orange cultivar. Daylily (3)

F. Hemerocallis, cream or light yellow cultivar. Daylily (2)

G. Hemerocallis 'Black-eyed Stella'. Daylily (3)

H. Oenothera fruticosa (O. tetragona) 'Fireworks' ('Feuerwerkeri', 'Fyrverkeri'). Sundrops (2)

I. Gaillardia × grandiflora 'Tokajer'. Blanket flower (4)

J. Coreopsis auriculata 'Nana' (4)

K. Potentilla atrosanguinea 'Gibson's Scarlet'. Cinquefoil (6)

L. Tithonia rotundifolia (T. speciosa). Mexican sunflower (5)

M. Tagetes patula. French marigold (10)

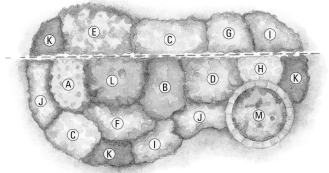

Planting area: 15' x 8'

Berberis thunbergii 'Aurea'

WHO NEEDS FLOWERS?

When foliage forms a vivid patchwork like this, flowers are irrelevant! From the start of the growing season until leaf-fall in autumn, the planting is consistently colorful, presenting a striking combination of wine red, glowing yellow, chartreuse, steely blue, silver gray, and green-and-cream (in the variegated foliage of cotoneaster and eulalia grass). Dominating the plan is a golden privet that's almost too bright to believe; its vivid hue is repeated more subtly in the 'Aurea' barberry and the spiraea, forming a yellow thread that weaves throughout the foliage tapestry. All the plants are tough customers, suited to a sunny site in Zones 2–11, 14–21, 32–41.

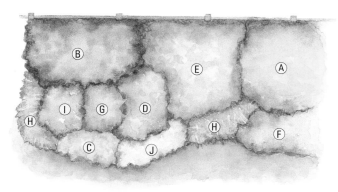

Planting area: 28' x 13'

PLANT LIST

A. **Ligustrum × vicaryi.** Vicary golden privet (1)

B. **Berberis thunbergii 'Atropurpurea'.** Red-leaf Japanese barberry (2)

C. **Berberis thunbergii 'Aurea'.** Japanese barberry (2)

D. **Spiraea × bumalda 'Goldflame'** (2)

E. **Cotoneaster horizontalis 'Variegata'.** Rock cotoneaster (3)

F. **Juniperus sabina 'Blue Danube'.** Savin juniper (4+)

G. **Miscanthus sinensis 'Morning Light'.** Eulalia grass (1)

H. **Festuca 'Elijah Blue'.** Blue fescue (10)

I. **Salvia officinalis 'Berggarten'.** Common sage (1)

J. **Artemisia stellerana 'Silver Brocade'.** Beach wormwood (4)

Say it with foliage

If the plan on the facing page is a bold quilt, this one is more like a needlepoint design, featuring more variety and a greater number of plants. The red-leafed Japanese maple sets the lightly shaded scene, where a host of shrubs and perennials sparkle in yellow, blue, silver, burgundy, and white-and-green. The focus is on foliage: the flowers of the lady's-mantle are subtle, while those of the hostas are so fleeting as to be immaterial. Only the daphne has conspicuous blossoms—but you'll forgive their showiness when you breathe in their heady scent. This grouping grows best where there's a bit of atmospheric moisture: Zones 3–6, 14–17, 32, 34, 35, 37, 39. Gardeners in Zones 33, 36, 40, and 41 can use the plan as well by replacing the holly (C in the list below) with *Euonymus fortunei* 'Canadale Gold'.

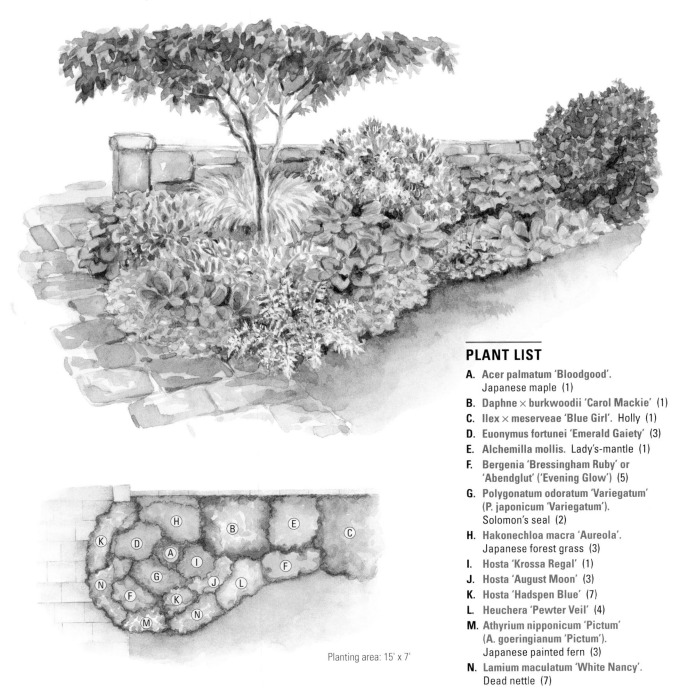

Planting area: 15' x 7'

PLANT LIST

A. **Acer palmatum 'Bloodgood'.** Japanese maple (1)

B. **Daphne × burkwoodii 'Carol Mackie'** (1)

C. **Ilex × meserveae 'Blue Girl'.** Holly (1)

D. **Euonymus fortunei 'Emerald Gaiety'** (3)

E. **Alchemilla mollis.** Lady's-mantle (1)

F. **Bergenia 'Bressingham Ruby' or 'Abendglut' ('Evening Glow')** (5)

G. **Polygonatum odoratum 'Variegatum' (P. japonicum 'Variegatum').** Solomon's seal (2)

H. **Hakonechloa macra 'Aureola'.** Japanese forest grass (3)

I. **Hosta 'Krossa Regal'** (1)

J. **Hosta 'August Moon'** (3)

K. **Hosta 'Hadspen Blue'** (7)

L. **Heuchera 'Pewter Veil'** (4)

M. **Athyrium nipponicum 'Pictum' (A. goeringianum 'Pictum').** Japanese painted fern (3)

N. **Lamium maculatum 'White Nancy'.** Dead nettle (7)

SUNSET'S GARDEN CLIMATE ZONES

A plant's performance is governed by the total climate: length of growing season, timing and amount of rainfall, winter lows, summer highs, humidity. *Sunset*'s climate zone maps take all these factors into account—unlike the familiar hardiness zone maps devised by the U.S. Department of Agriculture, which divide the U.S. and Canada into zones based strictly on winter lows. The U.S.D.A. maps tell you only where a plant may survive the winter; our climate zone maps let you see where that plant will thrive year-round. Below and on page 648 are brief descriptions of the zones illustrated on the maps on pages 646–648. For more information, consult *Sunset*'s regional garden books.

ZONE 1A. Coldest Mountain and Intermountain Areas in the West

All zone is west of Continental Divide. Growing season mid-June to early September, with mild days, chilly nights. Average lows to –0°F/–18°C, extreme lows to –40F/–40C; snow cover (or winter mulch) key to perennials success.

ZONE 1B. Coldest Eastern Rockies and Plains Climate

All zone is east of Continental Divide. Growing season mid-May to late September: warm days, warmer nights than 1A. Summer rainfall present, wind a constant. Winter Arctic cold fronts create sudden temperature shifts; average lows to 0°F/–18°C, extreme lows to –50°F/–46°C.

ZONE 2A. Cold Mountain and Intermountain Areas

Growing season mid-May to mid-September. Occurs at lower elevation than Zone 1A; summers are mild, winters to 10°F/–12°C (extremes to –30°F/–34°C) with snow. The coldest zone for growing sweet cherries, hardiest apples.

ZONE 2B. Warmer-Summer Intermountain Climate

Growing season mid-May to October. Premier fruit- and grain-growing climate with long, warm to hot summers. Winters to 12°F/–11°C (extremes to –20°F/–23°C) with snow.

ZONE 3A. Mild Areas of Mountain and Intermountain Climates

Growing season May to mid-October. Long, dry, warm summers favor a variety of warm-season crops, deciduous fruits, many ornamentals. Occurs at higher elevation the farther south it is found. Winter temperatures drop to 15°F/–9°C with extremes to –18°F/–28°C; snow is possible.

ZONE 3B. Mildest Areas on Intermountain Climates

Growing season early April to late October. Compared to Zone 3A, summers are warmer, winters milder: to 19°F/–7°C with extremes to –15°F/–26°C. Snow is possible. Excellent climate for vegetables, also a wide variety of ornamentals that prefer dry atmosphere.

ZONE 4. Cold-winter Western Washington and British Columbia

Growing season: early May to early Oct. Summers are cool, thanks to ocean influence; chilly winters (19° to –7°F/–7° to –22°C) result from elevation, influence of continental air mass, or both. Coolness, ample rain suit many perennials and bulbs.

ZONE 5. Ocean-influenced Northwest Coast and Puget Sound

Growing season: mid-April to Nov., typically with cool temperatures throughout. Less rain falls here than in Zone 4; winter lows range from 28° to 1°F/–2° to –17°C. This "English garden" climate is ideal for rhododendrons and many rock garden plants.

ZONE 6. Oregon's Willamette Valley

Growing season: mid-Mar. to mid-Nov., with somewhat warmer temperatures than in Zone 5. Ocean influence keeps winter lows about the same as in Zone 5. Climate suits all but tender plants and those needing hot or dry summers.

ZONE 7. Oregon's Rogue River Valley, California's High Foothills

Growing season: May to early Oct. Summers are hot and dry; typical winter lows run from 23° to 9°F/–5° to –13°C. The summer-winter contrast suits plants that need dry, hot summers and moist, only moderately cold winters.

ZONE 8. Cold-air Basins of California's Central Valley

Growing season: mid-Feb. through Nov. This is a valley floor with no maritime influence. Summers are hot; winter lows range from 29° to 13°F/–2° to –11°C. Rain comes in the cooler months, covering just the early part of the growing season.

ZONE 9. Thermal Belts of California's Central Valley

Growing season: late Feb. through Dec. Zone 9 is located in the higher elevations around Zone 8, but its summers are just as hot; its winter lows are slightly higher (temperatures range from 28° to 18°F/–2° to –8°C). Rainfall pattern is the same as in Zone 8.

ZONE 10. High Desert Areas of Arizona, New Mexico, West Texas, Oklahoma Panhandle, and Southwest Kansas

Growing season: April to early Nov. Chilly (even snow-dusted) weather rules from late Nov. through Feb., with lows from 31° to 24°F/–1° to –4°C. Rain comes in summer as well as in the cooler seasons.

ZONE 11. Medium to High Desert of California and Southern Nevada

Growing season: early April to late Oct. Summers are sizzling, with 110 days above 90°F/32°C. Balancing this is a 3½-month winter, with 85 nights below freezing and lows from 11° to 0°F/–12° to –18°C. Scant rainfall comes in winter.

ZONE 12. Arizona's Intermediate Desert

Growing season: mid-Mar. to late Nov., with scorching midsummer heat. Compared to Zone 13, this region has harder frosts; record low is 6°F/–14°C. Rains come in summer and winter.

ZONE 13. Low or Subtropical Desert

Growing season: mid-Feb. through Nov., interrupted by nearly 3 months of incandescent, growth-stopping summer heat. Most frosts are light (record lows run from 19° to 13°F/–17° to –11°C); scant rain comes in summer and winter.

ZONE 14. Inland Northern and Central California with Some Ocean Influence

Growing season: early Mar. to mid-Nov., with rain coming in the remaining months. Periodic intrusions of marine air temper summer heat and winter cold (lows run from 26° to 16°F/–3° to –9°C). Mediterranean-climate plants are at home here.

ZONE 15. Northern and Central California's Chilly-winter Coast-influenced Areas

Growing season: Mar. to Dec. Rain comes from fall through winter. Typical winter lows range from 28° to 21°F/–2° to –6°C. Maritime air influences the zone much of the time, giving it cooler, moister summers than Zone 14.

ZONE 16. Northern and Central California Coast Range Thermal Belts

Growing season: late Feb. to late Nov. With cold air draining to lower elevations, winter lows typically run from 32° to 19°F/0° to –7°C. Like Zone 15, this region is dominated by maritime air, but its winters are milder on average.

ZONE 17. Oceanside Northern and Central California and Southernmost Oregon

Growing season: late Feb. to early Dec. Coolness and fog are hallmarks; summer highs seldom top 75°F/24°C, while winter lows run from 36° to 23°F/2° to –5°C. Heat-loving plants disappoint or dwindle here.

ZONE 18. Hilltops and Valley Floors of Interior Southern California

Growing season: mid-Mar. through late Nov. Summers are hot and dry; rain comes in winter, when lows reach 28° to 10°F/–2° to –12°C. Plants from the Mediterranean and Near Eastern regions thrive here.

ZONE 19. Thermal belts around Southern California's Interior Valleys

Growing season: early Mar. through Nov. As in Zone 18, rainy winters and hot, dry summers are the norm—but here, winter lows dip only to 27° to 22°F/–3° to –6°C, allowing some tender evergreen plants to grow outdoors with protection.

ZONE 20. Hilltops and Valley Floors of Ocean-influenced Inland Southern California

Growing season: late Mar. to late Nov.—but fairly mild winters (lows of 28° to 23°F/–2° to –5°C) allow gardening through much of the year. Cool and moist maritime influence alternates with hot, dry interior air.

ZONE 21. Thermal Belts around Southern California's Ocean-influenced Interior Valleys

Growing season: early Mar. to early Dec., with same tradeoff of oceanic and interior influence as in Zone 20. During winter rainy season, lows range from 36° to 23°F/2° to –5°C—warmer than Zone 20, since colder air drains to the valleys.

ZONE 22. Colder-winter Parts of Southern California's Coastal Region

Growing season: Mar. to early Dec. Winter lows seldom fall below 28°F/–2°C (records are around 21°F/–6°C), though colder air sinks to this zone from Zone 23. Summers are warm; rain comes in winter. Climate here is largely oceanic.

ZONE 23. Thermal Belts of Southern California's Coastal Region

Growing season: almost year-round (all but first half of Jan.). Rain comes in winter. Reliable ocean influence keeps summers mild (except when hot Santa Ana winds come from inland), frosts negligible; 23°F/–5°C is the record low.

ZONE 24. Marine-dominated Southern California Coast

Growing season: all year, but periodic freezes have dramatic effects (record lows are 33° to 20°F/1° to –7°C). Climate here is oceanic (but warmer than oceanic Zone 17), with cool summers, mild winters. Subtropical plants thrive.

ZONE 25. South Florida and the Keys

Growing season: all year. Add ample year-round rainfall (least in Dec. through Mar.), high humidity, and overall warmth, and you have a near-tropical climate. The Keys are frost-free; winter lows elsewhere run from 40° to 25°F/4° to –4°C.

ZONE 26. Central and Interior Florida

Growing season: early Feb. to late Dec., with typically humid, warm to hot weather. Rain is plentiful all year, heaviest in summer and early fall. Lows range from 15°F/–9°C in the north to 27°F/–3°C in the south; arctic air brings periodic hard freezes.

ZONE 27. Lower Rio Grande Valley

Growing season: early Mar. to mid-Dec. Summers are hot and humid; winter lows only rarely dip below freezing. Many plants from tropical and subtropical Africa and South America are well adapted here.

ZONE 28. Gulf Coast, North Florida, Atlantic Coast to Charleston

Growing season: mid-Mar. to early Dec. Humidity and rainfall are year-round phenomena; summers are hot, winters virtually frostless but subject to periodic invasions by frigid arctic air. Azaleas, camellias, many subtropicals flourish.

ZONE 29. Interior Plains of South Texas

Growing season: mid-Mar. through Nov. Moderate rainfall (to 25" annually) comes year-round. Summers are hot. Winter lows can dip to 26°F/–3°C, with occasional arctic freezes bringing much lower readings.

ZONE 30. Hill Country of Central Texas

Growing season: mid-Mar. through Nov. Zone 30 has higher annual rainfall than Zone 29 (to 35") and lower winter temperatures, normally to around 20°F/–7°C. Seasonal variations favor many fruit crops, perennials.

ZONE 31. Interior Plains of Gulf Coast and Coastal Southeast

Growing season: mid-Mar. to early Nov. In this extensive east-west zone, hot and sticky summers contrast with chilly winters (record low temperatures are 7° to 0°F/–14° to –18°C). There's rain all year (an annual average of 50"), with the least falling in Oct.

ZONE 32. Interior Plains of Mid-Atlantic States; Chesapeake Bay, Southeastern Pennsylvania, Southern New Jersey

Growing season: late Mar. to early Nov. Rain falls year-round (40" to 50" annually); winter lows (moving through the zone from south to north) are 30° to 20°F/–1° to –7°C. Humidity is less oppressive here than in Zone 31.

ZONE 33. North-Central Texas and Oklahoma Eastward to the Appalachian Foothills

Growing season: mid-April through Oct. Warm Gulf Coast air and colder continental/arctic fronts both play a role; their unpredictable interplay results in a wide range in annual rainfall (22" to 52") and winter lows (20° to 0°F/–7° to –18°C). Summers are muggy and warm to hot.

ZONE 34. Lowlands and Coast from Gettysburg to North of Boston

Growing season: late April to late Oct. Ample rainfall and humid summers are the norm. Winters are variable—typically fairly mild (around 20°F/–7°C), but with lows down to –3° to –22°F/–19° to –30°C if arctic air swoops in.

ZONE 35. Ouachita Mountains, Northern Oklahoma and Arkansas, Southern Kansas to North-Central Kentucky and Southern Ohio

Growing season: late April to late Oct. Rain comes in all seasons. Summers can be truly hot and humid. Without arctic fronts, winter lows are around 18°F/–8°C; with them, the coldest weather may bring lows of –20°F/–29°C.

ZONE 36. Appalachian Mountains

Growing season: May to late Oct. Thanks to greater elevation, summers are cooler and less humid, winters colder (0° to –20°F/–18° to –29°C) than in adjacent, lower zones. Rain comes all year (heaviest in spring). Late frosts are common.

ZONE 37. Hudson Valley and Appalachian Plateau

Growing season: May to mid-Oct., with rainfall throughout. Lower in elevation than neighboring Zone 42, with warmer winters: lows are 0° to –5°F/–18° to –21°C, unless arctic air moves in. Summer is warm to hot, humid.

ZONE 38. New England Interior and Lowland Maine

Growing season: May to early Oct. Summers feature reliable rainfall and lack oppressive humidity of lower-elevation, more southerly areas. Winter lows dip to –10° to –20°F/–23° to –29°C, with periodic colder temperatures due to influxes of arctic air.

ZONE 39. Shoreline Regions of the Great Lakes

Growing season: early May to early Oct. Springs and summers are cooler here, autumns milder than in areas farther from the lakes. Southeast lakeshores get the heaviest snowfalls. Lows reach 0° to –10°F/–18° to –23°C.

ZONE 40. Inland Plains of Lake Erie and Lake Ontario

Growing season: mid-May to mid-Sept., with rainy, warm, variably humid weather. The lakes help moderate winter lows; temperatures typically range from –10° to –20°F/–23° to –29°C, with occasional colder readings when arctic fronts rush through.

Continued on page 648

Sunset's Garden Climate Zones

| Climate Zones | / | 1A | 1B | 2A | 2B | 3A | 3B | 4 | 5 | 6 | 7 | 8 | 9 | 10 | 11 | 12 | 13 | 14 | 15 | 16 | 17 | 18 | 19 | 20 | 21 | 22 |

James Bay

ONTARIO 45

45

QUÉBEC

NEW BRUNSWICK

43

42 Québec

Presque Isle

Lake of the Woods

43

Lake Superior

44 MAINE 38

Bangor

MINNESOTA 45

Duluth 35

MICHIGAN 43

43 Ottawa

St. Lawrence River

43 Burlington

42 VERMONT 87 NEW HAMPSHIRE 38

95 Portland

94 Montréal

44

94

Minneapolis

WISCONSIN 94

Lake Huron

75

43

40 Lake Ontario

Toronto

39

90 Albany 88

38

Boston 91 MASSACHUSETTS

43

90

MICHIGAN 41

NEW YORK 42

RHODE ISLAND 34

35

94 90

43 Lake Michigan

Milwaukee

39

Detroit 39

Lake Erie 40

Buffalo 90

81 87 CONNECTICUT 37

34

Dubuque 41

IOWA

94

Chicago 80

Cleveland 80 90

Akron 71 77

79

PENNSYLVANIA 40

78

Newark New York 95

Des Moines 80

80

55

69

OHIO 41

70 Columbus

Pittsburgh

76

Philadelphia 34 NEW JERSEY

74

65 INDIANA

32

29

35

41

55 Springfield

Indianapolis 71

70 Cincinnati

WEST VIRGINIA 36

79

66 Washington, D.C. MARYLAND

DELAWARE

Missouri River

70 St. Louis 70

35

Louisville

64 Charleston

64 VIRGINIA 95 Richmond

Kansas City 70

MISSOURI

57

65

KENTUCKY 36

81 32 85 31

44

35

44

40 Nashville 75

36 77 85 NORTH CAROLINA 40

95 Raleigh

33

TENNESSEE 24 75

36

40

85

31

ARKANSAS 40 Memphis

32

SOUTH CAROLINA

Columbia 95

Arkansas River

35

Little Rock 30

65 59

85 32

26

Red River 30

33

55

20 59 Birmingham

Atlanta 20

16

75

44

49

MISSISSIPPI ALABAMA

GEORGIA 31

Savannah

65

10 LOUISIANA 31

Jackson 59

28 Jacksonville

Houston 45 10

28

Mobile 10

Lake Pontchartrain

New Orleans

75 95

Atlantic Ocean

FLORIDA

Orlando

Tampa 4

26

Gulf of Mexico

75 Lake Okeechobee

25

Miami

0 100 200 300 miles

Shreveport 20

| 23 | 24 | 25 | 26 | 27 | 28 | 29 | 30 | 31 | 32 | 33 | 34 | 35 | 36 | 37 | 38 | 39 | 40 | 41 | 42 | 43 | 44 | 45 | **Climate Zones** |

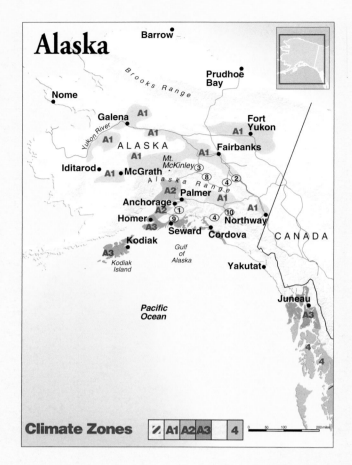

Alaska

Barrow
Brooks Range
Prudhoe Bay
Nome
Galena A1
Fort Yukon A1
A1 A1
A1 ALASKA A1 Fairbanks
Iditarod A1 Mt. McKinley ③ A1
McGrath Alaska Range ⑧ ④ ②
A2 Palmer
Anchorage A2 A1
Homer ⑨ ① ④
A3 Seward Northway
Kodiak Cordova
Gulf of Alaska CANADA
A3
Kodiak Island Yakutat
Pacific Ocean Juneau
A3
4
4

Climate Zones A1 A2 A3 4   0 50 100 200 miles

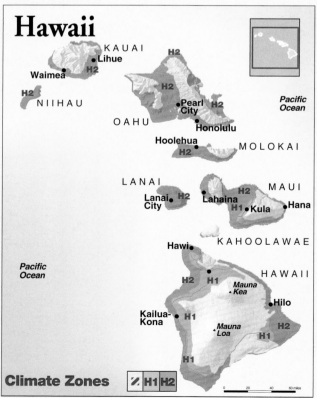

Hawaii

KAUAI
Lihue H2
Waimea H2
H2
NIIHAU
Pearl City H2
OAHU Honolulu
Hoolehua H2 Pacific Ocean
MOLOKAI
LANAI MAUI
Lanai City H2 Lahaina H2 Hana
H1 Kula
KAHOOLAWE
Hawi
HAWAII
H1 Mauna Kea
Pacific Ocean Hilo
Kailua-Kona H1 Mauna Loa H2
H1
H1

Climate Zones H1 H2   0 20 40 60 miles

ZONE 41. Northeast Kansas and Southeast Nebraska to Northern Illinois and Indiana, Southeast Wisconsin, Michigan, Northern Ohio

Growing season: early May to early Oct. Winter brings average lows of −11° to −20°F/−23° to −29°C. Summers in this zone are hotter and longer west of the Mississippi, cooler and shorter nearer the Great Lakes; summer rainfall increases in the same west-to-east direction.

ZONE 42. Interior Pennsylvania and New York; St. Lawrence Valley

Growing season: late May to late Sept. This zone's elevation gives it colder winters than surrounding zones: lows range from −20° to −40°F/−29° to −40°C, with the colder readings coming in the Canadian portion of the zone. Summers are humid, rainy.

ZONE 43. Upper Mississippi Valley, Upper Michigan, Southern Ontario and Quebec

Growing season: late May to mid-Sept. The climate is humid from spring through early fall; summer rains are usually dependable. Arctic air dominates in winter, with lows typically from −20° to −30°F/−29° to −34°C.

ZONE 44. Mountains of New England and Southeastern Quebec

Growing season: June to mid-Sept. Latitude and elevation give fairly cool, rainy summers, cold winters with lows of −20° to −40°F/−29° to −40°C. Choose short-season, low heat-requirement annuals and vegetables.

ZONE 45. Northern Parts of Minnesota and Wisconsin, Eastern Manitoba through Interior Quebec

Growing season: mid-June through Aug., with rain throughout; rainfall (and humidity) are least in zone's western part, greatest in eastern reaches. Winters are frigid (−30° to −40°F/−34° to −40°C), with snow cover, deeply frozen soil.

ZONE A1. Alaska's Coldest Climate—Fairbanks and the Interior

Growing season mid-May to early September. Summer days are long, mild to warm; permafrost usually recedes below root zone. Winter offers reliable snow cover. Season extenders include planting in south and west exposures, boosting soil temperature with mulches or IRT plastic sheeting. Winter lows drop to −20°F/−29°C, with occasional extremes to −60°F/−51°C.

ZONE A2. The Intermediate Climate of Anchorage and Cook Inlet

Growing season mid-May to mid-September. Climate is moderated by mountains to the north and south, also by water of Cook Inlet. Microclimates reign supreme: winter lows may be 5°F/−15°C but with extremes of −40°F/−40°C possible. Summer days are cool to mild and frequently cloudy.

ZONE A3. Mild Southern Maritime Climate from Kodiak to Juneau

Growing season mid-May to October. Summers are cool and cloudy, winters rainy and windy. Typical lows are to 18°F/−8°C with extremes to −18°F/−28°C. Winter-spring freeze-thaw cycles damage plants that break growth early. Cool-weather plants revel in climate but annual types mature more slowly than usual.

ZONE H1. Cooler Volcanic Slopes from 2,000 to 5,000 Feet Elevation

Found only on Hawaii and Maui, this zone offers cooler air (and cooler nights) than lower Zone H2; temperatures here are better for low-chill fruits (especially at higher elevations) and many non-tropical ornamentals. Warm-season highs reach 65° to 80°F/19° to 27°C; cool-season lows drop to around 45°F/7°C.

ZONE H2. Sea Level to 2,000 Feet: the Coconut Palm Belt

The most heavily populated region in the islands, this has tepid climate with high temperatures in the 80° to 90°F/27° to 32°C range, low temperatures only to about 65°F/18°C. Rainiest period is November through March, the remaining months, on leeward sides, being relatively dry. Windward sides of islands get more precipitation than leeward sides from passing storms and year-round tradewind showers.

ANNUALS AND PERENNIALS PHOTOGRAPHY CREDITS

Em Ahart: 72 top; **Max Badgley:** 76 top right; **Paul Bousquet:** 26 bottom; **Marion Brenner:** 11 middle left, 24 center, 42 bottom right, 87 bottom, 94 bottom, 103 top, 119 bottom, 124 bottom, 153 middle, 176 bottom left; **Rob Cardillo:** 27 bottom left, 28 top left, 29 top, 31 top left, 36 top, middle, 40 bottom left, 42 bottom left, 89 bottom, 92 top left, 93 top, 94 top, 99 bottom, 106 top left, 113, 114 middle, 124 top, 125 bottom, 134 right, 141 top, 175 middle, 183 bottom left; **David Cavagnaro:** 9 top right, 17 bottom left, 19 bottom left, 37 bottom, 88 top left, 89 top, 91 top, 95 middle, 95 bottom, 96 bottom, 97 bottom, 98 middle, 103 bottom, 106 bottom left, 110 bottom, 123 bottom, 127 bottom left, 128 left, 129 top right, 130 bottom right, 153 top right, 158 top left, 167 top, 171 bottom, 175 top, 178 left, 180 left, 182 bottom, 183 bottom right; **Peter Christiansen:** 79 right; **Richard Cowles:** 79 left; **Rosalind Creasy:** 10 top, 10 bottom right, 11 top left, 82, 90 bottom left, 107 bottom, 108 bottom, 153 bottom, 155; **Claire Curran:** 38 bottom right, 40 top right, 116 right; **Robin B. Cushman:** 8 top left, 14 top, 32 bottom, 43 top right, 67 top right, 151 right; **Janet Davis:** 15 bottom; **R. Todd Davis:** 23 top right, 111 top, 147 top, 150 top right; **Alan & Linda Detrick:** 17 bottom right, 20 top, 22 bottom right, 25 top left, 27 bottom right, 32 top, 39 middle right, 98 top right, 99 top, 105 bottom, 120 top, 121 top, 130 bottom left, 132 top, 139 top, 145 right, 150 bottom, 163 left, 167 middle, 169 top, 172 bottom, 179 top, 179 bottom, 180 right, 181 top, 185 top right; **William Dewey:** 162 bottom; **Ken Druse:** 70 top; **Philip Edinger:** 143 top; **Derek Fell:** 9 top left, 92 bottom left, 129 middle right, 148 bottom; **Roger Foley:** 19 top, 22 bottom left, 172 top; **Steven W. George:** 112 bottom; **David Goldberg:** 77 center left, 137 top, 150 top left, 161 bottom; **Goldsmith Seeds:** 35 top; **Steven Gunther:** 45 bottom, 101 bottom; **Jamie Hadley:** 83; **Lynne Harrison:** 91 bottom, 100 middle left, 109 middle, 122, 125 top, 132 bottom, 133 bottom, 135 top, 139 middle, 142 top, 166 bottom, 173 top, 178 right; **Jessie M. Harrison:** 138 top; **Philip Harvey:** 48 bottom, 64; **Saxon Holt:** 18 bottom right, 19 bottom center, 20 bottom, 29 bottom, 31 top right, 36 bottom, 71, 73, 88 middle right, 109 bottom, 118 bottom left, 130 top left, 131 top right, 133 top, 133 middle, 137 bottom, 142 bottom, 145 left, 160 top, 161 middle, 162 top, 163 top right, 163 bottom right, 166 top, 171 middle, 185 bottom right; **Dency Kane:** 90 top left, 131 bottom left, 152 bottom; **Janet Loughrey:** 21, 27 top, 42 top, 144 bottom, 156 bottom; **Mary-Kate MacKay:** 41 bottom; **Allan Mandell:** 3 top left, 6, 10 bottom left, 11 bottom left, 23 top left, 128 center; **Charles Mann:** 14 bottom left, 18 top left, 28 bottom left, 33 bottom, 39 bottom left, 55, 87 top, 95 top, 96 top, 106 right, 114 bottom, 115 top, 119 top, 120 bottom, 127 top right, 129 left, 131 top left, 135 bottom, 140 bottom, 143 bottom, 148 top, 151 left, 154 top left, 164 bottom, 184 left; **Mayer/Le Scanff, The Garden Picture Library:** 22 top left; **David McDonald:** 118 right, 176 top left, 183 bottom right; **Baldassare Mineo:** 126 top; **Jerry Pavia:** 5 bottom left, 35 middle, 86, 92 top right, 107 top, 108 top, 109 top, 110 top, 114 top, 121 bottom, 123 top, 129 bottom right, 134 left, 139 bottom, 140 top, 154 bottom, 159 top, 159 bottom, 168 top, 171 top, 174 top, 176 right, 177 bottom right, 182 top right; **Joanne Pavia:** 24 right, 33 top left, 57; **Pam Peirce:** 77 left; **Norman A. Plate:** 8 right, 11 top center, 11 bottom right, 32 middle, 40 bottom right, 44 top, 44 bottom, 45 top left, 45 top right, 48 top, 65 top, 67 top left, 68, 70 bottom, 81 all, 84, 101 top, 102 top, 112 top, 141 bottom, 157 bottom, 184 right, 185 top left; **Rob Proctor:** 9 bottom right; **Howard Rice, The Garden Picture Library:** 147 bottom; **John Rizzo:** 173 bottom; **Susan A. Roth:** 5 top right, 5 middle, 5 bottom right, 8 middle left, bottom left, 10 top left, 12, 14 bottom right, 16 right, 17 top, 18 bottom left, 23 bottom right, 24 left, 25 top right, 26 bottom left, 26 top right, 28 bottom right, 29 middle, 30 top, 31 bottom right, 33 top right, 38 middle left, 40 top, 43 top left, 46, 62, 100 top left, 104 bottom, 105 top, 107 middle, 111 bottom, 115 bottom, 128 right, 130 middle left, 136 top, 146 top, 152 top, 160 bottom, 165 top, 167 bottom, 170 top, 177 top, 181 bottom, 182 top left; **Mark Rutherford:** 35 bottom, 93 bottom; **Richard Shiell:** 38 top left, 90 right, 102 bottom, 117 all, 136 bottom, 141 middle, 144 top, 149 top, 154 top right, 157 top, 161 top, 175 bottom; **Malcolm C. Shurtleff:** 77 center right; **Chad Slattery:** 25 bottom, 136 middle; **Lauren Springer:** 4; **Randy & Kara Stephens-Flemming:** 118 top left, 131 top center; **Thomas J. Story:** 41 middle left, middle right; **J. G. Strauch, Jr.:** 77 right; **Michael S. Thompson:** 19 bottom right, 30 bottom right, 37 top, 38 bottom left, 39 bottom right, 43 bottom, 53, 72 bottom, 97 top, 98 bottom right, 100 bottom right, 104 top, 116 left, 126 bottom, 127 bottom right, 130 top right, 138 bottom, 146 bottom, 156 top, 158 bottom, 164 top, 165 bottom, 170 bottom, 174 bottom; **Ron West/Nature Photography:** 76 top left, 76 center left, 76 center right, 76 bottom left, 76 bottom right, 78 all; **Rick Wetherbee:** 169 bottom; **Didier Willery, The Garden Picture Library:** 149 bottom; **Doug Wilson:** 39 top right, 58; **Tom Woodward:** 16 bottom, 88 bottom, 168 bottom, 177 middle; **Cynthia Woodyard:** 15 top, 59, 158 top right.

GARDEN DESIGNS CREDITS

GARDEN DESIGNERS
Philip Edinger for all illustrated gardens except the following: **Kathleen Norris Brenzel:** 620; **Gary Patterson:** 582, 601, 624; **Truxell & Valentino Landscape Development:** 562.

ILLUSTRATORS
Gwendolyn Babbitt: 572, 573, 604–605, 612–613, 632, 633, 634, 635; **Marcie Hawthorne:** 550 top, 554, 555, 574, 575, 614, 615, 630, 631; **Lois Lovejoy:** 556, 557, 560, 561, 577, 580, 581, 582, 584, 585, 601, 602, 603, 606, 620, 621, 622, 623, 624, 625; **Mimi Osborne:** 550 bottom left; **Erin O'Toole:** 540, 546, 548, 552, 553, 562, 563, 564, 565, 566, 567, 570, 571, 576, 578, 579, 586, 587, 588, 589, 590, 591, 592, 593, 594, 595, 596, 600, 607, 608, 609, 610, 611, 616, 617, 618, 619, 628, 629, 636, 637, 638, 639, 640, 641, 642, 643; **Lucy Sargeant:** 545 bottom; **Elayne Sears:** 551, 558, 559, 568, 569, 583, 598, 599, 626–627; **Jenny Speckels:** all plot plan illustrations.

PHOTOGRAPHERS
Dariel Alexander: 541 bottom, 596; **Marion Brenner:** 568, 571; **Gay Bumgarner:** 626 bottom; **David Cavagnaro:** 595 bottom, 605 bottom, 608, 612, 618, 620; **Claire Curran:** 567 bottom; **Daybreak Imagery, Richard Day:** 626 top; **Derek Fell:** 547 top; **Philip Harvey:** 547 bottom; **Saxon Holt:** 544, 545 top, 569, 594, 621, 642; **Allan Mandell:** 541 top, 542; **Charles Mann:** 554 top, 567 top, 581, 595 top, 600, 624; **Jerry Pavia:** 584, 626 center; **Joanne Pavia:** 574, 605 center; **Norman A. Plate:** 588; **Lauren Springer:** 541 center, 548; **Michael S. Thompson:** 570, 572, 578, 579, 633; **Wayside Gardens:** 554 bottom; **Doug Wilson:** 562; **Cynthia Woodyard:** 556, 580, 601; **Tom Wyatt:** 605 top.

Roses photography credits

Syl Arena: 293 bottom, 362, 365 bottom right, 368 bottom left, 368 bottom middle right, 370 bottom middle right, 371 top left, 381 top middle, 384 top left, 384 bottom middle left, 385 bottom left, 386 top left, 391 bottom middle left, 393 top left, 393 bottom left, 394 top middle, 394 bottom right, 399 top right, 401 bottom left, 403 top left; **Scott Atkinson:** 335 middle left, 335 bottom left, 335 bottom right, 374 bottom right, 375 bottom left, 397 top right, 402 bottom middle right; **Marion Brenner:** 317; **Patricia J. Bruno/Positive Images:** 299 top right, 302 top right; **Gay Bumgarner/Positive Images:** 305 bottom right; **Karen Bussolini:** 293 top, 294, 299 top left, 306 top right, 345 middle, 348 bottom left, 351, 352, 377 bottom left; **Karen Bussolini/Positive Images:** 317 bottom; **R. S. Byther:** 336 middle right; **Rob Cardillo:** 345 left, 368 top left, 370 top left, 372 top middle right, 379 top right, 382 bottom middle, 383 top middle, 388 top left, 396 top middle left, 396 bottom left, 397 top left, 398 bottom right, 403 bottom right; **David Cavagnaro:** 307 top; **Van Chaplin:** 311 top right; **The Conrad-Pyle Co.:** 400 bottom right; **Ken Conway:** 337 bottom left; **Eric Crichton/The Garden Picture Library:** 301 bottom; **Claire Curran:** 292, 335 top right, 365 top middle right, 366 top right, 371 bottom right, 373 bottom right, 374 top middle, 381 top right, 382 bottom left, 385 bottom middle, 390 top left, 399 bottom left, 402 top left, 412; **Robin B. Cushman:** 308 left, 367 bottom middle, 371 top middle left, 371 top right, 372 bottom middle left, 378 bottom middle left, 389 bottom right; **R. Todd Davis:** 375 top middle, 388 bottom left, 402 top right, 413; **Alan and Linda Detrick:** 314, 320, 336 bottom right, 337 right, 348 bottom right, 370 top right, 406 top right, 406 top middle, 407 bottom right; **Andrew Drake:** 366 bottom left, 414; **Ken Druse:** 401 top left, 401 top right; **Philip Edinger:** 392 top middle right,

395 top middle; **Derek Fell:** 368 top right, 407 bottom left, 408 bottom right; **Roger Foley:** 304 left inset, 305 top, 357; **Steven Gunther:** 300 bottom right; **Lynne Harrison:** 296 top left, 372 bottom right, 379 top middle left, 391 bottom right, 395 bottom left, 396 top left, 400 top middle right, 400 top right; **Heirloom Roses, Inc.:** 392 bottom left, 408 top left; **Saxon Holt:** 298 left inset, 304 top right, 307 bottom, 309 top, 345 right, 348 top right, 353, 361, 364 bottom middle, 371 top middle right, 373 top middle, 379 bottom right, 380 bottom middle left, 382 bottom right, 383 bottom right, 384 bottom middle left, 384 bottom right, 385 top left, 386 bottom left, 387 top middle, 390 bottom middle left, 391 bottom left, 391 bottom middle right, 392 bottom middle, 392 bottom right, 393 top right, 394 bottom middle, 397 top middle, 397 bottom middle, 398 bottom left, 398 bottom middle right, 405 top left, 405 top middle, 407 top right, 408 top middle left, 409 bottom right; **Jerry Howard/Positive Images:** 310 top right; **Jackson & Perkins:** 408 bottom left, 415 top right; **Dency Kane:** 308 left inset, 348 top left, 377 top middle left, 377 bottom middle right, 378 top right, 378 bottom middle right, 382 top middle; **Kathryn Kleinman:** 319 bottom right, 364 bottom left, 398 bottom middle left; **Janet Loughrey:** 293 upper middle, 300 bottom left, 310 bottom right, 312, 365 top middle left, 365 bottom middle, 368 bottom left, 370 bottom middle left, 376 middle, 376 right, 377 top right, 379 bottom middle, 380 bottom left, 381 top right, 381 bottom right, 384 top right, 384 bottom left, 385 top right, 385 bottom right, 388 bottom right, 389 top left, 396 bottom right, 399 bottom middle, 402 bottom middle left, 402 bottom right, 403 bottom middle, 407 top left; **Charles Mann:** 299 bottom right, 306 top left, 307 bottom inset, 318 top left, 395 bottom middle; **Ells Marugg:** 404 bottom middle, 408 bottom

middle right; **Mayer/Le Scanff/The Garden Picture Library:** 300 top left; **David McDonald/Photo Garden:** 309 bottom left, 366 top left, 376 left, 377 bottom middle left, 399 bottom right; **Andrew McKinney:** 335 top left, 384 top middle right; **Nor'East Mini Roses:** 404 bottom left, 408 top middle right, 408 top right, 410 bottom right; **Jerry Pavia:** 296 top middle right, 298 left, 303 top, 304 left, 305 bottom left, 306 bottom, 308 top right, 309 middle left, 318 top right, 318 bottom right, 328, 343, 365 top right, 365 bottom left, 366 top middle, 366 bottom middle right, 367 bottom left, 368 bottom middle left, 368 top middle, 368 top right, 370 bottom right, 372 top left, 372 top right, 372 bottom middle right, 373 top left, 373 top right, 373 bottom left, 375 top right, 378 top middle, 379 top middle right, 386 top middle, 386 bottom middle right, 386 bottom right, 387 top right, 387 bottom right, 390 bottom left, 390 bottom middle right, 393 bottom right, 395 top right, 395 bottom right, 396 top middle right, 399 bottom right, 400 top middle left, 402 bottom left, 403 top middle, 405 top right, 405 bottom right, 406 bottom left, 406 bottom middle, 406 bottom right, 407 top middle left, 408 bottom middle left, 410 bottom left, 415 bottom left; **Pamela Peirce:** 338; **Ben Phillips/Positive Images:** 368 bottom right; **Norman A. Plate:** 29 top right, 326, 349, 359, 367 top left, 385 top middle, 388 top middle, 404 bottom right; **Howard Rice/The Garden Picture Library:** 302 top left; **Susan A. Roth:** 293 lower middle, 296 bottom middle, 299 bottom left, 300 top right, 309 middle right, 310 middle right, 346, 364 top right, 365 top left, 367 top right, 367 bottom left, 368 top middle right, 368 top left, 370 top left, 370 top middle right, 371 bottom left, 372 top middle left, 372 bottom right, 374 bottom left, 374 bottom middle left, 375 top left, 377 top left, 377 top middle right, 378 bottom right, 379 top left, 380 top

right, 380 bottom right, 382 top left, 382 top right, 383 top left, 383 bottom left, 384 top middle left, 386 top right, 386 bottom middle left, 387 top left, 388 top right, 388 bottom middle, 389 top middle, 389 top right, 389 bottom left, 390 bottom right, 391 top, 392 top middle left, 393 top middle right, 395 top left, 396 top right, 397 bottom left, 397 bottom right, 398 top, 399 top middle, 400 top left, 400 bottom left, 401 top middle right, 402 top middle, 403 bottom left, 409 top left, 410 bottom middle; **Kjell Sandved/Visuals Unlimited:** 336 top right; **Richard Shiell:** 296 top right, 309 bottom right, 366 bottom middle left, 368 bottom right, 374 top right, 374 bottom middle right, 375 bottom middle, 375 bottom right, 380 top left, 381 bottom left, 392 top left, 393 top middle left, 394 top left, 404 top, 406 top left, 407 bottom middle, 409 top middle, 410 top right; **Southern Progress Corp.:** 303 bottom left; **Anthony Tesselaar:** 380 bottom middle right; **Michael S. Thompson:** 296 bottom left, 296 bottom middle right, 310 left, 311 middle left, 344, 360, 368 top middle left, 377 bottom middle, 378 top left, 379 bottom left, 383 bottom, 387 bottom left, 390 top middle, 390 top right, 392 top right, 394 top right, 394 bottom left, 396 bottom middle right, 401 top middle left, 401 bottom right, 403 top right, 405 bottom left, 407 top middle right, 409 top right, 409 bottom left, 410 top right, 410 top middle; **Mark Turner:** 307 middle, 318 bottom left, 336 top left, 336 bottom left, 355, 366 bottom right, 374 top left, 378 bottom left, 381 bottom middle; **Juliette Wade/The Garden Picture Library:** 302 bottom; **Ron West:** 337 top left; **judywhite/GardenPhotos.com:** 301 top, 303 bottom right, 311 top left, 311 bottom right, 337 top right, 396 bottom middle left, 401 bottom middle; **Lee Anne White:** 311 bottom left; **Tom Wyatt:** 364 bottom right, 370 bottom left, 405 bottom middle.

Roses acknowledgments

Special thanks to the six regional consultants—Russ Bowermaster, Kathleen Brenzel, Larry Parton, Michael Ruggiero, Peter Schneider, and Peggy Van Allen (see page 411)—who gave us lists of their favorite roses, from which we wrote chapter 4, and to the American Rose Society for its help with the manuscript.

CONTAINER GARDENING
PHOTOGRAPHY AND DESIGN CREDITS

PHOTOGRAPHY

A–Z Botanical Collection Ltd.: 427 bottom; **William D. Adams:** 447 top; **Max E. Badgley:** 534 top left; **Matthew Benson:** 423 top right, 472 bottom, 477 left, 480 top right; **Marion Brenner:** 423 top middle, 424 top, 425 bottom, 426, 427 top right, 427 top left, 427 middle left, 427 middle right, 432 bottom, 438 all, 439 all, 451 top, 460 top, 460 bottom, 461 left, 461 right, 468 top left, 482 top, 482 bottom, 483 left, 483 right, 492 top, 492 bottom, 496 top, 496 bottom, 498 all, 499 all, 502 top, 503 bottom, 515 top, 515 middle, 515 bottom, 523 top, 523 bottom; **Roger Brooks/A–Z Botanical Collection Ltd.:** 487 top; **David Cavagnaro:** 452 right, 526 top left, 529 bottom right; **Robin B. Cushman:** 440, 448, 524, 527 top left; **Janet Davis:** 435 bottom, 444 top, 459, 526 upper left; **Alan and Linda Detrick:** 497 bottom; **Andrew Drake/ Garden Image:** 443 top, 451 bottom, 462, 476 top; **Liz Eddison:** 445 bottom, 457 top right, 466 top, 469 bottom, 476 bottom, 509 top, 538 bottom right; **Derek Fell:** 514 top; **Roger Foley:** 489, 494 top; **John Glover:** 417 top, 422 top, 423 middle right, 425 top, 430 left, 454 right, 467 bottom right, 474 left, 474 right, 475 bottom right, 477 top right, 478 right, 479, 480 bottom left, 484, 486, 490 bottom, 494 bottom, 495 left, 513 bottom, 527 bottom left, 538 top right; **John Glover/Garden Picture Library:** 488 bottom; **David Goldberg:** 428, 450 bottom, 464 top left, 473 left, 480 bottom right; **Arthur Gray:** 514 bottom; **Steven Gunther:** 422 top, 431 top, 477 bottom right; **Jamie Hadley:** 471 top right, 528 top; **Mick Hales:** 442 bottom; **Lynne Harrison:** 420 left, 431 bottom right, 449 left; **Saxon Holt:** 430 right, 443 bottom, 445 top, 446 top, 449 right, 455 top, 457 bottom, 471 bottom right, 472 top, 502 bottom, 503 top, 506; **Holt Studios/Nigel Cattlin:** 526 top, 526 bottom right; **Holt Studios/Bob Gibbons:** 525 top right, 525 bottom left; **Holt Studios/John Veltom:** 437 bottom; **Dency Kane:** 454 left, 525 middle, 526 lower left, 526 bottom left, 527 right, 529 top left; **Holt Studios/M. Szadzuik and R. Zinck:** 529 top middle; **Allan Mandell:** 434 right, 444 bottom; **Charles Mann:** 434 left, 453 top left, 470, 478 bottom left; **David McDonald:** 420 right, 455 bottom, 465 bottom, 466 bottom; **Clive Nichols:** 416, 423 bottom left, 436 top, 446 bottom, 450 top, 453 top right, 453 bottom, 464 bottom left, 467 top, 468 top right, 471 top left, 473 right, 475 top, 475 bottom left, 480 top left, 487 bottom, 488 top, 539 top; **Marie O'Hara/Garden Picture Library:** 432 top; **Jerry Pavia:** 431 bottom left, 436 bottom, 437 left, 467 bottom left, 529 bottom left; **Julia Pazowski/ A–Z Botanical Collection Ltd.:** 507 bottom; **Norman A. Plate:** 418, 433 bottom, 442 top, 447 bottom, 458, 465 top, 468 bottom, 504, 505 top, 510 all, 511, 512, 513 top, 528 bottom; **Harry Smith Collection:** 539 bottom; **Thomas J. Story:** 417 middle, 417 bottom, 423 bottom right, 424 bottom, 435 top, 437 right, 500, 505 bottom, 507 top, 508, 516, 518, 519 left, 519 right, 520, 521, 530, 533 all; **Friedrich Strauss/Garden Picture Library:** 421, 452 left, 497 bottom, 509 bottom, 538 bottom left; **Ron Sutherland/ Garden Picture Library:** 469 top, 490 top, 495 right; **Bjorn Svensson/A–Z Botanical Collection Ltd.:** 433 top; **Mark Turner:** 456, 457 top left, 525 top left, 525 bottom right, 526 upper right, 526 lower right, 529 top right; **Ron West:** 534 bottom left, bottom right, top right; **Steven Wooster/Garden Picture Library:** 478 top left.

DESIGN

Bill and Dana Anderson: 477 bottom right; **Mark Ashmead:** 454 right; **Jonathan Baillie:** 474 left; **Rob Benoit Associates:** 435 top; **Susan Blevins:** 478 bottom left; **Kathleen N. Brenzel:** 502 bottom, 503 top, 505 top; **Susanna Brown:** 476 bottom; **Ralph Cade/Robin Greene:** 436 top, 450 top, 467 top; **Natalie Charles:** 457 top right; **Stephen Crisp:** 488 bottom, 490 bottom; **Robin B. Cushman:** 527 top left; **Scott Daigre:** 514 bottom; **Tina Dixon:** 442 top, 444 bottom, 447 bottom; **Ann Frith:** 467 bottom right; **Teena Garay:** 504; **Sonny Garcia:** 443 bottom; **John Glover:** 513 bottom; **Karen Guzak:** 449 left; **Ben Hammontree:** 455 bottom; **Mark Henry:** 466 bottom; **Tom Hobbs:** 420 right; **Lynn Hollyn:** 417 middle, 500, 508 (concrete containers); **Raquel Hughes:** 434 left; **Chris Jacobson:** 423 right, 457 bottom; **Ann Kelly:** 456; **Joan Kropf:** 448; **Land Art:** 475 bottom right; **Randy Lancaster:** 433 bottom; **Stonie Lewenhaupt:** 480 top left; **Little & Lewis Design:** 431 bottom right; **Emma Lush:** 453 top right; **Jean Manocchio:** 458; **Patti McGee:** 465 bottom; **Callie McRoskey:** 473 left; **Claire Mee/Candy Bros.:** 468 top right; **Carol Mercer/Lisa Verderosa:** 454 left; **Clive and Jane Nichols:** 471 top left, 475 top, 475 bottom right; **Oehme, van Sweden & Associates:** 489, 494 right; **Anthony Paul:** 469 top, 486, 495 right; **Ellen Pearce:** 450 bottom; **Lisette Pleasance:** 464 bottom left; **Suzanne Porter:** 432 bottom; **Nan Raymond:** 453 top left, 470; **Sarah Robertson:** 440; **Charlotte Sanderson:** 473 right; **Hilda Schwerin:** 513 top; **Candra A. Scott:** 428; **Randle Siddeley:** 488 top; **Jill Slater:** 417 middle (plants), 417 bottom, 423 top middle, 425 bottom, 438 bottom; 439 all, 460 bottom, 461 left, 461 right, 482 bottom, 483 left, 483 right, 498 bottom, 499, 500 (plants), 502 top, 503 bottom, 505 bottom, 507 top, 508 (plants), 515, 516; **Jill Slater/Jan Smith:** 451 top; **Billy Spratlin:** 431 top; **Robert and Judith Stitzel:** 457 top left; **Stonesmith Garden Vessels:** 505 top (container); **Diana Stratton:** 446 top; **Bud Stuckey:** 437 right, 512; **Martin Summers:** 478 top left; **Joe Swift:** 423 bottom left; **Bernard Trainor:** 464 top left; **Greg Trutza:** 465 top; **Ron Wagner/Nani Waddoups:** 434 right; **Tisa Watts:** 468 bottom; **Geoff Whitten:** 453 bottom; **Paul Williams:** 432 top; **Stephen Woodhams:** 416, 446 bottom, 487 bottom, 539 top; **Kay Yamada:** 445 bottom.

BULBS PHOTOGRAPHY CREDITS

Scott Atkinson: 225 bottom; Max E. Badgley: 202 bottom left-1, middle right-2, bottom right-1; R. S. Byther: 202 bottom left-2, bottom left-3, bottom right-3; Marion Brenner: 285 top; Richard L. Carlton/Visuals Unlimited: 202 top right-2; David Cavagnaro: 192 top right, middle, bottom right, 202 top right-1, 229 bottom right, 245 top right, 252 top, 257 top, 261 top, 266 top, 281 left; Peter Christiansen: 193 bottom; R. Cowles: 202 top right-3; Charles Cresson: 206 bottom, 291 bottom; Claire Curran: 265 top, 267 top; R. Todd Davis: 190 top, 199 top right, 251 bottom left, 271 bottom; Dr. Auguste DeHertogh: 254 top; Ken Druse: 219 top right, 222 bottom, 231 left, 273 left, 278 bottom, 283 right; Derek Fell: 187 top, 187 middle bottom, 188, 190 middle, 192 top left, 202 middle right-3, 208, 217 top, 226 bottom, 233

right, 245 bottom right, 251 top right, 253, 256 bottom, 262 bottom left, 280 bottom, 286 right; William E. Ferguson: 198 bottom; David Goldberg: 202 bottom right-2, 261 bottom; William Grenfell/Visuals Unlimited: 202 middle right-1; Thomas Hallstein: 225 top; Lynne Harrison: 192 bottom left, 224 top, 231 bottom right, 237 left, 238 top, 240 top, 244 top, 249 top, 250 top, 255 middle right, 269 top, 272 top, 288 top left; Saxon Holt: 190 bottom left, 198 top, middle, 201 bottom, 205 middle right, 207 top, 210 top right, 211 top, 212 left, 216 top, 218, 219 left, 219 bottom right, 220, 221 bottom, 228, 229 top right, 230, 237 bottom right, 240 bottom, 249 bottom, 268 right, 282, 287 bottom right; Horticultural Photography: 241 bottom; David McDonald/Photo Garden: 213 middle, 226 top; Kevin Miller: 260 top; N. and P. Mioulane/

M.A.P.: 187 bottom, 214; Netherlands Flowers: 285 bottom; Don Normark: 227 top; Hugh Palmer: 199 bottom, 247, 262 top left, 284 right; Park Seed Co.: 268 left; Jerry Pavia: 190 bottom right, 199 top left, 244 bottom, 246, 248 bottom, 252 bottom, 259 bottom right, 265 bottom, 266 bottom, 271 top, 275 top, 276 right, 283 left, 288 bottom right, 291 top; Joanne Pavia: 192 middle left, 243 bottom, 254 bottom, 263 bottom; Pamela K. Peirce: 207 bottom, 256 top, 289 right; Norman A. Plate: 186, 192, 193 top, 197 bottom, 200 top and bottom left, 201 top, 204, 205 top, bottom left, bottom center, bottom right, 210 bottom left, 216 bottom, 236 bottom, 255 bottom right, 257 bottom, 258 left, 259 top right, 269 bottom, 270, 276 left, 289 left, 290 left; Susan A. Roth: 224 bottom, 251 bottom right, 255 left, 284 bottom left; Eric Tankesley-

Clark: 258 right, 260 bottom; Michael S. Thompson: 197 top, 210 bottom right, 211 bottom, 212 right, 213 bottom, 221 top, 222 top, 223, 229 left, 231 top right, 232 top, 233 left, 234 top, 236 top, 237 top right, 238 bottom, 242, 250 bottom, 255 top right, 259 bottom left, 262 top right, 264, 274, 277, 278 top, 279, 280 top, middle, 286 left, 287 top right, 290 right; VISIONS-Holland: 187 middle top, 194, 206 top, 213 top, 227 bottom, 232 bottom, 234 bottom, 235, 239, 243 top, 248 top, 263 top, 272 bottom, 281 right; Darrow M. Watt: 241 top, 267 bottom; Wayside Gardens: 275 bottom; Peter O. Whiteley: 200 top right, 271 middle, 287 top left; Tom Woodward: 217 bottom, 245 bottom left, 284 top left; Tom Wyatt: 196, 273 right.

Glossary of Gardening Terms

Acid soil. A soil with a pH that is below 7. Acid soil is most common in regions that have heavy rainfall and is often associated with sandy soils and those high in organic matter. Though most plants grow well in acid soil, highly acid soils are inhospitable. Adding calcium carbonate is one way to raise pH in the soil.

Alkaline soil. A soil with a pH that is above 7. Alkaline soil, which is high in calcium carbonate, is found in many regions where rainfall is light. Many plants grow well in moderately

ALTERNATE/OPPOSITE LEAVES

Alternate   Opposite

SOIL PH

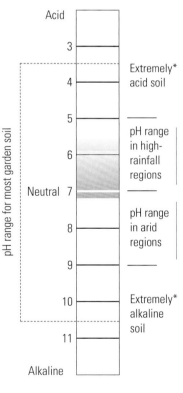

pH range preferred by acid-loving plants

pH range preferred by most garden plants

*Soils nearing extremes require professional intervention to modify pH.

alkaline soil. Others, notably camellias, rhododendrons, and azaleas, do not. Sulfur can be used to lower soil pH. You can also lower pH over time with regular (at least annual) applications of organic amendments such as compost.

Alternate leaves; opposite leaves. Alternate leaves arise from different nodes on opposite sides of the stem. Leaves are opposite when they spring from the same node on a stem, but on opposite sides.

Annual. A plant that completes its life cycle in 1 year or less.

Anther. *See* Flower.

Axil. The inner angle between a leaf (or other organ of a plant) and the stem from which it springs. Organs in the axil, such as flowers and buds, are called axillary.

Balled-and-burlapped (B-and-B). Specimen shrubs and trees sold for planting with a ball of soil around the roots, wrapped in burlap or a synthetic. Usually available from late fall to early spring.

Bare-root. Refers to deciduous shrubs and trees and some perennials sold for planting with the soil removed from their roots. Usually sold in winter and early spring.

Bedding plant. Any plant suitable for massing in beds for its colorful flowers or foliage. Most bedding

plants are annuals or perennials that are grown as annuals.

Biennial. A plant that germinates and produces foliage and roots during its first growing season, then blooms, produces seed, and dies during its second growing season.

Blanching. The process of blocking light from parts of certain vegetables to keep them paler in color or milder in flavor (or both). With cauliflower and the central leaves of endive or cardoon (an artichoke relative), the outer leaves are tied over the inner head or leaves. Asparagus is blanched by mounding soil over the emerging spears.

Bolt. To produce seeds or flowers prematurely; the term usually refers to annual flowers and vegetables. Bolting most frequently occurs when cool-season plants (lettuce, for example) are set out in hot weather that rushes growth.

Bonsai. The word bonsai is Japanese for "tray planting": growing and training dwarf plants in containers selected to harmonize with them. The objective is to create a tree or landscape in miniature.

Bracts. Modified leaves growing on some plants below a flower or flower cluster. Bracts are usually green, but may be colorful enough to resemble flowers or petals. Bougainvillea, dogwood *(Cornus)*, and poinsettia *(Euphorbia pulcherrima)* all have showy bracts.

Broad-leafed. Refers to evergreen trees and shrubs that have foliage year-round—camellia, for example—but are not conifers (such as juniper). Also refers to any weed that is not a grass.

Bud. A rudimentary organ or shoot of a plant. A flower bud develops into a blossom; a growth bud produces shoots of leafy growth. Terminal (apical) buds are produced at the end of a shoot. Lateral (axillary) buds are produced in the axil of a plant. Latent buds lie dormant until the branch is cut or breaks near it; then the bud will develop into a new shoot.

Budding. A method of propagation in which a bud (scion) from one plant is inserted beneath the bark of another related plant.

Bud union. The point at which a shoot or bud (scion) unites with the rootstock.

Bulb. A plant that grows from a thickened underground structure. A true bulb consists of an underground stem base that contains an embryonic plant surrounded by scales—modified leaves that overlap one another. Bulblike structures include corms, rhizomes, tubers, and tuberous roots.

Calyx. Collectively, the sepals of a flower.

Cambium. The layer of growing cells between the xylem and phloem.

Cane. An elongated flowering or fruiting stem, usually arising directly from the roots. Examples of cane-producing plants include barberry *(Berberis)*, forsythia, rose, raspberry, and grape.

Cane pruning. A method of pruning grapevines.

Catkin. A slender, spikelike, often drooping flower cluster. Alder *(Alnus)*, birch *(Betula)*, and willow *(Salix)* are familiar trees that produce catkins.

Chill requirement. Many bulbs, perennials, and deciduous shrubs and trees (fruit trees in particular) need cold weather (as measured in hours required at temperatures below 45°F/7°C) to produce well. Many varieties of such plants—apples and lilacs (*Syringa*), for example—have been developed that require less winter chill. Bulbs can be refrigerated in warm-winter areas.

Composite head. *See* Inflorescence.

Compound leaf. *See* Leaf.

Conifer. A precise term for certain evergreens—such as cedar (*Cedrus*), juniper (*Juniperus*), and pine (*Pinus*). Conifers have leaves that are narrow and needlelike or tiny and scalelike. A few conifers, including larch (*Larix*) and dawn redwood (*Metasequoia*), are deciduous. All conifers bear seeds in cones or in modified conelike structures (juniper berries, for example). Yew (*Taxus*) and Podocarpus bear single seeds on fleshy bases, but because of their needlelike foliage, they are sometimes considered conifers.

Corm. A bulblike, swollen underground stem base composed of solid tissue.

Corm

Corolla. Collectively, the petals of a flower.

Crown. A tree's crown is its entire branch structure, including foliage. Also refers to the point at which a plant's roots and top structure join, usually at or near the soil line.

Cultivar. Shorthand for "cultivated variety." These are genetically distinct plants, maintained in cultivation by human effort; they may be of hybrid origin or selected varieties of plants that occur in the wild. Cultivars are propagated by divisions, cuttings, or (in some cases) seed. Cultivar names are enclosed in single quotation marks and are not italicized, as in *Lobelia erinus* 'Crystal Palace'. In

general usage and throughout this book, the term "variety" (*see also* Variety) refers both to cultivars and to varieties found in nature.

Deadhead. To remove spent flowers, neatening a plant, preventing it from setting seed, and prolonging its bloom.

Deadheading

Deciduous. Any plant that naturally sheds all of its foliage at any one time (usually in fall).

Defoliation. The unnatural loss of foliage, which may result from high winds, intense heat, drought, unusually early or late frosts, or severe damage caused by chemicals, insects, or diseases.

Dieback. When a plant's stems die for part of their length, beginning at the tips. Causes include inadequate moisture, nutrient deficiency, poor climate adaptation, or severe injury from pests or diseases.

Dormancy. The annual period when a plant's growth slows down. For many plants, dormancy commences as days grow shorter and temperatures colder.

Drainage. The downward movement of water through the soil.

Drip line. The circular area of soil around a tree directly under its outermost branch tips; rainwater tends to drip from the tree at this point. Roots of established trees usually extend beyond the drip line.

Epiphyte. Epiphytes grow on another plant for support but take no nourishment from the host plant. Examples include cattleya orchids and staghorn ferns (*Platycerium*). Epiphytes are sometimes mistakenly considered parasites, but true parasites draw nourishment from the host, while epiphytes live on nutrients drawn from the air, rainwater, and organic debris on the supporting plant.

Espalier. The act of training a tree or shrub to grow more or less flat against a wall or fence, espalier is a classic space saver. Dwarf, potted fruit trees make good candidates, as do berry-bearing shrubs such as firethorn (*Pyracantha*) and cotoneaster.

Evergreen. Plants that never lose all their leaves at one time. *See also* Broad-leafed; Conifer.

Family. Every plant is classified in a family whose members share certain broad characteristics that set them apart from plants in other families. Family names are in Latin and typically end in "-aceae"; examples include *Rosaceae* (the rose family) and *Iridaceae* (the iris family). Botanists often reclassify family names, so reference works may differ in their classifications.

Fertilization. The fusion of male and female gametes (fertile reproductive cells) following pollination.

Fertilize. To apply nutrients in the form of fertilizer to a plant.

Flower. The part of a seed-bearing plant that contains the reproductive organs.

Forcing. Hastening an out-of-season plant to maturity or to a flowering or fruiting stage. Usually occurs in a greenhouse, where temperature, light, and humidity can be controlled.

Foundation plant. Originally, a plant used to hide the foundation of a house. Since many of today's homes lack high or even visible foundations,

ESPALIER FORMS

Double U-shaped

Candelabra

Fan

Belgian fence

Belgian arch

Belgian doublet

BASIC FLOWER FORMS

Single

Semidouble

Double

The basic flower form is single (top), with one row of petals (usually four, five, or six). Semidouble flowers (center) have two or three times the minimum number of petals, usually in several rows. Double flowers (bottom) have many densely packed petals that often produce a rounded blossom shape.

COMPLETE FLOWER

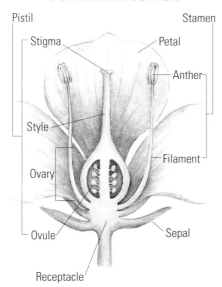

Pistil
Stamen
Stigma
Petal
Anther
Style
Filament
Ovary
Ovule
Sepal
Receptacle

the term has come to refer to any shrub planted near house walls.

Frond. In the strictest sense, fronds are the foliage of ferns. Often, however, the word is used to describe the leaves of palms or any foliage that looks fernlike.

Fruit. The mature ovary of a plant, containing one to many seeds. Fruits may be soft and fleshy, as in the case of peaches or apples, or dry, like an acorn or dried pea pod.

Genus (plural: genera). Plant families are subdivided into groups of more closely related plants called genera; the first word in a plant's botanical name is the genus. Some families contain only a single genus; for example, the family *Ginkgoaceae* includes only the genus *Ginkgo*. Others contain hundreds of genera; *Asteraceae* (the daisy family), for instance, comprises over 900 genera. The second word in a botanical name is the species (*see also* Species). Both the genus and species are written in italics, with just the name of the genus capitalized—as in *Rosa moschata* (musk rose) and *Hemerocallis lilio-asphodelus* (lemon daylily).

Girdling. The removal of bark all around a stem or branch, cutting off water and nutrients and possibly killing the plant. Girdling can occur when a woody plant has been tied tightly to a support and the growing plant becomes constricted. Gnawing rodents can also cause girdling. In

some cases, a gardener may girdle a plant deliberately, removing a narrow ring of bark to reduce overly vigorous growth or to kill an unwanted plant.

Growing season. The number of days between the average dates of the last killing frost in spring and the first killing frost in fall. Also used to describe the period of time a plant is actively growing and not dormant.

Harden off. Exposing a plant that has been growing indoors to increasing periods of time outside, so that when it is planted in the garden it can make the transition with a minimum of shock.

Hardy. A plant's hardiness is its resistance to, or tolerance of, frosts or freezing temperatures. A plant hardy to −20°F/−29°C will survive undamaged by a temperature that low, for example. The word does not mean tough, pest-resistant, or disease-resistant.

Herbaceous. A plant with soft or fleshy (nonwoody) tissue—which might be an annual, perennial, or bulb. In the strictest sense, the term refers to plants that die to the ground each year and regrow stems the following growing season.

Humus. The soft dark substance formed when animal or vegetable matter decomposes. The term is also commonly used to describe organic materials that will eventually decompose into humus—such as sawdust, ground bark, leaf mold, and animal manure.

Hybrid. A plant that results from a cross between two species, subspecies, varieties, cultivars, strains, or any combination of the above; or, less commonly, between two plants from different genera. Hybrids may occur naturally, but more often they are deliberately bred. Hybrids are indicated with the symbol ×, as in *Buddleja × weyeriana*, a cross between the two butterfly bush species *B. davidii* and *B. globosa*.

Hydroponics. A method of gardening with a water-based solution rather than soil. In some systems, an inert medium such as rockwool is used to anchor plant roots.

Inflorescence. A group of individual flowers on a single stem, which can take many forms. A spike has flowers attached to the main stem without stalks, as in bottlebrush *(Calliste-mon)* or montbretia *(Crocosmia)*. In an umbel, individual flowers spring from approximately the same point, as in the blossoms of dill *(Anethum graveolens)*. In a raceme, flowers form on stalks arising from the main stem, as in foxglove *(Digitalis)*. The flowers of lilac *(Syringa)* and privet *(Ligustrum)* are panicles; they have groups of flowers borne on stalks (racemes) arising from the main stem. A composite head refers to small, closely packed, stalkless flowers; these may include central disk flowers and outer ray flowers, as in sunflower *(Helianthus)*.

Internode. *See* Node.

Lath. Any overhead structure (originally a roof of spaced laths) that reduces the amount of sunlight reaching plants beneath its cover or protects them from frost.

INFLORESCENCES

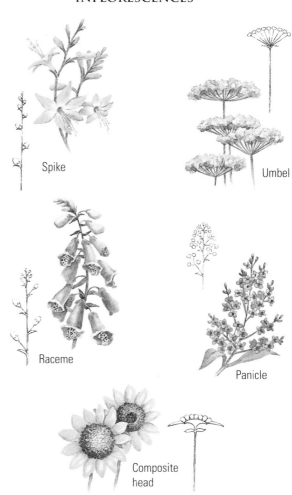

Spike

Umbel

Raceme

Panicle

Composite head

LEAF TYPES

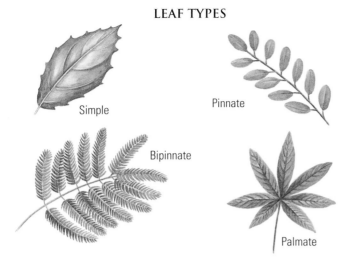

Simple

Pinnate

Bipinnate

Palmate

STEM NODES

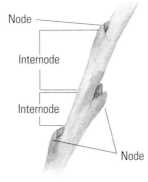

Node

Internode

Internode

Node

Leader. The central upward-growing stem of a single-trunked tree or shrub.

Leaf. The main photosynthetic organ of most plants. A simple leaf is a single unit, whereas a compound leaf is divided into separate segments called leaflets. In a palmately compound leaf, the leaflets grow from one point at the end of a stem. In a pinnately compound (once-divided) leaf, the leaflets are arranged along a central axis; a bipinnately compound leaf is twice-divided, or twice pinnate.

Leafburn. Damage of a leaf's tissues from sunlight, chemicals, strong wind, or lack of water. Leafburn usually starts as brownish, dried-out tissue around the edge of the leaf; sometimes the whole leaf dries out. Plants sensitive to leafburn include Japanese maples *(Acer palmatum)* and azaleas *(Rhododendron)*.

Leafburn

Leaflet. A division or segment of a compound leaf. *See also* Leaf.

Leaf mold. Partially decomposed leaves used as an organic amendment.

Leaf scar. A rounded or crescent-shaped mark on a branch where a leafstalk once was attached.

Lip. Irregular flowers (those with unequal segments) often have an upper and a lower division (each known as a lip), each bearing one or more segments. Honeysuckle *(Lonicera)* is an example.

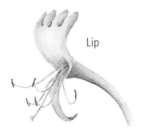

Lip

Microclimate. A small area (such as a backyard or even a portion of it) with a slightly different climate than that of its larger surroundings. Microclimates are determined by factors such as hills, hollows, and the location of structures. Plants that might not survive in a specific climate zone may grow well in the right microclimate.

Naturalize. To set out plants (especially bulbs) randomly, without a precise pattern, and allow them to spread at will. Also refers to plants that become established in an area where they are not native, such as foxglove *(Digitalis purpurea)*, for example, which has naturalized in parts of the Pacific Northwest.

Node. The joint in a stem where a bud, branch, or leaf starts to grow. The area of stem between nodes is the internode.

Offset. A young plant that develops at or near the base of the parent plant. Hen and chicks *(Echeveria)* and strawberry readily produce offsets. The word also refers to the increases of bulbs and corms.

Open-pollinated plants. Varieties or cultivars of plants produced from natural, random pollination. In contrast with hybrids, these are the result of deliberate crosses (controlled pollination).

Opposite leaves. *See* Alternate leaves.

Organic matter. Any material originating from a living organism—peat moss, ground bark, compost, or manure, for example—used as a soil amendment.

Ovary. *See* Flower; Fruit.

Panicle. *See* Inflorescence.

Peat moss. A water-retentive organic soil amendment, peat moss is the partially decomposed remains of mosses. It increases soil acidity. Sphagnum peat moss is generally considered the highest in quality.

Perennial. A nonwoody plant that lives for more than 2 years (often for many years).

Petal. *See* Flower.

Pistil. *See* Flower.

Pleaching. A training method in which branches are interwoven to form a hedge or arbor. Subsequent

pruning keeps a neat, rather formal pattern.

Pollarding. A training method in which the main limbs of a young tree are drastically cut back. In each subsequent dormant season, the growth from these branch stubs is cut back to one or two buds. In time, the branch ends become large and knobby. The result is a compact, leafy dome during the growing season and a somewhat grotesque branch structure during the dormant months. London plane tree *(Platanus × acerifolia)* is the tree most often subjected to this treatment.

Pollenizer. A plant that provides pollen for another plant, such as an apple variety planted to provide pollen for a nearby second variety that does not produce fertile pollen.

Pollination. The transfer of pollen from the male reproductive organs to the female ones, which leads to fertilization and seed production.

Pollinator. An insect or animal that transfers pollen from one part of a flower to another or from flowers on one plant to flowers on another.

Pseudobulb. A modified aboveground stem that serves as a storage organ. Some orchids have pseudobulbs.

Raceme. *See* Inflorescence.

Rhizome. A modified, horizontally growing stem. It may be long and slender, as in some perennials (and in perennial weeds like blackberry), or thick and fleshy, as in many irises.

Rhizome

Rootbound. Plants grown in the same container for too long develop tangled, matted roots.

Rootstock. The part of a budded or grafted plant that furnishes the root system and sometimes part of the branch structure (also known as an understock).

Rosette. Leaves closely set around a crown or center, usually at or close to ground level. Hen and chicks (*Echeveria*) and partridge-breast aloe (*Aloe variegata*) both grow in rosettes.

Runner. *See* Stolon.

Scion. A shoot or bud cut from one plant to graft or bud onto the rootstock of another.

Self-seed, self-sow. When a plant sheds fertile seeds that produce seedlings.

Semidouble flower. *See* Basic flower forms.

Sepal. *See* Flower.

Simple leaf. *See* Leaf.

Single flower. *See* Basic flower forms.

Species. Each genus is subdivided into groups of individual species—generally distinct entities (though they may closely resemble other species in the genus) that reproduce from seed with only a small amount of variation. The second word in a plant's botanical name designates the species; the first word designates the genus. Both genus and species are italicized; the name of the genus is capitalized. For example, French marigold is, in botanical terms, *Tagetes patula*—genus *Tagetes*, species *patula*. *See also* Genus.

Specimen. A tree or shrub that makes a significant impact in a planting or in a conspicuous location in the garden.

Sphagnum. Various mosses native to bogs. Much of the peat moss sold in the West contains decomposed sphagnum. These mosses also are collected live and packaged in whole pieces, fresh or dried. In this form, they are used for lining hanging baskets and for air layering.

Spike. *See* Inflorescence.

Spore. A simple reproductive cell. Algae, fungi, mosses, and ferns reproduce by spores.

Sport. A spontaneous mutation (variation) from the normal pattern, often a branch that differs from the rest of the plant. Examples include spurred apple varieties that occur as limb sports on standard apple varieties, and camellias propagated from branches that have shown changes in flower color or form.

Spur. In grapevines and fruit trees (particularly apples and cherries), a specialized short twig that bears the plant's fruit. Also refers to short and saclike or long and tubular projections from a blossom's petals or sepals. Most species of columbine (*Aquilegia*), for example, have flowers with pronounced spurs.

Spur pruning. In winter, grapevine canes that grew and fruited in the past season are pruned from a framework of permanent arms, leaving a series of spurs (short twigs, each with two buds). These buds will produce fruit in the following summer or fall.

Stamen. *See* Flower.

Standard. A plant trained to a single, upright trunk topped by a rounded crown of foliage. In some standards, the trunk and top are joined by grafting.

Stolon. A stem that creeps and roots along the soil surface, forming new plants where it roots. Bermuda grass spreads by stolons.

Strain. Many popular annuals and some perennials are strains (sometimes referred to as series). Examples include State Fair zinnias and Pacific delphiniums. Plants in a strain are similar but vary in some respect—usually in flower color.

Stress. Stress may result from inadequate or excess water, wind, or excessively high or low temperatures. It can cause wilting, dulling of foliage color, and browning of leaf edges.

Subshrub. A low-growing plant with woody stems—a small shrub. Also describes a perennial with a woody base but soft, herbaceous stems in its upper part.

Subspecies. A simple botanical name consists of two words in italics, denoting genus and species. When a third name in italics appears, it denotes a subspecies—a major division within a species. An example is *Eucalyptus mannifera maculosa*, red-spotted gum. (The name of the subspecies may be preceded by the abbreviation "ssp."; for example,

Eucalyptus mannifera ssp. *maculosa*.) A third italicized name may also denote a variety (*see also* Variety).

Sucker. In a grafted or budded plant, suckers grow from the rootstock rather than from the grafted or budded part of the plant. *See also* Water sprout.

Taproot. A thick central root that may penetrate deeply into the ground. In some plants, such as carrots and parsnips, taproots are storage organs.

Tender. The opposite of hardy; tender plants have a low tolerance for frost or freezing temperatures.

Tendrils. Specialized growths along the stems or at the ends of leaves on some vines. Tendrils wrap around supports, enabling the vine to climb.

Thin. To prune out entire branches, large or small, cutting back to the main trunk, a side branch, or the ground. Seedlings or developing fruits are thinned by removing excess plants or fruits so that the remaining ones have enough room to grow well.

Topiary. The technique of pruning and training shrubs and trees into shapes—either geometric forms (cones, spheres, pyramids) or fanciful animals or objects.

Truss. A typically compact cluster of flowers at the end of a stem, branch, or stalk. Many rhododendrons bear their flowers in trusses.

Tuber. A swollen underground stem with multiple growth points, such as the potato.

Tuberous root. A true root, thickened to store nutrients.

Umbel. *See* Inflorescence.

Underplanting. Planting one plant beneath another, such as setting out a ground cover under a tree.

Understock. *See* Rootstock.

Variegation. Striping, edging, or other markings in a color different from the primary color of a leaf or petal.

Variety. A variant of a basic species as it occurs in nature. Like a subspecies name, a botanical variety

SUCKER AND WATER SPROUTS

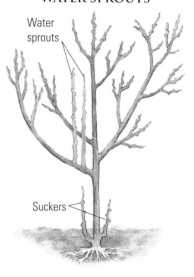

Water sprouts

Suckers

name is written in italics as the third word in a plant's botanical name; it may be preceded by the abbreviation "var." (such as *Ilex pernyi veitchii* or *Ilex pernyi* var. *veitchii*). The word "variety" is also used to include cultivated varieties (*see also* Cultivar).

Water sprout. In trees, any strong vertical shoot growing from the main framework of trunk and branches; also referred to as sucker.

Whorl. Three or more leaves, branches, or flowers growing in a circle from a node on a stem or trunk.

Woody. A plant with hardened (woody) stems or trunks. An herbaceous plant, in contrast, has soft stems.

Tuber

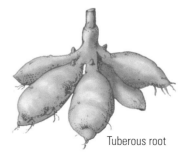

Tuberous root

INDEX

Pages listed in **bold** include photographs.